D1555079

The Pictorial Life of
George
Washington

THE PICTORIAL LIFE OF
GEORGE
WASHINGTON

Embracing a Complete History of
THE SEVEN YEARS WAR, THE REVOLUTIONARY WAR,
THE FORMATION OF THE FEDERAL CONSTITUTION,
and
THE ADMINISTRATION OF WASHINGTON

JOHN FROST, LL.D.

WHITE HALL PRESS
WHITE HALL, WEST VIRGINIA
&
AMERICAN VISION PRESS
POWDER SPRINGS, GEORGIA

THE PICTORIAL LIFE OF GEORGE WASHINGTON

Embracing a Complete History of The Seven Years War,
The Revolutionary War, The Formation of the Federal Constitution,
and the Administration of Washington

by John Frost, LL.D.

Facsimile printing.
Originally published by Leary & Getz, Philadelphia, 1859.

White Hall Press
44 Mountain Park Drive
White Hall, West Virginia 26554
www.WhiteHallPress.com

The American Vision, Inc.
3150 Florence Road
Powder Springs, Georgia 30127
www.AmericanVision.org
1-800-628-9460

Printed in The United States of America

Cover design by Luis Lovelace

ISBN13: 978-1-61658-939-4

GEORGE WASHINGTON.

THE
PICTORIAL
LIFE OF
GENERAL WASHINGTON

BY JOHN FROST, L. L. D.

See Page 85

PHILADELPHIA

LEARY & GETZ.

PICTORIAL LIFE

OF

GEORGE WASHINGTON:

EMBRACING

A COMPLETE HISTORY

OF

THE SEVEN YEARS' WAR, THE REVOLUTIONARY WAR, THE
FORMATION OF THE FEDERAL CONSTITUTION, AND
THE ADMINISTRATION OF WASHINGTON.

BY J. FROST, LL. D.

AUTHOR OF "PICTORIAL HISTORY OF THE WORLD," "PICTORIAL HISTORY
OF THE UNITED STATES," AND "PICTORIAL HISTORY OF MEXICO AND
THE MEXICAN WAR, WITH FIVE HUNDRED ENGRAVINGS."

WITH UPWARDS OF ONE HUNDRED ENGRAVINGS,

BY CROOME & DEVEREUX.

PHILADELPHIA:
PUBLISHED BY LEARY & GETZ,
No. 224 NORTH SECOND STREET.
1859.

PREFACE

WASHINGTON was so completely a public man, that his biography is necessarily a history of the period in which he lived. In compiling the following narrative I have, therefore, endeavoured not only to bring into view the transactions in which he was personally concerned, but all those contemporary events which were of sufficient importance to deserve attention in a general history of the period. The volume will, consequently, if I have succeeded in my design, present a history of Washington and his times.

The authorities on which I have chiefly relied, besides the biographies of Washington by Ramsay, Marshall, Paulding, Sparks, and others, are the general histories of the Revolution by Ramsay, Gordon, Allen, Botta, and others; the correspondence of Washington and his cotemporaries, state papers and documents, and

3

a history of the United States, entitled the Western
World. In using these authorities I have not hesitated to adopt their phraseology, where it was not too
diffuse for a work of so limited extent as the present.
This general acknowledgment, and the frequent references in the foot notes, are considered sufficient to
enable the reader to recognise the grounds of authenticity upon which the narrative rests.

My thanks are due to many literary friends for the
assistance they have rendered me in the present undertaking; and in particular to Dr. Thomas R. Maris,
for the obliging loan of the sketch by Volozan, from
which Mr. Croome's drawing was made for the full-
length portrait of Washington; and to my accomplished friend, Mr. J. Russel Smith, for the use of his
original sketches of Braddock's Field, and the scenery
in the neighbourhood of Mount Vernon.

Whoever has occasion to examine carefully into the
history of the period in which Washington lived, will
find his reverence for the character of that illustrious
man always increasing. The more intimately one becomes acquainted with the facts, the more firmly he
becomes convinced that Washington was, throughout
the whole forming period of the republic, the grand
moving power. Every thing seems to have depended
on him. The leaders of popular opinion looked to
him for advice; the Congress for direction. While
the war was raging he guided every movement, re

pressed all discontent, infused the breath of life into inert masses, and created the means of efficient warfare. When the war was ended, and a new form of government became necessary, he guided the deliberations on which it was founded. When its strength and efficiency were to be tested by experiment, the sovereign power was placed in his hands, which steered the new ship of the state through the most perilous storms, and conducted her into the secure haven of national prosperity. He was present in every creative movement. The impress of his mind is stamped upon every great national institution. Never did any great benefactor of mankind more faithfully earn his titles, than the FATHER OF HIS COUNTRY—THE FOUNDER OF THE REPUBLIC.

CONTENTS

8 CONTENTS.

Within this Enclosure
Rest
the Remains of
GEN^L GEORGE WASHINGTON

CHAPTER I.

Early Life.

HEN in the progress of the world's affairs, a great work is to be accomplished, the reformation of religion, the discovery of a new world, the subjection of barbarous nations to the mild sway of civilization, the resistance of political oppression, or the founding of a great republic, it appears to be the order of Divine Providence to raise up and prepare a great man for effecting the object. Such a man was GEORGE WASHINGTON. He was the chosen instrument for laying the foundations of the republic on whose prosperity and perpetuity the hopes of human freedom rest. Born and educated in the ranks

B   13

of the people, early trained to the endurance of hardship, endowed with extraordinary courage, circumspection, foresight and self-reliance, he found himself placed, by the suffrages of his fellow-citizens, at the head of that grand movement which was to detach his country from her state of colonial dependence, and render her the noblest empire of modern times; and having by deliberate examination convinced himself of the justice of her cause, he devoted his whole life to the great work which he had been raised up to accomplish, the successful assertion of her independence and the complete organization of her free institutions. No man was ever charged with a higher mission. None ever performed his mission with more complete success. Every step in the onward march of the republic affords a new proof of the greatness of its founder. Our future glories can never exceed the grandeur of his conceptions; for we have only to examine his actions and his writings in order to see that he anticipated all—believed all—provided for all—and that he laid the foundations deep enough, broad enough, to sustain any superstructure of national greatness that can ever be raised upon them.

As our country advances in prosperity and power, it becomes more and more interesting and important for us to recur to those trying times in which its institutions were formed, and its liberties defended; and to recognise in the exalted character of its acknowledged FATHER, the elements of its greatness and strength. The life of Washington has already furnished a subject for some of the most distinguished writers in America; but it still offers a fertile theme; it presents new aspects as the country continues to fulfil the destinies which he foresaw; it is hoped and believed, therefore, that a new attempt to recount the actions of his life, to recommend his virtues to the imitation of his countrymen, and to enforce his principles of conduct in public and private life, may be regarded with indulgence, even though this attempt should be supported by little more than a sincere reverence for his character and an earnest desire to do justice to his merits.

Many of the most illustrious benefactors of mankind have been not less remarkable for the obscurity of their origin than for the greatness of their destiny; but Washington sprung from a family whose name had already become known to history. Mr. Sparks has traced his ancestry back to the thirteenth century, and has recognised the name in the local records of the county histories as belonging to men of ample fortunes and respectable characters. Sir Henry Washington was a colonel in the army of Charles I.

and his good conduct at the capture of Bristol, in 1643, is noticed by Clarendon. Hume, in his account of the same event, (as quoted by Paulding,) has the following passage:—"One party, led by Lord Grandison, was beaten off, and its commander mortally wounded. Another, conducted by Lord Bellasis, met with a like fate. But Washington, with a less party, finding a place in the curtain weaker than the rest, broke in, and quickly made room for the horse to follow." He was afterwards governor of Worcester, and defended the place bravely for three months against the parliamentary forces. Two uncles of this Colonel Washington, John and Lawrence Washington, emigrated to Virginia about the year 1657, and settled at Bridge's Creek, afterwards called Pope's Creek, on the Potomac River, in the county of Westmoreland. John married Anne Pope of the same county, and gave his name to the parish in which he lived. He served as lieutenant-colonel in the wars against the Indians. He had two sons, Lawrence and John, and a daughter, Ann. To Lawrence Washington, the elder son, he bequeathed the estate on which he lived, then called the Pope's Creek Farm.

Lawrence Washington married Mildred Warner, daughter of Colonel Augustine Warner, by whom he had two sons, John and Augustine, and a daughter, Mildred.

Augustine Washington, the second son of Lawrence, was twice married. By his first wife, Jane Butler, he had four children, Butler, Lawrence, Augustine and Jane. Of these, Butler and Jane died in infancy. Lawrence and Augustine attained to manhood. His second wife was Mary Ball, a young lady of fortune, from one of the first families in Virginia. To her he was married on the 6th of March, 1730, being then in his thirty-seventh year. Of this union GEORGE was the first fruit. He was the eldest of six children, by the second marriage of his father, viz.: GEORGE, Betty, Samuel, John Augustine, Charles, and Mildred. Mildred died when sixteen months old.

GEORGE WASHINGTON was born in the parish of Washington, Westmoreland county, Virginia, on the 22d of February, 1732, being the great-grandson of John Washington, the founder of the family in America. The house in which he was born stood on Pope's Creek, about half a mile from the Potomac; but it was either burned or pulled down some time before the commencement of the Revolution. Its site is now designated by a stone, placed there by Mr. Custis, bearing this inscription—"Here on

THE BIRTHPLACE OF WASHINGTON.

the 11th of February, (Old Style) 1732, GEORGE WASHINGTON was born." Mr. Paulding thus describes the place:

"A few scanty relics alone remain to mark the spot, which will ever be sacred in the eyes of posterity. A clump of old decayed fig trees, probably coeval with the mansion, yet exists; and a number of vines, and shrubs, and flowers still reproduce themselves every year, as if to mark its site, and flourish among the hallowed ruins. The spot is of the deepest interest, not only from its associations, but its natural beauties. It commands a view of the Maryland shore of the Potomac, one of the most majestic of rivers, and of its course for many miles towards the Chesapeake Bay. An aged gentleman, still living in the neighborhood, remembers the house in which Washington was born. It was a low-pitched, single-storied, frame building, with four rooms on the first floor, and an enormous chimney at each end on the outside. This was the style of the better sort of houses in those days, and they are still occasionally seen in the old settlements of Virginia."*

Washington's parents were members of the Episcopal Church, the prevailing form of religion at that time in Virginia; and, according to its forms, he was baptized on the 16th of April, 1732. His early instruction appears to have been of a religious, but by

* Paulding's Life of Washington.

no means of a bigoted or ascetic character. That his father was extremely anxious to imbue his mind with the love of truth, has been illustrated by several anecdotes; and that he was successful is evident, not less in the conduct of George's youth, than in the frankness of his political course, when, as President of the United States, he insisted on sincerity in all the diplomatic declarations of his public envoys.

From the indications which we have of George's earliest studies, the books presented to him by his father must have been carefully chosen with reference to their moral and religious tendency. The direction thus given to young aspirations, was towards that elevated character which his subsequent life exhibited; and the fact should not escape the attention of those parents who are desirous to train up their children in the paths of virtue and honour. "The child is father of the man." The moral tendencies, good or bad, of childhood, are seldom eradicated in after life. It is with this conviction, and at the risk perhaps of being considered as detracting from the dignity of our subject, that we give some incidents of Washington's life, which illustrate his father's system of early training.

Mr. Weems, the Rector of Mount Vernon parish, relates the following anecdote of an old lady who had spent many years of her youthful days in the Washington family.

"On a fine morning in the fall of 1737, Mr. Washington, having little George by the hand, came to the door and asked my cousin Washington and myself to walk with him to the orchard, promising he would show us a fine sight. On arriving at the orchard we were presented with a fine sight indeed. The whole earth, as far as we could see, was strewed with fruit, and yet the trees were bending under the weight of apples, which hung in clusters like grapes, and vainly strove to hide their blushing cheeks behind the green leaves. 'Now, George,' said his father, 'look here, my son! Don't you remember when this good cousin of yours brought you that fine large apple last spring, how hardly I could prevail on you to divide with your brothers and sisters, though I promised you that if you would but do it, the Almighty would give you plenty of apples this fall?' Poor George could not say a word, but hanging down his head, looked quite confused, while, with his little naked toes, he scratched the soft ground. 'Now look up, my son,' continued his father, 'look up George, and see there, how richly the Almighty has made good my promise to you! Wherever you turn your eyes, you see the

3

trees loaded with fine fruit; many of them, indeed, breaking
down, while the ground is covered with mellow apples, more than
you could ever eat, my son, in your lifetime.' George looked
in silence on the wide wilderness of fruit; then lifting his eyes,
filled with shining moisture, to his father, he softly said, 'Well,
pa, only forgive me this time, see if I ever be so stingy any
more.' "

It was also the purpose of Mr. Washington to create in his
son an early love of truth, and an abhorrence of every thing like
deception. He often talked with him on this subject, and that his
lectures were not wasted, but sown on good ground, is evident
from the following anecdote, which rests on the same authority
as the one recorded above.

"When George was about six years old, he became the happy
owner of a hatchet, of which, like most little boys, he was immo-
derately fond, and was constantly going about chopping every thing
that came in his way. One day in the garden, where he often
amused himself, he unluckily tried the edge of his hatchet on the
body of a beautiful young English cherry-tree, which he barked
so terribly, that I believe the tree never got the better of it. The
next morning, the old gentleman, finding out what had befallen his
tree, which, by-the-by, was a great favourite with him, came into
the house, and with much warmth asked for the mischievous
author, declaring at the same time, that he would not have taken
five guineas for his tree. Nobody could tell him any thing about
it. Presently George and his hatchet made their appearance.
'George,' said his father, 'do you know who killed that beautiful
little cherry-tree yonder in the garden?' George was taken by
surprise, and for a moment staggered under the question; but he
quickly recovered himself, and looking at his father with the
sweet face of youth brightened with the inexpressible charm of
all-conquering truth, he bravely cried out, 'I can't tell a lie, pa,
you know I can't tell a lie; I cut it with my hatchet.' 'Run to
my arms, my dearest boy,' cried the delighted father, 'run to my
arms. Glad am I, George, that you killed the tree, for you have
paid me for it a thousand fold! Such an act of heroism in my
son, is worth more than a thousand trees, though their blossoms
were silver and their fruits the purest gold.' " Such lessons,
communicated in such a way, it is not easy to eradicate.

At an early age George was sent to a school kept by a man
named Hobby, who not only exercised the responsible functions
of schoolmaster, but also those of sexton and grave-digger to the

parish of Washington. Accomplished teachers were not so common in those days as at present; and the practice which prevailed before the Revolution, of sending boys to England to be educated, was by no means favourable to the encouragement of good schools in the colonies. George's first schoolmaster appears to have been one of the humblest pretensions; and he was soon surpassed by his pupil. The old man lived, it is said, to see Washington in the meridian of his glory, and in his latter days he used to boast with a pardonable complacency, that "it was he who laid the foundation of George Washington's greatness."

When George was about seven years old, his father removed from his farm on Pope's Creek, to another owned by him in Stafford county, on the eastern side of the Rappahannoc river, directly opposite Fredericksburg. There he lived till the 12th of April, 1743, when he died, after a short illness, at the age of forty-nine years.

Mr. Washington was taken sick during the Easter holidays, when George was absent on a visit to some of his acquaintances in Chotanct, King George's County. As soon as his sickness became serious, George was sent for, and he arrived in time to receive the parting, though silent blessing of his beloved parent. His father was speechless when he arrived, and the parting between them was extremely affecting. The moment he alighted, he ran into the chamber in which his father lay expiring; but who can paint the feelings that darted through his mind, as he beheld the change before him! Those eyes, lately so loving and bright, now robbed of all their lustre, were fixed on him from the depths of their sunken sockets; and, through swelling tears, in mute, but melting language, seemed to bid him a *last farewell*. With sobs and cries, he fell upon his father's neck, kissed him many times, and bathed his cold, pale face, with tears.

Though in the death of his father, George lost his best friend, his more immediate and hourly adviser, yet the event seems to have been consecrated to his good, by strengthening in his heart and memory the salutary lessons which that friend had taken so much care early to inculcate. It also threw him more into the society of his excellent mother, who completed the moral training which we have seen so happily commenced by his father.

Mr. Washington left to each of his sons a separate plantation. To Lawrence, the eldest, he bequeathed an estate near Hunting Creek, afterwards called Mount Vernon, and shares in productive

iron works, situated in various parts of Virginia and Maryland
To Augustine, the second son, he left an estate in Westmoreland
County.   To George, the lands and mansion in Stafford County,
where his father died; and to each of his other sons an estate of
six or seven hundred acres.   Betty, his only surviving daughter,
was handsomely provided for; and every thing was placed in the
hands of Mrs. Washington, until her children should respectively
become of age.*   Thus was George Washington, at the early age
of eleven years, left to the guardianship of his mother.

Well did Mrs. Washington fulfil her trust.   It is impossible for
the human race to estimate the debt which they owe her for the
manner in which she trained the young hero.   Mrs. Mary Washington has been described by those who were intimately acquainted with her, as being of the ordinary stature, and possessing great personal beauty; indeed, her beauty was so great that
she was known throughout the colony as "the belle of the Northern
Neck."   She was high-spirited, and possessed uncommon strength
of mind and decision of character, coupled with great simplicity
of manners.   Washington's inflexible regard to the performance
of the minute duties of life, on which the happiness of himself
and all who were connected with him depended; and his strict
punctuality in keeping his word, and discharging all the obligations of justice, may be traced back to the early influence and
example of his mother.   She was remarkable for her truth of
purpose, her hospitality, and for all those domestic habits and qualities which are so much more becoming to women than the most
fashionable accomplishments of the present day.   She was distinguished for her good sense, the control which she exercised
over her children, her great and exemplary piety; and she was
well calculated to complete that work which her husband had
commenced, the religious training of her offspring.   She had
always, no doubt, united cordially with him in his attempt to
"bring up her children in the nurture and admonition of the
Lord;" but now the whole burden falling upon her, the fidelity
with which she exercised her trust, and her fitness for the delicate
office, approved by her success, stand out in bolder characters.
Of the harmony of sentiment existing in this respect between her
and Mr. Washington, and of the high estimate in which she held
the virtue of truth, let the following incident, resting on undoubted
authority, bear witness.

Mrs. Washington was at all times fond of fine horses.   Shortly

* Sparks's Life of Washington.

after the death of her husband she owned a colt, which, on account of its many fine qualities, was a particular favourite, and had never been broken to the saddle, though it was old enough to have been broken long before. George had frequently admired this colt, as it pranced around the field, proudly snuffing up the air, wheeling and halting, and displaying its fine proportions, and more than once he wished that he was upon its back. It happened one day, that he told his wishes to some of his companions, and engaged them to meet him early the next morning, when, with their assistance, he would have a ride. Accordingly, the little party assembled the following day, soon after sunrise, and repaired to the field where the young Arabian was kept, at no great distance from the house. With some effort they contrived to pen him, and with still more effort to put a bridle upon him. Several took hold of the bridle, while the athletic youngster, with a single leap, vaulted upon his back. The necessary consequences of such an undertaking now took place. A desperate struggle followed between the horse and his rider. For a long time, the contest continued doubtful, till at length in the fury of his plunges, the noble animal falling headlong, burst a blood-vessel, which produced almost instant death. By this fall, George received no injury. But it grieved him to see lying before him the lifeless body of the spirited animal, whose death he was now sensible had been occasioned by his censurable folly and rashness. His mother too, and her fondness for this animal, came crowding upon him, to render his trouble still more distressing. Shortly after, a call to breakfast was heard. Some of the companions of George had been invited to breakfast with him that morning; and now, however much they might have desired to have been excused, they went in, and were soon seated at the table. For a time, little was said, less than usual. At length, Mrs. Washington, breaking the silence, inquired whether they had seen her fine sorrel colt in their rambles. To this none of the boys replied, and the question was repeated. There was now no escape. The case was to be met, and met at once. The integrity of George had been tried in still younger days; and now, that it was again tried, it nobly stood the test. He replied to the question put by his mother. "Your sorrel colt is dead, mother." "Dead, George," exclaimed Mrs. Washington, with much surprise, "dead, do you say?" her hands relaxing from some service which she was performing at the table. "Yes, he is dead." "How happened it, George?" "I will tell you, mother. I am the only one in fault." And then he proceeded to give her a circumstantial and correct account of the whole transaction. Before the story was ended, the flush, which had for a short time arisen upon the cheek of Mrs. Washington, an evidence of her displeasure, had all passed away, and in conclusion, she observed, quite kindly and calmly: "While I regret the loss of my favourite, *I rejoice in my son who always speaks the truth.*"

Such was the mother of our great Washington. She daily laboured to teach her children the first principles of religion, as laid down and established in the Bible, and in the formularies of the Church of England, and to inculcate upon them the fear of God, and the strict observance of the moral virtues, such as truth, justice, charity, humility, temperance, and industry. In these laudable and pious efforts she was aided by the daily use of a volume with the title of *"Contemplations, Moral and Divine, by Sir Matthew Hale, Knight, late Chief Justice of the King's Bench."* She made it her daily practice to read extracts from that book to her children. From her the book passed to George, but at what time is not known. It was found after his death, in his library at Mount Vernon, with his mother's name, "Mary Washington," written in it with her own hand, and is now in the possession of the owner of Mount Vernon. It bears the marks of having been much used, and particular chapters are designated by marks of reference. This book, filled with lessons of virtue and wisdom, clothed in the language of sincerity and truth, is the work of a pious and enlightened sage, whose whole life exemplified his precepts; and without doubt it contributed much in forming the character of a man whose actions, great as they were, scarcely conferred greater benefit upon his country than posterity is now deriving, and will always continue to derive, from his example. In contemplating this circumstance, we feel that a debt of gratitude is due to the illustrious man who gave himself to the labour of writing such a book in the midst of the duties of his high office. Though he had been abundantly rewarded by the fruits which have been gathered from the good seed which he has sown, even if his work had been blessed in but this single instance, yet the debt of gratitude which America owes him can never, till the end of time, be fully paid. Neither should we forget what we owe to the mother of Washington, who stored the mind of her son with the inestimable wisdom contained in this book, and then gave it to him, to constitute, along with his Bible, "a light to his feet and a lamp to his path."

She also had her reward: for she lived to see all her children filling the stations allotted to them, with honor to themselves and her.

A few months after the death of his father, George was sent to Westmoreland to reside with his half-brother, Augustine, principally for the purpose of attending a respectable school in the neighbourhood, kept by Mr. Williams. While a pupil of Mr. Williams, he maintained the good character which he had already gained. He soon acquired such a reputation for veracity, impartiality, and sound judgment, among his schoolmates, that he was

WASHINGTON A PEACEMAKER.

made umpire in all their disputes; and his decision was almost always satisfactory. He never quarreled with any of them, nor would he consent to see them fight among themselves; if he could prevent it in no other way, he would notify the teacher of their brutal design. For this the boys were often angry with him, but his reputation for courage and firmness, being as well founded as it was for veracity, he never received either insult or injury. His companions, afterwards, when the anger of the moment had passed away, and their passions had time to cool, felt doubly grateful to him for preventing them from whipping each other; and their love for him was continually on the increase. He inherited from his father great bodily strength and activity, and not only while at school, but long afterwards, did he delight in the sports which strengthen the frame and swell the muscles. It was a favourite amusement, during the hours of relaxation at Mr. Williams's school, for the boys to divide themselves into two parties, which they dignified with the name of armies; and calling the one French, and the other American; with cornstalks for muskets, and calabashes for drums, they would form into line, and march and counter-march, and file off, or fight their harmless battles with great interest. George always led the American army, and there was no sport in which he so much delighted as training his young soldiers.

But there was something besides playing to be done at Mr. Williams's school. That gentleman was an excellent teacher, and by him George was instructed in mathematics and in surveying. While studying these important branches of education, he kept a blank book in which he entered the examples in a fair round hand. These manuscripts have been preserved from the time of his thirteenth year. They occupy several quires of paper, and are remarkable for the care with which they were kept, the neatness of the handwriting, the clearness and beauty of the diagrams, and the precise method in which tables and columns of figures were copied.* They also contain what he calls *Forms of Writing*, such as notes of hand, bills of exchange, bonds, indentures, deeds, mortgages, wills, bills of sale, land warrants, leases, and receipts, written out with care. Then follow selections in rhyme, distinguished for their religious character. But the most interesting and significant part of these books was that which he called *Rules of Behaviour in Company and Conversation.* This contained maxims or rules of conduct for the government of young persons, drawn from sources which are not known, and arranged with much care. We present the reader with a specimen of these rules, that it may be seen upon what principles certain parts of the character of Washington were formed.

"1. Every action in company ought to be with some sign of respect to those present.

"2. Be no flatterer.

"3. Let your countenance be pleasant; but in serious matters, somewhat grave.

"4. Show not yourself glad at the misfortune of another, though he were your enemy.

"5. When you meet with one of greater quality than yourself, stop and retire; especially, if it be at a door, or any strait place, to give way for him to pass.

* Sparks.

"6. They that are in dignity or in office, have in all places precedency; but whilst they are young they ought to respect those that are their equals in birth, or other qualities, though they have no public charge.

"7. It is good manners to prefer them to whom we speak before ourselves; especially, if they be above us, with whom in no sort we ought to begin.

"8. Let your discourse with men of business be short and comprehensive.

"9. In writing, or speaking, give to every person his due title, according to his degree and the custom of the place.

"10. Strive not with your superiors in argument, but always submit your judgment to others with modesty.

"11. Undertake not to teach your equal in the art himself professes; it savours to arrogancy.

"12. When a man does all he can, though it succeeds not well, blame not him that did it.

"13. Being to advise, or reprehend any one, consider whether it ought to be done in public or in private, presently or at some other time, in what terms to do it; and in reproving, show no signs of choler, but do it with sweetness and mildness.

"14. Take all admonition thankfully, in what time or place soever given; but afterwards, not being culpable, take a time or place convenient to let him know it that gave them.

"15. Mock not, nor jest at any thing of importance; break no jests that are sharp-biting, and if you deliver any thing that is witty and pleasant, abstain from laughing thereat yourself.

"16. Wherein you reprove another be unblamable yourself, for example is more prevalent than precepts.

"17. Use no reproachful language against any one; neither curse nor revile.

"18. Be not hasty to believe flying reports to the disparagement of any.

"19. In your apparel be modest, and endeavour to accommodate nature rather than to procure admiration; keep to the fashion of your equals, such as are civil and orderly with respect to times and places.

"20. Play not the peacock, looking everywhere about you to see if you be well decked, if your shoes fit well, if your stockings sit neatly, and clothes handsomely.

"21. Associate yourself with men of good quality, if you

4   C

esteem your own reputation; for it is better to be alone than in bad company.

"22. Let your conversation be without malice or envy, for it is a sign of a tractable and commendable nature; and in all causes of passion, admit reason to govern.

"23. Utter not base and frivolous things among grave and learned men; nor very difficult questions or subjects among the ignorant: nor things hard to be believed.

"24. Be not immodest in urging your friend to discover a secret.

"25. Break not a jest where none takes pleasure in mirth; laugh not aloud, nor at all without occasion. Deride no man's misfortune, though there seem to be some cause.

"26. Speak not injurious words neither in jest nor in earnest; scoff at none, though they give occasion.

"27. Be not forward, but friendly and courteous; the first to salute, hear, and answer; and be not pensive when it is time to converse.

"28. Detract not from others; neither be excessive in commending.

"29. Go not thither, where you know not whether you shall be welcome or not. Give not advice without being asked, and when desired, do it briefly.

"30. Reprehend not the imperfections of others; for that belongs to parents, masters, and superiors.

"31. Gaze not on the marks or blemishes of others, and ask not how they came. What you may speak in secret to your friend, deliver not before others.

"32. When another speaks, be attentive yourself, and disturb not the audience. If any hesitates in his words help him not, nor prompt him without being desired; interrupt him not, nor answer him till his speech be ended.

"33. Make no comparisons; and if any of the company be commended for any brave act of virtue, commend not another for the same.

"34. Be not apt to relate news if you know not the truth thereof. In discoursing of things you have heard, name not your author always. A secret discover not.

"35. Undertake not what you cannot perform, but be careful to keep your promise.

"36. Speak not evil of the absent, for it is unjust.

"37. Set not yourself at the upper end of the table, but if it ɒe your due, or that the master of the house will have it so, contend not lest you should trouble the company.

"38. When you speak of God, or his attributes, let it be seriously in reverence. Honour and obey your natural parents although they be poor.

"39. Let your recreations be manful, not sinful.

"40. Labour to keep alive in your breast that little spark of celestial fire, called conscience."

These rules of conduct claim the reader's special attention, because we are able to trace in the subsequent life of Washington their influence on his character and conduct. Not less worthy of notice are certain extracts which we shall take the liberty of making from Sir Matthew Hale's "Contemplations," to which we have already referred as forming a subject of Washington's early study, and as exerting a direct influence in the formation of his principles of action. His well-known habits of private devotion, as well as his frequent public acts of reverence to the Deity, we may suppose to have been influenced in some measure by his imprinting on his mind such passages of this excellent work as the following:

"But on the other side, an humble man leans not to his own understanding; he is sensible of the deficiency of his own power and wisdom, and trusts not in it; he is also sensible of the all-sufficient power, wisdom, and goodness of almighty God, and commits himself to him for counsel, guidance, direction, and strength. It is natural for any man or thing that is sensible of his own deficiency, to seek out after that which may be a support and strength to him, and as Almighty God is essentially good and perfect, so he is (if I may use the expression) most naturally communicative of it to any that seek unto him for it in humility and sincerity. The air does not more naturally yield to our attraction in respiration, or to insinuate itself into those spaces that are receptive of it, than the Divine assistance, guidance, and beneficence does, to the desires, and exigencies, and wants, of an humble soul, sensible of its own emptiness and deficiency, and imploring the direction, guidance, and blessing, of the most wise and bountiful God. I can call *my own experience* to witness, that even in the external actions, occurrences, and incidences of my whole life, I was never disappointed of the best guidance and direction, when in humility and sense of my own deficiency, and diffidence of my ability to direct myself, or to grapple with the difficulties of my life, I have with humility and sincerity implored the secret direction and guidance of the Divine Wisdom and Providence

And I dare therein appeal to the vigilant and strict observation of any man's experience, whether he has not found the same experience in relation to himself, and his own actions and successes; and whether those counsels and purposes which have been taken up after an humble invocation of the Divine direction, have not been always most successful in the end.

"Consider what it is thou pridest thyself in, and examine well the nature of the things themselves, how little and inconsiderable they are; at least how uncertain and unstable they are.

"Thou hast fine gay clothes, and this makes children and young men and women proud, even to admiration. But thou art not half so fine and gay as the peacock, ostrich or parrot; nor is thy finery so much thine own as their's is, but it is borrowed from the silk-worm, the golden mines, the industry of the embroiderer, weaver, tailor, and is no part of thyself. And hast thou the patience to suffer thyself to be abused into this childish, pitiful, foolish pride?

"Thou hast, it may be, wealth, stores of money, but how much of it is of use to thee? That which thou spendest is gone; that which thou keepest is as insignificant as so much dirt or clay; only thy care about it makes thy life the more uneasy.

"Thou hast honour, esteem; thou art deceived, thou hast it not, he hath it that gives it thee, and which he may detain from thee at pleasure . . . . . But suppose it were as fixed and stable a reputation and honour as a rock of marble or adamant, and that it were the best kind of honour imaginable, namely, the result of thy virtue and merit; yet still it is but a shadow, a reflection of that virtue or worth, which, if thou art proud of, thou degradest into vanity and ostentation; and canst thou think it reasonable to be proud of the shadow, where thou oughtest not to be proud of that worth that causeth it.

"Again; thou hast power, art in great place and authority; but thou art mistaken in this; the power thou hast is not inherent in thyself. One of the meanest of those whom it may be thou oppressest, is inherently as powerful as thee, and could, it may be, overmatch thee in strength, wit, or policy; but the power thou hast is, (next to the dispensation of Divine Providence,) from those men, that either by their promises, faith, or voluntary assistance, have invested thee with this power. This power is nothing inherent in thee, but it depends upon the fidelity or assistance of others, which, if they, either by perfidiousness to thee, or resistance against thee, or withdrawing their assistance from the shall call again home to themselves, thou art like Samson, having lost his locks. *' Thy strength will go from thee, and thou wilt become weak, and be like another man.'* "

Washington's punctuality and his rigid economy of time, as well as his habitual sense of religion, seem but the natural consequences of his attention to such passages as the following:—

"How time is to be redeemed. The particular methods of husbanding time under both the former relations, viz., in relation to opportunity, and in relation to our time in life, shall be promiscuously set down. Now the actions of our lives may be distinguished into several kinds, and in relation to those several actions, will the employments of our time be diversified. 1. There are *actions natural;* such as eating, drinking, sleep, motion, rest. 2. Actions *civil;* as provision for families, bearing of public offices in time of peace or war; moderate recreations and diversions, employments in civil vocations, as agriculture, mechanical trades, liberal professions. 3. Actions *moral.* Whether relating to ourselves, as sobriety, temperance, moderation; or relating to others, as acts of justice, charity, compassion, liberality; 4. or lastly, Actions *religious;* relating to Almighty God, as invocation, thanksgiving, inquiring into his works, will, obedience to his law and commands, observing the solemn seasons of his worship and service, which must go through and give a tincture to all the rest, a habit of fear of him, love of him, humility and integrity of heart and soul before him; and, in sum, a habit of religion towards God in his Son Jesus Christ, which is the one thing necessary and overweighs all the rest.

* * * * * * *

"Much time might be saved and redeemed, in retrenching the unnecessary waste thereof in our ordinary sleep, attiring and dressing ourselves, and the length of our meals, as breakfasts, dinners, suppers; which, especially in this latter age, and among people of the better sort, are protracted to an immoderate and excessive length.

"Beware of too much *recreation.* Some bodily exercise is necessary, for sedentary men especially; but let it not be too frequent or too long. Gaming, taverns, and plays, as they are pernicious, and corrupt youth; so, if they had no other fault, yet they are are justly to be declined in respect to their excessive expense of time, and habituating men to idleness and vain thoughts, and disturbing passions, when they are past, as well as while they are used. Let no recreation of any long continuance be used in the morning, for they hazard the loss or discomposure of the whole day after.

"Be obstinately constant to your devotion at certain set times, and be sure to spend the Lord's day entirely in those religious duties proper for it; and let nothing but an inevitable necessity divert you from it.

"Be industrious and faithful to your calling. The merciful God has not only indulged us with a far greater portion of time for our ordinary occasions than he has reserved for himself, but also enjoins and requires our industry and diligence in it. And remember, that you observe that industry and diligence, not only as the means of acquiring a competency for yourself and your family, but also as an act of obedience to his command and ordinance, by means whereof, you make it not only an act of civil conversation, but of obedience to Almighty God; and so it becomes in a manner spiritualized into an act of religion.

"Whatever you do, be very careful to retain in your heart a *habit of religion*, that may be always about you, and keep your heart and life always as in His presence, and tending towards him. This will be continually with you, and put itself into acts, even though you are not in a solemn posture of religious worship, and will lend you multitudes of religious applications to God, upon all occasions and interventions, which will not at all hinder you in any measure, in your secular concerns, but better and further you. It will make you faithful in your calling, through reflection of the presence and command of Him you fear and love. It will make you thankful for all successes and supplies; temperate and sober in all your natural actions; just and faithful in all your dealings; patient and contented in all your disappointments and crosses; and actually consider and intend His honour in all you do; and will give a tincture of religion and devotion upon all your secular employments, and turn those very actions which are materially civil or natural, into the very true and formal nature of religion, and make your whole life to be an unintermitted life of religion and duty to God. For this habit of piety in your soul will not only not lie sleeping and inactive, but in almost every hour of the day will put forth actual exertings of itself in applications of short occasional prayers, thanksgivings, dependence, resort unto that God that is always near you, and lodgeth in a manner in your heart, by his fear, and love, and habitual religion towards him. And by this means you do effectually, and in the best manner, redeem your time."

The part of the volume, quoted by Mr. McGuire, in his Religious Opinions and Character of Washington, as having exerted the most perceptible influence on Washington's mind and character, is that in which the author supposes all mankind to be standing before the bar of God, who submits to each a charge, and receives from the "good steward" an account of his life.

The following passages form a portion of the charge.

"1. I have given unto you all your senses, and principally those two great senses of discipline, your sight and your hearing.

"Item. I have given unto you all, understanding and reason, to be a guide of your actions, and to some of you more eminent degrees thereof.

"Item. I have given you all, memory, a treasury of things past, heard, and observed.

"Item. I have given you a conscience to direct you, and to check you in your miscarriages, and to encourage you in well-doing; and I have furnished that conscience of yours with light, and principles of truth and practice, conformable to my will.

"Item. I have given you the advantage of speech, whereby to communicate your minds to one another, and to instruct and advantage one another by the help thereof.

"Item. I have given over to you the rule and dominion over my creatures, allowing you the use of them for your food, raiment, and other conveniences.

"Item. Besides these common talents, I have enriched some of you with special and eminent talents above others. I have given such great learning and knowledge in the works of nature, art, and sciences; great prudence and wisdom in the conduct of affairs; elocution, excellent education. I have given you a firm and healthy constitution, strength, beauty, and comeliness; also great affluence of wealth and riches, eminence of place, and power and honour; great reputation and esteem in the world; great success in enterprises and undertakings, public and private. Christian and liberal education you have had; counsel and advice of faithful and judicious friends; good laws in the place and country where you live; the written word of God acquainting you with my will, and the way to eternal life; the word preached by able and powerful ministers thereof; the sacraments both for your initiation and confirmation:" &c. &c.

The good steward is represented as giving his answer to this charge. The following passages form a part of what he is represented as saying:

"As to all the blessings and talents wherewith thou hast intrusted me, I have looked up to thee with a thankful heart, as the only Author and Giver of them. I have looked on myself as unworthy of them. I have looked upon them as committed to my trust and stewardship, to manage them for the ends that they were given, the honour of my Lord and Master. I have therefore been watchful and sober in the use and exercise of them, lest I should be unfaithful in them. If I have at any time, through weakness or inadvertence, or temptation, misemployed any of them, I have been restless till I have in some measure rectified my miscarriage, by repentance and amendment.

"As touching my conscience and the light thou hast given me in it: It has been my care to improve that natural light, and to furnish it with the best principles I could. Before I had the knowledge of thy word, I got as much furniture as I could from the writings of the best moralists, and the examples of the best men; after I had the light of thy word, I furnished it with those most pure and unerring principles that I found in it. I have been very jealous either of wounding, or grieving, or discouraging, or deadening my conscience. I have therefore chosen rather to forbear that which seemed but indifferent, but there might be somewhat in it that might be unlawful; and would rather gratify my conscience with being too scrupulous, than displease or dis quiet it, by being too venturous. I have still chosen rather to forbear what might probably be lawful, than to do that which might be possibly unlawful; because I could not err in the former, I might in the latter. If things were disputable whether they might be done, I rather chose to forbear because the lawfulness of my forbearance was unquestionable.

"Concerning my speech, I have always been careful that I offend not with my tongue; my words have been few, unless necessity or thy honour required more speech than ordinary; my words have been true, representing things as they were; and sincere, bearing conformity to my heart and mind . . . . . I have esteemed it the most natural and excellent use of my tongue to set forth thy glory, goodness, power, wisdom and truth; to instruct others, as I had opportunity, in the knowledge of thee, in their duty to thee, to themselves and others; to reprove vice and sin, to encourage virtue and good living, to convince of errors, to maintain the truth, to call upon thy name, and by vocal prayers to sanctify my tongue, and to fix my thoughts to the duty about which I was : to persuade to peace and charity and good works.

"Touching thy creatures, and the use of them, and the dominion over them, I have esteemed them thine in propriety; thou ast committed unto me the use, and a subordinate dominion over them ; yet I ever esteemed myself accountable to thee for them, and therefore I have received them with thankfulness unto thee, the great Lord both of them and me. When the earth yielded me a good crop of corn, or other fruits; when flocks increased; when my honest labours bought me in a plentiful or convenient supply, I looked up to thee as the giver, to thy providence and blessing as the source of all my increase. I did not sacrifice to my own net, or industry, or prudence, but I received all as the gracious and bountiful returns of thy liberal hand; I looked upon every grain of corn that I sowed as buried and lost, unless thy power quickened and revived it; I esteemed my own hand and industry but impotent, unless thou hadst blessed; for it is thy blessing that maketh rich, and it is thou that givest power to get wealth.

"I esteemed it my duty to make a return of this my acknowledgment, by giving the tribute of my increase in the maintenance of thy ministers, and the relief of the poor ; and I esteemed the practice enjoined to thy ancient people of giving the tenth of their increase, not only a sufficient warrant, but instruction to me, under the gospel, to do the like. . . . .

"Concerning human prudence, and understanding in affairs, and dexterity in the management of them, I have always been careful to mingle justice and honesty with my prudence ; and have always esteemed prudence, actuated by injustice and falsity, the arrantest and most devilish practice in the world, because it prostitutes thy gift to the service of hell, and mingles a beam of thy Divine excellence with an extract of the devil's furnishing, making a man so much the worse by how much he is wiser than others. I always thought that wisdom, which in a tradesman and in a politician was mingled with deceit, falsity, and injustice, deserved the same name, only the latter is so much the worse, because it was of the more public and general concernment; yet because I have often observed great employments, especially public affairs, are sometimes under great temptations of mingling too much craft with prudence, and then to miscall it policy, I have, as much as may be, avoided such temptations, and if I have met with them, I have resolutely rejected them.

5

"I have always observed, that honesty and plain dealings in transactions, as well public as private, is the best and soundest prudence and policy, and commonly at the long-run overmatches craft and subtlety; for the deceived and deceiver are thine, and thou art privy to the subtlety of one, and the simplicity of the other; and as the great observer and ruler of men dost dispense success and disappointments accordingly.

"As human prudence is abused if mingled with falsity and deceit, though the end be ever so good, so it is much more debased, if directed to a bad end; to the dishonour of thy name, the oppression of thy people, the corrupting of thy worship or truth, or to execute any injustice towards any person. It hath been my care as not to err in the manner, so neither in the end, of the exercising of thy Providence. I have ever esteemed my prudence then best employed, when it was exercised in the preservation and support of thy truth, in the upholding of thy faithful ministers, in countermining, discovering, and disappointing the designs of evil and treacherous men, in delivering the oppressed, in righting the injured, in preventing of wars and discords, in preserving the public peace and tranquillity of the people where I live; and in all those offices incumbent upon me by thy providence under every relation.

"When my end was most unquestionably good, I ever then took most heed that the means were suitable and justifiable. Because the better the end was, the more easily are we cozened into the use of ill means to effect it. We are too apt to dispense with ourselves in the practice of what is amiss, in order to the accomplishing of an end that is good; we are apt, while with great intenseness of mind we gaze upon the end, not to take care what course we take so we attain it; and we are apt to think that God will dispense with, or at least overlook, the miscarriages in our attempts, if the end be good. Because many times, if not most times, thy name and honour do more suffer by attempting a good end by bad means, than by attempting both a bad end and by bad means. For bad ends are suitable to bad means; they are alike; and it doth not immediately as such concern thy honour. But every thing that is good hath somewhat of thee in it; thy name, and thy nature, and thy honour is written upon it; and the blemish that is cast upon it, is, in some measure, cast upon thee; and the evil, and scandal, and infamy, that is in the means, is cast upon the end, and doth disparage and blemish it, and consequently it dishonours thee. To rob for burnt offerings, and to lie for God, is a greater disservice to thy majesty, than to rob for rapine or to lie for advantage.

"Whensoever my prudence was successful, in the attainment of a good end, I ever gave thy name the glory and that in sincerity. I have known some men, (and if a man will observe his own heart, he will find it there also, unless it be strictly denied,) that will give God the glory of the success of a good enterprise, but yet with a kind of secret reservation of somewhat of praise for themselves, their prudence, conduct, and wisdom; and will be glad to hear of it, and secretly angry and discontented if they miss it; and many times give God the glory, with a kind of ostentation and vanity in doing so. But I have given thee the glory of it because of my very judgment, that it is due, and due only to thee. I do know that that prudence that I have comes from thee; and I do know that it is thy providential ordering of occurrences that makes prudential deliberations successful; and more is due unto thy ordering, disposing, fitting, timing, directing of all in seeming casualties, than there is to that human counsel by which it is moved or seems to be moved; the least whereof, if not marshalled by thy hand, would have shattered and broken the counsel into a thousand pieces. Thou givest the advice by thy wisdom, and dost second it by thy providence; thou dealest by us, as we do by our children, when we set them to lift up a heavy weight, and we lift with them; and we again are too like those children that think we moved the weight, when we moved not a grain of it.

"In reference to my health, I always avoided these two extremes: I never made it my idol, I declined not the due employment of my body in the works of charity or necessity, or my ordinary calling, out of a vain fear of injuring my health; for I reckoned my health given me in order to these employments. And as he is over careful, that will not put on his clothes, for fear of wearing them out, or use his axe, for fear of hurting it; so he gives but an ill account of a healthy body, that dares not employ it in a suitable occupation, for fear of hurting his health. Nor was I vainly prodigal of it, but careful in a due manner to preserve it. I would decline places of infection, if I had no special duties that brought me to them, also unnecessary journeys, exposing myself to unnecessary dangers, especially intemperance in eating and drinking.

"Touching my eminence of place or power in this world, this is my account. I never sought or desired it, and that for these reasons. First, because I easily saw that it was rather a burden than a privilege. It made my charge and my account the greater, my contentment and my rest the less. I found enough in it to make me decline it in respect of myself, but not any thing that could make me seek or desire it. That external glory and splendour that attended it, I esteemed as vain and frivolous in itself, a bait to allure vain and inconsiderate persons, not valuable enough to invite a considerate judgment to desire to undertake it. I esteemed it as the gilding that covers a bitter pill, and I looked through the dress and outside, and easily saw that it covered a state obnoxious to danger, solicitude, care, trouble, envy, discontent, disquietude, temptation, and vexation. I esteemed it a condition, which, if there were any distempers abroad, they would infallibly be hunting and pushing after it; and if it found any corruptions within, either of pride, vain-glory, insolence, vindictiveness, or the like, it would be sure to draw them out and set them to work. And if they prevailed, it made my power and greatness, not only my burden but my sin; if they prevailed not, yet it required a most watchful, assiduous, and severely vigilant labour and industry to suppress them.

"When I undertook any place of power or eminence, first, I looked to my call thereunto, to be such as I might discern to be thy call, not my own ambition. Second, that the place were such as might be answered by suitable abilities, in some measure, to perform. Third, that my end in it might not be the satisfaction of any pride, ambition, or vanity in myself, but to serve thy providence and my generation faithfully. In all which my undertaking was not an act of my choice, but of my duty.

"In the holding or exercising these places, I kept my heart humble; I valued not myself one rush the more for it. First, because I easily found that that base affection of pride, which commonly is the fly that haunts such employments, would render me dishonourable to thy majesty and disserviceable in the employment. Second, because I easily saw great places were slippery places, the mark of envy. It was, therefore, always my care so to behave myself in them, as I might be in a capacity to leave them, and so to leave them, that when I had left them I might have no scars and blemishes stick upon me. I carried, therefore, the same evenness of temper in holding them, as might become me if I were without them. Third, I found enough in great employments, to make me sensible of the danger, trouble, and cares of them, enough to make me humble, but not enough to make me proud and haughty.

"I never made use of my power or greatness to serve my own turns, either to heap up riches, or to oppress my neighbour, or to revenge injuries, or to uphold injustice. For, though others thought me great, I knew myself to be still the same, and in all things, besides the due execution of my place, my deportment was just the same as if I had been no such a man; for first, I knew that I was but thy steward and minister, and placed there to serve thee, and those ends which thou proposedst in my preferment, and not serve myself, much less my passions or corruptions. And further, I very well and practically knew, that place, and honour, and preferment, are things extrinsical, and form no part of man. His value and estimate before, and under, and after his greatness, is still the same in itself, as the counter that now stands for a penny, anon for sixpence, and then for twelve-pence, is still the same counter, though its place and extrinsical denomination be changed.

"I improved the opportunity of my place, eminence, and greatness, to serve thee and my country in it, with all vigilance, diligence, and fidelity. I protected, countenanced, and encouraged thy worship, name, day, and people. I did faithfully execute justice according to that station I had. I rescued the oppressed from the cruelty, malice, and insolence of their oppressors. I cleared the innocent from unjust calumnies and reproaches. I was instrumental to place those in offices, places, and employments of trust and consequence, that were honest and faithful. I removed those that were dishonest, irreligious, false, or unjust, &c.

"Touching my reputation and credit, I never affected the reputation of being rich, great, crafty, or politic; but I esteemed much a deserved reputation, of justice, honesty, integrity, virtue, and piety.

"I never thought that reputation was the thing primarily to be looked after in the exercise of virtue, for that were to affect the substance for the sake of the shadow, which had been a kind of levity and weakness of mind; but I looked at virtue, and the worth of it, as that which was the first desirable, and reputation, as a fair and useful accession to it.

"The reputation of justice and honesty, I was always careful to keep untainted, upon these grounds. First, because a blemish in my reputation would be dishonourable to thee. Second,

D

it would be an abuse of a talent which thou hadst committed to me. Third, it would be a weakening of an instrument which thou hadst put into my hands, upon the strength whereof much good might be done by me.

"Though I have loved my reputation, and have been vigilant not to lose, or impair it, by my own default or neglect, yet I have looked upon it as a bitter thing, a thing that the devil aims to hit in a special manner, a thing that is much in the power of a false report, a mistake, a misapprehension, to wound and hurt; and notwithstanding all my care, I am at the mercy of others, without God's wonderful, overruling providence. And as my reputation is the esteem that others have of me, so that esteem may be blemished without my default. I have, therefore, always taken this care, not to set my heart upon my reputation. I will use all fidelity and honesty, and take care it shall not be lost by any default of mine; and if, notwithstanding all this, my reputation be soiled by evil, or envious men, or angels, I will patiently bear it, and content myself with the serenity of my own conscience.

"When thy honour, or the good of my country, was concerned, I then thought it was a seasonable time to lay out my reputation for the advantage of either, and to act with it, and by it, and upon it, to the highest, in the use of all lawful means. And upon such an occasion, the counsel of Mordecai to Esther was my encouragement—'Who knoweth whether God hath not given thee this reputation and esteem for such a time as this?'"

In these striking selections from this excellent production, our readers will doubtless see reason for the belief, that no small influence was contributed thereby toward the formation of Washington's character. Here we might stop in the assurance that such a persuasion would be general. But we cannot forbear another quotation, because of the singular coincidence of its sentiments with those which are known to have distinguished the Father of his country. We cite the discourse in which the author treats "Of Wisdom and the Fear of God." His language is:—

"Sincerity, uprightness, integrity, and honesty, are certainly true and real wisdom. Let any man observe it where he will, an hypocrite, or dissembler, or a double-hearted man, though he may shuffle it out for awhile, yet at the long run he is discovered, and disappointed, and betrays very much folly at the latter end; when a plain, sincere, honest man, holds it out to the very last, so that the proverb is most true, that 'Honesty is the best Policy.'

Now the great privilege of the fear of God is, that it makes the heart sincere and upright, and even that will certainly make the words and actions so. For he is under the sense of the inspection and animadversion of that God who searches the heart; and therefore, he dares not lie, nor dissemble, nor flatter, nor prevaricate, because he knows the pure, all-seeing, righteous God, that loves truth and integrity, and hates lying and dissimulation, beholds, and sees, and observes him, and knows his thoughts, words and actions. . . . .

"Another great cause of folly in the world is, inadvertence, inconsideration, precipitancy, and over-hastiness in speeches or actions. If men had but the patience, many times, to pause but so long in actions and speeches of moment as might serve to repeat but the Creed or Lord's Prayer, many follies in the world would be avoided that do very much mischief, both to the parties themselves and others. And therefore, inadvertence and precipitancy in things of great moment, and that require much deliberation, must needs be a very great folly, because the consequence of miscarriage in them is of greater moment. Now the fear of God, being actually present upon the soul, and exerting itself, is the greatest motive and obligation in the world to consideration and attention, touching things to be done or said. . . . .

"It mightily advanceth and improveth the worth and excellency of most human actions in the world, and makes them a nobler kind of a thing, than otherwise, without it, they would be. Take a man that is employed as a statesman or politician, though he have much wisdom and prudence, it commonly degenerates into craft, and cunning, and pitiful shuffling, without the fear of God; but mingle the fear of Almighty God with that kind of wisdom, it renders it noble, and generous, and staid, and honest, and stable. Again, take a man that is much acquainted with the subtler kind of learning, as philosophy for instance, without the fear of God upon his heart, it will carry him over to pride, arrogance, self-conceit, curiosity, presumption; but mingle it with the fear of God, it will ennoble that knowledge, carry it up to the honour and glory of that God, who is the author of nature, to the admiration of his power, wisdom, and goodness; it will keep him humble, modest, sober, and yet rather with an advance than detriment to his knowledge."

We should not have ventured to copy such long extracts from Sir Matthew Hale's Contemplations, even though they may with propriety be denominated Washington's Manual, so far as religion and morals are concerned, had we not been desirous to com mend them to the notice of the reader as suitable for general use and observance. These principles of conduct are as worthy the attention of those occupying the humbler stations in life as of those who are called to direct the movements of armies and preside over the destinies of nations.

While Washington was at school, he studied surveying, and reduced it to practice in the neighbourhood of his residence. His masterly style of composition was not the result of any instruction in the Greek and Latin classics, for he never studied them. It was acquired as he advanced in life, by self-instruction, reflection, practice, and intercourse and correspondence with men of superior classical attainments. Nor was it in composition alone that Washington was his own instructor. Never did any one better deserve to be called a self-taught man. All that may with most propriety be denominated education, all that forms the character for great enterprises, and exalted stations, appears in his case to have been the result of self-directed study, reflection, and practice. And such is the education of all truly great men. If we run over the list of those who have distin guished themselves signally on the great theatre of human affairs, those who have advanced science by inventions and discoveries, who have conducted armies to conquest, or who have successfully guided the masses of their fellow-men in political affairs, we shall find that they have been, almost without exception, self-taught men. An art, a trade, or a science, may be taught by instructors—learnt by imitation; but the ability to invent, to originate new views and laws of action, to combine parts into a system, to meet new and unexpected emergencies, to grasp and manage the helm of power, is derived only from self-instruction. A man may be taught any thing but to be great.

By this view of the matter, it is not intended to detract in any degree from the value of instruction derived from others, and least of all in the case of Washington, to whose early moral and religious instruction we have already referred as forming his principles of conduct. But this training served merely as the basis upon which he himself, by study, reflection, and earnest activity, built up that exalted and masculine character which has no parallel among men.

Washington left school for the last time in the autumn preceding his sixteenth birthday; and from that time, leaving his brother Augustine, he resided partly with his mother opposite to

Fredericksburg, and partly with his brother Lawrence, at Mount Vernon. He still spent much of his time in the study of mathematics, and in the exercise of practical surveying for the purpose of becoming familiar with the use of the instruments and the application of the principles. His leisure hours were spent in athletic exercises; and he excelled, in an especial manner, in running, wrestling, jumping, and riding. This habit of vigorous exercise continued with him through life, and gave such strength and activity to his body as enabled him afterwards to sustain all those hardships which it was his duty to encounter in his country's cause.

CARTHAGENA.

CHAPTER II.

Washington a Surveyor.

I N 1739, war had been declared by Great Britain against Spain, and Admiral Vernon was sent to take the command of a small fleet in the West Indies, with orders to operate against the Spanish possessions in that quarter. In November, he sailed with six men-of-war from Jamaica and attacked the fortress of Porto Bello. The Spanish governor was compelled to capitulate; and Vernon, blowing up the fortifications, returned to Jamaica. During the next year, with thirty sail of the line and 15,000 sailors, he undertook an expedition against Carthagena. The land forces accompanying this expedition amounted to 12,000, and were under the command of General Wentworth. Carthagena was besieged by this force, the greatest that had ever been seen in America, but such was the bravery and determination of the Spaniards that the English officers were compelled to abandon the siege. Lawrence Wash-

ADMIRAL VERNON.

ington, George's eldest brother, served as an officer in this expedition. So well had he conducted himself that he had procured the approbation and confidence of the two commanders, Admiral Vernon and General Wentworth. This friendship continuing, a correspondence was kept up between them and him for many years after the conclusion of the war. At George's desire, before he left school, in the year 1746, Lawrence procured for him a midshipman's warrant in the British navy, which was then considered the best road to preferment. George, though he was then only in his fifteenth year, prepared with pleasure for his departure; for the vessel in which he was to embark was lying almost ready to sail, in the Potomac, within sight of Mount Vernon—so called by Lawrence in compliment to his friend, the Admiral.

In the mean time the mother of Washington had felt and expressed much concern at the prospect of parting with her son, and his entering on a career which would effectually separate him from the soil of his native country. This was not the effect of mere maternal fondness. George was her eldest son, and in her widowed state he was her natural stay and support. His connections and prospects were such as to render his permanent residence on shore an object of great importance; and although the proposed scheme apparently afforded the best prospect of promotion, the result proved that it would really have marred for ever his brilliant fortunes. What arguments she used in order to convince, or what solicitations to persuade her son to relinquish his favourite project, of course cannot be known; but it will always be considered one of the wisest actions of his life that he yielded to her wishes and abandoned his hopes of fame and fortune as a naval officer. Such self-denial in a boy of sixteen is equally creditable as a proof of good sense, and of filial affection.

WASHINGTON RELINQUISHING HIS PLAN OF ENTERING THE NAVY.

Though Washington thus relinquished his station on the deck of a man-of-war, he did not the less cultivate that military talent which had been given him for higher uses. Adjutant Muse, of the county of Westmoreland, who had accompanied his brother Lawrence in the expedition against Carthagena, taught him the manual exercise. The same gentleman also lent him certain treatises on the art of war, by the aid of which he obtained some knowledge of the theory of tactics, and of the movements and evolutions of troops. The art of fencing he learnt from Monsieur Van Braam, who subsequently acted as his interpreter in his intercourse with the French on the Ohio.

Soon after leaving school, George went to reside with his brother Lawrence, at Mount Vernon, where he became acquainted with Lord Fairfax, and other members of the Fairfax family then established in Virginia. Lawrence Washington had married a sister of William Fairfax, a distant relation of Lord Fairfax, and at that time a member of the Virginia council. This gentleman was at Mount Vernon on a visit to his sister while George was there, and being very much pleased with his young acquaintance, he invited him to his residence at Belvoir, a short distance from

Mount Vernon. There he made George acquainted with his sons and daughters, and soon became his friend and adviser. Hearing him one day express a wish to get employment as a surveyor, Mr. Fairfax introduced and recommended him to his relative, Lord Fairfax, the inheritor of a vast tract of country lying between the Potomac and Rappahannoc Rivers, and stretching across the Alleghany Mountains.

This immense tract of land had never been surveyed; and the important and responsible office of surveying it was now intrusted to Washington, who entered on his first expedition for this purpose at the age of sixteen. He was accompanied by George Fairfax, a son of William Fairfax. (1748.) The duty, as usual, in a wild country, was extremely arduous, exposing the young surveyors to all the inclemencies of the weather, and bringing them into frequent contact with the Indians. It was performed, however, to the entire satisfaction of the proprietor; and it undoubtedly led to Washington's subsequent appointment as public surveyor, an office which kept him actively and laboriously employed for three years.

The business of practical surveying undoubtedly formed a very important part of Washington's preparation for the office of military commander. It not only hardened and invigorated his already robust frame, but it educated his eye, and accustomed him to judge respecting distances and advantages of position. By making him an able civil engineer, it laid the foundation of his future eminence in a military capacity. It was more immediately advantageous to him by procuring for him the acquaintance of the principal landholders of the state, and by making known to them his remarkable judgment, good sense, and ability in the conduct of affairs. The effect of this last circumstance was seen in his appointment, at the age of nineteen, to the office of adjutant-general with the rank of major. This gave him the charge of a district, with the duty of exercising the militia, inspecting their arms, and superintending their discipline.

Soon after entering upon the duties of this office, Washington's fraternal affection induced him to accompany his brother Lawrence in a voyage to Barbadoes, whither he had been ordered by the physicians, in consequence of a pulmonary attack which threatened his life. The brothers were strongly attached to each other, and the office of cheering and nursing the invalid could not have been confided to better hands. The voyage, however, was made too late. The disease had already made such progress that the

VOYAGE TO BARBADOES.

change of air and scene was insufficient to effect a cure.   After
remaining some time in Barbadoes, Lawrence determined to proceed to Bermuda after sending his brother back to Virginia with
instructions to accompany his wife, who was to join her husband
at Bermuda.   While in Barbadoes, George had the small-pox,
with which he was slightly marked during the rest of his life.

Finding, soon after his arrival at Bermuda, that his health was
not essentially benefited, Lawrence Washington returned to Virginia without waiting for his relations to meet him at that island ;
and soon after his return he sunk rapidly to the grave.   " Few
men," says Mr. Sparks, " have been more beloved for their amiable qualities, or admired for those higher traits of character
which give dignity to virtue, and a charm to accomplishments of
mind and manners."

In his will, Lawrence appointed George one of his executors,
and the estate of Mount Vernon, bequeathed to his daughter, was
to pass to George in case of her demise without issue.   The new
responsibilities thus devolved upon him, together with his public
duties, afforded ample employment for all his active energies.

The Northern military division of Virginia, which was now
assigned to Major Washington, included several counties, each
of which, in the discharge of his duties as adjutant-general, he
visited at stated times.   Here it was that he first tried, and learned

to place confidence in those military manœuvres in which he afterwards became so skilful. Nor was his vigilance useless to the
officers under his command, at this early period. Animated and
encouraged by the example of one, younger than most of them,
they learned to love him, to place unlimited confidence in his
knowledge and abilities, and to render that strict and active obedience to superiors in command, whatever may be their age, which
is absolutely necessary to success in all military enterprises. It
was by the courage, the perseverance, and the obedience of some
of these very officers, that Washington was, some time afterwards,
enabled to save the remnant of the army of the unfortunate Braddock.

CHAPTER III.

Commencement of the Seven Years' War.

HE course of events being now such as to call Washington into a more extended field of operations, it is thought neces- sary to trace the causes which led to his taking an active part in public affairs.

Canada, since the year 1608, when the first permanent settlement was made, had been in the undisputed possession of the French. Both the French and English claimed the lands in the Western Continent, by the right of prior discovery, and possession or settlement, without any regard to the right of the native inhabitants. The claims founded on discovery and actual occupation had hitherto covered but a small portion of the continent, and the European nations, by the Treaty of Aix-la-Chapelle, adjusted, in a superficial manner, the distribution of North America between the three dominant powers, England, France, and Spain. This agreement was very imperfect, however, inasmuch as the colonies of these three powers occupied but a narrow band along the Atlantic coast; and though their charters claimed the whole country from sea to sea, yet as they were entirely unacquainted with those vast regions, it was not improbable that they would soon be again involved in new difficulties respecting boundaries.

In 1673, a party of French from Canada discovered the upper waters of the Mississippi River, at the spot at which it is joined by the Wisconsin; and sailing down it as far as the Arkansas, they decided from its course that it emptied into the Gulf of Mexico. They then returned by land to Canada. On this discovery, the French nation based its right to the great Mississippi Valley. Having sailed down the river, they claimed all the lands watered by its tributaries. They afterwards took possession of the country lying near the mouth of the river, and about the year 1722, a small colony was planted at New Orleans. In ten or twelve years their settlements in Louisiana increased and began to extend up the Mississippi. Thus the French possessed two considerable colonies, one of them north, and the other south, of the English possessions. Their settlers from Canada approaching the Ohio River, and those of Louisiana manifesting a disposition to occupy the Valley of the Mississippi, the project was formed of connecting these two colonies by means of a chain of forts, running along the Ohio, and down the Mississippi. This plan interfered with the chartered rights of the English, extending from sea to sea, and would have confined them to the eastern side of the Alleghany Mountains. The Indians, too, who had hitherto been friendly to the English settlers of Virginia, becoming alarmed for their safety, began to side with their nearer neighbours, and by them they were soon instigated to make depredations on their former friends.

Already had the French, by the erection of a strong fort at Crown Point, secured the command of Lake Champlain, and a connected chain of posts was maintained from Quebec, up the St. Lawrence, and along the great lakes; until at last they approached the Ohio, and entered on the territory which had been actually granted, by charter, to the colony of Virginia. The English traders were warned not to enter the country claimed by the French to trade with the Indians. A few, disregarding the warning, were captured and carried as prisoners to Presque Isle, on Lake Erie, where the French were then erecting a strong fort. This was done, too, when the two nations were at peace with each other. A. D. 1753.

HE Indians, instigated it is supposed by French 'emissaries, commenced their savage warfare. The great valley of the Shenandoah was then but thinly peopled. The farmers who had ventured so far from the civilized world seemed to be careless about the society of their species, and took up their positions out of sight of even the smoke from their neighbours' chimneys. These isolated families often suffered from the incursions of the savages, who spared neither age nor sex, but committed their wanton cruelty on the persons of all alike, often wreaking their fiendish hatred on the unoffending and lifeless body after the soul had been released from sufferings too horrible to be narrated. The near approach of their old enemies, the French, and the ascendency which they were known to possess over the wild savages of the forest, naturally filled these desolate families with fear. They called upon the governor for aid. Governor Dinwiddie had already despatched a messenger over the mountains, with presents for the Indians, and instructions to ascertain their temper and designs, and, if possible, to find out the intentions of the French. He, however, became alarmed at the tales told him by the Indians, to whom he delivered his presents, and returned without effecting his object.

Orders now arrived from the British ministry, for the Governor of Virginia to build two forts near the Ohio River, to prevent the encroachments of the French, and to hold the Indians in check. But the orders arrived too late. The French had already taken possession of the territory bordering on the Ohio.

Thus commenced the Seven Years' War in America, called, by the provincial soldiers who were engaged in it, the Old French War. It was destined to develope the military talents and energies of Washington, and to transfer the possession of Canada and the other northern provinces of America, from France to Great Britain.

The French having taken possession of the country and built forts in different places on the Ohio, Governor Dinwiddie, in obedience to the orders of the British ministry, determined to assert the right of his king, as well as that of the province of Virginia, to the stations thus occupied, and if possible effect their dislodgment. For this purpose, he deemed it advisable, at first, to de

spatch an envoy to the French commandant, ordering him to retire
from the territories of the British. This service was one of great
delicacy, and full of danger and difficulty. "The envoy would
be under the necessity of passing through an extensive and almost
unexplored wilderness, intersected with rugged mountains and
considerable rivers, and inhabited by fierce savages, who were
either hostile to the English or of doubtful attachment."[*]

Such were the difficulties and dangers of the service that not
one of the many aids and immediate attendants on the governor
offered to undertake it, and Dinwiddie began to fear that it
would be necessary to abandon the project.

N this crisis Washington, then only twenty-one years
of age, volunteered his services. This was not
done at the instigation of ambition : the service was
dangerous, and no honour would accrue on its successful issue. He did it not from poverty, nor from
the want of employment ; we have seen him actively
and usefully engaged, and in possession of a competent fortune. But at the voice of his country he cheerfully resigned the ease and comforts of home, to enter on a journey in the
depth of winter, through a savage wilderness which exposed him
to the severest fatigue and privation, and the most imminent dangers. The acceptance of the office, therefore, can only be regarded as an act of devoted patriotism.

The governor, a kind-hearted old Scotsman, thankfully accepted
the offer of Washington's services, saying, at the same time, that
if he conducted himself to his satisfaction and that of the council,
he would have no cause to repent having undertaken the service.

On the 30th of October, he received his commission and instructions from the governor, together with a letter to the French commander, inquiring into his designs and the authority by which he
had dared to invade the dominions of the King of England, and
ordering him forthwith to evacuate the territory of Virginia. Besides delivering this message, his instructions required him to
obtain information of the position, force, and designs of the
French through the aid of the friendly Indians on the borders.

With these instructions and a passport, Washington commenced
his journey on the 31st of October, 1753. He was accompanied
by John Davidson, as Indian interpreter, and Jacob Van Braam,
his old fencing-master, as French interpreter. Passing through
Fredericksburg, Alexandria, and Winchester, they arrived on the

* Marshall.

E 2

14th of November at Wills' Creek, beyond which no road extended, and where it was necessary to hire a guide. For this purpose, the services of Mr. Gist were secured. This person was eminently qualified for the post thus given to him, for having made a settlement between the northwestern ridge of the Alleghanies and the Monongahela River, he had often traversed the country between his settlement and the Ohio, and was well acquainted with the habits of the Indians in the neighbourhood through which their route lay.* Four other men were here added to the little expedition, to act as attendants, and take charge of the horses and baggage. Their names were Currin, McQuire, Steward and Jenkins, the two former being Indian traders. The number of the party being thus increased to eight, they proceeded on their way. They now entered on the great western wilderness, through which it was necessary to follow Indian trails or direct their course by the compass. Excessive rains, aided by the melting of the snows with which the tops of the mountains were already covered, had so swelled the streams which crossed their course, as to render their journey one of continued labour and difficulty.

On the 22d they arrived at the settlement of Mr. Frazier, an Indian trader on the Monongahela River, about ten miles from the forks of the Ohio. The streams being impassable except by swimming the horses, or on rafts, they were obliged to borrow a canoe from the trader, and to send Currin and Steward down the Monongahela with the baggage, to meet the rest of the party at the forks. Washington, arriving at that place before the canoe, spent some time in viewing the rivers and land in the fork, which he thought extremely well situated for a fort, as it had the absolute command of both rivers. He thus speaks of the spot where the French soon after erected Fort Du Quesne, and where the great manufacturing city of Pittsburg has since sprung up so rapidly. The words are taken from his journal, published by the order of the governor on his return from the expedition. "The land at the point is twenty or twenty-five feet above the common surface of the water; and a considerable bottom of flat, well-timbered land all around it, very convenient for building. The rivers are each a quarter of a mile or more across, and run here very nearly at right angles, Alleghany bearing northeast, and Monongahela south-east. The former of these is very rapid, running water, the other deep and still, without any perceptible fall." The next day he examined a spot about two miles down

* Sparks.

the Ohio, where the Ohio Company intended to erect a fort, and he declared it to be greatly inferior, either for defence or advantages, to the position at the forks. He says, "A fort at the fork would be equally well situated on the Ohio, and have the entire command of the Monongahela, which runs from the Virginia settlement, and is extremely well designed for water carriage, as it is of a deep, still nature. Besides, a fort at the fork might be built at much less expense than at the other place. Nature has well contrived this lower place for water defence; but the hill whereon it must stand being about a quarter of a mile in length, and then descending gradually on the land side, will render it difficult and very expensive to make a sufficient fortification there. The whole flat upon the hill must be taken in, the side next the descent made extremely high, or else the hill itself cut away; otherwise, the enemy may raise batteries within that distance, without being exposed to a single shot from the fort."

Such was Washington's opinion, at the age of twenty-one, of the advantages and capabilities of a position, the importance of which soon became manifest to the French, who there, as we have already remarked, soon after erected Fort Du Quesne. The correctness of his opinion is further demonstrated by the importance attached to the fort in two wars, and by the flourishing condition of the city which now stands at the forks of the Ohio. On the 25th day after his departure from Williamsburg, Washington reached Logstown, where he was instructed to convene as many Indian chiefs as possible, and solicit a guard to the French forts. He immediately called a council of the principal sachems, to be held on the 26th. Tanacharison, or the Half-King, the principal chieftain, being absent on an embassy from the others to the French commandant, it was necessary to make this short delay in order that time might be allowed for his return. He returned on the afternoon of the 25th. This chief, thinking that the English only desired to trade with the Indians and not to dispossess them of their lands, favoured them in preference to the French, whom he saw building forts and houses, and taking forcible possession of the country. This forcible entry of the French upon their territories was deprecated by several tribes, and the Half-King was sent by them as their deputy to remonstrate with the intruders, on the injustice of their course. From this embassy he had just returned, when a private interview was solicited by Major Washington. After informing him of the nature of the business which had brought the party to his village, he de-

TANACHARISON, OR THE HALF-KING

sired the chief to relate some of the particulars of his journey to
the French encampment, and of his reception there, and to give
him an account of the ways and distances. He told him that
"the nearest and levelest way was at that season impassable, on
account of the many large miry savannas through which it passed,
that he would be obliged to go by Venango, and could not get to
the nearest fort in less than five or six nights' sleep, good travelling."* Tanacharison said, that when he visited the fort, he had
been received in a very stern manner by the late commander,
(who had since died,) who asked him very abruptly, what he had
come about, and what was his business. He said that he had
answered in the following words :

"Fathers, I am come to tell you your own speeches; what
your own mouths have declared. Fathers, you in former days
set a silver basin before us, wherein there was the leg of a beaver,
and desired all the nations to come and eat of it, to eat in peace
and plenty, and not to be churlish to one another ; and that if any
person should be found to be a disturber, I here lay down by the
edge of the dish a rod, which you must scourge him with; and
if your father should get foolish in my old days, I desire you
may use it upon me as well as others.

"Now, fathers, it is you who are the disturbers in this land, by
coming and building your towns ; and taking it away unknown
to us, and by force.

* Washington's Journal.

"Fathers, we kindled a fire long time ago, at a place called Montreal, where we desired you to stay, and not to come and intrude upon our land. I now desire you may despatch to that place; for be it known to you, fathers, that this is our land, and not yours.

"Fathers, I desire you may hear me in civilness; if not, we must handle that rod which was laid down for the use of the obstreperous. If you had come in a peaceable manner, like our brothers, the English, we would not have been against your trading with us as they do; but to come, fathers, and build houses upon our land, and to take it by force, is what we cannot submit to.

"Fathers, both you and the English are white; we live in a country between; therefore, the land belongs to neither one nor the other. But the Great Being above allowed it to be a place of residence for us; so, fathers, I desire you to withdraw, as I have done our brothers the English; for I will keep you at arm's length. I lay this down as a trial for both, to see which will have the greatest regard to it, and that side we will stand by, and make equal sharers with us. Our brothers the English have heard this, and I come now to tell it to you; for I am not afraid to discharge you off this land."

This patriotic and heroic, though simple speech, was answered by the general. The following is the substance of his speech as reported by the Half-King to Major Washington, and published by him in his interesting journal of this expedition.

"Now, my child," the general said, "I have heard your speech; you spoke first, but it is my time to speak now. Where is my wampum that you took away, with the marks of towns in it? This wampum I do not know which you have discharged me off the land with: but you need not put yourself to the trouble of speaking, for I will not hear you. I am not afraid of flies or musquitoes, for Indians are such as those; I tell you down that river I will go, and build upon it according to my command. If the river was blocked up, I have forces sufficient to burst it open, and tread under my feet all that stand in opposition, together with their alliances; for my force is as the sand upon the sea-shore; therefore here is your wampum; I sling it at you. Child, you talk foolishly; you say this land belongs to you, but there is not the black of my nail yours. I saw that land sooner than you did, before the Shannoahs and you were at war. Lead was the man who went down and took possession of that river. It is my land and I will have it, let who will stand up for, or say against it

8

I will buy and sell with the English! (mockingly.) If people will be ruled by me, they may expect kindness, but not else."

The sachems met in council on the 26th of November. Major Washington addressed them and explained the objects of his mission in the following speech:

"Brothers," said he, "I have called you together in council, by order of your brother, the governor of Virginia, to acquaint you that I am sent with all possible despatch, to visit and deliver a letter to the French commandant, of very great importance to your brothers the English, and I dare say to you their friends and allies.

"I was desired, brothers, by your brother the governor, to call upon you, the sachems of nations, to inform you of it, and ask your advice and assistance to proceed the nearest and best road to the French. You see, brothers, I have gotten thus far on my journey.

"His honour likewise desired me to apply to you for some of your young men to conduct and provide provisions for us on our way; and be a safeguard against those French Indians who have taken up the hatchet against us. I have spoken thus particularly to you, brothers, because his honour our governor treats you as good friends and allies, and holds you in great esteem. To confirm what I have said, I give you this string of wampum."

The chiefs received the token of friendship and alliance, and after a short consultation, deputed Tanacharison to answer in the name of the whole. He said,

"Now, my brother, in regard to what my brother the governor had desired of me, I return you this answer.

"I rely upon you as a brother ought to do, as you say we are brothers, and one people. We shall put heart in hand, and speak to our fathers, the French, concerning the speech they made to me; and you may depend that we will endeavour to be your guard.

"Brother, as you have asked my advice, I hope you will be ruled by it, and stay until I can provide a company to go with you. The French speech belt is not here; I have it to go for to my hunting cabin. Likewise, the people whom I have ordered in are not yet come, and cannot until the third night from this; until which time, brother, I must beg you to stay.

"I intend to send the guard of Mingos, Shannoahs, and Delawares, that our brothers may see the love and loyalty we bear them."

The young men did not arrive on the third night, as the Indian had said, and the business being pressing, Major Washington determined to set out with what escort could be immediately furnished. Having made known his intention to the chiefs, they met at their council-house, and deputed Tanacharison and three others to attend him to the French fort. With this small escort he started on the 30th of November; and on the 4th of December reached Venango, an old Indian town, at the mouth of French Creek, on the Ohio, about sixty miles north of Logstown. This town was occupied by the French under Captain Joncaire, as an outpost. The French commandant affected to treat the young officer with great respect, though he used every means in his power to detain him. The Indians were intoxicated, and rendered incapable of attending to their business or proceeding on their journey. When that could not be kept up, Joncaire pretended that he was intrusted with the management of Indian affairs; and Tanacharison found it necessary to spend another day to hold a council and have a talk about the incursions of the French on his hunting-grounds. The council ended, as Washington knew it would, where it began, Joncaire referring the Indian to the commander at the fort. Washington, during this short delay, succeeded, however, in gaining from Captain Joncaire information of the real designs of the French in building their forts and extending their settlements along the Ohio. Professing the greatest respect and friendship for Washington, and concern for the success of his journey, Joncaire, while holding him back, pretended to use all his power and the greatest expedition to accomplish his business with the Indians and send him forward. He told him where he would find the commandant, and gave him as many directions about the route as if he were going to travel alone and without guides.

Washington succeeded with great difficulty in leaving Venango, about noon on the 7th; but in consequence of excessive rains, followed by snow, and the bad travelling through many mires and swamps, he did not reach the station of the French commandant until the 11th, forty-one days after his departure from Williamsburg.

The commandant, Legardeur de St. Pierre, received him kindly, and in two days gave him an answer to the governor's letter. During the two days spent at the fort, Washington embraced every opportunity of making himself acquainted with the defences of the place. He thus describes the fort in his journal: "It is situ-

ated on the south or west fork of French Creek, near the water.
and is almost surrounded by the Creek, and a small branch of it
which forms a kind of island. Four houses compose the sides.
The bastions are made of piles driven into the ground, standing
more than twelve feet above it, and sharp at the top; with port-
holes cut for the cannon, and loop-holes for the small arms to fire
through. There are eight six-pound pieces mounted in each
bastion, and one piece of four pound before the gate. In the
bastions are a guard house, chapel, doctor's lodging, and the
commander's private store: round which are laid platforms for
the cannon and men to stand on. There are several barracks
without the fort, for the soldiers' dwelling, covered, some with
bark, and some with boards, made chiefly of logs. There are
also several other houses, such as stables, smith's shop, &c. I
could get no certain account of the number of men here; but
according to the best judgment I could form, there are an hundred, exclusive of officers, of which there are many. I also gave
orders to the people who were with me, to take an exact account
of the canoes which were hauled up to convey the forces down
in the spring. This they did, and told fifty of birch bark, and
an hundred and seventy of pine; besides many others which were
blocked out, in readiness for being made."*

A plan which Washington afterwards made of this fort, was forwarded to the British government.

Monsieur de St. Pierre, having consulted with Captain Reparti,
the next officer in rank, prepared an answer to the letter of the
governor, couched in a determined and firm, but respectful tone;
in which he said that as he acted by instructions from the governor
of Canada, he could not comply with the summons to retire; and
that it was not his province nor his duty to discuss treaties, which
should be referred to his superior.

The weather continuing very inclement, and the horses of the
party becoming daily weaker, Washington sent them with haste to
Venango, intending, as M. de St. Pierre had offered him a canoe
or two, to return to that place by water. The French commandant
again endeavoured to detain the Indians, by means of presents
and various artifices. But Washington succeeded in getting the
whole party embarked, on the 16th of December.

The passage down the creek was very tedious and fatiguing.
"Several times," says Washington in his journal, "we had like
to have been staved against rocks; and many times all hands

* Marshall's Notes, p. 8.

WASHINGTON'S EXPEDITION TO THE FRENCH POST.

were obliged to get out, and remain in the water half an hour or more, in getting over the shoals. At one place the ice had lodged, and made it impassable by water; we were therefore obliged to carry our canoe across a neck of land a quarter of a mile over." They reached Venango on the 22d, which was distant from the fort, by the winding of the stream, about one hundred and thirty miles, and there found their horses. The proceedings of Washington for the next five or six days will be best related in the words of his journal. They furnish a noble example of resolution and hardihood.

"Our horses were now so weak and feeble, and the baggage so heavy, (as we were obliged to provide all the necessaries which the journey would require,) that we doubted much their performing it. Therefore, myself and others, except the drivers, who were obliged to ride, gave up our horses, for packs to assist along with the baggage. I put myself in an Indian walking-dress, and continued with them three days, until I found there was no probability of their getting home in a reasonable time. The horses became less able to travel every day; the cold increased very fast; and the roads were becoming much worse by a deep snow, continually freezing; therefore, as I was uneasy to get back to make report of my proceedings to his honour the governor, I determined to prosecute my journey, the nearest way through the woods on foot. Accordingly, I left Mr. Van Braam in charge of our baggage, with money and directions to provide necessaries from place to place for themselves and horses, and to make the most convenient despatch in travelling.

"I took my necessary papers, pulled off my clothes, and tied myself up in a watch-coat. Then, with gun in hand, and pack on my back, in which were my papers and provisions, I set out with Mr. Gist, fitted in the same manner, on Wednesday, the 26th. The day following, just after we had passed a place called Murdering Town, (where we intended to quit the path and steer across the country for Shanapin's Town,) we fell in with a party of French Indians who had lain in wait for us. One of them fired at Mr. Gist or me, not fifteen steps off, but fortunately missed. We took this fellow into custody, and kept him until about nine o'clock at night, then let him go, and walked all the remaining part of the night without making any stop, that we might get the start so far as to be out of the reach of pursuit the next day, since we were well assured they would follow our track as soon as it was light. The next day we continued travelling until quite dark, and got to the river about two miles above Shanapin's. We expected to have found the river frozen, but it was not, only about fifty yards from each shore. The ice, I suppose, had broken up above, for it was driving in vast quantities.

"There was no way for getting over but on a raft, which we set about making with but one poor hatchet, and finished just after sunsetting. This was a whole day's work. We next got it launched, then went on board and set off, but before we were half way over, we were jammed in the ice in such a manner that we expected every moment our raft to sink, and ourselves to perish. I put out my setting pole to try to stop the raft, that the ice might pass by, when the rapidity of the stream threw it with so much violence against the pole, that it jerked me out into ten feet water; but I fortunately saved myself by catching hold of one of the raft logs. Notwithstanding all our efforts, we could not get to either shore, but were obliged, as we were near an island, to quit our raft and make to it.

"The cold was so extremely severe, that Mr. Gist had all his fingers and some of his toes frozen, and the water was shut up so hard that we found no difficulty in getting off the island the next morning on the ice, and went to Mr. Frazier's. We met here with twenty warriors who were going to the southward to war; but coming to a place at the head of the Great Kenawha, where they found seven people killed and scalped, (all but one woman with very light hair,) they turned about and ran back, for fear the inhabitants should rise, and take them as the authors of the murders. They report that the bodies were lying about the house, and some of them much torn and eaten by the hogs. By the marks which were left, they say they were French Indians of the Ottowa nation, &c., who did it. As we intended to take horses here, and it required some time to find them, I went up about three miles to the mouth of the Yohogany, to visit Queen Alliquippa, who had expressed great concern that we had passed her in going to the fort. I made her a present of a watch-coat and a bottle of rum, which latter was thought much the best present of the two."

They left Mr. Frazier's on Tuesday the first day of January, 1754, and the next day arrived at Mr. Gist's, at Monongahela. On the 6th they arrived at Wills's Creek, after a very fatiguing and disagreeable journey. "From the 1st of December to the 15th," says Washington, "there was but one day on which it did not rain or snow incessantly; and throughout the whole journey, we met with nothing but one continued series of cold, wet weather, which occasioned very uncomfortable lodgings."

On the 16th, Major Washington arrived at Williamsburg, where he waited on the governor, delivered the letter of the French commandant, and gave him an account of his proceedings since his departure. This he did by presenting his journal to the governor, who expressed his entire approbation of every act of the young officer. The journal was published by Governor Dinwiddie, with Washington's consent, and copied into nearly every newspaper in the Colonies and Great Britain. It was the first authentic information of the designs of the French against the British American Colonies which was ever made public.

GRENADIER. TIME OF GEORGE

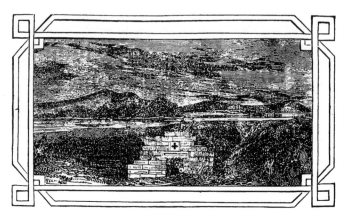

REMAINS OF THE MAGAZINE OF FORT DUQUESNE.

CHAPTER IV.

Campaign against Fort Duquesne.

HE intentions and acts of the French being made known by Major Washington to Governor Dinwiddie, and by him reported to the British ministers, they, seeing the danger which menaced their American colonies, took immediate measures to repel the French, and ordered their officers, in case of invasion, to oppose force by force, promising the aid of the mother country if it should be necessary. The danger being equally great to all the colonies, a confederacy for mutual defence was recommended, and each one was urged to contribute its proportion to the general defence, in case of need.

The governor of Virginia, having no doubt that his territory was actually invaded, now called upon the governors of New York and North Carolina to aid him in repelling the French invaders. He was authorized by the Earl of Holdernesse to call for two independent companies from New York and one from North Carolina.

Conceiving the danger to be imminent, and of too urgent a nature to admit of the delay which would be consequent upon a call of the House of Burgesses, Governor Dinwiddie laid the subject before his council, who issued an order for the immediate raising of two companies of volunteers, of one hundred men each, and their confidence in Major Washington was so great that he was appointed to the command of these two companies, apparently without a dissenting voice.*

The principal object of the council in these hasty proceedings, was to send forward a force, to act upon Washington's recommendation and build a fort at the junction of the Alleghany and Monongahela Rivers. Accordingly, while Major Washington was stationed at Alexandria to receive the volunteers and forward supplies and cannon for the intended fort, the command of one of the companies was given to Captain Trent, who was sent forward to raise men among the back-settlers and traders, and proceed at once to occupy the position before the French parties from the south and the north could unite, and set up the claim of prior possession.

The governor, in his instructions to Major Washington on this occasion, ordered him, after having every thing in readiness, to proceed with all expedition to the fork of the Ohio, and there act on the defensive; but in case any person attempted to interrupt or obstruct the completion of the works, to restrain all such offenders, or, in case of resistance, to make prisoners of, or kill and destroy them. For the rest, he was to conduct himself as the circumstances of the service should require, and to act as he should think best for the furtherance of his majesty's service and the good of Virginia.

Having made these preliminary arrangements, Governor Dinwiddie summoned the legislature to meet at an early day, to take into consideration the critical state of the colony. When they assembled, they were found to be in what the governor called "a republican way of thinking," and far from being as zealous as himself in the prosecution of violent measures. It was with the greatest difficulty that he obtained from them an appropriation of ten thousand pounds, and even that was voted "for the encouragement and protection of the settlers on the Mississippi;" the legislators wishing, if possible, to prevent a rupture with France, and restrain the prerogatives of the crown.

With the aid thus granted, the governor was induced to increase the military force to six companies of fifty men each. With a modesty, the more rare because unaffected, and which in after-life was never lost, Washington declined being a candidate for the command of this regiment. In a conversation with Colonel Corbin, a member of the council, which had taken place some time previously, Washington was led to hope for a commission

* Sparks.

above that of major; but now, fearing that the friendship of the colonel might lead him to neglect the true interests of his country, the future commander-in-chief of the American armies thus addressed him. "The command of the whole forces is what I neither look for, expect, or desire; for I must be impartial enough to confess, it is a charge too great for my youth and inexperience to be intrusted with. Knowing this, I have too sincere a love for my country to undertake that which may tend to the prejudice of it. But, if I could entertain hopes that you thought me worthy of the post of lieutenant-colonel, and would favour me so far as to mention it at the appointment of officers, I could not but entertain a true sense of the kindness.

"I flatter myself that under a skilful commander, or man of sense, (which I most sincerely wish to serve under,) with my own application and diligent study of my duty, I shall be able to conduct my steps without censure, and, in time, render myself worthy of the promotion that I shall be favoured with now."

On this, as on every other occasion of his life, Washington, though well qualified for the highest stations, was extremely unwilling to seek them. His request was granted. Colonel Joshua Fry was appointed to the chief command, and Washington was made lieutenant-colonel.

Both these officers now made the greatest exertions to hasten the necessary preparations, and Governor Dinwiddie, in order to give alacrity to the recruiting service, issued a proclamation, granting two hundred thousand acres of land, on the Ohio River, to be distributed among the officers and soldiers who should engage in this expedition. This grant was approved by the king, but it was not until some time after the close of the war, that the government, instigated principally by Washington, caused the land to be surveyed and divided.

While Lieutenant-Colonel Washington was stationed at Alexandria, an incident took place, which brought to light the moral strength of his character, while, at the same time, it unfolded his opinion with respect to the practice of duelling, a practice suitable only to the dark ages in which it originated. This occurrence took place during an election for members of the House of Burgesses, the opposing candidates being Colonel George Fairfax and Mr. Elzey. The warm friendship which existed between Washington and Colonel Fairfax, led him to speak in strong terms of the fitness of his friend for the office, and in the course of his remarks he gave offence to a man named Payne, who raised his stick and struck Washington with such force that he knocked him down. This naturally excited the indignation of such of the officers as were present, and a tumult ensued, which it required all the authority of Washington to subdue. When he had in some degree restored order, and pacified the incensed feelings of his officers, he retired to his lodgings in the public house. He immediately wrote a note to Mr. Payne, asking to see him at the tavern in the morning. Payne, expecting nothing but a challenge, repaired accordingly to the place appointed, but found Washington prepared to make a full apology, and ask his pardon for an offence given in an unguarded moment. Payne, admiring the great courage of the man who dared to face the reproach of his fellow-man, instantly apologized for his cowardly assault, and a friendship was formed between the two men, which is said to have lasted as long as they lived. "How noble and becoming was this conduct. It was especially admirable in a youthful soldier, whose very profession exposed him to peculiar temptations on such an occasion. How many would have been driven by the fear of reproach, and dread of unfavourable insinuations, to incur the hazards of a duel; thus offering up at the shrine of honour the costly sacrifice of human life. It was not possible that a man like Washington, so endowed with moral courage and regard for virtue, should be moved by the fear of man to such a course. He dreaded not the charge of cowardice from the mouths of fools. In his own bosom he had its ample refutation. He was conscious of a fortitude which no dangers could shake. To display it in murdering a fellow-citizen was not his ambition. He had before him the tented field and the enemies of his country, and he was pledged for the hazards of a mortal conflict in her defence. Here he was willing to show his courage, and lay down his life. He would not do so to gratify revenge, or win applause from the vain."[*]

So impatient was Washington to be engaged in active service, that early in April, 1754, he solicited and obtained permission to advance, with two of the companies which were completed, to a place called the Great Meadows, in the Alleghany Mountains, where he would be better able to protect the frontier of Virginia, act as a check upon the incursions of hostile savages, and also form a connecting link between the principal recruiting station at Alexandria, and the advanced company under Captain Trent.

He reached Will's Creek on the 24th of April, where he found

[*] McGuire.

Captain Trent actively engaged in raising recruits for his company, which at the time was thought to be at the new fort, at the junction of the Alleghany and Monongahela Rivers; but great was the disappointment of Washington, when, on the evening of the same day, Ensign Ward, who had been left in command by Captain Trent, entered his camp and informed him, that on the 17th instant the fort had been surrendered to the French. This work had out lately been commenced, and was not, when threatened, in a fit condition for defence. It was garrisoned by but forty-one men, and the captain and lieutenant were both absent. Mr. Ward reported that on the 17th of April, Captain Contrecœur advanced against the incomplete works, with a thousand men and eighteen cannon, which had been transported from Venango in three hundred canoes and sixty batteaux. The French captain planted his artillery against the fort, drew up his men, and sent a summons to the English, demanding their surrender within an hour. Seeing no alternative, Mr. Ward surrendered the works, and was permitted to retire with his men, arms, and working tools.

 HE capture of this military post by the French was considered by Washington as an actual invasion of the frontiers of the colony, a commencement of the war, and he conceived it to be his duty, in compliance with his instructions, to march forward, and prepare to meet the invaders wherever they might appear.

This opinion was confirmed by a council of war; and it was resolved to proceed immediately to the mouth of the Red Stone Creek, which enters the Monongahela about thirty-seven miles above the fort taken by the French, and there to construct such defences as circumstances would admit, and await the reinforcements which were expected under Colonel Fry. Accordingly, on the 1st of May, the little army, having been reinforced by the company of Captain Stephens, and now numbering three companies of fifty men each, set out from Will's Creek, and advanced by slow marches through the wilderness, making the roads as they advanced fit for the transportation of stores and cannon. In this way they advanced until they arrived at the Great Meadows, where, having certain information of the advance and near approach of the French, Washington cleared a space of its brush and underwood, and threw up a slight intrenchment. On the morning of the 27th of May, Mr. Gist arrived in camp and reported that he had seen the trail of a party which he was sure were French within five miles of the Great Meadows. Leaving a strong guard at the intrenchment, Washington advanced with forty men in search of the French. He started about ten o'clock at night, and arrived at the French encampment a short time before sunrise. Tanacharison, or the Half-King, accompanied Washington in this expedition with a few Indians. When they arrived in sight of the French camp, which was in a retired position, Washington made his dispositions for the attack, placing his men on the right and the Indians on the left. Advancing in this manner, they were soon discovered by the French, who ran to their arms and prepared for their defence. Washington then ordered his men to fire, and a skirmish commenced, which continued for about fifteen minutes, when the French, to the number of twenty-one, surrendered. The number of their killed was ten, including their commander Jumonville. Washington's loss was one man killed and two or three wounded.

A loud clamor was raised on this occasion by the French, who declared that Jumonville was merely the bearer of a summons, and that his death was an act of positive assassination. Washington did not deign to reply to such an absurd charge; but his friends have observed, that the great numbers of the French, and their cautious mode of approaching, did not at all accord with the representation of their being political envoys, but, coupled with the previous violence, gave every ground to believe that they intended to make good their pretensions by force.

Colonel Fry had at length raised three additional companies, and was advancing to take the command, but died suddenly on the way. The command then devolved upon Washington, who was soon after reinforced by two companies of regulars under Captain Mackey, increasing the forces at the Great Meadows to about four hundred men. Having enlarged the entrenchments at the Great Meadows, and erected palisades, Washington, leaving the regulars under Captain Mackey to defend the post, advanced with the remainder of his forces towards the fort at the forks, which the French had named Du Quesne. He had proceeded but thirteen miles, when he was met by some friendly Indians, who informed him that a body of eight hundred French and four hundred Indians were advancing rapidly to meet him. In this extremity, a council of war was held, and the great superiority of the enemy, which had been clearly ascertained, leaving no hope of successful resistance, a retreat was determined upon. In two days they reached the Stockade fort at the Great Meadows, and the soldiers being excessively fatigued and the horses weak for want of food, it was found impossible to retreat farther. Accordingly, Washington had no choice but to strengthen the defences of the small fort, which was now named, from the circumstances of its use, Fort Necessity, and wait the arrival of reinforcements, or meet the enemy behind the enclosure, imperfect as it was.

 HOSE of the soldiers who were not completely worn out by their incessant duties were immediately employed in felling trees to increase the height of the breastwork, and digging a ditch around the entrenchment. Their labours, however, were far from being completed, when, on the morning of the 3d of July, a wounded sentinel ran into the enclosure and gave information of the near approach of the French, with their savage allies. They appeared before Fort Necessity about eleven o'clock, in number between nine hundred and a thousand, and commanded by Monsieur de Villiers.

Washington having stationed his small body of men on the outside of the trenches, bravely awaited the approach of the enemy, who without leaving the woods commenced firing at the distance of six hundred yards. As they showed no intention of approaching nearer, Washington withdrew his men to the enclosure, with orders to fire at discretion. The French kept their position behind the trees and among the high grass, where they maintained an incessant fire of musketry till eight o'clock in the evening. The Americans fought with intrepidity, firing wherever an enemy presented himself, or aiming at the flash or smoke caused by the discharge of their muskets. During the greater part of the day the rain fell in torrents, rendering the position of the small garrison very uncomfortable, and making it difficult to use their arms with precision or certainty. In this way the battle continued with no signal advantage on either side until dark, when De Villiers demanded a parley. This was at first refused by Washington, who thought it only a feint to introduce a Frenchman within the enclosure to discover and report the weakness of the garrison; but it being soon after renewed, with the request that he would send an officer to the French camp, to confer with the commanding officer, at the same time giving the strongest assurances of the safety of the officer, Washington hesitated no longer, but sent out his old interpreter Captain Van Braam, who soon returned with proposed articles of capitulation. The proposals first made were rejected by Washington, but some changes having been effected by mutual agreement, both parties signed the articles of capitulation about midnight.*

By the terms of capitulation, the English were allowed to march out of the fort the next morning with all the honours of war, with drums beating and colours flying. They were permitted to retain their baggage, and every thing in their possession except their artillery ; and were assured of a safe retreat into the inhabited parts of the country. As the greater part of the horses had been killed, Washington was allowed to leave his baggage, under a guard, until he could forward horses to remove it, while he on his part agreed to restore the prisoners who had been taken in the skirmish with Jumonville.

About 10 o'clock, on the morning of the 4th of July, 1754, Washington, at the head of his regiment, and with the honours of war, evacuated Fort Necessity, and took up the line of march in perfect order for Virginia. Fifty-eight of the Virginians, and two hundred of the French had been killed and wounded during the engagement. The safe conduct granted by De Villiers was violated, he suffering the Indians which were attached to his army to plunder the retreating soldiers.

The courage and ability of Washington, in thus successfully resisting for a whole day an army of more than twice his number, and then obtaining honourable terms of capitulation, raised him in the estimation of the whole country, and he received the cordial approbation of the governor, as soon as he returned to Williamsburg. When the House of Burgesses assembled, they unanimously voted the thanks of the assembly to Colonel Washington and his officers and soldiers, "for their bravery, and the gallant manner in which they had conducted themselves in the defence of the country." A resolution was also passed, granting an appropriation of four hundred pistoles to be distributed among the soldiers who had aided the expedition.

The assembly met in October, 1754, and made an appropriation of twenty thousand pounds for the public service, and soon after ten thousand pounds, in specie, was forwarded from England for the same purpose. The governor immediately enlarged the army to ten companies of one hundred men each, and reduced the whole to the establishment of independent companies, thus making captains the highest officers in the Virginia regiments. And even

* Sparks.

10   G

.hey, inferior to those of the same grade holding the commission
of the king. This new arrangement, reducing Colonel Washington
to the rank of captain, and placing him under officers whom he
was accustomed to command, rendered his continuance in the
army very disagreeable.*   .

Professional pride and dignified self-respect were always among
Washington's most marked characteristics. Notwithstanding his
ardent devotion to a military life, he resolved at once to resign
a station which he believed was no longer to be held without
personal dishonour, and his commission was immediately returned
into the hands of the governor of Virginia. He retired to Mount
Vernon, and there resided until a new call was made upon his
services, in that name to whose appeal he was never deaf or
wanting.†

After the unsuccessful expedition of Washington, the colonists
began seriously to feel the want of some general system of co-
operation against their formidable enemy. Those who were most
immediately exposed to attack, complained that upon them alone
was thrown the whole burden of repelling it; and the English
government was at length induced to recommend the meeting of
a convention of delegates at Albany, to form a league with the
Six Nations of Indians, and to concert among themselves a plan
of united operations for defence, against the common enemy.
The New England States, together with New York, Pennsylvania,
and Maryland, adopted the advice, and appointed deputies, who
assembled in June, 1754, and after a pacific treaty with the Six
Nations undertook the more important subject committed to their
deliberations. The delegates were unanimous in resolving that a
union of the colonies was essential to the general safety, and ought
to be accomplished as speedily as possible. But then the difficulty
of proposing such a plan of union as would be at the same time
acceptable to the colonies and the British government, arose,
and put an end to unanimity. Among the delegates from Pennsylvania, appeared Benjamin Franklin, who even at this early
date ranked as one of the most intelligent and distinguished citizens of America. Rising from the humble station of journeyman
printer, he had already acquired a paramount influence in his
own state of Pennsylvania, and had been appointed postmaster-
general of America, a situation which he retained until near the
commencement of the Revolution, when he was displaced by the
British court. He proposed to his fellow-members of the con-

* Sparks, p. 56, 57   † Ed. Cyclo.

FRANKLIN

vention the Albany plan of union, which provided for a general government, consisting of a president, appointed by the crown; and of a council of repretatives from the several colonies. To this government was to be intrusted the general direction of war, peace, treaties, and transactions with the Indians. They were to have the power of imposing such taxes as might be deemed necessary for these purposes, and their acts, if not disallowed by the king within three years, were to acquire the force of law. They might also levy troops, the commanding officers being nominated by the president, and approved by the council. Civil offi cers were to be appointed by the counsel with the consent of the president.

This scheme gained the approbation of all the delegates except those from Connecticut, who objected to the authority conferred on the president, and the power of general taxation ; but when submitted to the legislatures of the several colonies, they all, without exception, considered the powers which it proposed to grant to the new government, especially that of direct taxation, as far too great to be placed in the hands of a body over whom each had so little control. It was accounted by them far too favourable to the royal prerogative. Its reception was equally unfavourable in the British cabinet, who viewed it, not without reason, as conceding too much power to the representatives of the people, and rendering America almost entirely independent. Thus the plan, recommended as it was by such high authority, proved wholly abortive, though its discussion undoubtedly had some effect in preparing the minds of the people for a similar union, in the struggle which resulted in the independence of the United States.*

The plan of thus uniting the colonies failing, the British ministry determined to take the conduct of the war into their own

* Murray. Grahame.

hands. First, making warm remonstrances to the court of France, and receiving, in return, nothing but pacific promises, they resolved to employ such a force in America as would compel the French to retire from their present advanced position, and, for the future, keep within their own acknowledged territory.

 CCORDINGLY, in January, 1755, General Braddock was despatched from Ireland, with two regiments of infantry, to co-operate with the Virginian forces in recovering the command of the Ohio. The arrival of Braddock excited enthusiastic hopes among the colonists. The different provinces seemed to forget their disputes with each other, and with Great Britain, and to enter into a resolution to chastise the French, at whatever cost. At the request of the British commander, a meeting of the governors of five of the colonies was held at Alexandria, at which they determined to undertake three simultaneous expeditions. The first of these was to be conducted by Braddock, with the British troops against Fort Duquesne; the second, under the command of Governor Shirley, now honoured with the commission of a general from the king, was intended for the reduction of the French fort of Niagara, and was composed of American regulars and Indians; the third, was an expedition against Crown Point, to be undertaken by a regiment of militia.

General Braddock brought with him an order of the king, dated November 12th, 1754, the design of which was to regulate the comparative rank of the regular and provincial officers. The general and field-officers of the colonies were divested of all rank while serving with officers of the same grade commissioned by the king, or his general commanding in America, and company officers of the same rank were directed to give precedence to the regulars without regard to seniority in the date of their commissions. This order rendered the separation of Washington from the army wider than ever. His passion for a military life, however, was not in the least degree weakened, and could he have held his rank, he would have hastened to join the army which in February ascended the Potomac.

His wishes were soon favoured; for General Braddock considering his military talents and local knowledge essential to the success of the expedition, he invited him to join it with the rank of aide-de-camp in his military family.

Though Washington found himself, at this juncture, greatly embarrassed with his private affairs, having no person in whom he could confide to intrust with the management of them, he gladly accepted the appointment, with the proviso that the general would permit his return, as soon as the active part of the campaign should be over, if he desired it; or if there should be a space of inaction long enough to permit him to visit home, he might be allowed to take advantage of it.*

Braddock gladly acceded to the desire expressed by Washington, and marching towards the interior, was joined by him at Frederic Town. The army then proceeded in two columns to Winchester, and thence to Will's Creek, where they arrived about the middle of May.

As soon as Washington arrived in the British camp, he was appointed one of the general's aides-de-camp, and this appointment was proclaimed to the army, in general orders, on the 10th of May.

The army was detained three weeks at Will's Creek, by the failure of the Virginian contractors to furnish the wagons and horses, which, according to the European rules of warfare, were indispensable. This evil was finally obviated by the exertions of Benjamin Franklin, who was then postmaster-general of America, and had visited the camp for the purpose of facilitating the transmission of the mail to and from the army and the settlements. He, by great exertions, and by using his influence with the farmers of Pennsylvania, succeeded in procuring these supplies. In the mean time, Washington, conscious of the fact that the success of the expedition would, in a great degree, depend upon the celerity with which they advanced, advised the general to make use of pack-horses in conveying the baggage, and not to wait for the wagons. In support of this advice, he stated that the French were known to be weak on the Ohio, but they were hourly expecting reinforcements, and, at the same time, the continued drought had so dried up the streams that neither troops nor provisions could be conveyed by them to Venango, or Fort Duquesne. This prudent advice was overruled by a council of war, by which it was declared extremely rash, and contrary to established custom.

While the army was thus constrained to remain in inactivity,

* Washington's Writings, vol. ii. p. 71.

G 2

Washington received with pleasure an order from General Braddock, to return to Williamsburg, and bring to the camp four thousand pounds, for the use of the army. He executed this commission with promptness and effect, and arrived with his charge safe in camp, on the 30th of May, though he had been compelled to wait a day in Winchester, in expectation of an escort of cavalry. This escort not arriving in time, he was obliged to make use of a small guard of the militia.

One hundred and fifty wagons, the number promised by Franklin, having arrived, the army, on the 10th of June, commenced the march for the Ohio; but now, new obstacles sprung up before them. The nature of the road which they were traversing made it necessary to double the teams of horses, which over an ordinary road would have been sufficient to drag the wagons. This caused unavoidable delay, and the general, becoming impatient, began to think, and not without reason, that the season for military operations would be consumed before he would be able to reach Fort Duquesne. He called a council of war to consider what was to be done, but before the meeting of the council, he privately asked Washington's opinion concerning the expedition. "I urged him," says Washington in a letter to his younger brother, "in the warmest terms I was able, to push forward, if he even did it with a small but chosen band, with such artillery and light stores as were necessary; leaving the heavy artillery, baggage, and the like, with the rear division of the army, to follow by slow and easy marches, which they might do safely, while we were advanced in front."

This advice prevailed in the council, and being approved by the general, he advanced on the 19th of June, with twelve hundred chosen men, and officers from all the different corps, leaving the remainder, with most of the wagons, under the command of Colonel Dunbar, with instructions to follow as fast as he could. Notwithstanding this arrangement, Braddock advanced very slowly, "halting to level every mole-hill, and to erect bridges over every brook, by which means he was four days in advancing twelve miles."

At this time Washington was suffering from the effects of a severe fever. On the 14th, but three days after the army commenced its march from Will's Creek, he was attacked by a violent fever and pain in the head, which continued without intermission for nine days. On the 23d, the fever and pain began to abate. His illness was too violent to suffer him to ride on horseback, and he soon found it necessary to make use of a covered wagon; but the jolting was so great that he could continue in it but a short time, at the rate of the advanced detachment. He was accordingly advised, by the general, to wait the arrival of Colonel Dunbar's detachment, which was two days' march behind. On his manifesting a strong disinclination to be left behind, the doctor declared that if he persevered in his determination to go on, in the condition in which he then was, his life would be endangered. This, with the promise of the general, that he should be brought up before he reached the French fort, induced him to halt and await Dunbar's detachment. He continued with the rear division two weeks, when he was so far recovered as to bear the fatigue of quick travelling in a covered wagon. In this way, on the 8th of July, he rejoined the advanced division, and on the next day, the day of the battle, attended the general on horseback, though still very weak.

N joining Braddock's division on the 8th, at the mouth of the Youghiogany, Washington was surprised to find them, though within fifteen miles of the fort, marching in regular European order, in as perfect security as if they were on the wide plains of the Eastern Hemisphere; or in a peaceful review, on a field day, in England. They marched without advanced guards or scouts; and the offer of Washington to scour the woods, in front and on the flanks, with his Virginian provincials, was haughtily rejected.

A considerable bend in the Monongahela river, and the nature of the banks, made it necessary for the army to cross it twice before they reached the fort. On the morning of the ninth of July, every thing being in readiness, the whole train crossed the river in perfect order, a short distance below the mouth of the Youghiogany, and took up their line of march along its southern bank, in high spirits. The garrison of the fort was understood to be small, and quite inadequate to resist the force now brought to bear upon it; exulting hope filled every heart; and no one doubted that he should see the British flag waving, next day, over the battlements; and the enemy obliged to retire to Canada, or surrender themselves prisoners of war. The march on that morning is described as a splendid spectacle; being made in full military array, in exact order, the sun glancing from the burnished bayonets to the scarlet uniform of the regulars, with a majestic river on the right, and dark, deep woods on the left. Not an enemy appeared, and

BATTLE-GROUND OF THE MONONGAHELA.

the most profound silence reigned over this wild territory.   The
only countenance among them which was clouded with care or
concern was that of Washington, who, as he rode beside the
general, vainly represented that the profound silence and apparent
solitude of the gloomy scenes around them afforded no security
in American warfare against deadly and imminent danger.
Again, and still vainly, did he offer to scour the woods in front
and on the left with the provincial troops.   The general treated
his fears as the effects of fever upon his brain, and the provincials
were ordered to form the rear-guard of the detachment.

About noon they reached the second crossing-place, within ten
miles of Fort Duquesne, and at one o'clock had all crossed the
river in safety.   Three hundred men under Colonel Gage formed
the advanced party, which was closely followed by a party of two
hundred ; and last of all followed the general with the main body,
consisting of about seven hundred men, the artillery and baggage.

After crossing the river, the road along which they marched led
for about a half a mile through a low plain, and then commenced
a gradual ascent of about three degrees, the prospect being shut
in by hills in the distance.   About a hundred and fifty yards from
the bottom of this inclined plain, and about equi-distant from the
road leading to the fort, commenced two ravines, from eight to ten
feet deep, which led off in different directions until they terminated in the plain below.   Covered as these ravines were with

trees and long grass, and the British having no scouts, it was impossible for them to discover their existence without approaching within a few feet of them. Up this inclined plain, between these ravines, General Braddock led his army on the afternoon of the 9th of July.

While the English were thus leisurely advancing, the scouts of the French kept the commandant of Fort Duquesne accurately informed of their motions and their numbers. Believing the small force under his command wholly inadequate to the defence of the fort against three thousand men, with a formidable park of artillery, as his scouts had represented them, he was hesitating what course to pursue, when Captain de Beaujeu offered to lead a small party of French and Indians to meet the enemy and harass his march. It required a great deal of persuasion to induce the Indians to engage in what they considered an impossible undertaking, but possessing their confidence, he finally subdued their unwillingness, and induced about six hundred of them to accompany him. With these and about two hundred and fifty French and Canadians, he intended to occupy the banks of the Monongahela, and harass the English as they crossed the river. It was only on the morning of the 9th, that he was ready to start on this expedition, and when he arrived near the river his spies reported that Braddock had already crossed. Finding that he was too late to pursue his original plan, De Beaujeu placed his followers in the ravines before mentioned, between which the English were seen advancing along the road.

When the three hundred under Gage came near the head of the ravines, a heavy discharge of musketry was poured in upon their front, and immediately after another upon their left flank. This was the first notice which they had of the presence of an enemy. Braddock was completely surprised. Gage ordered his men to fire, and though no enemy was visible, yet they poured such a discharge upon the spot where the smoke of the first fire was still to be seen, that the Indians, believing that it proceeded from artillery, were upon the point of retreating. Their indecision was but for an instant, for the advance falling back on the main body, threw them into confusion; and instead of following the example of the Indians and taking to the trees, or opening upon their invisible foe a discharge of grape, they were ordered by Braddock to maintain their ranks and advance. Captain De Beaujeu was killed by the first discharge of Gage's men, and Captain Dumas, who succeeded him in the command, immediately rallied the Indians,

11

and sending them down the ravines, ordered them to attack the enemy on each flank, while he, with the French and Canadians, maintained his position in front. Then commenced a terrible carnage. The British, panic-struck and bewildered, huddled together in squads, heeded not the commands of their officers, who were riding about madly urging them to advance, but they only fled from one side of the field to be met by the fire of an invisible foe on the other side; and then they would gather in small parties as if they hoped to shield themselves behind the bodies of their friends; firing without aim, oftener shooting down their own officers and men than Indians. Their only hope would now have been to separate, rush behind the trees, and fight man to man with their assailants; but Braddock insisted on forming them into platoons and columns, in order to make regular discharges, which struck only the trees, or tore up the ground in front. The Virginians alone seemed to retain their senses. Notwithstanding the prohibition of the general, they no sooner knew the enemy with whom they had to deal, than they adopted the Indian mode of fighting, and each for himself, behind a tree, manifested bravery worthy of a better fate.

Meanwhile the French and Indians, secure behind their natural breastworks, aimed deliberately, first at the officers on horseback, and then at others, each shot bringing down a man. The leaders, selected by unerring aim, fell first. Captains Orme and Morris, two of the three aides-de-camp, were wounded early in the action, and Washington was the only person left to distribute the general's orders, which he was scarcely able to do, as he was not more than half recovered from his illness. Notwithstanding the neglect with which his warnings had been treated, he still aided his general with his mental as well as his physical powers; though the troops lay thick around him in slaughtered heaps, he still gave the aid of salutary counsel to his ill-fated chief, and urged it with all the grace of eloquence, and all the force of conviction. Riding in every direction, his manly form drew the attention of the savages, and they doomed him to destruction. The murdering rifles were levelled, the quick bullets flew winged with death, and pierced his garments; but, obedient to the Sovereign will, they dared not shed his blood. One chieftain especially singled Washington out as a conspicuous mark, fired his rifle at him many times, and ordered his young warriors to do the same, until they became convinced that he was under the especial protection of the Great Spirit, and would never die in battle, when they

BATTLE OF MONONGAHELA.

desisted.   Although four balls passed through Washington's coat, and two horses were shot under him, he escaped unhurt.

Washington's conduct in the action is described by an eye-witness whose verbal account is thus given by Mr. Paulding. "I saw him take hold of a brass field-piece, as if it had been a stick. He looked like a fury; he tore the sheet-lead from the touch-hole; he placed one hand on the muzzle, the other on the breach; he pulled with this, and he pushed with that, and wheeled it round as if it had been nothing.   It tore the ground like a bar-share.*   The powder monkey rushed up with the fire, and then the cannon began to bark, I tell you.   They fought and they fought, and the Indians began to *holla*, when the rest of the brass cannon made the bark of the trees fly, and the Indians come down. That place they call Rock Hill, and there they left five hundred men dead on the ground."†

After the slaughter had thus continued for three hours, General Braddock, after having three horses killed under him, received a shot through the right arm and the lungs, and was borne from the field by Colonel Gage.   More than one half of the soldiers who had so proudly crossed the river, three hours before, were now killed or wounded, and the rest, on the fall of the general, fled precipitately.   The provincials, who were among the last to leave the ground, were kept in order by Washington, and served to cover the retreat of the regulars.   The officers in general remained on the field while there seemed any hope of rallying their troops, and consequently, out of eighty-six engaged, sixty-three were killed or wounded.   Of the privates, seven hundred and fourteen fell.   The rout was complete, and the more disgraceful in that it was before an inferior enemy, who attacked without the least hope of such success, and during the whole battle lost but forty men. Most of these were Indians killed in venturing out of the ravine to take scalps.

Captain Dumas thought his force too weak to pursue the fugitives, who fled precipitately until they had recrossed the Monongahela, when being no longer in immediate danger, they again formed.   Colonel Washington hastened forward to bring up wagons and other conveyances for the wounded.

General Braddock, under the particular charge of Captain Stewart of the Virginia forces, was at first conveyed in a tumbril; afterwards he was placed on horseback, but being unable to ride, he was obliged to be carried by soldiers.   In this way he was

---

* A kind of plough.   † See vignette on the title page.

H

transported until, on the night of the 13th, when they arrived within a mile of Fort Necessity, where he died, and was buried in his cloak, in the road, to elude the search of the Indians. Washington, by the light of a torch, read the funeral service over his remains.

The news of the defeat soon reached the rear division under Colonel Dunbar. The greatest confusion for a time reigned in his camp. The artillery stores were destroyed, the heavy baggage burned, and as soon as the fugitives arrived he took up the line of march with all speed for Philadelphia. Colonel Washington proceeded to Mount Vernon, justly indignant at the conduct of the regulars in the late engagement, though his own bravery and good conduct in the action gained him the applause of all his countrymen.

BURIAL OF BRADDOCK.

LAKE GEORGE.

CHAPTER V.

Northern Campaign. Battle of Lake George.

HE expeditions against Niagara and Crown Point also failed, though their failure was not attended with such disastrous consequences as that against Fort Duquesne. The troops destined for both these expeditions assembled at Albany. Governor Shirley of Massachusetts took the command of that against Niagara. Various causes operating to prevent the commencement of his march, the season was well advanced before he left Albany. His army was composed of certain regiments of regulars from New England, New York, and New Jersey, and a few Indians. At last, in the month of July, (1755,) he commenced his march for Oswego, but before he arrived at that place, the news of the defeat of Braddock overtook him, and spread such a consternation through his army, that many deserted, and the Indians, always vacillating and inclined to favour the stronger party, began to manifest great unwillingness to proceed. The necessity of securing the good will and co-operation of his savage allies, made some farther delay inevitable, so that it was not until the 21st of August that he arrived at Oswego.

After remaining there for some time, in the hope of filling up his army, and waiting till all the Indians had left him, he made a vigorous effort to reach Niagara, but was prevented by a succession of heavy rains, and the increasing sickness of the few soldiers who remained with him. Considering these obstacles insurmountable, he left a garrison of seven hundred men at Oswego, under the command of Colonel Mercer, and instructing him to build two other forts, to secure the command of the lake, he returned with the remainder of the army to Albany.

The army destined for the reduction of Crown Point consisted of about five thousand men. The command was given to William Johnson, an Irishman, who began life as a common soldier, but whose uncommon bodily strength, with a rude energy of character, had enabled him to acquire the friendship of some of the most powerful chiefs of the Six Nations. During a residence of several years on the banks of the Mohawk, he cultivated this friendship with such assiduity, that now, on his being appointed commander of the expedition, he was immediately joined by Hendrick, one of the chiefs of that confederacy, with three hundred picked warriors.

Impatient to commence the campaign, Johnson made all haste in collecting the artillery and military stores, and in the mean time sent the troops forward under General Lyman, the second in command, to the carrying place, about sixty miles above Albany, where he soon after joined them, and began to build a fort on the eastern side of the Hudson, which he called Fort Edward. Leaving a few men to garrison the new fort, he advanced with the main body of his army to the southern extremity of Lake George, where he learned that the enemy were erecting a fort at Ticonderoga, at the other extremity of the lake, and about fifteen miles below Crown Point. He resolved to push forward, hoping by so doing to reduce the new fort before it could be put in a state of defence, but before he advanced he received information which obliged him to stand on the defensive.

This intelligence, which changed the whole character of the campaign, was, that Baron Dieskau, an able commander, had recently arrived in Canada from France, with a large reinforcement, and that, having collected a considerable body of Canadians and Indians, he was now advancing with great speed to attack the English settlements.

Johnson transmitted this intelligence to the colonies, and began with haste to fortify his camp. He could gain no definite idea of the numbers of Dieskau's army, the Indian spies uniformly reporting them as innumerable, by pointing to the stars in the sky, or the hairs of the head. It was impossible from their accounts to discover whether they fell short of a thousand, or exceeded ten thousand in number. Thus, left in doubt, and not knowing the destination of the enemy, Johnson secretly conveyed a few cannon from Fort Edward to his camp, and doubling his spies and scouts awaited the expected attack.

Dieskau at first proceeded towards Oswego, but on learning the advance of Johnson with an inferior army towards Crown Point, hastened to direct his operations against him; and so confident was he of an easy victory, that he made known his intention after the capture of Fort Edward to destroy Albany, ravage the neighbouring settlements, and cut off the English from all communication with Oswego, which would soon be compelled to surrender. His superior strength and skill rendered this result very probable; but victory does not always smile on the strong, and the wisdom of the most experienced may sometimes fail them.

Dieskau's hopes were raised to a high pitch, and his contempt for his English enemy greatly increased by a blunder of Johnson's; who, deceived by the information that the van of the enemy was advancing incautiously, on the sixth of September, sent forward a party of a thousand men under Colonel Williams, together with Hendrick and his Indians, to attack them. Scarcely had this party advanced three miles, when they found themselves almost surrounded by the whole French army. Nothing daunted, they commenced a spirited but hopeless conflict, which resulted in the death of their gallant leader, Colonel Williams; and Hendrick, with many of his followers, was also among the slain. The greater part of the detachment escaped to the camp, closely pursued by the victorious French.

Having heard, a few days before, that Johnson had no artillery at his camp, Dieskau was confident of victory, and consequently, instead of attacking the entrenchments at once, permitted his soldiers to pause at some distance, that they might be regularly formed, and advance with decency and in the true European style, to take possession of the fort.

Johnson, though now convinced of his great inferiority, bu.

having the courage of an Irishman, determined to resist to the last; and uncovering his cannon, effectually disturbed the repose of the enemy, and spread such consternation among the Canadian militia and the Indians, that they fled precipitately to the woods, leaving the ranks of Dieskau in more confusion than when pursuing the retreating foe. The French regulars, however, maintained their position, and opening a brisk fire upon the camp, continued the assault with spirit for several hours. Johnson being severely wounded, reluctantly resigned the command to General Lyman, who carried on the defence with such resolution and spirit that the French were finally obliged to retire with the loss of nearly a thousand men. Dieskau himself was mortally wounded, and made prisoner; and his retreating forces, rallying at some distance, and preparing to refresh themselves with food, were suddenly attacked by a small detachment of militia from New York, when they abandoned their baggage and ammunition, and fled in confusion.

Johnson did not follow up his victory, but spent the time in lingering and irresolute deliberations until October, when a council of war decided that it was inexpedient to attempt any further military operations in that quarter during that year. He built Fort William Henry at the southern extremity of Lake George, and leaving six hundred men to garrison it and Fort Edward, disbanded the remainder of his army. It was thought by many that if he had followed up his victory by an immediate attack on Crown Point, or even on Ticonderoga, he would have succeeded; but he did not choose to hazard his reputation, by exposing himself to the chance of defeat. For his services in this campaign, Johnson received from the king the dignity of a baronet, and from the parliament a grant of five thousand pounds.

Thus did the three main expeditions projected by the council of governors at Alexandria, in the beginning of the year, all signally fail; and at the end of 1755, the French were more firmly planted in their North American possessions than at its commencement. The brilliant engagement at Lake George produced no lasting good, because it was not followed up with alacrity; and the French gained time to strengthen and complete their fortifications. Besides, the fact that they still held all their works, and were hastening forward to construct others, and the great victory gained at the Monongahela, operated powerfully on the minds of the Indians, who began, in great numbers, to flock to their standard.

Encouraged by this seeming willingness of the Indians to join them, the French attempted, by bribes and promises, to allure to their side the powerful nation of Cherokees, who had hitherto been the firmest allies of Great Britain; but the attempt only caused these Indians to enter into a closer alliance with the English colonists; and by a treaty concluded with the governor of South Carolina, they voluntarily ceded to the king of Great Britain a large portion of their territory.

CHAPTER VI.

𝕭𝖔𝖗𝖉𝖊𝖗 𝖂𝖆𝖗.   𝕱𝖆𝖑𝖑 𝖔𝖋 𝕱𝖔𝖗𝖙 𝕯𝖚𝖖𝖚𝖊𝖘𝖓𝖊.

HE defeat of Braddock, and the flight of Dunbar, left the frontier of Virginia exposed to all the horrors of Indian warfare. The Assembly then in session saw the danger to which the colony was exposed, and the necessity of protecting it. For this purpose, they voted forty thousand pounds, and the governor ordered the regiment to be increased to sixteen companies. The courage and good conduct shown by Colonel Washington at the battle of the Monongahela, pointed him out as the only person in the colony who was capable of affording the desired protection, and he was accordingly appointed, on the 14th of August, 1755, commander-in-chief of the Virginia forces. This commission was accompanied by a letter from Governor Dinwiddie, giving him the unusual power of naming his field-officers, and appointing an aide-de-camp and secretary.

This command was cheerfully accepted by Washington, though well aware of the nature of the charge which it imposed upon him. With very few men, nominally one thousand, but seldom exceeding seven hundred, he was expected to defend a frontier of upwards of three hundred miles in extent, against hordes of savages, who were instigated to the most barbarous murders by men calling themselves civilized, Christians, and subjects of his majesty, the king of the French.

Possessing a knowledge of the nature of his duties, Washington felt that there was no time to be lost, and accordingly after appointing as the next officers in rank under him, Lieutenant· Colonel Adam Stephen, and Major Andrew Lewis, and issuing the necessary orders for the recruiting service, he proceeded personally to inspect the condition of the defences on the frontier. He fixed his head-quarters at Winchester, where he arrived on the 14th of September, and then visited and took the command of the principal forts. He found many posts, but few soldiers to garrison. Such as he found, however, he disposed in the most efficient manner, and then started for Williamsburg to arrange a plan of operations with the governor. He passed through Fredericksburg on the 5th of October, but he had not reached Williamsburg when he was overtaken by an express from Colonel Stephen, informing him that a large body of Indians had fallen upon the inhabitants of some of the back settlements, and were murdering and capturing men, women, and children, burning their houses and destroying their crops, and that the few soldiers who were stationed there for their protection had fallen back upon the stockade forts, where they were hourly in expectation of destruction.

Colonel Washington immediately changed his course from Williamsburg to Winchester, where he used every exertion to induce the terrified and flying settlers to unite in the defence of their families and possessions. Too much frightened to care for any thing but the safety of their own families, they took very little thought for the general welfare, and fled in confusion towards the more thickly settled portions of the colony. Such was the consternation and confusion that prevailed, that before a force sufficient to stand before the enemy could be collected, they had recrossed the Alleghany Mountains, and retired with their plunder ·and captives to the protection afforded by the guns of Fort Duquesne.

Colonel Washington well knew that the only security against the repetition of such incursions was the capture of the French fort on the Ohio; but that was an absolute impossibility with the small means which the government of Virginia thought fit to place at his disposal. The governor and council considered it better to act on the defensive; and Washington was ordered to establish a line of small stockade forts along the frontier. This was soon done, and the principal part of the forces under Washington being stationed in them, he, with the remainder, traversed the frontier, for the purpose of preventing or punishing the aggressions of the enemy.

The force at his command was too small to accomplish the intended object, and the enemy with whom he had to deal, too active and cunning to suffer from the forts. If Washington appeared with a force at any one part of his extended line, the enemy knew that the remainder of the line was proportionally weakened, and they would accordingly divide themselves into small parties, and, avoiding the forts, assail solitary farm-houses, by night or by day, and after plundering them and murdering their inmates, set them on fire and retire. The approach of a respectable force was the signal for the incendiaries to disappear. The distress of the inhabitants, caused by these incursions, exceeded all description. If they continued on their farms, they retired to rest every night under the apprehension of being murdered before the morning; if they fled, they abandoned the conveniences of home, and all means of support; and if they took refuge in the stockade forts, they suffered from famine, and were always liable to be cut off and murdered by strong parties. Death, too, was not the greatest of the evils to which they were exposed. Captivity, or torture, by which death was rendered a thousand times more terrible, and yet often welcome, was often their portion. Nor was it the men alone, who were liable to these evils, but the women and children; for the savages and their inhuman allies made little distinction on account of age or sex.

The vigilance and authority of Washington at last succeeded in restoring a little of the confidence of the inhabitants, and in opposing a slight barrier to the incursions of the enemy.

Some of the difficulties with which Colonel Washington was surrounded at this period, exclusive of those naturally to be expected from an active and vigilant enemy, and the smallness of his numbers, compared with the services expected from him, may be gathered from the tenor of his letters to Governor Dinwiddie.

In one dated from Fredericksburg, about two months after he had assumed the command, speaking of the difficulties which met him at the very outset, he says:

"In all things I meet with the greatest opposition.

"No orders are obeyed, but such as a party of soldiers or my own drawn sword enforces. Without this, not a single horse, for the most earnest occasion, can be had, to such a pitch has the insolence of these people arrived, by having every point hitherto submitted to them. However, I have given up none, where his majesty's service requires the contrary, and when my proceedings are justified by my instructions; nor will I, unless they execute what they threaten, that is, 'blow out our brains.'"

In the same letters, complaining of his inadequate authority to enforce military discipline, he says:

"I would again hint the necessity of putting the militia under a better regulation, had I not mentioned it twice before, and a third time may seem impertinent. But I must once more beg leave to declare, for here I am more immediately concerned, that unless the Assembly will pass an act to enforce military law in all its parts, I must, with great regret, decline the honour that has been so generously intended me. I am urged to this, by the foreknowledge I have of failing in every point that might justly be expected from a person invested with full power to execute his authority. I see the growing insolence of the soldiers, and the indolence and inactivity of the officers, who are all sensible how limited their punishments are, compared with what they ought to be. In fine, I can plainly see, that under the present establishment, we shall become a nuisance, an insupportable charge to our country, and never answer any one expectation of the Assembly. And here I must assume the freedom to express some surprise, that we alone should be so tenacious of our liberty as not to invest a power where interest and policy so unanswerably demand it, and whence so much good must consequently ensue. Do we not know that every nation under the sun finds its account therein, and that without it, no order or regularity can be observed? Why then should it be expected from us, who are all young and inexperienced, to govern and keep up a proper spirit of discipline without laws, when the best and most experienced can scarcely do it with them? If we consult our interest, I am sure it loudly calls for them. I can confidently assert, that recruiting, clothing, arming, maintaining and subsisting soldiers who have since deserted, have cost the country an immense sum, which might have been prevented, were we under restraints that would terrify the soldiers from such practices."

Strictly punctilious in yielding deference and obedience to those who by the laws and usages of the army, were entitled to exact it, Washington, as we have already seen, was peculiarly sensitive when any portion of his rights as an officer were invaded. And now, to add to the difficulties by which he was surrounded, the old difficulty between the provincial officers and those holding the king's commissions was revived. A certain Captain Dagworthy, who had received his commission from the king, and had served in the Canada expedition, was now at Fort Cumberland, at the head of thirty volunteers, raised by the colony of Maryland, and acting under the authority of that province. Dagworthy refused to obey the orders of any provincial officer, no matter how high his rank might be. This led to wranglings and the formation of parties among the inferior officers, and Washington complained. The governor of Maryland, wishing to consider Fort Cumberland under his authority, refused to interfere. The governor of Virginia contended, from the fact that the fort had been built by him, under an order from the king, that Maryland had no authority over it, though it was situated within the bounds of that province. He considered it as an absurdity for a captain of thirty men, acting under a commission from the governor of Maryland, to claim precedence of the commander-in-chief of all the Virginia forces. The governor, now beginning to vacillate in his conduct towards Washington, and not wishing to risk his authority in deciding a doubtful question, went no farther. He hinted that Washington might arrest Dagworthy, but evaded giving any positive order on the subject.

The conduct of Dinwiddie only increased the embarrassments of Washington, and he immediately sent a forcible remonstrance to him and the council, informing them that he would not hold his commission, unless this difficulty were removed. In a letter to the governor, dated 5th December, 1755, he says: "I never can submit to the command of Captain Dagworthy, since you have honoured me with the command of the Virginia regiment."

In order to put an end to the difficulty, Governor Dinwiddie wrote to General Shirley, then commander-in-chief of his majesty's forces in North America, soliciting brevet commissions for Colonel Washington and the officers under him. This solicitation was not answered in January, 1756, when Colonel Washington wrote to the governor:—"As I have not yet heard how General Shirley has answered your request, I fear for the success of it, especially as it is next to an impossibility (since Governor Sharpe* has been there to plead Captain Dagworthy's cause) to make the general

* Of Maryland.

acquainted by writing with the nature of the dispute. The officers have drawn up a memorial to be presented to the general, and, that it may be properly strengthened, they humbly beg your solicitation to have us put upon the establishment, as we have certain advices that it is in his power. This would, at once, put an end to the contention, which is the root of evil, and destructive to the best operations; and it would turn all our movements into a free and easy channel.

"They have urged it to me in the warmest manner, to appear personally before the general, for that end. This I would gladly do, even at this disagreeable season, if I had your permission; which I the more freely ask, since I am determined to resign a commission, which you were generously pleased to offer me, and for which I shall always retain a grateful sense, rather than submit to the command of a person, who has not such superlative merit as to balance the inequality of rank. However, he adheres to what he calls his rights, in which I know he is supported by Governor Sharpe. He says, that he has no commission from the province of Maryland, but acts by virtue of that from the king; this was the condition of his engaging in the Maryland service; and that when he was sent up there, the first of last October, he was ordered by Governor Sharpe and Sir John St. Clair not to give up his right. To my certain knowledge his rank was disputed before General Braddock, who gave it in his favour; and he accordingly took place of every captain upon the expedition, except Captain James Mercer and Captain Rutherford, whose commissions were older than his; so that I should not by any means choose to act, as your honour hinted in your last, lest I should be called to an account myself.*

"I have during my stay at Winchester, from the 20th of December to this time, disposed of all the men and officers that are not recruiting, and can be spared from the fort, in the best manner I could for the defence of the inhabitants, and they will need no further orders till I could return. And the recruiting officers are allowed till the first of March to repair to their rendezvous, which leaves at present nothing to do at the fort, but to train and disci pline the men, and prepare and salt the provisions. For the better perfecting both these, I have left full and clear directions.

"Besides, in other respects, I think my going to the northward might be of service, as I should thereby become acquainted with

* This passage relates to the hint cautiously thrown out by Dinwiddie, that Washington might safely arrest Dagworthy.

13   I

the plan of operations, so far as it may be thought proper to be communicated."

The permission thus asked was granted, and Washington commenced a journey of five hundred miles on the 4th of February, 1756. He, accompanied by Captains Mercer and Stewart, travelled to Boston on horseback, passing through the cities of Philadelphia, New York and New London on the route. At New York he was politely received and entertained by Mr. Beverly Robinson, at whose house he became acquainted with Miss Mary Phillips, a sister of Mrs. Robinson, a young lady whose rare accomplishments made a deep impression on his heart. He arrived in Boston towards the end of February, where he was well received by General Shirley, who made him acquainted with the plan of operations lately agreed on by a council of governors assembled at New York. He remained in Boston ten days, when, having accomplished the object of his mission, and obtained from the general his order in writing that Dagworthy should be subject to his command, he set out on his return. It is worthy of remark, that Washington only partially succeeded in the original object for which he set out. Had he succeeded in obtaining for himself and his field-officers a commission from the king of Great Britain, it is impossible to conceive what would have been its effect on the future destinies of the provinces. In returning, he again stopped at New York, as long as he could consistently with his duty, and it was with some reluctance, that, on the near approach of the day of meeting of the Virginia Assembly, he tore himself away; taking care to intrust his secret to a confidential friend who promised to keep him informed of every thing that happened in relation to the lady to whom he had become attached. From this friend he soon learned that his old companion in arms, Captain Morris, had appeared as a rival, and claimed the hand of Miss Phillips, and his correspondent further said that it was impossible to divine the result if he delayed to revisit New York and press his suit. This information found Washington busily engaged in his public duties, and even an affair of the heart was not enough to make him neglect his duty to his country. The lady was soon after married to Captain Morris, and it is supposed that Washington never saw her more. He arrived at Williamsburg on the 23d of March, having been absent but seven weeks.

The Assembly met about the time of his return, and determined on another defensive campaign. They passed an act increasing the army to fifteen hundred men, but it was found impossible, under the laws then in force, to get more than one half of them into service at any one time.

While Washington was at Williamsburg, an express arrived with the intelligence that the enemy had recommenced their predatory incursions, and that they now came with greater assurance, having committed several murders within a short distance of Winchester, and spread great alarm among the inhabitants of that region. He immediately hastened to Winchester, where he found that the French and Indians were so emboldened by the impunity with which they had hitherto carried on their operations, that they hesitated not to attack the small forts in the day-time. In a letter which he wrote to the governor, on the 7th of April, he says:—"However absurd it may appear, it is nevertheless certain, that five hundred Indians have it more in their power to annoy the inhabitants than ten times their number of regulars. Besides the advantageous way they have of fighting in the woods, their cunning and craft, their activity and patient sufferings, are not to be equalled. They prowl about like wolves, and, like them, do their mischief by stealth. They depend upon their dexterity in hunting and upon the cattle of the inhabitants for provisions."

Colonel Washington had always represented to the government of the province that the only way to prevent the incursions of the savages, and effectually to protect their extended frontier, was to capture Fort Duquesne, whence they obtained aid and protection. But the colony had no cannon, and they thought that in their situation it was enough to station the small force under Washington along the frontier, to ward off the blows which they might have prevented. The sufferings to which these errors gave rise were strongly and pathetically represented to the governor in a letter to him from Washington, under the date of Winchester, 22d April, 1756.

"Your honour," he says, "may see to what unhappy straits the distressed inhabitants and myself are reduced. I am too little acquainted, sir, with pathetic language to attempt a description of the people's distresses, though I have a generous soul, sensible of wrongs, and swelling for redress. But what can I do; I see their situation, know their danger, and participate their sufferings, without having it in my power to give them further relief than uncertain promises. In short, I see inevitable destruction in so clear a light, that unless vigorous measures are taken by the Assembly, and speedy assistance sent from below, the poor inhabitants that are now in forts must unavoidably fall, while the remainder are flying before the barbarous foe. In fine, the melan-

choly situation of the people, the little prospect of assistanre, the
gross and scandalous abuses cast upon the officers in general,
which is reflecting upon me in particular, for suffering misconduct
of such extraordinary kinds,* and the distant prospect, if any, of
gaining honour and reputation in the service, cause me to lament
the hour that gave me a commission, and would induce me, at
any other time than this of imminent danger, to resign, without
one hesitating moment, a command from which I never expect to
reap either honour or benefit; but on the contrary, have almost an
absolute certainty of incurring displeasure below, while the murder
of helpless families may be laid to my account here!

"The supplicating tears of the women, and moving petitions of
the men, melt me into such deadly sorrow, that I solemnly declare,
if I know my own mind, I could offer myself a willing sacrifice to
the butchering enemy, provided that would contribute to the
people's ease."

Two days afterwards he again addressed the governor in the
same strain of humanity and sympathy with the distressed people.
"Not an hour," he says, "nay scarcely a minute passes, that does
not produce fresh alarms and melancholy accounts. Nor is it possible to give the people the necessary assistance for their defence,
on account of the small number of men we have, or that are likely
to be here for some time. The inhabitants are removing daily,
and in a short time will leave this country as desolate as Hampshire, where scarce a family lives.

"Three families were murdered the night before last, at the distance of less than twelve miles from this place ; and every day we
have accounts of such cruelties and barbarities as are shocking
to human nature. It is not possible to conceive the situation and
danger of this miserable country. Such numbers of French and
Indians are all around, that no road is safe ; and here we know
not the hour we may be attacked."

But the fullest statement of the disadvantage under which he
laboured, is to be found in his memorial to Lord Loudoun, who
had been appointed commander-in-chief of the North American

---

* This relates to certain false reports which the governor received of the immorality
of the Virginia regiment, their habits of gaming, drinking, swearing, and such reprehensible irregularities. These reports were spread by certain Scotchmen, who from
interested motives poisoned the mind of the governor, and greatly influenced him in
withholding the aid which was so necessary for the army. Washington firmly but
modestly repelled these charges, calling for the names of his accusers. The governor
denied that any accusations were made against him; but the breach, which had for
some time been opening between them, continued to grow wider and wider while
Dinwiddie remained in Virginia.

LOUDOUN.

forces, and which bears date Fort Loudoun, February, 1757. In this communication he strikingly shows the absurdity of expecting him to defend a frontier of three hundred miles with fifteen hundred men. He details the most convincing reasons for adopting aggressive operations, more particularly upon the stronghold of the enemy, Fort Duquesne. He complains loudly of the utter insufficiency and folly of existing military regulations, of the incompetency of the soldiers' pay, and the want of punctuality in remitting it, and of any provision for those who might be wounded or disabled in the service. He depicts the uselessness of the militia, the indifference of the people at large, and finally crowns the catalogue of his complaints with some of a personal kind.

"And now, before I conclude, I must beg leave to add that my unwearied endeavours are inadequately rewarded. The orders I receive are full of ambiguity. I am left, like a wanderer in the wilderness, to proceed at hazard. I am answerable for consequences, and blamed without the privilege of defence.' This, my Lord, I beg leave to declare, is at present my situation. Therefore, it is not to be wondered at, if, under such peculiar circumstances, I should be sick of a service which promises so little of a soldier's reward. I have long been satisfied of the impossibility of continuing in this service, without loss of honour. Indeed, I was fully convinced of it before I accepted the command the second time, seeing the cloudy prospect before me ; and I did, for this reason, reject the offer until I was ashamed any longer to refuse, not caring to expose my character to public censure. The solicitations of the country overcame my objections, and induced me to accept it."

The attention of Lord Loudoun, however, was so much directed to the north, that he could pay but little regard to the affairs of the middle and southern provinces. The result of this state of things was, that until 1758, all the remonstrances of Colonel Washington

were disregarded; and the history of the war during that period
is the history of continual and successful irruptions made by the
French and Indians across the least defended parts of the frontier;
in which they massacred all the inhabitants without regard to age
or sex, burned and destroyed such property as they could not
remove, and returned across the mountains almost with impunity,
loaded with spoil and sated with slaughter.

Towards the close of 1757, Washington, under a severe attack
of dysentery and fever, was reduced so low that he was obliged
to retire to Mount Vernon, and it was not till about the 1st of
April that he was able to resume his command at Fort Loudoun.
In the mean time Governor Dinwiddie returned to England, and
Lord Loudoun was superseded in the supreme command by
Major-general Abercrombie; who, to the inexpressible joy of
Washington, determined to attempt the reduction of Fort Du-
quesne, and while he carried on the operations in the North,
intrusted the defence of the Middle and Southern colonies to
Brigadier-general Forbes.

The forces of Virginia were increased to two regiments of about
eight hundred men each. Besides these, the troops under the
command of General Forbes consisted of twelve hundred Highlanders, three hundred and fifty Royal Americans, about two
thousand seven hundred provincials from Pennsylvania, and two
or three hundred from Maryland; making in all over six thousand
men. Part of this force was at Philadelphia, part at Raystown,
and part dispersed over the frontiers of Virginia. Though Washington urged the necessity of an early campaign, he did not receive
orders to assemble his regiment at Winchester, till the 24th of
May; nor to march to Fort Cumberland, till the 24th of June;
nor to join the main body at Raystown till the 21st of September.
To Washington, who knew the value of time thus lost, these delays
were exceedingly vexatious. As if studiously seeking delay,
General Forbes, instead of marching by Braddock's road, which
was open to within seven or eight miles of the fort, determined
to cut a new road through the wilderness from Raystown. Washington urgently and repeatedly remonstrated against this waste of
precious time and labour, but to no effect. His superiors in
command determined on making the new road, and Washington
quietly submitted. He was put in command of the advanced
division, and was ordered to act in concert with Colonel Bouquet
in opening the new route.

General Forbes arrived at Loyal Hanna on the 5th of November,

OLD BLOCK-HOUSE AT FORT DUQUESNE.

and calling a council of war, it was resolved, on account of the lateness of the season, to abandon the attempt on Duquesne for that campaign. Some prisoners being soon afterwards brought in, gave such an account of the weakness of the garrison, that the resolution was reconsidered, and the general determined to push forward at all hazards. At length, after the greatest labour and difficulty, they reached Fort Duquesne on the 25th of November, which, to their great surprise, they found evacuated, the enemy having set fire to the buildings the preceding evening, and closed the war by retreating down the Ohio in boats. The neighbouring tribes of Indians now deserted their ancient allies and joined the English.

The name of the fort was changed to Fort Pitt, and being repaired, it was garrisoned by two hundred men. Thus Washington had the satisfaction of seeing the object of his wishes and efforts accomplished. His health being seriously impaired by the arduous service he had performed, and his domestic affairs needing his attention, he resigned his commission, and retired again to domestic life at Mount Vernon. Perhaps the clearest view of the character which he left behind him, and of the feelings with which the army suffered the loss of his services, may be obtained from the following address, presented to him by the officers on his resigning the command. Though inferior as a literary composition, it evinces those warm sentiments of admiration and love for Washington which were shared with them by the great majority of his countrymen. The address is as follows: "Sir, we your most obedient and affectionate officers, beg leave to express our great concern, at the disagreeable news we have received of your determination to resign the command of that corps in which we have so long under you served. The happiness we have enjoyed, and the honour we have acquired, together with the mutual regard which has always subsisted between you and your officers, have implanted so sensible an affection in the minds of us all, that we cannot be silent on this critical occasion.

"In our earliest infancy you took us under your tuition, trained us up in the practice of that discipline, which alone can constitute good troops, from the punctual observation of which you never suffered the least deviation.

"Your steady adherence to impartial justice, your quick discernment, and invariable regard to merit, wisely intended to inculcate those genuine sentiments of true honour and passion for glory, from which the greatest military achievements have been derived, first heightened our natural emulation and our desire to excel. How much we improved by those regulations and our own example, with what alacrity we have hitherto discharged our duty, with what cheerfulness we have encountered the severest toil, especially while under your particular directions, we submit to yourself, and flatter ourselves that we have in a great measure answered your expectations.

"Judge, then, how sensibly we must be affected with the loss of such an excellent commander, such a sincere friend and so affable a companion. How rare it is to find those amiable qualifications blended together in one man! How great the loss of such a man! Adieu to that superiority which the enemy have granted us over other troops, and which even the regulars and provincials have done us the honour publicly to acknowledge! Adieu to that strict discipline and order which you have always maintained! Adieu to that happy union and harmony, which have been our principal cement! It gives us additional sorrow, when we reflect, to find our unhappy country will receive a loss no less irreparable than our own. Where will it meet a man so experienced in military affairs—one so renowned for patriotism, conduct, and courage? Who has so great a knowledge of the enemy we have to deal with?—who so well acquainted with their situation and strength?—who so much respected by the soldiery?—who, in short, so able to support the military character of Virginia?

"Your approved love to your king and country, and your uncommon perseverance in promoting the honour and true interest of the service, convince us that the most cogent reasons only could induce you to quit it; yet we, with the greatest deference, presume to entreat you to suspend those thoughts for another year, and to lead us on to assist in the glorious work of extirpating our enemies, towards which so considerable advances have been already made. In you, we place the most implicit confidence. Your presence only will cause a steady firmness and vigor to actuate in every breast, despising the greatest dangers and thinking light of toils and hardships, while led on by the man we know and love.

"But if we must be so unhappy as to part, if the exigencies of your affairs force you to abandon us, we beg it as our last request that you will recommend some person most capable to command, whose military knowledge, whose honour, whose conduct, and whose disinterested principles we may depend upon.

"Frankness, sincerity, and a certain openness of soul, are the true characteristics of an officer, and we flatter ourselves that you do not think us capable of saying any thing contrary to the purest dictates of our minds. Fully persuaded of this, we beg leave to assure you, that, as you have hitherto been the actuating soul of our whole corps, we shall at all times pay the most invariable regard to your will and pleasure, and will always be happy to demonstrate by our actions with how much respect and esteem we are, &c."

Thus had Washington, in his twenty-sixth year, secured for himself the love and esteem of all who knew him. He was the boast of Virginia; and his name was blessed in all her families and settlements as the saviour of her land from pillage, her property from destruction, and her sons and daughters from the bloody war-knife of the savage.

The same high opinion of his character and merits had been adopted by the British officers with whom he had come in contact. "The duties he performed, though not splendid, were arduous; and were executed with zeal, and with judgment. The exact discipline he established in his regiment, when the temper of Virginia was extremely hostile to discipline, does credit to his military character; and the gallantry the troops displayed, whenever called into action, manifests the spirit infused into them by their commander.

"The difficulties of his situation, while unable to cover the fron-

14

tier from the French and Indians who were spreading death and desolation in every quarter, were incalculably great; and no better evidence of his exertions under these distressing circumstances can be given, than the undiminished confidence still placed in him, by those whom he was unable to protect.

"The efforts to which he incessantly stimulated his country for the purpose of obtaining possession of the Ohio; the system for the conduct of the war which he continually recommended; the vigorous and active measures always urged on those by whom he was commanded; manifested an ardent and enterprising mind tempered by judgment, and quickly improved by experience."*

* Marshall.

BRITISH INFANTRY.　TIME OF GEORGE II.

FORT TICONDEROGA.

CHAPTER VII.

Conquest of Canada.

HILE the gigantic efforts and slow movements of the English in Virginia and Pennsylvania were accomplishing the expulsion of five hundred men from the wilderness fortress of Du quesne, the same policy, on a proportionate scale, was pursued against the stronger French posts in Canada. In the council of governors, already mentioned as having been held at New York, in 1756, three expeditions were planned, in which twenty-one thousand men were to be employed against Crown Point, Niagara, and Fort Duquesne. The operations of Generals Abercrombie and Loudoun, who arrived successively as commanders-in-chief, were retarded by their own want of energy, and disputes with the provincial officers concerning rank. While the British were deliberating on the best mode of opening the campaign, the Marquis de Montcalm, an officer of high spirit, who and succeeded Baron Dieskau in the chief command of the French forces in Canada, suddenly disconcerted all their plans by commencing offensive operations.

He made a rapid march at the head of five thousand men to Lake Ontario, and invested one of the forts occupied by the British at Oswego. He began the siege on the 10th of August. The scanty supply of ammunition possessed by the besieged was soon exhausted, when Colonel Mercer, the commandant, spiked his guns, and carried his troops without the loss of a man to the other fort. Montcalm immediately opened a heavy fire upon the remaining fort, and the brave Mercer having been killed by a cannon-ball, the garrison, dismayed by his loss, demanded a capitulation, and surrendered themselves, to the number of fourteen hundred, prisoners of war. By the surrender of the fort at Oswego, the French obtained possession of one hundred and twenty-one cannon, fourteen mortars, a great quantity of military stores and provisions, as well as several sloops and boats.

In consequence of this disastrous event, the British abandoned all their plans of offensive operations, and confined their attention to the strengthening of the posts which still remained to them on the Northern and Western frontiers. In 1757, Montcalm, always watchful and active, took advantage of a blunder made by Lord Loudoun. That nobleman withdrew his main army to Halifax, with the intention of attempting the reduction of Louisburg. No sooner was this movement known to the French general than he marched with nine thousand men, and in the beginning of August laid siege to Fort William Henry, which was garrisoned by three thousand men under Colonel Monroe. Montcalm pressed the siege with such vigour and skill, that he compelled the garrison to surrender on capitulation in six days. The defenders stipulated that they should be allowed to march out of the fort with the honours of war, and be escorted to Fort Edward by French troops, as a security against the savages. These terms, however, were violated by the Indians; for no sooner had the British laid down their arms, than they began to strip them of their clothing, killing and scalping whoever made the slightest resistance. Scarcely one half of the garrison of Fort William Henry reached Fort Edward, and they arrived in small squads and in the most miserable condition. The neglect of Montcalm, on this dreadful occasion, kindled through the colonies a deep thirst for vengeance; and such was the number of determined volunteers that began to arm in the New England colonies, and pour into Fort Edward, and the exposed strongholds in the neighbourhood,

AMHERST.

that the French thought it inexpedient to pursue their victory farther during that year.

This massacre, manifesting the insensibility of the French to the barbarous conduct of their Indian allies, may be considered as the pivot on which the fortunes of the war turned. Hitherto, it had been an almost uninterrupted series of disasters and disgrace to the British arms. In Europe similar results followed the feeble measures of the cabinet. But the spirit of the nation being now aroused, forced into power William Pitt, afterwards Earl of Chatham, the most able and accomplished statesman that Britain had yet produced. Disapproving military operations on the continent of Europe, he turned his main attention to the North American colonies, and by vigorously announcing his resolution of speedily bringing the war to a successful termination, drew from them the most powerful aid. Lord Loudoun was recalled, and superseded by General Amherst, a more able commander; while a subordinate command was assigned to General Wolfe, a young officer in whom the discerning eye of Pitt discovered a rising military genius.

In the campaign of 1758, three expeditions were again determined on; the first against Louisburg, under the command of Generals Amherst and Wolfe, aided by the fleet under Admiral Boscawen; the second against Ticonderoga and Crown Point, under the command of General Abercrombie; and the third against Fort Duquesne, under General Forbes.

We have already witnessed the success of the last of these, in which Washington was personally engaged.

General Abercrombie, at the head of sixteen thousand men, marched towards Ticonderoga. On the road he fell in with a detachment of the enemy, who attacked Abercrombie, and by their first fire killed Lord Howe, a young officer of high promise, and much beloved in America. The superior numbers of the British, however, bore down all opposition, and defeating their

K

opponents, they proceeded onward to Ticonderoga. The British commander, hearing that the French were inconsiderable in number, but that they were daily expecting large reinforcements, made a premature attack on the fort and was repulsed with considerable loss, when, notwithstanding the remonstrances of his officers, he raised the siege and precipitately retreated. Colonel Bradstreet, a provincial officer distinguished for his valour, intelligence, and activity, unwilling to participate in the disgrace of his commander, solicited his permission with a few men, to make an attempt on Fort Frontignac, a post of some consequence on Lake Ontario. Bradstreet succeeded in his enterprise. He laid siege to the fort on the 25th of August, and compelled the garrison to surrender at discretion on the 27th. He destroyed the fort, and nine armed vessels lying in the harbour, and such of the stores as he could not carry away.

The formidable expedition against Louisburg, succeeded chiefly through the exertions of the gallant Wolfe, and it was surrendered to the fleet and army of Great Britain towards the end of July.

Uninterrupted success henceforward attended the British arms during the remainder of the French war. In 1759, General Amherst marched against Ticonderoga and Crown Point, which were evacuated on his approach.

General Prideaux, meantime, with a strong detachment advanced and laid siege to Fort Niagara. He was accidentally killed by the bursting of a cohorn ; but Sir William Johnson, his successor, pushing operations with increased vigour, completely defeated a large force which had been collected against him, added new laurels to those already won by him, and finally obliged the garrison to surrender. He conveyed them in safety as prisoners of war to New York.

But the most brilliant action of the whole war was the capture of Quebec by General Wolfe. He embarked at Louisburg with an army of eight thousand men, and, towards the end of June, landed on the Isle of Orleans, and immediately commenced opera tions against the city. Quebec was principally built on a steep rock on the northern bank of the St. Lawrence, while the river St. Charles, which flowed past it on the east, and united with the St. Lawrence immediately below the town, defended it on that side, and gave it the security of a peninsular locality. There was a boom thrown across the mouth of the St. Charles, immediately within which the French fleet was moored. A formidable French army, commanded by the experienced Montcalm, was strongly intrenched on the eastern side of this river, their encampment extending along the shore to the falls of the Montmorency, while their rear was defended by an impenetrable forest. With a force far inferior in numbers to the enemy, Wolfe laid vigorous siege to the place, secure of the means of retreat while the British fleet remained in the river.

Perceiving that he could effect but little at the Isle of Orleans, General Wolfe, after a successful skirmish, took posession of Point Levi, on the opposite side of the St. Lawrence, and there erected batteries to annoy the town. This position was, however, at too great a distance to make any useful impression on the enemy's works, and feeling that the season for active operations was fast flying, and his own bodily strength diminishing, he determined to make use of every expedient to entice Montcalm from his defences. He accordingly planned an attack upon a redoubt at the mouth of the Montmorency; but the garrison, instead of offering resistance, retreated towards the encampment, while the French opening a tremendous fire upon his forces, he thought it best to retreat, with the loss of nearly five hundred men killed or wounded.

Finding it impossible to approach the city on its eastern side, Wolfe now turned his eyes to the apparently inaccessible cliffs above, and which, on account of the difficulty of ascending them, were but feebly defended. He assembled a council of his principal officers, and it was resolved to make an attempt to gain the heights of Abraham, a lofty plain just above Quebec. "It was proposed to land the troops by night, at the foot of the rocks, a small distance above the city, and to climb to the summit before daybreak. This attempt manifestly involved extreme difficulty and hazard. The stream was rapid, the shore shelving, the bank of the river lined with French sentinels, the landing-place so narrow as easily to be missed in the dark, and the cliff which must afterwards be surmounted so steep that it was difficult to ascend it even in open day and without opposition. Should the design be promulgated by a spy or deserter, or suspected by the enemy; should the disembarkation be disordered, through the darkness of the night or the obstructions of the shore ; the landing-place be mistaken, or but one sentinel alarmed,—the Heights of Abraham would instantly be covered with such numbers of troops as would render the attempt abortive and defeat inevitable. Though these circumstances of danger could not escape the penetration of Wolfe, yet he hesitated not a moment to embrace a project so congenial to his ardent and enterprising disposition, as well as to

GENERAL TOWNSHEND.

the hazardous and embarrassing predicament in which he was placed, and from which only some brilliant and soaring effort could extricate him to his own and his country's satisfaction. He reposed a gallant confidence in the very magnitude and peril of his attempt, and fortune extended her proverbial favour to the brave. His active powers revived with the near prospect of decisive action; he soon recovered his health, so far as to be able to conduct the enterprise on which he was resolved to stake his fame; and in the execution of it, displayed a force of judgment, and a deliberate valour and intrepidity that rivalled and vindicated the heroism of its conception.*

On the night of the 12th of September, the attempt to land was successfully made, and by daybreak, on the 13th, the whole army was arrayed on the summit of the Heights of Abraham. Montcalm, though astonished at the temerity and boldness of the British, instantly quitted his encampment, crossed the St. Charles, and the two armies were drawn up in battle array opposite to each other. About nine o'clock in the morning, the action was commenced, by the French advancing vigorously to the charge, and in a few moments the conflict became general along the whole line. Wolfe having been wounded in the wrist and in the groin, continued to lead on his troops without manifesting any signs of pain, until a third bullet pierced his breast, and he fell mortally wounded. General Monckton, who succeeded to the command, was soon obliged by a dangerous wound to resign the command to General Townshend. Montcalm was about the same time mortally wounded, and the second in command, General Senezergus, also fell. The loss of their general only incited the English to fresh acts of the most daring heroism, while the death of Montcalm seemed to produce a contrary effect upon the French; who soon began to retreat on all sides. A thousand of the enemy were killed in the

* Grahame's Colonial History.

battle and pursuit, and about the same number captured; the remainder of the army fled, some to Quebec, and others to Trois Rivières and Montreal. The English lost, in killed and wounded, less than six hundred men.

On the 17th of September, five days after the battle, the city of Quebec, the capital of New France, was surrendered to the English, and garrisoned by five thousand men under General Murray.

Quebec was in great danger of being retaken during the winter, but was saved by the good conduct of General Murray. In the summer of 1760, he concerted with General Amherst a combined attack upon Montreal, which was still held for France, by the Marquis de Vandreuil. The march of the two armies was planned with such precision that they both, by different routes, arrived before Montreal on the same day. The French general, perceiving from the skilful movements and superior numbers of the British armies that resistance would be ineffectual, demanded a capitulation, and on the 8th of September, 1760, he surrendered Montreal and all Canada to the British; which was finally secured to them by the treaty of Paris, concluded February 10, 1763. Thus ended the colonial empire of France in North America; for though she still possessed the infant colony of Louisiana and the growing town of New Orleans, yet this settlement was so thinly peopled, and possessed such meagre resources, that had it not been for the supplies of provisions which it received from the British colonies, it could scarcely have maintained itself for a year.

K 2

PARISH CHURCH OF WASHINGTON AT ALEXANDRIA.

CHAPTER VIII.

Marriage of Washington.

HE marriage of Washington took place in 1759. It was in the month of May, 1758, that he undertook a journey from Fort Loudoun to Williamsburg, in the course of which he first became acquainted with Mrs. Custis, his future wife. The Virginia regiment being in want of many of the necessary munitions of war, and the Assembly not seeming to heed the representations of the commanding officers, Sir John St. Clair, the quarter-master of the army under General Forbes, thought it expedient to despatch Colonel Washington, to represent to the president of the council, then acting as governor, the posture of affairs at Winchester, and to obviate, by personal explanation, any doubts that might arise from the best written narrative; with instructions to urge upon the council and Assembly the necessity of putting the Virginia troops in a fit condition to proceed and aid in the capture of Fort Duquesne. Washington's first interview with Mrs. Custis, as well as her character during the remainder of her life, is thus truly and beautifully described by Mrs. Sigourney :—

It was in the spring of 1758, that two gentlemen, attended by a servant, were seen riding through the luxuriant scenery with which the county of New Kent, in Virginia, abounds. The most striking figure of the group was tall, graceful, and commanding, in a rich military undress, and apparently twenty-five or twenty-six years of age. He would have been held a model for the statuary when Rome was in her best days. His companion was an elderly man, in a plain garb, who, by the familiarity with which he pointed out surrounding objects, would seem to be taking his daily round upon his own estate. As they approached the avenue to an antique mansion, he placed his hand upon the rein of his companion :

"Nay, Colonel Washington, let it never be said that you passed the house of your father's friend without dismounting. I must insist on the honour of detaining you as my guest."

"Thanks to you, my dear sir, but I ride in haste, the bearer of despatches to our governor in Williamsburg, which may not brook delay."

"Is this the noble steed which was given you by the dying Braddock, on the fatal field of the Monongahela? and this the servant which he bequeathed you at the same time?"

Washington answered in the affirmative.

"Then, my dear colonel, thus mounted and attended, you may well dine with me, and by borrowing somewhat of this fine moonlight, reach Williamsburg ere his excellency shall have shaken off his morning slumbers."

"Do I understand that I may be excused immediately after dinner?"

"Immediately, with all the promptness of military discipline."

"Then, sir, I accept your hospitality;" and gracefully throwing himself from his spirited charger, he resigned the reins to his English servant, giving, at the same time, strict orders as to the hour when he must be ready with the horses to pursue their journey.

"I am rejoiced, Colonel Washington," said the hospitable old gentleman, "thus fortunately to have met you on my morning ride; and the more so, as I have some guests who will make the repast pass pleasantly, and will not fail to appreciate our young and valiant soldier."

Washington bowed his thanks, and was introduced to the company. Virginia's far-famed hospitality was well set forth in that spacious baronial hall. Precise in his household regulations, the social feast was closed at the time the host had predicted. The servant also was punctual. He knew the habits of his master. At the appointed moment, he stood with the horses caparisoned at the gate. Long did the proud steed champ his bit, and curve his arching neck, and paw the broken turf. And much did the menial marvel, as, listening to every footstep that paced down the avenue, he saw the sun sink in the west, and yet no master appear. When was he ever before known to fail in an appointment? The evening air breathed cool and damp, and soothed the impatience of the chafing courser. At length, orders came that the horses should be put up for the night. Wonder upon wonder! when his business with the governor was so urgent! The sun rode high in the heavens the next day, ere Washington mounted for his journey. No explanation was given. But it was rumoured, that among the guests was a beautiful and youthful widow, to whose charms his heart had responded. This was further confirmed, by his tarrying but a brief space at Williamsburg, and retracing his route with unusual celerity, and becoming a frequent visiter at the house of the late Colonel Custis, in that vicinity, where, the following year, (January 6, 1759,) his nuptials were celebrated. "And rare and high," says G. W. P. Custis, Esq., the descendant and biographer of the lady, "rare and high was the revelry, at that palmy period of Virginia's festal age; for many were gathered to that marriage, of the good, the great, the gifted, and the gay; while Virginia, with joyful acclamation, hailed in the prosperous and happy bridegroom her favourite hero."

Henceforth, the life of the lady of Mount Vernon is a part of the history of her country. In that hallowed retreat, she was found entering into the plans of Washington, sharing his confidence, and making his household happy. There, her only daughter, Martha Custis, died in the bloom of youth; and a few years after, when the troubles of the country drew her husband to the post of commander-in-chief of her armies, she accompanied him to Boston, and witnessed its siege and evacuation. For eight years he returned no more to enjoy his beloved residence on the banks of the Potomac. During his absence she made the most strenuous efforts to discharge the added weight of care, and to endure, with changeless trust in Heaven, continual anxiety for the safety of one so inexpressibly dear. At the close of each campaign, she repaired, in compliance with his wishes, to head-quarters, where the ladies of the general officers joined her in forming such a society, as diffused a cheering influence over even the gloom of the winter at Valley-Forge and Morristown. The opening of every campaign was the signal of the return of Lady Washington (as she was called in the army) to her domestic cares at Mount Vernon. "I heard," said she, "the *first* and the *last* cannon of the revolutionary war." The rejoicings which attended the surrender of Cornwallis, in the autumn of 1781, marked for her a season of the deepest private sorrow. Her only remaining child, Colonel John Custis, the aide-de-camp of Washington, became, during his arduous duties at the siege of Yorktown, the victim of an epidemic fever, and died at the age of twenty-seven. He was but a boy of five years, at the time of her second marriage, and had drawn forth strongly the affection and regard of her illustrious husband, who shared her affliction for his loss, and by the tenderest sympathy strove to alleviate it.

After the close of the war, a few years were devoted to the enjoyment and embellishments of their favourite Mount Vernon. The peace and returning prosperity of their country gave pure and bright ingredients to their cup of happiness. Their mansion was thronged with guests of distinction, all of whom remarked, with admiration, the energy of Mrs. Washington, in the complicated duties of a Virginia housewife, and the elegance and grace with which she presided at her noble board.

The voice of a free nation, conferring on General Washington the highest honour in its power to bestow, was not obeyed without a sacrifice of feeling. It was in the spring of 1789, that, with his lady, he bade adieu to his tranquil abode, to assume the responsibilities of the first presidency. In forming his domestic establishment, he mingled the simplicity of a republic with that degree of dignity, which he felt was necessary to secure the respect of older governments. The furniture of his house, the livery of his servants, the entertainment of his guests, displayed elegance, while they rejected ostentation. In all these arrangements, Mrs. Washington was as a second self. Her Friday evening levees, at which he was always present, exhibited that perfect etiquette which marks the intercourse of the dignified and high-bred Commencing at seven, and closing at ten, they lent no more sanction to late hours than to levity. The first lady of the nation still preserved the habits of early life. Indulging in no indolence, she left her pillow at dawn, and, after breakfast, retired to her chamber an hour, for the study of the Scriptures and devotion. This practice, it is said, during the long period of half a century, she never omitted. The duties of the Sabbath were dear to her. The President and herself attended public worship with regularity, and in the evening he read to her, in her chamber, the Scriptures, and a sermon."

Receiving with his wife an addition to his fortune of more than a hundred thousand dollars, it became necessary for Washington to devote a considerable portion of his time to the care and management of his estate. Accordingly, in April, 1759, he retired with Mrs. Washington to Mount Vernon; having spent the three months intervening from the time of his marriage, in arranging the affairs of his wife's estate, and in attending the session of the House of Burgesses, which was convened in February. For, during the last campaign, while advancing upon Fort Duquesne, he was chosen by the people of Frederic County to represent them in the Assembly.

When he first took his seat in the house, an incident occurred, of sufficient interest to require a notice in this place. The House of Burgesses resolved to return their thanks to him in a public manner for the services he had rendered his country, and this duty devolved on his friend, Mr. Robinson, the speaker of the House. As soon as Colonel Washington had taken his seat, the speaker discharged the duty imposed upon him with all the warmth of panegyric which personal regard and a full appreciation of his merits could dictate. This unwonted and unexpected honour completely robbed the young warrior of his self-possession. He rose to express his acknowledgment, but such was his trepidation and confusion that he could not give distinct utterance to a syllable. For a moment he blushed, stammered, and trembled, when the speaker relieved him with a stroke of address that would have done honour to Louis the Fourteenth in his proudest and happiest moments : "Sit down, Mr. Washington," said he with a conciliating smile, " your modesty is equal to your valour, and that surpasses the power of any language that I possess."*

From this period until he was called upon to take part in the revolution, a period of fifteen years, Washington was constantly a member of the Virginia House of Burgesses, being returned at every election, with large majorities over every opponent. During the first half of this period he represented the county of Frederic

* Wirt's Life of Patrick Henry.

in conjunction with another gentleman, and during the remainder of the time, the county of Fairfax in which he resided.

In the House of Burgesses, Washington was by no means distinguished for his eloquence. He " had none of those brilliant and extraordinary qualities which strike at once upon the human imagination. He was not one of those ardent spirits, eager to explode, driven onwards by the energy of their thoughts or of their passions, and scattering about them the exuberance of their own natures, before either opportunity or necessity has called forth the exercise of their powers. Unacquainted with aught of inward agitation, untormented by the promptings of splendid ambition, Washington anticipated none of the occurrences of his life, and aspired not to win the admiration of mankind. His firm intellect and his high heart were profoundly modest and calm. Capable of rising to the level of the highest greatness, he could, without a pang, have remained ignorant of his own powers, and he would have found in the cultivation of his estate enough to satisfy those vast faculties which were equal to the command of armies and the foundation of a government. But when the opportunity occurred, when the need was, without an effort on his part, and without surprise on that of others, or rather, as has just been shown, in conformity with their expectations, the wise planter shone forth a great man. He had, to a very high degree, the two qualities which, in active life, fit men for great achievements ; he trusted firmly in his own thoughts, and dared resolutely to act upon them, without fear of responsibility."*

The interest with which his remarks were always listened to, arose out of the importance of the subjects which elicited them, the manifest soundness of his views, and the unbiassed directness of his political course. Even at this early period of life, the sobriety of his judgment anticipated the claims of advanced age ; and though he rarely generated enthusiasm in his hearers, yet he almost invariably convinced their minds and obtained their concurrence. He evidently acted in his own person, upon the advice which he subsequently gave to his nephew on his first appearance in the Assembly. " If you have a mind to secure the attention of the House," he said, "speak seldom but on important subjects, except such as particularly relate to your constituents ; and in the former case, make yourself completely master of the subject. Never exceed a decent warmth, and submit your sentiments with

* Guizot.

diffidence. A dictatorial style, though it may carry conviction, is always accompanied with disgust.''*

On his estate at Mount Vernon, Washington engaged extensively in the business of agriculture, and is said to have been remarkable for the judgment he displayed in the improvement of his lands. On his farm he displayed the same general features of character, by which he was distinguished, when he led the army and fought the battles of his country. The fixedness and tenacity of purpose which we have seen marking his military operations, now re-appeared in the systematic energy with which he reduced to order those complicated interests which had long been endangered by irregularity and neglect; while the same imperturbable sobriety of judgment which had contributed equally with his martial valour to the preservation of his country, was again exhibited in the prudential care of minor interests, and in unvarying seemliness of deportment. Every branch of business was conducted upon system. Exact method and economy were carried into every department of his domestic concerns. He personally inspected the account of his overseers every week; the divisions of his farms were numbered, and the expense of cultivation, and the produce of each lot, were exactly registered; so that at one view he could determine the profit or loss of any particular crop, and ascertain the comparative advantage of various modes of husbandry. He became one of the largest landholders in North America. Besides other tracts of great extent and value, his Mount Vernon estate consisted of nine thousand acres, whic were entirely under his own management; and from it alone, he in one year raised seven thousand bushels of wheat, and ten thousand of Indian corn. His establishments, agricultural and domestic, consisted of no fewer than a thousand persons; and though the greater part of his farming implements were obtained from London, the linen and woollen cloth required in his business were chiefly manufactured on the estate.

It was during this period of Washington's life that he officiated as judge of the county court. He was also elected a vestryman in Truro parish, and there, as in the House of Burgesses, exercised his powers, and spent his time in seeking the good of his constituents, his fellow-parishioners. On one occasion, about the year 1765, he gained a triumph of some moment, which has often been cited by the venerable Mr. Massey, then the clergyman of the parish, as an instance of characteristic address. "The dilapida-

* Sparks.

tion of the old church rendering it expedient either to repair or rebuild, the subject was agitated in the vestry, of which Colonel Washington was a member. It having been determined after due consideration, that a new church should be built, the question of location next presented itself. George Mason, a prominent member of the vestry, was in favour of the old situation, in the neighbourhood of which he had his residence. Others maintained that its site was not sufficiently central. George Mason supposed the place, if not perfectly central, yet not seriously inconvenient of access to any; and especially thought that the sacred associations which belonged to it, as the place of worship for several generations, and as hallowed by the sepulchres of their fathers, should induce a preference for the spot. Colonel Washington differed with George Mason, 'objecting to the distance and the inconvenience to which his plan would subject the parishioners. He, moreover, could not see the force of the consideration derived from the contiguity of the grave-yard. He thought churches were erected for the living, and not for the dead. Nor was it necessary that any desecration of the place should occur. The ashes of the dead could be preserved inviolably secure by a proper enclosure.' The vestry, however, adjourned, without coming to any settled conclusion, another meeting being appointed with a view to a final decision.

"In the mean time Colonel Washington occupied himself in surveying the parish, ascertaining its limits, and the relative position of the old church. Having done this, and prepared a draught of the survey with his usual accuracy and neatness, he awaited the meeting of the vestry. On that occasion, George Mason again urged, and with increased vehemence, the claims of the old situation. Having done so, Colonel Washington repeated his former objections, and dwelt upon the remoteness of the place, took from his pocket the plan which he had prepared, in which the old church was found to be in an extreme corner of the parish. This ocular demonstration soon settled the matter, and brought about a decision against the old and in favour of the new location, which would bring the church in the centre of the parish.

"Here it was, at the new or Pohick Church, that Washington habitually attended, from the period of its erection, till the commencement of the Revolutionary War. Here he offered his adorations to the God and Father of all, and here received the symbols of a Saviour's love at the hands of the consecrated servant of the altar.

16   L

"The Rev. Lee Massey was the rector of the parish here referred to. He was a highly respectable man, and shared much of the esteem of Washington. In regard to the religious deportment of his distinguished friend, especially in the house of God, he has often been heard to express himself in the following strain: 'I never knew so constant an attendant on church as Washington. And his behaviour in the house of God was ever so deeply reverential, that it produced the happiest effects on my congregation; and greatly assisted me in my pulpit labours. No company ever withheld him from church. I have often been at Mount Vernon, on the Sabbath morning when his breakfast table was filled with guests; but to him they furnished no pretext for neglecting his God, and losing the satisfaction of setting a good example. For instead of staying at home, out of false complaisance to them, he used constantly to invite them to accompany him.' "

* McGuire.

GEORGE GRENVILLE.

CHAPTER IX.

Opening of the Revolution.

NALTERABLY mindful as he was of his religious, domestic, and parish duties, Washington still continued to watch with a jealous eye the progress of public events, especially as occurring in the intercourse of the colonies with the mother country. The French war having occasioned a heavy increase of expense to the British government, the ministers began to look for remuneration to the American colonies, for whose immediate benefit the increased expense had been incurred. Resolutions had previously passed the British parliament, declaring the expediency of laying a stamp duty in America; but, before 1765, they had not been followed by any legislative act. The mere declaration, however, of a right denied by the colonists, of imposing on

them a tax without their consent, was sufficient to call from them innumerable remonstrances, and strong constitutional objections were urged to the passage of such an act by statesmen of both England and America.

Notwithstanding the remonstrances and the powerful reasons offered against this unjust and hazardous experiment, in March, 1765, George Grenville, the first commissioner of the Treasury, introduced a bill into the House of Commons for imposing a stamp duty on the American colonies. By this act, the instruments of writing in daily use among a commercial people were to be null and void, unless executed upon parchment or paper stamped with a specific duty. Law documents and leases, articles of apprenticeship and contracts, protests and bills of sale, newspapers and advertisements, almanacs and pamphlets, all must contribute to the British treasury. The unjust and oppressive nature of this bill raised up for it opponents, even in the British parliament. Its passage was eloquently opposed by Colonel Barré, an officer who had served with the British army in America, and who was distinguished in the House of Commons, as one of the firmest and strongest supporters of civil liberty. The celebrated Charles Townshend, who afterwards succeeded to Grenville's office, replied in support of the bill, and after severely reprobating the attacks made upon it by Colonel Barré, concluded by indignantly demanding: " And now, will these Americans—children planted by our care, nourished by our indulgence till they are grown up to a degree of strength and opulence, and protected by our arms— will they grudge to contribute their mite to relieve us from the heavy weight of that burden which we lie under ?"

To this invidious appeal to the pride and prejudices of the members of the House of Commons, Colonel Barré, after repelling the censure personally addressed to him, thus energetically replied to the conclusion of his opponent's remarks:

" *They planted by your care!* No, your oppressions planted them in America. They fled from your tyranny to a then uncultivated and inhospitable country, where they exposed themselves to almost all the hardships to which human nature is liable ; and among others to the cruelties of a savage foe, the most subtle, and, I will take upon me to say, the most formidable of any people upon the face of God's earth; and yet, actuated by the principles of true English liberty, they preferred all hardships to those which they had endured in their own country from the hands of men who should have been their friends. *They nourished by your indulgence!* They grew by your neglect of them. As soon as you began to care about them, that care was exercised in sending persons to rule them in one department or another, who were, perhaps, the deputies of deputies to some members of this house, sent to spy out their liberties, to misrepresent their actions, and to prey upon them,—men, whose behaviour, on many occasions, has caused the blood of those sons of liberty to recoil within them,—men, promoted to the highest seats of justice, some of whom to my knowledge were glad, by going to a foreign country, to escape being brought to the bar of a court of justice in their own. *They protected by your arms!* They have nobly taken up arms in your defence; and have exerted a shining valour, amidst their constant and laborious industry, for the defence of a country whose frontier was drenched in blood, while its interior parts yielded all their little savings to your emoluments. And believe me,—remember, I this day told you so, that the same spirit of freedom which actuated that people at first will accompany them still; but prudence forbids me to explain myself farther. God knows I do not at this time speak from motives of party spirit; what I deliver are the genuine sentiments of my heart. However superior to me in general knowledge and experience the respectable body of this house may be, yet I claim to know more of America than most of you; having seen and been conversant with that country. The people, I believe, are as truly loyal as any subjects the king has,—but they are a people jealous of their liberties, and will vindicate them, if ever they should be violated. But the subject is too delicate, I will say no more."

Though the act was further opposed by General Conway, Alderman Beckford, and a few others, it passed the Commons by a majority of two hundred and fifty to fifty. In the House of Lords it met with no opposition; and on the 22d of March received the royal assent, though it was not to take effect until the first of November following. The night after the bill passed, Dr. Franklin, then in London, wrote to Mr. Charles Thomson: "The sun of liberty is set; you must light up the candles of industry and economy." Mr. Thomson replied: "I was apprehensive that other lights would be the consequence, and I foresee the opposition that will be made."

The intelligence of the passage of the Stamp Act was received in America with feelings of stupified amazement. Had its authority and operation come close upon the announcement, it is impossible to imagine what wonder and terror might have done.

Happily for liberty, there was time given for its consideration and discussion. The Assembly of Virginia was in session when the heavy tidings arrived. On the 28th of May, Patrick Henry introduced into that body a series of resolutions, which, after some opposition, was finally passed. The tenor of these resolutions may be gathered from two of them, which were as follows :—"Resolved, that his majesty's most liege people of this his most ancient colony, have enjoyed the right of being thus governed by their own Assembly in the article of taxes and internal police, and that the same have never been forfeited, nor in any other way yielded up, but have been constantly recognised by the king and people of Great Britain.

"Resolved, therefore, that the General Assembly of this colony, together with his majesty, or his substitute, have, in their representative capacity, the only exclusive right and power to lay taxes and impositions upon the inhabitants of this colony; and that every attempt to vest such a power in any person or persons whatsoever, other than the General Assembly aforesaid, is illegal, unconstitutional, and unjust, and bears a manifest tendency to destroy British as well as American freedom."

The opponents of Henry's resolutions loaded him with abuse, and so galled him with menaces, that, at one stage of the discussion, he was provoked to a tone of defiance, and his words, memorable as they are in themselves, were made immortal by the remarkable scene produced by them. "Cæsar," he exclaimed, "had his Brutus, Charles the First his Cromwell, and George the Third," here he was interrupted by the cry of *Treason*, repeated by the Speaker, and echoed from every part of the House; but, drowning the startling cry with his commanding voice, he continued, "George the Third, I say, *may profit by their example!* If this be treason, make the most of it."

Washington was a member of the Assembly which passed these resolutions, and though his name does not appear on the minutes, yet that he was arrayed on the side of liberty may be safely and surely inferred from his letter to his wife's uncle in London, written a short time afterwards.

"At present," he says, "there are few things among us that can be interesting to you. The Stamp Act imposed on the colonies by the parliament of Great Britain, engrosses the conversation of the speculative part of the colonists, who look upon this unconstitutional method of taxation as a direful attack upon their liberties, and loudly exclaim against the violation. What may be the result

of this, and of some other (I think I may add ill-judged) measures, I will not undertake to determine; but this I may venture
to affirm, that the advantage accruing to the mother country will
fall greatly short of the expectations of the ministry; for certain it
is, that our whole substance already in a manner flows to Great
Britain, and that whatsoever contributes to lessen our importations
must be hurtful to her manufacturers. The eyes of our people
already begin to be opened; and they will perceive, that many
luxuries, for which we lavish our substance in Great Britain, can
well be dispensed with, whilst the necessaries of life are mostly to
be had within ourselves. This, consequently, will introduce frugality, and be a necessary incitement to industry. If Great Britain, therefore, loads her manufactures with heavy taxes, will it
not facilitate such results? They will not compel us to give our
money for their exports, whether we will or not; and I am certain that none of their traders will part with them without a valuable consideration. Where, then, is the utility of these restric-
tions?

"As to the Stamp Act, regarded in a single view, one and the
first bad consequence attending it is, that our courts of judicature
must inevitably be shut up; for it is impossible, or next to impossible, under our present circumstances, that the act of parliament
can be complied with, were we ever so willing to enforce its execution. And, not to say (which alone would be sufficient) that
we have not money to pay for the stamps, there are many other
cogent reasons which prove that it would be ineffectual. If a stop
be put to our judicial proceedings, I fancy the merchants of Great
Britain, trading to the colonies, will not be among the last to wish
for a repeal of the act."

When the governor became acquainted with the work upon
which the Assembly was engaged, it was dissolved, and writs for
new elections were issued; but so entirely did the people take
part with the opposition to the scheme of taxation proposed by the
British ministry, that, in almost every instance, those members
who had voted in favour of the above resolutions were re-elected,
while those who had voted against them were generally excluded
in favour of candidates who favoured the popular opinions.

Similar sentiments flew like lightning through the other colonies, but the representatives of Massachusetts originated a still
more momentous innovation, by recommending a congress of
deputies to meet at New York, in order to consult upon the position in which the colonies at large were placed. Nine colonies

responded to this call; Virginia, North Carolina, and Georgia, being prevented by the difficulty of convoking their assemblies, when opposed by the governors. New Hampshire was not represented, from some unknown cause. This convention adopted a series of fourteen resolutions, in which they denounced the injustice and ruinous consequences of their being taxed without being represented: a privilege, which, from their distance, it was impossible to enjoy. They prepared an address to the throne, and petitions to both houses of parliament, in which this sentiment was forcibly expressed, while they declared that their connection with the empire formed their greatest happiness and security.

The people of the colonies, in the mean time, everywhere formed combinations against the execution of the Stamp Act. It was resolved to dispense with stamps upon the various instruments, to the validity of which they had previously been considered necessary, to abandon litigation for the settlement of disputes, as well as to abandon, as far as possible, the importation of British manufactures. The day on which the Stamp Act was to come into force, was ushered in by the general tolling of bells, and by other demonstrations of popular regret.

Meanwhile, in England, affairs began to take a favourable turn for the colonists, through circumstances wholly independent of the merits of the question. A turn of the political wheel brought into power the Marquis of Rockingham, a nobleman professing principles decidedly liberal. The colonial department was intrusted to General Conway, who had stood forward as the zealous advocate of the Americans. His views were seconded by petitions from London, Liverpool, Manchester, Birmingham, Newcastle, Glasgow, and other great commercial towns, deprecating the loss of their lucrative commerce. Yet ministers were beset with considerable difficulties, having to maintain the honour of the British government, which would be seriously compromised and its authority weakened by yielding to a resistance thus violently urged. In the debate on the address, Mr. Grenville maintained that if the government yielded, their power over America was lost; what was now almost rebellion would become a revolution. "The seditious spirit in the colonies owed its birth, he said, to factions in the House. We were bid to expect disobedience; what was this but telling the Americans to resist—to encourage their obstinacy with the expectation of support?" This argument, however, seems untenable, when we consider the apathy shown in parliament till the disturbances had actually arisen. Mr. Nugent, afterwards Lord Clare, insisted that the colonies should at least be obliged to own the right of taxation, and to solicit the repeal of the late act as a favour. The opposite cause was most strenuously advocated by Mr. Pitt, who, after a long illness, reappeared on the scene. On the proposal to tax America, so great he said had been his agitation for the consequences, that if he could have been carried in his bed, and placed on the floor of the House, he would have come to bear testimony against it. He maintained the supremacy of Great Britain in all matters of government and legislation; the greater must rule the less; but taxes were a gift or grant from the people; and how could any assembly give or grant what was not their own. "I rejoice," said he, "that America has resisted. Three millions of people, so dead to all the feelings of liberty as voluntarily to submit to be slaves, would have been fit instruments to make slaves of the rest. In a good cause, on a sound bottom, the force of this country can crush America to atoms. But on this ground your success would be hazardous. America, if she fell, would fall like the strong man; she would embrace the pillars of the state, and pull down the constitution along with her."

These debates resulted in the passage of a "declaratory act," on the 24th of February, 1766, which asserted "that the parliament have, and of right ought to have, power to bind the colonies in all cases whatsoever;" and was followed on the 19th of March by another, repealing the Stamp Act. Notwithstanding the unpalatable ingredient with which this act was accompanied, the joy of America, on receiving the intelligence, was unbounded. The assertion of the abstract principle of right gave the colonists but little concern, because they considered it as merely intended to save the honour of the nation, and believed confidently, that no future attempt would be made to reduce it to practice. The highest honours were everywhere decreed to those members of parliament who had been strenuous in obtaining a repeal of the obnoxious act, and in Virginia, an act passed the House of Burgesses, for erecting a statue to his majesty, as an acknowledgment of their high sense of his attention to the rights and petitions of his people.

The opinions of Washington, on this occasion, may be perceived from a letter written at the time, to a friend in London, in which, after glancing at the unhappy consequences which might have followed from the prosecution of the designs of the Grenville government, he says:

17

"Those, therefore, who wisely foresaw such an event, and were instrumental in procuring a repeal of the act, are, in my opinion, deservedly entitled to the thanks of the well-wishers to Britain and her colonies, and must reflect with pleasure, that, through their means, many scenes of confusion and distress have been prevented. Mine they accordingly have, and always shall have, for their opposition to any act of oppression ; and that act could be looked upon in no other light by every person who would view it in its proper colours."

In the joy of the colonists on the retraction of the sentiments and designs indicated in the Stamp Act, all past jealousies were merged, and it may safely be said that the union of the colonies with the mother country was never more complete than at this moment. This disposition, however, was not suffered long to continue. An entirely new cabinet came into power, at the head of which was, nominally, Mr. Pitt, the friend of America ; but his health was so broken that he was unable to take part in public affairs, and the lead was taken by Charles Townshend, now chancellor of the Exchequer, a man of the most brilliant wit and eloquence, whom we have already seen advocating measures in opposition to the interests of America.

The power of Townshend over the House of Commons was almost unbounded, but he was destitute of those solid qualities which are so necessary to statesmen, while he suffered himself to be impelled by an inordinate vanity to the vain attempt to please both parties. Finding that concession to America was in bad odour among the majority of the House, he determined to attempt the perilous measure of imposing a tax on the colonies, which would be less offensive to them as well as more efficacious than the Stamp Act.

With artistic hand he avoided the vexed question, and called the imposition of revenue a regulation of trade. The right to make regulations of trade had been exercised by Britain, and acceded to by the colonists ; consequently he thought himself safe in 1767, in bringing forward a bill which was quickly passed into a law, for granting duties on glass, paper, tea, and painters' colours, exported from Britain to British colonies.

But England had now to deal with a strong and enlightened people. They would have borne this load without a murmur, before their jealousy was aroused and the integrity of their liberty questioned ; but now they recognised in it the first fruit of the Declaratory Act, and it was met immediately by bold and animated discussions as to the distinction between tax bills, and bills for the regulation of trade. To add to the alarm of the colonists, a board of resident commissioners of customs was established at each of the principal sea-ports. The principle of these arrangements, as the prime minister well knew, could not be objected to, but they pressed with such severity upon the colonists that their indignation was tenfold stronger than before. The new regulations were spoken of as a burden, and a curse. "Nothing," said they, "is left us but to complain and pay." They soon discovered another alternative, of which they made noble use.

Redress was at first sought through constitutional channels. Memorials, petitions, remonstrances, were all tried, but in vain. A harder necessity suggested bolder remedies. The Assembly of Massachusetts, in January, 1768, drew up a petition to the king, asserting, in decided, though not violent terms, the right of exemption from all taxes imposed without their consent; and soon after they took the more obnoxious measure of entering a resolution on their minutes, directing that a circular letter should be written to the speakers of the different Assemblies throughout the colonies, requesting their co-operation and assistance in seeking for "a legal and constitutional redress of their grievances." This resolution was violently resisted at first, and decided in the negative; but, on its being renewed the next day, it was passed by a large majority. This proceeding displeased the governor, and the Earl of Hillsborough, the colonial secretary of England, being informed of it, directed Governor Bernard to call upon the Assembly to rescind the resolution, or, in case of non-compliance, to dissolve it. Accordingly, in June, the governor, as if rescinding the resolution could unwrite the letter, demanded its erasure from the records of the house. A strong confirmatory resolution, passed by a vote of 92 to 17, was its answer. This resolution, however, was not adopted until after several ineffectual attempts at explanation, which resulted only in recrimination and defiance. The governor immediately dissolved the Assembly, and sent a counter circular to the other Assemblies, warning them not to follow the example of that of Massachusetts.

At Boston fresh grounds of irritation continually arose. When the commissioners of customs arrived, they met with undisguised resentment from the populace. Associating them with a wide scheme of subjugation, the people shunned them as evil things. But as the preparation for exacting the revenue proceeded, the gloom of the people deepened into anger, and threatened revenge.

Some slight disturbances took place. The vessels of war in the bay shifted their moorings; and on land and water every thing wore an alarming aspect. The seizure of the sloop Liberty—an ominous name—belonging to John Hancock, a popular leader, for an infringment of the revenue laws, incited the people to renewed acts of violence, which drove the commissioners of customs for shelter to Castle William. To suppress this spirit of insubordination, the ships of war were brought nearer to the town, and two regiments of soldiers were ordered from New York to Boston. The intention of the British government to send this force to Boston having been announced, the selectmen of ninety-six towns of the colony of Massachusetts met in Faneuil Hall, and disclaiming legislative authority, merely recommended moderate measures, and then dissolved itself. The day after the adjournment of this convention, the troops arrived, and landed without opposition under the protection of the armed vessels in the harbour.

The intelligence of the refractory spirit manifested by the inhabitants of Boston, produced such irritation in the British parliament, that in February, 1769, resolutions were adopted, prompting the king to vigorous measures against all persons guilty of what they were pleased to denominate treasonable acts; and pledging the faith of the kingdom to second the most vigorous measures his majesty could adopt. They went so far as to beseech him, in pursuance of powers contained in an obsolete law, to seize the offenders, and bring them to England, to be tried under a special commission.

Previous to this impolitic action of parliament, (in March, 1768,) the people of Massachusetts had entered into an agreement for the non-importation of British goods until the objectionable taxes should be removed. These agreements were now renewed, and observed with increased rigour. With the speed of evil tidings, the resolutions of parliament reached the colony of Virginia. The Assembly of that province being then in session, guided by the genius of Patrick Henry, counter-resolutions were proposed and carried, by which the principles of American liberty were again asserted. Other colonies adopted similar resolutions; and when cargoes of British goods arrived, they were packed up in storehouses, and there left to rot, or, in some instances, reshipped and sent back to England. This occasioned great distress among the British manufacturers, who, thus losing their most profitable market, earnestly petitioned the ministers to repeal the duties which were ruining them. A change in the ministry at this crisis seemed to

favour the colonists and manufacturers.   Lord North was placed
at the head of affairs.   He commenced his administration by
obtaining the passage of a bill repealing all the American duties,
except that on tea.   This reservation was extremely odious to the
American colonists, as it was a practical assertion of the right of
parliament to impose internal taxes without their consent, the
very right which they had so long opposed.   Not ungrateful,
however, for the removal of a part of the burden ; they so far
relaxed their associations, as to allow the importation of all articles except tea ; while they entered into a further agreement for
the non-consumption of that commodity.

The views of Colonel Washington on the subject of the non-
importation agreements at this time were most distinct and decisive.   They were stated at large in a letter dated 5th April, 1769,
and addressed to George Mason, an intimate friend and neighbour.   The letter was written after receiving the resolutions of
the merchants of Philadelphia, in favour of the non-importation of
articles of British manufacture; which resolutions he had received
from Dr. Ross, and then forwarded to Mr. Mason.

"Herewith," he said, "you will receive a letter and sundry
papers, which were forwarded to me a day or two ago, by Dr.
Ross, of Bladensburg.   I transmit them with the greater pleasure,
as my own desire of knowing your sentiments upon a matter of
this importance exactly coincides with the doctor's inclinations.

"At a time when our lordly masters in Great Britain will be
satisfied with nothing less than the deprivation of American freedom, it seems highly necessary that something should be done to
avert the stroke, and maintain the liberty which we have derived
from our ancestors.   But the manner of doing it, to answer the
purpose effectually, is the point in question.

"That no man should scruple, or hesitate a moment, to use
arms in defence of so valuable a blessing, is clearly my opinion,
yet arms, I would beg leave to add, should be the last resource,
the *dernier ressort*.   We have already, it is said, proved the inefficacy of addresses to the throne, and remonstrances to parliament.
How far, then, their attention to our rights and privileges is to be
awakened or alarmed, by starving their trade and manufacturers,
remains to be tried.

"The northern colonies, it appears, are endeavouring to adopt
this scheme.   In my opinion it is a good one, and must be attended with salutary effects, provided it can be carried generally
into execution.   But to what extent it is practicable to do so, I

M

will not take upon me to determine.   That there will be a diffi
culty attending the execution of it everywhere, from clashing interests, and selfish, designing men, ever attentive to their own gain,
and watchful of every turn that can assist their lucrative views,
cannot be denied; and in the tobacco colonies, where trade is so
diffused, and in a manner wholly conducted by factors for their
principals at home, [in England,] these difficulties are certainly
enhanced, but I think not insurmountably increased, if the gentlemen in their several counties will be at some pains to explain
matters to the people, and stimulate them to cordial agreements
to purchase none but certain enumerated articles out of any of the
stores after a definite period, and neither import nor purchase any
themselves.

"This, if it should not effectually withdraw the factors from
their importations, would at least make them extremely cautious
in doing it, as the prohibited goods could be vended to none but
the non-associators, or those who would pay no regard to their
association; both of whom ought to be stigmatized, and made
the objects of public reproach.

"The more I consider a scheme of this sort, the more ardently
I wish success to it, because I think there are private as well as
public advantages to result from it; the former, certain, however
precarious the other may prove.   In respect to the latter, I have
always thought that by virtue of the same power, which assumes
the right of taxation, the parliament may attempt at least to
restrain our manufactures, especially those of a public nature, the
same equity and justice prevailing in one case as in the other, it
being no greater hardship to forbid my manufacturing, than it is
to order me to buy goods loaded with duties, for the express purpose of raising a revenue.   But as a measure of this sort would
be an additional exertion of arbitrary power, we cannot be placed
in a worse condition, I think, by putting it to the test.

"On the other hand, that the colonies are considerably indebted
to Great Britain is a truth universally acknowledged.   That many
families are reduced almost, if not quite, to penury and want by
the low ebb of their fortunes, and that estates are daily selling for
the discharge of debts, the public papers furnish too many melancholy proofs.   That a scheme of this sort will contribute more
effectually than any other that can be desired to extricate the
country from the distress it at present labours under, I most firmly
believe, if it can be generally adopted.   And I can see but one
class of people, the merchants excepted, who will not, or ought

not, to wish well to the scheme, namely, they who live genteelly
and hospitably on clear estates.   Such as these, were they not to
consider the valuable object in view, and the good of others,
might think it hard to be curtailed in their living and enjoyments.
As to the penurious man, he would thereby save his money and
his credit, having the best plea for doing that, which before, perhaps, he had the most violent struggles to refrain from doing.
The extravagant and expensive man has the same good plea to
retrench his expenses.   He would be furnished with a good pretext to live within bounds, and would embrace it.   Prudence dictated economy before, but his resolution was too weak to put it
in practice.   'For how can I,' says he, 'who have lived in such
and such a manner, change my method?   I am ashamed to do it,
and, besides, such an alteration in the system of my living will
create suspicions of the decay of my fortune, and such a thought
the world must not harbour.'   He continues his course, till at last
his estate comes to an end, a sale of it being the consequence of
his perseverance in error.   This, I am satisfied, is the way that
many, who have set out in the wrong track, have reasoned, till
ruin has stared them in the face.   And in respect to the needy
man, he is only left in the same situation he was found in, better,
I may say, because, as he judges from comparison, his condition
is amended in proportion as it approaches nearer to those above
him.

"Upon the whole, therefore, I think the scheme a good one,
and that it ought to be tried here, with such alterations as our
circumstances render absolutely necessary.   But in what manner
to begin the work, is a matter worthy of consideration.   Whether
it can be attempted with propriety or efficacy, further than a communication of sentiments to one another before May, when the
court and Assembly will meet at Williamsburg, and a uniform
plan can be concerted, and sent to the different counties to operate
at the same time, and in the same manner everywhere, is a thing
upon which I am somewhat in doubt, and I should be glad to
know your opinion."

The reply of Mr. Mason to this letter of Colonel Washington
may safely be regarded as an exposition of the feelings and intentions of the great mass of the colonists.

"I entirely agree with you," he replies, "that no regular plan
of the sort proposed can be entered into here, before the meeting
of the general court at least, if not of the Assembly.   In the mean
time, it may be necessary to publish something preparatory to it in

our gazettes, to warn our people of the impending danger, and to induce them the more readily and cheerfully to concur in the proper measures to avert it; and something of this sort I had begun, but am unluckily stopped by a disorder which affects my head and eyes.   As soon as I am able, I shall resume it, and then write you more fully, or endeavour to see you.   In the mean time, pray commit to writing such hints as may occur.

"Our all is at stake, and the little conveniences and comforts of life, when set in competition with our liberty, ought to be rejected, not with reluctance, but with pleasure.   Yet it is plain, that in the tobacco colonies we cannot at present confine our importations within such narrow bounds as the northern colonies. A plan of this kind, to be practicable, must be adapted to our circumstances, for if not steadily executed it had better have remained unattempted.   We may retrench all manner of superfluities, finery of all descriptions, and confine ourselves to linens, woollens, &c., not exceeding a certain price.   It is amazing how much this practice, if adopted in all the colonies, would lessen the American imports, and distress the various traders and manufacturers in Great Britain.

"This would awaken their attention.   They would see, they would feel the oppressions we groan under, and exert themselves, to procure us redress.   This once obtained, we should no longer discontinue our importations, confining ourselves still not to import any articles that should hereafter be taxed by act of parliament for raising revenue in America; for, however singular I may be in my opinion, I am thoroughly convinced, that, justice and harmony happily restored, it is not the interest of these colonies to refuse British manufactures.   Our supplying our mother country with gross materials, and taking her manufactures in return, is the true chain of connection between us.   These are the bands, which, if not broken by oppression, must long hold us together, by maintaining a constant reciprocation of interest.   Proper caution should, therefore, be used in drawing up the proposed plan of association.   It may not be amiss to let the ministry understand, that, until we obtain a redress of grievances, we will withhold from them our commodities, and particularly refrain from making tobacco, by which the revenue would lose fifty times more than all their oppressions could raise here.

"Had the hints which I have given with regard to taxation of goods imported into America, been thought of by our merchants

before the repeal of the Stamp Act, the late American revenue acts
would probably never have been attempted."

Mr. Mason drew up a series of resolutions, otherwise called
associations, or non-importation agreements, which he, not being
a member of the Assembly, gave to Colonel Washington, who
carried them with him to Williamsburg, whither he went in May,
to attend to his duty as a member of the House of Burgesses.
That body had been in session only a few days when they passed
a series of strong resolutions, asserting their rights alone to impose
taxes upon the people of the province of Virginia ; and declaring
that it was the privilege of the inhabitants to request the other
colonies to unite with them in petitioning the king for a redress
of grievances. They also prepared a petition to the king, remonstrating in strong and feeling language against the execution of
the old law, by which persons accused of any crime whatever
might be seized, and sent to places beyond the seas to be tried.

Lord Botetourt, the governor of Virginia, being informed of
the proceedings of the house, immediately dissolved the Assembly.
As soon as the burgesses left the public hall, they met at a private
house, and choosing their late speaker, Peyton Randolph, mode-
rator, adopted, with a slight modification, the agreement which
had been drawn up by George Mason, and intrusted by him for
presentation and support to Colonel Washington. These resolutions against the importation of any articles that were taxed by
the parliament of Great Britain were signed by every member of
the Assembly present, and then sent through the country for the
signatures of the people.

That Washington was sincere in the support of the principles
which were now generally adopted by his countrymen, will be
clearly seen from the following extract from a letter to his London
correspondent, in sending out his customary orders :—"You will
perceive, in looking over the several invoices, that some of the
goods there required are upon condition that the act of parliament,
imposing a duty on tea, paper, &c., for the purpose of raising a
revenue in America, is totally repealed, and I beg the favour of you
to be governed strictly thereby, as it will not be in my power to
receive any articles contrary to our non-importation agreement,
which I have subscribed, and shall religiously adhere to, and
should, if it were as I could wish it to be, ten times as strict."

Thus did Washington heartily join with the colonists in every
measure of opposition to the encroachments of the British ministry
from 1769, until, in 1773, more active and warlike proceedings

18   M 2

were required by America from all her children.   While engaged
in the House of Burgesses in resisting the claim of Great Britain
to tax the colonies at pleasure, and during the recesses of the
Assembly, at his plough, he did not forget his old friends, the officers and soldiers who had served with him in the French War.
Governor Dinwiddie, as a reward for their services, had promised
these men two hundred thousand acres of land on the Ohio.   This
claim was long opposed, first by the English ministry, and afterwards by the authorities of Virginia, and it was only by the unwearied exertions of Washington, that the matter was finally, in
1773 or 1774, adjusted.

Washington even undertook a journey, in the autumn of the year
1770, for the express purpose of selecting such tracts of land as
would be most valuable to the future owners, when the government should think fit to fulfil its pledge to his fellow-soldiers.
Some months afterwards, Lord Dunmore, then governor of the province, solicited his company in an excursion to the western country,
and Washington began his preparations for once more visiting the
scenes of his early renown.   The death of Mrs. Washington's
only daughter, however, prevented him from accompanying the
governor.

The crisis of the Revolution was now fast approaching.   Already
had blood been shed in the sacred cause of liberty.   The two royal
regiments stationed at Boston, had, from the first, been a source of
constant annoyance to the inhabitants.   Frequent quarrels arose between them and the townsmen ; and at length, on the 5th of March,
1770, an affray took place in which a party of soldiers fired upon their
opponents, and four men were killed.   The alarm-bells were immediately rung, a mob assembled, who became infuriated at the sight of
the dead bodies, and far more serious mischief might have been the
result, had not the lieutenant-governor assured them, that the law
should be strictly enforced on the perpetrators of the offence.
Accordingly, Captain Preston, who had commanded, and several
soldiers who had fired, were brought to trial ; on which occasion
Mr. Quincy and Mr. Adams, two of the most zealous patriots,
actuated by a sincere regard to justice, undertook the defence.
The accused were honourably acquitted, it having been proved
that the people first insulted the soldiers, and then commenced an
attack, while the officer made every exertion to prevent the catastrophe.   Such urgent representations, however, were now made by
the council and the citizens, that the commander agreed to remove

the troops, quartering them in Castle William and in barracks erected near it.

At this time public indignation was excited against Governor Hutchinson, and Oliver the lieutenant-governor of Massachusetts, in consequence of the publication of letters written by them to a secretary of the treasury in England.   These letters, which had been transmitted to Boston by Dr. Franklin, contained a strong reprobation of the course pursued by the popular leaders, and recommendations that they should be put down at once, by coercive measures if necessary.   Such was the public resentment excited by the publication of these letters, that the government chose rather to recall Hutchinson, and appoint General Gage as his successor, than run the risk of submitting to the fury of the populace.*

* The following account of the affair of the letters is from the Pictorial History of England :—

" Before these proceedings, and even before the arrival of the intelligence of the tea riot, Dr. Franklin, the agent for the colony or house of representatives of Massachusetts, had met with a severe castigation from the sharp tongue of a crown lawyer, for his conduct in the affair of the letters.   That affair, moreover, had led to bloodshed in England, for a duel had been fought in Hyde Park, between Mr. Whately, banker in Lombard street, and brother to Mr. Thomas Whately, late secretary to the treasury, and member for Castle Rising, and Mr. (afterwards Sir) John Temple, lieutenant-governor of New Hampshire; and the unfortunate banker had been dangerously wounded.   Upon this event, which caused considerable excitement, Franklin wrote and published a letter, declaring that neither Mr. Whately nor the lieutenant-governor of New Hampshire had any thing to do with the mischievous letters, and that both of them were totally ignorant and innocent of that transaction.   'I think it incumbent on me,' wrote Franklin, ' to declare, for the prevention of further mischief, that I alone am the person who obtained and transmitted to Boston the letters in question.   Mr. Whately could not communicate them, because they were never in his possession ; and, for the same reason, they could not have been taken from him by Mr. Temple.   They were not of the nature of *private letters between friends ;* they were written by public officers to persons in public stations, on public affairs, and intended to procure public measures ; they were, therefore, handed to other public persons, who might be influenced by them to produce those measures: their tendency was to incense the mother country against her colonies, and, by the steps recommended, to widen the breach, which they effected.   The chief caution expressed with regard to privacy was, to keep their contents from the colony agents, who, the writers apprehended, might return them, or copies of them, to America.   That apprehension was, it seems, well founded; for the first agent who laid his hands on them thought it his duty to transmit them to his constituents.'

" This letter was signed ' B. Franklin, agent for the house of representatives of Massachusetts Bay,' and was dated Craven street, December 25th, 1773.   As a matter of course, it left in mystery the means by which the philosopher had got possession of the letters.   But the secret has since transpired.   ' It is only within these seven years,' says the writer of the History of the American Revolution, published by the Society for the Diffusion of Useful Knowledge, in 1830, ' that it has been ascertained that Governor Hutchinson's letters were put into Franklin's hands by a Dr. Williamson, who, without any suggestion on his part, had procured them by stratagem from the office where they had been deposited.   This curious fact is stated, with many particulars, in a Memoir of Dr. Williamson, by Dr. Hosack of New York.'

" On Saturday, the 29th of January, Franklin, with Mr. Dunning as counsel to speak

In the mean time, the other colonies were not undisturbed. In Rhode Island, the revenue schooner Gaspee was seized and burned with all her cargo. A special commission, appointed to inquire into the matter and try the offenders, found it impossible to procure any evidence. We have already seen that the legislature of Virginia was alarmed by the rumor that the plan of transporting accused persons to Britain for trial was to be adopted. In March, 1773, they appointed a standing committee of correspondence and inquiry, with instructions to communicate with the other colonies, a measure which met with their zealous co-operation.

While the colonies were in this state, seemingly balancing

to the Bostonian petition for the removal of the governor and lieutenant-governor, which petition was got up in consequence of the letters he had transmitted, appeared before the privy council, where thirty-five lords were assembled, besides those in office. Wedderburn, the solicitor-general, attended as counsel for the governor. Mr. Dunning having asked, on the part of his clients, the reason of being ordered to attend, and having spoken shortly on the general object of the petition, was replied to by Wedderburn, whose naturally sharp tongue was made sharper on this occasion by his friendship and sympathy for Mr. Whately, the banker, who was at that moment lying between life and death. After entering largely into the constitution and temper of the province of Massachusetts, he concluded with a most scurrilous invective against the double dealing and malice of Franklin. According to another great philosopher, (Priestley,) whose sympathy with Franklin and his cause was perfect, and whose affection for his native country had been nearly extinguished at the time he wrote, by a popular and brutal persecution—'Mr. Wedderburn had a complete triumph: at the sallies of his sarcastic wit, all the members of the council, the president himself (Lord Gower) not excepted, frequently laughed outright; and no person belonging to the council behaved with decent gravity, except Lord North, who came in late.' The Earl of Shelburne, who conveyed to Chatham an ample account of what passed, taxes Wedderburn with violence and indecency of language; but he does not mention that the members of the council misbehaved themselves so grossly. It was no laughing matter: Wedderburn was no buffoon, and his invective was calculated to arouse the violent passions, to provoke any thing rather than laughter. It concluded with this indignant burst of feeling:—'Amidst tranquil events, here is a man who, with the utmost insensibility of remorse, stands up and avows himself the author of all. I can compare him only to Zanga, in Dr. Young's Revenge:—

> "———Know, then, 'twas I.
> I forged the letter—I dispos'd the picture—
> I hated—I despis'd—and I destroy!"

I ask, my lords, whether the revengeful temper attributed to the bloody African is not surpassed by the coolness and apathy of the wily American?' Whatever may have been the effect upon the members of the council, the invective sunk deep into the soul of Franklin. It is said that he controlled his feelings in that presence, standing in a corner of the room without the least apparent emotion; but it is added, that, when he got back to his lodgings, he took off the suit of clothes he had worn, and vowed he would never wear it again until he should sign the degradation of England and the independence of America. On the following morning he is said to have told a friend who breakfasted with him, that he had never before been so sensible of the power of a good conscience; that he had been accused of clandestinely procuring the letters, and sending them to America with a view to excite animosities and embroil the two countries; but that, in fact, he did not even know that such letters existed, till they were brought to him as agent of the colony, in order to be sent to his constituents. He never would name the person from whom he got the letters, but said, some time after that he had received them from a gentleman that was since dead."

between patriotism and right on the one hand, and loyalty and submission on the other, a new scheme entered the mind of Lord North, as if to hasten on the great catastrophe by which Britain was in a few years to be deprived of the brightest gems in her diadem. In consequence of the pertinacious and successful exclusion of tea from the American colonies, that article had accumulated in the warehouses of the East India Company. It was accordingly proposed that the British duty of a shilling a pound should be drawn back on the importation of the article into America, where a duty of only three pence was to be imposed. The colonists, who would thus procure it cheaper than the English, might, it was thought, be gently manœuvred out of the principle for which they so obstinately contended. It was almost madness to renew in any shape a contest in which the government had been so repeatedly worsted; though this was really a small measure to issue in a vast rebellion,—a slender spark to kindle such a mighty conflagration. We must also again reproach the parliamentary friends of America, that they sounded no note of alarm, and this momentous vote passed in the usual silent and unregarded manner.

The intelligence, when it reached the colonies, strongly roused the determination of the popular leaders. They were sensible, as is admitted by all their advocates, that if the tea were once landed and offered for sale at the cheap rate which these arrangements allowed, nothing could prevent its being bought and consumed; a circumstance which by no means indicates a very fervid zeal among the mass of the people. Large vessels, however, were already crossing the Atlantic, laden with this commodity, the introduction of which, on so extensive a scale, would completely break up their grand principle of non-taxation. They therefore determined to exert their utmost efforts to prevent the landing; and possessing a paramount influence in the mercantile ports, extorted a promise from the consigners to refuse it, and thus oblige the vessels to carry back their lading. Unfortunately, the agents at Boston rejected this demand, and appealed to the governor, who promised protection; but a mob was quickly collected, their houses were broken into, and themselves compelled to take refuge in Castle William. On the other hand, the governor and custom-house officers even refused to permit the vessels which had arrived to depart without landing the tea. A general meeting of the inhabitants was then called, when resolutions were entered into to oppose the landing of the tea; and a guard was appointed, who watched night and day to prevent any portion of the cargo from being sent ashore. Some time after, another great assemblage met at Faneuil Hall, where one party recommended moderate measures; but the majority discovered a violent spirit, and some undoubtedly desired to urge on steps which might issue in a total rupture. Mr. Quincy warned them, that a spirit was now necessary, different from any hitherto displayed; they were advancing to "measures which must bring on the most trying and terrible struggle this country ever saw." The captain of one of the tea-ships, who now sought to extricate himself from the affair, was allowed to make a last application to the governor for permission to depart; but having returned and reported a refusal, the meeting separated. Immediately after, the harbour was thronged by a vast multitude, seventeen of whom, disguised as Mohawk Indians, went on board the ships, took full possession of them, and deliberately emptied the whole of their cargoes into the sea.

This daring outrage hurried affairs to a crisis. On the intelligence arriving in England, the determination was immediately formed to proceed to extreme measures. These were not akin to Lord North's disposition; but he was probably goaded on by others, reproached for his previous concessions, and keenly sensible to this total failure of his own favourite scheme. Now, he said, was our time to stand out, to defy them, to proceed with firmness, and without fear. Boston was the centre whence all the present disorders emanated. It had been the ringleader in every riot, and set always the example which others only followed. To inflict a signal penalty on this city would be to strike at the root of the evil. He quoted several instances, as the murder of Dr. Lamb in London, under Charles II., and the execution of Captain Porteous by the Edinburgh mob, in which a whole city had been punished for an offence committed by a large body of its inhabitants. It was proposed, therefore, that the port of Boston should be closed, and no goods allowed to be either shipped or landed. This interdict was to continue, till the citizens should express a due sense of their error, and make full compensation to the company; when the crown, if it should see sufficient reason, might restore its lost privileges. This motion, so big with war and disaster, when made to the House of Commons, met with such eager concurrence, that the very few who attempted opposition could not without extreme difficulty obtain a hearing. Alderman Sawbridge was obliged to tell them that though he could not speak long, he could sit long. Even Colonel Barré, the standing advocate of

America, said he approved of this measure for its moderation. Some zealous supporters of authority indulged the most imprudent violence in invective against the Americans. Mr. Herbert described them as a strange set of people, from whom it was in vain to expect any degree of reasoning; they always chose tarring and feathering. Mr. Montague, second son of Lord Sandwich, attributed their boldness to the tame councils, the weak and unmanly character of ministers, who allowed themselves to be swayed by a faction seeking popularity by clamour, and composed of "the vilest excrement of the earth." Mr. Van drew still greater attention, by declaring that the port ought to be knocked about their ears and destroyed, adding the quotation, "*delenda est Carthago.*"

The second reading passed without a division; but a petition was then presented by the lord mayor, from a number of American settlers resident in London. It urged that the citizens of Boston had not been heard in their own defence, nor redress sought at common law. The place was not walled, nor held by any executive power, and the offence had not even been committed within its limits. They proceeded in very bold language to observe that the attachment of their countrymen could not survive the justice of Great Britain, a violation of which might extinguish the filial sentiments hitherto cherished. Some opposition was now mustered, Mr. Fuller proposing merely the imposition of a fine. Mr. Burke began that series of splendid orations, which he devoted to the cause of American liberty. He denounced this confounding of the innocent and the guilty, and expressed his heartfelt sorrow at the general aspect of affairs; the universal resistance of all America; one town in proscription, the rest in rebellion; not a port on its coast where goods could be landed and vended. The consequences would be dreadful, nay, he was afraid, destructive; and he gave the prophetic warning, that ministers would draw upon themselves a foreign enemy at a time they little expected. Two former governors, Johnstone and Pownall, expressed themselves earnestly in favour of the Americans; the former declaring he had advised the company against sending the tea, and was sure the affair would issue in rebellion. The latter excited the laughter of the house, by extolling the people for their love of order and peace. But it is remarkable, that none of their advocates now disputed the right of taxation. Mr. Dowdeswell referred to a time when this had been doubted by persons of great knowledge; now there was no such opinion; the policy only was questioned. It is remarkable that Mr. Fox, on this occasion, made his first appearance in parliamentary life, by objecting to the power vested in the crown of re-opening the port; a suggestion which was not supported by either party.

The bill passed without a division. In the House of Lords, however, it encountered a stronger opposition from certain noblemen of eminence and talent, particularly Rockingham, Shelburne, and Richmond; but the debates have not been preserved, and it passed finally without any protest.

General Gage, the governor, was directed to transfer his residence to Salem, along with the custom-house, and all the courts which were by law removable. But he arrived at a most inauspicious moment; the Boston port bill having just preceded him. He was received with the ordinary marks of respect, while, at the same time, a hope was expressed, that his government might present a contrast to that of his predecessor.

The day after the arrival of the new governor, a town meeting was called to deliberate on the tenor of the Boston port bill, at which resolutions were passed, recommending the immediate renunciation of all commercial intercourse with Britain and the West Indies until the repeal of the act. "The impolicy, injustice, inhumanity, and cruelty of this act," they declared, "exceed all our powers of expression. We therefore leave it to the just censure of others, and appeal to God and the world." Mr. Quincy published a paper, in which he said: "A whole people are accused, prosecuted by they know not whom, tried they know not where, proved guilty, they know not how, and sentenced to suffer inevitable ruin." Reports of this meeting, together with copies of the new act, were immediately sent to all the provincial Assemblies.

A feeling of indignation at the conduct of the government, and sympathy with the people of Boston, spread with incredible rapidity throughout the continent. The legislative Assembly of Virginia was in session when the intelligence of the Boston port bill reached that province. They immediately appointed the first of June, the day on which the operation of the bill was to commence, to be set apart as a day of fasting, humiliation and prayer, in order "devoutly to implore the divine interposition to avert the heavy calamity which threatened destruction to their civil rights, and the evils of a civil war; and to give them one heart and one mind firmly to oppose, by all just and proper means, every injury to American rights." When Lord Dunmore, who had been recently appointed to supersede the popular Lord Botetourt as governor of Virginia, heard of this proceeding, he immediately dissolved the Assembly; but before their separation, eighty-nine of the members signed a declaration, in which they declared that "an attack made upon one of our sister colonies to compel submission to arbitrary taxes is an attack made upon all British America, and threatens ruin to the rights of all, unless the united wisdom of the whole be applied." They also instructed the committee of correspondence to propose to similar committees in the other colonies the appointment of delegates to a general congress, to meet annually, in order to watch over the g meral interests of the whole people.

The opinions of Colonel Washington, if further proof of them than the proceedings of a public body of which he was a member be required, may be learned from a letter written at the time to Bryan Fairfax, who was strongly opposed to violent measures, and anxious that time should be given for the repeal of the obnoxious acts. In the course of the letter, Washington writes:

"As to your political sentiments, I would heartily join you in them, so far as relates to an humble and dutiful petition to the throne, provided there was the most distant hope of success. But have we not tried this already? Have we not addressed the Lords, and remonstrated to the Commons? And to what end? Did they deign to look at our petitions? Does it not appear as clear as the sun in its meridian brightness, that there is a regular, systematic plan formed to fix the right and practice of taxation upon us? Does not the uniform conduct of parliament for some years past confirm this? Do not all the debates, especially those just brought to us, in the House of Commons, on the side of government, expressly declare that America must be taxed in aid of the British funds, and that she has no longer resources within herself? Is there any thing to be expected from petitioning after this? Is not the attack upon the liberty and property of the people of Boston, before restitution of the loss to the India Company was demanded, a plain and self-evident proof of what they are aiming at? Do not the subsequent bills (now I dare say acts) for depriving the Massachusetts Bay of its charter, and for transporting offenders into other colonies or to Great Britain for trial, where it is impossible from the nature of the thing that justice can be obtained, convince us that the administration is determined to stick at nothing to carry its point? Ought we not, then, to put our virtue and fortitude to the severest test?

"With you I think it a folly to attempt more than we can execute, as that will not only bring disgrace upon us, but weaken our cause; yet I think we may do more than is generally believed, in respect

19   N

to the non-importation scheme. As to the withholding of our remit
tances, that is another point, in which I own I have my doubts on
several accounts, but principally on that of justice; for I think,
while we are accusing others of injustice, we should be just ourselves; and how this can be, whilst we owe a considerable debt,
and refuse payment of it to Great Britain, is to me inconceivable.
Nothing but the last extremity, I think, can justify it. Whether
this is now come is the question."

The conjectures expressed in this letter were speedily realized.
An act soon arrived, by which the charter of the province of Massachusetts Bay was nullified, and the appointment of all magistrates
and officers of every kind vested in the crown. This act was
speedily followed by another, professing to secure the *impartial
administration of justice* in the province, which provided, "That
in case any person should be indicted in that province for murder,
or any other capital offence, and it should appear by information
given on oath to the governor that the fact was committed in the
exercise and aid of magistracy in suppressing riots, and that a fair
trial could not be had in the province, he should send the person so
indicted to any other colony, or to Great Britain to be tried."

In the mean time the General Assembly of Massachusetts met
on the 31st of May, and were immediately adjourned by the
governor to meet at Salem on the 7th of June. Having there
organized, they proceeded to revive a project formerly proposed
by them and lately suggested by the legislature of Virginia. They
accordingly declared a general congress of delegates from all the
provinces to be highly expedient, and necessary to concert measures for the recovery of the just rights and liberties of Americans,
and "for the restoration of that union and harmony between Great
Britain and the colonies, most ardently desired by all good men."
In order to carry out this resolution, a committee of five of the
most distinguished patriots of Massachusetts was elected to meet
the delegates which might be sent from the other colonies, at
Philadelphia, in the month of September. Apprised of their proceedings, General Gage sent his secretary to dissolve the Assembly;
but they kept the door of the room, in which they met, locked until
these measures were completed.

The effect of the tyranical acts of the British parliament upon
the town of Boston, was most calamitous. Silent streets, deserted
arsenals, closed warehouses, unemployed workmen and starving
families, testified that the spirit of commercial industry had taken
its departure. At the same time, the sympathy of their fellow-

countrymen contributed materially to mitigate their sufferings, and evinced itself in acts of disinterested patriotism, of which old Rome would have been proud. The Boston port bill, instead of fomenting jealousy and disunion within the province, as had been wished and expected by its originators, produced only a closer union and greater firmness of purpose among the inhabitants. The people of Marblehead offered the use of their harbour to the Boston merchants, together with free store-room in their stores and warehouses, as well as their personal services in lading and unlading goods. The people of Salem, which, by the removal of the seat of government, became the capital of the province, in a memorial presented at the dissolution of the last Assembly, addressed the governor in the following highly honourable and patriotic strain :—

"We are deeply afflicted with the sense of our public calamities; but the miseries that are now rapidly hastening on our brethren in the capital of the province greatly excite our commiseration; and we hope your excellency will use your endeavours to prevent a further accumulation of evils on that already sorely distressed people."——"By shutting up the port of Boston some imagine that the course of trade might be turned hither, and to our benefit; but nature, in the formation of our harbour, forbids our becoming rivals in commerce with that ancient mart; and, were it otherwise, we must be dead to every idea of justice, and lost to all feelings of humanity, could we indulge in one thought to seize on wealth, and raise our fortunes on the ruin of our suffering neighbours."

The ancient privilege of holding town-meetings was next attacked, and the governor issued his proclamation, prohibiting, in obedience to act of parliament, the calling of town-meetings after the 1st of August. As soon as this proclamation was issued, an assembly of this kind was called, which adjourned till after the day mentioned, and then met. The governor ordered them to disperse, but he was told that the holding of the meeting was no violation of the act of parliament, which only forbade the calling of town-meetings; and that no such call had been made, a legal meeting, held before the 1st of August, having since adjourned themselves from time to time. At one of these adjourned meetings, "a solemn league and covenant" was adopted by which the signers of the paper bound themselves "to suspend all commercial intercourse with Great Britain until the late obnoxious laws were repealed, and the colony of Massachusetts restored to its chartered rights."

The governor next attempted to form the government under the new constitution ; but he could find none to act as jurors under the direction of judges appointed by the crown, and very few to accept the offices now in the gift of the king.   Finding himself thus involved in difficulties, which daily assumed a more threatening aspect, he began to fortify Boston Neck, and increase the garrison, and he soon had such a force at his command, and was so well entrenched as to commence aggressive and coercive measures.

In the midst of the gathering storm, when black clouds seemed to be fast hiding the heavens, the solemnity of the crisis, and the responsibilities imposed by it were felt by none more than by George Washington.   On the 18th of July, 1774, he presided at a general meeting of the freeholders and inhabitants of the County of Fairfax, at which a series of resolutions were passed, which may be considered as imbodying his sentiments at the commencement of the revolutionary contest, as well as the predominant opinions of the province of Virginia.   They are chiefly expressive of a determined denial of the right claimed by Great Britain to tax the American colonies, of determination to suspend all commercial intercourse with England until the claim should be abandoned, and with all parties in America who should refuse to enter into a similar agreement.   They contain a luminous statement of the constitutional rights of America, and many earnest exhortations to the use of those expedients which should enable the colonies to dispense with the commerce of England, and to consolidate their strength by union.   It is remarkable that one of these resolutions condemns the importation of slaves as "a wicked, cruel, and unnatural trade."   George Washington and Charles Broadwater were chosen by this meeting to represent the county of Fairfax at the convention which was called to meet at Williamsburg on the 1st day of August.

The Virginia convention appointed Peyton Randolph, Richard Henry Lee, *George Washington*, Patrick Henry, Richard Bland, Benjamin Harrison, and Edmund Pendleton, to meet the delegates from the other colonies, which were to assemble at Philadelphia in September.   In a session of six days, the convention gave instructions to these deputies, and adopted a series of resolutions, which they called an association, similar in tenor and temper to those adopted two weeks before in Fairfax county.

Before noticing the acts of the first continental Congress, it may be important to understand the precise state of Washington's mind respecting the dispute between the two countries. This is important for two reasons; first, because the sentiments of Washington may be considered as a fair exponent of those of his countrymen at large; and next, because these sentiments have been much misunderstood, in consequence of the circulation of a series of spurious letters bearing his name, and tending to show that he did not enter heartily into the defence of the cause of his country. The statements of these letters were believed by many. They even crept into history, and were, a little before the close of his life, revived against him by his political opponents.

The utter falsehood of these representations will best be shown by three of his letters written about this time. The first was addressed to Bryan, afterwards Lord Fairfax, dated July 20, 1774, and contains the following passages.

"That I differ very widely from you in respect to the mode of obtaining a repeal of the acts so much and so justly complained of, I shall not hesitate to acknowledge; and that this difference in opinion probably proceeds from the different constructions we put upon the conduct and intention of the ministry, may also be true; but as I see nothing, on the one hand, to induce a belief that the parliament would embrace a favourable opportunity of repealing acts, which they go on with great rapidity to pass, in order to enforce their tyrannical system; and, on the other, I observe, or think I observe, that government is pursuing a regular plan at the expense of law and justice to overthrow our constitutional rights and liberties, how can I expect any redress from a measure which has been ineffectually tried already? For, sir, what is it we are contending against? Is it against paying the duty of three pence per pound on tea because burdensome? No, it is the right only that we have all along disputed; and to this end we have already petitioned his majesty in as humble and dutiful a manner as subjects could do. Nay, more, we applied to the House of Lords and House of Commons in their different legislative capacities, setting forth, that, as Englishmen, we could not be deprived of this essential and valuable part of our constitution. If, then, as the fact really is, it is against the right of taxation that we now do, and, as I before said, all along have contended, why should they suppose an exertion of this power would be less obnoxious now than formerly? And what reason have we to believe that they would make a second attempt, whilst the same sentiments fill the breast of every American, if they did not intend to enforce it if possible?

"The conduct of the Boston people could not justify the rigour of their measures, unless there had been a requisition of paymen. and refusal of it; nor did that conduct require an act to deprive the government of Massachusetts Bay of their charter, or to exempt offenders from trial in the places where offences were committed, as there was not, nor could there be, a single instance produced to manifest the necessity of it. Are not all these things evident proofs of a fixed and uniform plan to tax us? If we want further proofs, do not all the debates in the House of Commons serve to confirm this? And has not General Gage's conduct, since his arrival, in stopping the address of his council, and publishing a proclamation more becoming a Turkish bashaw than an English governor, declaring it treason to associate in any manner by which the commerce of Great Britain is to be affected, has not this exhibited an unexampled testimony of the most despotic system of tyranny that ever was practised in a free government? In short, what further proofs are wanting to satisfy any one of the designs of the ministry than their own acts, which are uniform and plainly tending to the same point, nay, if I mistake not, avowedly to fix the right of taxation? What hope have we then from petitioning, when they tell us that now or never is the time to fix the matter? Shall we, after this, whine and cry for relief, when we have already tried it in vain? Or shall we supinely sit and see one province after another fall a sacrifice to despotism?

"If I were in any doubt, as to the right which the parliament of Great Britain had to tax us without our consent, I should most heartily coincide with you in opinion, that to petition, and to petition only, is the proper method to apply for relief; because we should then be asking a favour, and not claiming a right, which, by the law of nature, and by our constitution, we are, in my opinion, indubitably entitled to. I should even think it criminal to go further than this, under such an idea; but I have none such. I think the parliament of Great Britain have no more right to put their hands into my pocket without my consent, than I have to put my hands into yours; and this being already urged to them in a firm but decent manner, by all the colonies, what reason is there to expect any thing from their justice?

"As to the resolution for addressing the throne, I own to you, sir, I think the whole might have been expunged. I expect nothing from the measure, nor should my voice have sanctioned it, if the non-importation scheme was intended to be retarded by it; for I am convinced, as much as I am of my existence, that there is no relief for us but in their distress ; and I think, at least I hope, that there is public virtue enough left among us to deny ourselves every thing but the bare necessaries of life to accomplish this end. This we have a right to do, and no power upon earth can compel us to do otherwise, till it has first reduced us to the most abject state of slavery. The stopping of our exports would, no doubt, be a shorter method than the other to effect this purpose; but if we owe money to Great Britain, nothing but the last necessity can justify the non-payment of it ; and, therefore, I have great doubts upon this head, and wish to see the other method first tried, which is legal, and will facilitate these payments.

"I cannot conclude without expressing some concern that I should differ so widely in sentiment from you, on a matter of such great moment and general import; and I should much distrust my own judgment upon the occasion, if my nature did not recoil at the thought of submitting to measures, which I think subversive of every thing that I ought to hold dear and valuable, and did I not find, at the same time, that the voice of mankind is with me."

The second letter was addressed to the same gentleman, about a week before he left Mount Vernon to attend the first meeting of Congress. It is dated Mount Vernon, 24th August, 1774, and is as follows :—

"DEAR SIR—Your letter of the 5th instant came to this place, forwarded by Mr. Ramsey, a few days after my return from Williamsburg, and I delayed acknowledging it sooner, in the hope that I should find time, before I began my journey to Philadelphia, to answer it fully, if not satisfactorily ; but as much of my time has been engrossed since I came home, by company, by your brother's sale and the business consequent thereupon, in writing letters to England, and now in attending to my own domestic affairs previous to my departure, I find it impossible to bestow as much attention on the subject of your letter as I could wish, and, therefore, I must rely upon your good nature and candour in excuse for not attempting it. In truth, persuaded, as I am, that you have read all the political pieces which compose a large share of the gazettes at this time, I should think it, but for your request, a piece of inexcusable arrogance in me, to make the least essay towards a change in your political opinions; for I am sure I have no new light to throw upon the subject, nor any other arguments to offer in support of my own doctrine, than what you have seen ; and I could only in general add, that an innate spirit of freedom first told me, that the measures which the administration have for some time been, and now are most violently pursuing, are opposed to every principle of natural justice; whilst much abler heads than my own have fully convinced me, that they are not only repugnant to natural right, but subversive of the laws and constitution of Great Britain itself, in the establishment of which some of the best blood in the kingdom has been spilt.

"Satisfied, then, that the acts of the British parliament are no longer governed by the principles of justice, that they are trampling upon the valuable rights of Americans, confirmed to them by charter, and by the constitution they themselves boast of, and convinced, beyond the smallest doubt, that these measures are the result of deliberation, and attempted to be carried into execution by the hand of power, is it a time to trifle, or risk our cause upon petitions, which with difficulty obtain access, and afterwards are thrown by with the utmost contempt? Or should we, because heretofore unsuspicious of design, and then unwilling to enter into disputes with the mother country, go on to bear more, and forbear to enumerate our just causes of complaint? For my own part, I shall not undertake to say where the line between Great Britain and the colonies should be drawn; but I am clearly of opinion, that one ought to be drawn, and our rights clearly ascertained. I could wish, I own, that the dispute had been left to posterity to determine; but the crisis is arrived when we must assert our rights, or submit to every imposition that can be heaped upon us, till custom and use shall make us tame and abject slaves.

"I intended to write no more than an apology for not writing; but I find I am insensibly running into a length I did not expect, and therefore shall conclude with remarking, that, if you disavow the right of parliament to tax us, unrepresented as we are, we only differ in respect to the mode of opposition, and this difference principally arises from your belief, that they (the parliament I mean) want a decent opportunity to repeal the acts; whilst I am fully convinced, that there has been a regular, systematic plan formed to enforce them, and that nothing but unanimity and firmness in the colonies, which they did not expect, can prevent it. By the best advices from Boston it seems that General Gage is exceedingly disconcerted at the quiet and steady conduct of the people of the Massachusetts Bay, and at the measures pursuing by the other governments. I dare say he expected to force those oppressed people into compliance, or irritate them to acts of violence before this, for a more colourable pretence of ruling that and the other colonies with a high hand.

" I shall set off on Wednesday next for Philadelphia, where, if you have any commands, I shall be glad to oblige you in them; being, dear sir, with real regard,

Your most obedient servant."

The third letter was addressed to Captain Robert Mackenzie, formerly a captain in the Virginia regiment, in answer to one received from him. He was then an officer in the forty-third regiment of foot, of the regular British army stationed at Boston. The following extract from his letter to Washington called forth the reply which is given below.

"Mr. Atcheson can sufficiently inform you of the state of this unhappy province, of their tyrannical oppression over one another, of their fixed aim at total independence, of the weakness and temper of the mainsprings that set the whole in motion, and how necessary it is, that abler heads and better hearts should draw a line for their guidance. Even when this is done, it is much to be feared that they will follow it no further than it coincides with their present sentiments. Amidst all these jarrings we have until lately lived in a camp of pleasure ; but the rebellious and numerous meetings of men in arms, their scandalous and ungenerous attacks upon the best characters in the province, obliging them to save themselves by flight, and their repeated, but feeble threats to dispossess the troops, have furnished sufficient reasons to General Gage to put the town in a formidable state of defence, about which we are now fully employed, and which will be shortly accomplished to their great mortification."

Colonel Washington, who was then at Philadelphia, attending the first Congress, answered as follows, under date of the 9th October, 1774.

"Dear Sir—Your letter of the 13th ultimo, from Boston, gave me pleasure, as I learnt thereby, that you are well, and might be expected at Mount Vernon in your way to or from James River, in the course of the winter.

"When I have said this, permit me, with the freedom of a friend, (for you know I always esteemed you,) to express my sorrow, that fortune should place you in a service that must fix curses to the latest posterity on the contrivers, and if success (which, by-the-by, is impossible) accompanies it, execrations upon all those who have been instrumental in their execution.

"I do not mean by this to insinuate, that an officer is not to discharge his duty, even when chance, not choice, has placed him in a disagreeable situation ; but I conceive, when you condemn

20

the conduct of the Massachusetts people, you reason from effects, not from causes; otherwise you would not wonder at a people who are every day receiving fresh proofs of a systematic assertion of an arbitrary power, deeply planned to overturn the laws and constitution of their country, and to violate the most essential and valuable rights of mankind, being irritated, and with difficulty restrained from acts of the greatest violence and intemperance. For my own part, I confess to you candidly, that I view things in a very different point of light from the one in which you seem to consider them, and though you are led to believe by venal men,— for such I must take the liberty of calling those new-fangled counsellors who fly to, and surround you, and all others, who, for honours or pecuniary gratifications, will lend their aid to overturn the constitution, and introduce a system of arbitrary government,—although you are taught, I say, by discoursing with such men, to believe that the people of Massachusetts are rebellious, setting up for independency, and what not,—give me leave, my good friend, to tell you that you are abused, grossly abused. This I advance with a degree of confidence and boldness which may claim your belief, having better opportunities of knowing the real sentiments of the people you are among, from the leaders of them in opposition to the present measures of the administration, than you have from those whose business it is not to disclose truths, but to misrepresent facts, in order to justify, as much as possible, to the world their own conduct. Give me leave to add, and I think I can announce it as a fact, that it is not the wish or interest of that government, or any other upon this continent, separately or collectively, to set up for independence; but this you may at the same time rely on, that none of them will ever submit to the loss of those valuable rights and privileges which are essential to the happiness of every free state, and without which, life, liberty, and property are rendered totally insecure.

"These, sir, being certain consequences, which must naturally result from the late acts of parliament relative to America in general, and the government of Massachusetts Bay in particular, is it to be wondered at, I repeat, that men who wish to avert the impending blow, should attempt to oppose it in its progress, or prepare for their defence, if it cannot be averted? Surely, I may be allowed to answer in the negative; and again, give me leave to add as my opinion, that more blood will be spilled on this occasion, if the ministry are determined to push matters to extremity, than history ever yet furnished instances of in the annals of North America, and such a vital wound will be given to the peace of this great country, as time itself cannot cure, or eradicate the remembrance of.

"But I have done. I was involuntarily led into a short discussion of this subject, by your remarks on the conduct of the Boston people, and your opinion of their wishes to set up for independency. I am well satisfied that no such thing is desired by any thinking man in all North America. On the contrary, that it is the ardent wish of the warmest advocates for liberty, that peace and tranquillity upon constitutional grounds may be restored, and the horrors of civil discord prevented."

The language of Washington in this last letter, respecting the ulterior designs of his countrymen, naturally leads us to inquire what were the predominant sentiments of the American statesmen on this point. More especially is it important to ascertain the views with which the first congress assembled; whether they regarded themselves as an independent parliament, or whether they simply designed to consult for the interest of their constituents, subject to the legislative control of the parent government. Upon this subject, the industrious and untiring editor of Washington's writings has bestowed a singular degree of research, which has brought to light some very interesting details regarding the notions of the American patriots, and the country at large, upon the subject of independence.

"It is not easy to determine," says this accomplished author,* "at what precise date the idea of independence was first entertained by the principal persons in America. English writers, arguing from the conduct of the colonists, have commonly charged them with secretly harbouring such designs at a very early period. This is not probable. The spirit and form of their institutions, it is true, led them to act frequently as an independent people, and to set up high claims in regard to their rights and privileges, but there is no sufficient evidence to prove, that any province, or any number of prominent individuals, entertained serious thoughts of separating entirely from the mother country, till very near the actual commencement of the war of the revolution.

"Gordon relates the following anecdote of a conversation, said to have taken place in the year 1759, between Mr. Pratt, afterwards Lord Camden, and Dr. Franklin, but he cites no authority. 'For all what you Americans say of your loyalty,' observed Mr. Pratt, 'I know you will one day throw off your dependence upon this country; and, notwithstanding your boasted affection to it, will

* Appendix to Sparks's Writings of Washington, vol. ii. p. 496.

set up for independence.' Franklin answered, 'No such idea is entertained in the mind of the Americans ; and no such idea will will ever enter their heads, unless you grossly abuse them.' 'Very true,' replied Mr. Pratt, 'that is one of the main causes I see will happen, and will produce the event.'*

"As early as the year 1774, Dr. Franklin began to talk of a 'total emancipation,' or independence.† And Mr. Wirt represents Patrick Henry, as uttering the same sentiment anterior to the meeting of the first continental Congress. Yet the manner in which it was received by his hearers indicates that it was to them a novel and unexpected doctrine ; 'at the word *independence*, the company appeared to be startled, for they had never heard any thing of the kind before even suggested.'‡

"Washington, in his letter to Captain Mackenzie, denies, in very strong terms, that such was the design of any person, so far as his knowledge extended. No man, perhaps, was better informed on the subject by mingling in the society of others ; and it may hence be confidently inferred, that the topic of independence was not openly broached by the members of the first Congress, even in their private discourse among themselves. That he and his immediate friends had no such object in view is manifest from a clause in the *Fairfax County Resolves*, passed on the 18th of July preceding, at a public meeting over which he presided. It is there stated as a cause of complaint, 'that the British ministry are artfully prejudicing our sovereign, and inflaming the minds of our fellow-subjects in Great Britain, by propagating the most malevolent falsehoods, *particularly that there is an intention in the American colonies to set up for independent states.*' It was the opinion of Washington, and of the framers of these resolves, that the colonies had the power, by withholding their support of British commerce, to inflict so much distress on the people of Great Britain, as to rouse the government to a sense of the colonial wrongs, and produce a speedy change in their measures. And it was moreover supposed, that spirited resolutions, showing the almost universal sense of the people, that the acts of the British parliament in regard to them were oppressive and unjust, would tend to hasten so desirable a result. Such were, no doubt, the views entertained by all classes of people, and the motives actuating them in the primary movements of the Revolution.

"The subject being somewhat curious, as well as interesting in

* Gordon's History of the American Revolution, vol. i. p. 136.
† Memoir of Josiah Quincy, jun., p. 250.   ‡ Life of Patrick Henry, p. 94.

its historical aspect, I thought it not amiss to obtain the impressions of Mr. Madison, who could not fail to have a vivid recollection of the popular feeling and principal events in Virginia at the period in question, and to know the sentiments of the political leaders.   The following is an extract from his letter, dated January 5th, 1828.

"'You wish me to say whether I believe that at the beginning of the Revolution, or at the assembling of the first Congress, the leaders of that day were resolved on independence.   I readily express my entire belief, that they were not ; though I must admit that my means of information were more limited than may have been the case with others still living to answer the inquiry.   My first entrance on public life was in May, 1776, when I became a member of the convention in Virginia, which instructed her delegates in Congress to propose the Declaration of Independence. Previous to that date I was not in sufficient communication with any under the denomination of leaders, to learn their sentiments or views on that cardinal subject.

"'I can only say, therefore, that so far as ever came to my knowledge, no one of them ever avowed, or was understood to entertain a pursuit of independence, at the assembling of the first Congress, or for a considerable period thereafter.   It has always been my impression, that a re-establishment of the colonial relations to the parent country, as they were previous to the controversy, was the real object of every class of the people, till despair of obtaining it, and the exasperating effects of the war, and the manner of conducting it, prepared the minds of all for the event declared on the 4th of July, 1776, as preferable, with all its difficulties and perils, to the alternative of submission to a claim of power at once external, unlimited, irresponsible, and under every temptation to abuse, from interest, ambition, and revenge.   If there were individuals who aimed at independence, their views must have been confined to their own bosoms, or to a very confidential circle.'

"It was the belief, before the meeting of the Congress, particu-.arly of the more cautious and moderate, that petitions to the king and parliament by a body of representatives assembled from all parts of the colonies, would be respected, and in the end procure redress.   They, on the contrary, who, like Washington, had no confidence in the success of this measure, looked forward to the probable issue of arms, but still without any other anticipations than, by a resolute vindication of their rights, to effect a change in the conduct and policy of the British government, and restore

O

the colonies to their former condition. It was not till these petitions were rejected with a show of indifference, if not of contempt,
that the eyes of all were opened to the necessity of unconditional
submission, or united resistance. From that time the word *independence* was boldly pronounced, and soon became a familiar sound
to the ears of the whole people.

"On the 10th of November, 1775, Mr. Richard Penn, who had
been governor of Pennsylvania, and had left Philadelphia in the
preceding July, was examined before the House of Lords, while
the petition from Congress, which had been brought over and presented by Mr. Penn, in conjunction with the agents for the colonies, was under discussion. The following questions and answers
occur in the examination.

" *Question.* Are you personally acquainted with many of the
members of Congress?

" *Answer.* I am acquainted with almost all the members of Congress.

" *Question.* Do you think they levy and carry on this war for the
purpose of establishing an *independent empire*?

" *Answer.* I think they do not carry on the war for independency.
I never heard them breathe sentiments of that nature.

" *Question.* For what purpose do you believe they have taken
up arms?

" *Answer.* In defence of their liberties.*

"It is a curious fact, that the ministers had at this moment in
their hands two intercepted letters, written by Mr. John Adams in
Congress, which expressed sentiments quite at variance with the
testimony of Mr. Penn. These letters were dated on the 24th of
July, only two weeks later than the petition to the king, taken to
England by Mr. Penn, which was approved in Congress on the
8th. They were intercepted in crossing the ferry at Newport, and
sent on board Admiral Graves's fleet, whence they found their
way to Lord Dartmouth. The originals are now in the State Paper
Office. One of these letters was from Mr. Adams to his wife, in
which he said:

"'The business I have had on my mind has been as great and
important as can be intrusted to one man, and the difficulty and
intricacy of it are prodigious. When fifty or sixty men have a
constitution to form for a great empire, at the same time that they
have a country of fifteen hundred miles in extent to fortify, millions
to arm and train, a naval power to begin, an extensive commerce

* Parliamentary Debates, November, 1775.

to regulate, numerous tribes of Indians to negotiate with, a standing army of twenty-seven thousand men to raise, pay, victual, and officer, I really shall pity those fifty or sixty men.'

" The other letter was to James Warren, at that time speaker of the Massachusetts Assembly, and contained the following declarations :

" 'We ought to have had in our hands a month ago the whole legislative, executive, and judicial power of the whole continent, and have completely modelled a constitution ; to have raised a naval power and opened all our ports wide; to have arrested every friend to government on the continent, and held them as hostages for the poor victims in Boston ; and then opened the door as wide as possible for peace and reconciliation. After this, they might have petitioned, and negotiated, and addressed, if they would. Is all this extravagant? Is it wild? Is it not the soundest policy?'

" With sentiments like these, coming from a prominent member of Congress, it is no wonder that the ministry should be puzzled to reconcile the doctrines and assertions of the petitions to the king, in which that body express their loyalty, and desire an opportunity ' of evincing the sincerity of their professions, by every testimony of devotion becoming the most dutiful subjects and the most affectionate colonists.' No charge of insincerity, however, can attach to Mr. Adams. It is well known that he had little sympathy with the party who insisted on this last petition, and that he and others yielded to their associates, with the view of preserving peace and harmony within the walls of Congress, as the only means of ultimate union and success. At this stage of affairs, they hoped nothing from petitions, and anticipated a remedy of evils from no other sources, than strong and determined measures on the part of the representatives of the people. Whatever may have been the opinions or wishes of other members of Congress, it is hardly possible, that Mr. Adams could have written the above letters without looking forward at least to the possibility of a speedy separation, and an independent form of government. The fact of their being in the hands of the ministry when the petition came under the notice of parliament, may serve as a key to some of the proceedings on the subject.

" In tracing this matter farther, we shall find the opinions of Washington, Madison, and Penn, in regard to a scheme of independence among the colonists anterior to the beginning of the Revolution, confirmed by other testimony of the highest order. In a letter which Dr. Franklin wrote to his son, dated March 22,

JAY.

1775, he relates a conversation he had held in the August preceding with Lord Chatham, in which that statesman spoke of the prevailing belief in England, that the colonists aimed at setting themselves up as an independent state. 'I assured him,' said Franklin, 'that having more than once travelled almost from one end of the continent to the other, and kept a great variety of company, eating, drinking, and conversing with them freely, I never had heard in any conversation from any person, drunk or sober, the least expression of a wish for a separation, or a hint that such a thing would be advantageous to America.'*

"Again, Mr. Jay, remarking on certain parts of Botta's History of the American Revolution, in a letter to Mr. Otis, January 13th, 1821, thus expressed himself: 'During the course of my life, and until after the second petition of Congress in 1775, I never did hear an American of any class, or of any description, express a wish for the independence of the colonies.' 'It has always been, and still is my opinion and belief, that our country was prompted and impelled to independence by *necessity*, and not by *choice*. They who knew how we were then circumstanced, know from whence that necessity resulted.'†

"We have likewise the opinions uttered on the same occasion, of two other persons not less qualified to judge than any that have been mentioned. 'That there existed a general desire of independence of the crown,' says Mr. John Adams, 'in any part of America, before the Revolution, is as far from the truth as the zenith from the nadir.' 'For my own part, there was not a moment during the Revolution, when I would not have given every thing I possessed for a restoration to the state of things before the contest

* Franklin's Works, vol. i. p. 278.   † Life of John Jay, vol. ii. p. 412

began, provided we would have had a sufficient security for its continuance.'*

"And Mr. Jefferson affirmed, ' What eastward of New York, might have been the disposition towards England before the commencement of hostilities, I know not; before that I never had heard a whisper of a disposition to separate from Great Britain ; and after that, its possibility was contemplated with affliction by all.'†

" This mass of testimony, derived from separate sources, coincident in every particular, vouched by the first names in American history, and the principal actors in producing a separation, is perfectly conclusive on this point. It is moreover established, as Mr. Jay has remarked, by all the public documents and proceedings of the colonial legislatures, in which assurances of loyalty and allegiance are uniform and cordial. Any opinion, therefore, that the spirit of independence had an early origin, and a progressive growth, with a direct aim to a separation, or the prospect of such an event, must be a mere inference, sanctioned only by the circumstances of the free institutions of the colonies, and the tendency of a people under such institutions to self-government and a system independent of foreign control."

After citing the opinion of Mr. Sparks, that independence was not sought by the leading American patriots at the beginning of the contest, it is but fair to show, by a quotation from a respectable English authority, (the Pictorial History of England,) that a contrary opinion was entertained by the ministry, and to exhibit the grounds afforded for that opinion, by the conduct of Dr. Franklin. Whatever views may have been entertained by leading men in this country, Franklin, then in England, seems to have anticipated and desired a total separation of the colonies from the parent state.

Franklin's sending Governor Hutchinson's letters to Boston was one of the facts which influenced the author of the above-mentioned work to say : " We believe that by nature, by habit, by the whole course of his life, Franklin was disposed to be a republican ; and that, from the very beginning of the troubles, he aimed at nothing short of revolution, independence, and the establishment of a commonwealth in his native country." For his agency in the affair of the letters, Franklin was dismissed from his office of postmaster-general. The quotation in the note below refers to a subsequent transaction.‡

* Life of John Jay, vol. ii. p. 416.   † Ibid. p. 417.
‡ " In England, meanwhile, Franklin had not been idle. As instructed by his constituents, he had given all possible publicity to the addresses of the general congress to

The Congress destined to change the face of America, met at Carpenter's Hall, Philadelphia, on the 5th of September, 1774; and if any further evidence were necessary to show that they assembled with an almost universal desire to heal, and not to widen the

the king and to the people of Great Britain—the first to show how loyal were the Americans—the second (Jay's composition) to excite the popular body. Moreover, the philosopher, assisted by numerous agents, and by some of the members of opposition in parliament, had been extremely active in some of the principal manufacturing towns of the north of England, particularly among the dissenters, who were urged to petition the throne in favour of the colonies and of their own trade, which must suffer immensely from the non-importation agreements. To counteract these agencies, to show that Franklin's scheme was in reality nothing less than to dismember the British empire, to check the petitions, or get up counter-petitions, Adam Smith, the author of the ' Wealth of Nations,' applied to Dr. Roebuck, the eminent physician of Birmingham, and the intimate friend of Shenstone, the poet, imploring him, without loss of time, to make a journey through the manufacturing districts, Manchester, Leeds, Sheffield, Birmingham, &c., to see his friends, to communicate with the people, and to explain to them the real motives and objects of the Americans. This was done in concurrence with Wedderburn, the solicitor-general, who at the same time adopted other measures to check or throw discredit on the petitions Franklin was procuring. Soon after Adam Smith's letter was written, an attempt was made to disarm Franklin's hostility, or to ascertain his intentions, by an English lady, and by that lady's brother, Admiral Lord Howe, who had probably been already designated for the American command, which he afterwards held with so little glory. The philosopher, being introduced by Mr. Raper, a member of the Royal Society, played a few games at chess with the lady, whom he found of very sensible conversation and pleasing behaviour; and the lady, on Christmas day, made him acquainted with Lord Howe, saying that he was a very good man, and that she was sure they would like each other. According to Franklin, Lord Howe behaved in the most courteous manner, said that, beside the general motives for his desiring an acquaintance with so eminent a man, he had a particular motive at this time, arising out of the alarming situation of American affairs, which no one understood better than Dr. Franklin. The philosopher further says that Howe confessed that he (Franklin) had been very ill treated by the English ministry; that he had much disapproved of their conduct towards him; that some of the ministers themselves were ashamed of it, and sorry it had happened. But even in this account, which is Franklin's own, it is certainly not said that Howe expressed his disbelief of the charges, touching the letters, which Wedderburn had made against Franklin before the privy-council. From the nature of his mission, from his inward conviction that in winning over Franklin he would have won over America, Howe, in spite of his habitual taciturnity, may, no doubt, have made use of many conciliatory and flattering expressions (and, without flattery, there was much to applaud and reverence in Franklin's history, character, and intellectual performances;) but we cannot discover that, either on this or any other occasion, Howe gave the lie to Wedderburn, however much he may have disapproved of that functionary's injudicious violence. After a few general observations as to the possibility of bringing about a reconciliation through the medium of a communication by himself (Lord Howe) with the ministry, his lordship, says Franklin, concluded by observing that "being himself upon no ill terms with ministers, he thought it not impossible that he might, by conveying my sentiments to them, and theirs to me, be the means of bringing on a good understanding, without committing either them or me, if his negotiation should not succeed; and that I might rely on his keeping perfectly secret every thing I should wish to remain so." Franklin's account—*and we have no other*—goes on to state that he told Lord Howe that his manner was such as had already engaged his confidence; that he requested his lordship to give him credit for a sincere desire of healing the breach between the two countries, assuring him that he would do every thing in his small power to accomplish it, though he apprehended, from the king's last speech, and from the measures talked of, no intention or disposition of the kind existed in the present breach between the colonies and the parent state, it would be found in the measures they first adopted, and which were so important, so characteristic, and so conclusive upon many points of party discussion, as to have ever since claimed the attention of the historical student.

It is related in the life of Peyton Randolph, on the authority of the venerable Charles Thomson, that on the first day of the session, the house having been summoned to prayers, and after the chaplain had commenced the service, it was perceived that of the fifty-five members present, George Washington was the only one who was upon his knees. This was characteristic. He was truly religious, and, in every circumstance and relation, strictly moral and blameless. In Washington, the sense of duty always prevailed over all other feelings or considerations.

The Congress then determined that their deliberations should be secret, that the result should be given to the world as unanimous, and no difference of opinion be allowed to transpire. A committee

cabinet. He said that, as to the *personal injuries* his lordship had spoken of, they were not worth mentioning; and that, besides, it was a fixed rule with him not to mix his private affairs with those of the public. This first interview ended by Lord Howe obtaining a promise from Franklin, that he would draw up in writing a series of propositions on which he thought a good understanding between the mother country and the colonies might be based. They agreed to meet again at the same place—the house of Lord Howe's sister—in the course of a few days, in order to discuss those propositions. When Howe saw the paper, he must have been convinced that the British government would not pay the least attention to it, and that Franklin never intended they should; for his propositions, without periphrasis, were :—that all the laws and acts of parliament, or all parts of them requested to be repealed in the petition of the general congress to the king, should be repealed forthwith ; that orders should be given to withdraw all the ships of war from Boston, and remove all the troops, that the colonies might be left at liberty in all their future speculations, &c. They scarcely admitted even of a private discussion, and Lord Howe merely told Franklin he would lay them before ministers, without any hope that such propositions were likely to produce any good effect. His lordship, however, brought about a meeting in private between Franklin and Lord Hyde ; but this was equally void of effect. The philosopher expressed, indeed, on all occasions, a tender anxiety for the preservation of peace and good fellowship ; but he would never pledge himself to a single sacrifice or concession, continuing to ask for extreme conditions, which would have left the English government scarcely the shadow of authority, and which would have given the colonies virtually an entire independence, although he persisted in declaring that independence was neither their object nor their wish. Lord Howe saw him again for the last time a little before his return to his constituents in America, apologized for the trouble he had given him, but hoped, if he should chance to be sent out by his government to attempt an arrangement with the colonists, he might still expect his assistance. Franklin assured him of his readiness at all times to co-operate with him in so good a work. ' And so,' says he, ' taking my leave, and receiving his good wishes, ended the negotiation with Lord Howe.' We shall meet the philosopher again before his departure, giving assurances of his good intentions to Lord Chatham, who appears to have been determined not to doubt in the slightest degree of his sincerity, and not to diminish the blame due to the king and Lord North's cabinet by layirg any portion of it upon Franklin and his countrymen."

was then appointed to draw up a report upon the rights violated
the injuries sustained, and the means of redress. The committee
soon made their report, and on the 1st of October the Congress
entered into an unanimous declaration of rights, protesting against
the various acts passed during the preceding years, for the purpose
of taxing and interfering with the charters of the various colonies,
as an infringement and violation of those rights, and binding themselves and their constituents to the minute observance of a series
of agreements, calculated to cut off all commercial intercourse
between themselves and Great Britain, till redress of their grievances should be obtained.

HEY next framed a petition to the king,
a memorial to the people of Great Britain,
an address to the colonists at large, and
another to the people of Canada. " To
the king they appealed, as a sovereign
whose true interest and glory were inseparable from the liberty and happiness of
which his ministers were attempting to
bereave them."* "We ask," said they,
"but for peace, liberty, and safety. We wish not a diminution
of the prerogative, nor do we solicit the grant of any new right in
our favour. Your royal authority over us, and our connection with
Great Britain, we shall always carefully and zealously endeavour
to support and maintain." They concluded this address to the
sovereign in the following pathetic terms: "We implore your
majesty, for the honour of Almighty God, whose pure religion our
enemies are undermining; for your glory, which can be advanced
only by rendering your subjects happy, and keeping them united;
for the interests of your family, depending on the principles which
enthroned it; for the safety and welfare of your kingdom and
dominions, threatened with almost unavoidable dangers and distresses; that your majesty, as the loving father of your whole people, connected by the same bonds of law, loyalty, faith, and blood,
though dwelling in various countries, will not suffer the transcend-
ent relations formed by these ties to be further violated, in uncertain expectation of effects that, if attained, never can compensate
for the calamities through which they must be gained.

"We, therefore, most earnestly beseech your majesty, that your
royal authority and interposition may be used for our relief, and
that a gracious answer may be given to this petition."

* Grahame, 494.

To the people of Britain, they earnestly declared the high value which they attached to a full share in the system of the British constitution, and represented the danger portended to the whole system by the extinction of liberty, its vital principle, in so large and flourishing a department of the empire. "Place us," they said, "in the situation in which we were at the close of the last war, and our former harmony will be restored."

The address to their constituents is replete with serious and temperate argument. In this paper, the several causes which had led to the existing state of things were detailed at large, and great care was taken thoroughly to convince their judgments, that their liberties must be destroyed and the security of their property and persons annihilated, by submission to the pretensions of Great Britain. Their greatest object being to unite the people of America, by demonstrating to them the sincerity with which their leaders had sought for reconciliation, on terms compatible with liberty; the conduct of the colonists was contended to have been uniformly moderate, and entirely exempt from blame, while the system of administration was treated as equally dangerous to them all, although it insidiously professed to be particularly aimed at Massachusetts. They stated the measures of commercial resistance which had been recommended, and after having declared their confidence that they would prove efficacious if persisted in with fidelity and virtue, they concluded with saying:

"Your own salvation, and that of your posterity, now depends upon yourselves. You have already shown that you entertain a proper sense of the blessings you are striving to retain against the temporary inconvenience you may suffer from a stoppage of trade; you will weigh in the opposite balance the endless miseries you and your descendants must endure from an established arbitrary power; you will not forget the honour of your country, that must, from your behaviour, take its title, in the estimation of the world, to glory or to shame; and you will, with the deepest attention, reflect, that if the peaceable mode of opposition recommended by us be broken and rendered ineffectual, as your cruel and haughty ministerial enemies, from a contemptuous opinion of your firmness, insolently predict will be the case, you must inevitably be reduced to choose either a more dangerous contest, or a final, infamous, and ruinous submission.

"Motives thus cogent, arising from the emergency of your unhappy condition, must excite your utmost diligence and zeal to give all possible strength and energy to the pacific measures calculated for your relief. But we think ourselves bound in duty to observe to you, that the schemes agitated against these colonies have been so conducted as to render it prudent that you should extend your views to mournful events, and be in all respects prepared for every contingency. Above all things, we earnestly entreat you, with devotion of spirit, penitence of heart, and amendment of life, to humble yourselves, and implore the favour of Almighty God; and we fervently beseech his Divine goodness to take you into his gracious protection."

They called upon the Canadians to make common cause with their fellow-colonists, and to elect delegates to the Continental Congress.

After directing these several addresses to be distributed, and recommending that another Congress should be held at Philadelphia on the 10th of May following, unless a redress of grievances should, before that time, be obtained, they, on the 26th of October, dissolved their assembly, and the members returned to their respective homes. Shortly after Patrick Henry returned to Virginia, he was asked by a friend, who was the first man in the Congress which had met at Philadelphia. He replied, "If you speak of eloquence, Mr. Rutledge of South Carolina is by far the greatest orator; but if you speak of solid information and sound judgment, Colonel Washington is unquestionably the greatest man on that floor.*

HE proceedings of this Congress were viewed throughout America with enthusiastic admiration. Though they claimed no authority as a legislative assembly, yet their resolutions were almost unanimously received as the most binding enactments. A thorough conviction of the rectitude of their cause awakened the whole community to the most vigorous exertions. Independent military companies were formed throughout the provinces, and a presentiment of an approaching war spread itself through the length and breadth of the land.

The petition from Congress to the king arrived in England, when his majesty was just about to meet a new parliament. In the speech from the throne, he announced, "that a most daring spirit of resistance and disobedience to the laws unhappily prevailed in the colony of Massachusetts;" and, at the same time, intimated the steps which he considered necessary to repress it. A short delay, however, occurred before active measures were

* Wirt's Life of Patrick Henry, p. 113.

THE EARL OF CHATHAM.

adopted, and hopes began to revive in the breasts of the friends of American liberty. Lord Chatham yet lived. "That splendid orb had not yet set for ever. The Western horizon yet blazed with his descending glory;"* and in the House of Lords, to which he had lately been raised, he once more threw the whole force of his mighty eloquence into the balance of liberty, which was now vibrating fearfully between peace and war.

He began by offering a motion that an humble address be presented to his majesty, most humbly advising and beseeching him to withdraw the royal forces from Boston; and he supported his motion by one of the most eloquent and impressive speeches ever delivered in the British parliament. He told the House that in this distracted state of affairs, though bowed down with a cruel disease, he had crawled thither to offer them his best counsel and experience. He urged the necessity of the step he recommended, as the means of opening a way for settling the dangerous troubles in America, by beginning to allay ferments and soften animosities there. He said, an hour now lost might produce years of calamity.

* Burke.

His object was to put his foot upon the threshold of peace. His present motion was only the introduction to a comprehensive plan; and he pledged himself to the House, that he would not desert, for a moment, the conduct of this mighty business. Unless nailed to his bed by the extremity of sickness, he would give it his unremit ted attention; he would knock at the door of a sleeping and confounded ministry, and rouse them to a sense of their imminent danger. He described the situation of the troops at Boston as truly unworthy, being penned up, and pining in inglorious inactivity. He called them an army of impotence and contempt; and to make the folly equal to the disgrace, they were an army of irritation.

After stating that the Americans had been "abused, misrepresented, and traduced, in the most atrocious manner, in order to give colour, and urge on the most precipitate, unjust, cruel, and vindictive measures that ever disgraced a nation," he asks, "but how have this respectable people behaved under their grievances? With unexampled patience, with unparalleled wisdom. They chose delegates by their free suffrages; no bribery, no corruption, no influence there, my lords. Their representatives meet with the sentiments, and temper, and speak the sense of the continent. For myself, I must avow, that in all my reading and observation— and I have read Thucydides, and have studied and admired the master states of the world—I find nothing recorded in antiquity, which, in genuine sagacity, in singular moderation, in solid wisdom, manly spirit, sublime sentiments, and simplicity of language, in every thing respectable and honourable, that can rival the despised Congress of Philadelphia. This wise people speak out. They do not hold the language of slaves; they tell you what they mean. They do not ask you to repeal your laws as a *favour;* they claim it as a *right*, they demand it. They tell you they will not submit to them; and I tell you the acts must be repealed; they will be repealed; you cannot enforce them. The ministry are checkmated; they have a move to make on the board; yet not a move, they are ruined. Repeal, therefore, my lords, I say. But bare repeal will not satisfy this enlightened, and spirited people. It is not repealing this or that act of parliament; not the annihilation of a few shreds of parchment, that can restore America to your bosom. You must go through the work— you must declare you have no right to tax—you must repeal her fears and resentments; and you may then hope for her love and gratitude.

"The cause of America is the cause of every true Whig. This

glorious spirit animates three millions of men in our colonies. What shall oppose this spirit, aided by the congenial flame, glowing in the breast of every whig in England, to the amount, I hope, of double the American numbers? Ireland, they have to a man. Nay, what dependence can you have upon your soldiery, the unhappy instruments of your wrath? They are Englishmen, who must feel for the privileges of Englishmen; and their carrying muskets and bayonets about them surely does not exclude them from the pale of the civil community. Foreign war hangs over your heads, by a slight and brittle thread. France and Spain are watching your conduct, and waiting for the maturity of your errors."

HIS animated harangue was concluded in the following emphatic manner. "My lords, if the ministers thus persevere in misadvising the king, he will be undone. He may, indeed, still wear his crown, but, the American jewel out of it, it will not be worth the wearing. I must not say the king is betrayed; but this I will say, the nation is ruined."

It was all in vain. The motion of Lord Chatham, though supported by Lord Camden, Lord Shelburne, and the Marquis of Rockingham, was rejected by a large majority. Parliament seemed determined on coercion.

The crisis was at hand. On the 9th of February, 1775, a joint address of both houses of parliament was presented to the king, declaring that " a rebellion actually existed in the province of Massachusetts." This was followed by a vote, adding 4400 land troops and 2000 seamen to the military and naval forces of the kingdom; and this, in close succession, was followed by the passage of an act restraining the commerce of all the colonies, except New York, Delaware, and North Carolina, to Great Britain, Ireland, and the West Indies, and to prevent them from fishing on the banks of Newfoundland, under certain conditions, and for a limited time. The exceptions in this case may have been designed to create disunion among the colonies; but it only served to draw them closer together.

After this series of coercive measures, Lord North, the premier, surprised the House by a conciliatory proposition. He procured the passage of an act, declaring that parliament would forbear to tax any colony which should tax itself to such an amount as govern-

22   P

ment might deem satisfactory. On the introduction of this measure. Lord North exposed himself to a hot fire from his usual supporters, who branded the attempt as grossly inconsistent with all his former measures. So warmly was he opposed by his friends, that he was compelled to give them an explanation, which he did in the following words: "If this bill does no good in the colonies, it will do good here; it will unite the people of England, by holding out to them a distinct object of revenue." He added further, "As it tends to unite England, it is likely to disunite America; for if only one province accept the offer, their confederacy, which alone makes them formidable, will be broken."

This bill, which was thus unblushingly advocated, passed into a law, but as it remedied no grievance but that of taxation, and even on that head contained nothing specific, it was received in America with mingled indignation and derision.

Mr. Burke, on the 25th of March, brought forward, and eloquently supported, a series of resolutions, in which, without entering into any question of speculative right, a complete practical concession was made of all the points in dispute. His resolutions were negatived. The general tendency of his speech may be learned from the language of Mr. Fox respecting it. "Let gentlemen," he said, "read this speech by day, and meditate on it by night; let them peruse it again and again, study it, imprint it on their minds, impress it on their hearts. They would then learn that representation was the sovereign remedy for every evil."

Dr. Franklin, who was then in London, endeavoured to effect a reconciliation by drawing up seventeen propositions, which, with permission, he submitted to the ministry. Two months after their delivery an answer was returned virtually granting all that he asked, except the abolition of the new constitution of Massachusetts. Franklin answered, that the claim of altering the charters and rights upon which the governments were founded, without the consent of the parties to whom they were granted, was one to which Americans could never submit. The obstinate refusal of the cabinet to restore the ancient charter of Massachusetts, broke off the communications, and Franklin, despairing of the continuance of peace, returned to America, resolved to share in her trials, and devote his talents to the maintenance of her rights.

In the mean time, affairs in America were inevitably hurried on in the course to which they had long been tending. General Gage, who had summoned the Massachusetts Assembly, to meet at Salem, on the 5th of October, 1774, felt that in the tumultuary state of the country, he could not with safety repair thither to open it. Learning also that of thirty-six counsellors named by him, though twenty-four had at first accepted, the greater number were induced or compelled to resign, he issued a proclamation countermanding the writs ; but the members, treating it as illegal, repaired at the time appointed to Salem. There they went through the form of waiting a day, as if for the governor, and then removed their sittings to Concord, about twenty miles in the interior. Hence they sent out directions for all the branches of administration, the disciplining of the militia, the retaining of the taxes in the hands of the revenue-officers for patriotic purposes, and the collection of arms and ammunition. They remonstrated with Gage on the increase of troops, the fortifying of Boston, and other hostile proceedings ; but he repelled their complaints, and warned them that their own meeting was altogether illegal. He had again recourse to a proclamation enjoining that no regard should be paid to their usurped authority, instead of which, his mandates were entirely disregarded, while theirs met with implicit obedience. They adjourned, but met again by appointment at Cambridge, on the 4th of February. They then announced to the people that the tenor of the king's speech, and other information, afforded little prospect of compliance with their reasonable demands ; on the contrary, numerous reinforcements were expected, in order to compel ignominious submission. The most strenuous invitations were therefore employed to induce them to improve their military discipline, and to collect fire-arms and bayonets.

General Gage had hitherto, probably under instructions from home, avoided every movement which would bring on a collision and lead to a commencement of actual war. Yet, remaining almost besieged at Boston, he began to experience scarcity of provisions ; and an impression was felt, that something must be done to check these extensive preparations and seize the military stores now collected all over the country. He formed the injudicious plan of sending out secretly small detachments to capture them by surprise. Even if successful, which was not very probable, the adoption of such a scheme must have lowered the impression of British power. If the troops were to march into the country, it should have been in such large bodies as would overpower, and even deter resistance. A small party sent towards Salem, were induced to return, owing to the mere obstacles raised by the country people against their march.*

* Murray's History of the United States.

The governor having learned that a considerable magazine of stores had been formed at Concord, determined on an attempt to seize them. He employed a larger force, but trusted still to secrecy and surprise. On the night of the 18th of April, 1775, he detached from his garrison for this purpose, eight hundred picked men, under the command of Lieutenant-colonel Smith, who sought the more effectually to conceal his march, by sending forward horsemen to arrest all travellers on the road. But, notwithstanding every precaution, startling indications of wakefulness presented themselves on every side. Dr. Warren, of Boston, had, by some means, obtained information of the intended expedition, and no sooner had the detachment started, than the intelligence was borne, as quick as light could carry it, from the steeple of the old town-house, glancing from every hill-top, and confirmed by the ringing of alarm-bells, until it reached every point within a circle of thirty miles around Boston. As the British troops marched along the road in the early morning twilight, they saw men on horseback hurrying along from point to point, with determination and indignation stamped upon their countenances. As no one offered any opposition to their march, their courage soon revived, and they arrived at the village of Lexington about five o'clock on the morning of the 19th, in high spirits. There they found about a hundred militia-men drawn up under arms, on the green before the meeting-house. Major Pitcairn, galloping up, in no very courteous terms, ordered them to disperse; and, on their hesitating to obey his commands, he discharged his pistol, and ordered his soldiers to fire. By the discharge which followed, three or four of the militia were killed, and the rest retreated behind the church and dispersed. After this slight skirmish, this opening of the tragedy, Lieutenant-colonel Smith proceeded on his march until he reached the town of Concord, of which he took possession unopposed. He then detached parties to guard the approaches to the town, while the main body proceeded to destroy the arms, ammunition, and provisions, which were found in store. A detachment, sent forward to occupy a bridge, was surrounded by a body of militia and minute-men, who, having approached in the guise of travellers, were opposed and fired upon. A general skirmish commenced, which ended in the confused retreat of the detachment towards the main body in the town. Smith immediately ordered a retreat. The militia, increasing in numbers, commenced a series of desultory attacks; and, without concert, organization, or orders, maintained a galling fire upon the front, flanks, and rear of the retreating column, from behind houses, walls, and trees. When the British arrived at Lexington, they found themselves in a most exhausted state; and they would, no doubt, have been totally destroyed, had not General Gage, apprehensive for the fate of the expedition, sent forward Lord Percy, in the morning, with sixteen companies of foot, a corps of marines, and two pieces of artillery, to support Lieutenant-colonel Smith. The retreating and advancing detachments entered Lexington at opposite points, at the same time, and the latter, with their field-pieces, checked the fierce pursuit of the provincials, while the former were resuming order, and putting themselves in a better posture of defence. All together then proceeded towards Boston, while the assailants, without attempting to obstruct their march, kept up an incessant fire, both in front and rear, from behind stone walls, which lined the road along the greater part of the route. The British forces arrived, exhausted and wearied, at Bunker's Hill, near Boston, a little after sunset, having sustained a loss of sixty-five killed, one hundred and eighty wounded, and twenty-eight prisoners. The loss of the Americans was fifty killed and thirty-four wounded.

The intelligence of this event excited the utmost enthusiasm throughout Massachusetts, and the whole country was soon put in warlike array. The first blood was shed in defence of American rights, and without adequate provocation. The militia had met in open conflict with the proud army of England and overthrown it. They had come to that conflict on a sudden summons, without arrangement, discipline, or experience, every one obeying the impulse of his own patriotism and courage; and though some were roused from their sleep at the dead of night, others hurried, half-armed, from long distances, and others mingled in the affray, without well knowing how it commenced, or what was its object; all fought almost without thinking, certainly without shrinking, until the night closed upon vanquished and victors; when the first had time to take counsel, or consider the consequences of the unforeseen battle in which they had engaged, and the unhoped-for triumph which they had won. Out of victory thus gained in the first encounter, arose a new hope for the whole land. The British cannon at Lexington dispelled the apathy, as it kindled the indignation of every man from the St. Lawrence to James's River; and though peace was still assumed to be the condition of the colonies, and England's acts and language were becoming more conciliatory, both felt that their differences were, from that hour, committed to the arbitrement of the sword, and each prepared, at once, with the utmost diligence, for the bloody trial which appeared imminent and inevitable.

The sentiments of Washington, in reference to these events, may be gathered from a letter written by him to George William Fairfax, in England, dated at Philadelphia, May 31, 1775, while he was there attending the Second Continental Congress. It is as follows :

"DEAR SIR,—Before this letter will come to hand, you must undoubtedly have received an account of the engagement in the Massachusetts Bay, between the ministerial troops (for we do not, nor can we yet prevail upon ourselves to call them the king's troops) and the provincials of that government. But as you may not have heard how that affair began, I enclose you the several affidavits* which were taken after the action.

"General Gage acknowledges that the detachment under Lieutenant-colonel Smith was sent out to destroy private property ; or, in other words, to destroy a magazine, which self-preservation obliged the inhabitants to establish. And he also confesses, in effect at least, that his men made a very precipitate retreat from Concord, notwithstanding the reinforcement under Lord Percy ; the last of which may serve to convince Lord Sandwich and others of the same sentiment, that the Americans will fight for their liberties and property, however pusillanimous, in his lordship's eye, they may appear in other respects.

"From the best accounts I have been able to collect of that affair, indeed from every one, I believe, the fact, stripped of all colouring, to be plainly this, that if the retreat had not been so precipitate as it was, and God knows it could not well have been more so, the ministerial troops must have surrendered, or been totally cut off. For they had not arrived in Charlestown (under cover of their ships) half an hour, before a powerful body of men from Marblehead and Salem was at their heels, and must, if they had happened to be up one hour sooner, inevitably have intercepted their retreat to Charlestown. Unhappy it is, though, to reflect, that a brother's sword has been sheathed in a brother's breast, and that the once happy and peaceful plains of America are either to be drenched with blood, or inhabited by slaves. Sad alternative ! but can a virtuous man hesi tate in his choice ?"

The Provincial Congress of Massachusetts being in session at the time of the battle of Lexington, passed a vote for raising thir-

---

* These depositions were intended to prove that the British were the aggressors, and had commenced the action at Lexington.

teen thousand six hundred men, and called upon the other New England colonies to increase this number to thirty thousand. These acts were almost unnecessary, for the provincials crowded to the standard raised in defence of their rights, in numbers greater than could be maintained in the field; and placed themselves under the command of Generals Ward, Stark, Putnam, and other officers, as chance or their inclination suggested. The fortifications of Boston were considered sufficiently strong to preclude the hazard of an attack; and the number of the British in garrison was increased by the addition of ten thousand men, who arrived about the same time as Lord North's conciliatory resolution.

The provincials, however, formed a line of thirty miles in extent around the peninsula on which the town is built, entirely cutting off its connection with the surrounding country.

Thus stood these two armies in front of each other; the one on the heights of the town, and the other on the surrounding hills, each animated by powerful, but different impulses to begin that contest which was to decide the fate of American liberty. The British, weary of inactivity, thirsted to become participators in the glory which their new generals—Howe, Burgoyne, and Clinton—had won on every debated field in Europe, over the most disciplined and tried valor, and which they did not think could be perilled in open conflict with the raw, unorganized mobs of the colonies. Even those who shared in the former short struggle and sudden flight, could not admit that, on a fair field, and in battle order, they would not be an over-match for ten times their number of the provincials. Surrounding them was the ocean, over whose vast space spread their undisturbed dominion, while their enemies had not a single shallop or a mounted gun along their extended line of coast. Between them and their country, profuse in wealth, valor, and the munitions of war, there rose no barrier, nor could even coward's fear suggest the apprehension that a country without a single ship would attempt to intercept their convoys on that highway of nations, where the angry elements alone were supposed to be their rivals. The army was well provided with stores, and every thing necessary for aggression or defence. Their vessels of war were moored around the town, and so placed as not only to render the narrow accesses thereto impassable, but, if need be, to reduce the town itself to ashes in a single hour. And this fair and growing town was the capital of the province, contained most of its wealth, was the seat of its provincial assembly, and inhabited by thirty thousand Americans; so that, if ever they were, as it seemed, blockaded in their city camp, they had in their power the lives of nearly twice their own number of the enemy, and not a shell could be thrown into their intrenchments without imminent risk of a conflagration, which would lay in ruins that proud, rising, though, as they thought, rebellious city, so justly an object of pride and love to the besieging army.

And, on the other hand, what was that army? By this time several officers had assumed the command of its different divisions; but they were independent of each other, and subject to no superior; nor did they derive their rank from any civil authority. They neither received nor expected pay for that dangerous service, and were kept together solely by virtuous patriotism. The troops, if such they might be called, acknowledged no control, and though they sat down before the city, prepared to brave danger and death, they were bound by no obligation, save their own courageous purpose. The army was, in fact, a multitude of men brought together by the impulsive enthusiasm of sudden emergency; but there was no instance of devotion in ancient or modern times to suggest a hope that, without provisions, ammunition, clothing, or pay, beyond the uncertain supplies which patriotism might furnish, they could be maintained, after the first flush of victory subsided, or necessity began to press upon them. They had scarcely any of the agencies, which, in all ages, enabled nations to wage successful war. Their first impulse to resistance arose from their aversion to taxation; and no one man in all the colonies would be bold enough to counsel the heavier tax necessary to meet the expenses of the country's defence; nor was there any constitutional or delegated authority competent to impose it. Perhaps that great struggle presented, in all its vicissitudes, no feature so singular and admirable as the mutual faith and trust which kept those thousands, with their chiefs, knit together, during the doubtful period that intervened between the battle of Lexington and the appointment by Congress, of a commander-in-chief, who was to reduce to order, discipline, and efficiency, the elements of resistance which his country presented, and lead these raw troops, at first to desperate struggles, sure of defeat, and finally to victory and glory.

In the provincial army there were many men of eminent abilities and tried patriotism. There were generals, and colonels, and captains; but among them all, there was not one moulding mind, having confidence and power to undertake the management of the whole, so as to secure the means of making a permanent stand for the liberties of the country. The salvation of America, at this juncture, depended on the cordiality of co-operation which prevailed in the camp. Each chief confined the sphere of his action to his own immediate duties, and none thought of supplanting or overruling his brother officer, while every man in the army must have felt that his personal responsibility extended to the entire defence of his country. Hence, he was indifferent where, or under whom he served, and was eager to perform any duty, the only emulation between him and his fellows being, who could do the best service and incur the greater peril. There is no trial of a man's courage so severe as uncertainty; nor was there ever on earth an instance when uncertainty prevailed to as great an extent, as during the first struggle of the people of Massachusetts. They knew not what resolution the other states had come to. From the great extent of the country, and the delays and difficulties of holding communications, the people of New England might have been scattered by the invading army long before those of Virginia or the Carolinas had intelligence of their first resistance, or could even determine either on giving or refusing aid; yet was there none found to falter or to hesitate; and all trusted that the same just cause, in defence of which they took up arms, would find volunteers throughout every part of the continent. They calculated truly, for while the camp was recruited by almost every young man in Massachusetts, and even the old and feeble attended them with whatever means they could spare, and drove to the camp, from hamlet and farm, cart loads of provisions, which were bestowed not merely without a price, but with a benediction; the committees of corre spondence in every other colony were actively engaged in preparing for the common defence.*

Meantime, while the British were thus penned up in Boston, an adventurous scheme was formed by two determined provincial leaders, Colonels Arnold and Allen. Collecting a small body of men in Connecticut, they proceeded against the fortresses of Crown Point and Ticonderoga, the keys of Canada; those against which so many expeditions were planned during the French War. Traversing, undiscovered, the immense wilderness which then stretched across the north of New England, they completely surprised and captured, without the loss of a man, both these important places,

---

* Doheny's History of the American Revolution.

23

each containing a valuable and much needed supply of military stores.   Colonel Arnold was equally successful against a sloop of war lying at St. John's, and thus obtained the command of Lake Champlain, by the capture of the first vessel that ever belonged to the American Navy.

COSTUME OF THE BRITISH INFANTRY, 1775.

STATE HOUSE AND CONGRESS HALL, PHILADELPHIA.

CHAPTER X.

The Second Continental Congress.

EANWHILE the alarming state of the country, and the prospect of war at no very distant day, had led the people of the different provinces to form various schemes for the defence of their liberties and property. In Virginia, they resorted to the practice pursued by Pennsylvania and Maryland during the French war, of forming themselves into independent companies, throughout the different counties, for the purpose of military training, and to secure some degree of organization. These companies acted independently of each other, choosing their own officers, from the rank of captain down. They adopted such uniforms as they pleased, and provided themselves with arms, ammunition, drums, and colours. As soon as war was apprehended, several of these companies solicited Colonel Washington to take them under his command. He always acceded to these requests, and aided them materially in procuring equipments, and in perfecting their discipline. On one occasion he was very near being brought into an active command of these companies. The hasty step of Governor Dunmore, in causing the powder to be secretly removed from the magazine in Williamsburg, and placed on board one of his majesty's ships in the river, roused the indignation, and kindled the martial spirit of the whole colony The independent companies flew instantly to their arms, and resolved to march to Williamsburg, and compel the governor, by force, to restore the powder.* For this purpose upwards of seven hundred men assembled at Fredericksburg; but the governor, having promised to arrange the affair to the satisfaction of the people, a council of deputies from the several companies was held, in which, after much warm discussion, it was resolved that they should all return home, but hold themselves in readiness to march at any future alarm at a moment's warning.

In the mean time, the Second Virginia Convention met at Richmond on the 20th of March. They had scarcely come together when Patrick Henry introduced a series of resolutions for putting the colony in a state of defence, and for imbodying, arming, and disciplining for that purpose a sufficient number of men. The boldness of these resolutions caused many of the ablest patriots of the province to oppose them. It was in support of them that Henry was led to utter that memorable declaration : "We must fight! I repeat it, sir, we must fight! An appeal to arms and to the God of hosts is all that is left us!" The resolutions were carried, and Washington was appointed on a committee to report a plan for putting them in execution. The former deputies were appointed to the Continental Congress, which was summoned to meet on the 10th of May, except that Thomas Jefferson was substituted for Peyton Randolph, in case the latter should not be able to attend.

Four days after the return of the independent companies from Fredericksburg, Colonel Washington left Mount Vernon to attend the meeting of the Second Continental Congress; which assembled at Philadelphia, on the 10th of May, 1775. Twelve of the colonies were represented, and before the close of the session, they had the satisfaction of admitting delegates from Georgia, the thirteenth, to a participation in their deliberations. The prudence and caution with which these deliberations were conducted, show that the object of this justly celebrated council was not an open rupture with England. Peyton Randolph was again unanimously chosen president, but urgent business soon after requiring his presence

* Note to Washington's Writings, by Jared Sparks, vol. ii. p. 507.

at home, he was succeeded by John Hancock. Charles Thomson was re-elected secretary.

Early in the session, an official account of the hostilities at Lexington and Concord, and of the capture of Crown Point and Ticonderoga, was laid before them. Some of the members were unprepared for so serious a result; but the majority, seeing no other way of preserving their liberties inviolate, urged the necessity of defensive operations. Accordingly, on the 26th of May, after stating the dangerous and critical situation of the colonies, from the attempts to carry into execution, by force, several unconstitutional acts of parliament, from the actual hostilities committed in Massachusetts, and from the large number of troops daily expected, with the same hostile views, Congress unanimously determined, " that for the express purpose of securing these colonies, and preserving them in safety, against all attempts to carry said acts into execution, by force of arms, the colonies be placed in a state of defence." Still, before attempting any active measures, they determined, though with a few dissentient voices, to make another attempt at reconciliation, by a second solemn appeal to the king. Nor did they confine themselves to a petition to his majesty; they again addressed the people of Great Britain, and of the province of Quebec; and also sent an address to the inhabitants of Ireland, and a letter to those of the island of Jamaica.*

 O the king, † they expressed, as strongly as ever, their devotion to his person, family, and government; their deep regret at any event which could weaken their connection with his crown, and their ardent desire for the restoration of harmony.

The address to the people of Great Britain ‡ is eminently distinguished for its magnanimity and eloquence. Even its opening, which is as follows, is remarkable:

" THE TWELVE UNITED COLONIES, BY THEIR DELEGATES IN CONGRESS, TO THE INHABITANTS OF GREAT BRITAIN.

" Friends, countrymen, and brethren,—

" By these, and by every other appellation that may designate the ties which bind us to each other, we entreat your serious

* Pitkin, vol. i. 330.
† The address to the king was drawn up by Mr. Dickinson.
‡ Said to have been written by R. H. Lee.

Q

attention to this, our second attempt to prevent their dissolution. Remembrance of former friendships, pride in the glorious achievements of our common ancestors, and affection for the heirs of their virtue, have hitherto preserved our mutual connection. But when that friendship is violated by the grossest injuries, when the pride of ancestry becomes our reproach, and we are no otherwise allied than as tyrants and slaves, when reduced to the melancholy alternative of renouncing your favour or our freedom, can we hesitate about the choice? Let the spirit of Britons determine."

After again recapitulating former injuries, and stating the recent acts of hostility by the wanton destruction of their lives, as well as property, they seriously ask, "whether the descendants of Britons could tamely submit to this? No," they add, "we never will,—while we revere the memory of our gallant and virtuous ancestors, we never can surrender those glorious privileges, for which they fought, bled, and conquered."

"Admit," they tell them, "that your fleets and armies can destroy our towns, and ravage our coasts; these are inconsiderable objects, things of no moment to men whose bosoms glow with the ardour of liberty. We can retire beyond the reach of your navy, and without any sensible diminution of the necessaries of life, enjoy a luxury, which, from that period, you will want,—the luxury of being free."

They again repel the charge of aiming at independence.

"Our enemies charge us with sedition. In what does it consist? In our refusal to submit to unwarrantable acts of injustice and cruelty? If so, show us a period in your history, in which you have not been equally seditious.

"We are accused of aiming at independence; but how is this accusation supported? By the allegations of your ministers, not by our actions. Abused, insulted, and contemned, what steps have we pursued to obtain redress? We have carried our dutiful petitions to the throne. We have applied to your justice for relief. We have retrenched our luxury, and withheld our trade.

"The advantages of our commerce were designed as a compensation for your protection: when you ceased to protect, for what were we to compensate?

"What has been the success of our endeavours? The clemency of our sovereign is unhappily diverted; our petitions are treated with indignity; our prayers answered by insults. Our application to you remains unnoticed, and leaves us the melancholy apprehension of your wanting either the will or the power to assist us.

"Even under these circumstances, what measures have we taken that betray a desire of independence? Have we called in the aid of those foreign powers, who are the rivals of your grandeur? When your troops were few and defenceless, did we take advantage of their distress, and expel them our towns? Or have we permitted them to fortify, to receive new aid, and to acquire additional strength?

"Let your enemies and ours persuade you, that in this we were influenced by fear, or any other unworthy motive. The lives of Britons are still dear to us. They are the children of our parents, and an uninterrupted intercourse of mutual benefits had knit the bonds of friendship. When hostilities were commenced; when, on a late occasion we were wantonly attacked by your troops, though we repelled their assaults, and returned their blows, yet we lamented the wounds they obliged us to give; nor have we yet learned to rejoice at a victory over Englishmen.

"As we wish not to colour our actions, or disguise our thoughts, we shall, in the simple language of truth, avow the measures we have pursued, the motives upon which we have acted, and our future designs.

"When our late petition to the throne produced no other effect than fresh injuries, and votes of your legislature, calculated to justify every severity; when your fleets and your armies were prepared to wrest from us our property, to rob us of our liberties or our lives; when the hostile attempts of General Gage evinced his designs, we levied armies for our security and defence. When the powers vested in the governor of Canada gave us reason to apprehend danger from that quarter,—and we had frequent intimations that a cruel and savage enemy was to be let loose upon the defenceless inhabitants of our frontiers,—we took such measures as prudence dictated, or necessity will justify.

"We possessed ourselves of Crown Point and Ticonderoga; yet, give us leave most solemnly to assure you, that we have not lost sight of the object we have ever had in view,—a reconciliation with you on constitutional principles, and a restoration of that friendly intercourse which, to the advantage of both, we till lately maintained."

After reminding them, that the loss of liberty in America would be only a prelude to its loss in Great Britain, they conclude, "A cloud hangs over your head and ours,—ere this reaches you, it may probably burst upon us; let us then (before the remembrance of former kindness is obliterated) once more repeat these appellations, which are ever grateful to our ears; let us entreat Heaven to avert our ruin, and the destruction that threatens our friends, brethren, and countrymen on the other side of the Atlantic."

The address to the inhabitants of Canada was drawn up by Messrs. Jay, Adams, and Deane, and is distinguished by so much manliness of sentiment and force of expression, that it is not unworthy of a more particular notice in this place. Its general tenor is the same as that of the addresses to the people of Ireland and the West Indies. "Since the conclusion of the war," its writers say, "we have been happy in considering you as fellow-subjects; and from the commencement of the present plan for sub-jugating the continent, we have viewed you as fellow-sufferers with us. As we are both entitled by the bounty of an indulgent Creator to freedom, and being both devoted by the cruel edicts of a despotic administration to common ruin, we perceived the fate of the Protestant and Catholic colonies to be strongly linked toge-ther, and therefore invited you to join with us in resolving to be free, and in rejecting with disdain the fetters of slavery, however artfully polished.

"We most sincerely condole with you on the arrival of that day in the course of which the sun shall not shine on a single freeman in all your extensive dominions. Be assured that your unmerited degradation has engaged the most unfeigned pity of your sister colonies, and we flatter ourselves you will not, by tamely bearing the yoke, suffer that pity to be supplanted by contempt.

"When hardy attempts are made to deprive men of rights be-stowed by the Almighty; when avenues are cut through the most solemn compacts for the admission of despotism; when the plighted faith of government ceases to give security to dutiful subjects; and when the insiduous stratagems and manœuvres of peace become more terrible than the sanguinary operations of war; it is high time for them to assert those rights, and with honest indignation oppose the torrent of oppression rushing in upon them."

After assuring them that the capture of the forts of Ticonderoga and Crown Point was only dictated by self-preservation, they strongly represented the subservient condition to which they would be reduced by closing with the claims of Great Britain, and con-cluded with the following animated expressions: "We yet enter-tain hopes of your uniting with us in the defence of our common liberty; and there is yet reason to believe that should we join in

imploring the attention of our sovereign to the unmerited and unparalleled oppressions of his American subjects, he will at length
be undeceived, and forbid a licentious ministry any longer 'to riot
in the ruins of the rights of mankind."

THESE papers, breathing the same ardent love
of liberty, containing the same dignified sentiments, evincing the same determined purpose of soul, and the same consciousness of
the justice of their cause, as those of the
former session ; drawn up in language no
less bold and energetic on the subject of their
rights, or less affectionate towards those to
whom they were addressed, were sent forth
as a last effort "to accommodate the unhappy disputes between
Great Britain and her colonies."

Having issued these addresses, Congress proceeded at once to
the adoption of such measures as they considered necessary to
carry into effect their resolution, to put all the colonies in a defensive position. All the troops within their limits, and acknowledging their authority, were now to be called the Continental Army :
committees were appointed to devise ways and means for raising
and supporting it, supplying it with arms and stores, and preparing
regulations for its government. An issue of paper money was
voted, to the amount of three millions of dollars ; and a resolution
was passed appropriating five hundred dollars a month, as the pay
of the commander-in-chief of the Continental Army. The next
object was considered to be the choice of a commander, and on
this point, as on a pivot, the liberties of America now rested.
Hitherto, the enthusiasm of the men had received no check, from
their ability to calculate the chances, hazards, or duration of a war,
or to balance against them their own feeble resources and total
want of military establishments. It is to be supposed that a general, appointed to so precarious and dangerous a command, be his
experience ever so limited, must see and measure at least the
apparent difficulties of his situation, and his dim prospect of being
able to resist, for any length of time, the operations of one of the
bravest, best disciplined, and best prepared armies in the world.
The appointment of a commander easily discouraged, or of one
possessing but an ordinary degree of firmness, would have been
irretrievably fatal to the cause.

There was still another difficulty in the way of selecting a commander. This difficulty did not arise from the want of ability in

24   Q 2

the candidates suggested; but serious apprehensions were entertained whether any person whom they might select would be acceptable to all the colonies. The remarkable weight of talents in Virginia, and its wealth and forwardness in the great project, were circumstances not to be overlooked, and which pointed to the policy, if not the necessity, of securing that powerful province by this mark of distinction; and which of the sons of Virginia was more deserving the honour than Colonel Washington? On the other hand, the existing army had been raised wholly by the New England provinces, and to put it under the command of an officer of a distant province, was thought to be a delicate and hazardous experiment. It was, however, of the utmost importance to secure unanimity in the choice, and to unite the whole continent in the support of the commander-in-chief.

Great, therefore, was the relief felt by the members, when John Adams, the leading representative of Massachusetts, "in discussing the question respecting the army then lying before Boston, made a motion that it should be adopted by the continent, and in enforcing his motion, said it was his intention to propose for the office of commander-in-chief, a gentleman from Virginia, and one of their own body. His remarks on the qualifications of this gentleman were so pointed, that they were known to apply only to Colonel Washington, who, upon hearing this reference to himself, immediately withdrew. The appointment was deferred to a succeeding day, when Washington was nominated by Thomas Johnson, a delegate from Maryland. The choice was by ballot, and, on counting the votes, it was found that he was unanimously elected."* This was on the 15th of June, 1775. When the Congress assembled the next morning, the president informed him officially that he was unanimously chosen by the Continental Congress to be general and commander-in-chief of all the forces raised, or to be raised, for the defence of the country.

He immediately arose in his place, and accepted the appointment with his usual and characteristic modesty, diffidence, and disinterestedness, in the following address to the president :—" Though I am truly sensible of the high honour done me in this appointment, yet I feel great distress, from a consciousness that my abilities and military experience may not be equal to the extensive and important trust. However, as the Congress desire it, I will enter upon the momentous duty, and exert every power I possess in their service, and for the support of the glorious cause. I beg they

* Note to Washington's Writings, by Sparks, vol. iii. 480, 481.

will ac.ept my most cordial thanks for this distinguished testimony of their approbation.

"But, lest some unlucky event should happen, unfavourable to my reputation, I beg it may be remembered by every gentleman in the room, that I this day declare, with the utmost sincerity, I do not think myself equal to the command I am honoured with.

"As to pay, sir, I beg leave to assure the Congress, that, as no pecuniary consideration could have tempted me to accept this arduous employment at the expense of my domestic ease and happiness, I do not wish to make any profit from it. I will keep an exact account of my expenses. Those, I doubt not, they will discharge; and that is all I desire."

"Having thus placed one of their own body, a gentleman of ample fortune, and great distinction, in a situation so new, so replete with difficulties and dangers; having called him to be principal in support of a cause in which, in case of failure, not only his fortune but his life, must be the certain forfeiture, those patriots did not leave him without the most solemn pledge of their support. With his commission, they presented him a resolution, declaring that they would *maintain* him, and *assist* him, and *adhere* to him, with their *lives* and *fortunes*, in the same cause. With respect to instructions for the conduct of the commander, in the untried scenes before them, Congress could do little more than direct him, as the Roman senate formerly did their consuls in times of danger, to take care 'that the republic should receive no detriment.' In their letter to him on this subject, they say: 'And whereas all particulars cannot be foreseen, nor positive instructions for such emergencies so beforehand given, but that many things must be left to your prudent and discreet management, as occurrences may arise upon the place, or from time to time befall you, and therefore, upon all occasions that may happen, to use your best circumspection, and advising with your council-of-war to order and dispose of the army under your command, as may be most advantageous for attaining the end for which those forces have been raised; making it your special care, in the discharge of the great trust committed unto you, *that the liberties of America receive no detriment.'* "

General Washington, with his usual promptness, immediately began his preparations to proceed to the seat of war. His private opinions and reasons for accepting the command, as well as the tender affection which he always felt for his beloved wife, are well

* Pitkin, vol. i. 334, 335

expressed in the following letter to her, dated Philadelphia, June 18, 1775.

"My Dearest,—I am now set down to write to you on a subject which fills me with inexpressible concern, and this concern is greatly aggravated and increased, when I reflect upon the uneasiness I know it will give you. It has been determined in Congress that the whole army raised for the defence of the American cause shall be put under my care, and that it is necessary for me to proceed immediately to Boston to take upon me the command of it.

"You may believe me, my dear Patsy, when I assure you, in the most solemn manner, that, so far from seeking this appointment, I have used every endeavour in my power to avoid it, not only from my unwillingness to part with you and the family, but from a con sciousness of its being a trust too great for my capacity, and that I should enjoy more real happiness in one month with you at home, than I have the most distant prospect of finding abroad, if my stay were to be seven times seven years. But as it has been a kind of destiny that has thrown me upon this service, I shall hope that my undertaking it is designed to answer some good purpose. You might, and I suppose did perceive from the tenor of my letters, that I was apprehensive I could not avoid this appointment, as I did not pretend to intimate when I should return. That was the case. It was utterly out of my power to refuse this appointment, without exposing my character to such censures as would have reflected dishonour upon myself, and given pain to my friends. This, I am sure, would not, and ought not, to be pleasing to you, and must have lessened me considerably in my own esteem. I shall rely, therefore, confidently, on that Providence, which has heretofore preserved and been bountiful to me, not doubting but that I shall return safe to you in the fall. I shall feel no pain from the toil or the danger of the campaign; my unhappiness will flow from the uneasiness I know you will feel from being left alone. I therefore beg that you will summon your whole fortitude, and pass your time as agreeably as possible. Nothing will give me so much sincere satisfaction as to hear this, and to hear it from your own pen. My earnest and ardent desire is, that you would pursue any plan that is most likely to produce content, and a tolerable degree of tranquillity; as it must add greatly to my uneasy feelings to hear that you are dissatisfied or complaining at what I really could not avoid.

"As life is always uncertain, and common prudence dictates to every man the necessity of settling his temporal concerns, while it

is in his power, and while the mind is calm and undisturbed, I
have, since I came to this place, (for I had not time to do it before
I left home,) got Colonel Pendleton to draft a will for me, by the
directions I gave him, which will I now enclose; the provision
made for you in case of my death will, I hope, be agreeable."

The Congress afterwards chose Artemas Ward, Charles Lee,
Philip Schuyler, and Israel Putnam, major-generals, and Horatio
Gates, adjutant-general.   On the 22d of June, they appointed Seth
Pomeroy, Richard Montgomery, David Wooster, William Heath,
Joseph Spencer, John Thomas, John Sullivan, and Nathaniel Green,
brigadier-generals.

HESE appointments gave universal satisfaction.   General Washington used the utmost
expedition in preparing to start for the seat of
war.   Before he left Philadelphia he reviewed
several independent companies of volunteers,
amounting in all to about two thousand men,
under arms.   One of these companies, a troop
of light-horse, accompanied him as far as New
York.   He was also accompanied to that city
by General Schuyler, whom he left there in
charge of the troops of the province, and by General Lee, who continued with him to Cambridge.   He was met, at Newark, by a
committee from the Provincial Congress of New York, and escorted
by them to that metropolis, where he arrived on the 25th of June.
An address presented by the New York Congress to Washington,
on this occasion, was remarkable for its tone of timidity and luke-
warmness, and for the broad hint contained in its concluding paragraph; as well as for the delicate and appropriate answer which it
drew from Washington; leading him, as it did, to avow sentiments, at this early period of the war, which were closely adhered
to throughout its whole progress, and in an especial manner at its
close.

The address of the New York Congress contained this paragraph :

"Confiding in you, sir, and in the worthy generals immediately
under your command, we have the most flattering hopes of success
in the glorious struggle for American liberty, and the fullest assurance, that whenever this important contest shall be decided by that
fondest wish of each American soul, an accommodation with our
mother country, you will cheerfully resign the important deposit

committed into your hands, and re-assume the character of our worthiest citizen."

The following was General Washington's reply :

" Gentlemen, at the same time that with you I deplore the unhappy necessity of such an appointment, as that with which I am now honoured, I cannot but feel sentiments of the highest gratitude for this affecting instance of distinction and regard.

" May your every wish be realized in the success of America, at this important and interesting period ; and be assured, that every exertion of my worthy colleagues and myself will be equally extended to the re-establishment of peace and harmony between the mother country and the colonies, as to the fatal, but necessary operations of war. When we assumed the soldier, we did not lay aside the citizen ; and we shall most sincerely rejoice with you in that happy hour, when the establishment of American liberty, upon the most firm and solid foundations, shall enable us to return to our private stations in the bosom of a free, peaceful, and happy country."

On the 26th of June, General Washington departed from New York, under the escort of several military companies, passed the night at Kingsbridge, and the next morning proceeded on his journey. He arrived at Cambridge on the 2d of July. During the whole of this journey, he met with the most flattering attentions from the people, as well as the public authorities, of the districts through which he passed. He was continually escorted by companies of volunteers ; and at Springfield, a hundred miles from Boston, a committee of the Massachusetts Assembly met, and accompanied him to head-quarters. On his arrival at Watertown, where the Provincial Congress of Massachusetts was then sitting, an address was presented to him by that body, pledging themselves to the most cordial co-operation with his measures. His reply was simple and dignified.

" Gentlemen," said he, " your kind congratulations on my appointment and arrival, demand my warmest acknowledgments, and will ever be retained in grateful remembrance. In exchanging the enjoyments of domestic life for the duties of my present honourable but arduous station, I only emulate the virtue and public spirit of the whole province of Massachusetts Bay, which, with a firmness and patriotism without example in modern history, has sacrificed all the comforts of social and political life, in support of the rights of mankind, and the welfare of our common country. My highest ambition is to be the happy instrument of vindicating those rights, and to see this devoted province again restored to peace, liberty, and safety."

On arriving at the head quarters, at Cambridge, he was welcomed by the troops with joyful acclamations. He found the army, consisting of about sixteen thousand men, so disposed as to beleaguer the enemy within Boston; but they were much distressed on account of the necessary munitions of war, and the want of subordination manifested by the greater number of them towards their officers. He, accordingly, first turned his attention to the remedying of these evils, the disciplining of the army, and the closer investment of the city.

COSTUME OF BRITISH TROOPS, 1775.

WARREN.

CHAPTER XI.

Battle of Bunker Hill.

IN the mean time, the spark which had been lighted at **Lexington**, and fanned at Concord, had been blown up into a blazing fire at Bunker Hill. On the arrival of reinforcements from Europe, General Gage prepared for more decisive operations than he had thought it prudent, previously, to attempt. In the midst of his preparations, he issued a proclamation, as a last warning to the people, before a final appeal to arms. He placed before them the dread alternative of war or submission; if they still persisted in their rebellion, he would commence a war of extermination; but if they would submit, he offered a free pardon to all, for past offences against the government, except Samuel Adams and John Hancock, whom he described as "firebrands,"

out who were objects of confidence and respect to the American people. This proclamation only aroused the Americans to more vigorous exertions. Rightly judging that the proclamation was the herald of immediate hostility, and regarding it as the last aggression on their civil liberties, for it contained the promulgation of martial law, they boldly prepared for the worst.

A council of war was called, and the Provincial Congress suggested to them the great importance to either army of the possession of Bunker Hill, a commanding eminence on the north side of the peninsula of Charlestown, and nearly opposite to the British camp. The council immediately adopted the suggestion, and on the night of the sixteenth of June, a detachment of one thousand men, under the command of Major Prescot, was ordered to take possession of Bunker Hill, and throw up, with the greatest expedition, field fortifications for the defence of the position. By some mistake, the detachment took up their station on Breed's Hill, another eminence to the right, and still nearer to the enemy's lines. Here they began their field-works, and so silently and sedulously did they labour, that at dawn of day the British were alarmed to discover a small redoubt constructed on the brow of the hill, nearly under the guns of their vessels. Orders were instantly given to the batteries and vessels to commence a simultaneous fire upon the works and workmen. But this heavy cannonade seemed only to stimulate the young soldiers' activity and zeal; nor did they pause until they had constructed a line of breastwork from the right of the redoubt to the bottom of the hill. Towards noon, General Gage, finding all his efforts to arrest these formidable preparations unavailing, determined on dislodging the Americans; and gave orders that two squadrons, under command of Generals Howe and Pigot, should undertake that duty. They were landed at Moreton's, the north-east point of Charlestown peninsula. To their left was the village of that name, consisting of about five hundred houses; in front of them the American works; and to their right, the valley between Breed's and Bunker Hills. Beyond the Americans, the peninsula gradually narrowed till it ended at Charlestown neck, at the left of which, as you enter the peninsula, was stationed the Glasgow man-of-war; and, at the right, two floating batteries. The Americans continued their works while the British forces formed on the shore. Slowly and steadily the latter proceeded up the hill, under cover of their guns, which poured into the American intrenchments a continuous and destructive fire, pausing occasion-

R

ally to give their field-pieces time to play on the newly constructed works. Meantime, orders were given by the British general to set Charlestown on fire, lest it might serve as a cover for the provincials. It was built, for the most part, of wood; suddenly one wild flame enveloped the whole town, and, curling high in air, shed its unnatural light over the scene of havoc, adding to the heat and suffocation of the sultry summer day. The inhabitants of Boston, the unengaged soldiers, the American army from their camp, witnessed this terrible spectacle; but they soon lost all interest in the burning houses and temples, to watch the progress of the advancing columns, while, amid the roar of cannon, and the glare of the blazing town, they moved up the declivity where so many of them were to find gory graves. The Americans calmly and unmovedly regarded the steady onset of discipline and courage. Major Putnam, a veteran soldier of the colonies, charged his untrained warriors to withhold their fire until they could distinguish "the whites of their assailants' eyes," and then to fire low. Well was that order obeyed;—their first fire was so deadly that the advancing troops reeled under the shock, wavered, and suddenly fled. They were again rallied by the courage of their officers, and again advanced to the charge; but again the same unerring stream of fire continued to pour in upon them from the redoubt and breastwork, until, a second time, their lines broke, and they fled precipitately. General Clinton seeing this disaster from the camp, and burning with shame at the defeat of the British arms, volunteered to lead a fresh detachment to their aid. His presence once more inspired the British officers, and, by wonderful exertions, amounting, in some cases, to goading the men, they prevailed upon them again to face those terrible and immovable lines. This third attack was even more cautious than the others, and the artillery had raked the entire length of the breastwork before the troops reached it. By this time, the ammunition of its defenders was nearly exhausted; but they reserved their last fire until the enemy was at the works. This fire was true and telling as the former, but it had not the same effect, for the British soldiers, charging fiercely, attacked the redoubt on three sides, and carried it by storm; the Americans, who had been ordered to retire when their powder was spent, continuing to defend it, and dealing death around them with the butt end of their muskets, until the redoubt was filled with the enemy. While the ground at the redoubt and intrenchments was thus contested and won, a detachment of the British right, ordered to turn the left flank of the Americans, was received by the defenders of that pass, where they sheltered themselves with hay, and the rails of a fence, hastily thrown together during the early part of the conflict, with equal coolness, firmness, and precision of fire. There, too, the British troops staggered beneath the well-directed aim of the provincials, who retired only from their post of danger when they saw the works on the hill abandoned by the main body. Then they joined the retreat, and the British remained masters of the field of battle. But though the victory was theirs, the retreat of their enemy was unmolested, and they were allowed time to form, for crossing at their own convenience the terrible passage of the Neck, exposed to the double fire of the batteries and the Glasgow man-of-war. The British halted on Bunker Hill, where they hastily threw up defences; and the Americans took their position immediately opposite them, on Prospect Hill, and began that line of fortifications which was never more approached by the attacking army.

The British encamped that evening about a mile in advance of their position in the morning; but dearly did they pay for the advantage. Nineteen of their bravest officers, and two hundred and twenty-six men lay dead in the disputed way, while eight hundred and twenty-eight of the remainder were wounded. Of the Americans, two hundred and seventy-eight were wounded, thirty-six missing, and one hundred and thirty-nine slain. Among the latter was Doctor Warren, a man whom his country deeply loved, and long mourned. He commanded that day for the first time, with the rank of major-general, a rank which he only held four days, and which was conferred on him for the purity of his patriotism, and his eminent abilities.

The disproportion of killed and wounded will appear still more strange, on a comparison of the numbers actually engaged. Almost all accounts agree in stating these numbers thus:—British, three thousand; Americans, one thousand five hundred.

Although the ground was lost, the Americans claimed the victory. Their confidence in themselves was greatly increased, and it was universally asked, "How many more such triumphs the British army could afford?" This battle was, in fact, one of the most bloody and destructive which we find recorded in the annals of war.

CARLETON

CHAPTER XII.

Invasion of Canada.

FTER the capture of Ticonderoga and Crown Point by Colonels Allen and Arnold, the former returned home, leaving Arnold in garrison at Ticonderoga. His impetuous spirit, however, ill brooked inactivity, and early in June he proposed the bolder design of invading the Canadas, which he promised to reduce with four thousand men. To this proposal Congress refused then to accede. But the governor of Canada, Sir Guy Carleton, engaging in active preparations for retaking the forts, and the military spirit of the colonies rising with each successive event, the invasion of Canada was, two months afterward, voted to be practicable, just, and necessary.

Its practicability was based upon the courage and success of the provincials; its justice, on the preparations of Sir Guy Carleton, which, in the eyes of Congress, amounted to indications of aggressive war, and invasion; and its necessity, on the overruling law of self-preservation.

The responsibility of the northern expedition devolved on General Montgomery, who with a thousand men effected a landing at St. John's, to which he laid siege. His want of ammunition forbade the hope of speedy success, but succeeding in an attack on a small fort, called Chamble, about six miles off, he obtained six tons of gunpowder, which enabled him to prosecute the siege with vigor. The garrison maintained themselves with great bravery; but learning that the governor, who was marching to their aid from Montreal, with eight hundred men, was attacked and routed ly Colonel Allen, the victor of Crown Point, they surrendered on terms of honourable capitulation. Montgomery here obtained thirty-nine pieces of cannon, nine mortars, two howitzers, and eight hundred stand of arms. During the siege of St. John's, Colonel Allen was taken prisoner, on an expedition planned by his general, and sent to England, loaded with irons. Montgomery hastened from St. John's to Montreal, which was evacuated, on his approach, by the few troops stationed there, who, with General Prescott, the governor of St. John's, attempted to escape down the river, but were captured by some troops and an armed gondola, at the junction of the Sorel. One hundred and twenty prisoners here surrendered themselves on terms of capitulation. Montgomery, scarcely delaying to count the immense advantages, in food, clothing, and necessaries of all kinds, placed in his hands by the evacuation of this rich commercial town, pushed rapidly on, and with his small, but victorious army, set down before the capital of the province. And here, for the first time, the full extent of his difficulties and perils arose upon his hopes, and checked them. He was a soldier by profession, accustomed to strict obedience. His troops were, for the most part, the champions of liberty, who carried into armed service the spirit which animated them to undertake their country's defence. To them the charm of that service was, that honour and courage were its only obligations; nor would they brook the idea, that, undertaken on those terms, it should be prolonged by other authority than their own will. Many a time of danger, as well as this, saw the cause for which the colonists took up arms, reduced to the verge of ruin by a similar spirit; nor was it until after many perilous escapes from a final overthrow, that sanguine men, in Congress and out of it, admitted the stern necessity of maintaining a regular army for the defence of the country. Some, who were engaged for no term, and some whose term had nearly expired, when unsustained by military movements, and exposed to unaccustomed severity of weather, united in claiming their dismissal from the service; and the situation of thei. general was rendered precarious and most difficult; but the genius of Montgomery prevailed over greater obstacles. During his brief but bright career, he endeavoured to maintain himself without once sinking the humanity and honour of the man, in the sternness of the hard-set commander. And a daring ally hastening to his relief by a route hitherto unattempted by the steps of civilized man, was now approaching the colony, from a quarter, in whose depths the inhabitants thought that not even the savages shared the solitude of the bear and the wolf.

About the time of Montgomery's invasion, Arnold, at the head of one thousand men, left the camp at Cambridge, by the order of General Washington, with the design of penetrating Canada by the streams of the Kennebec and Chaudière, and through the intervening wilderness. In the ascent, of the former, they had often to land and haul their boats up rocks down which roared the precipitous river. And when this weary task was done, they but exchanged the labours of the waters for greater labours on the land. They had to carve their slow way through forests at the rate of five miles a day, to cross deep swamps, and creep over rough crags, which it seemed that neither man nor beast ever before clambered. Their numbers were daily thinned by sickness and hunger, many of them consuming their dogs, shoes, leathern breeches, and cartouches. When yet one hundred miles from a human habitation, they divided their last remaining stores, which amounted to four pints of meal to each man. With thirty miles of yet untrodden pathway to march over, they had eaten their last morsel. But in this trying journey, they were sustained by the hope of completing an enterprise unrivalled, save by the most dazzling achievements of the heroes of antiquity. After a march of nearly two months of unexampled hardships and difficulty, the Hannibal of the New World reached the first inhabited settlement on the borders of the Chaudière, which emptied itself into the St. Lawrence, a few miles above Quebec. Here his delay was shorter than required by the broken spirits and worn-out energies of his feeble but unshrinking band. With the rapidity of ambition did he speed, leaving the inhabitants to conjecture whether he had issued from the wilderness or descended from the clouds. His welcome and reception were in proportion to their wonder and awe; and he circulated among them the proclamations of the commander-in-chief, offering liberty, security, and peace, should they aid the common object of the united colonies. But Arnold relied on sterner agencies than these, and his sudden appearance near Quebec caused as much consternation in the garrison as if his had been an army of demons, so little could they calculate upon the approach from that quarter of such a foe. Arnold found the town, as he had anticipated, completely deserted, the governor being absent, endeavouring to turn the storm of war, raging upon another side of the province. The mighty river rolled between him and his certain prey, and vessels of war, moored in the stream, checked his first bold and prompt design of crossing the river, and entering at once the undefended gates of Quebec. But the passage would have been attempted in the night, were it not for a storm which raged for several days and nights, sweeping with angry, but protecting surge, between the panting Arnold and the unguarded town. While he was thus delayed, the panic in the garrison abated, and Colonel McLean, with his Scotch volunteers, threw himself into it to protect its fate, or share its fall. Arnold, chafing at further delay, moved his force down the river to Wolfe's Cove, and resolved to imitate the daring, and share the glory of the hero of that name. At dead of night his intrepid band crossed the flood and ascended the precipitous banks at the other side. Here a council-of-war was held, in which Arnold proposed to storm the town; but this counsel was overruled as desperate; and, after a short delay before the walls, he was obliged to retire to a position of greater safety, twenty miles up the river, there to await a junction with Montgomery.

Meantime the governor of Canada arrived in Quebec, and took the promptest and most decisive measures for its defence; so that by the time the junction of the two American generals was effected, it was fully prepared to resist their joint assault. Ere Arnold reluctantly abandoned the storming of Quebec, or retired from its walls, he was forced to admit to himself, that all his toil, his waste of time and treasure, and the stupendous undertaking he had accomplished, had been in vain. He sighed to think, that the storm which averted from the city his long collected blow, or being a day or two behind the propitious time, should interpose between him and his crowning fame, and give to Quebec and Canada a different destiny. But thus does fortune play with the prospects of the wisest and the boldest. The spirit of Arnold was not, however, to be depressed by this mischance. He warmly seconded Montgomery's prompt resolution of investing Quebec; a resolution at once executed. But Quebec was defended by superior resources and a valor equal to their own. Sir Guy Carleton was a man of great daring and the sagest prudence. By his presence and virtue he infused his own indomitable spirit into the bosoms of all the inhabitants; and every day the siege was continued gave fresh proofs of the strength and security of his position. The besiegers, fearing delay, and sorely urged by the season, the climate, and the uncertainty of the service subordinate to their authority, resolved to risk the storming of the garrison at every hazard. That attempt was made at five o'clock in the morning, on the last day of the year, their forces being divided into four parties, the two principal of which were led in person by Montgomery and Arnold. A heavy snow-storm enveloped besiegers and besieged, amid the fury of which the devoted bands and their gallant leaders groped their way to the destined points of attack. These were, for the two main divisions, the two opposite sides of the lower town—Montgomery choosing that around Cape Diamond, by the banks of the river, which was guarded by an outpost. The pathway leading to this post was narrow and difficult, being under the steep precipices, and covered by large masses of ice, washed in upon it by the overgorged river. Along this the storming party advanced with extreme difficulty in single file, and the general himself leading the way, had more than once to halt for those that followed. Reaching the outpost, its guards, after a few random shots, fled to the battery; but being in advance of his men, the general again halted to give time to his followers to collect, and as soon as about two hundred were collected, he rushed forward, animating them by his voice and example, when one of the sentinels who had fled, astonished at the delay, returned to his post, and slowly applying a match to a gun mounted there, fired it without any immediate design. This single and chance shot decided the fate of the assault; its first victim was General Montgomery. He fell dead where he stood; and two young and gallant officers who shared his peril and daring, shared also his untimely fate. Colonel Campbell, on whom devolved the command, hesitated to advance; and the troops, whom no danger could deter, when following their beloved general, seeing him lying dead, retraced their steps with confusion and consternation. Arnold, to whom this disaster was unknown, approached the opposite battery, along the suburb of St. Rogers, about the same time. He, too, found all in readiness to meet him, and in assaulting the first battery, received a wound and retired to have it dressed. The battery was, however, taken, and Captain Morgan, of the Virginia riflemen, who were leading the assault, was called on by a unanimous shout to assume the command and rush forward. That dauntless officer accepted with eagerness the post of danger and of honour; at the same moment, Lieutenant Anderson, issuing from the gate, with the view of attacking the Americans, who were supposed to be plundering the exposed part of the town, challenged Captain Morgan, and received a ball through his head from Morgan's hand in reply. His troops fell back and closed the gate. The besiegers instantly scaling the wall, saw inside a large force, with their guns fixed to the earth, ready to receive any who descended on their bayonets, and at the same time a most destructive fire was poured upon them from windows and port-holes, beneath which they retired into the stone houses outside the barrier, where the dawning day discovered them endeavouring to answer, but ineffectually, the terrible fire from the barrier and surrounding posts. To appear even an instant outside their precarious shelter was certain death; and so depressed were the men by defeat, disaster, and cold, that they refused to attempt a retreat in the face of the murderous barrier. Meantime, troops issuing from another gate made their rear-guard prisoners, and completely surrounded them. But, even in this situation, the resolution which still upheld the American leaders, prompted the desperate attempt of cutting their way, sword in hand, through the town backwards. While preparing, however, for this last enterprise, they were entirely encompassed, and surrendered prisoners of war. Many officers of this detachment were killed, and all the rest, including the intrepid Morgan, except a few who accompanied Arnold, were taken prisoners. Thus ended this assault upon Quebec, which many have described as rash and desperate, but which all admit to be one of the most gallant upon record. Its failure supplies the readiest proof that it was ill-advised and unmilitary; but if, as it is on the other hand averred, the shot which deprived the army of its general was a random one, discharged by a trembling hand at a forsaken post, success might have changed the reasoning, and generated a host of critics, stout to assert that the enterprise was as wisely and surely planned as it was daring and chivalrous.

Upon Arnold's camp, the new year opened with gloomy prospects; yet, himself badly wounded, the army dispirited by defeat and suffering, his bravest chiefs dead or captured, and the winter closing around him with its frozen terrors, he did not hesitate to prosecute boldly the blockade. And the distress to which he reduced the garrison, which once or twice barely escaped falling into his hands, ere he was superseded in command, proves that his

26

energy was indomitable, and his operations those of a consummate military genius.

But in all that surrounded it of gloom and horror, in this season of snow and storms, nothing pressed so heavily on the American army as the fate of their too gallant general. No thought had they for calculating harshness in judging the enterprise which cost his life. And indeed, if want of foresight, to any extent, dimmed the lustre of that stupendous undertaking, it was amply redeemed by his personal contempt for danger, and his chivalrous fall. Nor does it well become the nation on whose arms victory smiled, to insult his memory on this ground; for, had he lived to divide their strength, or share in the encounter, history may be compelled to restrict the praises which British valour justly claims from the triumph of that eventful day. Nor was the voice of unkind criticism much heeded by the generous ear. No man fell in, or perhaps survived the war, save one, to whose virtue and courage so large and liberal a tribute of homage was offered, of hearty admiration by his enemies, of deepest mourning by his adopted country. His monument, the first voted by Congress, attests the estimation in which they held his eminent services, his purity, and his genius. But, perhaps, the most solid testimony to his worth and valour was, the cheer which echoed through the British senate when the baffled minister "cursed his virtues for having undone his country."

Let us not pass to other subjects without doing justice to the humanity and clemency of Sir Guy Carleton, and the garrison of Quebec. The prisoners who fell into their hands, and the wounded who were left to their mercy, were treated with the kindest solicitude, and most delicate respect. Whether in the hour of danger or of triumph, the garrison never lost sight of the honourable duties which brave men ever discharge towards those whom the chances of war deliver into their power.

The fate of the northern army claimed the early and anxious care of the commander-in-chief, and of Congress. The largest supplies that could be afforded were generously voted to its command. Nor was the hope abandoned, even yet, of arousing in the breasts of Canadians the love of liberty, and a community of purpose with the other states. Franklin, then the literary star of the continent, arrived on this mission with two able coadjutors, having means and authority to establish a free press. But the task of thoroughly conciliating a province with different habits, tastes, and religion, and a priesthood averse to the union, was then hopeless;

or the spirit that could accomplish it was hushed for ever. Fortune's current was turned backwards. The army, though greatly
reinforced, was unable to maintain itself against the still more
numerous army now hotly pressing it, and commanded by the
accomplished soldier who saved Quebec. Advantages of a trifling
character were occasionally gained by the continental troops; but
a series of reverses, thickening upon their scattered forces, and
increasing their difficulties at every step, with a victorious army
hovering in their rear, compelled them, early in the summer, to
evacuate the province, and abandon an expedition from which so
much was hoped, and which, at one time, was justly regarded as
nearly crowned with success.

GENERAL MONTGOMERY.

HEAD-QUARTERS AT CAMBRIDGE

CHAPTER XIII.

Siege and Evacuation of Boston.

HEN General Washington arrived at Cambridge, on the 2d of July, he found a mixed multitude of people there, under very little discipline, order, or government; the enemy in possession of Bunker Hill, on Charlestown Neck, strongly intrenched, and fortifying themselves. He found part of the Continental Army on Winter and Prospect Hills, about a mile and a quarter from the enemy on Bunker Hill, in a very insecure state; another part at the village of Cambridge, which he made his head-quarters; and a third part at Roxbury, guarding the passage in and out of Boston. He immediately began to throw up lines of defence at these places, for the double purpose of securing his troops from any attempts of the enemy, and

cutting off all communication between the latter and the surrounding country.   The enemy's strength, including marine forces, was
estimated at about twelve thousand ; that of the Americans, present
and fit for duty, thirteen thousand seven hundred, or including the
sick and absent on leave, sixteen thousand seven hundred.   With
this number, Washington had to guard a semicircle of eight or
nine miles, to every part of which he found it necessary to be
equally attentive; whilst the enemy, situated as it were in the
centre of the semicircle, and having the entire command of the
water, could bend their whole force against any one part with equal
facility.   Several circumstances, however, concurred to render the
American forces very inadequate to active operations.   Many of
the soldiers were ill-provided with arms, particularly with bayonets ;
and the general soon became acquainted with the alarming fact,
that the quantity of powder in the camp would only supply nine
rounds to each man.   Much distress was also occasioned by the
want of tents and clothing.   The urgency and continuance of these
wants were increased by causes which General Washington thus
stated in a letter to Congress :   "I should be extremely deficient in
gratitude as well as justice, if I did not take the first opportunity
to acknowledge the readiness and attention which the Congress
and different committees have shown to make every thing as convenient and agreeable as possible ; but there is a vital and inherent
principle of delay incompatible with military service in transacting
business through such various and different channels.   I esteem it
my duty, therefore, to represent the inconvenience that must unavoidably ensue from a dependence on a number of persons for supplies, and submit it to the consideration of Congress whether the
public service will not be best promoted by appointing a commissary-general for that purpose."
    The fact that no such officer had been appointed, and that the
army wanted a paymaster and a quarter-master-general, will give
some idea of the labours and difficulties to which the general was
subjected.   The want of arms and ammunition was one which it
was extremely difficult to supply.   A successful voyage was, however, made to the coast of Africa, where every pound of gunpowder
for sale in the British factories was purchased, and a magazine was
seized in the island of Bermudas.
    The absolute importance of a maritime force now began to be
extensively felt throughout the country, and this sentiment was
daily increased by the aggressions of British ships of war, whose
commanders had received orders from the king to proceed against

any sea-port towns where troops might be raised, or military work erected. Under these directions, a small naval force arrived before Falmouth, in Maine, commanded by Captain Mowatt, who, on his arrival, gave notice that he was directed to burn every sea-port town between Boston and Halifax,* and demanded of the inhabitants all their arms and ammunition, and four of their citizens as hostages. This order being of course refused, a furious cannonade and bombardment was commenced, by which the whole town was speedily reduced to ashes. This brutal measure may be said to have originated the American navy. Ships of war were immediately fitted out, and, at the urgent suggestion of General Washington, courts were established to take cognisance of prizes, whose proceedings were conducted on the soundest principles of international law.†

In September, 1775, a committee of Congress was appointed, who repaired to head-quarters for the purpose of consulting with the commander-in-chief " on the most effectual method of continuing, supporting, and regulating the army." On their return, it was determined by Congress, that the new army, intended to lie before Boston, should consist of twenty thousand three hundred and seventy-two men, whose officers were to be raised chiefly from the troops already stationed there. There was one result of the report of this committee, and the deliberations of the Congress upon it, which, for years, entailed the most pernicious and embarrassing effects, and which was nearly fatal to the cause of American independence.

The members of this body had suddenly sprung into political importance. Their practical knowledge of the means of conducting a war was, in general, as scanty as their notions of political justice, and their spirit of freedom and patriotism were exemplary. Their caution, as was natural, increased with the peril of their cause, until, in this particular instance, it realized the proverbial effect of fear, by creating a danger almost as serious as any which it strove to avoid. The example of a Cromwell, afforded by the annals of their ancestors, and of a host of military despots, supplied by universal history, inspired in their minds a fear, lest, having thrown off the restraints of the parent government, their liberties should fall a prey to the ambition of a military faction, whose power would unquestionably exceed that of any other portion of the community. After the ample opportunities they had had of

---

* No orders were issued by the British ministry for the destruction of these towns.
† See Washington's Writings, vol. iii. 155.

acquainting themselves with the character of Washington, it is next to impossible that these fears should have had reference to him; certain it is, however, that they extensively prevailed, and dictated the measure which perpetually thinned the numbers, and relaxed the discipline of their army. This great error consisted in enlisting soldiers—not for the duration of the war, but—for the term of one year only. Its lamentable consequences will be seen hereafter.

As soon as the measure was determined on, the general issued his orders, that all officers who intended to decline the further service of their country at the expiration of the term for which they were engaged, should signify their intentions, in writing, to their respective colonels; and "those brave men and true patriots who resolved to continue to serve and defend their brethren, privileges, and property," were also requested to signify their intentions in the same manner.

But the comparative inactivity of the army, as it lay before Boston, engaged in strengthening its position, with now and then an inconsiderable skirmish, allowed time for that ardor to cool, which had been so gloriously evinced at Lexington and Bunker Hill. Many were unwilling to continue in the service after the brief term of their first enlistment. Some consented under inadmissible conditions; while some suspended their decision.

The general, therefore, repeated his orders for an explicit and unconditional declaration. "The times," said he, "and the importance of the great cause we are engaged in, allow no time for hesitation and delay. When life, liberty, and property are at stake; when our country is in danger of being a melancholy scene of bloodshed and desolation; when our towns are laid in ashes, and innocent women and children driven from their peaceful habitations, exposed to the rigor of an inclement season, to depend, perhaps, on the hand of charity for support;—when calamities like these are staring us in the face, and a brutal, savage enemy (more so than ever was found in a civilized nation) are threatening us, and every thing we hold dear, with destruction from foreign troops, it little becomes the character of a soldier to shrink from danger, and condition for new terms. It is the general's intention to indulge both officers and soldiers who compose the new army, with furloughs, for a reasonable time; but this must be done in such a manner as not to injure the service, or weaken the army too much at once."

In this state of things, several officers, supposing that commissions and rank might depend on recruiting men, began, without permission, to enlist soldiers to serve particularly under them This practice it was necessary to stop. All further enlistments under particular officers were forbidden, till directions to that effect should be given. "Commissions in the army," say the orders, " are not intended for those who can raise the most men, but for such gentlemen as are most likely to deserve them. The general would not have it even supposed, nor our enemies encouraged to believe, that there is a man in his army (except a few under particular circumstances) who will require to be twice asked to do what his honour, his personal liberty, the welfare of his country, and the safety of his family, so loudly demand of him. Where motives powerful as these, conspire to call men into service, and when that service is rewarded with higher pay than private soldiers ever yet received in any former war, the general cannot, nor will not, until convinced to the contrary, harbour so despicable an opinion of their understanding and their zeal for the cause, as to believe they will desert it."

At the same time that General Washington urged these appeals upon the troops, he communicated his sentiments with equal earnestness to Congress.

" The disadvantages," he observed, " attending the limited enlistment of troops are too apparent to those who are eye-witnesses of them, to render any animadversions necessary; but to gentlemen at a distance, whose attention is engrossed by a thousand important objects, the case may be otherwise. That this cause precipitated the fate of the brave, and much-to-be-lamented General Montgomery, and brought on the defeat which followed thereupon, I have not the most distant doubt; for had he not been apprehensive of the troops leaving him at so important a crisis, but continued the blockade of Quebec, a capitulation, from the best accounts I have been able to collect, must inevitably have followed. And that we were not at one time obliged to dispute these lines, under disadvantageous circumstances, proceeding from the same cause, to wit, the troops disbanding of themselves before the militia could be got in, is to me a matter of wonder and astonishment, and proves, that General Howe was either unacquainted with our situation, or restrained by his instructions from putting any thing to hazard, till his reinforcements should arrive.

" The instance of General Montgomery (I mention it because it is a striking one, for a number of others might be adduced) proves, that, instead of having men to take advantage of circumstances,

you are in a manner compelled, right or wrong, to make circum
stances yield to a secondary consideration. Since the 1st of December, (upwards of two months previously,) I have been devising
every means in my power to secure these encampments; and
though I am sensible that we never have, since that period, been
able to act upon the offensive, and at times not in a condition to
defend, yet the cost of marching home one set of men, bringing
in another, the havoc and waste occasioned by the first, the repairs
necessary for the second, with a thousand incidental charges and
inconveniences which have arisen, and which it is scarcely possible either to recollect or describe, amount to nearly as much as
the keeping up a respectable body of troops the whole time, ready
for any emergency, would have done. To this may be added,
that you never can have a well-disciplined army.

" To bring men to be well acquainted with the duties of a soldier, requires time. To bring them under proper discipline and
subordination, not only requires time, but is a work of great difficulty, and, in this army, where there is so little distinction between officers and soldiers, requires an uncommon degree of
attention. To expect, then, the same service from raw and undisciplined recruits, as from veteran soldiers, is to expect what
never did, and perhaps never will happen. Men who are fami-
liarized to danger, meet it without shrinking; whereas, troops
unused to service often apprehend danger where no danger is.
Three things prompt men to a regular discharge of their duty in
time of action; natural bravery, hope of reward, and fear of punishment. The two first are common to the untutored, and the disciplined soldier; but the last most obviously distinguishes the one
from the other. A coward, when taught to believe, that, if he
breaks his ranks and abandons his colours, he will be punished
with death by his own party, will take his chance against the
enemy; but a man who thinks little of the one, and is fearful of
the other, acts from present feelings, regardless of the consequences.

" Again, men of a day's standing will not look forward; and
from experience we find, that, as the time approaches for their
discharge, they grow careless of their arms, ammunition, and
camp utensils. Nay, even the barracks themselves have felt uncommon marks of wanton depredation, and lay us under fresh
trouble and additional expense in providing for every fresh set,
when we find it next to impossible to procure such articles as are
absolutely necessary, in the first instance. To this must be added,

27   s 2

the seasoning which new recruits must have to a camp, and the loss consequent thereupon. But this is not all. Men engaged for a short and limited time only, have the officers too much in their power ; for, to obtain a degree of popularity in order to induce a second enlistment, a kind of familiarity takes place, which brings on a relaxation of discipline, unlicensed furloughs, and other indulgences incompatible with order and good government; by which means the latter part of the time for which the soldier was engaged is spent in undoing what you were aiming to inculcate in the first.

" To go into an enumeration of all the evils we have experienced in this late great change of the army, and the expenses incidental to it, to say nothing of the hazard we have run, and must run, between the discharging of one army and the enlistment of another, unless an enormous expense of militia is incurred, would greatly exceed the bounds of a letter. What I have already taken the liberty of saying, will serve to convey a general idea of the matter ; and therefore I shall, with all due deference, take the freedom to give it as my opinion, that, if the Congress have any reason to believe that there will be occasion for troops another year, and consequently for another enlistment, they would save money, and have infinitely better troops, if they were, even at a bounty of twenty, thirty, or more dollars, to engage the men already enlisted till January next, and such others as may be wanted to complete the establishment, for and during the war. I will not undertake to say that the men can be had upon these terms ; but I am satisfied that it will never do to let the matter alone, as it was last year till the term of service was near expiring. The hazard is too great, in the first place ; in the next, the trouble and perplexity of disbanding one army, and raising another at the same instant, and in such a critical situation as the last was, are scarcely in the power of words to describe, and such as no man who has experienced them once will ever undergo again.

"If Congress should differ from me in sentiment upon this point, I have only to beg that they will do me the justice to believe, that I have nothing more in view, than what to me appears necessary to advance the public weal, although, in the first instance, it will be attended with a capital expense."

The semblance of inactivity which General Washington was compelled to preserve while blockading Boston, was matter of considerable annoyance to him, anxious as he was, by some great exploit, to show himself worthy of the honourable post to which he had been advanced. As the winter approached, the army suffered severely for want of fuel, clothes, and provisions. The period of enlistment was drawing to a close, and recruits came in but slowly to occupy the places of those who insisted upon returning home. Some discontent prevailed, at what was considered the sluggishness and undue caution of the commander-in-chief, in permitting the enemy to remain so long unmolested. Under these painful circumstances, the general wrote to the Congress, in terms which will convey some idea of their incapacity to conduct a war :

"It gives me great pain," he said, "to be obliged to solicit the attention of the honourable Congress to the state of this army, in terms which imply the slightest.apprehension of being neglected. But my situation is inexpressibly distressing, to see the winter fast approaching upon a naked army, the time of their service within a few weeks of expiring, and no provision yet made for such important events. Added to these, the military chest is totally exhausted ; the paymaster has not a single dollar in hand ; the commissary-general he assures me has strained his credit for the subsistence of the army to the utmost. The quarter-master-general is precisely in the same situation ; and the greater part of the troops are in a state not far from mutiny, upon the deduction from their stated allowance. I know not to whom I am to impute this failure ; but I am of opinion, if the evil is not immediately remedied, and more punctuality observed in future, the army must absolutely break up. I hoped I had so fully expressed myself on this subject, both by letter, and those members of the committee who honoured the camp with a visit, that no disappointment could possibly happen. I therefore hourly expected advice from the paymaster, that he had received a fresh supply in addition to the two hundred and seventy-two thousand dollars delivered to him in August ; and thought myself warranted to assure the public creditors, that in a few days they should be satisfied. But the delay has brought matters to such a crisis as admits of no farther uncertain expectation. I have therefore sent off this express with orders to make all possible despatch. It is my most earnest request, that he may be returned with all possible expedition, unless the honourable Congress have already forwarded what is so indispensably necessary."

The innumerable difficulties under which General Washington was compelled to labour, by the culpable neglect, or too great caution of Congress, are thus succinctly stated by Monsieur Guizot in his introduction to the translation of Washington's writings into French. "From the first," he says, "the task of Washington lay before him in all its extent and its complexity. To carry on the war, he not only had to create an army; for, however difficult such an operation must at all times be, there the creative power was itself wanting; the United States were as destitute of a government as of an army. The Congress, a mere phantom, a delusive point of union, had no right and no power to act, and neither dared nor did any thing. Washington, from his camp, was obliged, not only unceasingly to solicit support, but to suggest to Congress what was required to be done in order to accomplish its work, and to prevent both Congress and the army from becoming a mere dead letter. His letters were read in the House, and formed the subject of their debates, but those debates were characterized by inexperience, timidity, and mistrust. Promises and pretences were all that could be obtained : matters were referred to the local governments ; and the power of the army was an object of constant dread. Washington replied respectfully, obeyed orders, and then insisted to demonstration upon the fallacy of pretences, and the necessity of supporting by real power that titular authority with which they had invested him, and that army to which they looked for victory. Men of intellect, courage, and devotion to the cause, were not wanting in that Assembly, however unaccustomed to govern it had hitherto been. Some of them visited the camp, saw with their own eyes, conversed with Washington, and brought back with them, on their return, the authority of their own observations and of his advice. The Assembly became better informed, more resolute, more confiding in its resources and in the general of its choice. The measures he required were passed ; the powers he needed were conferred upon him. He then entered into correspondence and negotiation with the local governments, with the local assemblies, with committees, with magistrates, with private citizens, pointing out facts to their observation, calling upon their good sense and patriotism, turning his own private friendships to the advantage of the public service, carefully avoiding all umbrage to the spirit of democracy or the sensitiveness of personal vanity, preserving his rank, speaking with authority, but without offence, and with the persuasiveness of moderation : wonderfully skilled in ruling men by their sense of what was right and virtuous, whilst he observed the most prudent treatment of the frailties of human nature.

"But when he had succeeded thus far ; when first the Congress, and afterwards the different states had given him the materials of an army, his task was yet unaccomplished ; the work of war was scarcely begun, the army itself not yet in existence. Here, again, he was met by complete inexperience, by the same absence of unity, the same passion for individual independence, the same conflict between patriotic intentions, and anarchical propensities. Here, again, he had to rally the most discordant elements, to hold together elements which threatened immediate dissolution, to instruct, to persuade, to act by every means of precaution and of influence, to obtain, in short, without compromising his dignity or his power, the moral support and free co-operation of his officers, and even of his soldiers.

"Then first could Washington act as a general, and turn his thoughts to the conduct of the war; say rather, that during the war itself, amidst its incidents, its chances, and its perils, he had constantly to recommence in the country, as well as in the army, the laborious task of organizing and directing the administration."

Washington had, early in the autumn, called the attention of Congress to the imminent danger which threatened the army, in consequence of the troops having enlisted but for one year, which term would expire at the end of December. A committee was accordingly appointed to repair to head-quarters to provide for the enlistment of the army for the year 1776. They found, at the expiration of the year, the names of only nine thousand, six hundred and fifty soldiers on the general's muster-roll. In consequence of their exertions, the numbers were increased by accessions from the militia to seventeen thousand. This dissolution of one army and the assemblage of another, in the face of a superior enemy, placed the commander-in-chief in a critical situation. In allusion to this he wrote to Congress:—"It is not in the pages of history, perhaps, to furnish a case like ours—to maintain a post within musket-shot of the enemy for six months together without powder; and, at the same time, to disband one army and recruit another within that distance of twenty odd British regiments, is more, probably, than was ever attempted. But if we succeed as well in the last as we have heretofore in the first, I shall think it the most fortunate event of my whole life."

Though the centre of resistance to British encroachments was in New England, it extended to the other colonies, as we have already incidentally mentioned. Virginia, from the first, had taken a prominent part. Lord Dunmore, the governor, soon forfeited his popularity, by his efforts against the colonists; and their resentment was heightened by ministers laying before parliament some letters, in which he mentioned their proceedings with extreme bitterness. Then attempting to remove some powder on board of a vessel in the harbour, he was compelled to restore it, and take refuge himself on shipboard. Finding his power on the continent entirely at an end, he endeavoured to restore it by partial and detached landings, with inadequate forces, which only irritated, without overawing. He had then recourse to the extreme measure of not only summoning all capable of bearing arms to join his standard, but offering liberty to all slaves who should follow their example; a step tending to exasperate the proprietary classes. Having thus, however, collected a small force, he took possession of Norfolk, the principal port of Virginia. The provincials assembled a considerable body of troops, and assumed a fortified position on the river Elizabeth; while the English were intrenched on the opposite bank. Captain Fordyce, sent to dislodge them, advanced briskly to the attack, but was warmly received both in front and flank, and his column retreated, though without being pursued. Lord Dunmore was then obliged to retire on board the vessels, where he was still annoyed by discharges from the houses nearest the water. He effected a landing, set them on fire, and the whole town was soon reduced to ashes. Dunmore, however, being unable to make any serious impression, or even to procure provisions, sailed to the West Indies, where he left the negroes, and proceeded to join the main army.

HIGHLAND OFFICER.

Governor Martin, in North Carolina, was involved in similar controversies with the provincial convention, which also led to his retirement on board a ship of war. In the interior, however, a number of Highlanders, recently emigrated from Scotland, were mustered by General McDonald, who was at first master of the field, but allowed himself to be amused by Colonel Moore, the opposite commander, till the country had risen around him. He then attempted a retreat, but was forced into action; several of the best officers, and many of the private soldiers, were brought down in the first onset by the American rifles, and the rest fled in confusion.

Lord William Campbell, governor of South Carolina, was equally obliged to seek security on shipboard, and joined Martin in the vicinity of Cape Fear.

Governor Tryon, also, at New York, betook himself to a similar refuge, but still retained command of the harbour, and preserved an intercourse with the numerous loyalists in that quarter.

Governors Eden and Franklin, in Maryland and New Jersey, contrived to maintain their places, but not to exercise any jurisdiction.

In the mean time, General Washington, before Boston, was informed that the prisoners taken by Governor Gage were treated by him in the most cruel and insulting manner. He affected to consider them as rebels and traitors, who had taken up arms against their king without cause, and without justice. Accordingly, when they fell into his hands, he treated them as felons, throwing them into the common prison, and making no distinction between the officers and soldiers, the dangerously wounded and unwounded. General Washington immediately wrote to him, deprecating such a course, and threatening retaliation.

"Let your opinion, sir, of the principle which actuates them," he says, "be what it may, they suppose that they act from the noblest of all principles,—a love of freedom and their country. My duty now makes it necessary," he continues, "to apprize you, that, for the future, I shall regulate all my conduct towards those gentlemen who are or may be in our possession, exactly by the rule you shall observe towards those of ours now in your custody. If severity and hardship mark the line of your conduct, painful as it may be to me, your prisoners will feel its effects. But, if kindness and humanity are shown to ours, I shall with pleasure consider those in our hands only as unfortunate, and they shall receive from me that treatment to which the unfortunate are ever entitled."

General Gage, in his answer, denied the charge of cruelty or barbarity, but acknowledged that the prisoners were lodged indiscriminately, "for," says he, "I acknowledge no rank that is not derived from the king." Washington replied, but not producing the desired effect, he resolved to adopt the same mode of treatment towards the British prisoners in his hands. Accordingly, he gave orders that the officers at Watertown and Cape Ann, who were prisoners, should be removed to Northampton, and confined in the jail in that town, along with the other prisoners. This order was obeyed, so far as related to the removal, but Washington could not bring his mind to an act so cruel and harsh as their imprisonment would appear to be, and the next day, by his secretary, wrote to the committee of Northampton, requiring them to allow the officers, on their parole, to enjoy the liberty of walking about the town.

When the command of the British forces devolved upon General Howe, he adopted a milder course towards his prisoners, and relieved Washington from a fruitful source of trouble and anxiety.

In the mean time, the besieging army laboured under accumulated difficulties. The scarcity of ammunition, notwithstanding every effort, continued almost unabated; while the want of money, as well as of necessary equipments, was severely felt through all that rigorous winter. Washington describes his situation as inexpressibly distressing, and declares, that unless some remedy were devised, the force must be broken up. Amidst all his distresses, it was necessary to keep up a good face towards the enemy, while many on the American side, exaggerating both the numbers and efficiency of his troops, wondered he should remain inactive, and not have already driven the English out of Boston. Extremely sensitive to troubles and opposition, these criticisms touched him sensibly; yet, as a true patriot, he carefully concealed the explanation, which, reaching the opposite party, would have produced fatal effects.

In February, 1776, having collected nearly seventeen thousand men, Washington thought it possible to destroy the British army in Boston, and in that way bring the war to a conclusion at one blow. "No man on earth," said he to the President of Congress, "wishes more ardently to destroy the nest in Boston, than I do; no person would be willing to go greater lengths than I shall to accomplish it, if it be thought advisable." Three successive councils of war induced him to give up the plan, but his conviction was not altered, and he spoke of this adverse decision with great regret.*

The counsel of war which decided the inexpediency of attacking the troops in Boston, unanimously advised the occupation of Dorchester heights, to the extreme right of the American lines. These heights commanded the bay, Roxbury neck, and Boston harbour. On the night of the 4th of March, during a brisk cannonade and

* See his letter to the President of Congress, dated 26th of February, 1776.

bombardment from a distant point of the American lines, a detachment of twelve hundred men, who worked all night, guarded by about seven hundred under arms, occupied and fortified this important position. The British, whose attention was directed, during the time, to the cannonade, were startled to find, at dawn of day, a powerful host, strongly intrenched in a position incompatible with the longer safety of the fleet in the bay, or the army in their intrenchments. Pressed by the alternative of a sudden and perilous evacuation, or an attempt to dislodge the detachment on the heights, bravery, and perhaps necessity, determined them to adopt the latter course.

The 5th of March, a day ominous for the soldiers of the king, arrived. It had memories of blood connected with it, and blended with the zeal for liberty, the thirst and strength of vengeance. Both parties prepared for the final struggle, conscious that success, at that early period of the contest, would go far to determine the fortune of the war. As on the day of Bunker Hill, every eminence in and around Boston was covered with anxious spectators, watching for the terrible fray, in whose event so many public and individual feelings were involved. In the American bosom were gathered resentment, coupled with a patriotic ardour to expel from the soil the arms and presence of its enslavers, and the powerful, though new impulses of a rising ambition. In that of the long cooped-up army swelled the yet unabated confidence in the superiority of British arms, and a desire, at every hazard, of escaping from the ignominy of inaction under the insulting menaces of a blockading army, as well as a stinging memory of the former fields in which they had encountered them. With these feelings inflaming all the martial passions of the two hostile forces, now nearly on an equality—for the one was superior in numbers as the other was in discipline and military resources—the encounter would have been a terrible and bloody one. But it was their fate not to meet. The British detachment ordered to dislodge the Americans, not intending to commence the assault before the morning of the 6th, were embarked on board their transports, and fell down to Castle William, to be in readiness to make the attack by daylight, from that point. But a storm arose during the night which completely scattered their boats, so as to render it impossible to make the intended attack. Washington prepared, at the other side, to lead four thousand picked men into the heart of the British camp, as soon as any considerable detachment should be engaged in the enterprise which they had planned, and now saw, with mortifica-

28   T

tion, that once more he was disappointed in his anxiety to bring on a general action.

General Howe, finding his situation rendered more precarious by this mischance, determined in a council of war, hurriedly called, to evacuate the town. Information of this determination, and of the fact that the safety of Boston depended on the inactivity of the American forces, being conveyed to General Washington, he determined to offer no interruption to the departure of the British ; but, at the same time, he prepared by fortifying Nook's Hill, and drawing his lines closer around Boston, to attack them at a moment's notice, should they manifest the least disposition to injure the town. It was reported that they were bound for Halifax, but General Washington thought that this report was propagated by them, in order to conceal their real course, while they actually intended to proceed to New York, or some more southern port. With this idea he immediately despatched Brigadier-general Heath with six regiments, and before the end of March, Brigadier-general Sullivan, with six more, for the defence of that city ; intending to follow himself with the remainder of the army, as soon as the British had entirely gone.

About nine o'clock, on the morning of the 17th of March, the British troops precipitately embarked, without attempting the destruction of Boston, but they remained within sight of the town ten days longer, and then steered for Halifax.

General Washington entered Boston, as the vessels of the enemy were yet sluggishly and, as if reluctantly, struggling through the bay, not without regret, even though he acquired so signal and cheap an advantage, that he was not able to prevent this army of invasion from transferring its operations to another part of his devoted country. The citizens of Boston received their countrymen with exulting shouts, which all America fervently echoed. The General Assembly of Massachusetts, in an address to the general, on this happy occasion, tendered him their grateful thanks for his attention to the civil constitution of the colony, whilst acting in the line of his department, and expressed their unrestrained joy in the delivery of the colony from the hateful presence of their enemies.

When the Congress at Philadelphia received intelligence of the evacuation of Boston, they resolved, "That the thanks of this Congress, in their own name, and in the name of the thirteen united colonies, whom they represent, be presented to his excellency, General Washington, and the officers and soldiers under his command, for their wise and spirited conduct at the siege and acquisition of Boston; and that a medal be struck in commemoration of this great event, and presented to his excellency; and that a committee of three be appointed to prepare a letter of thanks, and a proper device for the medal."

The following was accordingly addressed to General Washington by the president of Congress.

"*Philadelphia, April* 2, 1776.

"Sir,—It gives me the most sensible pleasure to convey to you, by order of Congress, the only tribute which a free people will ever consent to pay, the tribute of thanks and gratitude to their friends and benefactors. The disinterested and patriotic principles which led you to the field, have also led you to glory; and it affords no little consolation to your countrymen to reflect, that, as a peculiar greatness of mind induced you to decline any compensation for serving them, except the pleasure of promoting their happiness, they may, without your permission, bestow upon you the largest share of their affections and esteem.

"Those pages in the annals of America will record your title to a conspicuous place in the temple of fame, which shall inform posterity, that, under your direction, an undisciplined band of husbandmen, in the course of a few months, became soldiers; and that the desolation meditated against the country by a brave army of veterans, commanded by the most experienced generals, but employed by bad men in the worst of causes, was, by the fortitude of your troops, and the address of their officers, next to the kind interposition of Providence, confined for near a year within such narrow limits as scarcely to admit more room than was necessary for the encampments and fortifications they lately abandoned. Accept, therefore, sir, the thanks of the United Colonies, unanimously declared by their delegates to be due to you, and the brave officers and troops under your command; and be pleased to communicate to them this distinguished mark of the approbation of their country. The Congress have ordered a golden medal adapted to the occasion to be struck, and when finished to be presented to you.

"I have the honour to be, with every sentiment of esteem, sir, your most obedient and very humble servant,

"John Hancock, President."

This letter was received by General Washington at New York, on the 17th of April, when he immediately in general orders communicated the thanks of Congress to the officers and soldiers under his command; and in his letter to Congress, informing them that he had executed their order, in so doing, he observes: "They were indeed, at first, *a band of undisciplined husbandmen;* but it is, under God, to their bravery and attention to their duty, that I am indebted for that success which has procured me the only reward which I wish to receive, the affection and esteem of my countrymen."

The intelligence of these proceedings excited in England that spirit which former examples might lead us to expect. The ministry determined upon the most vigorous measures to put down a movement which had now assumed the character of open insurrection. The nation poured in addresses, which appear to have expressed decided assurances of public support. Penn, the hereditary governor of Pennsylvania, arrived with the address from Congress to the king, and endeavoured to second it, declaring his positive belief that the sentiments expressed in it were sincere. It was rejected, however, as coming from an illegal body, and consisting only of a series of empty professions, which their actions belied. The royal speech at the opening of parliament, on the 26th October, 1775, lamented that a desperate faction, by gross misrepresentations, had inflamed the mind of the people, overawed the well-affected, and amid protestations of loyalty and attachment to the parent state, openly raised the standard of rebellion. It was added that these persons now obviously aimed at total independence, and hence clemency as well as prudence called for decisive exertions speedily to put down such disorders; that those of the misled multitude who should repent of their error would experience the utmost lenity, and be received into favour, as if they had never revolted; and that individuals on the spot would be invested with discretionary powers to grant immediate pardon and indemnity to any province or colony which should return to its allegiance. Offers of aid had been received from several foreign powers; and there was no reason to apprehend hostility or impediment from any quarter.

The debates then followed in their usual train, ministers retaining their inflexible majority, while the opposition displayed unabated energy, and even a small increase of numbers. The Duke of Grafton, who had hitherto taken the side of the government, declared himself to have been misled by the supposition that their measures would issue in the peaceful adjustment of differences. He now urged a liberal course of conciliation, by repealing all the obnoxious acts passed since 1763; but unable to procure the concurrence of the cabinet, he resigned the seals, and took a decided place in the opposite ranks. The thunders of indignant eloquence were no longer heard from Chatham, who was confined with illness; but Camden, Richmond, and Shelburne, declared Great Britain to have been in every instance the aggressor, and stigmatized her proceedings as oppressive, cruel, unjust, and unrelenting, while they acquitted America of any design of aiming at independence. Wilkes asserted that ministers had wrested the sceptre out of the hands of the sovereign. Colonel Barré severely censured the conduct of the campaign, and held out the most gloomy prospects. The British army, he said, was a mere wen, a little excrescence on the vast continent of America. Fox characterized Lord North as the blundering pilot who had brought the vessel of the state into its present difficulties; in one campaign he had lost a whole continent. The provincials, he admitted, were not justifiable to the extent they had gone; yet, if they had not resisted at all, he would have thought them still more culpable. Mr. Adam, praising his lordship for ability and public virtue, accused him of indolence. The minister admitted this charge, but declared he had been forced into the situation, and had been deceived in events, never imagining that all America would have risen in arms. He pathetically lamented his own situation, under the weight of which, amid all its power and pageantry, he felt himself ready to sink. The rejection by the provincials of his conciliatory plan, proved the necessity of using force, yet without the least intention of reducing them to slavery. It was his object, immediately on their submission, to establish a most just, mild, and equitable government.

The address to the king, forming a regular echo to the speech, was carried in the Commons by one hundred and seventy-six to seventy-two, and in the Lords by seventy-five to thirty-two.

The Duke of Grafton, in the Lords, moved for accounts of the troops serving and to be employed in America. This was objected to, as giving information to the enemy, and was not pressed. The Duke of Richmond introduced the petition from Congress to the king, as an opening for pacification, and seeing in the house Mr. Penn, from Pennsylvania, obtained, with much difficulty, permission that he should be examined. That gentleman, as we have before seen, declared his belief that the colonies were willing to acknowledge the legislative authority of Britain, and did not aim at independence; but they were determined to resist arbitrary taxation, and all the obnoxious acts, so that if no concessions were made, they would probably not hesitate in seeking the aid of foreign powers. The duke's motion, that the petition afforded a ground for conciliation, was, after a warm debate, rejected, by eighty-six to thirty-nine.

In the Commons, Mr. Burke brought forward a plan, which, avoiding all extremes, would, he hoped, conciliate both parties. It included the repeal of the Boston and Massachusetts acts ; a declaration that Britain would not tax America ; a general amnesty ; and the calling of a congress by royal authority to adjust the remaining differences. Lord George Germain, who had recently joined the ministry, strenuously argued that concession must be preceded by submission. Lord North could not believe that it would lead to conciliation. Even Pownall insisted that any thing short of repealing every measure since 1763, would not now avail, and would uselessly present Great Britain in an humbled aspect as suing for peace. This motion, however, which some writers suppose might have saved America to England, commanded a larger minority than any former question, being not less than one hundred and five to two hundred and ten. Mr. Hartley followed, with a proposal for a much larger concession, but could only command twenty-one against one hundred and twenty-three.

Meantime, Lord North was carrying through a bill prohibiting all trade or intercourse with the colonies till they should submit. The Boston port, and other restraining acts were repealed, as being all merged in this greater measure ; and the regulations for the trial of the malecontents became unnecessary, when the country was to be subjected to martial law. Commissioners were to go out with full powers, not only to restore any colony, on submission, to all its privileges, but to inquire into and redress its well-founded complaints. This measure was opposed with extreme warmth in all its stages, as ruinous to Great Britain, and, in fact, proceeding on the principle adopted by the colonists themselves. The opposition, justifying the resistance of the latter, were branded by ministry as defenders, and little better than adherents of rebellion. The bill was carried by sweeping majorities, one hundred and twelve to sixteen ; seventy-eight to nineteen.

The determination being thus formed to employ force, the requisite means were to be provided. In the estimates, the number of seamen was fixed at twenty-eight thousand, of land forces at fifty-five thousand ; but the difficulty lay in making up this latter number. The troops at Boston, amounting to seven thousand four hundred, were manifestly inadequate ; while in Britain there was merely the small peace establishment considered necessary for the security of the country. The levying of a new army by voluntary enlistment was difficult and tedious ; while an additional time would be required for its training. In this exigency, ministers saw no expedient, except that of having recourse to several German princes, who on former occasions had been induced, partly by alliance, but more by pecuniary motives, to hire out their soldiers for temporary service. In the beginning, therefore, of 1776, treaties were concluded with the Landgrave of Hesse-Cassel, for twelve thousand one hundred and four men, the Duke of Brunswick, for four thousand and eighty-four, the Prince of Hesse, for six hundred and sixty-eight, and the Prince of Waldeck, for six hundred and seventy ; in all, seventeen thousand five hundred and twenty-six. These petty princes, keeping in view the extreme necessity of the British government, extorted very advantageous terms. The sum of £7, 4s. 4d. (about $36) was to be paid for each man ; and besides being relieved from the whole burden of their maintenance, they were to receive compensation for all extraordinary losses, in addition to certain stipends, amounting in all to about £135,000, not only during the whole period of their engagement, but considerably longer. Besides this heavy charge, the employment of foreign mercenaries, subjects of despotic princes, greatly aggravated the odium of the undertaking.

These treaties, being in the end of February laid before parliament, afforded ample room for invective. Their enormous expense, with the unconstitutional and dangerous tendency of introducing into the empire such vast bodies of mercenaries, were dwelt on at great length. The most gloomy views were taken of the condition and prospects of the British force. The Duke of Manchester observed, that the defection from government was total,—" total, my lords, besides the desolated prison of English troops, the devoted Boston." He saw little prospect of success with bands of German mercenaries and raw English recruits, said to be partly drawn from prisons. Earl Temple, however, while he deeply felt the imbecility of ministers, and the deplorable condition of the country, would not now obstruct their plan of making peace sword in hand. He hoped the first opportunity of doing so would be seized ; at present the die of war was cast; it was time to act, not talk. Townshend saw no reason to doubt the war being ended in a single campaign. The measures were carried, and the adverse motion negatived by the usual majorities.

The news of the evacuation of Boston arrived in England about the 1st of May. The intelligence was published by the ministry on the 3d of May, in a short paragraph, merely announcing that "his majesty's forces had embarked from Boston with the greatest order and regularity, and without the least interruption from the rebels," and were destined for Halifax. One week afterwards, the Duke of Manchester moved an address to the king, praying him to order that the despatches of General Howe and Admiral Shuldham, relating to the operations of the army and fleet in the neighbourhood of Boston, should be laid before the House of Lords. A long and warm debate ensued, in the course of which the ministers were most severely censured for the part which they had taken in the recent occurrences in America.

The Duke of Manchester complained of the scantiness of the information vouchsafed by the ministers, and said that he believed, as he was informed by private intelligence, that General Howe quitted Boston, not of his own free will; but that a superior enemy, by repeated efforts, by extraordinary works, by the fire of their batteries, rendered the place untenable. The Earl of Suffolk defended the ministry, saying, that orders had been sent out for a removal of the troops when the commander should think proper, and that after securing Halifax, it was the intention of General Howe, to penetrate by that way into the interior of the country, and thence pursue his future intended operations.

The Marquis of Rockingham, however, came nearest to the true state of the case. After stating certain particulars, which he had received through a private channel, he said :—"If those accounts are true, of which I have very little doubt, your lordships will perceive, though possibly there might have been no formal convention or capitulation signed, which I understood was avoided by the generals on both sides, for particular reasons, that, in whatever manner the business might have been negotiated, it had every substantial requisite of a treaty or compromise, as much as if it had been ever so solemnly authenticated or subscribed. The troops were permitted to evacuate the town without interruption, because they engaged on the other hand not to burn or destroy it, either previous to their departure, or after they had got on board their ships." The same sentiments were expressed by Lord Shelbourne, and other lords in the opposition, but the minister persisted that he had no knowledge or belief of any such agreement.

BATTLE-GROUND OF TRENTON.

CHAPTER XIV.

Campaign of 1776.

HE British General Howe, when he sailed from Boston, left some cruizers to watch the entrance of the bay, and to give notice of the evacuation to such British vessels as were destined for that port. Notwithstanding this precaution, however, several ships and transports sailed into the harbour, and became prizes to the Americans, who now began with the vessels, arms, and ammunition thus obtained to fit out privateers to act in some degree in the place of a regular naval force. Lieutenant-colonel Campbell of the British army, with about two hundred and seventy men, and a considerable quantity of military stores, was thus captured, while entering the harbour.

29

Anxious for the safety of New York, General Washington sent forward his whole army to that place except five regiments, which he left under the command of General Ward, for the defence of Boston. As soon as he was sure that the British vessels had certainly sailed from Nantasket Roads, where they had lain for ten days after the evacuation, he proceeded to join his army, and passing through Providence, Norwich, and New London, arrived in New York on the 13th of April. That city was but ill prepared for defence in case of the arrival of General Howe. The state troops were as deficient in arms as many of the citizens were in patriotism. Many of the most influential citizens were loyalists, and the city itself lay open to attack at any time, on the side of the ocean. Washington's first care, therefore, was to erect such forts as would command the approaches to the city, and in some degree overawe the inhabitants, while vessels were sunk in the North and East Rivers to obstruct the navigation.

Though it was soon ascertained that General Howe, instead of sailing to the southward, had steered for Halifax, Washington did not allow himself to lose time, or give his enemies an advantage which skill or activity could prevent. As the command of the Hudson River was necessary, as well to facilitate the transmission of supplies to the northern army, then under the command of General Schuyler, as to secure that intercourse between the northern and southern colonies which was of so much consequence to the Americans, he immediately began to fortify the passes in the Highlands bordering on that river. It was thus that the American army was actively employed until General Howe appeared with the British off Sandy Hook, about the end of June.

As early as December, 1775, the attention of the British was drawn to the importance of establishing a strong post in the south, with the double object in view of overawing the southern colonists, and distracting the attention of General Washington. For this purpose a large fleet was fitted out in Ireland, under the command of Admiral Sir Peter Parker, and General Clinton was detached from Boston with instructions to use the utmost diligence, so as to accomplish his object before the opening the next campaign at the north, when he was ordered at all events to join General Howe at New York. He sailed from Boston in December, and, after touching at New York, joined Governor Martin, near Cape Fear.

In the beginning of June, the British fleet, under Sir Peter Parker, came to anchor in the harbour of Charleston, where it was joined by General Clinton. Fortunately, an official letter had been inter-

cepted early in the year, announcing the departure of this armament, and its destination against the southern colonies. This gave
the colonists an opportunity to be prepared for its reception. On
Sullivan's Island, at the entrance of Charleston harbour, a fort
had been constructed of the wood of the palmetto tree, which in its
nature very much resembles the cork. Major-general Lee had
already been sent by Washington to take the command of any
forces which might be collected in the neighbourhood. His popularity soon collected a force of from five to six thousand men ; and
his high military reputation gave confidence to the citizens as well
as soldiers. Under him were Colonels Gadsden, Moultrie, and
Thompson. Colonel Gadsden commanded a regiment stationed
on the northern extremity of James Island ; two regiments under
Colonels Moultrie and Thompson occupied the opposite extremities
of Sullivan's Island. The remainder of the troops were posted at
various points. General Clinton landed a number of his troops on
Long Island, separated from Sullivan's Island on the eastern side
by a small creek. The fort on Sullivan's Island was garrisoned
by about four hundred men commanded by Colonel Moultrie.
The attack on this fort commenced on the morning of the 28th of
June. The ships opened their several broadsides upon it ; and
General Clinton attempted to cross the creek from Long Island and
attack it in the rear. The discharge of artillery upon this little
fort was incessant, but Moultrie and his brave Carolinians returned
the fire with such skill and spirit that many of the ships suffered
severely ; one of them ran aground and was burned the next morning. The British, after persisting in the attack until dark, were
repulsed and forced to abandon the enterprise. Their loss amounted
to about two hundred, that of the Americans to twenty. The palmetto wood, in this instance, proved an effectual defence, as the
enemy's balls did not penetrate, but sunk into it as into earth.

In the course of the engagement, the flag-staff of the fort was shot
away ; but Serjeant Jasper leaped down upon the beach, snatched
up the flag, fastened it to a sponge staff, and while the ships were
incessantly directing their broadsides upon the fort, he mounted the
merlon and deliberately replaced the flag. Next day, President
Rutledge presented him with a sword, as a testimony of his respect
for his distinguished valour. Colonel Moultrie, and the officers and
troops on Sullivan's Island, received the thanks of their country for
their bravery, and in honour of the gallant commander the fort
was named Fort Moultrie.

The failure of the attack on Charleston was of great importance

U

MOULTRIE.

to the American cause, and contributed much to the establishment of the popular government. The friends of Congress triumphed; and numbers of them, ignorant of the power of Britain and of the spirit which animated her counsels, began to think that their freedom was achieved. The diffident became bold; the advocates of the irresistibility of British fleets and armies were mortified and silenced; and they who, from interested motives, had hitherto been loud in their professions of loyalty, began to alter their tone. The brave defence of Fort Moultrie saved the Southern States from the horrors of war for several years.*

Congress having requested the presence of General Washington to advise with them on the state of the country, and such measures as it might be necessary to adopt for the coming campaign, he repaired to Philadelphia, stopping by the way to view the capabilities of Staten Island, with regard to fortifications. He left the troops in New York under the command of Major-general Putnam, and passing through New Jersey, arrived at Philadelphia on the 22d of May, 1776, where he remained about two weeks. Congress, as well as all the people of the country, were at this time in a high state of excitement. Affairs seemed to be hurrying to a crisis. News had lately arrived that their petition to the king had been rejected; that they had been declared rebels; that large armies were preparing to subdue them; and that their whole commerce was utterly prohibited. A large majority of the leading men, spurning the very thought of abandoning all that they had been so long contending for, and descending without a struggle from the proud rank of freemen, to be the slaves of the servants of the British empire, immediately formed the determined purpose of asserting independence. There were many, however, who still shrunk from entire separation; and even whole provinces contended against it.

* Western World, vol. i. 179, 180.

The partisans of independence, however, were bold and indefatigable. They laboured incessantly to render the subject more familiar to the popular mind and ear. It was at that time that the notorious Thomas Paine published his pamphlet called Common Sense, which had a very powerful effect upon the multitude, in bringing them over to the side of those who thought that America ought to declare herself a free and independent state, and sever for ever her unprofitable connection with Great Britain. Congress, as a preliminary step, authorized the immediate suppression of royal jurisdiction in all the colonies, and the formation of governments emanating from the people; while they met the prohibition of the British parliament against their trade, by throwing it open to the whole world except Britain. The provincial assemblies of the different colonies took the matter up. On the 22d of April, the Convention of North Carolina empowered their delegates to concur with the others in the establishment of independence. That of Virginia went farther, instructing theirs to propose it. Boston was now somewhat less forward, merely intimating that if Congress should think it necessary, they would willingly concur. To add to the difficulties of Congress, it was known from the late proceedings in parliament that commissioners were coming out with proposals for an accommodation. It is supposed that the presence and arguments of Washington had some influence in inducing them to vote an increase of the army, by the addition of twenty-three thousand eight hundred militia, ten thousand of whom were to form a flying camp.

While General Washington was in Philadelphia, he received a letter from his brother, John Augustine Washington, informing him of the resolution of the convention of Virginia, in relation to independence. He replied:

"I am very glad to find that the Virginia Convention have passed so noble a vote, and with so much unanimity. Things have come to such a pass now, as to convince us, that we have nothing more to expect from the justice of Great Britain; also, that she is capable of the most delusive arts; for I am satisfied, that no commissioners ever were designed, except Hessians, and other foreigners; and that the idea was only to deceive, and throw us off our guard. The first has been too effectually accomplished, as many members of Congress, in short, the representation of whole provinces, are still feeding themselves upon the dainty food of reconciliation; and though they will not allow that the expectation of it has any influence upon their judgment, with respect to their

preparations for defence, it is but too obvious that it has an operation on every part of their conduct, and is a clog to their proceedings. It is not in the nature of things to be otherwise; for no
man that entertains a hope of seeing this dispute speedily and
equitably adjusted by commissioners, will go to the same expense,
and run the same hazard, to prepare for the worst event, as he who
believes that he must conquer, or submit to unconditional terms,
and the concomitants, such as confiscation, hanging, and the
like."

He returned to New York on the 7th of June, and lost no time
in hastening his preparations to receive the enemy, whose fleet
was daily expected.

On the very day of Washington's arrival in New York, Richard
Henry Lee, one of the representatives of Virginia, in the Congress,
submitted a resolution for dissolving all connection with Great
Britain, and constituting the united colonies free and independent
states. This resolution was referred to a committee of the whole,
but, it appearing that six of the thirteen colonies were not yet prepared to close the door of reconciliation with the mother country,
on the 10th of June it was laid on the table until the 1st of July,
when the discussion was resumed. On the evening of that day,
the question being put in the committee, it was decided in the
affirmative, by the votes of nine colonies; the representatives of
New York, Pennsylvania, Delaware, and South Carolina, acting
under instructions from provincial conventions, did not feel themselves at liberty to concur, though the delegates, as individuals,
were mostly in favour of the measure. At the request of Mr. Rutledge, one of the representatives from South Carolina, the report of
the committee was postponed one day, and in that interval, instructions arrived from conventions in Pennsylvania and South Carolina,
and the arrival of other members from New York and Delaware,
gave majorities in those two colonies in favour of the resolution.
In the mean time, a committee, consisting of Thomas Jefferson,
John Adams, Benjamin Franklin, Roger Sherman, and R. R. Livingston, had been appointed to draw up a formal declaration of
independence. A draft was prepared by Thomas Jefferson, which,
without any amendment by the committee, was reported to Congress on the 3d of July. On the 4th, this declaration, after being
slightly modified, received the sanction of Congress, by the unanimous vote of the colonies; and it was unanimously declared that
"the united colonies were, and of right ought to be, free and independent states."

This declaration was ordered to be engrossed, and on the 2d of August, it was signed by every member then present. Copies nad, in the mean time, been sent to all the states, and one was sent to Washington, to be proclaimed at the head of the army. The news of independence was everywhere received with demonstrations of joy.

" This measure entirely altered the character of the contest, and gave a clear and definite view of the point at issue between the contending parties. We no longer see colonists complaining and petitioning with arms in their hands, and vigorously resisting an authority which they did not disavow; but a people asserting their independence, and repelling the aggressions of an invading foe."*

On receiving intelligence of this important declaration, General Washington wrote as follows, to the President of Congress :

" I perceive that Congress has been employed in deliberating on measures of the most interesting nature. It is certain that it is not with us to determine, in many instances, what consequences will flow from our counsels ; but yet, it behooves us to adopt such, as, under the smiles of a gracious Providence, will be most likely to promote our happiness. I trust the late decisive part they have taken is calculated for that end, and will secure to us that freedom and those privileges, which have been and are refused to us, contrary to the voice of nature and the British constitution. Agreeably to the request of Congress, I caused the *Declaration* to be proclaimed before all the army under my immediate command ; and have the pleasure to inform them, that the measure seemed to have their most hearty assent; the expressions and behaviour, both of officers and men, testifying their warmest approbation of it. I have transmitted a copy to General Ward, at Boston, requesting him to have it proclaimed to the continental troops in that department."

Before this, the British army had made its appearance off New York. The abrupt departure of General Howe from Boston had considerably deranged his plans, as all the supplies were directed to that city, and some, consequently, fell into the hands of the Americans. After waiting two months at Halifax, in expectation of the arrival of reinforcements from England, General Howe sailed with the force he had previously commanded in Boston . and directing his course towards New York, arrived on the 25:h

* Western World, vol. i. 188.

of June, off Sandy Hook, and, on the 3d of July, disembarked his troops on Staten Island. Admiral Howe, to whom the command of the fleet had been intrusted, touched at Halifax soon after the departure of his brother, the general, and, without dropping anchor, followed, and joined him at Staten Island, on the 12th of July. One month afterwards, General Clinton arrived with the troops brought back from the expedition against Charleston, South Carolina; and about the same time Commodore Hotham also appeared with the reinforcement under his escort; so that, at the middle of August, the invading army amounted to about twenty-four thousand men.

Admiral Howe had brought out with him letters-patent from the king, constituting him, with his brother, joint commissioners for effecting a reunion between Great Britain and her colonies. Accordingly, his first act was to send ashore to Amboy, under the protection of a flag, a circular letter addressed to the several late governors of the colonies, announcing his pacific powers, and requesting them to publish the declaration or proclamation which accompanied the letters. He promised pardon to all who had lately deviated from their allegiance, on condition that they speedily returned to their duty; and in case of their compliance encouraged them to hope for future marks of favour from their sovereign. In his declaration he observed, "that the commissioners were authorized in his majesty's name, to declare any province, colony, county, district, or town, to be at peace with his majesty; and that due consideration should be had to the meritorious services of any who should aid or assist in restoring the public tranquillity; that their dutiful representations should be received, pardons granted, and suitable encouragement to such as would promote the measures of legal government and peace, in pursuance of his majesty's most gracious purpose."

A letter containing this declaration, addressed to Governor Franklin of New Jersey, was intercepted by General Mercer and forwarded to General Washington, and by him transmitted to Congress. Washington's opinion of them may be gleaned from his letter to the President of Congress, dated July 22, 1776. He there says: "When the letter and declaration from Lord Howe to Mr. Franklin and the other late governors come to be published, I should suppose the warmest advocates for dependence on the British crown must be silent, and be convinced beyond all possibility of doubt, that all that has been said about the commissioners was illusory, and calculated expressly to deceive and put off their guard, not only the good people of our own country, but those of the English nation that were averse to the proceedings of the king and ministry. Hence we see the cause why a specification of their powers was not given to the mayor and city of London, on their address requesting it. That would have been dangerous, because it would then have been manifest that the line of conduct they were to pursue would be totally variant from that which they had industriously propagated, and amused the public with. The uniting of the civil and the military offices in the same persons, too, must be conclusive to every thinking person that there is to be but little negotiation of the civil kind."

Congress resolved that these papers should "be published in the several gazettes, that the good people of the United States might be informed of what nature were the commissioners, and what the terms, with the expectation of which the insidious court of Britain had sought to amuse and disarm them ; and that the few who still remained suspended by a hope, founded either in the justice or moderation of their late king, might now at length be convinced, that the valour alone of their country is to save its liberties."

On the 14th of July, the same day on which Admiral Howe attempted to circulate his proclamation, he sent, with a flag, a letter directed " *To George Washington, Esq.*," which the general refused to receive, it not being addressed to him with the title and in the form due to the rank which he held under the United States. This course was approved by Congress, in a resolution passed three days afterwards, by which they directed "that no letter or message be received on any occasion whatsoever from the enemy, by the commander-in-chief, or others, the commanders of the American army, but such as should be directed to them in the characters they respectively sustain."

The commissioners not wishing to recognise any officer created by the existing powers in America, and yet having strong reasons inducing them to open a negotiation with General Washington, were at first unable to determine upon any measure likely to remove this preliminary obstacle. At length, Colonel Patterson, adjutant-general of the British army, was sent to New York, by General Howe, with a letter addressed " *To George Washington, &c., &c., &c.*" He was received with great politeness, and the usual cere-mony of blindfolding, in passing through the fortifications, was dispensed with in his favour. He was introduced to the commander-in-chief, whom he addressed by the title of "excellency;" and, after the usual compliments, entered upon the business, by regretting in the name of his principals the difficulties which had arisen with respect to addressing the letters, and declaring their high esteem for his person and character, and that they did not mean to derogate from the respect due to his rank, and thus it was hoped that the *et ceteras* would remove the impediments to their correspondence. The general replied, that a letter directed to any person in a public character should have some description or indication of it, otherwise it would appear a mere private letter; that it was true the *et ceteras* implied every thing, but they also implied any thing, and that he should absolutely decline any letter directed to him as a private person, when it related to his public station. Colonel Patterson then said that General Howe would not urge his delicacy farther, and repeated his assertions that no failure of respect was intended.

A long conference ensued on the subject of prisoners, and the complaints which were made on both sides, particularly by the Congress, relative to the treatment they received. The adjutant then observed that the commissioners were armed with great powers, that they would derive the greatest pleasure from effecting an accommodation, and that he (Colonel Patterson) wished to have that visit considered as making the first advance towards that desirable object. He received for answer, among other things, that, by what had appeared, their powers were only to grant pardons; that those who had committed no fault wanted no pardons; and that the Americans were only defending what they considered their indisputable rights. Colonel Patterson was soon after introduced to the general officers, and refusing to stay and partake of some refreshments provided for him, he was conducted to his boat, which waited for him. The general had received him with honour and respect, and he had behaved with the greatest politeness and attention during the whole business, and expressed strong acknowledgments that the usual ceremony of binding his eyes had been dispensed with.

The substance of this interview was transmitted to Congress and published by their order.

The disparity existing between the numbers of the British and American forces at the siege of Boston, still existed, though in a reversed condition. General Howe, in the month of August, commanded a force of twenty-four thousand men, well disciplined, and abundantly supplied with every thing necessary to success in the field; he daily expected to be reinforced by another detachment of

German troops, and he was supported by a fleet well fitted to its destined service.

The state of General Washington's forces may be best inferred from the following letter from him to the president of Congress, dated August 8. "In my letter of the 5th, I enclosed a general return of the army under my immediate command, but I imagine the following statement will give Congress a more perfect idea, though not a more agreeable one, of our situation :—For the several posts on New York, Long, and Governor's Islands, and Paulus Hook, we have, fit for duty, ten thousand five hundred and fourteen; sick present, three thousand and thirty-nine; sick absent, six hundred and twenty-nine; on command, two thousand nine hundred and forty-six; on furlough, ninety-seven: total, seventeen thousand two hundred and twenty-five. In addition to these, we are only certain of Colonel Smallwood's battalion in case of an immediate attack. Our posts, too, are much divided, having waters between many of them, and some distant from others many miles. These circumstances, sufficiently distressing of themselves, are much aggravated by the sickness that prevails throughout the army. Every day more or less are taken down, so that the proportion of men that may come in cannot be considered as a real and serviceable augmentation on the whole. These things are melancholy, but they are nevertheless true; I hope for better. Under every disadvantage my utmost exertions shall be employed to bring about the great end we have in view, and so far as I can judge from the professions and apparent disposition of my troops, I shall have their support. The superiority of the enemy, and the expected attack, do not seem to have repressed their spirits; these considerations lead me to think, that though the appeal may not terminate so happily in our favour as I could wish, yet they will not succeed in their views without considerable loss. Any advantage they may get, I trust will cost them dear."

Soon after the date of this letter, the American army was reinforced by the arrival of Smallwood's battalion, two regiments from Pennsylvania, and a number of militia, which increased it to twenty-seven thousand, of whom but three-fourths were fit for duty. A part of these forces were stationed on Long Island, and, during the illness of Major-general Greene, was commanded by Major-general Sullivan; the remainder occupied New York, Governor's Island, and Paulus Hook.

From the time of the first appearance of the British forces, the Americans were in daily expectation of an attack. General Washington was therefore strenuous in preparing his troops for action. He was untiring in his efforts to improve their discipline, to inspire them with some of his own enthusiasm, and love of country, and high-toned indignation against the invaders of the soil. Soon after the landing of the enemy on Staten Island, he addressed them in general orders, as follows :

"The time is now near at hand which must probably determine whether Americans are to be free men or slaves; whether they are to have any property they can call their own; whether their houses and farms are to be pillaged and destroyed, and themselves consigned to a state of wretchedness, from which no human efforts will deliver them. The fate of unborn millions will now depend, under God, on the courage and conduct of this army. Our cruel and unrelenting enemy leaves us only the choice of a brave resistance, or the most abject submission. We have therefore to resolve to conquer, or to die. Our own, our country's honour, calls upon us for a vigorous and manly exertion; and if we now shamefully fail, we shall become infamous to the whole world. Let us then rely on the goodness of our cause, and the aid of the Supreme Being, in whose hands victory is, to animate and encourage us to great and noble actions. The eyes of all our countrymen are now upon us, and we shall have their blessings and praises, if happily we are the instruments of saving them from the tyranny meditated against them. Let us, therefore, animate and encourage each other, and show the whole world that a freeman contending for liberty, on his own ground, is superior to any slavish mercenary on earth. The general recommends to the officers great coolness in time of action, and to the soldiers, a strict attention and obedience, with a becoming firmness and spirit. Any officer, or soldier, or any particular corps distinguishing itself by any acts of bravery and courage, will assuredly meet with notice and rewards, and, on the other hand, those who behave ill, will as certainly be exposed and punished; the general being resolved, as well for the honour and safety of the country, as of the army, to show no favour to such as refuse or neglect to do their duty at so important a crisis."[*]

While the general was thus actively employed in organizing and disciplining his army, and preparing them to meet an enemy superior both in numbers and appointment, he did not forget or neglect his duties as a Christian; he did not neglect to admonish his followers against the commission of sinful acts, nor to encou-

* Orderly Book, July 2, 1776.

rage them, by every means in his power, to follow the path of virtue. He was unceasing in efforts to induce Congress to order the appointment of a chaplain to each regiment. His wishes in this respect were complied with in the beginning of July. He con cludes his orders, communicating this fact, by saying, that " the blessing and protection of Heaven are at all times necessary, but especially so in times of public distress and danger. The general hopes and trusts, that every officer and man will endeavour so to live and act, as becomes a Christian soldier, defending the dearest rights and liberties of his country."

In an order issued on the 3d of August, he says he " is sorry to be informed that the foolish and wicked practice of profane cursing and swearing, a vice heretofore little known in an American army, is growing into fashion; he hopes the officers will, by example as well as influence, endeavour to check it, and that both they and the men will reflect, that we can have little hope of the blessing of Heaven on our arms, if we insult it by our impiety and folly; added to this, it is a vice so mean and low, without any temptation, that every man of sense and character detests and despises it."

In the midst of his preparations for the approaching conflict, the general received intelligence, through Congress, of the brilliant successes of the American arms in South Carolina; these he promptly announced, in his orders, for the encouragement of his army.

" This glorious example of our troops," he said, " under the like circumstances with ourselves, the general hopes, will animate every officer and soldier to imitate, and even out-do them, when the enemy shall make the same attempt on us. With such a bright example before us, of what can be done by brave and spirited men fighting in defence of their country, we shall be loaded with a double share of infamy if we do not acquit ourselves with courage, and manifest a determined resolution to conquer or die. With this hope and confidence, the general most earnestly exhorts every officer and soldier to pay the utmost attention to his arms and his health; to have the former in the best order for action, and by cleanliness and care to preserve the latter; to be exact in discipline, obedient to superiors, and vigilant on duty. With such preparation, and a suitable spirit, there can be no doubt, but, by the blessing of Heaven, we shall repel our cruel invaders, preserve our country, and gain the greatest honour."

When all the reinforcements of the enemy had arrived, General ashington, in expectation of an immediate attack, and in order to inspire them with his own feelings, again addressed his army, and repeated his earnest request that every officer and soldier should have his arms and ammunition in good order; keep within his quarters and encampments as far as possible; be ready for action at a moment's call; and when called to it, to remember that liberty, property, life, and honour, would all be at stake; that upon their courage and conduct rested the hopes of their bleeding and insulted country; that their wives, children, and parents, expected safety from them alone; and that there was every reason to believe, that Heaven would crown with success a cause so just. He added,—" The enemy will endeavour to intimidate by show and appearance, but remember they have been repulsed on various occasions by a few brave Americans. Their cause is bad; their men are conscious of it, and if opposed with firmness and coolness on their first onset, with our advantage of works, and knowledge of the ground, the victory is most assuredly ours. Every good soldier will be silent and attentive, wait for orders, and reserve his fire until he is sure of doing execution: of this the officers are to be particularly careful."

The possession of Long Island is necessary to the defence of New York. It had been determined in a council of war, to fortify a camp at Brooklyn, opposite New York, and stretching across that end of Long Island, from the East River to Gowan's Cove. The rear of this encampment was defended by batteries on Red Hook and Governor's Island, and by works on the East River, which secured the communication with New York. In front of the encampment ran a range of hills, from east to west, across the island. These were covered with wood, and were steep, but could anywhere be ascended by infantry. Over this range were three passes, leading by three roads to Brooklyn Ferry.

A strong detachment of the American army was posted on Long Island, under the command of General Greene, who made himself intimately acquainted with the passes on the hills, but unfortunately becoming sick, General Sullivan succeeded him in the command, only a few days before active operations commenced. The main body of the American army remained on York Island. A flying camp, composed of militia, was formed at Amboy, to prevent the depredations of the enemy in New Jersey; and a force was stationed near New Rochelle, and at East and West Chester, on the Sound, to check the progress of the enemy, should they attempt to land above Kingsbridge, and enclose the Americans on York Island. The head-quarters of General Washington were in the city, but he was daily over at Brooklyn, to inspect the state of that camp, and to make the best arrangements circumstances would admit. An immediate attack being expected on Long Island, General Sullivan was reinforced, and directed carefully to watch the passes.

On the 22d of August, the main body of the British troops, with a large detachment of Germans, landed under cover of the ships, on the south-western extremity of Long Island. A regiment of militia, stationed on the coast, retreated before them to the heights. A large reinforcement was sent to the camp at Brooklyn, and the command of the post given to General Putnam, who was particularly charged to guard the woods, and to hold himself constantly prepared to meet the assault of the enemy.

Confident that an engagement must soon take place, General Washington made still another effort to inspire his troops with the most determined courage. "The enemy," said he, on addressing them, "have now landed on Long Island, and the hour is fast approaching, on which the honour and success of this army, and the safety of our bleeding country depend. Remember, officers and soldiers, that you are freemen, fighting for the blessings of liberty, that slavery will be your portion, and that of your posterity, if you do not acquit yourselves like men." He repeated his instructions respecting their conduct in action, and concluded with the most animating and encouraging exhortations.

On the 26th, the British, in three divisions, took post upon the south skirt of the wood; General Grant upon their left, near the coast; the German General De Heister in the centre, at Flatbush; and General Clinton upon their right, at Flatland. The range of hills only now separated the two armies, and the different posts of the British were distant from the American camp from four to six miles. Upon their left a road to Brooklyn lay along the coast to Gowan's Cove, before General Grant's division. From Flatbush a direct road ran to the American camp, in which the Germans might proceed. General Clinton might either unite with the Hessians, or take a more eastern route, and fall into the Jamaica road, by the way of Bedford. These three roads unite near Brooklyn. On the pass of Flatbush, the Americans had flung up a small redoubt, mounted it with artillery, and manned it with a body of troops. Major-general Sullivan continued to command

31   X

on the heights. On the evening of the 26th of August, General Clinton, without beat of drum, marched with the infantry of his division, a troop of light-horse, and fourteen field-pieces, to gain the defile on the Jamaica road. A few hours before day he surprised an American party stationed there to give the alarm of an approaching enemy, and, undiscovered, seized the pass. At daylight he passed the heights, and descended into the plain on the side of Brooklyn. Early in the morning General De Heister, at Flatbush, and General Grant, upon the western coast, opened a cannonade upon the American troops, and began to ascend the hill; but they moved very slowly, as their object was to draw the attention of the American commander from his left, and give General Clinton opportunity to gain the rear of the American troops stationed on the heights. General Putnam, in the apprehension that the serious attack would be made by De Heister and Grant, sent detachments to reinforce General Sullivan and Lord Sterling, at the defiles through which those divisions of the enemy were approaching. When General Clinton had passed the left flank of the Americans about eight o'clock on the morning of the 27th, De Heister and Grant vigorously ascended the hill; the troops which opposed them bravely maintained their ground, until they learned their perilous situation from the British columns, which were gaining their rear.

As soon as the American left discovered the progress of General Clinton, they attempted to return to the camp at Brooklyn, but their flight was stopped by the front of the British column. In the mean time the Hessians pushed forward from Flatbush, and the troops in the American centre, under the immediate command of General Sullivan, having also discovered that their flank was turned, and that the enemy was gaining their rear, in haste retreated towards Brooklyn. Clinton's columns continuing to advance, intercepted them; they were attacked in front and rear, and alternately driven by the British on the Hessians, and by the Hessians on the British. Desperate as their situation was, some regiments broke through the enemy's lines and regained the fortified camp.

The detachment on the American right, under Lord Sterling, behaved well, and maintained a severe conflict with General Grant for six hours until the van of General Clinton's division having crossed the whole island, gained their rear. Lord Sterling perceived his danger, and found that his troops could be saved only by an immediate retreat over a creek near the cove. He gave orders to this purpose, and to facilitate their execution, he in person attacked Lord Cornwallis, who, by this time having gained the coast, had posted a small corps in a house just above the place where the American troops must pass the creek. The attack was bravely made with four hundred men, who, in the opinion of their commander, were upon the point of dislodging Cornwallis; but his lordship being reinforced from his own columns, and General Grant attacking Lord Sterling in the rear, this brave band was overpowered by numbers, and those who survived were compelled to surrender themselves prisoners of war; but this spirited assault gave opportunity for a large proportion of the detachment to escape.

The loss of the Americans on this occasion, compared with the number engaged, was great; General Washington stated it at a thousand men, but his returns probably included only the regular regiments. General Howe, in an official letter, made the prisoners amount to one thousand and ninety-seven. Among these were Major-general Sullivan and Brigadier-generals Sterling and Wood-hull. The amount of the killed was never with precision ascertained. Numbers were supposed to have been drowned in the creek, and some to have perished in the mud of the marsh. The British loss acknowledged by General Howe, was twenty-one officers, and three hundred and forty-six privates, killed, wounded, and taken.*

General Washington passed over to Brooklyn in the heat of the action; but unable to rescue his men from their perilous situation, was constrained to be the inactive spectator of the slaughter of his best troops. On this occasion, he is said for a moment to have lost his customary equanimity, and to have burst into the most violent exclamations of grief. He was now sensible of the imminent peril which would follow from his awaiting the regular approaches of the enemy. His troops were without tents, many were suffering from sickness, and all from fatigue. Moreover, the movements of the British fleet indicated an intention to force a passage into the East River, and thus cut off the retreat of the troops into New York. By this measure the whole army would, doubtless, have been lost. The general, therefore, determined on an immediate removal of the army from Long Island to New York. This seemed, at first sight, to be utterly impracticable. The East River, nearly a mile broad, and sufficiently deep to float vessels of war, was in the rear; the British had a strong fleet at hand; and the victorious enemy was in front. In the evening of the 27th, the British encamped in front of the American works; and on the morning of the 28th they broke

* Marshall. Bancroft. Edmonds.

ground about six hundred yards from the American redoubt on the right. In the face of all these difficulties, the Americans with their ammunition, artillery, provisions, horses, and carriages, on the evening of the 29th and morning of the 30th of August, by exer‑tions which any but Washington would have deemed impossible, passed over from Brooklyn to New York without the loss of a man. This retreat was conducted with such perfect silence and order, that although the sound of the intrenching tools of the British was distinctly heard, their escape, favoured by a heavy mist, was unper‑ceived until their rear was out of reach of the British fire.

This event was announced by General Washington to the Presi‑dent of Congress on the day after the evacuation of Long Island, by the following letter:

New York, August 31*st*, 1776.

"SIR,—Inclination as well as duty would have induced me to give Congress the earliest information of my removal and that of the troops, from Long Island and its dependencies to this city, the night before last; but the extreme fatigue which myself and family have undergone, as much from the weather since, as from the engagement on the 27th, rendered me and them entirely unfit to take pen in hand. Since Monday scarce any of us have been out of the lines till our passage across the East River was effected yes‑terday morning; and for forty-eight hours preceding that, I had hardly been off my horse, and never closed my eyes; so that I was quite unfit to write or dictate till this morning.

"Our retreat was made without any loss of men or ammunition, and in better order than I expected from troops in the situation ours were. We brought off all our cannon and stores, except a few heavy pieces, which, in the condition the earth was, by a long continued rain, we found upon trial impracticable; the wheels of the carriages sinking up to the hobs rendered it impossible for our whole force to drag them. We left but little provisions on the island, except some cattle which had been driven within our lines, and which, after many attempts to force across the water, we found it impossible to effect, circumstanced as we were. I have enclosed a copy of the council-of-war held previous to the retreat, to which I beg leave to refer Congress for the reasons, or many of them, that led to the adoption of that measure. Yesterday evening and last night a party of our men were employed in bringing our stores, cannon, and tents from Governor's Island, which they nearly com‑pleted. Some of the heavy cannon remain there still, but I expect they will be got away to-day.

"In the engagement on the 27th, Generals Sullivan and Sterling were made prisoners. The former has been permitted on his parole to return for a little time. From Lord Sterling I had a letter by General Sullivan, a copy of which I have the honour to transmit, that contains his information of the engagement with his brigade. It is not so full and certain as I could wish; he was hurried, most probably, as his letter was unfinished; nor have I yet been able to obtain an exact account of our loss; we suppose it from seven hundred to a thousand killed and taken.* General Sullivan says Lord Howe is extremely desirous of seeing some of the members of Congress; for which purpose he was allowed to come out and to communicate to them what has passed between him and his lordship. I have consented to his going to Philadelphia, as I do not mean or conceive it right to withhold or prevent him from giving such information as he possesses in this instance. I am much hurried and engaged in arranging and making new dispositions of our forces; the movements of the enemy requiring them to be immediately had; and therefore I have only time to add that I am, with my best regards to Congress, &c.,

"GEORGE WASHINGTON."

The retreat of General Washington from Long Island to New York was confessed, by the enemy themselves, to be a masterstroke of military skill, and to reflect the highest honour upon the man by whom it was planned and successfully executed. The defeat which occasioned it, however, though gained by immensely superior numbers, with all the advantages derived from an almost perfect state of discipline, threw a gloomy shade upon the affairs of America. The British were left in undisputed possession of Long Island. Their future operations were involved in uncertainty. With the largest fleet that had ever appeared on the coast of America, they could transfer the seat of war to any spot which they might deem advisable. To gain exact knowledge of their strength, and future movements, was of high importance. For this purpose, General Washington applied to Colonel Knowlton, who commanded a regiment of light-infantry, in the van of the American army, and desired him to adopt some mode of gaining the necessary information. Colonel Knowlton communicated this request to Captain Nathan Hale, of Connecticut, who was then serving in his regiment. This young officer, animated by a sense

* This is exclusive of General Woodhull and the militia under him, about two hundred, who were not in the action, but were captured afterwards at Jamaica

x 2

of duty, a hope that he might, in this way, be useful to his country, and a fixed opinion, that every kind of service necessary to the public good became honourable by being necessary, at once offered himself a volunteer for this hazardous enterprise. He passed, in the disguise of a schoolmaster, to Long Island, examined every part of the British army, and obtained the best possible information respecting their position and future operations. In his attempt to return, he was met by a tory in the British service, recognised, apprehended, and carried before General Howe. The proof of his object was so clear, that he frankly acknowledged who he was, and what his designs were, in visiting the British camp. The British general, without a trial, and without even the form of a court-martial, doomed him to be executed the next morning. This sentence was carried into execution in the most unfeeling manner. A clergyman, whose attendance he desired, was refused him; a Bible, for a moment's devotion, was not procured, though he requested it. Letters, which, on the morning of his execution, he wrote to his mother and sister, were destroyed; and this very extraordinary reason was given by the provost-martial: "that the rebels should not know that they had a man in their army who could die with so much firmness." Unknown to all around him, without a single friend to offer him the least consolation, as amiable and as worthy a young man as America could boast, was thus hung as a spy, with this as his dying observation, that he "only lamented he had but one life to lose for his country, in the cause of liberty and the rights of man." Though the incidents attending this execution will ever be abhorred by every friend to humanity and religion, yet there cannot be a question, but that the sentence was conformable to the rules of war, and the practice of nations in similar cases. Intelligence of this melancholy event was not received by General Washington for a long time.

The defeat of, and retreat from Long Island, inspired unmingled disappointment and apprehension in the minds of the American soldiers; who could not have acquired that power of sustaining ill-success without any diminution of spirit and energy which is peculiar to veteran troops. The manner in which the army was constituted, was, consequently, almost fatal to the cause. The limited period for which the troops were enlisted, and which with many was on the point of expiring, induced them, as far as possible, to shrink from active service.

This state of things was matter of the most painful concern to the commander-in-chief. Had he held in his own hands the disposal of the war, or possessed the powers which are ordinarily vested in officers of his rank, his decision of character would doubtless have soon manifested itself in the adoption of the admirable measures which he could at present only recommend. In his present position that decision of mind could only be exhibited in its rarest form, in the patient endurance of failure, with but a distant prospect of remedy, and in the maintenance of unwavering energy, in the absence of all the stimulants which usually incite to it. That he did not sink under the accumulated disappointments which now began to overtake him, may indeed be attributed, in part, to the robustness and insusceptibility of his physical and mental constitution; but far more to that all-absorbing patriotism which lightened every burden, and sweetened every suffering sustained in the cause of American freedom.

His views of the present condition of the army may best be given in his own words, as they are contained in a letter addressed to Congress on the 2d of September, 1776. The letter is as follows :

"As my intelligence of late has been rather unfavourable, and would be received with anxiety and concern, peculiarly happy should I esteem myself, were it in my power, at this time, to transmit such information to Congress as would be more pleasing and agreeable to their wishes; but, unfortunately for me, unfortunately for them, it is not. Our situation is truly distressing. The check our detachment sustained on the 27th ultimo, has dispirited too great a proportion of our troops, and filled their minds with apprehension and despair. The militia, instead of calling forth their utmost efforts to a brave and manly opposition, in order to repair our losses, are dismayed, intractable, and impatient to return. Great numbers of them have gone off; in some instances, almost by whole regiments, by half ones, and by companies at a time. This circumstance, of itself, independent of others, when fronted by a well appointed enemy, superior in number to our whole collected force, would be sufficiently disagreeable; but, when their example has infected another part of the army, when their want of discipline, and refusal of almost every kind of restraint and government, have produced a like conduct, but too common to the whole, and an entire disregard to that order and subordination necessary to the well-doing of an army, and which had been inculcated before, as well as the nature of our military establishment would admit of, our condition becomes still more alarming; and, with the deepest concern, I am obliged to confess my want of confidence in the generality of the troops.

"All these circumstances fully confirm the opinion I ever entertained, and which I, more than once, in my letters, took the liberty of mentioning to Congress, that no dependence could be put in a militia, or other troops than those enlisted and imbodied for a longer period than our regulations heretofore have prescribed. I am persuaded, and as fully convinced as I am of any one fact that has happened, that our liberties must of necessity be greatly hazarded, if not entirely lost, if their defence is left to any but a permanent standing army; I mean, one to exist during the war. Nor would the expense incident to the support of such a body of troops as would be competent to almost every exigency, far exceed that which is daily incurred by calling in succour, and new enlistments, which, when effected, are not attended with any good consequences. Men who have been free, and subject to no control, cannot be reduced to order in an instant; and the privileges and exemptions which they claim and will have, influence the conduct of others; and the aid derived from them is nearly counterbalanced by the disorder, irregularity, and confusion they occasion.

"I cannot find that the bounty of ten dollars is likely to produce the desired effect. When men can get double that sum to engage for a month or two in the militia, and that militia frequently called out, it is hardly to be expected. The addition of land might have a considerable influence on a permanent enlistment. Our number of men at present fit for duty is under twenty thousand; they were so by the last returns and best accounts I could get after the engagement on Long Island; since which, numbers have deserted. I have ordered General Mercer to send the men intended for the flying camp to this place, about a thousand in number, and to try, with the militia, if practicable, to make a diversion upon Staten Island. Till of late, I had no doubt in my own mind of defending this place; nor should I have yet, if the men would do their duty; but this I despair of. It is painful, and extremely grating to me, to give such unfavourable accounts; but it would be criminal to conceal the truth at so critical a juncture. Every power I possess shall be exerted to serve the cause; and my first wish is, that, whatever may be the event, the Congress will do me the justice to think so."

The general's concern for the pecuniary resources of his country probably induced him to omit, in this letter, urging the Congress

to remedy a defect in the structure of the army, which was probably one of the causes of the late miscarriage. The American army
contained not a single corps of cavalry. "Had the general," says
Judge Marshall, "been furnished with a few troops of light-horse,
to serve merely as videts, it is probable that the movement, so
decisive of the fate of the day, could not have been made unnoticed."

The defeat of Long Island, followed up so closely by this serious
remonstrance, opened the eyes of Congress, dispelled the delusion,
which maintained that the defence of the country needed not a
regular army, and convinced all that an organized and permanent
army was essential to the defence of the republic, and soon after
the reception of Washington's letter, a resolution was adopted to
raise and equip eighty-eight battalions, to serve during the war.
Tardy resolution, when a great army had landed in the country,
and had obtained a signal victory!

Admiral Howe took advantage of the effect which that victory
had produced on the minds of the Congress, by opening a negotiation in the exercise of his power as a commissioner. For this purpose General Sullivan was sent on parole to Philadelphia, with a
verbal message from Admiral Howe, stating his powers, and saying that though he could not treat with them in the character which
they had assumed, yet he was desirous of a conference with some
of the members in the character of private gentlemen, for the purpose, if still possible, of adjusting the dispute between Great Britain and America. When General Sullivan reached Philadelphia,
he was instructed by Congress to present the message of Admiral
Howe to them in writing. This was done, and after much debate,
it was resolved that General Sullivan be requested to inform Lord
Howe, that, "being the representatives of the free and independent
states of America, they could not with propriety send any of their
members to confer with him in their private characters; but that,
ever desirous of establishing peace on reasonable terms, they would
send a committee of their body to know if he had any authority
to treat with persons appointed by Congress for that purpose, in
behalf of America, and what that authority was, and to hear such
propositions as he should think fit to make upon the subject."

Dr. Franklin, John Adams, and Edward Rutledge, were appointed the committee " to receive the communications of Admiral
Howe." They waited on his lordship on the 11th of September,
in Staten Island, and were received with great politeness, but as
the main condition on one side was " allegiance," and on the other

32

"independence," the conference proved fruitless. General Sullivan returned once more a captive to the British camp, and in the course of the month was exchanged for General Prescott. The committee of Congress returned to Philadelphia, and, on the 17th of September, made their report. They sum up their account of the conference in these words :

"Upon the whole, it did not appear to your committee, that his lordship's commission contained any other authority of importance than what is contained in the act of Parliament, viz.: that of granting pardon with such exceptions as the commissioners shall think proper to make, and of declaring America, or any part of it, to be in the king's peace, upon submission. For as to the power of inquiring into the state of America, which his lordship mentioned to us, and of conferring and consulting with any persons the commissioners might think proper, and representing the result of such conversations to the ministry, who (provided the colonies would subject themselves) might, after all, or might not, at their pleasure, make any alterations in the former instructions to governors, or propose in parliament any amendment of the acts complained of, we apprehend any expectation from the effect of such a power would have been too uncertain and precarious to be relied on by America, had she still continued in her state of dependence."

This conference, though ineffectual with respect to the object immediately in view, was of considerable service to the Americans. It arrested General Howe in the career of victory, and suspended, during its progress, the operations of the campaign. It afforded a pause to the dispirited Americans, and gave them time to rally their drooping spirits ; a matter, in their circumstances, of no slight importance.

The British army, now in complete possession of Long Island, fronted and threatened New York Island from its extreme southern point to the part opposite to the northren extremity of Long Island —a space of about nine miles. The two armies were thus separated only by the East River, which is, on an average, about thirteen hundred yards wide, and on both sides of which batteries were erected, which kept up an almost incessant cannonade upon each other. Immediately after the battle of Long Island, General Howe made preparations for the purpose of compelling Washington to evacuate New York. This he thought himself unable to accomplish by a direct attack upon the American lines, and accordingly he sought to affect it by a circuitous manœuvre. A part of the fleet sailed round Long Island, and appeared in the upper part of the Sound. Two frigates passed between Governor's Island and Red Hook, up the East River, without any apparent injury from the batteries, and were sheltered behind a small island from the American artillery, while the admiral, with the main body of the fleet, lay at anchor close in with Governor's Island, ready to pass up either the North or East River, or both, and act against any part of New York Island, as might be required. These movements indicated a disposition to land somewhere about Kingsbridge, and take a position which would cut off the communication of the American army with the country, and thereby force them to a battle, which, if unfortunate in its issue, would infallibly destroy them.

In this state of things General Washington called a counsel of the general officers, who, upon a full and comprehensive view of their situation, advised him to arrange the army in three divisions; five thousand men to remain for the defence of the city; nine thousand to take post at Kingsbridge and its dependencies, as well to possess and secure those important positions as to be ready to repel any attempt of the enemy to land on the island; and the remainder to occupy the intermediate space, and support either. A few days afterwards it was determined to withdraw the five thousand from New York, and with them strengthen the other posts.

"I am sensible," says the general, in a letter to Congress, "that a retreating army is encircled with difficulties; that declining an engagement subjects a general to reproach; and that the common cause may be affected by the discouragement it may throw over the minds of many. Nor am I insensible of the contrary effects, if a brilliant stroke could be made with any probability of success, especially after our loss upon Long Island. But, when the fate of America may be at stake on the issue, when the wisdom of cooler moments and experienced men have decided that we should protract the war, if possible, I cannot think it safe or wise to adopt a different system, when the season for action draws so near to a close. That the enemy mean to winter in New York, there can be no doubt; that with such an armament they can drive us out, is equally clear. The Congress having resolved that it should not be destroyed, nothing seems to remain, but to determine the time of their taking possession. It is our interest and wish to prolong it as much as possible, provided the delay does not affect our future measures."

When the evacuation of New York city was finally resolved on, General Washington immediately began to remove the sick, amounting to more than the fourth part of the whole army, together with the military stores and provisions, to a place of safety above Kingsbridge. The sick were removed, but before all the stores could be brought off, three ships of war ran up the North River on the morning of the 15th of September, and, though they were probably designed to draw the attention of the general from what was passing on the other side of the island, they also effectually prevented the removal of the remainder of the stores from the city by water. About the same time, General Sir Henry Clinton, detached by General Howe, with four thousand men, crossed the East River in flat-bottomed boats, and, under cover of the fire of six or seven ships of war which had ascended the East River some few days before, landed at Kipp's Bay. General Washington, who, from the movements of the enemy, had thought it probable they would soon attempt to land in the vicinity of Haerlem, had, on the evening of the 14th, proceeded to that place; the main body of his army being posted on the surrounding heights. Immediately on hearing the cannonade the next morning, he rode with all possible expedition towards the place of landing, where breastworks had been thrown up, and men stationed to oppose the enemy. To his great surprise and mortification, however, he found the troops which had been posted there, and those ordered to their support, consisting of eight regiments, notwithstanding the exertions of their generals to form them, running away in the most disgraceful manner. On the appearance of a small party of the enemy, not more than sixty or seventy, they fled with the greatest terror and precipitation, without firing a shot. General Washington met the fugitives on the road, drew his sword, threatened and endeavoured to rally them. But his efforts were ineffectual; they deserted their general-in-chief in the presence of the enemy, and it is said that he was "so vexed at the infamous conduct of his troops that he sought death rather than life."[*] To extricate him from his hazardous situation, his attendants found it necessary to seize the reins of his horse and turn him away from the enemy. General Clinton, not having a full knowledge of the nature of the field, took post on some high ground called the Inclenberg, about three miles north of the city, and on a portion of the island, where, if he had lengthened his lines, or passed over to Haerlem plains, he might have effectually cut off the retreat of the troops still in the city.

* General Greene's Letter, Sept. 17.

ASHINGTON immediately sent orders to General Putnam to evacuate the city and join him on the heights of Haerlem; while he secured those heights in the best manner he could with the troops which were on or near them. Putnam's retreat was effected with the loss of but few men, though most of the heavy cannon and part of the stores and provisions were left in the city.

The successive retreats which had followed the landing of the British on Long Island, had so dispirited the American troops, that they fled whenever the enemy appeared. The new position of the general's quarters on the heights of Haerlem, was such as to allow of frequent skirmishes with the enemy, which he thought might have some influence in accustoming the American militia to oppose the superior discipline of the British troops. Accordingly, he immediately formed the design of cutting off some of the enemy's light troops, who, encouraged by their successes, and the apparent cowardice of their opponents, had advanced to the extremity of the high ground opposite to the American camp. To effect this salutary purpose, on the morning of the 16th of September, the day after the landing of General Clinton, Colonel Knowlton and Major Leitch were detached with parties of riflemen and rangers to get in their rear, while a disposition was made, as if to attack them in front. A sharp conflict ensued; each party was reinforced; a severe firing was kept up for nearly four hours; the enemy were put to flight in open ground, and forced from posts which they had seized two or three times. In consequence of the attack being made on the flank rather than the rear, as had been directed, the British had an opportunity of retreating to their main body. The American loss was about twenty killed and forty wounded, but the greatest loss sustained was in the death of Colonel Knowlton, who fell bravely fighting, while Major Leitch was mortally wounded. These officers were killed near the beginning of the action, but their men, animated by the example of the inferior officers, persevered, and continued the engagement with the greatest resolution; and in some measure blotted out the stain of the preceding day. This and similarly successful skirmishes had the expected effect of raising the depressed spirits of the American forces, and accustoming them to the sound of the British cannon, and the sight and effects of British discipline.

In this way the American army remained encamped on the heights of Haerlem for upwards of three weeks in a state of com-

Y

parative inactivity.   The British took possession of New York on the 15th of September.

On the 21st of September, a destructive fire broke out in New York, and reduced about a fourth part of the city to ashes.   It began in a dram shop near the river, about one o'clock in the morning ; and, as every thing was dry, and the houses covered with shingles, the flames spread rapidly, and raged with great fury. Many of the citizens had removed from the town before the entrance of the British, the pumps and fire-engines were in bad order, and a brisk south wind fanned the flame.   Two regiments of soldiers and many men from the fleet were employed to arrest the progress of the devouring element, and at length succeeded in extinguishing the fire, but not till it had consumed about a thousand houses.

" The Americans have been accused of wilfully setting fire to the city.   Such accusations in similar circumstances have at all times been made ; but in the present instance the charge is wholly unfounded.   It is most likely that the fire was occasioned by the inconsiderate revelry of the British sailors, who had been permitted to regale themselves on shore."*

Convinced that no successful attack could be made upon the American camp from the side of New York, General Howe again attempted to cut off the communication of the army with the New England states, and by enclosing it on New York Island compel General Washington to a general engagement.   For this purpose, leaving a garrison in New York, early on the morning of the 12th of October, he embarked the remainder of his army in flat-bottomed boats, and, in the course of the same morning, landed at Frog's Neck, in West Chester county, and soon after advanced to New Rochelle, where he was joined by about five thousand foreign mercenaries.   To counteract the manifest object of these movements, General Washington extended the left of his army towards White Plains, beyond the right of the enemy, while he left a garrison for the protection of Fort Washington and the lines of Haerlem, and Kingsbridge, so that the main body of the American army formed a line of intrenched camps extending from twelve to thirteen miles, from the heights of Haerlem to White Plains.   The British moved with slowness and circumspection, towards the extreme left of the American lines.   The compactness which they endeavoured to preserve, did not, however, prevent some skirmishes, in which the Americans conducted themselves to the satisfaction of the commander-in-chief.   On the 26th of October, the main body of the

* Western World, London, 1830, vol. i. 198, 199.

American army, to the number of about seventeen thousand, took possession of the heights, on the east side of the river Brunx, in front of the British army. Following his usual plan, Washington entrenched his camp with the greatest rapidity, and in such a manner, that it drew from the British general, and contemporary British records, the highest praise for his military talents. A bend in the river covered his right flank, and he posted a body of about sixteen hundred, under General McDougall, on a hill in a line with his right, but on the western side of the Brunx.

 N the 28th of October, the British army advanced in two columns towards the American camp. The left column was led by General Howe in person, while the other was led by General Clinton. A distant cannonade was kept up with but little effect on either side. McDougall's detachment, on the American right, attracted the notice of General Howe, and he resolved to dislodge it. He ordered General Leslie, with the second British brigade, and Colonel Donop, with the Hessian grenadiers, on that service. On their advance, the American militia fled with precipitation ; but about six hundred regulars, animated by McDougall, vigorously defended themselves for some time. Being at last compelled to retreat, the British took possession of the hill ; but they were still at too great a distance to be able to annoy any part of the American line.

Three days afterwards, General Howe having received reinforcements from New York and other quarters, resolved to attack the American camp. A heavy rain, during the whole night preceding the day appointed for the attack, rendered the ground so slippery, that he deemed it unadvisable to persist in the attempt. He accordingly changed his plan, and began to move off his army by small detachments, in order, unobserved, if possible, to possess himself of the heights behind the American position. On perceiving this, Washington withdrew his forces, on the 1st of November, towards North Castle, and took a strong position behind the river Croton, about two miles above his former encampment ; and so strongly did he fortify this excellent position, that the British general, despairing of success in any attempt to force it, marched his army away, in order to attack Fort Washington ; in which a considerable garrison had been left. The design of this movement was at once conjectured by General Washington. In communicating the information to Congress, he observes :

"I cannot indulge an idea, that, supposing he is going to New York, he means to close the campaign, and to sit down without attempting something more. I think it highly probable, and almost certain, that he will make a descent, with a part of his troops, into Jersey; and, as soon as I am satisfied that the present manœuvre is real, and not a feint, I shall use every means in my power to forward a part of our force to counteract his designs." In a subsequent part of the same letter, he says, "I expect the enemy will bend their force against Fort Washington, and invest it immediately. From some advices, it is an object that will attract their earliest attention."

He wrote, the next day, to Governor Livingston, of New Jersey, advising him of the measures which he apprehended, recommending that the militia should be held in readiness, and that the stock, and every thing which could yield support to the British army, should be removed from the sea-coast, or destroyed. Hearing that three British vessels had sailed up the Hudson River, notwithstanding the obstructions which he had caused to be sunk in the channel; he was convinced that Fort Washington was no longer tenable, or if it could be retained, it would be of no use. He accordingly wrote to General Greene, who commanded on the Jersey shore, and was particularly intrusted with the defence of Forts Washington and Lee, "If we cannot prevent vessels from passing up, and the enemy are possessed of the surrounding country, what valuable purpose can it answer, to attempt to hold a post from which the expected benefit cannot be had? I am therefore inclined to think, that it will not be prudent to hazard the men and stores at Mount Washington; but, as you are on the spot, I leave it to you, to give such orders respecting the evacuation of Fort Washington as you may judge best."

General Greene, being thus left to use his discretion, being struck with the importance of the post, and the discouragement which the successive evacuation of posts was calculated to give, reinforced Colonel Magaw, who commanded at Fort Washington, and increased the garrison to two thousand men.

Convinced that the British general intended to move southward, General Washington, on the 11th and 12th of November, crossed the river with the greater part of his army. He was obliged to make a circuit of sixty-five miles, on account of the British shipping, which opposed his passage at all the lower ferries. In the mean time, General Howe appeared before Fort Washington, and, on the 15th of November, summoned the garrison to surrender.

Colonel Magaw replied that he would defend it to the last extremity. This summons and the colonel's answer were communicated to General Washington, who had arrived at Fort Lee. In the silent hour of midnight he left Fort Lee in a boat, and sailed for the besieged post. On his way, he was met by Generals Greene and Putnam, who assured him of the high probability of the miscarriage of the enemy's attempts, as well as the ability of the fort to stand a siege for a considerable time, and he returned again to Fort Lee.

On the following morning, Howe, with unusual boldness, determined to attempt the reduction of the fort by storm, and advanced against it in four divisions. In a few hours, after an obstinate resistance, they succeeded in surmounting the outworks, and driving the garrison within the fort. In this situation General Howe again demanded their surrender. The ammunition of the Americans being nearly expended, and the numbers being very unequal, Colonel Magaw surrendered himself and the soldiers under his command, prisoners of war. It was most unfortunate that this surrender was made so hastily, as, during the negotiation, a message was received from General Washington, that he would bring troops to his assistance in the evening, or, if the fortress could not be maintained, he would endeavour to bring off the garrison. This offer came too late. He had already entered too far into a treaty to retract. In the attack, the British lost about eight hundred men, in killed and wounded. That of the Americans was inconsiderable.

On the 20th of November, Lord Cornwallis was detached with a large force, to cross the Hudson, probably with the hope of surrounding the whole American army, which lay around Fort Lee, between the Hackinsac and Hudson Rivers. Retreat was now unavoidable. Already part of the stores had been removed, but the greater part fell into the hands of the enemy. The retreat of the army over the Hackinsac was effected without loss of men. These misfortunes were indeed disastrous, and almost insupportable. The troops taken at Fort Washington were the flower of the army, and the loss of the provisions captured at Fort Lee was most severely felt in an army which was at the best but scantily supplied. These two losses were the greatest that had ever befallen the American cause, and they may be considered as the commencement of a period of suffering, almost unexampled in the history of warfare. Of all the eras of Washington's career, this was the one which most severely tested his courage and patriotism. The prospect around him and before him, so far as human sagacity could penetrate the future, was gloomy and melancholy in the extreme. To add to his difficulties, now, when he needed numbers at his command, and enthusiasm in the minds of all, he saw his army on the eve of dissolution, the time of enlistment being nearly expired, and the soldiers themselves, unused to defeat, and weary of the service, anxious for nothing more than to return to their own homes. Under these depressing circumstances, he wrote to General Lee, who was still on the eastern side of the Hudson, desiring him to join him with his forces; but, unhappily, the same wretched system of short enlistments frustrated this design. His troops were daily vanishing on the expiration of their term of enlistment, and he urged this as a reason why it would be impolitic in him to hazard a march past the enemy to join his general. The forces stationed at Bergen, under General Mercer, were also fast melting away, and the newly-drafted militia but scantily supplied the places of the deserters. In addition to these adverse circumstances, the inhabitants of New Jersey were in a great measure indifferent to the cause of their country, and many of the most wealthy testified a desire to return to their allegiance to Britain. So high had this spirit run, in the county of Monmouth, that General Washington was obliged to detach some militia to suppress an insurrection of the royalists there. The danger of a majority of the people of the state deserting the cause of independence, when the enemy should come among them, and thus causing a disruption in the political union of America, gave him the most serious alarm.

Being liable to be enclosed between the Hackinsac and Passaic Rivers, and unable to prevent the crossing of the enemy, Washington retreated to Newark, where he remained some days, making the most earnest applications in every quarter for reinforcements, and pressing General Lee to hasten his march to the southward and join him. On the appearance of Cornwallis, on the 29th November, he retreated to Brunswick. While there, the term of service of the Maryland and Jersey troops expired, and he had the mortification of witnessing the gradual diminution of his feeble army in the very sight of a pursuing enemy. He continued in Brunswick until the advanced guards of the enemy showed themselves, when he again fell back, and leaving twelve hundred men under Lord Sterling at Princeton, he himself, with the remainder of the army, proceeded to Trenton, on the Delaware. Having taken the precaution of collecting and guarding all the boats on this river, from Philadelphia upwards for seventy miles, he first sent nis sick to Philadelphia, and his few remaining military stores and baggage across the Delaware, and then sent a detachment of twelve hundred men to Princeton, to keep up the appearance of opposition, and soon after followed with two thousand militia; but before he reached Princeton, he received intelligence that Lord Cornwallis was advancing from Brunswick by several routes, evidently with the intention of gaining his rear and cutting off his retreat across the Delaware. An immediate retreat was necessary. Lord Sterling was called in, and, on the 8th of December, he accomplished the passage at Trenton ferry, the van of the British army making its appearance just as his rear-guard had crossed.

General Washington was careful to secure all the boats in the river on the Pennsylvania side, so that the little army could now rest in some security, after a retreat of three weeks in front of an enemy six times their number. The distresses suffered by the troops in this retreat, have scarcely been surpassed since the celebrated retreat of the Ten Thousand. Dispirited by their recent losses and fatigues, these men marched almost naked and barefooted through the snows and extreme cold of November and December, before, and almost continually in sight of, a numerous, well-appointed, and victorious enemy, through a desponding country; the inhabitants of which were much more disposed to secure safety by submission, than to seek it by manly resistance. It is said, that the march through New Jersey could actually be traced by the blood which their lacerated feet left upon the snow or the soil.

"While General Washington was retreating through New Jersey, he almost daily earnestly desired General Lee to hasten his march towards the Delaware, and join the main army. But that officer, notwithstanding the critical nature of the case, and the pressing orders of his commander, was in no haste to obey. Reluctant to give up his separate command, and subject himself to superior authority, he marched slowly to the southward at the head of between three and four thousand men; and his sluggish movements and unwary conduct proved fatal to his own personal liberty, and excited a lively sensation throughout the whole country. Lying carelessly, and with but a small guard, at some distance from his troops, at a house called White's Tavern, near Baskenbridge, in Morris County, he was surprised by Colonel Harcourt, and carried off a prisoner to New York. For some time he was closely confined, and considered, not as a prisoner of war, but as a deserter from the British army. The command of his division devolved

upon General Sullivan, who, towards the end of December, conducted it across the Delaware to General Washington's army. At
the same time, General Gates, with part of the army of Canada,
arrived in camp."

Before Washington retreated across the Delaware, a proclamation
was issued by Admiral and General Howe, as commissioners
appointed on the part of the crown for restoring peace to America;
commanding all persons assembled in arms against his majesty's
government, to disband and return to their homes; and all civil
officers to desist from their treasonable practices, and relinquish
their usurped authority. A full pardon was also offered to every
person who would, within sixty days, appear before certain civil
or military officers of the crown, and claim the benefit of that proclamation, and, at the same time, testify his obedience to the laws,
by subscribing a declaration of his submission to the royal authority. Copies of this proclamation were immediately dispersed
through the country, after which, many sought peace and pardon
by accepting the offers of the British commissioners.

The firmness of Washington's mind was undisturbed by the
misfortunes which had befallen him, or by the defection of those
who ought to have supported the cause of freedom with their arms.
The inflexible firmness, the majesty of his demeanor, at this critical
juncture, exerted a powerful influence over the minds of many
who would otherwise have despaired of the republic. The temporary inaction which followed his retreat over the Delaware, was
embraced to lay again before Congress reiterated remonstrances
against the fatal system of short enlistments. That body had adjourned from Philadelphia on the 12th, to meet at Baltimore on the
20th of December, leaving a committee of three members in Philadelphia, with powers to transact such continental business as required attention in that city. Before their adjournment they resolved, that, until Congress should otherwise order, full power
should be conferred on General Washington, to order, and direct
all things relative to the department, and to the operations of war.
Under this resolution, the general ventured to order three battalions
of artillery to be immediately recruited; but, thinking the exercise
of the powers necessary to the existence of the army, and the prosecution of the war, not fully authorized by this hasty resolution,
passed in the hurry of adjournment, he addressed a letter to the
President of Congress, on the 20th of December, in which he urged
upon him the necessity of more particularly specifying the powers
with which he was intrusted, and enabling him to execute important

measures without consulting them. He says, "I think the design of General Howe is to possess himself of Philadelphia this winter, if possible; and, in truth, I do not see what is to prevent him, as ten days more will put an end to the existence of our army. That one great point is to keep us as much harassed as possible, with a view to injure the recruiting service, and hinder a collection of stores and other necessaries for the next campaign, I am as clear in as I am of my existence. If, therefore, in the short interval in which we have to provide for, and make these great and arduous preparations, every matter that in its nature is self-evident is to be referred to Congress, at the distance of a hundred and thirty or forty miles, so much time must necessarily elapse as to defeat the end in view.

" It may be said, that this is an application for powers that are too dangerous to be intrusted. I can only add, that desperate diseases require desperate remedies; and I, with truth, declare, that I have no lust after power; but I wish, with as much fervency as any man upon this wide-extended continent, for an opportunity of turning the sword into the ploughshare. But my feelings, as an officer and a man, have been such as to force me to say, that no person ever had a greater choice of difficulties to contend with than I have.

" It is needless to add, that short enlistments, and a mistaken dependence on militia, have been the origin of all our misfortunes, and the great accumulation of our debt. We find, sir, that the enemy are daily gathering strength from the disaffected. This strength, like a snow-ball, by rolling, will increase, unless some means can be devised to check effectually the progress of the enemy's arms. Militia may possibly do it for a little while; but in a little while, also, and the militia of those states which have been frequently called upon, will not turn out at all; or if they do, it will be with so much reluctance and sloth as to amount to the same thing. Instance New Jersey! Witness Pennsylvania! Could any thing but the river Delaware have saved Philadelphia? Can any thing (the exigency of the case indeed may justify it) be more destructive to the recruiting service, than giving ten dollars bounty for six weeks' service of the militia, who come in, you cannot tell how; go, you cannot tell when; and act, you cannot tell where; consume your provisions, exhaust your stores, and leave you at last, at a critical moment?

" These, sir, are the men I am to depend upon, ten days hence; this is the basis on which your cause will, and must for ever depend, till you get a large standing army, sufficient of itself to oppose the enemy. I therefore beg leave to give it as my humble opinion, that eighty-eight battalions are by no means equal to the opposition you are to make, and that a moment's time is not to be lost in raising a greater number—not less, in my opinion, and the opinion of my officers, than a hundred and ten. It may be urged that it will be found difficult enough to complete the first number. This may be true, and yet the officers of a hundred and ten battalions will recruit many more men than those of eighty-eight. In my judgment, this is not a time to stand upon expense; our funds are not the only object of consideration. The state of New York have added one battalion (I wish they had made it two) to their quota. If any good officers will offer to raise men upon continental pay and establishment in this quarter, I shall encourage them to do so, and regiment them when they have done it. If Congress disapprove of this proceeding, they will please to signify it, as I mean it for the best.

"It may be thought that I am going a good deal out of the line of my duty, to adopt these measures, or advise thus freely. A character to lose, an estate to forfeit, the inestimable blessings of liberty at stake, and a life devoted, must be my excuse."

On the reception of this letter, the Congress, notwithstanding the extreme jealousy which many of the members entertained of military supremacy, were constrained, by the alarming aspect of affairs, to vest in General Washington for six months such powers as would have rendered him, in the days of old Rome, a military *dictator*. On the 27th of December, depending on the "wisdom, vigour, and uprightness of General Washington," they passed a resolution vesting in him "full powers to raise and equip sixteen additional battalions of infantry; to appoint their officers; to raise, officer, and equip three thousand light horse, three regiments of artillery, and a corps of engineers, and to establish their pay; to apply to any of the states for such aid of the militia as he should judge necessary; to form such magazines of provisions, and in such places as he should think proper; to displace and appoint all officers under the rank of brigadier-general, and to fill up all vacancies in every other department of the American army; to take whatever he might want for the use of the army, (if the owners would not sell it,) allowing a reasonable price for the same; to arrest and confine persons who would refuse to take the continental money, or who were otherwise disaffected to the American cause; and return to the states of which they were citizens, their names, and the nature of their offences, together with the witnesses to prove them."

Congress then addressed a circular to each of the states, informing them of this resolution, and calling upon them to give all possible aid in raising such levies as the general should direct, and sending them with all possible despatch to head-quarters.

These proceedings were communicated to Washington on the night of the 31st of December, and, on the next day, he replied as follows:

" The confidence which Congress have honoured me with by these proceedings, has a claim to my warmest acknowledgments. At the same time, I beg leave to assure them, that all my faculties shall be employed to direct properly the powers they have been pleased to vest me with, and to advance those objects, and only those, which gave rise to this honourable mark of distinction. If my exertions should not be attended with the desired success, I trust the failure will be imputed to the true cause, the peculiarly distressed situation of our affairs, and the difficulties I have to combat, rather than to a want of zeal for my country, and the closest attention to her interest, to promote which, has ever been my study."

Before these Congressional proceedings, however, Washington had commenced active warfare. By the arrival of the troops under Sullivan and Gates, the army was increased to seven thousand men. It was stationed on the Pennsylvania side of the Delaware, near the falls of Trenton; while the British army, secure in its superior numbers, was cantoned in Burlington, Bordentown, Trenton, and other towns, in New Jersey. General Howe seemed to be waiting patiently until the ice, which is generally strong enough at that period of the year, should supply his want of boats, and enable his army to cross to victory, and the comfortable winter quarters which he expected to find in Philadelphia. Their situation in New Jersey was not as comfortable as they wished, nor as it had been when they first entered that province. The Hessians had indulged in such wanton cruelty and open licentiousness, that the friendship which many of the inhabitants were inclined to show them, was now changed to enmity, and a general desire for revenge, for injuries and atrocities committed, seemed now to be the feeling which predominated in that state. On receiving information of the numbers and different cantonments of the British troops, Washington observed: "Now is the time to clip their wings when they are so spread;" and he resolved to make a bold effort to check their

progress. For this purpose, he formed the bold design of recrossing the Delaware, and attacking the Hessian troops, which, to the
number of fifteen hundred, were posted at Trenton.

He formed his troops into three divisions, with orders simultaneously to pass the Delaware at three different places, on the evening of the 25th of December, hoping to surprise the enemy after the
festivities of Christmas. One division, under General Cadwallader,
was to cross the river in the vicinity of Bristol, but failed through
inattention to the state of the tide and of the river, as they could
not land on account of the heaps of ice accumulated on the Jersey
bank. The second division, under General Ewing, was to cross
at Trenton ferry, but was unable to make its way through the ice.
The third, and main division, under the command of Washington
in person, assisted by General Sullivan, and Greene, and Colonel
Knox of the artillery, consisting of about twenty-four hundred
men, accomplished the passage, with great difficulty, at McKonkey's,
about nine miles above Trenton. The general had expected to
reach the Jersey shore about midnight, and Trenton about five in
the morning. But the difficulties arising from the accumulation of
the ice were so great, that it was three o'clock in the morning before
the artillery could all be got over, and nearly four, before the troops
took up their line of march. He subdivided his detachment into
two divisions, one of which, under General Sullivan, proceeded
towards Trenton by the lower or river road, while the other, led
by the commander-in-chief, took the upper or Pennington road.

Washington's division reached the Hessian advanced posts at
eight o'clock, which he instantly drove in ; and so equal had been
the progress of the columns, that in three minutes afterwards, the
firing on the river road announced the arrival of the other division.
The advanced guards fell back in good order, keeping up a continual fire, which effectually alarmed their comrades. Colonel Rahl,
the commander, a very gallant officer, immediately drew out his
forces in order, and prepared for a brave defence ; but early in the
engagement he received a mortal wound, and his men, being severely
galled by the American artillery, attempted to file off towards
Princeton, but were checked by a body of troops thrown in their
way. About six hundred escaped by the road leading to Bordentown. The remainder, finding themselves completely surrounded,
and their artillery seized, laid down their arms and surrendered.
The number which submitted was twenty-three officers, and eight
hundred and eighty-six men. Between thirty and forty of the
Hessians were killed and wounded. Colonel Rahl was among the

WASHINGTON CROSSING THE DELAWARE

former, and several of his officers among the latter. Captain Washington, of the Virginia troops, and five or six of the Americans were wounded. Two were killed, and two or three were frozen to death. Had not the extreme severity of the weather forbidden the other divisions to cross the Delaware, the result of this masterly stroke would doubtless have been to sweep away the British from all their posts on the Delaware, and thus establish a firm footing in the Jerseys. As it was, the general concluded for the time to forbear further aggressions, and recrossed the river with his prisoners, six pieces of artillery, a thousand stand of arms, and some valuable military stores.

The effect of this victory was sudden and decisive. The spirits of the army revived, and with new confidence arose a new impulse. Those whose term of service was within four days of expiring, volunteered to continue ; and reinforcements began to arrive from the neighbouring towns of Pennsylvania and New Jersey. The rapine and dissoluteness of the British army, backed as it was by the daring of Washington, spurred to action all that there was of heart or virtue in the land. Washington, availing himself of every circumstance, quickened by such inspiring auguries, made a rapid provision for securing his prisoners, and in two days was again buffeting, as best he could, the sweeping waters of the Delaware with its burden of ice. He again marched to Trenton, and ordered Generals Mifflin and Cadwallader to join him on the 1st of January, 1777 ; by whom his force was on that day increased to five thousand men. His plan was now to recover as much as possible of the territory which the British had overrun.

The astonishment of the British general at this display of valour and enterprise in an army, which, in the midst of indigence and suffering, had been for weeks retiring, or rather flying, before his superior force, may be readily imagined. It taught him a useful lesson. He found that nothing short of absolute extermination would make them cease to be dangerous to him, and hostile to the government which he represented. Though in the depth of a severe winter, he found it necessary to recommence active operations, and Lord Cornwallis, who was on the point of sailing for England, was ordered to leave New York and resume his command in the Jerseys. A combination of the different detachments of the British army was the instantaneous result. By rapid movements, impelled by revenge, they concentrated upon Trenton, where they arrived on the afternoon of the 2d of January, 1777.

Washington, with his inferior force, drew up his men behind

Assumpinck Creek, a narrow stream running through the town of Trenton. The contending forces thus occupied the same village: both were posted on sloping ground, and were divided only by a creek, in many places fordable. This, Cornwallis attempted to cross at several places, but the vigilance of the guard frustrated his attempts, and he commenced a furious cannonade, which was deliberately returned by the Americans. The British, satisfied of their strength and security, were the first to desist; certain of engaging in a more decisive conflict at the dawn of the next day. But soon after midnight, General Washington silently decamped, leaving his fires burning, his sentinels advanced, and small parties to guard the fords of the rivulet, and, by a circuitous route, proceeded towards Princeton.

It was the most inclement season of the year, but the weather favoured his movement. For two days before, it had been warm, soft, and foggy; and great apprehensions were entertained, lest, by the depth of the roads, it should be found impossible to transport the baggage and artillery with the requisite celerity; but about the time the troops began to move, (one o'clock in the morning of January 3d,) a sudden change in the weather happened. The wind shifted to the north-west, while the council of war, which was to decide on the ulterior operations, was sitting. An intense frost set in, and, instead of being obliged to struggle through a miry road, the army marched as on a solid pavement. The common soldiers considered the change of weather as an interposition of Heaven in their behalf, and proceeded on their way with alacrity.

General Cornwallis, in his rapid march towards Trenton, had left three regiments, under Lieutenant-colonel Mawhood, at Princeton; with orders to advance on the 3d of the month, to Maidenhead, a village about halfway between Princeton and Trenton. General Washington approached Princeton towards daybreak, and shortly before that time, Colonel Mawhood's detachment had begun to advance towards Maidenhead, by a road a little to the left of that on which the Americans were marching. A small detached British guard discovered the advancing columns, and prevented a surprise. The British rushed forward, and a smart engagement instantly ensued. The Americans in the first shock quailed, and the head of the column fell back in disorder. The general hurried to the spot, broke through the mass of retreating men, and stood between pursuers and pursued—his horse's head towards the former. This daring aroused the Americans to a sense of their duty. They wheeled about and met their assailants; both fired while

WASHINGTON AT PRINCETON.

Washington stood between them; but, by a remarkable interposition of Providence, he remained unhurt. The conflict immediately became general; the Americans rushing headlong with the most desperate fury against the enemy, and the British defending themselves with equal obstinacy. The issue, however, did not long remain doubtful. A party of the British fled into the college, and the seat of the muses became the scene of action; but, after receiving a few discharges from the American field-pieces, they came out and surrendered themselves prisoners of war. Of the British, sixty were killed, among whom was Captain Leslie, son of the Earl of Leven; a great number were wounded, and about three hundred taken prisoners. The remainder made their escape, some by pushing on to Trenton, others by returning to Brunswick. The Americans had fewer men killed; but in this number was included General Mercer, a Scotch soldier who brought to the service of America a sterling devotion and rare abilities.

On the appearance of daylight, General Cornwallis discovered that the American army had again eluded his grasp, and the firing, which he soon afterwards heard in the direction of Princeton, revealed to him at once the plans which had been formed by Washington. The rapidity, success, and skill of the American evolutions filled his officers with a kind of awe. His fears were instantly excited for the safety of Brunswick, where magazines of great value had been collected. Breaking up his camp, he advanced with rapidity towards that place, and was close on the rear of the American army before they could leave Princeton.

General Washington now again found himself in a very perilous situation. His small army was exhausted with extreme fatigue, having been without rest, and almost without food for two days and two nights. He was closely pursued by an enemy, very superior in point of numbers, well clothed, not harassed by want of sleep, and who must necessarily overtake him before he could accomplish his designs on Brunswick, if the least opposition should there be offered to him. Under these circumstances, he wisely determined to resume his Fabian policy, and abandon the remaining part of his original design. Accordingly, he took the road leading up the country to Pluckemin, breaking down the bridges over Millstone Creek, and otherwise opposing obstacles to the pursuit of the enemy. Cornwallis, without attempting a pursuit of the retreating army, hastened to Brunswick, where he arrived the same day, and found that every exertion had been made for the removal of the baggage and the defence of the place.

z 2

On that retrograde march, notwithstanding its rapidity, the British began to reap the harvest of their own insolence and rapacity. Such had been the brutalities practised by them, that, with the first ebb of their prosperity, rolled upon them the swift vengeance of those whom they had wantonly outraged. The militia of Jersey, its husbandmen and labourers, hung upon the steps of the retiring troops, and on every possible opportunity, wreaked full vengeance on the stragglers, for the insults, injustice, and oppression which had been meted out to them.

After resting a few days at Pluckemin, General Washington fell back to Morristown, which is situated among hills difficult of access, having a fine country in the rear, and otherwise well situated for keeping open the communications with the New England states on the one side, and Philadelphia and Congress on the other.

From this point, as his centre of operations, though it has been called his winter-quarters, he threw out detachments which overran East and West Jersey, crossed the Raritan, and penetrated into the county of Essex, where they took possession of the coast opposite Staten Island. With a greatly inferior army, by judicious movements he thus wrested from the British almost all their conquests in the Jerseys. Brunswick and Amboy were the only posts remaining in their hands, and even in them they were not a little harassed and straitened. The American detachments were thus in a state of constant activity, frequently surprising and cutting off the British advanced guards, keeping them in perpetual alarm, and melting down their numbers by a desultory and indecisive warfare.

The successful and brilliant enterprises which closed the campaign commenced at Long Island, at once raised the spirits and stimulated the courage of the Americans, and impressed the mind of the British general with the necessity of the utmost circumspection, and with a high respect for the military talents of General Washington.

The favourable effect produced on the minds of his countrymen by these operations, induced General Washington to issue a proclamation, for the purpose of counteracting that issued by General Howe. This was a seasonable and necessary step. Intimidated by the desperate aspect of American affairs when the American army retreated into Pennsylvania, many of the inhabitants of the Jerseys had taken advantage of General Howe's proclamation, promising them protection in their persons and property, and submitted to the British authority; but with respect to the promised

BATTLE OF PRINCETON

BRICHER

protection, they had been entirely disappointed. Instead of protection and conciliation, they had been insulted by the rude insolence of a licentious soldiery, and plundered with indiscriminate and unsparing rapacity. General Washington's proclamation accordingly absolved the inhabitants from their engagements to Britain, and promising them protection on their submission to Congress. Many took advantage of this proclamation, and the militia of New Jersey afterwards did good service in the American cause.

"Thus terminated the eventful campaign of 1776, which witnessed the heroic defence of Charleston in the south ; the evacuation of Canada in the north ; the operations of Washington in the Middle States, first at the head of a respectable force in Long Island ; subsequently defeated there, and on York Island ; his soldiers leaving him as soon as their terms of service had expired; retreating through New Jersey, with what Hamilton has called the phantom of an army ; compelled to cross the Delaware ; turning, when it was confidently expected by the British that all his army would be disbanded, and inflicting severe wounds on their widely scattered forces ; and, in the end, acting on the offensive, and hunting them from place to place, until they are cooped up in New York, Amboy, and Brunswick. True, the British had taken possession of Rhode Island; but it was of no advantage to them yet, nor at any period of the war ; and they were compelled to weaken their armies for the purpose of keeping a garrison there. And finally, notwithstanding the joy of the British at the capture of General Lee, the effects which they anticipated were not produced on the American people ; and subsequent events showed them conclusively that they had not captured the American Palladium."

The success of Washington in the Jerseys enabled Congress to return to Philadelphia in the month of February. In the mean time, they had set in motion elsewhere agencies favourable to America. Convinced of the necessity of foreign relations, they resolved that commissioners should at once be sent to the courts of Spain, Vienna, Prussia, and Tuscany. The uneasiness, pride, jealousy, and hatred of England manifested by France, excited their strongest hopes. They used every means in their power to gain and cultivate the friendship of that great nation. They appointed Benjamin Franklin, Silas Deane, and Arthur Lee, commissioners to negotiate at Paris the preliminaries of friendly relations between the two countries. Mr. Deane had already been

35

some time in Paris, and had had audiences of the foreign minister, but was unable to effect any thing decisive. By great exertions, and after many difficulties, he concluded an agreement with a French merchant, M. Beaumarchais, to ship for the United States clothing for twenty thousand men, thirty thousand muskets, one hundred tons of powder, two hundred brass cannon, twenty-four mortars, and a large quantity of military stores of all kinds. He undertook to supply these on credit, accepting Mr. Deane's security as the agent of Congress. Many obstacles interfered to prevent the transportation of these stores. The remonstrances of the English minister, who kept spies on all the ports, constituted the chief difficulty. At length, Beaumarchais was able to despatch one vessel from Havre in the beginning of November. She arrived in New Hampshire in the following April, deeply needed, and loudly welcomed, as bearing a large supply of arms, ammunition, and clothing, for the opening campaign.

Mr. Deane had also undertaken and concluded another negotiation of far more brilliant results. The young and adventurous Marquis de Lafayette proposed to him to volunteer his services, on the sole condition of obtaining the rank of a brigadier-general in the republican army. The proposal was acceded to, and the name and sword of Lafayette soon shed glory, destined to be lasting, on the War of Liberty.

Early in December, Franklin and Lee arrived in Paris, to associate their address and ability with Mr. Deane, in obtaining the support, or at least the recognition of the court of Versailles. Hesitating assurances and equivocal promises were, however, all that could be then obtained. The commissioners, more than ever convinced that it is mature determination, aided by action and success, that can alone procure the sympathy and support of great powers, turned their thoughts elsewhere. They were even induced to dissuade from his purpose the generous young warrior, who was about to peril life, fortune, and fame, in a sinking cause, by representing to him that the scattered forces of America were flying through their native forests before the victorious and avenging army of England. But he was not to be disconcerted. At his own cost, he purchased a vessel to bear him from the land where he was born to greatness, that he might share in the success or fall of a weak, struggling people. In early spring, he gained the country of his ambition, and, with the rank of major-general, joined Washington's army.

Another illustrious name, too, graced that muster-roll of warriors—Count Pulaski, the gallant Pole, who, in the face of a Russian army, bore away the miserable monarch of his nation to reign over a free people. But Stanislaus was unworthy of the crown and the nation; and his deliverer now did battle in a better cause, and under happier auspices.

The British ministry, in the mean time, became conscicus of the wavering of France; they saw dark heavy clouds on the political horizon, and they began to prepare for the swiftly coming storm. A large increase was made in both the army and navy, and on the assembling of Parliament, on the 31st of October, 1776, the king, in his speech from the throne, stated to them that it would have given him much satisfaction to be able to inform them that the disturbances in the revolted colonies were at an end, and that the people of America, recovering from their delusion, had returned to their duty. Instead of this, however, so mutinous and determined was the spirit of their leaders, that they had openly abjured and renounced all connection and communication with the mother country, and had rejected every conciliatory proposition. Much mischief, he said, would accrue, not only to the commerce of Great Britain, but to the general system of Europe, if this treason were suffered to take root. The conduct of the colonies would convince every one of the necessity of the measures proposed to be adopted, and the past success of the British arms promised the happiest results; but preparations must be promptly made for another campaign. He expressed a hope of the general continuance of tranquillity in Europe, but, at the same time, he thought it advisable to increase the defensive resources at home.

The replies to the speech were in the usual form, but amendments were moved in both houses of parliament. After a violent debate, in which the animosity of party was more discernible than any thing else, the amendment was rejected, two hundred and forty-two to eighty-seven, and ninety-one to twenty-six. During the session of parliament, some other attempts were made for adopting conciliatory measures; but the influence of the ministry was so powerful that they were all completely defeated, and the plans of the administration received the approbation and support of parliament.

Forty-five thousand seamen were ordered to be raised; sixteen ships of war to be built; and between six and seven millions of pounds sterling were voted for the expenses of the army and navy during the coming year. Parliament then adjourned on the 13th of December, to meet again on the 21st of January, 1777.

HEAD-QUARTERS AT MORRISTOWN.

CHAPTER XV.

Campaign of 1777.

HE period while he was in winter quarters at Morristown, was passed by General Washington in making every exertion for a vigorous prosecution of the coming campaign. He urged Congress to appoint an additional number of general officers; he wrote to the governors of the different states, urging them to raise and forward to head-quarters, with as much despatch as possible, the quotas of troops assigned to their respective states; and at the same time he carried on a correspondence with General Howe, relating to exchange of prisoners. In February, at his earnest request, Congress appointed five additional major-generals,

PHILADELPHIA IN 1777

and ten brigadiers. He was not as successful in his applications to the states, for we find that on the 9th of June, he could muster no more than seven thousand two hundred and seventy-one men fit for duty. Before the capture of General Lee, it had been agreed between Generals Washington and Howe, that their prisoners should be exchanged officer for officer of equal rank, soldier for soldier, and citizen for citizen, but affecting to consider General Lee a deserter from the British army, in which he had formerly held a lieutenant-colonel's commission, he was treated with great severity, the commander refusing to exchange him, even for six officers, and threatening to bring him before a court-martial, to answer the crime of desertion. When intelligence of this conduct was received by Congress, they passed a resolution declaring that Lieutenant-colonel Campbell, who had been captured in the bay of Boston, together with five Hessian field-officers, should be detained, in order that the treatment which General Lee should receive might be exactly inflicted upon their persons. A copy of their resolution was sent to the council of Massachusetts Bay, and they were desired to detain Lieutenant-colonel Campbell and keep him in close custody till the further orders of Congress. Hitherto, this officer had been treated civilly, but on receiving the order of Congress, the council of Massachusetts Bay sent him to Concord jail, and lodged him in a filthy cell, denying him even the privilege of walking about the prison-yard, and neither permitting the visits of his friends nor the attendance of a servant.

Colonel Campbell, naturally conceiving that this rigorous treatment originated in some mistake of the local council, complained in dignified, but respectful terms, to General Washington, and, at the same time, sent through the Massachusetts council a statement of his treatment to General Howe. Washington immediately wrote to the council, enclosing them an extract of the colonel's letter, and the resolution of Congress respecting Colonel Campbell. Alluding to this resolution, he wrote : " By this you will observe, that *exactly the same treatment* is to be shown to Colonel Campbell and the Hessian officers, that General Howe shows to General Lee; and as he is only confined to a commodious house, with genteel accommodations, we have no right or reason to be more severe upon Colonel Campbell, who, I would wish, should immediately, upon the receipt of this, be removed from his present situation, and put into a house where he may live comfortably."

On the next day, March 1st, he wrote to the President of Congress a strenuous remonstrance against this hasty and premature attempt at retaliation. "Retaliation," he said, "is certainly just, and sometimes necessary, even where attended with the severest penalties; but, when the evils which may and must result from it exceed those intended to be redressed, prudence and policy require that it should be avoided.

"From the best information I have been able to obtain, General Lee's usage has not been so disgraceful and dishonourable as to authorize the treatment decreed to those gentlemen, were it not prohibited by many other important considerations. His confinement, I believe, has been more rigorous than has been generally experienced by the rest of our officers, or those of the enemy, who have been in our possession; but, if the reports received on that head be true, he has been provided with a decent apartment, and with most things necessary to render him comfortable. This is not the case with one of the officers comprehended in the resolves, if his letter, of which a copy is transmitted, deserves your credit. Here retaliation seems to have been prematurely begun; or, to speak with more propriety, severities have been and are exercised towards Colonel Campbell, not justified by any that General Lee has yet received.

"In point of policy, under the present situation of our affairs, this doctrine cannot be supported. The balance of prisoners is greatly against us; and a general regard to the happiness of the whole should mark our conduct. Can we imagine, that our enemies will not mete the punishments, the same indignities, the same cruelties, to those belonging to us in their possession, that we impose on theirs in our power? Why should we suppose them to possess more humanity than we have ourselves? Or why should an ineffectual attempt to relieve the distresses of one brave, unfortunate man, involve many more in the same calamities? However disagreeable the fact may be, the enemy at this time have in their power, and subject to their call, near three hundred officers belonging to the army of the United States. In this number there are some of high rank; and most of them are men of bravery and merit. The quota of theirs in our hands bears no proportion, being not more than fifty at most. Under these circumstances we should certainly do no act to draw upon the gentlemen belonging to us, and who have already suffered a long captivity, greater punishments than they have experienced and now experience. If we should, what will their feelings be, and those of their numerous and extensive connexions? Suppose the treatment prescribed for the Hessians should be pursued, will it not establish what the enemy have been aiming to effect by every artifice and the grossest misrepresentations; I mean, an opinion of our enmity towards them, and of the cruel conduct they experience when they fall into our hands—a prejudice which we on our part have heretofore thought it politic to suppress, and to root out by every act of lenity and kindness? It certainly will. The Hessians would hear of the punishment with all the circumstances of heightened exaggeration, would feel the injury without investigating the cause, or reasoning upon the justice or necessity of it. The mischiefs which may, and must inevitably flow from the execution of the resolves, appear to be endless and innumerable."

While the American general was thus advocating the cause of humanity, the soldiers who were captured at Fort Washington were confined during the winter in New York, ill-lodged and badly fed. The provisions which they received were deficient in quantity, and of the worst quality. Many of them died of cold and hunger, and diseases contracted by being confined in close and unhealthy situations. Thus ungenerously treated, and driven almost to desperation, large bounties and tempting offers were held out to others to induce them to enlist in the British service, but they generally remained faithful to their country and their engagements under all their privations and sufferings. In the spring, General Howe sent some of them out for exchange, but they were so emaciated and sickly, so totally unfit for service in the field or camp, that General Washington refused to release an equal number of healthy British and Hessian prisoners, and such had been the good treatment received by them, that but few sick could be found. General Howe said that the refusal of the American general to exchange prisoners was a violation of the rule mutually agreed on between them; and though he could not deny the facts, he contended that the prisoners were treated as well as his circumstances would permit, and so far from being barbarously used, they were provided with every thing which was necessary, and which their situation as prisoners of war allowed. Commissioners had been appointed on each side to settle the matter, but they could not agree. General Washington replied:

"You must be sensible, that our engagement, as well as all others of the kind, though in the letter it expresses only an equality of rank and number, as the rule of exchange; yet necessarily implies a regard to the general principles of mutual compensation and advantage. This is inherent in its nature, is the voice of reason, and no stipulation as to the condition in which prisoners should be returned, was requisite. Humanity dictated that their treatment should be such as their health and comfort demanded; and, where her laws have been duly respected, their condition has been generally good. Nor is this the language of humanity alone; justice declares the same. The object of every cartel, or similar agreement, is the benefit of the prisoners themselves, and that of the contending powers. On this footing, it equally exacts, that they should be well treated, as well as that they should be exchanged. The reverse is, therefore, an evident infraction, and ought to subject the party, on whom it is chargeable, to all the damage and ill consequences resulting from it. Nor can it be expected, that those unfitted for future service by acts of severity, in direct violation of a compact, are proper subjects for an exchange. In such case, to return others not in the same predicament, would be to give without receiving an equivalent; and would afford the greatest encouragement to cruelty and inhumanity. The argument, drawn from the mere circumstance of the prisoners having been received, is of no validity. Though, from their wretched situation, they could not, at that time, be deemed proper for an exchange, yet our humanity required that they should be permitted to return among us.

"It may, perhaps, be fairly doubted, whether an apprehension of their death, or that of a great part of them, did not contribute somewhat to their being sent out when they were.

"Such an event, whilst they remained with you, would have been truly interesting; because it would have destroyed every shadow of claim for a return of the prisoners in our hands, and therefore, policy, concurring with humanity, dictated that the measure should be adopted. Happy had it been, if the expedient had been thought of before these ill-fated men were reduced to such extremity. It is confessed, however, on all sides, that, after their delivery, they still continued your prisoners, and would be so till regularly exchanged.

"I acknowledge, that I should, and I have been always willing, notwithstanding this concession, to account for every man who was in a proper condition and fit to be exchanged at the time he came out, so far as the proportion of prisoners with us would extend. With what propriety, or upon what foundation of justice can more be demanded? This has been proposed, or, what is the same, was most clearly implied in the first article or objection made by Lieutenant-colonel Harrison, and illiberally rejected since, 'as inconsistent with any degree of reason or common sense.' Painful

as it is, I am compelled to consider it as a fact not to be questioned, that the usage of our prisoners whilst in your possession, of
the privates at least, was such as could not be justified. This was
proclaimed by the concurrent testimony of all who came out ; their
appearance sanctioned the assertion ; and melancholy experience,
in the speedy death of a large part of them, stamped it with infallible certainty."

These difficulties continuing, interrupted the free exchange of
prisoners until near the middle of the month of July, when an officer
fell into the hands of the Americans, of sufficient rank to induce
General Howe to exchange General Lee for him. This removing
one ground of the controversy between the two commanders, and
the British general being induced to pay more attention to the
condition of his prisoners, the causes of complaint were in some
measure removed, though not wholly eradicated, until the final
conclusion of the war.

As the spring opened, General Howe remained in some uncertainty with respect to reinforcements expected from Europe.
Arriving, as they did, later, and in smaller numbers than had been
anticipated, he was compelled, though he could number four times
as many men fit for duty as Washington, to remain for some time
in comparative inactivity ; and, when the season for action could
no longer be safely postponed, he was obliged to curtail the plans
which he had formed the preceding autumn.

In order somewhat to remove the appearance of entire idleness,
he determined to attempt the destruction of the stores collected by
the Americans at Peekskill, Danbury, and other points to the eastward. Colonel Bird, with five hundred men, was detached against
Peekskill on the 23d of March, under convoy of a frigate, two ships,
and two brigs, and some smaller armed vessels. The place was
garrisoned by two hundred and fifty men, under General McDougall, who receiving timely notice of the approach of the enemy,
and accurate information with respect to their numbers, he exerted
himself to remove the stores to places of greater safety ; but before
he had removed them all, the enemy landed with four pieces of
artillery, and he retreated to the hills beyond the town, giving directions for destroying such stores as could not be removed. At the same
time, he sent an express to Lieutenant-colonel Willett, ordering
him to leave a subaltern's command at Fort Constitution, and march
with the remainder of his small force to his assistance. The British
kept possession of the town until the next day, when they sent out
a detachment to take possession of a piece of high ground flanked

by a wood between the town and the position taken by General McDougall. There, in the afternoon, they were attacked by Colonel Willett's detachment, and a smart skirmish ensued, which ended in the retreat of the British party to the main body. In the evening, favoured by the light of the moon, but galled by the fire of the Americans, the whole party embarked, and returned down the river. Nine of the enemy were killed or wounded in the skirmish with Willett, and four were killed at the creek, while attempting to set fire to the boats. The Americans had one man mortally wounded by a cannon-ball. The loss of provisions and stores destroyed by order of General McDougall, was considerable, and in this way the British partly succeeded in their design.

Another expedition was projected soon after against Danbury, in Connecticut, where a considerable amount of military stores had been collected. Though this place was within twenty miles of the Sound, so much dependence was placed on the neighbouring militia, and the help which they would be able to obtain from detachments passing through the town from the eastward, that no regular guard was stationed there for the protection of the stores. There were actually but fifty regulars, and one hundred militia, under Colonel Huntington, in the place, when the British made their appearance on the afternoon of the 26th of April. They numbered two thousand men, and were commanded by Governor Tryon, who had recently been appointed major-general of the provincials in the British service. Being unable to make any effectual resistance, Colonel Huntington carried off part of the stores, and retired from the town. General Tryon landed his army of tories at Campo, between Fairfield and Norwalk. Being unexpected, he proceeded without opposition to Danbury, which, with the stores contained in it, they set on fire and destroyed. In the mean time the alarm had spread. General Silliman, an officer of the Connecticut militia, saw the landing, called together as many men as he could, and the same evening sent forward a small party, who came upon the enemy and had a smart skirmish with their advanced guard. The next morning, he marched in pursuit with all the men he could muster. Near Reading, he was joined by Generals Arnold and Wooster, who increased his numbers to six hundred men. They proceeded that night through a heavy rain to Bethel, about eight miles from Danbury, where, hearing that the town was destroyed, they rested their weary followers till daybreak. Then, hearing that the British were retreating towards the coast, they divided their forces, and Wooster, with two hundred men, took a route by which he might harass their rear. While Arnold and Silliman, crossing the country, took post in their front, at Ridgefield. General Wooster, being reinforced by Colonel Huntington, soon fell in with the rear of the enemy, and in a skirmish received a mortal wound. When Arnold arrived at Ridgefield, his numbers were increased to five hundred. Taking a position across the road, he threw up a breastwork, behind which he awaited the approach of the enemy. They arrived about three o'clock in the afternoon. A smart engagement ensued, which continued nearly an hour, when Arnold was compelled to give way; and the British troops, quite exhausted, spent the night on their arms at Ridgefield. During this engagement, Arnold's horse was killed under him, and he saved himself by drawing his pistol and shooting a soldier, who, having discharged his musket, was rushing upon him with his bayonet.

On the morning of the 28th, the British renewed their retreat, but they were immediately assailed by an irregular but destructive fire of musketry from houses, and from behind stone fences. Arnold being joined by some continental artillery and infantry, he kept up a continual skirmishing and cannonading until five in the afternoon, when the enemy reached a hill near their ships, and made a desperate stand. The Americans charged them with intrepidity, but were repulsed by superior numbers. The British, taking advantage of this, re-embarked in haste and sailed for New York. Nearly four hundred of the British were killed, wounded, or taken prisoners; while the loss of the Americans did not exceed one-third of that number. The loss of General Wooster was severely felt, and Congress ordered a monument to be erected to his memory. General Arnold also deserved and obtained the thanks of Congress. They resolved that a horse fully caparisoned should be presented to him in place of the one shot under him on the 27th, and another which had been wounded by a ball through his neck on the 28th. The people of New England gave no encouragement to the repetition of these hostile visits.

"The British troops were not permitted to carry on their sudden incursions and predatory attacks without retaliation. On the 8th of May, General Stevens, with a considerable force, attacked the British post at Piscataway, where the 42d regiment was stationed; but, after a furious engagement, he was repulsed. A considerable quantity of grain, forage, and other necessaries for the use of the royal army were collected at Sagg Harbour in Long Island, where they were but slightly guarded, as the number of British cruisers in the Sound seemed to secure them from all danger. Of these circumstances the American General Parsons gained information; and, on the 23d of May, he detached Colonel Meigs, with a party of one hundred and seventy men, who left Guilford in Connecticut, at one o'clock afternoon, crossed the Sound in thirteen whale boats, attended by three sloops; landed on the north part of the island near Southold, at six o'clock in the evening; carried his boats over a neck of land; re-embarked, and crossed the bay between the north and south parts of the island, and, at twelve o'clock at night, landed within four miles of Sagg Harbour. Leaving his boats under the protection of a slender guard, he advanced silently towards the place of destination, began the attack with fixed bayonets. The alarm soon became general, and a discharge of musketry on both sides ensued; but the Americans succeeded in burning the stores and twelve vessels. They also killed six men, took ninety prisoners, and only six of the party who guarded the place escaped. Colonel Meigs, without having a man either killed or wounded, returned with his prisoners to Guilford, where he arrived at two o'clock on the 24th; having, in the space of twenty-five hours, traversed by sea and land no less than ninety miles.

"When mentioning these achievements of desultory warfare, I may here relate another enterprise of the same kind, although it did not happen till the 10th of July,—the capture of General Prescott. That officer was commander of Rhode Island, and had his head-quarters on the west side of the island, near Narraganset Bay, about a quarter of a mile from the shore, and at some distance from any body of troops. He was but slightly guarded, trusting chiefly for security to the numerous cruisers, and to a guard ship which lay in a bay opposite to his quarters. Colonel Barton, at the head of forty men, officers and volunteers, passed by night from Warwick Neck to Rhode Island; and although they had a passage of ten miles by water, yet, by keeping near the land, they eluded the vigilance of the British ships of war and guard boats which surrounded the island. They conducted their enterprise with such silence and address, that, about midnight, they reached the general's quarters undiscovered, secured the sentinel, surprised the general in bed, and, without giving him time to put on his clothes, hurried him on board with one of his aids-de-camp, and conveyed him safely to Providence. This event was very mortifying to General Prescott, and to the royal army; but occasioned much exultation among the Americans. Hitherto, General Howe had absolutely refused to release General Lee, but he soon agreeᴅ to excʜange him for General Prescott; and General Lee again joined the American army."*

On the arrival of the time for active operations, the forces of General Howe amounted to about thirty thousand men, well equipped and provided; while the army under Washington numbered, as we have seen, only about seven thousand three hundred men fit for duty. During the winter his army had been extremely weak; but during the months of April and May, the new levies began to come in, and his numbers were so much increased that he advanced towards Brunswick, and posted his army upon the strong country about Middlebrook, in such a position that they would be able to move at a moment's notice, either towards the Hudson or the Delaware, or, if necessary, fall back without loss to their fortified encampment at Morristown. He took this position in the expectation that General Howe would either attempt to gain the North river, and by taking possession of the Highlands, cut off all supplies from the Eastern States, or renew the plan of the last campaign, and march through the Jerseys to Pennsylvania.

Calling in all his detachments, General Howe assembled his army at Brunswick on the 12th of June, but aware of the strength of the American position, and judging it unadvisable to attack his adversary there, he tried every expedient, and employed every artifice to draw him into less advantageous ground. For this purpose, he first formed his army into two strong columns, and marched towards the Delaware as far as Middlebush and Hillsborough. Washington saw through the designs of the British general, and kept possession of his camp, sending out skirmishing parties to harass and annoy his adversary's march.

Howe's next manœuvre was to commence an apparently precipitate retreat. Accordingly, on the night of the 19th of June, he abandoned his advanced position, returned to Brunswick, and in a short time, retiring to Amboy, he threw a bridge over the channel separating the main land from Staten Island, and conveyed over it his heavy baggage and part of his troops. Washington detached General Greene with some light parties to annoy the rear of the enemy, and moved his strong camp from Middlebrook to Quibbletown, which is six or seven miles nearer to Amboy. Lord Stirling's division was advanced a few miles lower, in order to cooperate with General Green, should the retreat from Amboy leave any point exposed.

In this sʼtate of things, General Howe thought it practicable ᴛʜ

* Western World, vol. i. 236—238.

bring the inferior force of Washington to an engagement in an open field, or at least to gain possession of the high lands to the left of his position, and thus compel him to abandon Middlebrook, and fall back towards Morristown. With this view, on the night of the 25th, he recalled the troops which had passed over to Staten Island, and very early the next morning the whole British army in two columns moved rapidly to Westfield. The right, under the command of Lord Cornwallis, fell in with Lord Stirling's division about seven o'clock in the morning, and a smart engagement ensued, which gave General Washington timely notice of his danger, and the whole army fell back hastily towards the mountains, regained the camp, and a detachment took possession of the heights to the left, which it was supposed the enemy had designed to seize. Lord Stirling's division, after some smart skirmishing, fell back with but little loss; and Lord Cornwallis, perceiving the passes in the mountains guarded, and the skilful plans of his commander again completely overturned by the American Fabius, returned to Amboy, and the whole army crossed over to Staten Island, and began to embark in transports, to proceed to some more assailable point of the coast.

It was difficult for Washington to ascertain the designs of the enemy. The whole coast of the United States was open to him, and he might sail to any part of it with far greater rapidity than he could be followed. To add to this uncertainty, a letter from General Schuyler informed him that Burgoyne was advancing from Canada with a large army against Ticonderoga. This seemed to render it probable that General Howe's intention was to move up the Hudson River, and co-operate with General Burgoyne, and under this impression he moved a part of his army towards the Highlands by the way of Morristown, and advancing as far as the Clove, detached Lord Stirling to occupy Peekskill. Another portion of the army was stationed at Trenton, to be in readiness, if necessary, to protect Philadelphia.

While in this state of uncertainty, he received information that General Howe had, on the 23d of July, sailed from Sandy Hook, having with him sixteen thousand men, in a fleet of two hundred and sixty-seven vessels. Still, the destination of this fleet was uncertain, some reporting that it had sailed towards the north, and others towards the south. Apprehending that the whole movement might be a feint, to put him off his guard, and open a passage up the Hudson, he prepared every thing for moving with celerity. At this juncture a letter purporting to be from Howe to Burgoyne was intercepted, and carried to head-quarters. It affected to give information that Howe's army was destined for New Hampshire, where a junction was advised; but so clumsily was the intended deception veiled on the face of this letter, that one hour after its reception, the army was in full march southward. The different divisions pursued different routes and concentrated on the banks of the Delaware, where the general was informed that the enemy's fleet had appeared off the capes of the Delaware. Its destination was no longer doubtful, and the troops were thrown across the Delaware, and stationed first at Germantown, where they would be at hand to defend Philadelphia, while Washington himself hastened forward to Chester. There he was informed that the fleet had left the Delaware Bay and steered towards the east. This again left him in suspense, and he naturally concluded from the reported course of the fleet, that General Howe would either go directly back to New York, or land at some port in New England, perhaps at Boston, and co-operate with Burgoyne. Till this point should be settled by certain information, nothing could be determined upon. Detaching Sullivan into New Jersey, Washington with the main army remained at Germantown, until the 22d of August, when he was relieved from his painful suspense by the intelligence that the fleet was ascending the Chesapeake.

It was during this period of comparative inaction that Washington first became acquainted with Lafayette. This young nobleman having offered his services as a volunteer without compensation, he was appointed by Congress, on the 31st of July, a major-general in the Continental army. His first interview with the commander-in-chief took place at a dinner-party in Philadelphia, where there were many officers and several members of Congress present. When the party was about to separate, Washington took him aside, invited him to consider himself as one of his family, and to make the head-quarters of the army his home during his residence in the country. The invitation was gladly accepted, and the young French nobleman immediately entered upon his duties, and ever after kept up a close intimacy with the commander-in-chief.

As soon as certain information of the destination of the British fleet was received, General Washington put his army in motion, and about seven o'clock on the morning of the 24th of August marched through Philadelphia, passing down Front Street, and up Chesnut Street, and proceeded without delay by the way of Chester, to Wilmington. From that time, for two weeks, he was incessantly

37   2 B

engaged in thoroughly reconnoitering the country between Phila delphia and the Chesapeake.

The British army debarked below the head of the Elk, a few days' march from Philadelphia. On landing, General Howe issued a proclamation, promising pardon and protection to all who would submit to him, but it seems to have produced but little effect. The American forces were thrown forward a few miles to Red Clay Creek, and their pickets advanced to Christiana bridge, towards which the enemy advanced on the 3d of September.

As the royal troops advanced, it became evident that Howe's design was to gain the right of the American army. To counteract this attempt, Washington fell back until he crossed the Brandywine Creek, and, taking post with his main body, opposite Chad's Ford, ordered General Sullivan, with a detachment, to watch the fords above. He sent General Maxwell with about a thousand light troops, to occupy the high ground on the other side of the Brandy-wine, to skirmish with the British, and retard their progress.

General Washington distinctly understood the nature of the con-test in which he was engaged ; and sensible of the inferiority of his raw and undisciplined army to the veteran troops under General Howe, he wished to avoid a general engagement; but aware of the effect which the fall of Philadelphia, without an effort to save it, would produce on the minds of the people, he determined to com-ply with the wishes of Congress in this instance, against his own judgment, to make a determined effort to retard the progress and defeat the aim of the royal army.

On the morning of the 11th of September, the British army advanced in two columns ; the right, under General Knyphausen, marched by the direct road towards Chad's Ford ; the left, under Lord Cornwallis, accompanied by the commander-in-chief, and Generals Grey, Grant, and Agnew, proceeded by a circuitous route towards the forks of the Brandywine, with the intention of turning the right of the Americans, and gaining their rear.

General Knyphausen's van soon found itself opposed to the light troops under General Maxwell. A smart conflict ensued. The British advanced guard being reinforced, drove the Americans across the creek, and Knyphausen commenced a heavy fire of artillery, which was returned with warmth by the American bat-teries. He made no attempt to cross, though small parties cross-ing over skirmished on both sides.

Meanwhile, the left wing of the British crossed the fords above the forks. Information of this movement was conveyed to Wash·

HEAD-QUARTERS AT BRANDYWINE.

ington by General Sullivan about noon, who immediately ordered Sullivan, with the right wing, to attack the enemy's column on its progress down the north side of the Brandywine, while he himself prepared for the daring measure of recrossing the creek with his centre and left, and attacking Knyphausen's division. While issuing orders for the execution of these plans, the information which had led to them was contradicted, and those already given were countermanded.

In the midst of this uncertainty, Lord Cornwallis crossed the creek by Trimble's and Jefferis' Fords, and took the road to Dilworth. The alarm reached Washington. The brigades of Stephen, Stirling, and Sullivan, under the command of the latter, were pushed forward to Birmingham meeting-house; General Wayne was left to defend the passage at Chad's Ford, while Washington, with General Green's division, took an intermediate position, in order to aid either Wayne or Sullivan, as circumstances might require. About two o'clock in the afternoon, Cornwallis's division reached Osborne's Hill, where they halted and dined, having in the course of the morning marched thirteen miles. Before they again fell in, the forces of the Americans were seen forming upon the brow of the opposite hill at Birmingham meeting-house. Their movements and manner of forming were admired and praised by Cornwallis, who, with Howe and the field-officers, occupied the summit of Osborne's Hill. Sullivan's left extended towards the Brandywine, his artillery was judiciously posted, and his right was forming across the road intended to be covered on the right flank by the woods. Before the right had fully formed, however, the attack was commenced with impetuosity by a party of Hessians, who crossed the street road in front of the American position, and resting their muskets upon the fence, fired upon the American outposts. In half an hour, about four o'clock, the attack became general; and for some time the Americans sustained it with intrepidity, but at length began to give way on the extreme right, where General Deborre, a French officer who had lately entered the service, commanded. In attempting to rally them, Lafayette was wounded in the leg. General Sullivan's brigade, which, on the retreat of the right, was in some degree outflanked also, began to give way. Sullivan, using every exertion to rally them, threw himself, with Stirling and Lafayette, personally into the conflict, and a most heroic stand was made, these officers continuing to maintain their ground until the American forces were completely broken, and the enemy within twenty yards of them, when they escaped by taking to the woods.

When General Washington heard the firing to the right, he ordered General Green, with his brigade, to support General Sullivan. Green marched four miles in forty minutes, but, on reaching the scene of action, he found Sullivan's division defeated and fleeing in confusion. He covered their retreat, and, taking an advantageous position, renewed the battle, arrested the progress of the enemy, and maintained his post until the darkness of night enabled him to withdraw, at the order of the commander-in-chief.

As soon as General Knyphausen heard the firing of Cornwallis's division, he forced the passage of Chad's Ford, attacked the troops opposed to him, and compelled them to make a precipitate retreat towards Chester.

The effective force of the Americans in this action did not exceed eleven thousand men, whilst Cornwallis's division alone amounted to thirteen thousand.

General Howe reported his own loss to be ninety killed, four hundred and eighty-eight wounded, and six missing; and that of

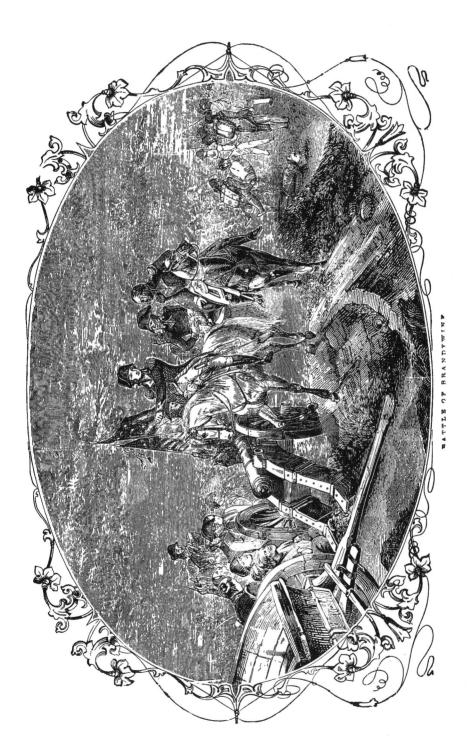

BATTLE OF BRANDYWINE

the Americans, three hundred were killed, six hundred were wounded, and four hundred were taken.

The American army retreated during the night to Chester, taking with them all their baggage and artillery, with the exception of ten small field-pieces and a howitzer. The next morning Washington retired to Philadelphia, where he remained one day, and then marched up the north side of the Schuylkill, crossed it at Swede's Ford, and proceeded again in the direction of the enemy. The two armies met on the 16th of September, twenty-three miles from Philadelphia, and the advanced parties had actually commenced an engagement, when a heavy rain rendered both parties unable to continue the action. Washington retired to the Yellow Springs, and on the 22d recrossed the Schuylkill near Pottsgrove. These operations will be best related in his own words, written in a letter to Congress on the 23d. That body had, after again increasing the powers of Washington, adjourned to Lancaster on the 18th, and on the 27th to York, where they met until the British evacuated Philadelphia.

"I have not had the honour of addressing you," he says, "since your adjournment to Lancaster, and I sincerely wish that my first letter was upon a more agreeable subject. The enemy, by a variety of perplexing manœuvres, through a country from which I could not derive the least intelligence, (being to a man disaffected,) contrived to pass the Schuylkill last night at Flatland, and other fords in the neighbourhood of it. They marched immediately towards Philadelphia, and I imagine their advanced parties will be near that city to-night. They had so far got the start before I received certain intelligence that any considerable number had crossed, that I found it in vain to think of overtaking their rear, with troops harassed as ours had been with constant marching since the battle of Brandywine ; and therefore concluded, by the advice of all the general officers, to march from this place to-morrow morning towards Philadelphia, and on the way endeavour to form a junction with the Continental troops under General McDougall from Peekskill, and the Jersey militia under General Dickinson, both of whom are, I hope, on this side of the Delaware. I am also obliged to wait for General Wayne and General Smallwood, who were left upon the other side of the Schuylkill, in hopes of falling upon the enemy's rear ; but they have eluded them as well as us.

"When I last recrossed the Schuylkill, it was with a firm intent of giving the enemy battle wherever I should meet them ; and accordingly, I advanced as far as the Warren Tavern upon the

Lancaster road, near which place the two armies were upon the point of coming to a general engagement, but were prevented by a most violent flood of rain, which continued all the day and following night. When it held up, we had the mortification to find that our ammunition, which had been completed to forty rounds a man, was entirely ruined, and in that situation we had nothing left for it but to find out a strong piece of ground, which we could easily maintain till we could get the arms put in order, and a recruit of ammunition. Before this could be fully effected, the enemy marched from their position near the White Horse Tavern, down the road leading to the Swedes' Ford. I immediately crossed the Schuylkill above them, and threw myself full in their front, hoping to meet them in their passage, or soon after they had passed the river. The day before yesterday they were again in motion, and marched rapidly up the road leading towards Reading. This induced me to believe that they had two objects in view, one to get round the right of the army, the other, perhaps, to detach parties to Reading, where we had considerable quantities of military stores. To frustrate those intentions, I moved the army up on this side of the river to this place, determined to keep pace with them; but early this morning I received intelligence that they had crossed the fords below. Why I did not follow immediately, I have mentioned in the former part of my letter; but the strongest reason against being able to make a forced march is the want of shoes. Messieurs Carroll, Chase, and Penn, who were some days with the army, can inform Congress in how deplorable a situation the troops are for want of that necessary article. At least one thousand men are barefooted, and have performed the marches in that condition. I was told of a great number of shoes in the hands of private people in Philadelphia, and sent down to secure them; but I doubt the approach of the enemy will prevent it.

"I have planned a method of throwing a garrison into Fort Mifflin. If it succeeds, and they, with the assistance of the ships and galleys, should keep the obstructions in the river, General Howe's situation in Philadelphia will not be the most agreeable, for if his supplies can be stopped by water, it may be easily done by land. To do both shall be my utmost endeavour; and I am not yet without hope that the acquisition of Philadelphia may, instead of his good fortune, prove his ruin."

On the 26th of September, General Howe entered and took possession of Philadelphia without further opposition; and on the same day, commenced the erection of batteries near the river, to protect

the place against such American vessels as might approach the shore. Commodore Hazlewood, being in command of two frigates, a sloop, and several galleys and gondolas on the river, commenced an attack on the unfinished batteries on the 27th. A warm cannonade was kept up for some time, but on the falling of the tide,)ne of the frigates, the Delaware, grounded within five hundred yards of the batteries, where, in her disabled condition, she was aken by the enemy. The other frigate, with the smaller vessels, returned to their former stations near Fort Mifflin; and Cornwallis opened a communication with the Jersey shore.

The main body of the British army encamped outside the city, throwing up strong lines of intrenchment reaching from the Schuylkill towards the Delaware, occupying principally the village of Germantown, about four miles above the city. Not twenty miles off was Washington, with an army of about eleven thousand men, once more elate with hope and fresh vigour. Along the line of the Delaware, between Philadelphia and the British fleet, which had left the Chesapeake immediately after the battle of Brandywine, formidable preparations were made, on the one hand to open the river, and on the other to resist the attempt. Throughout the entire distance, almost at the same moment, the shock of war was felt. Indeed, from the Delaware to the St. Lawrence, raged one wide, wasting flame of war; for, as Howe was approaching Philadelphia, Burgoyne, with a flushed army and savage allies, was descending the Hudson and threatening destruction to the Eastern States. But neither Congress nor Washington entertained the most distant thought of yielding. On the contrary, when the royal army was in a slight degree weakened by detachments sent to assist in removing the obstructions in the Delaware, General Washington made a warm attack on their encampment at Germantown. Germantown consisted of but one street about two miles long; the line of the British encampment bisected the village, almost at right angles and had its left covered by the Schuylkill. Washington marched from his encampment at Skippach Creek, about seven o'clock on the evening of the 3d of October, and the next morning approached the enemy in four divisions. By the order of battle, the divisions of Sullivan and Wayne, flanked by Conway's brigade, were to enter the town by way of Chestnut Hill; while Armstrong with the Pennsylvania militia should approach the enemy's left wing by the Manatawny road, which ran along the side of the Schuylkill. The divisions of Greene and Stephen, flanked by McDougall's brigade, were to take a circuit by way of the Lime-

38

CHEW'S HOUSE.

kiln road, and entering the village near the market-house, attack the right wing; while the militia of Maryland and Jersey, under Smallwood and Forman, were to march by the Old York road still further to the left, and fall upon the rear of the enemy's right. Stirling, with the brigades of Nash and Maxwell, advanced in the rear of Sullivan by the Chesnut Hill road, and acted as a *corps de reserve.*

The attack was commenced by General Sullivan about sunrise on the morning of the 4th of October. He drove in the advanced picket, and followed so close that he surprised the light infantry and fortieth regiment, which were encamped between Mount Airy and the village. After sustaining for a short time a sharp conflict, these forces, leaving their baggage, retreated into the village. In his retreat, Lieutenant-colonel Musgrave succeeded in throwing himself, with six companies of his regiment, into Chew's large stone house, which stood in front of Sullivan's column, and these two brigades were detained so long in endeavouring to dispossess them that the British had time to get under arms, and be in readiness to resist or attack, as occasion might require.

Green's division attacked the enemy's right wing about three quarters of an hour after the battle began in the centre, and he also drove back the forces opposed to him. He was on the point of forming a junction with Sullivan's division, when, actuated by some unaccountable impulse, the Americans began to give way, and retreated, carrying with them all their artillery.

General Washington gave the following account of this action to his brother. "The enemy crossed the Schuylkill by stratagem, though I do not know that it was in our power to prevent it, as their manœuvres made it necessary for us to attend to our stores, which lay at Reading, towards which they seemed bending their course, and the loss of which must have proved our ruin. After they had crossed, we took the first favourable opportunity of attacking them.

"This was attempted by a night's march of fourteen miles to surprise them, which we effectually did, so far as to reach their guards before they had notice of our coming; and if it had not been for a thick fog, which rendered it so dark at times that we were not able to distinguish friend from foe at the distance of thirty yards, we should, I believe, have made a decisive and glorious day of it. But Providence designed it otherwise; for, after we had driven the enemy a mile or two, after they were in the utmost confusion, and flying before us in most places, after we were upon the point, as it appeared to everybody, of grasping a complete victory, our own troops took flight and fled with precipitation and disorder. How to account for this, I know not; unless, as I before observed, the fog represented their own friends to them for a reinforcement of the enemy, as we attacked in different quarters at the same time, and were about closing the wings of our army when this happened. One thing, indeed, contributed not a little to our misfortune, and that was a want of ammunition on the right wing, which began the engagement, and in the course of two hours and forty minutes, which time it lasted, had, many of them, expended the forty rounds that they took into the field. After the engagement, we removed to a place about twenty miles from the enemy, to collect our forces together, to take care of our wounded, get furnished with necessaries again, and be in a better posture, either for offensive or defensive operations. We are now (October 15) advancing towards the enemy again, being at this time within twelve miles of them.

"Our loss in the late action, was in killed, wounded, and missing, about one thousand men,* but of the missing, many, I dare say, took advantage of the time and deserted. General Nash, of North Carolina, was wounded and died two or three days after. Many valuable officers of ours were also wounded, and some killed. In a word, it was a bloody day. Would to heaven I could add, that it had been a more fortunate one for us."

On the day after the battle, he wrote to Congress: "The morning was extremely foggy, which prevented our improving the advantages we gained so well as we should otherwise have done. This circumstance, by concealing from us the true situation of the enemy,

---

* One hundred and fifty killed, five hundred and twenty-one wounded, and about four hundred prisoners.

obliged us to act with more caution and less expedition than we could have wished ; and gave the enemy time to recover from the effects of our first impression ; and, which was still more unfortunate, it served to keep our different parties in ignorance of each other's movements, and hinder their acting in concert. It also occasioned them to mistake one another for the enemy, which, I believe, more than any thing else contributed to the misfortune that ensued. In the midst of the most promising appearances, when every thing gave the most flattering hopes of victory, the troops began suddenly to retreat, and entirely left the field, in spite of every effort that could be made to rally them."

The large numbers of prisoners taken by the British was also in consequence of the fog. Colonel Matthews, having routed a party of the British opposed to him, and captured a hundred and ten of them, lost sight of the brigade to which he belonged, and approaching a large body of men in good order, was deceived, and thinking they were the brigade to which he belonged, approached and was taken prisoner with his whole regiment, and the prisoners which he had previously taken were released.

The British had six hundred men killed or wounded; among the slain were Brigadier-general Agnew and Colonel Bird, both officers of distinguished reputation.

Notwithstanding the ill success of this expedition, Congress expressed their approbation both of its plan and execution, and voted their thanks to the general and his army.

Washington, having recruited his troops, returned towards the enemy and took a strong position at White Marsh before the end of October. His chief object was to attract the attention of the enemy to himself, and divert his strength from the operations against the forts on the Delaware. Howe understood and eluded this manœuvre, by withdrawing his entire force into the city, and thus concentrating his full power against the forts. For nearly two months the operations on the river were conducted with varied success, the British being sometimes repulsed, and sometimes partially successful in their attacks on the American forts, Mifflin, on Mud Island, in the river, and Mercer, on Red Bank, on the Jersey side. Count Donop was despatched with a strong body of Hessians against the latter place. Crossing the river, he marched rapidly to the assault at the head of two thousand men. The fort was defended by Colonel Greene, with about five hundred men. Not being sufficient in number to man the outworks, he ordered the garrison to retard the approach of the enemy until they came close to the outworks, and then to retire within the second barrier. The besiegers leaped upon the deserted barricades with loud huzzas, which the garrison answered with a terrific fire. Peal upon peal came in quick succession, and the enemy were compelled to stagger back over the corpses of their comrades. Count Donop remained on the ground mortally wounded. The second in command fell, and the detachment, so confident a few hours before, retreated in dismay, without effecting any serious injury, but leaving at least four hundred of their number behind them either killed or wounded.

Meanwhile, Fort Mifflin was attacked both by batteries on the shore and by shipping, and was battered incessantly from the 10th to the 16th of November. By that time, every defence was destroyed, and every cannon dismounted, so that ships could approach so near as to enable the sailors to throw hand-grenades from their tops. The garrison was then ordered to quit the post ; and Red Bank being now no longer useful, was abandoned on the approach of Lord Cornwallis, with five thousand men, to invest it. Thus the fortifications of the Delaware being destroyed, the obstructions in its channel were removed, and after six weeks of incessant effort and great loss, General Howe obtained command of the navigation of the Delaware, and thus opened a communication between the British fleet and his army in Philadelphia.

General Washington's army at Whitemarsh was, in November, reinforced by part of the northern army, the campaign having closed in that quarter, by the capture of Burgoyne. The arrival of militia further increased his numbers, in the beginning of December, to fourteen thousand men, which made it, in that respect, nearly equal to the British army under General Howe. But the difference in the quality and equipment of these two bodies gave an immense superiority to Howe. His men were veterans, accustomed to the most exact discipline and subordination, well armed, and abundantly supplied with military stores and other necessaries ; but the soldiers of Washington were mostly raw levies, and disorderly militia, ill-disciplined, imperfectly armed, and strangers to military subordination. This inferiority induced Washington still to keep on the defensive, unless circumstances should be so much in his favor as to counterbalance its effects. Consequently, when the British army, on the 4th of December, marched from Philadelphia, and took post on Chesnut Hill, fronting his camp, he had too much prudence and too much patriotism to hazard the permanent liberty of his country on a single action, how great soever might be the lustre which its success might reflect upon his

2 C

arms. The enemy took this position on the evening of the 4th, about three miles distant from the American right wing. On the 5th, both armies sent out light parties to skirmish, but Washington was not to be enticed from the advantageous position which he then occupied. During the night of the 5th, the enemy changed their ground, and moved to the left of the American line, where, strongly posted, they remained quiet the whole of the next day. On the 7th they advanced still farther towards the American left, and Colonel Morgan was detached to attack and skirmish with their advanced and flanking parties. About sunset, after various marches and countermarches, they halted, having taken such a position that General Washington concluded that they would attack him during the night, or early in the morning. Confident in the strength of his position, there was nothing which he desired more. In this, however, he was mistaken. On the morning of the 8th, they again began to move, but instead of advancing, they filed off from their right, and retreated in such haste to Philadelphia, that the parties detached by Washington to fall upon their rear, found it impossible to overtake them. In the several skirmishes which occurred during the three days on which the two armies lay in front of each other, the British lost twenty men killed, sixty-three wounded, and thirty-three prisoners. On the side of the Americans, there were forty-three or forty-four men killed or wounded; among the latter, Brigadier-general Irvine and Major Morris.

The winter now set in with great severity, and the Americans were badly clothed, and almost destitute of blankets. Notwithstanding these privations, which seemed to render good winter quarters absolutely necessary, Washington determined to sacrifice the comforts which his troops had a right to expect, to the welfare of his country. He therefore led them to Valley Forge, a strong position on the Schuylkill, about twenty miles from Philadelphia, where they arrived on the 19th of December, when they immediately commenced building for themselves log huts. These huts were each sixteen by fourteen feet, and were arranged in parallel lines, so far as the nature of the ground would admit. Twelve privates were quartered in one hut; while one was assigned to the commissioned officers of every two companies; one to the staff of each regiment; one to the field-officers of each regiment; one to the staff of each brigade; and one to each general officer.

On the 17th of December, General Washington issued his order for the retirement of his army to winter quarters. The concluding clause of this order deserves notice. It is in these words :

" To-morrow, being the day set apart by the honourable Congress for public thanksgiving and praise, and duty calling us devoutly to express our grateful acknowledgments to God for the manifold blessings he has granted us, the general directs that the army remain in its present quarters, and that the chaplains perform divine service with their several corps and brigades; and earnestly exhorts all officers and soldiers, whose absence is not indispensably necessary, to attend with reverence the solemnities of the day."

The army retired to Valley Forge, and the soldiers cut down the trees, built their huts, and fortified their position, which they occupied till June, 1778 ; but notwithstanding all their exertions, they suffered extremely during the winter, both for food and clothing. " It is with infinite pain and concern," said Washington, in a letter to Congress, as early as the 22d of December, " that I transmit the enclosed copies of sundry letters respecting the commissary's department. In these, matters are not exaggerated. I do not know from what cause this alarming deficiency, or rather total failure of supplies, arises ; but, unless more vigorous exertions, and better regulations take place in that line immediately, this army must dissolve. I have done all in my power, by remonstrating, by writing, by ordering the commissaries on this head, from time to time ; but without any good effect, or obtaining more than a present scanty relief. Owing to this, the march of the army has been delayed, upon more than one interesting occasion, in the course of the present campaign ; and, had a body of the enemy crossed the Schuylkill this morning, as I had reason to expect, from the intelligence I received at four o'clock last night, the divisions which I ordered to be in readiness to march and meet them could not have moved."

The following extracts from two of the letters to which the general alludes, and to which he referred the attention of Congress, and which he had received on the same morning on which he wrote the above letter, will give a sad but true account of the condition of the army at that early period of the winter cantonment.

" I received an order," writes General Huntington, " to hold my brigade in readiness to march. Fighting will be by far preferable to starving. My brigade are out of provisions, nor can the commissary obtain any meat. I am exceedingly unhappy in being the bearer of complaints to head-quarters. I have used every argument my imagination can invent, to make the soldiers easy, but I despair of being able to do it much longer."

The other extract is from a letter from General Varnum. He writes:

"According to the saying of Solomon, hunger will break through a stone wall. It is therefore a very pleasing circumstance to the division under my command, that there is a probability of their marching. Three days successively we have been destitute of bread. Two days we have been entirely without meat. The men must be supplied, or they cannot be commanded. The complaints are too urgent to pass unnoticed. It is with pain that I mention this distress. I know it will make your excellency unhappy; but, if you expect the exertion of virtuous principles, while your troops are deprived of the necessaries of life, your final disappointment will be great in proportion to the patience which now astonishes every man of human feeling."

On the next day, December 23d, the general again wrote to Congress:

"Full as I was in my representation of the matters in the commissary's department, yesterday, fresh and more powerful reasons oblige me to add, that I am now convinced, beyond a doubt, that, unless some great and capital change suddenly takes place in that line, this army must inevitably be reduced to one or other of these three things: starve, dissolve, or disperse, in order to obtain subsistence in the best manner they can. Rest assured, sir, this is not an exaggerated picture, and that I have abundant reason to suppose what I say.

"Yesterday afternoon, receiving information that the enemy, in force, had left the city, and were advancing towards Derby, with the apparent design to forage, and draw subsistence from that part of the country, I ordered the troops to be in readiness, that I might give every opposition in my power; when behold, to my great mortification, I was not only informed, but convinced, that the men were unable to stir on account of provisions, and that a dangerous mutiny, begun the night before, and which with difficulty was suppressed by the spirited exertions of some officers, was still much to be apprehended for want of this article. This brought forth the only commissary in the purchasing line in this camp; and, with him, this melancholy and alarming truth, that he had not a single hoof of any kind to slaughter, and not more than twenty-five barrels of flour! From hence form an opinion of our situation, when I add, that he could not tell when to expect any.

"All I could do, under these circumstances, was to send out a few light parties to watch and harass the enemy, whilst other parties were instantly detached different ways to collect, if possible, as much provision as would satisfy the present pressing wants of the soldiery. But will this answer? No sir; three or four days of bad weather would prove our destruction. What then is to become of the army this winter? And if we are so often without provisions now, what is to become of us in the spring, when our force will be collected, with the aid perhaps of militia to take advantage of an early campaign, before the enemy can be reinforced? These are considerations of great magnitude, meriting the closest attention; and they will, when my own reputation is so intimately connected with the event, and to be affected by it, justify my saying, that the present commissaries are by no means equal to the execution of the office, or that the disaffection of the people is past all belief. The misfortune, however, does, in my opinion, proceed from both causes; and, though I have been tender heretofore of giving any opinion, or lodging complaints, as the change in that department took place contrary to my judgment, and the consequences thereof were predicted; yet, finding that the inactivity of the army, whether for want of provisions, clothes, or other essentials, is charged to my account, not only by the common vulgar, but by those in power, it is time to speak plain in exculpation of myself. With truth, then, I can declare, that no man, in my opinion, ever had his measures more impeded upon than I have, by every department of the army.

"Since the month of July, we have had no assistance from the quartermaster-general, and to want of assistance from this department the commissary-general charges a great part of his deficiency. To this I am to add, that notwithstanding it is a standing order, and often repeated, that the troops shall always have two days' provisions by them, that they might be ready on any sudden call; yet an opportunity has scarcely ever offered, of taking an advantage of the enemy, that has not been either totally obstructed, or greatly impeded, on this account. And this, the great and crying evil, is not all. The soap, vinegar, and other articles allowed by Congress, we see none of, nor have we seen them, I believe, since the battle of Brandywine. The first, indeed, we have now little occasion for; few men having more than one shirt, many only the moiety of one, and some none at all.　In addition to which, as a proof of the little benefit received from a clothier-general, and as a further proof of the inability of an army, under the circumstances of this, to perform the common duties of soldiers, (beside a number of men confined to hospitals for want of shoes, and others in farmers' houses on the same account,) we have, by a field return, this day made, no less than two thousand eight hundred and ninety-eight men now in camp, unfit for duty, because they are barefoot, and otherwise naked.　By the same return, it appears, that our whole strength in continental troops, including the eastern brigades, which have joined us since the surrender of General Burgoyne, exclusive of the Maryland troops sent to Wilmington, amounts to no more than eight thousand two hundred in camp, fit for duty ; notwithstanding which, and that since the 4th instant, our numbers fit for duty, from the hardships and exposures they have undergone, particularly on account of blankets, (numbers having been obliged, and still are, to sit up all night by fires, instead of taking comfortable rest in a natural and common way,) have decreased near two thousand men."

A committee of Congress was appointed to proceed to Valley Forge, and take measures for the relief of these pressing wants, but during the whole winter and the ensuing spring, they continued almost unmitigated, until the army again moved in June.

While Washington was thus keeping up a show of resistance, and using his utmost endeavours to infuse courage and hope into the minds of the people in the Middle States, the northern army, at first repulsed, overawed, and driven back before a superior foe, was, under the guidance and superintendence of officers appointed by Congress, on the recommendation of Washington, and by his advice and aid, gaining for the country a most important triumph, and one which had no little influence on the minds of the French and English governments, and contributed greatly to the success of the campaign of 1778.

On the 30th of June, 1777, the British General Burgoyne issued the following order :

" The army embarks to-morrow to approach the enemy.　The services required on this expedition are actual and conspicuous. During our progress occasions may occur in which nor difficulty, nor labour, nor life are to be regarded.　This army must not retreat."

Such was the language of the ominous proclamation which heralded the operations of the British northern army.　And that army nad dread auxiliaries, to whose native passions might well be committed the execution of these sanguinary orders. It would be impossible to say whether Burgoyne, who led on this devastating force, addressed them, for the purpose of awakening the instincts of the savages, or by way of anticipating the acts of barbarity, which he knew it would be impossible to prevent them from perpetrating.

In the summer of 1776, the American army evacuated the province of Canada. From that time until the arrival of Burgoyne, the operations of Sir Guy Carleton were merely defensive ; and the Americans did not venture to disturb his repose. When Burgoyne, at the head of a large force destined to invade the northern states, began his march, the Americans had possession only of Ticonderoga and the several forts about it. He invested them on all sides ; and General St. Clair, first in command, finding his little force utterly inadequate to defend the extensive line of forts, the safety of which was essential to the fort of Ticonderoga itself, called a council of war, and submitted the humiliating proposal of evacuating the place, although the evacuation involved the loss of all the stores and baggage. The proposal received unanimous sanction, notwithstanding that step was one of great risk, and greater delicacy. The strength of Ticonderoga was a familiar boast with all America, and the general who abandoned it without an effort, was sure to be assailed with all the bitterness of popular odium. Time, however, and the verdict of a court-martial, bore testimony to the wisdom of St. Clair's resolution. An attempt was made to save some of the stores, which were shipped on board a few batteaux, which left the fort as the army commenced its retreat. Burgoyne's disposition to pursue them, both by land and water, was prompt and determined. The batteaux were overtaken, and, after a brief and bootless resistance, all the American vessels were sunk or fired. On the track of the army hung the avenging savages, who formed the van of Burgoyne's force.

The destruction of the little fleet, and the defeat of some regiments in St. Clair's rear, gave a new direction to his march ; his enfeebled resources suggesting the immediate necessity of forming a junction with Schuyler, at Fort Edward, on the Hudson. Marching south-west, he succeeded in reaching this point, when the joint forces of both generals were found to amount to only four thousand four hundred. On the approach of Burgoyne's victorious troops, this fort was abandoned, and the army fell back upon Albany. But in that quarter, too, a dangerous foe was in rapid march to intercept their retreat. St. Leger, with whom were the chief Indian auxiliaries, had made a circuit to the right, and was approaching Albany by Lake Ontario and the Mohawk River.

While Burgoyne was meditating on the surest means of capturing, or cutting off in the speediest way the American army, and his troops, in this hope, were surmounting all the difficulties of a march through the wilderness, St. Leger received an unexpected check on the banks of the Mohawk. While on rapid march with the Indians, athirst for blood and plunder, he laid siege to Fort Schuyler, on the Mohawk, the first place that presented any opposition. Colonel Herkimer, with a regiment of volunteers, hastily collected, determined to attack him in his intrenchments; but while on his route he was surprised by the Indians, and a detachment from St. Leger's camp. Herkimer was killed, and his army, after a desperate struggle, completely routed, leaving about one hundred and sixty of their comrades on the field, to glut the barbarity of the Indians. But in that unequal conflict, they made an impression on the red warriors which they never afterwards forgot. This short battle sorely thinned them, and its consequences were any thing but satisfactory to their cupidity. St. Leger, in his correspondence with the garrison, held out as a threat their uncontrollable ferocity, which, if the fort did not at once submit, would commit indiscriminate murder, " not alone on the garrison, but on every man, woman, and child in the Mohawk country."

The answer of Colonel Gavensfort to this inhuman menace, which it would be impossible to credit, did but one man then or since contradict it, is one of the noblest in any annals :—" I am determined," said he, " to defend the fort to the last extremity, against all enemies whatever, without any concern for the consequence of doing my duty."

Besieged and besiegers redoubled their efforts, and the extremity which the garrison had dared was quickly approaching, when a strange revolution in the British camp gave affairs a different turn. Two officers, Willet and Stockwell, undertook the desperate attempt of stealing through savages and soldiers to convey to Schuyler intelligence of the garrison's distress. They succeeded, and at the same time, a prisoner, acquainted with the language of the Indians, was prevailed on to enter their bivouacks, and dissuade them from the enterprise. They listened, and were convinced.

St. Leger employed all his address to change their resolutions, but in vain. At the same time other intelligence, still more gratifying, apprized them that Arnold was hurrying to their relief, with a speed such as but few besides him could employ when on errands of battle.

The siege was raised on the 22d of August, in the midst of the confusion caused by the departure of the Indians, the main body of whom only remained on condition of an instant abandonment of this tedious warfare. Ere yet Burgoyne was aware of this, he revolved in his mind, with deep anxiety, the prudence and glory of a rapid movement into the country, which, while it opened to him a dazzling prospect of triumph, involved the danger of removing a large army out of the reach of those shores whence he received his chief supply. Ambition prevailed. But he determined to try if he might not rely on the rich produce of Vermont, which he calculated that the panic of the inhabitants and their supposed disaffection to the American cause would place at his disposal. A detachment of five hundred men, with six hundred Indians, was directed to explore Vermont, disperse any scattered militia that might guard it, and enter into terms with the loyalists. They were rescued at the sword's point. Colonel Baum, their commander, found himself surrounded by forces vastly superior. He paused when too late, and despatched a messenger, demanding instant reinforcement. But before aid arrived, the militia fell upon him, at Bennington, and totally routed him. This was a signal and most timely advantage, and it was obtained by about eight hundred men without a single piece of artillery,—scarcely one man escaping. Colonel Brehman, despatched with a reinforcement by Burgoyne, arrived on the field too late to take part in the action, but not too late to engage in a fresh conflict with the elated Americans, now reinforced on their part by Colonel Warner's regiment. Brehman's force fought with obstinate bravery for a long time, though wearied with a forced march. At length they broke and fled, abandoning their artillery to the Americans, whose commanding officers received the just thanks of Congress for the important and gallant service they had rendered to their country. The British lost four brass field-pieces, two hundred and fifty dragoons' swords, and seven hundred prisoners.

This defeat checked the tide of British victory. Hitherto it had swept with wasting fury over lake, forest, and plain. Burgoyne reined in his impetuosity in deep chagrin. He reluctantly admitted that any further advance would expose his army to starvation. And, as perplexities thickened around him, while he delayed for a fresh supply, the courage and resolution of the American army were restored. General Gates arrived to assume its command. His abilities and daring supplied fresh impulses of enthusiasm in the American camp. The word went forth that Burgoyne was in their power, and the army was swelled by militia and volunteers until it far exceeded that of the royalists.

Meantime American enterprise did not sleep. The plan of retaking Ticonderoga was suggested and adopted. General Lincoln accepted the task. Dividing his squadrons into two divisions of five hundred men, under Colonels Brown and Johnson, he marched on Ticonderoga. Brown, arriving by the landing at Lake George, surprised all the outposts from that point to the fort. On the 13th of September, he stormed Mount Defiance and Mount Hope, took two hundred batteaux, an armed sloop, and two hundred and ninety prisoners, releasing, at the same time, one hundred Americans, detained in those forts. The two colonels met before Mount Independence; but finding an assault on the fort impracticable, did not attempt it.

On the same day that these proceedings were changing the posture of affairs far in his rear, Burgoyne, giving up all communications with his magazines, crossed the Hudson, and was in rapid march upon the American position, near Stillwater. Within two miles of Gates's intrenchments, on the 19th of September, he took possession of the heights which commanded the camp of the latter. The Americans, buoyant with recent victory, and reliance on their general, received him with alacrity. Scarcely were Burgoyne's positions formed, when the din of battle raged on the intervening plain. Detachment after detachment hurried from both camps to the scene of action. The outer posts at each side were repeatedly won and lost, and victory hovered over the field of battle for several hours, as if undecided which army to descend upon. Many a bloody corpse covered the plain; and among them were more than a proportion of the bravest officers. In the midst of the terrible din and carnage, the American riflemen took post in lofty trees, from which they poured a destructive fire on the enemy. Night fell upon the scene to close the work of havoc. There was no victory, and no defeat. The British lost five hundred men, and the Ameriçans little less than four hundred. But that was not the only result. The Indians in Burgoyne's camp, naturally disrelishing the service in which hunger and hard fighting were substituted for the plunder and vengeance, and revel they were promised, fled in numbers from the camp. His situation became most precarious. Every day dimmed his hopes, and accumulated his difficulties. From his anxious calculations, however, the idea of retreat was excluded. While in these difficulties, intelligence was brought him that General Clinton was advancing from New York to his relief. This was cheering. His answer was, that he could maintain himself till the 12th of October, and no longer. Whether this message reached Clinton we know not; but that general, having reduced Fort Montgomery, after a brave resistance, and thus opened an undisturbed passage to Albany, indulged his army of three thousand men in unrestrained rapine and devastation. Gates heard with pain, that the king's generals sank their profession in rapine and unlicensed libertinism. He remonstrated by letter, but in vain. The 12th of October, the day which was to close the fatal term beyond which there was no means of safety, was fast approaching. The rations of the men were stinted; the savage allies fled to the forests; there was no ray of hope from Clinton's army. Gates was sedulously occupying every favourable position for preventing his enemy's escape. But Burgoyne, brave in every extremity, determined to foil him. With this view, on the 7th of October, a movement was made towards the American left, so as to keep an open space at least at one side. One thousand chosen men attempted this movement. A sudden shock answered their first evolution. But it was met by equal bravery. The attack became general along the entire line of this division.

Fierce, and hot, and stubborn was that encounter, and meantime another division of the American army was forcing its way to the right of the British thus engaged, so as to intercept their retreat to the camp. Two more regiments ordered from the British camp, disputed this passage. Another charge on Burgoyne's left, under whose well-directed strength it reeled backward, threw the whole division into confusion, and its total ruin was only prevented by the bravery of the two regiments ordered out to secure its retreat. The entire British forces quickly formed behind the front lines of their entrenchments, upon which the impetuosity of Arnold was urging the concentrated strength of his brigade. The obstacles were too great even for him; but, baulked in his first attempt, he flew to a fresh regiment, which he led on to the redoubt defended by Breckman. Breckman fell at his post; and Arnold, now within the lines, was hotly pursuing their defenders as they retired still firing. Before they took shelter within the inner intrenchments, they wheeled round and discharged a joint volley. Arnold fell, wounded; but the battle, then becoming general, was interrupted by the darkness of night.

The Americans took two hundred prisoners, nine pieces of artillery, and the entire tents and stores of a German brigade. Among the British slain were Generals Frazer and Clarke; Burgoyne narrowly escaped, more than one ball having passed through his hat and clothes. The next day was one of deep anxiety to Burgoyne. His forces remained in order of battle and under arms, but no attack was made on them. He clearly saw his position was no longer tenable, and next morning the Americans discovered his camp completely abandoned. Instant precautions were taken, and his new position was soon more dangerous than the former.

The 12th of October came and went. Burgoyne, finding his hope of succour blasted, stood boldly at bay with his fate. Determined to break the armed circle that was closing around him, he retreated on Saratoga. Fatal field for that army that was "not to retreat." Here his first attempt was to clear a way for a further retreat on Lake George. Artificers and workmen were despatched to execute this task, but being abandoned by the regiments that protected them, they retired in confusion and gave up the works. Nothing remained but to escape by night to Fort Edward. This attempt was in preparation, when scouts brought intelligence that the Americans were posted in great force at the only ford on the river by which that retreat could be effected. Thus hemmed in, baffled, wasted, and defeated, Burgoyne sent a message to Gates, requesting to know on what honourable terms he would receive his capitulation. "On the terms," said that general, "of surrendering prisoners of war, grounding your arms." "Sooner," replied Burgoyne, "than ground our arms in our own encampment, we will rush on our enemy, determined to take no quarter." A more accommodating disposition, and a humane desire to avoid the effusion

of blood, induced him, on the 16th of October, to agree to terms of capitulation as follows:

"The troops under General Burgoyne to march out of their camp with the honours of war, and the artillery of the intrenchments to the verge of the river, where the arms and artillery are to be left. The arms to be piled by word of command from their own officers. A free passage to be granted to the army under Lieutenant-general Burgoyne to Great Britain, upon condition of not serving again in North America during the present contest; and the port of Boston to be assigned for the entry of the transports to receive the troops whenever General Howe shall so order. The army under Lieutenant-general Burgoyne to march to Massachusetts bay, by the easiest route, and to be quartered in, near, or as convenient as possible to Boston. The troops to be provided with provisions by General Gates's orders, at the same rate of rations as his own army. All officers to retain their carriages, bat-horses, and no baggages to be molested or searched. The officers to be permitted on their parol, and to be permitted to wear their side-arms."

On the night of the day that the British army paid this homage to American valour on the banks of the Hudson, thus redeeming the boast that retreat was not for them, Gates received at his table Burgoyne and his staff, and the officers who so often panted to cross each other on the field of death, exchanged the most cordial civilities, and paid each other that mutual honour and respect, in discharge of which there is, under every circumstance, a generous emulation between the brave.

The number of men contributing to that pile of arms was five thousand seven hundred and ninety, the remnant of the noble army, at least ten thousand strong, independent of the Indian auxiliaries, that crossed the States' boundary in search of sure conquest and glory. The northern American army now amounted to nearly fourteen thousand men.

This achievement led a few unthinking men to suppose that the arms of America might be more fortunate if General Gates was elevated to the supreme command. He himself seems not to have been hostile to the prevalence of such an opinion, and some parts of his conduct are sufficient to show that if it did not originate with him, he was not the last to adopt it. Not only did he neglect to communicate to General Washington the success of his army, after the victory of the 7th of October had opened to him the prospect of finally destroying the enemy opposed to him; but he carried on a correspondence with General Conway, in which that officer expressed himself with great contempt of the commander-in-chief; and on the disclosure of this circumstance, General Gates had demanded the name of the informer in a letter expressed in terms by no means conciliatory, and which was passed through the hands of Congress—a very extraordinary circumstance in the case of a general communicating with his commander. This letter, dated Albany, December 8th, 1777, was in the following words:

"I shall not attempt to describe what, as a private gentleman, I cannot help feeling, on representing to my mind the disagreeable situation in which confidential letters when exposed to public inspection may place an unsuspecting correspondent; but, as a public officer, I conjure your excellency to give me all the assistance you can, in tracing out the author of the infidelity, which puts extracts from General Conway's letters to me into your hands. Those letters have been stealingly copied; but which of them, when, and by whom, is to me, as yet, an unfathomable secret. There is not one officer in my suite, nor amongst those who have free access to me, upon whom I could, with the least justification to myself, fix the suspicion; and yet my uneasiness may deprive me of the usefulness of the worthiest men. It is, I believe, in your excellency's power to do me and the United States a very important service, by detecting a wretch who may betray me, and capitally injure the very operations under your immediate directions. For this reason, sir, I beg your excellency will favour me with the proof you can procure to that effect. But the crime being eventually so important, that the least loss of time may be attended with the worst consequences, and it being unknown to me, whether the letter came to you from a member of Congress or from an officer, I shall have the honour of transmitting a copy of this to the president, that the Congress may, in concert with your excellency, obtain as soon as possible a discovery which so deeply affects the safety of the states. Crimes of that magnitude ought not to remain unpunished. I have the honour to be, &c.   "HORATIO GATES."

General Washington sent the following answer to this letter to General Gates, through the hands of the President of Congress, saying that the unaccountable course of General Gates compelled him so to transmit it. It is dated Valley Forge, 4th January, 1778, and is as follows:—

"Sir, your letter of the 8th ultimo came to my hands a few days ago, and, to my great surprise, informed me that a copy of it had been sent to Congress, for what reason I find myself unable to

Designed by J. L. Morton.

Engraved by G B Ellis

SURRENDER OF GEN. BURGOYNE TO GEN. GATES 1777

account ; but as some end doubtless was intended to be answered by it, I am laid under the disagreeable necessity of returning my answer through the same channel, lest any member of that honourable body should harbour an unfavourable suspicion of my having practised some indirect means to come at the contents of the confidential letters between you and General Conway.

"I am to inform you, then, that Colonel Wilkinson, on his way to Congress, in the month of October last, fell in with Lord Stirling at Reading, and, not in confidence that I ever understood, informed his aide-de-camp, Major McWilliams, that General Conway had written this to you : ' Heaven has been determined to save your country, or a weak general and bad counsellors would have ruined it.' Lord Stirling, from motives of friendship, transmitted the account with this remark: ' The enclosed was communicated by Colonel Wilkinson to Major McWilliams. Such wicked duplicity of conduct, I shall always think it my duty to detect. In consequence of this information, and without having any thing more in view than merely to show that gentleman that I was not unapprized of his intriguing disposition, I wrote to him a letter in these words :—

" ' Sir, a letter which I received last night, contained the following paragraph :—" In a letter from General Conway to General Gates, he says, *Heaven has been determined to save your country, or a weak general and bad counsellors would have ruined it.*" I am sir, &c.'

" Neither the letter, nor the information which occasioned it, was ever, directly or indirectly, communicated to me by a single officer in this army, out of my own family, excepting the Marquis de Lafayette, who, having been spoken to on this subject by General Conway, applied for, and saw, under injunctions of secrecy, the letter which contained Wilkinson's information; so desirous was I of concealing every matter that could, in its consequences, give the smallest interruption to the tranquillity of this army, or afford a gleam of hope to the enemy by dissensions therein.

" Thus, sir, with an openness and candour which I hope will ever characterize and mark my conduct, have I complied with your request. The only concern I feel upon the occasion, finding how matters stand, is, that in doing this, I have necessarily been obliged to name a gentleman, who, I am persuaded, although I never exchanged a word with him upon the subject, thought he was rather doing an act of justice, than committing an act of infidelity; and sure I am, that till Lord Stirling's letter came to my hands, I never knew that General Conway, whom I viewed in the light of a stranger to you, was a correspondent of yours; much less did I suspect that I was the subject of your confidential letters. Pardon me then for adding, that so far from conceiving that the safety of the States can be effected, or in the smallest degree injured, by a discovery of this kind, or that I should be called upon in such solemn terms to point out the author, I considered the information as coming from yourself, and given with a friendly view to forewarn, and consequently to forearm me, against a secret enemy, or, in other words, a dangerous incendiary; in which character, sooner or later, this country will know General Conway. But in this, as in other matters of late, I have found myself mistaken."

Other letters passed between Washington, Gates, and Conway; but each succeeding one only the more clearly set forth the wickedness and ambition of those who, for their own aggrandizement, would not scruple to sacrifice the welfare or even the existence of their infant country. Lafayette, who was early made acquainted with the facts, warmly sympathized with Washington, and took every opportunity of expressing his undiminished confidence in him, though in the presence only of his opponents.

Anonymous papers, containing high charges against him, and urging the necessity of placing some more active and efficient person at the head of the army, were sent to Henry Laurens, the President of Congress, Patrick Henry, the Governor of Virginia, and others. These gentlemen forwarded the papers to the commander-in-chief, warning him to be on his guard against a dangerous plot, which, from their tenor, they conceived to be forming; expressing, at the same time, their high regard for him, and their sense of the injustice of the groundless censures contained in them. To Mr. Laurens, he replied:—"I cannot sufficiently express the obligation I feel to you, for your friendship and politeness upon an occasion in which I am so deeply interested. I was not unapprized, that a malignant faction had been for some time forming to my prejudice; which, conscious as I am of having ever done all in my power to answer the important purposes of the trust reposed in me, could not but give me some pain on a personal account. But my chief concern arises from an apprehension of the dangerous consequences which intestine dissensions may produce to the common cause.

"As I have no other view than to promote the public good, and am unambitious of honours not founded in the approbation of my country, I would not desire in the least degree to suppress a free spirit of inquiry into any part of my conduct, that even faction it-self may deem reprehensible. The anonymous paper handed to you exhibits many serious charges, and it is my wish that it should be submitted to Congress. This I am the more inclined to, as the suppression or concealment may possibly involve you in embarrass-ments hereafter, since it is uncertain how many or who may be privy to the contents.

" My enemies take an ungenerous advantage of me. They know the delicacy of my situation, and that motives of policy deprive me of the defence I might otherwise make against their insidious attacks. They know I cannot combat their insinuations, however injurious, without disclosing secrets which it is of the utmost mo-ment to conceal. But why should I expect to be exempt from censure—the unfailing lot of an elevated station ? Merit and ta-lents, with which I can have no pretensions of rivalship, have ever been subject to it. My heart tells me, that it has been my unre-mitted aim to do the best that circumstances would permit ; yet I may have been very often mistaken in my judgment of the means, and may in many instances deserve the imputation of error. I can-not forbear repeating, that I have a grateful sense of the favourable disposition you have manifested to me in this affair, and beg you will believe me to be, with sentiments of real esteem and regard, sir, &c."

His answer to Mr. Henry was of the same nature.

Not content with thus attempting to poison the minds of Wash-ington's firmest friends, by spreading malignant insinuations against his character as a general, his enemies industriously circulated a report that it was his intention to resign his commission of com-mander-in-chief of the American army, and retiring, to leave the people to fight their own battles. On this subject he wrote to Doctor Gordon, a gentleman of New England, as follows :

" I can assure you, that no person ever heard me drop an expres-sion that had a tendency to resignation. The same principles that led me to embark in the opposition to the arbitrary claims of Great Britain, operate with additional force at this day ; nor is it my de-sire to withdraw my services while they are considered of import-ance in the present contest ; but to report a design of this kind is among the arts which those who are endeavouring to effect a change are practising, to bring it to pass. I have said, and I still do say, that there is not an officer in the service of the United States, that would return to the sweets of domestic life with more heartfelt joy than I should   But I would have this declaration accompanied by these sentiments, that, while the public are satisfied with my endeavours, I mean not to shrink from the cause. But the moment her voice, not that of faction, calls upon me to resign, I shall do it with as much pleasure as ever the weary traveller retired to rest. This, my dear doctor, you are at liberty to assert ; but, in doing it, I would have nothing formal. All things will come right again, and soon recover their proper tone, as the design is not only seen through, but reprobated."

These machinations finally resulted in the shame and destruction of all concerned in them, and redounded to the honour of Washington. Even the troops who fought under General Gates indignantly resisted this attempt to raise him to the place of their beloved commander-in-chief. The resentment of the main army was such, that none of the known enemies of the general dared to show themselves in the camp. General Conway, in the spring of 1778, wrote an impertinent letter to Congress, in which he intimated a wish to resign his commission, unless they should give him a separate command, instead of serving under General McDougall. A motion to accept his resignation was carried, without a dissenting voice. The intelligence of this created such astonishment, that, after writing a letter, saying that he had been misunderstood, in supposing that he intended to resign, he himself proceeded to York, appeared before Congress, and claimed to be restored. It was in vain. His freedom of speech soon after involved him in difficulties with General Cadwallader of Philadelphia, with whom he fought a duel, and thinking himself mortally wounded, addressed the following confession to General Washington :

" I find myself just able to hold the pen during a few minutes, and take this opportunity to express my sincere grief for having done, written, or said any thing disagreeable to your excellency. My career will soon be over ; therefore, justice and truth prompt me to declare my last sentiments. You are, in my eyes, the great and good man. May you long enjoy the love, veneration and esteem of these states, whose liberties you have asserted by your virtues."

The end of Conway was not as near as he supposed. He recovered rapidly, and before the end of the year returned to France.

To add still more to the distresses of Washington, a pamphlet, lately published in England, was, during the encampment of the army at Valley Forge, republished in the papers of New York and

Philadelphia. The title of this pamphlet was, " Letters from General Washington to several of his friends, in the year 1776; in which are set forth a fairer and fuller view of American politics than ever yet transpired, or the public could be made acquainted with through any other channel." They purport to have been written in New York, in June and July, 1776, to Mr. Lund Washington, Mrs. Washington, and Mr. Custis, and to have been found in the possession of General Washington's servant, who had been left behind, sick, when Fort Lee was evacuated. The design of the fabrication of these letters seems to have been to disparage General Washington in the minds of his countrymen, by representing him as opposed to the war with Great Britain. One of these pamphlets was sent to General Washington by General Henry Lee, of Virginia, in the beginning of May, 1778. He had before heard of its existence, and had seen one or two of them which were published in New York. He acknowledged the receipt of the pamphlet, on the 25th of May, and wrote to General Lee :

" If any thing of greater moment had occurred, than declaring that every word contained in the pamphlet, which you were obliging enough to send me, was spurious, I should not have suffered your favour of the 6th instant to remain so long unacknowledged. These letters are written with a great deal of art. The intermixture of so many family circumstances (which, by the by, want foundation in truth) gives an air of plausibility which renders the villany greater ; as the whole is a contrivance to answer the most diabolical purposes. Who the author of them is, I know not. From information, or acquaintance, he must have had some knowledge of the component parts of my family; but he has most egregiously mistaken facts, in several instances. The design of his labours is as clear as the sun in its meridian brightness."

The author of these letters was never discovered ; and they would not have been noticed in this place, had they not been republished towards the close of his presidency, for party purposes, when he contented himself with denying their authenticity in a letter to the secretary of state.

During this year the Congress adopted articles of confederation for the government of the United States. After much discussion, at thirty-nine sittings, the articles were approved by Congress, transmitted to the several state legislatures, and, meeting with their approbation, were ratified by all the delegates on the 15th of No-

41

vember, 1777.   Though the affairs of the new government, during the greater part of the year, wore the most gloomy aspect, Congress maintained an erect posture, and after having thus united their several states into one confederacy, carried on the subsequent military operations under its provisions and authority.

The great powers of the continent of Europe had been attentive observers of the struggle between Great Britain and her American colonies, and to those powers the Americans made an early application for assistance.   But the strength and vengeance of Britain were not to be invoked on slight grounds.   The first power courageous enough to declare herself the friend and ally of the United States was France.   The battles of the Brandywine, Germantown, and the Convention of Saratoga, were already preparing the way for a treaty between France and the United States.

HEAD-QUARTERS AT VALLEY FORGE.

MONMOUTH BATTLE-GROUND.

CHAPTER XVI.

Campaign of 1778.

OON after the intelligence of the capture of Burgoyne's army reached Europe, the court of France concluded, at Paris, treaties of alliance and commerce with the the United States. Dr. Franklin, Mr. Deane, and Mr. Lee had been appointed commissioners to proceed to France for the purpose of concluding this treaty as early as September, 1776. Their efforts had hitherto been baffled by the vacillating counsels of the French court, which were affected by every intelligence and even report which arrived from America. Nothing could be effected towards the conclusion of an open and public treaty until December, 1777, when the momentous tidings of Burgoyne's surrender gave a decisive turn to the French cabinet.

On the 16th of December, M. Gerard intimated to the commissioners, that, after long deliberation, the king had determined to acknowledge the independence of the United States, and also to afford them support, though thereby involving himself in an expensive war. It was frankly admitted that he thus acted, not merely from a friendly disposition towards them, but for the promotion of his own political interests.

On the 8th of January, 1778, Louis XVI. wrote a letter to his uncle, the King of Spain, referring to Britain as their common and inveterate enemy. During the pending contest, he had afforded to the colonies supplies of money and stores, at which England had taken deep umbrage, and would no doubt seize the first opportunity of avenging herself.

The Americans had indeed shown that they were not to be subdued, but Britain might succeed in her present attempt to form a close and friendly alliance with them, and thus turn her arms undivided against her continental enemies: now, therefore, was the time to form such a connection as might prevent any re-union between them and the mother-country.

In pursuance of these views, there was concluded on the 6th of February, a treaty of commerce, accompanied by one of defensive alliance, in the well-foreseen case of war being the result. The allies were to make common cause with the States, and to maintain their absolute independence. Whatever conquests should be made on the continent, were to be secured to them; but those in the West Indies to the crown of France. The treaty between France and America, though soon generally known, was for some time studiously concealed from the British minister. On the 13th of March, however, the French ambassador at London delivered a note referring to the United States as already in full possession of independence, whence his majesty had concluded with them a treaty of friendship and commerce, and would take effectual measures to prevent its interruption. Professions were made of the king's anxiety to cultivate a good understanding with Britain and his sincere disposition for peace, of which it was ironically said that new proofs would be found in this communication. On the 17th, this document was laid before Parliament, with a message from the crown, stating that the British ambassadors had in consequence been ordered to withdraw from Paris, and expressing trust in the zealous and affectionate support of the people for repelling this unprovoked aggression, combined with insult. An address, echoing the message, was moved in both Houses; but the opposition reproached ministers with not having duly foreseen or prepared for this emergency ; while a few repelled as now hopeless the idea of holding America under any kind of dependence. It was carried, however, by majorities, in the Commons, of two hundred and sixty-three to one hundred and thirteen ; in the Lords, of sixty-eight to twenty-five. The message for calling out the militia was sanctioned without a division.*

Eleven days after the treaty between France and America had been concluded, 17th February, the British minister introduced into the house a project for conciliation, founded on the idea of obtaining a re-union of the new States with Great Britain. This consisted of two bills with the following titles : "A bill for declaring the intention of Great Britain, concerning the exercise of the right of imposing taxes within his majesty's colonies, provinces, and plantations in North America :" and a bill "to enable his majesty to appoint commissioners with sufficient power, to treat, consult, and agree upon the means of quelling the disorders now subsisting in certain of the colonies, plantations, and provinces of North America." These bills were hurried through both houses of Parliament, and before they passed into acts, were copied and sent across the Atlantic, to Lord and General Howe. On their arrival in America, they were sent by a flag to Congress at Yorktown. When they were received, 21st of April, Congress was uninformed of the treaty which their commissioners had lately concluded at Paris. For upwards of a year they had not received one line of information from them on any subject whatever. One packet had in that time been received ; but all the letters therein were taken out before it was put on board the vessel which brought it from France, and blank papers put in their stead. A committee of Congress was appointed to examine these bills, and report on them. Their report was brought in the day following, and was unanimously adopted. By it they rejected the proposals of Great Britain.

The vigorous and firm language in which Congress expressed their rejection of these offers, considered in connection with the circumstance of their being wholly ignorant of the late treaty with France, exhibits the glowing serenity of fortitude. While the royal commissioners were industriously circulating these bills in a partial and secret manner, as if they suspected an intention of concealing them from the common people, Congress, trusting to the good sense of their constituents, ordered them to be forthwith printed for the public information. Having directed the affairs of

* Murray.
2 E

their country with an honest reference to its welfare, they had nothing to fear from the people knowing and judging for themselves. They submitted the whole to the public. Their report, after some general remarks on the bill, concluded as follows: "From all which it appears evident to your committee, that the said bills are intended to operate upon the hopes and fears of the good people of these states, so as to create divisions among them, and a defection from the common cause, now, by the blessing of divine Providence, drawing near to a favourable issue: that they are the sequel of that insidious plan which, from the days of the stamp-act down to the present time, hath involved this country in contention and bloodshed : and that, as in other cases, so in this, although circumstances, may force them at times to recede from their unjustifiable claims, there can be no doubt they will, as heretofore, upon the first favourable occasion, again display that lust of domination, which hath rent in twain the mighty empire of Britain. Upon the whole matter, the committee beg leave to report it as their opinion, that as the Americans united in this arduous contest upon principles of common interest, for the defence of common rights and privileges, which union hath been cemented by common calamities, and by mutual good offices and affection, so the great cause for which they contend, and in which all mankind are interested, must derive its success from the continuance of that union. Wherefore, any man, or body of men, who should presume to make any separate or partial convention or agreement with commissioners under the crown of Great Britain, or any of them, ought to be considered and treated as avowed enemies of these United States.

"And further, your committee beg leave to report it as their opinion, that these United States cannot, with propriety, hold any conference with any commissioners on the part of Great Britain, unless they shall, as a preliminary thereto, either withdraw their fleets and armies, or else, in positive and express terms, acknowledge the independence of the said states.

"And inasmuch as it appears to be the design of the enemies of these states to lull them into a fatal security; to the end that they may act with a becoming weight and importance, it is the opinion of your committee that the several states be called upon to use the most strenuous exertions to have their respective quotas of continental troops in the field as soon as possible, and that all the militia of the said states be held in readiness to act as occasion may require."

The conciliatory bills were speedily followed by royal commissioners, deputed to solicit their reception. Governor Johnstone, Lord Carlisle, and Mr. Eden, appointed on this business, attempted to open a negotiation on the subject. They requested General Washington, on the 9th of June, to furnish a passport for their secretary, Dr. Ferguson, with a letter from them to Congress; but this was refused, and the refusal was unanimously approved by Congress. They then forwarded in the usual channel of communication a letter addressed, " To his excellency, Henry Laurens, the president, and other the members of Congress," in which they communicated a copy of their commission, and of the acts of parliament on which it was founded; and they offered to concur in every satisfactory and just arrangement towards the following among other purposes:

" To consent to a cessation of hostilities both by sea and land ;

" To restore free intercourse ; to revive mutual affection; and renew the common benefits of naturalization, through the several parts of this empire ;

" To extend every freedom to trade that our respective interests can require ;

" To agree that no military forces shall be kept up in the different states of North America without the consent of the general Congress, or particular assemblies ;

" To concur in measures calculated to discharge the debts of America, and to raise the credit and value of the paper circulation.

" To perpetuate our union by a reciprocal deputation of an agent or agents from the different states, who shall have the privilege of a seat and voice in the parliament of Great Britain; or, if sent from Britain, in that case to have a seat and voice in the assemblies of the different states to which they may be deputed respectively, in order to attend the several interests of those by whom they are deputed ;

" In short, to establish the power of the respective legislatures in each particular state ; to settle its revenue, its civil and military establishments ; and to exercise a perfect freedom of legislation and internal government, so that the British states throughout North America, acting with us in peace and war under one common sovereign, may have the irrevocable enjoyment of every privilege that is short of a total separation of interests, or consistent with that union of force, on which the safety of our common religion and liberty depend."

A decided negative having been already given, previous to the arrival of the British commissioners, to the overtures contained in the conciliatory bills, and the intelligence of the treaty with France having in the mean time arrived, there was no ground left for further deliberation. President Laurens, therefore, by order of Congress, on the 17th of June, returned the following answer :

"I have received the letter from your excellencies of the 9th instant with the enclosures, and laid them before Congress. Nothing but an earnest desire to spare the further effusion of blood could have induced them to read a paper containing expressions so disrespectful to his most Christian Majesty, the good and great ally of these states, or to consider propositions so derogatory to the honour of an independent nation.

"The acts of the British parliament, the commission from your sovereign, and your letter, suppose the people of these states to be subjects of the crown of Great Britain ; and are founded on the idea of dependence, which is utterly inadmissible.

"I am further directed to inform your excellencies that Congress are inclined to peace, notwithstanding the unjust claims from which this war originated, and the savage manner in which it hath been conducted. They will, therefore, be ready to enter on the consideration of a treaty of peace and commerce not inconsistent with treaties already subsisting, when the king of Great Britain shall demonstrate a sincere disposition for that purpose. The only solid proof of this demonstration will be, an explicit acknowledgment of the independence of these states, or the withdrawing his fleets and armies."

Though Congress could not, consistently with national honour, enter on a discussion of the terms proposed by the British commissioners, yet some individuals of their body ably proved the propriety of rejecting them. Among these, Gouverneur Morris and William Henry Drayton, with great force of argument and poignancy of wit, justified the decisive measures adopted by their countrymen.

As the British plan for conciliation was wholly founded on the idea of the states returning to their allegiance, it was no sooner known than rejected. In addition to the sacred ties of plighted faith and national engagements, the leaders in Congress and the legislative assemblies of America had tasted the sweets of power, and were in full possession of its blessings, with a fair prospect of retaining them without any foreign control. The war having originated on the part of Great Britain from a lust of power, had in its progress compelled the Americans in self-defence to assume and exercise its highest prerogatives. The passion of human nature which induced the former to claim power, operated no less forcibly with the latter, against the relinquishment of it. After the colonies had declared themselves independent states, had repeatedly pledged their honour to abide by that declaration, had by the smiles of Heaven maintained it for three campaigns without foreign aid, after the greatest monarch in Europe had entered into a treaty with them and guarantied their independence; after all this, to expect popular leaders, in the enjoyment of power, voluntarily to retire from the helm of government, to the languid indifference of private life; and while they violated national faith, at the same time to depress their country from the rank of sovereign states to that of dependent provinces, was not more repugnant to universal experience than to the governing principles of the human heart.

The high-spirited ardour of citizens in the youthful vigour of honour and dignity, did not so much as inquire whether greater political happiness might be expected from closing with the proposals of Great Britain, or by adhering to their new allies. Honour forbade any balancing on the subject; nor were its dictates disobeyed. Though peace was desirable, and the offers of Great Britain so liberal, that if proposed in due time they would have been acceptable; yet for the Americans, after they had declared themselves independent, and at their own solicitation obtained the aid of France, to desert their new allies and to leave them exposed to British resentment, incurred on their account, would have argued a total want of honour and gratitude. The folly of Great Britain in expecting such conduct from virtuous freemen, could only be exceeded by the baseness of America, had her citizens realized that expectation.

These offers of conciliation in a great measure originated in an opinion that the Congress were supported by a faction, and that the great body of the people was hostile to independence, and well disposed to reunite with Great Britain. The latter of these assertions were true till a certain period of the contest; but that period was elapsed. With their new situation, new opinions and attachments had taken place. The political revolution of the government was less extraordinary than that of the style and manner of thinking in the United States. The independent American citizens saw with other eyes and heard with other ears than when they were in the condition of British subjects. That narrowness of sentiment which prevailed in England towards France, no longer existed among the Americans. The British commissioners, unapprized of this real change in the public mind, expected to keep a hold on the citizens of the United States, by that illiberality which they inherited from their forefathers. Presuming that the love of peace, and the ancient national antipathy to France would counterbalance all other ties, they flattered themselves that, by perseverance, an impression favourable to Great Britain might yet be made on the mind of America. They therefore renewed their efforts to open a negotiation with Congress, in a letter of the 11th of July. As they had been informed, in answer to their preceding letter of the 10th of June, that an explicit acknowledgment of the independence of the United States, or a withdrawing of their fleets and armies, must precede an entrance on the consideration of a treaty of peace, and as neither branch of this alternative had been complied with, it was resolved by Congress that no answer should be given to their reiterated application.

In addition to his public exertions as a commissioner, Governor Johnstone endeavoured to obtain the objects on which he had been sent, by opening a private correspondence with some of the members of Congress, and other Americans of influence. He in particular addressed himself to Henry Laurens, Joseph Reed, and Robert Morris. His letter to Henry Laurens was in these words:

"DEAR SIR,—I beg to transfer to my friend Dr. Ferguson, the private civilities which my friends Mr. Manning and Mr. Oswald request in my behalf. He is a man of the utmost probity and of the highest esteem in the republic of letters.

"If you should follow the example of Britain in the hour of her insolence, and send us back without a hearing, I shall hope, from private friendship, that I may be permitted to see the country, and the worthy characters she has exhibited to the world, upon making the request any way you may point out."

The following answer was immediately written.

"*Yorktown, June 14th,* 1778.

"DEAR SIR,—Yesterday, I was honoured with your favour of the 10th, and thank you for the transmission of those from my dear and worthy friends, Mr. Oswald and Mr. Manning. Had Dr. Ferguson been the bearer of these papers, I should have shown that gentleman every degree of respect and attention that times and circumstances admit of.

"It is, sir, for Great Britain to determine whether her commissioners shall return unheard by the representatives of the United States, or revive a friendship with the citizens at large, and remain among us as long as they please.

"You are undoubtedly acquainted with the only terms upon

which Congress can treat for accomplishing this good end ; terms from which, although writing in a private character, I may venture to assert, with great assurance, they will never recede, even admitting the continuance of hostile attempts, and that from the rage of war the good people of these states shall be driven to commence a treaty westward of yonder mountains. And permit me to add, sir, as my humble opinion, the true interest of Great Britain in the present advance of our contest, will be found in confirming our independence.

" Congress in no hour have been haughty ; but to suppose that their minds are less firm at present than they were when destitute of all foreign aid, and even without expectation of an alliance ; when, upon a day of general public fasting and humiliation in their house of worship, and in the presence of God, they resolved ʻ to hold no conference or treaty with any commissioners on the part of Great Britain, unless they shall, as a preliminary thereto, either withdraw their fleets and armies, or in positive and express terms acknowledge the independence of these states,' would be irrational.

" At a proper time, sir, I shall think myself highly honoured by a personal attention, and by contributing to render every part of these states agreeable to you ; but until the basis of mutual confidence shall be established, I believe, sir, neither former private friendship, nor any other consideration, can influence Congress to consent, that even Governor Johnstone, a gentleman who has been so deservedly esteemed in America, shall see the country. I have but one voice, and that shall be against it. But let me entreat you, my dear sir, do not hence conclude that I am deficient in affection to my old friends, through whose kindness I have obtained the honour of the present correspondence, or that I am not with very great personal respect and esteem,

" Sir,

" Your most obedient, and most humble servant,

" HENRY LAURENS.

" The honourable George Johnstone, Esq., Philadelphia."

In a letter to Joseph Reed, of April 11th, Governor Johnstone said :

" The man who can be instrumental in bringing us all to act once more in harmony, and to unite together the various powers which this contest has drawn forth, will deserve more from the king and people, from patriotism, from humanity, and all the ten-

der ties that are affected by the quarrel and reconciliation, than
ever was yet bestowed on human kind."

On the 16th of June, he wrote to Robert Morris :

" I believe the men who have conducted the affairs of America
incapable of being influenced by improper motives; but in all such
transactions there is risk.   And I think, that whoever ventures
should be secured, at the same time, that honour and emolument
should naturally follow the fortune of those who have steered the
vessel in the storm, and brought her safely to port.   I think Washington and the president have a right to every favour that grateful
nations can bestow, if they could once more unite our interests,
and spare the miseries and devastations of war."

To Joseph Reed, private information was communicated, on the
21st of June, that it had been intended by Governor Johnstone, to
offer him, that in case of his exerting his abilities to promote a re-
union of the two countries, if consistent with his principles and
judgment, ten thousand pounds sterling, and any office in the colonies within his majesty's gift.   To which Mr. Reed replied : " I
am not worth purchasing : but such as I am, the king of Great
Britain is not rich enough to do it."

Congress, on the 9th of July, ordered all letters received by
members of Congress from any of the British commissioners, or
their agents, or from any subject of the king of Great Britain, of a
public nature, to be laid before them.   The above letters and information being communicated, Congress resolved, " that the same
cannot but be considered as direct attempts to corrupt their integrity, and that it is incompatible with the honour of Congress, to
hold any manner of correspondence or intercourse with the said
George Johnstone, Esquire, especially to negotiate with him upon
affairs in which the cause of liberty is interested."

Their determination, with the reasons thereof, was expressed in
the form of a declaration, a copy of which was signed by the president, and sent by a flag to the commissioners at New York.   This
was answered by Governor Johnstone, by an angry publication, in
which he denied, or explained away what had been alleged against
him.   Lord Carlisle, Sir Henry Clinton, and Mr. Eden denied
having any knowledge of the matter charged on Governor Johnstone.

The commissioners failing in their attempts to negotiate with
Congress, had no resource left but to persuade the inhabitants to
adopt a line of conduct, counter to that of their representatives.
To this purpose they published a manifesto and proclamation, ad-

dressed to Congress, the assemblies, and all others, the free inhabitants of the colonies, in which they observed :

" The policy, as well as the benevolence of Great Britain, have
so far checked the extremes of war, when they tended to distress a
people still considered as our fellow-subjects, and to desolate a
country shortly to become a source of mutual advantage ; but when
that country professes the unnatural design, not only of estranging
herself from us, but of mortgaging herself and her resources to our
enemies, the whole contest is changed : and the question is, how
far Great Britain may, by every means in her power, destroy, or
render useless a connection contrived for her ruin, and for the
aggrandizement of France. Under such circumstances, the laws
of self-preservation must direct the conduct of Great Britain ; and,
if the British colonies shall become an accession to France, will
direct her to render that accession of as little avail as possible to
her enemy."

Congress, upon being informed of the design of the commissioners to circulate these papers, declared that the agents employed
to distribute the manifestoes and proclamation of the commissioners
were not entitled to protection from a flag. They also recommended to the several states, to secure and keep them in close
custody : but that they might not appear to hoodwink their constituents, they ordered the manifestoes and proclamation to be
printed in the newspapers.

The proposals of the commissioners were not more favourably
received by the people than they had been by Congress. In some
places the flags containing them were not received, but ordered
instantly to depart ; in others, they were received and forwarded
to Congress, as the only proper tribunal to take cognisance of
them. In no one place, not immediately commanded by the British army, was there any attempt to accept, or even to deliberate
on the propriety of closing with the offers of Britain.

To deter the British from executing their threats of laying waste
the country, Congress, on the 30th of October, published to the
world, a resolution and manifestoes, in which they concluded with
these words :

" We, therefore, the Congress of the United States of America,
do solemnly declare and proclaim, that if our enemies presume
to execute their threats, or persist in their present career of barbarity, we will take such exemplary vengeance as shall deter others
from a like conduct. We appeal to that God who searcheth the
hearts of men, for the rectitude of our intentions ; and in his holy

presence we declare, that, as we are not moved by any light and hasty suggestions of anger and revenge, so, through every possible change of fortune, we will adhere to this our determination.''

This was the last effort of Great Britain, in the way of negotiation, to regain her colonies. It originated in folly and ignorance of the real state of affairs in America. She had begun with *wrong* measures, and had now got into *wrong* time. Her concessions, on this occasion, were an implied justification of the resistance of the colonists. By offering to concede all that they at first asked for, she virtually acknowledged herself to have been the aggressor in an unjust war. Nothing could be more favourable to the cementing of the friendship of the new allies, than this unsuccessful negotiation. The states had an opportunity of evincing the sincerity of their engagements, and France, abundant reason to believe, that, by preventing their being conquered, her favourite scheme of lessening the power of Great Britain would be secured beyond the reach of accident.*

The opening of the campaign of 1778 was marked by several expeditions undertaken by the British. Colonel Mawhood made an incursion into Jersey, at the head of twelve hundred men. Governor Livingston was immediately requested to call out the militia, in order to join Colonel Shreeve, whose regiment was detached for the protection of that state. This was found impracticable for want of funds ; and Mawhood was unchecked in his course of devastation. He returned to head-quarters at Philadelphia, after his incursion had lasted six or seven days.

Soon after, an expedition was undertaken against General Lacy, who, with a small body of Pennsylvania militia, watched the roads on the north side of the Schuylkill. Colonel Abercrombie, who commanded this expedition, avoided all Lacy's posts of security, and threw a detachment into his rear before he discovered the presence of an enemy. After a short resistance, Lacy escaped with the loss of a few men and all his baggage. His corps was entirely dispersed, and he was soon after replaced by General Potter.

To cover the country more effectually on the north of the Schuylkill, to form an advance guard for the security of the main army, and to be in readiness to annoy the rear of the enemy, should he evacuate Philadelphia, an event believed to be in contemplation, General Washington (May 18th) detached the Marquis

* Ramsay.

de Lafayette, with more than two thousand choice troops, to take post near the lines.* As this corps formed a very valuable part of the army, the commander-in-chief recommended, in his instructions to General Lafayette, the utmost attention to its safety ; and, particularly, to avoid any permanent station, as a long continuance in one position would facilitate the execution of measures which might be concerted against him.

The marquis crossed the Schuylkill, and took post near Barren Hill church, eight or ten miles in front of the army. Immediate notice of his arrival was given to Sir William Howe, who reconnoitred his position, and formed a plan to surprise or cut him off.

On the night of the 19th of May, General Grant, with five thousand select troops, took the road which leads up the Delaware, and consequently diverges from Barren Hill. After marching some distance, he inclined to the left, and passing White Marsh, where several roads unite, took one leading to Plymouth meeting-house, the position he was directed to occupy, something more than a mile in the rear of the marquis, between him and Valley Forge. He reached his point of destination rather before sunrise. Here the roads fork ; the one leading to the camp of Lafayette, and the other to Matson's ford over the Schuylkill.

In the course of the night, General Gray, with a strong detachment, had advanced up the Schuylkill on its south side, along the Ridge Road, and taken a post at a ford two or three miles in front of the right flank of Lafayette, while the residue of the army encamped on Chesnut Hill.

Captain McClane, a vigilant partisan of great merit, was posted on the lines some distance in front of Barren Hill. In the course of the night, he fell in with two British grenadiers at Three Mile Run, who informed him of the movement made by Grant, and also that a large body of Germans was getting ready to march up the Schuylkill. Immediately conjecturing the object, McClane detached Captain Parr, with a company of riflemen across the country to Wanderer's hill, with orders to harass and retard the column advancing up the Schuylkill, and hastened in person to the camp of Lafayette. He arrived soon after daybreak, and communicated the intelligence he had received. It was not long afterwards confirmed by the fire of Parr on the Ridge Road, and by an inhabitant who had escaped from White Marsh as the British column passed that place.

Thus surrounded with danger, Lafayette instantly put his troops

* Marshall.

in motion, and passed the Schuylkill at Matson's ford, which was rather nearer to Grant than himself, with the loss of only nine men.

General Grant followed his rear, and appeared at the ford, just after the Americans had crossed it. Finding them advantageously posted, he did not choose to attack them ; and the whole army returned to Philadelphia.

This was the last enterprise attempted by Sir William Howe. He resigned the command of the army to Sir Henry Clinton, and embarked for Great Britain.*

For the following graphic detail of the events which immediately followed, we are indebted to an able contemporary.†

" After the conclusion of the alliance between France and the United States, the vast fleet collected by the former, and the active part she proposed to take in the war, made it no longer safe for the British to remain in a port so easily blockaded as Philadelphia. Accordingly, orders were sent out by the ministry to evacuate the place. As soon as Washington learned this, and became satisfied that Sir Henry Clinton intended to reach New York by a march through the Jerseys, he consulted his general officers whether it would be advisable to attack the enemy during his retreat. With but two exceptions they opposed the measure. It was determined, however, to follow on the track of the foe, and seize every favourable opportunity for annoying him.

" The British general's first intention was to reach New York by the way of Brunswick, but after ascending the Delaware as far as Bordentown, he learned that Washington had already occupied the high grounds which commanded that route. He was accordingly forced to abandon his original design, and, turning off toward Croswick, he proceeded through Allentown to Monmouth court-house, intending to reach South Amboy in this more circuitous way. At Monmouth court-house he rested for several days, having chosen a wooded hill, surrounded by swamps, and almost inaccessible, for his encampment.

"During this retreat Washington had moved along the more elevated ground to the northward, in nearly a parallel line to his enemy, thus retaining the power to give or withhold battle. No means of annoying Sir Henry, meantime, were neglected. A strong corps hung on his left flank, a regiment followed on his rear, and Colonel Morgan watched his right. Washington appears to have secretly wished for a battle during the whole march, and as the

* Marshall.   † C. J. Peterson, in Graham's Magazine.

British approached the end of their journey he gradually drew his forces around them. He now again called a council of his officers, and proposed that battle should be given. But the measure was negatived a second time. It was, however, agreed that the corps on the left flank of the enemy should be strengthened, and that the main body of the army should move in close vicinity to it, so as to be at hand to support it in case of an emergency. Among those who opposed a battle were Generals Lee and Du Portail, and the venerable Baron Steuben. These officers considered the discipline of the Americans so inferior to that of the British, as to render defeat inevitable, in case the two armies should engage on equal terms; and the influence of their opinions brought over most of the junior officers to that side. Wayne, Cadwalader, Lafayette and Greene appear to have been the only ones who differed from the council; and the two first alone were openly in favour of a battle. When the council decided so much against his wishes, Washington resolved to act on his own responsibility. The British were already approaching Monmouth; twelve miles further on were the heights of Middletown; and if the enemy reached these latter, all hope of bringing him to an action, unless with his own consent, would be gone. The blow, if struck at all, must be given at once.

"To bring on a battle, Washington resolved to strengthen still further the force on the enemy's left flank, now the advanced corps and accordingly he detached Wayne to join it with a thousand men. This command, about four thousand strong, was thought of sufficient importance to be intrusted to one of the major-generals; and the post, of right, belonged to Lee. But having advised against the battle, and believing nothing serious was intended, he allowed Lafayette to take his place. Scarcely had he yielded, however, before he learned the importance of the post, and solicited Washington to restore it to him; 'otherwise,' to use his own phrase, 'both he and Lord Stirling (the seniors of Lafayette) would be disgraced.' To spare his feelings, Washington suggested a compromise. He sent Lee to join the marquis, with two additional brigades; but, in order that the feelings of Lafayette might not be wounded, he stipulated that if any scheme of attack had been formed for the day, Lee should not interfere with it. The intelligence of this change, and of the stipulation he had made, Washington communicated to Lafayette in a confidential letter, which shows the almost fatherly kindness the American chief entertained for the young marquis. No plan of attack, however, had been

formed, and by the night of the 27th Lee was in full command of
the advanced corps.

" His army lay at Englishtown, not five miles distant from Monmouth, where the British were encamped. Washington, with the
rear division, was but three miles behind ; and almost his last duty,
before he retired, was to send word for Lee to attack the enemy as
soon as he should have begun the march. This was known at the
outer posts, and during that short summer night, the sentry, as he
walked his round, speculated on the fortunes of the coming day.

" The morning had scarcely dawned before the British army
began their march, Knyphausen, with the baggage, going first,
while the flower of the army under Cornwallis, forming the rear
division, followed some distance behind. On the first intelligence
of the movement, Washington again sent orders for Lee to attack
the enemy's rear, ' unless there should be powerful reasons to the
contrary.' He accordingly put his troops in motion, and directly
after eight o'clock the glitter of his muskets flashed along the
heights of Freehold, where Cornwallis, less than an hour before,
had arrayed his men. As the Americans reached the brow of the
hill they beheld the splendid grenadiers of the enemy moving, in
compact masses, along the valley below ; while far in the distance,
toiling through the sandy plain, was visible the long line of baggage-wagons. A rapid glance decided Lee what to do. Pushing
Wayne forward, to press on the covering party of the British rear,
and thus engross their attention, he began a rapid march, by a
by-road, to gain the front of this party, and so cut it off from the
enemy. But he had advanced only a short distance when he learned
that this detachment was in greater force than he had thought ; and
galloping forward in person to reconnoitre, he saw the whole rear
division of the foe coming up to oppose him, their dense and glit-
tering columns darkening the plain.

" As Lee's opinion had been, on the general question, against a
battle, so now, in this peculiar position, his judgment appears to
have been opposed to the measure. He had a morass in his rear,
and a disciplined enemy in front, while aid was as yet distant. He
appears to have wanted confidence in his men ; to have regarded
victory as impossible ; yet he took his measures to prepare for
battle. Before, however, a shot had been fired, General Scott, who
commanded a portion of the detachment, mistook an oblique movement of one of the American columns for a retreat, and, without
waiting for orders, recrossed the morass in his rear. Lee did not
recall him, but giving up the contest as hopeless on his present

ground, followed Scott across the ravine, and so began that disastrous retreat which had wellnigh proved fatal to our army, and which led subsequently to his own disgrace.

" On the propriety of this movement there has been some difference of opinion. But an examination of all the authorities leaves the impression on our mind, that Lee, though a brave man, wanted, in his then circumstances, that reliance on himself without which success is impossible, even in the ordinary affairs of life. He at first resolved to stand his ground, but afterward suffered himself to be decided against it, by the comparatively trifling circumstance of Scott's retreat. This was certainly weak. Had he possessed the heroic determination which Washington evinced later in the day, he would have met the enemy with a firm front, and recalling Scott, endeavoured to keep his position, at every hazard, until the rear division, which he knew was advancing, could come up.

" His retreat to the heights was not effected without some skirmishing. Flushed with what they thought an easy victory, the British thundered hotly in pursuit, and Lee, still unable to find ground to suit him, continued retreating. Already he had left the heights of Freehold behind him in his flight, and, with the enemy close upon his rear, was approaching Englishtown, where he had lain the night before.

" Meanwhile the troops of our rear division, hearing the cannonade ahead, had cast aside their knapsacks and other impediments, and were hurrying to reinforce their brave companions in arms. What was the surprise and indignation of their leader to meet the retreating troops! Washington first came up with the van, and to his astonished inquiry received for answer that a retreat had been ordered without striking a blow. Mortified and alarmed, he galloped forward until he met Lee, whom he addressed with a warmth of manner unusual to him, and in terms of strong disapprobation. The crisis was indeed calculated to disturb even the equanimity of Washington. Of Lee's intention to stand his ground on the first favourable opportunity, he was ignorant. That general had been guilty of gross neglect in not sending word to his chief of the retrograde movement. Washington, in consequence, saw only what appeared an unnecessary and disgraceful flight, hazarding the safety, probably the very existence, of his army. But in this emergency he retained his self-composure. Never was he greater than now. His fine person appeared to grow more commanding ; his countenance, usually so calm, became animated with heroic resolution ; and forming the regiments of Stewart and Ram say, he brought them up to check the pursuit, while, at the same time, he ordered Lee, with the remainder of his corps, to hold the ground until the rear division could be brought into action. The sight of their beloved general, and the confidence that fired his aspect, inspired the drooping spirits of the troops, and they met the enemy with enthusiasm. For a time the pursuit was checked But Clinton's splendid legions, flushed with their success, poured on dauntlessly to the charge; and the advanced corps was at length driven back on the reserves, though not until it had stood its ground the required time. The fresh troops of the rear division were now drawn up, under the eye of the general, on an eminence, covered by a morass in front. With desperate courage a division of the British, disregarding their strong position, pressed on to the charge; but Lord Stirling galloped up with the artillery to the edge of the acclivity, unlimbered the guns and opened a galling fire, that soon drove them back. An attempt was now made to turn the left flank of our army; but this failed. Almost simultaneously a movement was seen among the enemy's masses, and directly a strong body appeared as if about to be thrown against our right. General Greene no sooner saw the movement than he hurried forward Knox to a high ground in front, whose heavy guns soon began to shake the plain, and make dreadful havoc not only among the advancing columns, but in the force opposed to the left wing, which they enfiladed. The enemy was just beginning to waver, when Wayne came dashing up with his veterans, and assailed him impetuously in front. Even the grenadiers of Cornwallis quailed before this terrible slaughter; and abandoning their ground, fell back behind the ravine, to the spot they had occupied when they received their first check, immediately after Washington met Lee.

" When the British were thus driven back, they seized an almost impregnable position, their flanks being secured by thick woods and morasses, and their front accessible only through a narrow pass. The day was now declining, and the excessive heat had destroyed numbers of the men, yet Washington determined on forcing the enemy from his position. Two brigades were accordingly detached to gain the right flank of the British, and Woodford with his gallant brigade was ordered to turn their left. Knox, with his artillery, was called to the front. With the opening of his terrible batteries the battle once more began. The British cannon replied, and soon the earth shook with the repeated reverberations of heavy artillery.

"No further decisive event, however, occurred. Night fell before

BATTLE OF MONMOUTH.

the brigades on either flank could conquer the obstacles in the way of gaining their positions, and, completely worn out, both combatants were glad of the reprieve afforded by darkness, and sank to rest on the ground they occupied. The troops of Washington slept on their arms, their leader slumbering, wrapt in his cloak, in the midst of his soldiers.

" It was the intention of the American general to renew the battle on the following day, but toward midnight the British secretly abandoned their position, and resumed their march. So fatigued were our men by the excessive heat, combined with the exertions of the day, that the flight of the enemy was not discovered until morning, when the ground he had occupied at nightfall was found deserted. Washington made no attempt at pursuit, satisfied that Sir Henry Clinton would reach the heights of Middletown before he could be overtaken. Accordingly, leaving a detachment to watch the British rear, the main body of the army was moved, by easy marches, to the Hudson. In this battle the enemy lost nearly three hundred men; the Americans did not suffer a third as much. Never, unless at Princeton, did Washington evince such heroism. His presence of mind alone probably saved the day. He checked the retreat, drove back the enemy, and remained master of the field; and this, too, with a loss very trifling when compared with that of the foe.

" The battle of Monmouth, won in this manner, when all the senior officers had declared a victory impossible, left a profound impression on the public mind of America and Europe. The discipline of our troops was no longer despised. Soldiers who, under such disastrous circumstances, could be brought to face and drive back a successful foe, were declared to be a match for the veteran troops of Europe; and their general, who had been called the Fabius, was now honoured with the new title of the Marcellus of modern history.

" We cannot dismiss this battle without referring to the subsequent disgrace of Lee. Though Washington had addressed him warmly in the first surprise of their meeting, it is probable that no public notice would have been taken of Lee's hasty retreat, but for the conduct of that general himself. Of a haughty, perhaps of an overbearing disposition, he could not brook the indignity which he considered had been put upon him; and almost his first act was to write an improper letter to Washington, demanding reparation for the words used towards him on the battle-field. The reply of the commander-in-chief was dignified, but severe. He assured his subordinate he should have a speedy opportunity to justify himself, and on Lee's asking for a court-martial, he was arrested. The verdict of that body was,

" First. That he was guilty of disobedience of orders in not attacking the enemy on the 28th of June, agreeably to repeated instructions. Second. That he was guilty of misbehaviour before the enemy on the same day, in making an unnecessary, and, in some few instances, a disorderly retreat. Third. That he was guilty of disrespect to the commander-in-chief in two letters. His sentence was, to be suspended from his rank for one year.

" We shall not go into a minute examination of the question whether this punishment was deserved. Our own opinion is that it was. We do not think Lee guilty in the retreat of any thing but an error in judgment, arising perhaps from want of confidence in his men. But he should have kept the commander-in-chief advised of his movements. It is probable that Lee considered himself a superior officer to Washington, for he was overbearing, proud, sullen, and dogmatical throughout the whole proceedings, both before and after the battle. This point of his character was well understood by the army, with whom he was unpopular, and who hailed his disgrace with secret satisfaction.

" The sentence proved the ruin of Lee. He passed, from that hour, out of men's minds. From having held the second rank in the army he sank to comparative obscurity. He never again figured in the war. In 1780, Congress intimated to him that they had no further need of his services; and two years later he died, in seclusion, at Philadelphia.

" The killed and wounded in the battle were not the only loss the British sustained. During their march through the Jerseys, about one thousand of their soldiers deserted them."

In the mean time, France had been preparing to assist the Americans. On the 14th of April, Count d'Estaing had sailed from Toulon with a strong squadron, and arrived on the coast of Virginia in the beginning of July, while the British fleet was employed in conveying the forces from Sandy Hook to New York. It consisted of twelve ships of the line, and four frigates, and brought M. Gerard, the first minister from France to the United States.

On being apprised of Count d'Estaing's arrival, General Washington sent him, by Colonel Laurens, a letter of congratulation, and proposals for co-operating in their attempts upon the common enemy. Their design of attacking the British in New York simultaneously, by land and water, was rendered abortive, by the pilots refusing to take the responsibility of conducting the heavy ships of the French fleet over the bar. D'Estaing, therefore, remained at anchor, four miles off Sandy Hook, till the 22d of July, without effecting any thing more than the capture of some vessels, which, through ignorance of his arrival, fell into his hands. The next attempt of the French admiral was in conjunction with the Americans, on Rhode Island, where the British had a force of six thousand men. General Washington anticipating the design of D'Estaing, Generals Greene and Lafayette were detached with two brigades from the main army, to co-operate with Count d'Estaing and General Sullivan, who was at Providence with a considerable force of New England troops. It was proposed that D'Estaing, with his troops, should make a descent on the south part of the island, and a body of Americans should take possession of the north, while the French squadron was to enter the harbour of Newport, and take or destroy the British shipping. On the 8th of August, the count entered the harbour, but found himself unable to do any material damage. Lord Howe instantly set sail for Rhode Island, and D'Estaing, confiding in his superiority, immediately came out of the harbour to attack him. A violent storm parted the two fleets, and did so much damage that they were rendered totally unfit for action. The French, however, suffered most ; and several of their ships being afterwards attacked singly, by the British, narrowly escaped being taken. On the 20th of August, he returned to Newport, in a very shattered condition, and sailed, two days after, for Boston. General Sullivan had landed, in the mean time, on the northern part of Rhode Island, with ten thousand men. On the 17th of August they began their operations, by erecting batteries, and making their approaches to the British lines. But General Pigot had taken such effectual care to secure himself on the land-side, that without the assistance of a marine force it was impossible to attack him with any probability of success. The conduct of D'Estaing, therefore, who had abandoned them when master of the harbour, gave the greatest disgust to the people of New England, and Sullivan began to think of a retreat ; but the garrison sallied out on him with such violence that it was not without difficulty that he effected it. He had not been long gone, when Sir Henry Clinton arrived with a body of four thousand men ; which, had it arrived sooner, would have enabled the British commander to have gained a decisive advantage over him.

The success of this expedition had been confidently anticipated,

44

and its failure caused great chagrin and vexation, which exhibited itself in the New England states and Boston particularly; this chagrin excited the fears of Washington, and he accordingly addressed letters to Generals Sullivan and Heath, the commandants at Boston, urging them to use their influence to restrain the intemperance of the moment. A letter from the Count d'Estaing, explaining the causes of the failure of the expedition, was received with such marks of esteem that it appears to have quieted all serious mischief. Congress also passed a resolution expressing their approbation of the conduct of the count. Lord Howe, in the mean time, had resigned his command to Admiral Gambier, and General Clinton had returned to New York, leaving his troops under the command of General Grey, with orders to conduct an expedition eastward, as far as Buzzard's Bay. Grey destroyed a number of vessels in Acushnet River, and having reduced Bedford and Fairhaven, re-embarked his troops and sailed to Martha's Vineyard. He soon after returned to New York, and the British army moved up the Hudson in great force, and encamped on both sides of the river; their ships of war maintaining the communication between their columns.

Colonel Baylor, with his cavalry, crossed the Hackensack early on the 27th of September, and took quarters at Herringtown, a small village near New Taupan, where some militia were posted. Lord Cornwallis, on hearing of this movement, formed a plan to cut off both the cavalry and the militia posted in the town. This was effected by a party under General Grey and Colonel Campbell. The militia saved themselves by flight, but the British completely surprised the cavalry, and cut them to pieces.

This act was in some measure retaliated by Colonel Richard Butler, with a detachment of infantry, assisted by Major Lee, with a part of his cavalry, who, falling in with a party of chasseurs and yagers commanded by Count Donop, charged and defeated them, killing ten men, and capturing one officer and eighteen privates.

After completing their forage, the British army returned to New York. Their movement had been designed to cover an expedition against Little Egg Harbour, where they succeeded in destroying works, store-houses, vessels, and merchandise to a large amount. Count Pulaski, who with his legion had been charged with the defence, was completely surprised, through the treachery of a deserter, and a considerable portion of his men were put to the bayonet with circumstances of barbarity very unusual in civilized warfare.

Admiral Byron arrived in New York and took command of the

British fleet in September.   He afterward sailed in October for Boston, but encountering a severe storm, he took shelter in Rhode Island.   Count d'Estaing seized this favourable moment and sailed, on the 3d of November, for the West Indies.

Lafayette, anticipating a war in Europe, was now desirous to return home; and General Washington, actuated not less by personal respect for this distinguished officer than by a regard for the public service, obtained from Congress an unlimited leave of absence for his friend.   "The partiality of America for Lafayette was well placed.   Never did a foreigner, whose primary attachments to his own country remained undiminished, feel more solicitude for the welfare of another than was unceasingly manifested by this young nobleman for the United States."*

A detachment of the British army, of five thousand men, commanded by General Grant, sailed, early in November, for the West Indies; and during the same month, a second detachment, commanded by Lieutenant-colonel Campbell, escorted by Sir Hyde Parker, was destined for the Southern States.

As Washington perceived that a force sufficient for the defence of New York still remained, the American army was ordered to retire into winter quarters.   The main army was cantoned in Connecticut, on both sides of the North River, about West Point, and at Middlebrook.   Light troops were stationed near the lines; and the cavalry were widely distributed, at Winchester in Virginia, at Frederick, Maryland, at Lancaster, Pennsylvania, and at Durham, Connecticut.   This was done with a view to facility in procuring forage.   In the whole distribution of the army, the protection of the country, the security of important points, and a cheap and convenient supply of provisions, were consulted.

The soldiers were again under the necessity of wintering in huts, to which they had in some measure become accustomed.   They were better clothed than in the preceding winter, in consequence of the supplies received from France; and their condition on the whole was far more comfortable than during any preceding winter of the war.

Towards the latter end of April, Congress had resolved to grant half-pay for life to the officers in their army, reserving to themselves the privilege of redeeming, at any time they might think proper, this annual stipend, by the payment of a sum equivalent to the half-pay for six years.   General Washington had repeatedly urged the necessity of adopting some measure of this sort, that men might find it to their *interest* to enter into the service.   No man was better

* Marshall.

acquainted with human nature than Washington. He knew tha.
"with far the greatest part of mankind, interest is the governing
principle, and motives of public virtue were not of themselves sufficient to keep the American army together for any extended period.
His letters to Congress on this subject are master-strokes of policy,
and evince a profoundness of wisdom, which shows how well he
knew how to profit by the lessons of experience. The letter which
seems to have been the immediate cause of the resolution of Congress, was that of April 21, in which he thus writes: "Men may
speculate as they will; they may talk of patriotism; they may draw
a few examples from ancient story of great achievements performed
by its influence; but whoever builds upon it as a sufficient basis
for conducting a long and bloody war, will find himself deceived
in the end. We must take the passions of men as nature has
given them, and those principles as a guide which are generally
the rule of action. I do not mean to exclude altogether the idea
of patriotism. I know it exists, and I know it has done much in
the present contest; but I will venture to assert, that a great and
lasting war can never be supported on this principle alone. It
must be aided by a prospect of interest or some reward. For a
time it may of itself push men to action, to bear much, to encounter
difficulties, but it will not endure unassisted by interest. Without
arrogance, or the smallest deviation from truth, it may be said,
that no history now extant can furnish an instance of an army's
suffering such uncommon hardships as ours has done, and bearing
them with the same patience and fortitude. To see men without
clothes to cover their nakedness, without blankets to lie on, without
shoes, so that their marches might be traced by the blood of their feet,
and almost as often without as with provisions, marching through
frost and snow, and at Christmas taking up their winter quarters
within a day's march of the enemy, without a house or hut to cover
them till they could be built, and submitting to all without a murmur,
is a mark of patience and obedience, which, in my opinion, can
scarcely be paralleled." Down to the date of this letter, no cartel
had been settled for the exchange of prisoners. A few instances
of exchange only had taken place, among which were those of Lee
for General Prescott, and Major Otho Williams for Major Ackland;
but Congress seemed unwilling to agree to any terms, until their
former resolution on the subject should be complied with, throwing
the blame, however, upon Sir William Howe and his commissioners.
Washington, on the contrary, thought the public faith and his own
honour pledged, as will be seen by his letter which follows. "It

may be thought," says he, "contrary to our interest to go into an exchange, as the enemy would derive more immediate advantage from it than we should: but on principles of genuine extensive policy, independent of the consideration of compassion and justice, we are under an obligation not to elude it. An event of this kind is the general wish of the country. I know it to be the wish of the army, and it must be the ardent wish of the unhappy sufferers themselves. Should the exchange be deferred till the terms of the last resolve of Congress on the subject are fulfilled, it will be difficult to prevent our being generally accused with a breach of good faith. Speculative minds may consider all our professions as mere professions, or at least, that interest and policy are to be the only arbiters of their validity. I cannot doubt that Congress, in preservation of the public faith and my personal honour, will remove all impediments that now oppose themselves to my engagements, and will authorize me, through commissioners, to settle as extensive and competent a cartel as may appear advantageous and necessary, any resolutions heretofore to the contrary notwithstanding." This letter produced the effect of relieving Washington in some measure from his unpleasant embarrassment, as Congress soon after resolved that he might proceed in his arrangements for an exchange without excluding those prisoners whose accounts remained unsettled. Commissioners were consequently appointed on both sides; but mutual objections arose to every thing like a general proposal, and the affair was left in its former state.

In the course of this summer, the western country had been the scene of most distressing events; the feuds between the independents and loyalists having raged with peculiar violence in this wild region. The latter complained, probably not without reason, that the rigorous laws enacted against them were enforced with severe aggravations, and many sought an asylum beyond the limits of the colonies. There they found themselves among the Indians, a race always bitterly hostile to the white borderers, and easily excited to the most daring enterprises. Unhappily the passions of the refugees were worked up to such violence, that instead of urging a milder mode of warfare, they stimulated these allies to deeds of more than their wonted barbarity. Wyoming, a flourishing settlement on the Pennsylvania frontier, was suddenly assailed, the slender militia force which defended it overpowered, and the inhabitants exposed to all the horrors of Indian vengeance and massacre. From the lateness of the season, only a few partial attempts could be made to retaliate. Next spring, however, General Sullivan was

2 G

VALLEY OF WYOMING.

despatched with four thousand men, and joined by General Clinton with another division from the Mohawk River. They entered the territory of the Indians, who, quite unable to resist so large a force, abandoned their homes and fled before them. The villages were then reduced to ashes, every trace of cultivation obliterated, and the region rendered as much as possible uninhabitable. This rigour is said to have been authorized by Washington, and justified on the ground, that without interposing a desert between the states and this savage race, no security could be enjoyed on the frontier.

The attention of Congress and of the commander was now called to plans for the campaign of 1779. The former, looking to their previous successes, and the powerful co-operation of France, cherished the most brilliant expectations, and had formed schemes truly magnificent. Concluding that the English would be speedily expelled, or would of their own accord depart from America, the chief object was to be the invasion of Canada from three different points, the French being invited to co-operate. Washington, on learning this vast design, took the utmost pains to prove its futility. He disclosed to them the painful truths, that the English were still so powerful both by land and sea, as to afford no speedy prospect of their complete expulsion; while the exhausted state of the finances, the imperfect organization of the army, and the extreme destitution under which it laboured, furnished no means whatever for carrying on such mighty operations. A committee of Congress, on further consideration, recommended that the project should be deferred; yet the members still clung to it, fondly contemplating its execution some time before the season closed, and wishing communications to be opened on that subject with the French court. The general, considering the project, even thus modified, as still quite inadmissible, repaired to Philadelphia, where he urged strongly all his former arguments, and confidentially pointed out to the leading statesmen the danger of admitting France into a country where she had so long ruled, and whose people bore still decided traces of her relationship. It appears, indeed, that, probably from the dread of embarrassment in some future negotiation, that power by no means favoured schemes of American conquest. Washington at last succeeded in convincing Congress, that instead of these grand measures of invasion, they must limit themselves, during the present campaign, to a course strictly defensive.

In fact, both the civil and military strength of the union was now at a lower ebb than at any time since the struggle commenced. The members of Congress had originally consisted of the ablest men in America, animated by the most ardent zeal, and implicitly obeyed by all the votaries of their cause. After the declaration of independence, however, a new modification of the government was considered necessary. A constitution was drawn up, and, after many delays and difficulties, brought into operation early in 1779, under which the state legislatures were invested with all the most important powers, resigning only a few which were judged indispensable for united action. Congress still retained the direction of foreign affairs, of the war, and consequently of the naval and military force; but to furnish men and supplies for these services, they had no resource, except requisitions, addressed to the state legislatures. The latter had the complete option, whether they should or should not comply, and had many motives which strongly inclined them to the latter alternative; indeed, compliance could only be afforded by measures very unpopular, and which would have much disobliged their constituents. The demands of Congress were thus only partially and unequally fulfilled, and the levies never approached the amount at which they were nominally fixed. The financial state of the country, too, was embarrassing in the extreme. The colonists, at the beginning of the war, had been very little accustomed to any serious taxation; and having taken arms expressly to resist it, would have ill brooked paying a larger amount for their expenses than Britain had ever demanded. It was not till November, 1777, that Congress ventured to make a requisition of five millions of dollars annually, to which the states but faintly responded. France and Spain gave some assistance, first in gift, and then in loan; but as their own finances grew embarrassed, these contributions became very stinted. The commissioners endeavoured to treat for loans with European capitalists, especially in Holland, and with this view drew a flattering picture of the future prosperity of the new republic, and her ultimate power to repay even the largest advances; but the Dutch were not inclined to be satisfied with such security, and money could be got only in small amounts, and on exorbitant terms. One house made a somewhat liberal offer, but on condition of carrying on the whole trade of the Union, and holding all its real and personal property in mortgage. In these circumstances, the states had no resource except paper money. In 1775, they issued three millions of dollars; and this moderate amount being easily absorbed in the circulation, proved an available resource. They were thus encouraged to pour forth repeated issues, which, at the beginning of 1779, had risen to above a hundred millions, and in the course of the year to double that amount, which they had pledged themselves not to exceed. The necessary consequence was a depreciation of the notes to about a fortieth part of their nominal value, and hence a miserable derangement in all mercantile and money transactions. The evil was aggravated, too, by preposterous remedies. The paper at its nominal value was made a legal tender for all debts; and by this iniquitous measure, which Washington deeply regretted, many creditors, both public and private, were defrauded, but no permanent relief could be afforded. As the articles furnished to the army, like all others, rose to an enormous nominal value, they were so ignorant as to fix a maximum, above which they should not be received. The consequence was, that at this inadequate rate none could be got; and the army would have perished had not these absurd regulations been rescinded.*

A naval action which took place this year excited considerable interest, from the distressing circumstances attending it. On the 7th of March, 1778, the Randolph, an American frigate of thirty-six guns, and three hundred and five men, commanded by Captain Nicholas Biddle, having sailed on a cruise from Charleston, fell in with the Yarmouth, of sixty-four guns, and engaged er in the night. Soon after the engagement commenced, Captain

* Allen.

Biddle was wounded in the thigh, and fell. He instantly ordered a chair to be brought; said he was only slightly wounded; and was carried forward to encourage his crew. Twenty minutes after the action commenced, the Randolph blew up. Four men only were saved upon a piece of her wreck. These men subsisted for four days on nothing but rain water, which they sucked from a piece of blanket. On the fifth day, Captain Vincent of the Yarmouth, though in chase of a ship, on discovering them, suspended the chase and took them on board. Captain Biddle, who perished on board the Randolph, was an officer of distinguished merit; and his loss was universally regretted.

BIDDLE

WAYNE.

CHAPTER XVII.

Campaign of 1779.

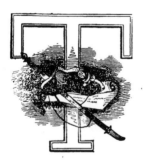

THE conquest of Canada being still a favourite scheme, General Washington was requested, by a resolution of Congress, to write to Dr. Franklin, the American minister at Paris, explaining to him the proposed expedition against that province, with a view to interest him in securing the co-operation of France In reply, he wrote to Congress a letter, from Middlebrook, dated 13th of December, 1778, in which he said:

"The earnest desire I have to render the strictest compliance in every instance to the views and instructions of Congress, cannot but make me feel the greatest uneasiness, when I find myself in circumstances of hesitation or doubt with respect to their directions. But the perfect confidence I have in the justice and candour of that honourable body emboldens me to communicate, without reserve, the difficulties which occur in the execution of their present order; and the indulgence I have experienced on every former occasion induces me to imagine, that the liberty I now take will not meet with their disapprobation.

"I have attentively taken up the report of the committee, respecting the proposed expedition into Canada. I have considered it in several lights, and sincerely regret, that I should feel myself under any embarrassment in carrying it into execution. Still, I remain of opinion, from a general review of things, and the state of our resources, that no extensive system of co-operation with the French, for the complete emancipation of Canada, can be positively decided on for the ensuing year. To propose a plan of perfect co-operation with a foreign power, without a moral certainty of our supplies, and to have that plan actually ratified by the court of Versailles, might be attended, in case of failure in the conditions on our part, with very fatal effects.

"If I should seem unwilling to transmit the plan as prepared by Congress, with my observations, it is because I find myself under a necessity, in order to give our minister sufficient ground on which to found an application, to propose something more than a vague and undecisive plan, which, even in the event of a total evacuation of these states by the enemy, may be rendered impracticable in the execution, by a variety of insurmountable obstacles ; or, if I retain my present sentiments and act consistently, I must point out the difficulties as they appear to me : which must embarrass his negotiations, and may disappoint the views of Congress.

"But, proceeding on the idea of the enemy's leaving these states, before the active part of the ensuing campaign, I should fear to hazard a mistake as to the precise aim and extent of the views of Congress. The line of conduct that I am to observe, in writing to our minister at the court of France, does not appear sufficiently marked. Were I to undertake it, I should be much afraid of erring, through misconception. In this dilemma, I should esteem it a particular favour to be excused from writing at all on the subject, especially as it is the part of candour in me to acknowledge, that I do not see my way clear enough to point out such a plan for co-operation as I conceive to be consistent with the ideas of Congress, and that will be sufficiently explanatory, with respect to time and circumstances, to give efficacy to the measure. But, if Congress still think it necessary for me to proceed in the business, I must request their more definitive and explicit instructions, and that they will permit me, previous to transmitting the intended despatches, to submit them to their determination.

"I could wish to lay before Congress more minutely the state of the army, the condition of our supplies, and the requisites necessary for carrying into execution an undertaking that may involve the most serious events. If Congress think this can be done more satisfactorily in a personal conference, I hope to have the army in such a situation, before I can receive their answer, as to afford me an opportunity of giving my attendance."

The personal interview requested in the latter part of this letter was agreed to, and the commander-in-chief, leaving the head-quarters of this army on the 22d of December, presented himself before Congress on the 24th. A committee was appointed to confer with him on the operations of the coming campaign. Such was the strength and cogency of the arguments which he used to convince this committee of the impracticability of the Canada expedition, that in five days they decided, and their decision was approved by Congress, to lay aside all thoughts of such an undertaking.

In this, and all other instances throughout the life of General Washington, it is not easy to determine wherein he was most essential to the welfare of his country; whether in the skill and bravery with which he led her armies to victory, or in the passive, but not less inflexible aspect of his character; in the unconquerable firmness with which he stood up under the severest complication of misfortunes; in the singular uprightness and wisdom by which he was qualified to compose the dissensions of men and parties, and the commanding but unobtruded influence with which he could sway the collective mind of a legislature or an empire.

Washington remained in Philadelphia about five weeks, during which time he submitted to the committee of Congress three plans of operations for the next campaign, with remarks on the mode of executing them. The first, proposed an attempt to drive the enemy from the posts which they then occupied at New York and Rhode Island; the second, an expedition against Niagara, which would give security upon the northern frontier, and open a door into Canada, which might be afterwards used or not, as policy might dictate; and the third plan proposed to hold the army entirely on the defensive, except such smaller operations against the Indians, as would be absolutely necessary to chastise them for depredations on the frontiers, and prevent them from a repetition of the same.

The advantages and disadvantages which were attendant upon each of these plans, were laid fully before the committee, and by them communicated to Congress.

" It is much to be regretted," he said, after discussing the two plans, " that our prospect of any capital offensive operations is so slender, that we seem in a manner to be driven to the necessity of adopting the third plan, that is, to remain entirely on the defensive, except such lesser operations against the Indians as are absolutely necessary to divert their ravages from us. The advantages of this plan are these : It will afford an opportunity of retrenching our expenses, and of adopting a general system of economy, which may give success to the plans of finance which Congress have in contemplation, and perhaps enable them to do something effectual for the relief of public credit, and for restoring the value of our currency. It will also give some repose to the country in general, and by leaving a greater number of hands to cultivate the lands, remove the apprehension of a scarcity of supplies.

" If this plan is determined upon, every measure of government ought to correspond. The most uniform principle of economy should pervade every department. We should not be frugal in one part, and prodigal in another. We should contract, but we should consolidate our system. The army, though small, should be of a firm and permanent texture. Every thing possible should be done to make the situation of the officers and soldiers comfortable, and every inducement offered to engage men during the war. The most effectual plan that can be devised for enlisting those already in the army, and recruiting in the country, ought to be carried into immediate execution.

"I shall not enter particularly into the measures that may be taken against the Indians, but content myself with the general idea thrown out, unless it should be the pleasure of the committee that I should be more explicit. The main body of the army must take a position so as to be most easily subsisted, and at the same time best situated to restrain the enemy from ravaging the country. If they should hereafter weaken themselves still more, so as to give a favourable opening, we should endeavour to improve it.

" This plan may perhaps have some serious disadvantages. Our inactivity will be an argument of our weakness, and may injure our credit and confidence with foreign powers. This may influence the negotiations of Europe to our disadvantage. I would not su:

pose it could alienate our allies, or induce them to renounce our interests. Their own, if well understood, are too closely interwoven with them; their national faith and honour are pledged. At home, too, it may serve to dispirit the people, and give confidence to the disaffected. It will give leisure for factious and discontented spirits to excite divisions. How far these inconveniences ought to influence us in our operations, Congress can alone be a competent judge."

Congress resolved to adopt the third plan, and in the beginning of February Washington returned to the head-quarters of his army at Middlebrook. Some of the evils which had been dreaded, and in some degree guarded against, soon began to manifest themselves. The vigilance of the people was lulled and their energies were paralyzed by the thought that their independence was now secure; that the powerful assistance of France, the second nation of Europe, would not fail to achieve at once a glorious victory for them over their ancient rival, England; and besides, there were whispers abroad that Spain was about to declare war against Great Britain, and that Russia refused or neglected to lend the latter nation aid, which she had promised her since the commencement of hostilities.

It is needless to show the fallacy of these hopes. Washington saw with great concern the origin and gradual spreading of this temper among his countrymen, and it is not too much to say that all hopes of American independence would, at this critical period, have ceased, but for the conduct of him who has well earned for himself the title of Father of his Country. He describes this period as the darkest and most critical that had occurred since the commencement of the contest. He knew enough of Britain to know that the war was not yet near its conclusion, and stimulated Congress and the states to exertion, by every consideration which he could suggest. Though the resolution empowering him to recruit the army was passed on the 23d of January, yet the requisition for the troops was not made upon the states until the 9th of March.

The apprehensions which these and other circumstances excited in the mind of General Washington, are thus fully stated in a letter to a friend, of great political influence. "I am particularly desirous of a free communication of sentiments with you at this time," he says, "because I view things very differently, I fear, from what people in general do, who seem to think the contest at an end, and that to make money and get places are the only things now remaining to be done. I have seen, without despondency even for a moment, the hours which America has styled her gloomy ones; but

I have beheld no day since the commencement of hostilities, when I have thought her liberties in such imminent danger as at present. Friends and foes seem now to combine to pull down the goodly fabric we have hitherto been raising at the expense of so much time, blood, and treasure."

After censuring with some freedom the prevailing opinions of the day, he added, "To me it appears no unjust simile to compare the affairs of this great continent to the mechanism of a clock, each state representing some one or other of the smaller parts of it, which they are endeavouring to put in fine order, without considering how useless and unavailing their labour is, unless the great wheel, or spring, which is to set the whole in motion, is also well attended to, and kept in good order. I allude to no particular state, nor do I mean to cast reflections on any one of them, nor ought I, it may be said, to do so on their representatives; but, as it is a fact too notorious to be concealed, that Congress is rent by party; that much business of a trifling nature and personal concernment withdraws their attention from matters of great national moment at this critical period; when it is also known that idleness and dissipation take place of close attention and application, no man who wishes well to the liberties of this country, and desires to see its rights established, can avoid crying out—where are our men of abilities? Why do they not come forth to save their country? Let this voice, my dear sir, call upon you, Jefferson, and some others. Do not, from a mistaken opinion that we are to sit down under our vine and our own fig-tree, let our hitherto noble struggle end in ignominy. Believe me when I tell you there is danger of it. I have pretty good reasons for thinking that administration, a little while ago, had resolved to give the matter up, and negotiate a peace with us upon almost any terms; but I shall be much mistaken if they do not now, from the present state of our currency, dissensions, and other circumstances, push matters to the utmost extremity. Nothing I am sure will prevent it but the intervention of Spain, and their disappointed hope from Russia."

Nor was this the only circumstance which called for the interposition of the general's influence. The depreciation of the paper currency had so affected the pay of the officers, that many were reduced to absolute indigence. Their sufferings led to desperate measures; and in the following May, when the New Jersey brigade was ordered to march, as a part of the western expedition against the Indians, the officers of the first regiment sent a memorial to the legislature of the state, demanding, in very strong language, some equitable provision for them and their men, and stating that unless their demand was acceded to, they would, in three days, resign their commissions. This proceeding was communicated by Brigadier-general Maxwell, and Washington at once foresaw the pernicious results which would ensue from such a proceeding to the army at large, and he endeavoured to obviate them by addressing a letter to General Maxwell, to be laid before the officers, exhorting them to order and obedience, and commanding them to march with the brigade in the first place to head-quarters, where they would receive further orders.

In the mean time, the legislature of New Jersey was embarrassed by the form of the application, as it assumed the air of menace, and some of the members said, that rather than yield to demands thus presented, however reasonable they might be, they would permit the brigade to be disbanded. To obviate this, the only difficulty which they perceived, they hit upon the expedient of persuading the officers to withdraw their memorial, with the understanding that the subject would then be instantly taken into consideration. The paper was withdrawn, and in a few hours resolutions were passed, granting nearly all that had been asked.

Washington improved this event, in communicating it to Congress, to urge upon them the absolute necessity of some general and adequate provision for the officers of the army; and observing "that the distresses in some corps are so great, either where they were not till lately attached to particular states, or where the states have been less provident, that officers have solicited even to be supplied with the clothing destined for the common soldiery. Coarse and unsuitable as they were, I had not power to comply with the request. The patience of men, animated by a sense of duty and honour, will support them to a certain point, beyond which it will not go. I doubt not Congress will be sensible of the danger of an extreme in this respect, and will pardon my anxiety to obviate it."

The endeavours of Washington, at this time, to stimulate the exertions of his countrymen, were so far effectual, that by the 1st of May, he found nearly sixteen thousand men under his command. It was, however, obviously out of his power to make any thing like a successful attack upon the strongholds of the British; and he therefore so disposed his forces as to protect the country from the incursions of the enemy, and guard the high lands on the Hudson river. Upwards of seven thousand men were stationed at Middlebrook, under the immediate command of Washington; the remainder were on both sides of the Hudson, under Generals McDougall and Putnam. ·

At the same time the British army at New York and Rhode Island amounted to about the same number, (sixteen thousand,) but they were assisted by a powerful fleet, which enabled them, with small detachments, to make sudden attacks on distant parts of the country, before the militia could be gathered together, or a company of regulars arrive.

It was in this way that General Matthews, with eighteen hundred men, gained such success in Virginia. He left Sandy Hook on the 5th of May, and, sailing up the Chesapeake bay, landed without opposition, and sending small parties to Portsmouth, Norfolk, Gosport, and Suffolk, took and carried off or destroyed a large quantity of naval and military stores, paying no respect to private property. Having thus accomplished the object of his expedition, he reimbarked his troops and returned to New York, before the end of the month.

Immediately on the return of this detachment, the British army, under Sir Henry Clinton, transported by the fleet, proceeded up the Hudson river. During the previous year, fortifications had been commenced at West Point, which was deemed more defensible than the positions lately occupied by Forts Clinton and Montgomery. The works at this place were yet far from being finished. It was a matter of the greatest importance to General Washington to preserve an uninterrupted communication between the Middle and Eastern States. The great road leading from one section of the country to the other crosses the Hudson at King's Ferry, some miles below West Point. Detachments of Washington's army now occupied positions on both sides of the river, commanding the ferry, and covering the incomplete works above. That on the western bank was stationed on a rough elevated piece of ground called Stony Point, where defences had been commenced, but were far from being completed. That on the eastern bank occupied a small fort called Lafayette on Verplanck's Point, a low flat peninsula, projecting some distance into the river, and extending towards the works on the other side. The works at Fort Lafayette were in a state of greater forwardness than those at Stony Point. The present movement of the British army and fleet was intended to effect the reduction of these two posts, the capture of West Point, the division of Washington's army, and perhaps that of the states of the confederacy.

Having arrived within eight miles of King's Ferry, Clinton

46   2 H

landed the largest division of his army on the eastern bank of the river, under the command of General Vaughan, while he himself accompanied the other division, five miles higher up the river, and there landed on the western side. The unfinished works at Stony Point, garrisoned by only forty men, were considered too weak for defence against the large army which they saw cautiously approaching. The garrison accordingly abandoned the place, after setting fire to a block-house on the top of the hill, taking with them their munitions and stores. Clinton took possession of it unopposed, on the afternoon of the same day, May 31st, and in the night dragged up some heavy cannon and mortars, which he planted on the brow of the hill, pointing towards the fort on the opposite side of the river.

At five o'clock the next morning, a heavy fire was opened upon Fort Lafayette, by the commanding battery at Stony Point, and the vessels in the river, two of which succeeded in passing the fort, and cutting off all chance of retreat by water. General Vaughan, having made a long circuit, completely invested the place by land. Thus surrounded and attacked on all sides by a vastly superior force, the small garrison of seventy men, commanded by Captain Armstrong, held out the whole day, and then capitulated, surrendering themselves prisoners of war, on honourable terms.

Sir Henry Clinton gave immediate directions for completing the fortifications of both posts, and putting them in a strong state of defence. But General Washington, having received early information of his advance up the river, had already strengthened West Point, and taken such a strong position with his main army at Smith's Clove, that he saw the impossibility, at that time, either of advancing further, or attacking with a chance of success the American camp. Besides, he heard that Staten Island was threatened in his absence. He deemed it most advisable to place such strong garrisons in the captured posts as would effectually prevent their being retaken, while he, with the main army, retired to a central position, from which he might give assistance, either to them on the one hand, or to New York and its dependencies on the other. A garrison of one thousand men was consequently left at Stony Point, one of five thousand at Fort Lafayette, and the main army retired to Phillipsburg.

Clinton next attempted by a diversion in Connecticut to draw General Washington from the strong positions which he had taken in the highlands. For this purpose Major-general Tryon, with two thousand six hundred men, sailed from New York on the 3d of

July, and landed on the coast of Connecticut. After pillaging New Haven, he proceeded to Fairfield, where, meeting with some opposition, he became infuriated, destroyed the public property, and then laid the village in ashes, and treated many unarmed persons with the greatest brutality. The towns of Norwalk and Greenfield, which were successively visited, shared the same unhappy fate with Fairfield. The ultimate object of the expedition was the town of New London, but the opposition of the people increased to such a degree, that Tryon thought it advisable not to attempt it for the present. He accordingly returned to New York, to boast of his exploits to General Clinton.

Intelligence of the invasion of Connecticut was late in reaching the commander-in-chief, as he was visiting the outposts in the vicinity of Stony Point, when the news of the sailing of the fleet was received at head-quarters. As soon as he learned it, however, he promptly despatched continental troops from the nearest encampments, and sent expresses to the governor of the state, and the militia officers in the vicinity of what he supposed would be the point of attack. He understood the design of the British general, however, and took care not to weaken his forces in the highlands to such an extent as to give him the desired advantage. On the contrary, he immediately planned a counter-attack against Stony Point, which, if successful, would so far alarm Clinton as to induce him to recall the detachment from Connecticut for the purpose of defending his own outposts.

" The execution of the plan was intrusted to General Wayne, who commanded the light infantry of the army. Secrecy was deemed so much more essential to success than numbers, that no addition was made to the force already on the lines. One brigade was ordered to commence its march, so as to reach the scene of action in time to cover the troops engaged in the attack, should any unlooked-for disaster befall them; and Major Lee of the light dragoons, who had been eminently useful in obtaining the intelligence which led to the enterprise, was associated with General Wayne, as far as cavalry could be employed in such a service. The night of the 15th, and the hour of twelve, were chosen for the assault.

" Stony Point is a commanding hill projecting far into the Hudson, which washes three-fourths of its base. The remaining fourth is, in a great measure, covered by a deep marsh, commencing near the river on the upper side, and continuing into it below. Over this marsh there is only one crossing-place; but at its junction with the river is a sandy beach, passable at low tide. On the summit of this hill stood the fort. In addition to these defences, several vessels of war were stationed in the river, and commanded the ground at the foot of the hill. The garrison consisted of about six hundred men, commanded by Colonel Johnson.

"General Wayne arrived about eight in the afternoon at Spring Steel's, one and a half miles from the fort; and made his dispositions for the assault.

"It was intended to attack the works on the right and left flanks at the same instant. The regiments of Febiger and of Meigs, with Major Hull's detachment, formed the right column, and Butler's regiment, with two companies under Major Murfree, formed the left. One hundred and fifty volunteers, led by Lieutenant-colonel Fleury and Major Posey, constituted the van of the right, and one hundred volunteers, under Major Stewart, composed the van of the left. At half-past eleven, the two columns moved to the assault, the van of each with unloaded muskets and fixed bayonets. They were each preceded by a forlorn hope of twenty men, the one commanded by Lieutenant Gibbon, and the other by Lieutenant Knox. They reached the marsh undiscovered; and, at twenty minutes after twelve, commenced the assault.

Both columns rushed forward under a tremendous fire. Surmounting every obstacle, they entered the works at the point of the bayonet; and, without discharging a single musket, obtained possession of the fort.

"The humanity displayed by the conquerors was not less conspicuous nor less honourable than their courage. Not an individual suffered after resistance had ceased.

"All the troops engaged in this perilous service manifested a degree of ardour and impetuosity which proved them to be capable of the most difficult enterprises; and all distinguished themselves whose situation enabled them to do so. Colonel Fleury was the first to enter the fort and strike the British standard. Major Posey mounted the works almost at the same instant, and was the first to give the watchword, 'The fort's our own.' Lieutenants Gibbon and Knox performed the service allotted to them with a degree of intrepidity which could not be surpassed. Of twenty men who constituted the party of the former, seventeen were killed or wounded.

"Sixty-three of the garrison were killed, including two officers. The prisoners amounted to five hundred and forty-three, among whom were one lieutenant-colonel, four captains, and twenty subaltern officers. The military stores taken in the fort were considerable.

"The loss sustained by the assailants was not proportioned to the apparent danger of the enterprise. The killed and wounded did not exceed one hundred men. General Wayne, who marched with Febiger's regiment in the right column, received a slight wound in the head, which stunned him for a time, but did not compel him to leave the column. Being supported by his aides, he entered the fort with the regiment. Lieutenant-colonel Hay was also among the wounded."[*]

An attempt was at the same time made on the opposite fort, but without success. This failure, together with the fact that it would require a garrison of fifteen hundred men to defend Stony Point against the enemy's shipping, induced General Washington to demolish and abandon it. He had no sooner retired than it was re-occupied and repaired by Sir Henry Clinton.

Though these transactions but slightly affected the general aspect of the war, yet they afforded to Congress an opportunity, which they gladly embraced, of passing a vote of thanks to the general, "for the wisdom, vigilance, and magnanimity with which he conducted the military operations of the nation, and particularly for the enterprise upon Stony Point." They also unanimously voted their thanks to General Wayne for his brave and soldier-like attack, and presented to him a gold medal commemorative of the event.

After replacing the garrison of Stony Point, Sir Henry Clinton descended the river, and took post above Haerlem, his line extending to Kingsbridge. General Washington established his head-quarters at West Point, on the 21st of July, and from that day, until the month of December, when the army retired to winter quarters, he gave his attention principally to the completion of the works at that post. His army was now posted for the purpose of defensive operations, on both sides of the Hudson. The right wing, under the command of General Putnam, on the western side, occupying the highlands to their southern point at King's Ferry; the left wing, under General Heath, was stationed on the east side of the river; while the centre, consisting only of the garrison, and companies on fatigue duty at West Point, was under the immediate command of General McDougall. From this strong position General Washington frequently detached skirmishing parties on both sides of the river, in order to check the British foragers, and to restrain their intercourse with the loyalists. Major Henry Lee, who com

* Marshall, 8vo, p. 310—312.

2 H 2

manded one of these parties, having received information that the garrison of the British post at Paulus Hook, on the Jersey bank of the Hudson, opposite the city of New York, was in a state of negligent security, planned a bold and hazardous enterprise for its surprise and capture. For this purpose he advanced against it silently, on the morning of the 19th of August, at the head of three hundred men, and a troop of dismounted dragoons. The sentinel at the gate, never dreaming that an enemy could advance so far within the lines, and supposing the force advancing so orderly and securely to be a detachment which had gone out on a foraging excursion the preceding evening, paid no further attention to them until they were within the enclosure, when, almost in an instant, they separated into parties and seized the block-house and two redoubts. Major Sutherland, the commandant of the post, with sixty Hessians, hastily entered another redoubt and commenced a brisk fire upon the assailants. This only served to spread the notice of the attack; and the firing of guns in New York, and by the vessels in the roads, proved that the alarm was general. The design of Major Lee, being not to keep possession of this post, but to carry off the garrison, to reflect credit on the American arms, and to encourage a spirit of enterprise in the army, he immediately complied with the verbal instructions of the commander-in-chief, given to him some days previously, and retired with the loss of two men killed, and three wounded, carrying with him one hundred and fifty-nine prisoners.

The manner of life of Washington, while he was thus effectually holding the enemy in check, defeating all their projects for getting possession of the highlands, and, by a few brilliant strokes, keeping the public mind from despondency, may be gathered from a letter, inviting a friend to dine with him at head-quarters, dated West Point, 16th of August, 1779. This letter, which was addressed to Dr. Cochran, surgeon and physician-general of the army, shows, that in the midst of the most harassing duties, when oppressed with public cares, he could still, when occasion required, be playful and facetious. The letter is as follows:

"Dear Doctor,—I have asked Mrs. Cochran and Mrs. Livingston to dine with me to-morrow; but, am I not in honour bound to apprize them of their fare? As I hate deception, even where the imagination only is concerned, I will. It is needless to premise, that my table is large enough to hold the ladies. Of this they had ocular proof yesterday. To say how it is usually covered.

is rather more essential; and this shall be the purport of my letter.

"Since our arrival at this happy spot, we have had a ham, sometimes a shoulder of bacon, to grace the head of the table; a piece of roast beef adorns the foot; and a dish of beans, or greens, almost imperceptible, decorates the centre. When the cook has a mind to cut a figure, which I presume will be the case to-morrow, we have two beef-steak pies, or dishes of crabs, in addition, one on each side of the centre dish, dividing the space, and reducing the distance between dish and dish, to about six feet, which, without them, would be near twelve feet apart. Of late he has had the surprising sagacity to discover that apples will make pies; and it is a question, if, in the violence of his efforts, we do not get one of apples, instead of having both of beef-steaks. If the ladies can put up with such entertainment, and will submit to partake of it on plates, once tin, but now iron, (not become so by the labour of scouring,) I shall be happy to see them; and am, dear doctor, yours," &c.

During the summer of 1779, Spain engaged in the war with Great Britain on the side of France, but though she received a minister from the United States, no definitive treaty was entered into between the two countries for some time. This delay was occasioned by the grasping policy of Spain, and some difficulties which arose in relation to the western boundary of the United States, and the free navigation of the Mississippi River, to its mouth. Notwithstanding this, substantial assistance was expected from her, in the obstacles and hindrances which she was able to lay in the way of Great Britain.

While the head-quarters of the army was at West Point, Washington was visited by Monsieur Gérard, the French minister to the United States, who informed him of the approach of a large French fleet, under the command of the Count d'Estaing. Congress having delegated to the commander-in-chief the power of arranging the manner in which the allies should co-operate with each other, various plans were agreed upon between him and Monsieur Gérard, which, however, the repulse of the fleet before Savannah, and its subsequent withdrawal, prevented from being carried into execution. While the French minister was at West Point, he wrote a letter to the Count of Vergennes, from which the following extract is taken, as showing the opinion which his visit led him to form of the commander-in-chief of the American armies. He says:

"I have had many conversations with General Washington, some of which have continued for three hours. It is impossible for me briefly to communicate the fund of intelligence which I have derived from him; but I shall do it in my letters, as occasions shall present themselves. I will now say only, that I have formed as high an opinion of the powers of his mind, his moderation, his patriotism and his virtues, as I had before from common report conceived of his military talents, and of the incalculable services he has rendered to his country."

The approach of D'Estaing alarmed Sir Henry Clinton for the safety of his garrison at Rhode Island. Apprehensive that he would come towards the north, and, with a strong preponderance of naval force, attack his troops at Newport, or, uniting with Washington, outnumber him and attack New York, he ordered the immediate evacuation of Rhode Island, and the concentration of the British forces at New York. Accordingly, the troops which for three years had occupied the former place, arrived at New York on the 27th of October. Clinton now meditated a southern expedition, and was actively engaged in completing some strong works at New York and Brooklyn, which might be defended by a few, while he, with the main army, should seek a more glorious scene of action than could be hoped for in the presence of Washington.

Washington, meanwhile, devoted the time which a comparative relaxation from active service in the field afforded him, to an object, the prosecution of which had been but little encouraged by past success. This was, to convince the Congress of the impolicy and danger of their present system, or rather want of system in the administration of their military affairs. It is really astonishing that the experience of such repeated evils as flowed from the existing arrangements, had not induced them long before to listen to the advice of their commander-in-chief. But at this period the evils of short enlistments were as heavy and embarrassing as they were before Washington exposed them, and prayed for their removal, in almost every communication, both public and private. In November of this year, he presented a minute report to Congress of the state of the army, by which it appeared that his whole force, the names which appeared on his muster-rolls, (which, as is universally the case, materially exceeded the real strength of his army,) was twenty-seven thousand and ninety-nine. This number included all sorts of troops, non-commissioned officers and privates, and drummers and fifers. That of this number about fifteen thousand were stated to be engaged for the war, while of the remainder, it appeared that between that time and the last of the following June, the time of service of ten thousand one hundred and fifty-eight would expire. To supply this deficiency he submitted a plan, founded upon the principle of temporary enlistment, which he had so long unsuccessfully laboured to supersede. It contained, as a leading provision, that each state be annually informed by Congress of the real deficiency of its troops, in such time that the men drafted might join the army on the first of January ; and that, on or before the first of October, annually, a return similar to that which he then presented should be transmitted to Congress, to enable them to make their demands with precision.

Notwithstanding the manifest expediency of following these suggestions, they were never carried into effect ; the number of independent authorities to be consulted, the want of a supreme executive, and of the power of Congress to raise the troops—these and similar defects paralyzed every effort of the commander-in-chief, and the result clearly demonstrated that whatever advantages the new confederation had conferred on the states, it was badly adapted for the despatch of business.

On the 1st of December, 1779, the American army retired into winter quarters. They were divided between West Point and Morristown, to which latter place Washington removed his head quarters. Here the army again suffered the extreme privations consequent upon wintering such a large body of men within narrow limits.

Towards the end of December, General Clinton having securely garrisoned New York, and received reinforcements from Europe, embarked about seven thousand men on board of the fleet now under the command of Admiral Arbuthnot, and sailed for South Carolina.

More important military operations took place in the southern states, which had hitherto escaped the scourge of war. Colonel Campbell, who had been detached from New York against Georgia, in the latter part of 1778, arrived at Savannah, about the end of December, and summoned the garrison to surrender. The Americans were commanded by General Howe, who, suffering the enemy to approach him in the rear, was attacked on all sides at once, and completely routed, with the loss of five hundred men who became the prisoners of the British. Howe retreated into South Carolina, leaving all lower Georgia in the hands of the enemy. Soon after,

47

General Prevost entered from Florida, reduced Sunbury, and taking upon himself the chief command, despatched Campbell against Augusta, the only remaining American post in the state. The fall of Augusta gave the British complete possession of Georgia.

Congress, in the mean time, had passed a resolution recalling General Howe, and General Lincoln was appointed to succeed him. He only arrived in South Carolina in time to cover that state against the advance of the victorious army under General Prevost. Soon after his arrival, a company of seven hundred Tory refugees, who had been compelled by the severities of their countrymen to take refuge among the Indians, attempted to rejoin the king's forces. They were met and attacked by a small body of militia under Colonel Pickens, their commander was killed, and upwards of three hundred of them were taken prisoners.

This success encouraged General Lincoln, who was daily receiving reinforcements, to send a detachment of fourteen hundred men under General Ashe across the Savannah river, to take post at its junction with Briar Creek, in the hope of cutting off the communication of the English at Augusta with the main army. On receiving information of this movement, General Prevost detached a party under the command of his brother, who, making a circuit of fifty miles, crossed Briar Creek, fifteen miles above its mouth, and coming unexpectedly on the rear of General Ashe's party, totally routed them; the regular troops, after a desperate resistance, being all either killed or taken.

Notwithstanding this disaster, Lincoln again reinforced, determined to proceed with his main body against Augusta. As he crossed the river above, Prevost crossed below, determined to recall him from Augusta by threatening Charleston. Intending only a feint, he proceeded very slowly at first, until he saw that his movement had not the desired effect upon Lincoln, and he heard of the defenceless state of the capital of South Carolina, when his feint was changed to a real invasion, and he advanced with celerity, driving Moultrie with the militia before him into the town. The alarm had been given as soon as he crossed the Savannah, and such active preparations had been made, that when he had crossed the Ashley river, advanced just beyond cannon shot from the walls, and summoned the governor to surrender, he did not venture an attack, but retired during the night to a safe distance, and finally, on the approach of the victorious Lincoln, took refuge on the islands on the coast, from and to which the British fleet formed an easy mode of conveyance. From these islands he began to transport his men to Georgia, about the middle of June; but before he had entirely completed their removal, his post at Stono Ferry was attacked by General Lincoln, who, after a warm engagement of an hour in length, apprehensive of the arrival of a reinforcement to the British from St. John island, drew off his men, and retired in good order, carrying his wounded along with him. The British loss in killed and wounded was about one hundred and thirty; that of the Americans, one hundred and ninety. During the greater part of the engagement the British were covered by their works, which accounts for their smaller number killed and wounded. The midsummer heat causing a suspension of military operations, the British retired by their shipping to Georgia.

The Count d'Estaing, then in the West Indies, being strongly importuned by Governor Rutledge and General Lincoln to repair to Savannah and aid in driving the British from Georgia, arrived on the coast in the month of September, and surprised and captured a fifty gun ship, and some other British vessels.

General Lincoln, with about a thousand men, marched to Zubly's Ferry on the Savannah, and took up a strong position on the heights of Ebenezer, about twenty-three miles from the city. On the 16th, D'Estaing landed three thousand men, and summoned the place to surrender. General Prevost, on the first appearance of the French fleet on the coast, had ordered all the British detachments and garrisons in Georgia to concentrate in Savannah, and had commenced, and still continued actively employed in strengthening the defences of the town. At the time of the summons to surrender, the works were still incomplete, and a strong detachment which had been in garrison at Beaufort had not yet arrived. Such being the state of affairs, it was of the utmost consequence to the British general to gain time, and he accordingly requested a suspension of hostilities for twenty-four hours, to consider the subject of capitulation. During this critical interval, the expected detachment under Colonel Maitland arrived from Beaufort, and taking some by-road unknown to the besiegers, succeeded in entering the town. About the same time, General Lincoln, reinforced by the garrison of Augusta and Pulaski's legion, arrived before the town and formed a junction with the French.

Encouraged by the arrival of Maitland, Prevost, at the expiration of the twenty-four hours, informed D'Estaing that he had concluded to defend the place to the last extremity. The allies deemed it imprudent to attempt the works by storm, and were obliged to wait a few days until the heavy ordnance and stores could be brought from the fleet. On the 23d of September, ground was broken in due form, and on the 1st of October, by regular approaches, they had advanced within three hundred yards of the walls ; but the defence was prosecuted with such vigour and skill by the British engineer, Major Moncrieff, that it was supposed a long time would still intervene before the garrison could be compelled to surrender D'Estaing, then strongly urged by his officers, refused any longer to adventure his fleet on the coast, as the tempestuous period was fast approaching, and, in the mean time, while he was spending time before Savannah, the French West Indies were left undefended to the mercy of the British. By continuing their regular approaches for a few days more, the besiegers would probably have made themselves masters of the place, and expelled or captured the only English army then in the Southern States ; but these few days D'Estaing could not spare. No alternative seemed to remain but to raise the siege or storm the place. General Lincoln, rather than give up the expedition, after having advanced so far, in opposition to his own judgment, accepted the offer of the French forces to make the attempt before their departure. For that purpose, on the morning of the 9th of October, a heavy cannonade and bombardment opened on the town. A hollow way being discovered by which the troops could advance within fifty yards of the wall, three thousand French and fifteen hundred Americans were led to the attack in three columns by D'Estaing and Lincoln. The party pushed on with great vigour ; they had even crossed the ditch, mounted the parapet, and planted their standards on the wall. Being here, however, exposed to a tremendous fire from works well-constructed and completely manned, they were checked. Count Pulaski, at the head of two hundred horsemen, galloped between the batteries towards the town, with the intention of charging the garrison in the rear ; but he fell, mortally wounded, and his squadron was broken. The vigour of the assailants began to abate ; and, after a desperate conflict of fifty minutes, they were driven from the works, and sounded a retreat.

The loss of the French in this unsuccessful attack was seven hundred ; that of the Americans, two hundred and thirty-four killed and wounded. The British, being mostly under cover, lost only fifty-five. D'Estaing immediately embarked and sailed for the West Indies, and the campaign was ended, to the disadvantage of the Americans, though the British had accomplished but little in its prosecution, and they were now confined within the wall of one town, Savannah.

Lincoln.

CHAPTER XVIII.

Campaign of 1780.

EANTIME the commander-in-chief of the British forces in America, Sir Henry Clinton, had determined to transfer the principal seat of war to the Southern States. Leaving, therefore, the command of the royal army in New York to General Knyphausen, he sailed from that city on the 26th of December, 1777, under convoy of Admiral Arbuthnot, but did not arrive at Savannah till the end of January. The passage was tempestuous, some of the transports and victuallers were lost, others shattered, and a few taken by the American cruisers. Most of the cavalry and draught-horses perished. One of the transports, which had been separated from the fleet, was captured by the Americans and brought into Charleston on the 23d of January, and the prisoners gave the first certain notice of the destination of the expedition.

2 I

On the 11th of February, 1780, Clinton landed on John's Island, thirty miles from Charleston; but so cautious were his approaches that it was not till the 29th of March, that he broke ground at\the distance of eight hundred yards from the American works, and commenced a formal siege.

The determination of the state authorities to defend the town was ill-advised. General Lincoln, who commanded the garrison, was not provided with sufficient means of defence; but the extreme reluctance of the citizens to abandon their capital to the enemy prevented him from availing himself of the ample opportunity afforded for evacuating it; and when, on the 9th of April, Clinton, having completed his first parallel, and mounted his guns in battery, sent him a summons to surrender, he answered: "Sixty days have passed since it has been known that your intentions against this town were hostile, in which time was afforded to abandon it; but duty and inclination point the propriety of supporting it to the last extremity."

The siege was now prosecuted with vigour, and on the 12th of May, General Lincoln found himself under the necessity of capitulating. The effective strength of the garrison had been only between two and three thousand men, while the besieging army consisted of nine thousand of the best of the British troops.

General Lincoln was loaded with undeserved blame by many of his countrymen; for he conducted the defence as became a brave and intelligent officer. The error lay in attempting to defend the town; but, in the circumstances in which General Lincoln was placed, he was almost unavoidably drawn into that course. It was the desire of the state that the capital should be defended; and Congress, as well as North and South Carolina, had encouraged him to expect that his army would be increased to nine thousand men; a force which might have successfully resisted all the efforts of the royal army. But neither Congress nor the Carolinas were able to fulfil the promises they had made; for the militia were extremely backward to take the field, and the expected number of continentals could not be furnished. General Lincoln was, therefore, left to defend the place with only about one-third of the force he had been encouraged to expect. At any time before the middle of April, he might have evacuated the town; but the civil authority then opposed his retreat, which soon afterwards became difficult, and ultimately impracticable.

The fall of Charleston was a matter of much exultation to the British, and spread a deep gloom over the aspect of American affairs. The southern army was lost; and, although small, it could not soon be replaced. In the southern parts of the Union there had always been a considerable number of persons friendly to the claims of Britain. The success of her arms drew over to the British cause all those who are ever ready to take part with the strongest, and discouraged and intimidated the friends of American independence.

After gaining possession of Charleston, General Clinton sent out detachments to complete the conquest of the state. One of these, under Lord Cornwallis, proceeded towards the frontiers of North Carolina. Soon after passing the Santee, Cornwallis, learning that Colonel Buford was lying, with four hundred men in perfect security near the border of North Carolina, detached Colonel Tarleton, with his cavalry, named the Legion, to surprise him. In this Tarleton was successful. Attacked by seven hundred men, Buford's party threw down their arms and made no resistance; but an indiscriminate slaughter ensued. Many begged for quarter, but no quarter was given. *Tarleton's quarter*, after this, became proverbial, and added much to the sanguinary spirit in which the subsequent operations in the south were conducted.

On the surrender of Charleston, the garrison had been permitted to return to their homes on parole. Clinton, having subsequently convinced himself that the state was completely restored to its allegiance, issued a proclamation, on the 3d of June, calling upon the people to take up arms in the royal cause. The people desired peace; but on finding that they must fight on one side or the other, they preferred the banners of their country, and thought they had as good a right to violate the allegiance and parole which Clinton had imposed upon them, as he had to change their state from that of prisoners to that of British subjects, without their consent. The proclamation, therefore, instead of raising up friends to the British cause, greatly increased the number of its open enemies.

On the 5th of June, Clinton sailed from Charleston for New York, leaving Lord Cornwallis in command of the southern army. In order to connect his operations in the south with those which led to his surrender to the allied army under Washington and Rochambeau, we shall hereafter give a rapid sketch of his movements, and those of Generals Gates and Greene in the Carolinas.

While the transactions just related were going on in the Southern States, some interesting events happened in the more northern parts of the Union, where General Washington was beset by pressing and formidable difficulties. The finances of Congress were in a most depressed condition, and the urgent wants of the army were but ill

supplied.   The evils of short enlistment, though distinctly understood and strongly felt, could not be remedied; and the places of
those men who were leaving the army on the expiration of their
stipulated term of service, could not easily be filled up.   Besides,
the troops were in danger of perishing by cold and famine.   During
the preceding year, General Green and Colonel Wadsworth had
been at the head of the quarter-master and commissary departments;
and notwithstanding their utmost exertions, the wants of the army
haᴅ been ill-supplied.   After being put into winter quarters, it was
in great danger of being dissolved by want of provisions.   The
colonial paper money was in a state of great and increasing depreciation; and, in order to check the alarming evil, Congress resolved
to diminish the circulation and keep up the value of their paper
currency, by withholding the necessary supplies from the public
agents.   This imprudent resolution threatened the ruin of the army.
Nobody was willing to make contracts with the public, and some of
those entered into were not fulfilled.

Congress, jealous of the public agents, because ignorant of what
was really necessary, repeatedly changed the form of its engagements with them; and at length, by its fluctuating policy, real wants,
and imprudent parsimony, brought matters to such extremities that
General Washington was compelled to require several counties of
the state of Jersey to furnish his army with certain quantities of
provisions, within six days, in order to prevent them from being
taken by force.   Although the provinces were much exhausted, yet
the people instantly complied with the requisition, and furnished a
temporary supply to the army.

Soon after Sir Henry Clinton sailed on his expedition against
Charleston, towards the end of the year 1779, a frost of unexampled severity began.   The Hudson, East River, and all the waters
round New York were so completely frozen that an army with its
artillery and wagons might have crossed them in all directions
with perfect safety.   The city was fortified by the British; but, on
account of its insular position, several parts being considered of
difficult access, were left undefended.   By the strength of the ice,
however, every point became exposed; and in that unforeseen emergency, General Knyphausen, who commanded in the city with a
garrison of ten thousand men, took every prudent precaution for his
own defence, and fortified every vulnerable part; but the inefficiency
of the American army was his best security.   General Washington
eᴀᴄily perceived the advantages which the extraordinary frost gave
ᴀm; but, from the destitute state of his army, he was unable to

avail himself of them, and was obliged to see an opportunity pass away which was probably never to return. The army under his immediate command was inferior in number to the garrison of New York; it was also ill clad, scantily supplied with provisions, and in no condition to undertake offensive operations.

The British had a post in Staten Island; and, as the ice opened a free communication between the island and the Jersey coast, General Washington, notwithstanding the enfeebled condition of his army, resolved to attack the garrison, and appointed Lord Stirling to conduct the enterprise. The night of the 14th of January was chosen for the attempt; but though the Americans used every precaution, yet the officer commanding on Staten Island discovered their intention, and took effectual measures to defeat it. The attack was repulsed, though but little loss was sustained on either side.

The extreme cold occasioned much suffering in New York, by want of provisions and fuel; for, as the communication by water was entirely stopped, the usual supplies were cut off. The demand for fuel, in particular, was so pressing, that it was found expedien to break up some old transports, and to pull down some uninhabited wooden houses, for the purpose of procuring that necessary article. As the British paid in ready money for provisions or firewood carried within the lines, many of the country people, tempted by the precious metals, so rare among them, tried to supply the garrison. The endeavour of the British to encourage and protect this intercourse, and the exertions of the Americans to prevent it, brought on a sort of partisan warfare, in which the former most frequently had the advantage. In one of the most important of those encounters, a captain and fourteen men of a Massachusetts regiment were killed on the spot, seventeen were wounded, and ninety, with Colonel Thompson who commanded the party, were made prisoners.

Congress found itself placed in very difficult circumstances. It always contained a number of men of talents, and manifested no small share of vigour and activity. Many of the members were skilful in the management of their private affairs, and having been successful in the world, thought themselves competent to direct the most important national concerns, although unacquainted with the principles of finance, legislation, or war. Animated by that blind presumption which often characterizes popular assemblies, they frequently entered into resolutions which discovered little

practical wisdom. In pecuniary matters they were dilatory, and
never anticipated trying emergencies, or made provision for pro
bable events, till they were overtaken by some urgent necessity.
Hence they were frequently deliberating about levying troops and
supplying the army, when the troops ought to have been in the
field and equipped for active service.   This often placed the
commander-in-chief in the most trying and perilous circumstances.

Congress had solemnly resolved not to exceed two hundred millions of dollars in continental bills of credit.   In November, 1779,
the whole of that sum was issued, and expended also.   The demand on the states, to replenish the treasury by taxes, had not been
fully complied with, and, even although it had been completely
answered, it would not have furnished a sum adequate to the expenses of the government.   Instead of maturely considering and
digesting a plan, adhering to it, and improving it by experience,
Congress often changed its measures ; and, even in the midst of
those distresses which had brought the army to the verge of dissolution, was busy in devising new and untried expedients for supporting it.   As the treasury was empty, and money could not be
raised, Congress, on the 25th of February, resolved to call on the
several states for their proportion of provisions, spirits, and forage,
for the maintenance of the army during the ensuing campaign ;
but specified no time within which these were to be collected ;
and consequently the states were in no haste in the matter.   In
order to facilitate compliance with this requisition, it was further
resolved, that any state which should have taken the necessary
means for furnishing its quota, and given notice thereof to Congress, should be authorized to prohibit any continental quarter-
master or commissary from purchasing within its limits.   Every
man who had a practical knowledge of the subject easily perceived
the defective nature and dangerous tendency of this arrangement.
It was an attempt to carry on the war rather by separate provincial
efforts, than by a combination of national strength ; and if the army
received from any state where it was acting the appointed quantity of necessaries, it had no right, though starving, to purchase
what it stood in need of.   Besides, the carriage of provisions from
distant parts was troublesome, expensive, and sometimes impracticable.

The troops were ill-clothed, their pay in arrear, and that of
the officers, owing to the great depreciation of the paper currency, was wholly unequal to their decent maintenance.   These

multiplied privations and sufferings soured the temper of the men ; and it required all the influence of their revered commander to prevent many of the officers from resigning their commissions. The long condition of want and hardship produced relaxation of discipline, which at length manifested itself in open mutiny.

On the 25th of May, two regiments belonging to Connecticut, whose pay was five months in arrears, paraded under arms, with the avowed intention of returning home, or of obtaining subsistence at the point of the bayonet. The rest of the soldiers, though they did not join in the mutiny, showed little disposition to repress it. At length the two regiments were brought back to their duty ; but much murmuring and many complaints were heard. While the army was in such want, the inhabitants of Jersey, where most of the troops were stationed, were unavoidably harassed by frequent requisitions, which excited considerable discontent.

Reports of the mutinous state of the American army, and of the dissatisfaction of the people of Jersey, probably much exaggerated, were carried to General Knyphausen ; who, believing the American soldiers ready to desert their standard, and the inhabitants of Jersey willing to abandon the union, on the 6th of June, passed from Staten Island to Elizabethtown, in Jersey, with three thousand men. That movement was intended to encourage the mutinous disposition of the American troops, and to fan the flame of discontent among the inhabitants of the province. Early next morning, he marched into the country towards Springfield by the way of Connecticut Farms, a flourishing plantation, so named because the cultivators had come from Connecticut. But even before reaching that place, which is five or six miles from Elizabethtown, the British perceived that the reports they had received concerning the Americans were incorrect; for, on the first alarm, the militia assembled with great alacrity, and, aided by some small parties of regulars, annoyed the British by an irregular but galling fire of musketry, wherever the nature of the ground presented a favourable opportunity ; and although those parties were nowhere strong enough to make a stand, yet they gave plain indications of the temper and resolution which were to be encountered in advancing into the country.

At Connecticut Farms the British detachment halted. The settlers were known to be zealous in the American cause, and therefore with an unworthy spirit of revenge, the British, among whom was General Tryon, laid the flourishing village, with its church and the minister's house, in ashes. Here occurred one of those affecting incidents which, being somewhat out of the ordinary course of the miseries of war, made a deep impression on the public mind. Mr. Caldwell, minister of the place, had withdrawn towards Springfield, but had left his wife and family behind, believing them to be in no danger. The British advanced to the industrious and peaceful village. Mrs. Caldwell, trusting to her sex for safety, and unsuspicious of harm, was sitting in her house with her children around her, when a soldier came up, levelled his musket at the window, and shot her dead on the spot in the midst of her terrified infants. On the intercession of a friend, the dead body was permitted to be removed, before the house was set on fire. This atrocious deed excited such general horror and detestation that the British thought proper to disavow it, and to impute the death of Mrs. Caldwell to a random shot from the retreating militia, though the militia did not fire a musket in the village. The wanton murder of the lady might be the unauthorized act of a savage individual; but can the burning of the house after the death be accounted for in the same way? Knyphausen was a veteran officer, and cannot be supposed capable of entering into local animosities, or of countenancing such brutality; but Tryon was present, and his conduct on other occasions was not unblemished.

After destroying the Connecticut Farms, Knyphausen advanced towards Springfield, where the Jersey brigade under General Maxwell, and a large body of militia, had taken an advantageous position, and seemed resolved to defend it. General Knyphausen, however, had met with a reception so different from what he expected, that without making any attempt on the American post, he withdrew during the night to Elizabethtown.

On being informed of the invasion of New Jersey, General Washington put his army in motion, early on the morning of the day in which Knyphausen marched from Elizabethtown, and proceeded to the Short Hills, behind Springfield, while the British were in the vicinity of that place. Feeble as his army was, he made the necessary dispositions for fighting; but the unexpected retreat of Knyphausen rendered a battle unnecessary. The British were followed oy an American detachment, which attacked their rearguard in the morning, but were repulsed. Instead of returning to New York, General Knyphausen lingered in the vicinity of Elizabethtown and in Staten Island; and General Washington, too weak to hazard an engagement, except on advantageous ground, remained on the hills near Springfield, to watch the movements of

the British army. At that time, the army under the immediate
orders of General Washington did not exceed four thousand effec
tive men.

On the 18th of June, Sir Henry Clinton returned from South
Carolina, with about four thousand men ; and, after receiving this
reinforcement, the British force in New York and its dependencies
amounted to twelve thousand effective and regular troops, most of
whom could be brought into the field for any particular service ;
as besides them, the British commander had about four thousand
militia and refugees for garrison duty. The British army directed
on any one point would have been irresistible ; therefore the Americans could only follow a wary policy, occupying strong ground,
presenting a bold front, and concealing their weakness as far as
possible.

Sir Henry Clinton embarked troops, and awakened the apprehensions of General Washington lest he should sail up the Hudson and
attack the posts in the highlands. Those posts had always been
objects of much solicitude with the American commander, and he
was extremely jealous of any attack upon them. In order to be in
readiness to resist any such attack, he left General Greene at Springfield, with seven hundred continentals, the Jersey militia, and some
cavalry, and proceeded towards Pompton with the main body of
the army.

Sir Henry Clinton, after having perplexed the Americans by his
movements, early on the morning of the 23d of June, rapidly
advanced in full force from Elizabethtown towards Springfield.
General Greene hastily assembled his scattered detachments, and
apprized General Washington of the march of the royal army, who
instantly returned to support Greene's division. The British
marched in two columns ; one on the main road leading to Springfield, the other on the Vauxhall road. General Greene had scarcely
time to collect his troops at Springfield, and make the necessary
dispositions, when the royal army appeared before the town, and
a cannonade immediately began. A fordable rivulet, with bridges
corresponding to the different roads, runs in front of this place.
Greene had stationed parties to guard the bridges ; and they
obstinately disputed the passage ; but after a smart conflict they
were overpowered and compelled to retreat. Greene then fell back
and took post on a range of hills, where he expected to be again
attacked. But the British, instead of attempting to pursue their
advantages, contented themselves with setting fire to the village,
and laying the greater part of it in ashes. Discouraged by the

obstinate resistance they had received, and ignorant of the detach
ment which opposed them, they immediately retreated to Eliza.
bethtown, pursued with animosity by the militia, who were provoked at the burning of Springfield.   They arrived at Elizabethtown about sunset ; and, continuing their march to Elizabeth
Point, began at midnight to pass over to Staten Island.   Before six
next morning they had entirely evacuated the Jerseys, and removed
the bridge of boats which communicated with Staten Island.

In the skirmish at Springfield the Americans had about twenty
men killed, and sixty wounded.   The British suffered a corresponding loss.   Sir Henry Clinton's object in this expedition seems
to have been to destroy the American magazines in that part of the
country.   But the obstinate resistance which he met with at Springfield deterred him from advancing into a district abounding in
difficult passes, where every strong position would be vigorously
defended.   He seems also to have been checked by the apprehension of a fleet and army from France.

General Washington was informed of Sir Henry Clinton's march
soon after the British left Elizabethtown ; but, though he hastily
returned, the skirmish at Springfield was over before he reached
that place.

After Sir Henry Clinton left the Jerseys, General Washington
planned an enterprise against a British post at Bergen Point, on
the Hudson, opposite New York, garrisoned by seventy loyalists.
It was intended to reduce the post, and also to carry off a number
of cattle on Bergen Neck, from which the garrison of New York
received occasional supplies of fresh provisions.   General Wayne
was appointed to conduct the enterprise.   With a respectable force
he marched against the post, which consisted of a block-house
covered by an abattis and palisade.   General Wayne pointed his
artillery against the block-house, but his field-pieces made no impression on the logs.   Galled by the fire from the loop-holes, some
of his men rushed impetuously through the abattis, and attempted
to storm the block-house, but they were repulsed with considerable
loss.   Though, however, the Americans failed in their attempt
against the post, they succeeded in driving off most of the cattle.

On the commencement of hostilities in Europe, the Marquis de
Lafayette, who had so early and so zealously embarked in the
cause of America, had returned home, as we have already seen, in
order to offer his services to his king, still, however, retaining his
rank in the army of Congress.   His ardour in behalf of the Americans remained unabated, and he exerted all his influence with

the court of Versailles to gain its effectual support to the United States : his efforts were successful, and the king of France resolved vigorously to assist the Americans both by sea and land. Having gained this important point, and perceiving that there was no need for his military services in Europe, he obtained leave from his sovereign to return to America and join his former companions in arms. He landed at Boston towards the end of April; and, in his way to Congress, called at the head-quarters of General Washington, and informed him of the powerful succour which might soon be expected from France. He met with a most cordial reception both from Congress and the commander-in-chief, on account of his high rank, tried friendship, and distinguished services.

The assistance expected from their powerful ally was very encouraging to the Americans, but called for corresponding exertions on their part. The commander-in-chief found himself in the most perplexing circumstances : his army was feeble, and he could form no plan for the campaign till he knew what forces were to be put under his orders. His troops, both officers and privates, were ill clothed, and needed to be decently appareled before they could be led into the field to co-operate with soldiers in respectable uniforms; for his half-naked battalions would only have been objects of contempt and derision to their better dressed allies. In order to supply these defects, and to get his army in a due state of preparation before the arrival of the European auxiliaries, General Washington made the most pressing applications to Congress, and to the several state legislatures. Congress resolved and recommended; but the states were dilatory, and their tardy proceedings ill accorded with the exigencies of the case, or with the expectations of those who best understood the affairs of the Union. Even on the 4th of July, the commander-in-chief had the mortification to find that few new levies had arrived in camp, and some of the states had not even taken the trouble to inform him of the number of men they intended to furnish.

In the month of June, the state of Massachusetts had resolved to send a reinforcement, but no part of it had yet arrived. About the same time a voluntary subscription was entered into in Philadelphia, for the purpose of providing bounties to recruits to fill up the Pennsylvania line ; and the president or vice-president in council was empowered, if circumstances required it, to put the state under martial law. A bank also was established for the purpose of supplying the army with provisions ; and a number of gentlemen engaged to support it to the amount of one hundred and eighty

OLD BANK OF THE UNITED STATES.

nine thousand pounds sterling, according to the sums affixed to their several names.   The ladies of Philadelphia were ambitious of sharing the honours of patriotism with their fathers, husbands, and brothers; a number of them visited every house in the city, in order to collect a sum of money to be presented to the army, in testimony of their esteem and approbation.   The money was expended on cloth for shirts, which the ladies made.

In the midst of this bustle and preparation, the expected succours from France, consisting of a fleet of eight ships of the line, with frigates and other vessels under the Chevalier de Ternay, having about six thousand troops on board, under General the Count of Rochambeau, arrived at Rhode Island on the evening of the 10th of July; and, in a few days afterwards, Lafayette arrived at Newport from the American head-quarters, to confer with his countrymen.

At the time of the arrival of the French in Rhode Island, Admiral Arbuthnot had only four sail of the line at New York; but, in a few days, Admiral Graves arrived from England with six sail of the line, which gave the British a decided superiority to the hostile squadrons, and, therefore, Sir Henry Clinton without delay prepared for active operations.   He embarked about eight thousand men, and sailed with the fleet to Huntington bay in Long Island, with the intention of proceeding against the French at Newport.

The militia of Massachusetts and Connecticut were ordered to join their new allies in Rhode Island, and the combined army there thought itself able to give the British a good reception.

As the garrison of New York was weakened by the sailing of the armament under the British commander-in-chief; General Washington, having received considerable reinforcements, suddenly crossed the North River, and advanced towards New York; that movement brought Sir Henry Clinton back to defend the place; and, consequently, Washington proceeded no farther in his meditated enterprise.*

The want of money and of all necessaries still continued in the American camp; and the discontent of the troops gradually increasing, was matured into a dangerous spirit of insubordination. The men, indeed, bore incredible hardships and privations with unexampled fortitude and patience; but the army was in a state of constant fluctuation; it was composed, in a great measure, of militia, harassed by perpetual service, and obliged to neglect the cultivation of their farms and their private interests in order to obey the calls of public duty, and of soldiers on short enlistments, who never acquired the military spirit and habits.

In consequence of an appointment, General Washington and suite set out to a conference with Count Rochambeau and Admiral Ternay, and, on the 21st of September, met them at Hartford, in Connecticut, where they spent a few days together, and conversed about a plan for the next campaign.

The season was now far advanced: no action of importance had been achieved on the Hudson by either party, and the campaign in that quarter seemed about to close without any thing remarkable, when both armies were suddenly roused, and the public mind both in Europe and America much agitated by one of those affecting events which deepen the gloom and give a melancholy and tender interest even to the calamities of war—the execution of Major Andre.*

In the early part of the month of August, when General Washington meditated an attack on New York, he proposed that General Arnold should have a command in the enterprise. This Arnold declined; alleging that his lameness disqualified him for camp duty. General Washington knew him to be a selfish man; but, having no suspicion of his infidelity to the American cause, for which he had professed so much zeal and made so many exertions, appointed him, at his own desire, to the command of West Point

* Western World.

49   2 K

and its dependencies, a most important post on the Hudson. Of the highland posts on that river, General Washington was extremely jealous, and exerted himself to prevent the British from establishing a communication between Canada and New York, by the Lakes Champlain and George, and the river Hudson. West Point was considered a principal key of that communication; and, by the appointment to the command of it, Arnold was put into a place of high trust and confidence. But that officer, impetuous and desperate, rather than cool and intrepid, and governed more by the violence of his passions than the dictates of his understanding, had secretly determined to abandon and betray the American cause; and entered into negotiations with the British commander-in-chief for that purpose. The surrender of West Point, he was well aware, would gratify his new friends; and he wished to inflict a deadly wound on his old associates, whom he hated the more because he intended to betray them. Ambitious and selfish, fond of ostentation and magnificence, his expenditure had exceeded his income; and, in order to supply his extravagance, he had engaged in trade and privateering. His speculations proved unsuccessful; his funds were exhausted, and his creditors became clamorous. About the month of July, 1779, he presented heavy accounts against the public; but the commissioners rejected about one-half of his demands; he appealed to Congress; but a committee of that body reported that the commissioners had allowed him more than he had any right to demand or expect. Irritated and inflamed by this treatment, embarrassed in his circumstances, and encumbered with an expensive family, he resolved to raise a fortune on the ruins of his character, and to commit the foulest treason in order to gratify at once his ambition and revenge.

In the course of the year 1779, Major André, adjutant-general of the British army, a young officer of distinguished talents and acquirements, had entered into a correspondence with Mrs. Arnold, on pretence of supplying her with millinery goods; that correspondence ripened into treason on the part of Arnold. After his nomination to the command of West Point, the Vulture sloop-of-war was stationed by Sir Henry Clinton, in the North River, at such a distance from the American works as to excite no suspicion, but near enough to facilitate the correspondence which was going on. Before that time, there had been a written correspondence through other channels between Arnold and André, under the assumed names of Gustavus and Anderson. In order to bring the negotiation to a speedy close, Arnold wished Clinton to send a confidential person to hold a conference with him; unhappily, the amiable and accomplished André was selected for the consummation of a work in which he was already too much implicated.

On the night of the 21st of September, a boat sent by Arnold carried André from the Vulture, and landed him on the bank of the river, where he met Arnold outside of the American posts. The day was about to dawn before the negotiation was finished; and André was told that it was necessary he should remain concealed till next night; for that purpose he was conducted within the American lines, contrary to his previous stipulation and intention, and without his knowledge. He spent the day with Arnold. Next night the boatmen refused to carry him back to the Vulture, because she had shifted her ground in order to be out of the reach of a cannon which had been mounted to annoy her; and he was obliged to attempt an escape by land. He now changed his uniform, which he had hitherto worn under a surtout, for a common coat; and, having procured a horse, was, under the name of John Anderson, furnished with a passport by Arnold to go to the lines at White Plains, or lower if he thought proper, as he was on public business.

Thus equipped, André set out alone, and proceeded on his journey towards New York. He passed the American guards and posts on the road without suspicion; but Arnold had a scouting party, chiefly militia, scouring the country between the outposts of the two armies. As André prosecuted his journey the next day, and flattered himself that all danger was past, a man suddenly sprung from a covert and seized his horse's bridle. Surprised by the unexpected onset, the major lost his presence of mind; mistaking the man for a British partisan, instead of presenting his passport, he declared himself a British officer, and asked permission to proceed; but two other militia-men coming up at the moment, the party refused to let him go, though he offered them the most tempting rewards. They conducted him to Colonel Jamieson, the officer commanding the scouting party, before whom he appeared as John Anderson; choosing rather to encounter every hazard, than, by a disclosure of his real character, to involve Arnold in jeopardy before he had a warning to provide for his safety. The names of the militia-men who captured André were John Paulding, David Williams, and Isaac Van Wart.

André had been disconcerted, and his presence of mind had forsaken him on his sudden and unexpected seizure; but, more alive to Arnold's danger than his own, he discovered his ingenuity in procuring Jamieson's permission to give that officer notice of his apprehension. Even before that time Jamieson had entertained suspicions of Arnold's fidelity; and although those suspicions must have been now strengthened or confirmed, yet he permitted a note to be sent to Arnold, giving him notice of John Anderson's detention.

Several papers were found in one of Major André's boots, all in Arnold's handwriting, which contained an exact account of the state of West Point and its dependencies, with remarks on the works, and estimate of the number of men ordinarily on duty in the place, and a copy of the state of matters which had been laid before a council of war by General Washington on the 6th of the month. All these papers Jamieson enclosed under cover to General Washington, with a letter from the prisoner, in which he avowed himself to be Major John André, adjutant-general of the British army, related the manner of his apprehension, and endeavoured to vindicate himself from the imputation of being a spy.

General Washington was then returning from his conference with the French commanders at Hartford; and Jamieson's messenger missed him, by taking a different road from that in which he was travelling.

Arnold received the notice of Anderson's detention some hours before Washington arrived at West Point; and immediately consulted his safety, by hastening on board the Vulture sloop of war, which lay in the river some miles below Verplanck's Point.

On opening the packet from Jamieson at West Point, General Washington discovered Arnold's treason, and took prompt and effectual measures for the security of the post, ordering two brigades from the nearest division of the army.

After allowing time for the notice of his detention to reach Arnold, Major André laid aside all disguise, and avowed who he was. His behaviour was frank and ingenuous; and he seemed anxious for nothing but the vindication of his character from the imputations which the circumstances of his apprehension appeared to cast upon him.

General Washington appointed a board of officers, of which General Greene was president, and Lafayette, Steuben, and others, were members, to inquire into the case of Major André, and to report in what character he was to be considered, and what punishment he deserved. Even during the short time that André was in the power of the Americans, and notwithstanding the unhappy circumstances in which he was placed, his behaviour and talents made a highly favourable impression on their minds; and when brought before the board, the members behaved towards him with the utmost respect and delicacy, and told him not to answer any questions that might embarrass his feelings. But in that crisis of his fate, André magnanimously disregarded every thing but his honour. He gave a candid recital of circumstances, concealing nothing that regarded himself; but making no disclosures to inculpate others. He acknowledged every thing that was reckoned essential to his condemnation; and the board of general officers, to whom his case was referred, without calling any witnesses, considered merely that he had been within their lines in disguise, and reported that in their opinion Major André was a spy, and ought to suffer death. The sentence was ordered to be carried into execution on the day after it was declared. The apprehension of Major André excited a lively sensation in the British army, which felt a strong interest in his fate; for he was dear to all his companions in arms, and especially to the commander-in-chief, who immediately, by a flag of truce, opened a correspondence with General Washington, and urged every consideration of justice, policy, and humanity in favour of André. Finding his letters ineffectual, he despatched General Robertson to confer with General Washington on the subject, or with any officer he might appoint. He was met by General Greene; but no mitigation of the doom could be procured. On the day before his execution, Major André wrote an affecting letter to General Washington, requesting to be put to death like a soldier, and not as a malefactor; but the board of general officers, to whom every thing respecting him was referred, did not grant his request. The 2d of October closed the tragical scene; on that day the major was led out and hanged, supporting his high character to the last moment. He suffered amidst the admirations and regrets even of the American officers; while his death was deeply lamented by the British army. He was a young man of an amiable character, engaging manners, and fine talents and acquirements. Sir Henry Clinton made every effort to save him, but his character as a spy was distinctly proved; and the circumstance of his being an officer of high rank, and a personal friend of Sir Henry Clinton, could not be regarded as any mitigation of his offence, much less a reason for absolving him from the penalty which a spy is never permitted to evade under any circumstances.

Even Arnold had the effrontery to write to General Washington, on the occasion, attesting such facts as he believed favourable to André. But what reliance could be placed on the testimony of a man capable of such foul treason? He also threatened the general, and reminded him that many of the inhabitants of South Carolina had rendered themselves liable to military execution. It was im pudent in Arnold to write, and imprudent in Sir Henry Clinton to transmit his letter; for it was the sure way to provoke André's fate ; even although there had been an inclination to spare him. Arnold endeavoured to vindicate his conduct, by pleading hostility to the alliance with France; and he attempted to induce others to imitate his example, if it be admitted that he had a right to abandon the American standard; no plea can justify the attempt to employ the power committed to him for the ruin of those who had trusted him; some of whom, perhaps, had been encouraged by his example and incitement to take up arms against the British authority. The name of Arnold must go down to posterity, loaded with all the infamy of a traitor : and it were for the honour of human nature, and the common advantage of nations, if all governments would unite in manifesting their detestation of such villanies.

After the melancholy event now related, no military transactions of much importance were carried on in the north during the remainder of the campaign. On the 21st of November, indeed, Major Talmadge performed a brilliant exploit of desultory warfare. Being informed that the British had a large magazine of forage, at Coram on Long Island, protected by a small garrison at Fort St. George on South Haven, in its vicinity, he crossed the Sound where it was upwards of twenty miles broad; and, with nearly one hundred men, surprised the fort; made the garrison, upwards of fifty in number, prisoners; burnt the magazines at Coram; and, escaping the British cruisers, recrossed the Sound without losing a man. On the other hand, Major Carleton, at the head of one thousand men, Europeans, Indians, and loyalists, made a sud- den irruption into the northern parts of the state of New York, took forts Anne and George, and made the garrisons prisoners. At the same time, Sir John Johnson, at the head of a body of a similar description, appeared on the Mohawk.

On the approach of winter, both armies went into winter quarters. General Washington stationed the Pennsylvania line near Morris- town; the Jersey line, about Pompton, on the confines of New York and New Jersey; the troops of New England, in West Point and its vicinity, on both sides of the North River; while the troops of New York remained at Albany, whither they had been sent to oppose the invasion of Carleton and Johnson.*

* Western World.

Towards the close of the year, an agreement for the exchange of prisoners was entered into between Generals Lincoln and Philips. Philips had been an American prisoner since the convention of Saratoga, and the former in the power of the British since the surrender of Charleston. Hitherto Congress had shown no forwardness to enter into arrangements for a general exchange of prisoners. That body was aware of the great expense of recruiting the British army from Europe, and the slender accession of strength which, owing to short enlistments, their own military force would derive from a release of prisoners. They considered a general exchange unfavourable to their cause; but many of the regular troops had fallen into the hands of the British, by the capitulation of Charleston, and the defeat of Gates at Camden. The complaints of the prisoners and of their friends were loud; and for that reason Congress found it expedient to agree to a general exchange; but the convention troops of Saratoga were detained prisoners till the end of the war. ·

We must now fulfil our promise to take a rapid view of those movements in the south which led to Lord Cornwallis's invasion of Virginia. That officer, it will be recollected, was left in command of the British army in the south, when General Clinton returned to New York (June 5th.) His force was four thousand men; his position the borders of North and South Carolina; his object the complete subjection of the southern states, which he considered a natural consequence of the fall of Savannah and Charleston.

Active hostilities were recommenced on July 12th, two months after the fall of Charleston, when one hundred and thirty-three of Colonel Sumpter's corps routed a detachment of royal forces and militia at Williamson's plantation. In consequence of this first advantage over the British since their landing, the inhabitants of South Carolina flocked to the American standard in such numbers, as in a few days to swell Sumpter's force to six hundred men. With these, he attacked a party of British at Rocky Mount; but being destitute of artillery, and the enemy well defended by their works, he was obliged to retreat. Sensible of the influence which action and excitement have upon militia, he fell upon another party, consisting of the Prince of Wales's regiment and some Tories. The British force was reduced from two hundred and seventy-three to nine, and the royalists dispersed.

UT while the southern people were gratified by these desultory victories, and by the news that a respectable continental force was marching to their assistance, difficulties arose from another source. The necessary supplies for the army were so long delayed that fears began to be entertained of their complete failure. This arose from the refusal of the manufacturers to deliver their articles without immediate payment. At length, after great exertions the Maryland and Delaware troops were enabled to move. Under the command of the Baron de Kalb, they marched through Pennsylvania and Jersey, embarked at the head of Elk, April 16th, landed at Petersburg, and thence proceeded toward South Carolina. Before commencing this last part of the route, the command was transferred to Major-general Gates, who, in consequence of his brilliant success in the north, had been selected by Congress to conduct the southern war. On assuming the command, this officer altered the baron's plan of a circuitous route, and decided upon taking the shortest road to Camden. This led through an open pine barren ; and in their march the army were obliged to suffer under a burning sun, want of water and provisions, and the ravages of a wasting disease. Although there was, at first, some murmuring, and even indications of mutiny, yet, in general, the soldiers bore their sufferings patiently. On the 13th of August, they reached Clermont, thirteen miles from Camden, and were next day joined by a body of Virginia militia under General Stephens.

The first operation of General Gates was to publish a proclamation, inviting all citizens of the south to join the standard of their country, and promising forgiveness to those who, under the pressure of adverse circumstances, had united their arms with the British. This proclamation had considerable effect. The people had been insulted and ground down by a ruthless conqueror ; and although prior to the arrival of the American army they had been to a great degree dormant, yet it was merely for want of an opportunity to display their real disposition. That opportunity they now improved.

On the approach of Gates, Lord Cornwallis hastened from Charleston to Camden, which he reached on the 14th. He found there a force of seventeen hundred infantry and three hundred cavalry. That of his adversary, including militia, was nearly four thousand men ; but the regular force numbered only nine hundred infantry and seventy cavalry. Notwithstanding this disparity in numbers,

Cornwallis determined to give battle, and on the night of the 15th marched from Camden with his whole force. The same night, Gates also left his camp, for the purpose of occupying a favourable position about eight miles from Camden. On the route, the advanced cavalry of Colonel Arnaud, flanked by light infantry, encountered the advance guard of the British, and a skirmish ensued in the early part of which the Maryland regiment was broken, and the whole line thrown into confusion. The Americans, however, rallied, and both armies continued to skirmish through the night. In this affair, Colonel Potterfield, commander of the light infantry and a very able officer, was wounded.

The general engagement was reserved for the next morning. At the first onset the American left wing, composed of Virginia militia, throwing down their arms, fled, and were followed by a part of those from North Carolina. The whole battle was now directed against the continental troops, who, notwithstanding the unworthy example of their comrades, coolly maintained their ground, and at one time had actually secured a number of prisoners.

On that disastrous day, the Americans lost the finest army ever concentrated in the Southern States. The enemy captured two hundred and ninety prisoners, only eighty-six of whom were militia, all the artillery, consisting of eight field-pieces, more than two hundred wagons, and the greater part of the baggage. Every American corps was broken and dispersed, and every officer separated from his command. The Baron de Kalb, while bravely fighting at the head of his command, was wounded and taken prisoner into Camden, where he next day died.

The loss of the royal army was also severe; and they owed the completeness of their victory solely to the cowardice of the militia, and to their own superiority in cavalry.

The defeat of Gates was followed by that of Sumpter, whose troops, being attacked by Colonel Tarleton, lost all their artillery, and a number of recently captured prisoners, and were themselv either killed, captured, or dispersed.

Toward the end of August, the wretched remains of the American army commenced their retreat towards Salisbury. That retreat was one of complicated sufferings. The wounded were too numerous to be carried. Even those who had escaped the sword were drooping with sickness; pain, anxiety, hurry, and confusion, brooded over their gloomy journey. Soon after their arrival at Salisbury, General Gates went to Hillsborough to devise plans, in

50

concert with the North Carolina authorities, for the renewal of operations.

Though the victory at Camden had given Lord Cornwallis complete ascendency over the south, yet, from the heat of the season and the sickness of his troops, he was restrained from improving it by active hostilities. Determined, however, to punish the temerity and rebellion of those who had resisted the royal forces, he issued orders "that all the inhabitants of the province who had submitted, and who had taken part in this revolt, should be punished with the greatest rigour; that they should be imprisoned, and their whole property taken from them or destroyed," and that "every militia-man who had borne arms with the British, and afterwards joined the Americans, should be put to death." These were the results of the favourite theory of his lordship, that his contest was not with an independent nation, but with outlaws and rebels.

Notwithstanding the execution of several, under these orders, together with a large confiscation of property, many most respectable citizens resisted every temptation to resume the character of British subjects. They were consequently deprived of their homes and property, and shipped to St. Augustine. General Moultrie remonstrated against their removal, as contrary to the terms of the capitulation of Charleston; but his remonstrance was disregarded.

Thus, the cause of southern freedom had become one of poverty, exile, and ruin. But though numbers forfeited their patriotism, there were some illustrious characters, whom losses could not dishearten, threats intimidate, nor suffering change. To make their country happy, they sacrificed their own happiness; to redeem her from poverty, they themselves became poor; and cheerfully embraced chains and exile, that their example might assist in the emancipation of America.

Even the ladies became martyrs. They visited the prison-ships in order to solace the suffering captives. At the evening assemblies, the gay conqueror was passed by unheeded; but the American officer, though a prisoner, was loaded with marks of attention and respect; and when, in the progress of the war, they, as well as their husbands and brothers, were commanded from their native country, they cheerfully followed them even to distant regions.

The success of Lord Cornwallis once more inspired the British ministry with the hope of subjugating America. That body confidently asserted that such troops as fought at Camden, conducted by the same general, would soon extirpate rebellion so effectually as to leave no vestige of it in America. But a second Saratoga

PICKENS.

was soon to deliver them from this fond error, by the defeat and surrender of those very troops.

The severities of the British toward defenceless citizens, instead of attaining the desired end, after some time began to foster a spirit of hatred and revenge. Those who had been deprived of their homes fled into the interior and united themselves with Marion, Pickens, and Sumpter, who, subsequently to the defeat of Gates, had been elevated, by Governor Rutledge, to the rank of brigadier-generals. The parties thus formed, though entirely destitute of artillery, and often of provisions and small arms, tended by their presence to keep alive a feeling of opposition in American bosoms. From their retreats in forests and deep swamps, they sallied out as often as opportunity presented, and besides sometimes obtaining slight advantages, they continually annoyed the enemy.

With a view to destroy these partisans, as well as to render their authority more congenial to the inhabitants, the British had long been endeavouring to form the Carolinians into a royal militia. Major Ferguson, of the 71st regiment, having by very active exertion raised such a corps, advanced toward North Carolina, in order that his presence might there promote the royal cause. Upon approaching Augusta, he learned that a Colonel Clark had recently made an unsuccessful attack upon that place, and resolving to intercept his retreat, he took up a position on King's Mountain. Here he was attacked on the 7th of October, by about a thousand republicans, who had formed themselves into three parties, and advanced alternately to the charge. The British fought principally with the bayonet, and overthrew each division of their opponents as it presented itself. But instead of fleeing, the discomfited Americans either retired to a short distance, rallied, and renewed their charge, or entered the surrounding thickets, from whence they poured forth a most galling fire.

Ferguson, after displaying the greatest bravery, received a mortal wound. Two hundred and twenty-five of his men were killed or wounded, and the remainder, amounting to eight hundred, obliged to surrender. The assailants lost but few; yet among these was the brave Colonel Williams, a militia officer who had been very active in opposing the re-establishment of British authority.

The army thus signally successful was of the most heterogeneous nature. They had not collected in obedience to superior orders, but from a spontaneous desire to resist their oppressors. Among their number, were Colonel Campbell of Virginia, Colonels Cleveland, Shelby, Sevier, and McDowell of North Carolina, and Colonels Lacey, Hawthorn, and Hill, of South Carolina. These, by common consent, commanded each day alternately. Their hardships were equal to their patriotism. Some of them subsisted for weeks without tasting bread, salt, or spirituous liquors. At night the earth was their bed and the trees their covering. Such was the fare of the heroes of King's Mountain.

Ferguson was a most able officer, possessing an uncommon spirit of enterprise and distinguished talents as a partisan. His unexpected defeat filled the Americans with exultation, and proportionably damped the spirit of the Tories.

Soon after the battle of King's Mountain, Cornwallis left Camden with his main army and moved toward Salisbury. On the way he met with many confirmations of the fact that South Carolina was not conquered. Groups of riflemen hung upon his march, annoying him so perseveringly that it became hazardous for his companies to leave the main body. Together with the Ferguson catastrophe, this convinced him that much of the labour which he had supposed to be accomplished, was yet to be encountered. Under these circumstances, his lordship abandoned the design of penetrating into North Carolina, and retreated to Hillsborough.

Meanwhile Sumpter had collected a respectable force, with which he so harassed the British parties, that intercourse between their different posts could be effected only with caution and difficulty. He was in consequence attacked on November 12th, at Broad River, by Major Wemyss, but defeated the British and captured their commander. Eight days after he had a second battle with Lieutenant-colonel Tarleton, at Black Stocks, near Tyger River. The enemy charged with one hundred and seventy dragoons and eighty men; but Sumpter, having thrown his force into a large log barn, met the charge with firmness, and Tarleton was obliged to retreat, with the loss of three officers and a considerable number of men. In this affair General Sumpter was wounded.

While these events were transpiring, General Gates had been

endeavouring to raise a force sufficient to enable him again to take the field, and retrieve the consequences of his former defeat. This, however, he was not permitted to accomplish. Public opinion loudly condemned his conduct at Camden; and Congress, obeying its influence, resolved to supersede him, and submit his case to a court of inquiry. This was pursuant to a former resolve, that whoever lost a post should be subjected to such examination. On his way home the feelings of the unfortunate general were soothed by a testimonial from the Virginia House of Burgesses, assuring him that "the remembrance of former glorious services could not be obliterated by any reverse of fortune, and that they would omit no opportunity of testifying to the world the gratitude which the country owed to him in his military character."

Thus closed the southern campaign of 1780. Though British conquests had rapidly succeeded each other, yet no advantages accrued to the victors. Such was the disposition of the people, that the expense of retaining them in subjection exceeded the profits of their conquest. British garrisons kept down open resistance in the vicinity of the places where they were established; but as soon as they were withdrawn, and the people left to themselves, a spirit of revolt always displayed itself, and the standard of independence never wanted the active and spirited partisan to defend it.

GENERAL GATES.

KOSCIUSKO.

CHAPTER XIX.

Campaign of 1781.

OTHING now seemed to interfere with the British projects of conquest in the south; their general good fortune since the reduction of Savannah and Charleston caused them to plan an invasion of North Carolina, as the business of the winter following Gates's defeat. Every circumstance seemed to favour the project. The Southern army was too weak to take the field, nor had Congress or the northern forces the means of strengthening it; and even could Washington have spared part of his troops, the time necessary to transport them seven hundred miles would have been amply sufficient to enable the enemy to execute their plans, and thus frustrate the object of their arrival. All therefore that Congress could do, was to appoint a general to supersede General Gates. At the earnest recommendation of Washington, they elected General Greene, who was soon to prove that the confidence of the commander-in-chief was not misapplied.

Upon the reception of his commission, Greene immediately proceeded to Charlottestown, where General Gates had concentrated the remnant of his forces. He there received the transfer of that general's authority, and entered upon his official duties.

The same day the army received news of the success of Lieutenant-colonel Washington, in an attack on Clermont, eighteen miles from Camden, and station of Lieutenant-colonel Rugely of the British militia. The plan of attack was somewhat novel. Having no artillery, the colonel planted the trunk of a pine tree so that it resembled a field-piece, and parading it in front of a blockhouse, in which were the enemy, peremptorily demanded a surrender. The ruse succeeded, and without firing a gun one hundred men, defended by a guard-house and abbatis, became prisoners.

Upon assuming the southern command, Greene found himself encompassed with difficulties. The late disasters had been no less fatal to the subordination than to the success of the American arms. The regulars were without pay, and often wanted proper clothing and provisions; while the continental currency, their only money, was so depreciated as to be no longer an article of exchange. Beside these difficulties, the sufferers from exile and loss of property were clamorous for immediate action, and the militia, though generally so inefficient when in battle, were still more so while idle. In a word, at the head of two thousand defeated men, one-half of whom were raw militia, he was to oppose a superior force of the best troops on the western continent. His first care was to enforce discipline; and he effected it, by promptly executing a few of the glaringly mutinous. To raise necessaries for the army, he was obliged to resort to impressment; and this he conducted in so delicate a manner as to effect his object without alienating the affections of the inhabitants. With regard to his operations, after mature deliberation had manifested the folly of an attempt at immediate open warfare, he determined to harass the enemy in detail, until the successes of a partisan struggle would swell the number of his army so as to enable him to risk a pitched battle.

Soon after the adoption of this plan, he sent General Morgan, with a respectable detachment, to the western part of South Carolina, and marched with the main body of his army to Hick's Creek, on the north bank of the Pedee.

Morgan was joined by a considerable number of militia, who, since the establishment of the British at Ninety-Six, had been ground down with cruel oppression, and were now burning for revenge.

As soon as the intelligence of this movement reached Lord Cornwallis, he despatched Colonel Tarleton, with eleven hundred men and two field-pieces, to "push the Americans to the utmost." Tarleton advanced with celerity, confident that his superiority, both in cavalry and infantry, together with the undisciplined condition of his opponents, would secure an easy victory.

The engagement took place on the 17th of January at the Cowpens. The Americans formed two lines; the first composed of one hundred and ninety North Carolina militia, under Colonel Pickens; and the second, of light infantry and a corps of Virginia riflemen. These were some hundred yards behind the others; and in the rear of both was the cavalry of Lieutenant-colonel Washington with about forty-five mounted militia. Though the British were exhausted with fatigue, Tarleton immediately ordered a charge, which he conducted in person. The first line, after some resistance, was broken, and the second shared a similar fate. Tarleton had begun to cut down the militia, when he was stopped by an unexpected charge of Colonel Washington, which was almost immediately seconded by one from Howard, with fixed bayonets. The militia, elated with this success, rushed on in great numbers, driving back the British advance-guard, and seizing their artillery. Amid the wild confusion of these simultaneous victories, Howard called to the enemy to surrender. The greater part obeyed, and of all Tarleton's army but one small party escaped, to carry the news to Cornwallis. Morgan's loss was twelve killed and sixty wounded; while that of the British was three hundred killed and wounded, five hundred prisoners, eight hundred muskets, one hundred dragoon horses, thirty-five baggage-wagons, and two field-pieces.

For their conduct in this brilliant affair, the officers received testimonials from Congress; and the whole army the thanks of that body. In its consequences, it was one of the most important actions of the Revolution; and the circumstances under which it was fought, challenge our utmost astonishment at its success.

The news of this misfortune, though it mortified, did not discourage Cornwallis. He determined, by a vigorous movement to the South, to nullify the impressions of defeat, and intercept Morgan, who, with his prisoners, was proceeding to Virginia. Notified of these movements, General Greene, after marching from Hick's Creek, left his army with General Huger, and rode one hundred and fifty miles, to join Morgan, that he might be in front of Cornwallis, and make the junction of his two commands more easy. Immediately on his arrival, he ordered the prisoners to Charlotteville, and his troops to Guilford court-house, to which place General Huger had been directed to proceed.

In their retreat, the Americans underwent almost incredible hardships. Besides being exhausted by fatigue and hunger, they were obliged to march bare-foot over the frozen ground, and often to ford deep creeks, yet far from murmuring, they submitted to all this, cheerfully. The royal army fared little better than their adversaries; for being obliged to destroy their baggage, in order to facilitate their progress, they encountered many privations hitherto almost unknown.

So active were the movements of the British general, that he reached the Catawba on the evening of the same day that the Americans had crossed it. Here his progress was for a while arrested by a heavy rain, which rendered the river impassable. When the freshet subsided, the enemy crossed by wading, and having dispersed a small company of militia who had opposed them, pushed forward, in hopes of overtaking Morgan before he could cross the Yadkin. They were again disappointed. The elements again favoured the Americans, and the British were again detained by the swelling of the river. These hair-breadth escapes were considered by the Americans as proof that their cause was favoured by Heaven, and impressed religious people with such sentiments as added fresh vigour to their exertions.

Cornwallis now marched to the upper fords of the Yadkin, but before he could cross, Greene had united his forces at Guilford court-house. Even now his numbers were so inferior to that of his antagonist, that a council of officers unanimously agreed that he ought to retire over the Dan, and by no means risk an engagement. Apprized of this, his lordship determined to keep the upper country, where the streams were fordable, so that his opponent being unable to cross below, and having his supplies and reinforcements intercepted, would be obliged to give battle under many disadvantages. In this expectation he was deceived; Greene, by good

management, eluded the snare. By the most indefatigable exer
tions he transported his army artillery and baggage over the Dan
into Virginia; yet, with so narrow an escape that the van of the
British arrived just as the rear of the Americans had crossed. To
the royal army this escape appeared almost incredible; and their
mortification must have been unbounded. They had cheerfully
submitted to fatigue, starvation, and every other hardship; and
when their object seemed within grasp, their hopes were destined
to a bitter disappointment.

Cornwallis, however, consoled himself by the reflection that he
could improve the opportunity offered by the absence of the Americans in assembling the royalists and establishing a constitutional
government. He therefore published a proclamation to that effect,
and afterwards erected the king's standard at Hillsborough. The
experiment was, however, attended with so little success that he
found it necessary to despatch Tarleton, with four hundred and
fifty men, to the Deep River, in order to incite a loyal spirit among
the inhabitants of that region. Hearing of this movement, and
apprehensive that the absence of the American army would be fatal
to their cause in the south, Greene determined to re-enter North
Carolina at all hazards. Accordingly, he crossed the Dan, and
immediately dismissed General Pickens and Lieutenant-colonel
Lee, in pursuit of Tarleton. On their way they met with a body of
three hundred and fifty Tories, who mistook the Americans for British, and were cut down while making protestations of their loyalty.
Tarleton was about a mile from this scene of slaughter, and upon
hearing the alarm, crossed the Haw River, and returned to Hillsborough. On his retreat, he killed several of the royalists who
were on their way to join the British, and whom he mistook for
American militia.

These movements of General Greene entirely disconcerted the
plans of Cornwallis, and so damped the spirit of the Tories, that
they left him in large numbers.

Though the American commander had resumed the field, he did
not wish to risk a general action, but to keep alive the courage of
his army by harassing the foragers and detachments of the enemy.
So artful were his movements, that for seven days he lay within ten
miles of the hostile camp; changing his position every night, and
keeping it a profound secret where the next one would be. At the
end of three weeks, he was joined by two brigades of militia from
North Carolina, one from Virginia, and four hundred regulars.
Having now a superiority in numbers, he gave battle on the 15th

of March at Guilford Court-house. His army consisted of four thousand four hundred men, more than one half of which were militia; that of Cornwallis, two thousand four hundred, chiefly veteran troops. The former were drawn up in three lines; the front, composed of North Carolina militia, the second of Virginia militia, the third of continentals under General Huger, and Colonel Williams. The British advanced in three columns; the Hessians on the right, the guards in the centre, and Lieutenant-colonel Webster's brigade on the left. The American front gave way almost as soon as attacked, in consequence of the indiscretion of a colonel, who called out to an officer that he would be surrounded. The Virginia militia maintained their ground with great spirit, but were also obliged to retreat. The continental troops were last engaged, and fought bravely for an hour and a half; but the discipline of veterans gained the day. They broke the second Maryland brigade, turned the left flank, and were endeavouring to encircle the American regulars. A retreat therefore became indispensable. It was ably conducted by Greene, who retired but three miles.

In this battle the Americans lost about four hundred killed and wounded; among the latter were Generals Huger and Stephens. The loss of the British was severe. Besides several hundred privates, Colonel Webster, an able and much beloved officer, Colonel Stuart, and three captains were killed; and Generals O'Hara and Howard, and Colonel Tarleton wounded.

Though Cornwallis had gained a victory, he was in no condition to improve it. The long-sought interview with his adversary ill repaid the toil and anxiety which he had expended to accomplish it. So effectually had it crippled his abilities, that on the 19th, he broke up his camp and retreated towards Wilmington. Greene having re-collected his forces, and provided for the wounded of both armies, immediately pursued as far as Ramsey's Mill, on the Deep River. From Wilmington his lordship marched towards Virginia; but instead of pursuing him, Greene formed the bold design of returning to South Carolina. Hazardous as was this attempt, circumstances afterwards proved that it was the very best one which could have been devised, as well as demonstrated the sagacity of the man who planned and executed it.

Before Greene commenced his march, he sent orders to General Pickens, to prevent supplies from going to the British garrisons at Augusta and Ninety-Six, and soon after proceeded towards the latter station. No sooner was his approach known than the friends of Congress were filled with exultation. The spirit of opposition had ever been sustained by Sumpter, Marion, and other partisans, who now hailed the coming campaign as the reward of their long exertions. Before the arrival of the American army, the latter general, accompanied by Lieutenant-colonel Lee, invested Fort Watson, between Camden and Charleston, and obliged it to surrender.

On the arrival of General Greene, he encamped before Camden, which was defended by Lord Rawdon with nine hundred men. In consequence of his force being insufficient for an assault, he took a good position about a mile distant, in order to allure the garrison from their works. He was successful, and an engagement ensued, in which the Americans were worsted; but they retreated in such good order as to save most of their wounded, artillery, and prisoners. The British retired to Camden, and the Americans to about five miles above their former position.

Lord Rawdon, on the 7th of May, received a considerable reinforcement under Colonel Watson. He, therefore, on the next day, endeavoured to give battle to General Greene. But failing in this, and having all his supplies intercepted, he returned to Camden, burned the jails, mills, and his own baggage, and evacuated the post. Soon after, the British were obliged to contract their extended chain of communication, and retire within the Santee. This measure greatly animated the friends of Congress, as well as the partisan militia, and was immediately followed by the surrender of a post at Orangeburg to General Sumpter, and of Fort Motte on the following day. Three days after, the garrison of Fort Granby, consisting of three hundred and fifty-two men, surrendered to Colonel Lee. About the same time, Marion compelled the garrison of Georgetown to evacuate that post.

But few stations now remained in possession of the British. One of these, Fort Cornwallis, was attacked by Lieutenant-colonel Lee, and Colonel Pickens, and, after an obstinate resistance, compelled to capitulate. The Americans took three hundred prisoners, and had about forty killed and wounded.

Some acts of retaliation took place about this time, which became a source of uneasiness to the officers. By strenuous exertions some of the perpetrators were discovered and received summary punishment.

Meanwhile, General Greene, with the main army, laid siege to Ninety-Six, in which was Lieutenant-colonel Crugar, with five hundred men. On the left of the besiegers was a work in the form of a star; on the right a strong stockade fort, containing two blockhouses. The town was also defended with strong pickets, and surrounded by a ditch and high bank. The Americans pushed

the siege with vigour, erecting four batteries, the last within a hundred lines of the main fort. The abattis was turned, and a mine and two trenches extended to within six feet of the ditch, when news arrived that Lord Rawdon was hastily approaching at the head of two thousand men. This at once blasted the fair prospects of the Americans, and after an unsuccessful assault, they raised the siege, and retreated over the Saluda. In this siege the Polish general, Kosciusko, particularly distinguished himself. His devotion to the American cause had already won him the confidence and esteem of Washington, Greene, and the other leading generals of the Revolution.

The disappointment of the American general was as bitter as it was unexpected; yet still his elastic spirit refused to despond; and when advised to retire to Virginia, his reply was: " I will recover South Carolina, or die in the attempt." As on a former occasion, he determined to attack the enemy in detail, and intercept their supplies. He therefore declined battle, when offered by Rawdon, until that general had divided his forces, when he showed himself with such effect that his lordship retreated to Orangeburg, closely pursued by his indefatigable opponent.

At Orangeburg, Lord Rawdon was joined by Lieutenant Crugar, who had evacuated Ninety-Six; and General Greene, unable to resist their combined force, retired to the high hills above Santee. In order to carry out his plan, and compel the evacuation of Orangeburg, Marion and Sumpter were despatched against Monk's Corner, and Dorchester. They took different roads, and commenced separate and successful attacks on convoys and detachments in the vicinity of Charleston. In this manner was the war conducted. While the British forces were compact they could neither cover the country, nor force the Americans to action; and when divided, the detachments were attacked separately, and defeated. The consequence was, that the spirit of revolt became general, and the royal interest daily declined.

Lord Rawdon now took post near the junction of the Wateree and Congaree; but upon the approach of Greene retired to the Eutaw Springs, forty miles nearer Charleston. Here he was attacked by the Americans, and a severe engagement ensued. Greene's front line was composed of militia, who commenced the attack on some advance parties of the enemy, and behaved with great courage. The continentals next engaged, rushing to the charge through a heavy cannonade and shower of musketry. They were led by Colonels Williams and Campbell, the latter of whom

was mortally wounded, but survived long enough to learn the com
plete success of the Americans. The British fled to a large brick
house, from which it was found impracticable to dislodge them.
Their loss, inclusive of prisoners, was one thousand one hundred
men ; that of the Americans, five hundred, of whom sixty were
officers.

General Greene was honoured by Congress with a British standard and gold medal ; and the thanks of that body were voted to
the different corps and commanders.

This battle closed the active warfare in the south. The Americans retired to their former position above Santee, and the British
stationed themselves near Monk's Corner. Both armies subsequently moved to the lower country. A few excursions were
afterwards made by the enemy, and sundry small enterprises executed ; but nothing of more general consequence than the loss of
property and a few individual lives.

Thus closed the campaign of 1781, in the south. Upon reviewing its operations, we are forcibly impressed by the talents of the
man who, during that gloomy period, redeemed and strengthened
the American cause. With an unpaid and half naked army, he
had to contend with veteran soldiers, who were supplied with
every thing that the wealth of Britain and the plunder of Carolina
could furnish ; yet he compelled superior numbers to retire from
the extremity of the state, and confine themselves in the capital
and its vicinity. Neither defeat nor difficulties could overcome
his indomitable perseverance ; and for him to lose a battle was but
to gain a store of experience, some day to be exercised to the dis-
comfiture of his enemies.

The year 1781 had opened with very gloomy prospects for the
cause of American independence. Vigorous and united efforts on
the part of the United States were needful to meet the co-operation of the succours from France ; but the states seemed feeble
and irresolute. The people were heartily tired of the war ; but
though no better affected towards Great Britain than before, yet
they earnestly desired deliverance from the multiplied miseries of
the long protracted struggle. At first they had rushed impetuously
into the contest ; but their early ardour had begun to cool. In the
Eastern States particularly, since the theatre of war had been transferred to the south, the greatest apathy prevailed.

Congress had called for an army of thirty-seven thousand men,
to be in camp on the first of January. The resolution, as usual,
was too late ; but even, although it could have been promulgated rea-

sonably, so large a force could not have been brought into the field under the imperfect organization of the government. The deficiencies and delays on the part of the several states exceeded all reasonable anticipation. At no time during this active and interesting campaign did the regular force drawn from Pennsylvania to Georgia, inclusive, exceed three thousand men. So late as the month of April, the states, from New Jersey to New Hampshire inclusive, had furnished only five thousand infantry; but this force was slowly and gradually increased; till, in the month of May, including cavalry and artillery, which never exceeded one thousand men, it presented a total of about seven thousand, of whom four thousand might have been relied on in active service. A considerable part of this force arrived in camp too late to acquire, during the campaign, that discipline which is essential to military success. Inadequate as this army was for asserting the independence of the country, the prospect of being unable to support it was still more alarming. The men were in rags: clothing had been long expected from Europe, but had not arrived, and the disappointment was severely felt.

The diary of Washington, as well as his correspondence, bears ample evidence of the destitute condition of the army, and of the severe trials to which, as commander-in-chief, he was consequently exposed. The magazines were ill supplied; the troops were often almost starving; and the army was ready to be dissolved for want of food. The arsenals were nearly empty. Instead of having the requisites of a well-appointed army, every thing was deficient; and there was little prospect of being better provided; for money was as scarce as food and military stores. Congress had resolved to issue no more bills on the credit of the Union; and the care of supplying the army was devolved upon the several states, according to a rule established by that body. Even when the states had collected the specified provisions, the quartermaster-general had no funds to pay for the transportation of them to the army, to accomplish which, military impressment was resorted to in a most offensive degree. Congress was surrounded with difficulties: the several states were callous and dilatory; and American affairs wore an aspect of debility and decay. To deepen the general gloom, there were portentous rumours of preparations for savage warfare along the whole extent of the western frontier; of an invasion on the side of Canada; and of strong disaffection in Vermont. In the midst of financial difficulties and apprehensions of attack both from foreign and domestic enemies, a new and alarming danger appeared, in a

quarter where it was little expected, and which threatened to consummate the ruin of American independence. The privations and
sufferings of the troops had been uncommonly great. To the usual
hardships of a military life, were added nakedness and hunger,
under that rigour of climate which whets the appetite and renders
clothing absolutely necessary. By the depreciation of the paper
currency, their pay was little more than nominal, and it was many
months in arrear.

Besides those evils which were common to the whole army, the
troops of Pennsylvania imagined that they laboured under peculiar
grievances. Their officers had engaged them for three years, or
during the war. On the expiration of three years, the soldiers thought
themselves entitled to a discharge ; the officers alleged that they
were engaged for the war. The large bounties given to those who
were not bound by previous enlistment, heightened the discontent
of the soldiers, and made them more zealous in asserting what they
thought their right. In the first transports of their patriotism they
had readily enlisted ; but men will not long willingly submit to
immediate and unprofitable hardships in the prospect of distant and
contingent rewards.

The discontents engendered by the causes now mentioned had
for some time been increasing ; and, on the 1st of January, 1781,
broke out into open and almost universal mutiny of the troops of
Pennsylvania. On a signal given, the greater part of the non-commissioned officers and privates paraded under arms, declaring
their intention of marching to the seat of Congress to obtain a
redress of grievances or to abandon the service. The officers made
every exertion to bring them back to their duty, but in vain ; in
the attempt, a captain was killed and several other persons wounded.
General Wayne interposed ; but on cocking his pistols at some of
the most audacious of the mutineers, several bayonets were at his
breast, the men exclaiming, "We respect you, we love you; but
you are a dead man if you fire ! Do not mistake us ; we are not
going to the enemy ; on the contrary, were they to come out, you
should see us fight under you with as much resolution and alacrity
as ever ; but we wish a redress of grievances, and will no longer
be amused." Such of the Pennsylvania troops as had at first taken
no part in the disturbance, were prevailed on to join the mutineers ;
and the whole, amounting to thirteen hundred men, with six field-
pieces, marched from Morristown under temporary officers of their
own selection. General Washington's head-quarters were then at
New Windsor, on the North River.

Next day, General Wayne and Colonels Butter and Stewart, officers who, in a high degree, enjoyed the confidence and affection of
the troops, followed the mutineers; but though civilly received, they
could not succeed in adjusting the differences or in restoring subordination.   On the third day, the mutineers resumed their march,
and in the morning arrived at Princeton.   Congress and the Pennsylvania government, as well as General Washington, were much
alarmed by this mutiny, fearing that the example might be conta-
gious and lead to the dissolution of the feeble American army.
Therefore a committee of Congress, with the governor, and some
members of the executive council of Pennsylvania, set out from
Philadelphia for the purpose of allaying this dangerous commotion.

 REVIOUS to this, Sir Henry Clinton, who heard
of the mutiny, on the morning of the 3d, was
equally active in endeavouring to turn it to the advantage of the British.   He ordered a large corps
to be in readiness to march on a moment's notice,
and sent two spies by way of Amboy, and two by
way of Elizabethtown, as agents from himself to treat with the mutineers.   But two of the persons employed were actually spies on
himself, and soon disclosed his proposals to the American authorities.   The two real spies, on reaching Princeton, were seized by
the mutineers, and afterwards delivered up to General Wayne, who
had them tried and executed on the 10th.

At first the mutineers declined leaving Princeton; but finding
their demands would be substantially complied with, they marched
to Trenton on the 9th, and before the 15th the matter was so far
settled that the committee of Congress left Trenton and returned
to Philadelphia.   All who had enlisted for three years, or during
the war, were discharged; and in cases where the terms of enlistment could not be produced, the oath of the soldier was to be received as evidence on the point.   They were to receive immediate certificates for the depreciation on their pay, and their arrears were to be settled as soon as circumstances would admit.
On these terms, about one-half of the Pennsylvania troops obtained their discharge; numbers of them having, as afterwards
appeared, made false declarations concerning the terms of their
enlistment.

Washington's agency in removing this alarming danger was
felt in the advice which he gave to General Wayne to proffer his
mediation between the soldiers and Congress, and to exert himself
in obtaining a redress of grievances.   That body, in this instance,

was compelled, by the circumstances, to grant much more than what, if well timed, would have prevented this dangerous mutiny.

The success of the Pennsylvania troops, in exacting their pay by threats of violence, produced a similar spirit of insubordination in another division of the army.   On the night of the 20th of January, about one hundred and sixty of the Jersey brigade, which was quartered at Pompton, complaining of grievances similar to those of the Pennsylvania line, and hoping for equal success, rose in arms, and marched to Chatham, with the view of prevailing on some of the troops stationed there to join them.   Their number was not formidable; and General Washington, knowing that he might depend on the fidelity of the greater part of his troops, and determined at all hazards to crush this mutinous spirit, detached General Robert Howe with six hundred men against the insurgents, with orders to force them to unconditional submission, and to execute some of the most turbulent of them on the spot.   These orders were promptly obeyed, and two of the ringleaders were put to death.   This summary proceeding put an end to the mutiny, and restored the army to its usual discipline.

Sir Henry Clinton, as in the case of the Pennsylvanians, endeavoured to take advantage of the mutiny of the Jersey brigade.   He sent emissaries to negotiate with them, and detached General Robertson with three thousand men to Staten Island, to be in readiness to support them, if they should accede to his proposals; but the mutiny, by Washington's promptness, was so speedily crushed, that Clinton's emissaries had no time to act.

These commotions among the soldiers awakened Congress to a sense of the public danger, and rendered it more attentive to the wants of the army than it had hitherto been.   It raised three months' pay in specie; and even that small sum was gratefully received by the troops, who considered it a token that the civil authorities were not entirely regardless of their sufferings, or indifferent to their comfort.   But, in attempting to escape one danger, Congress felt itself exposed to another scarcely less alarming.   The means used to soothe the army irritated the people.   The troops were scantily supplied; and yet the inhabitants murmured loudly at the contributions levied upon them; and the dissatisfaction which pervaded the mass of the community was almost as alarming as the mutinous spirit of the army.*

* Western World.

REVIOUS to these disturbances, the United States had been held together by a very slender bond. The powers of Congress were limited; and it was not to be expected that thirteen independent states, each jealous of its liberty, power, and property, would promptly, harmoniously, and vigorously combine their strength during a protracted, expensive, and bloody struggle. But though every man of discernment was sensible of the propriety of increasing the powers of Congress, and consequently of leaving less in the hands of the state legislatures; yet the several states, having once been in the possession of power, felt no inclination to relinquish any part of their authority, how incompetent soever they might be to the advantageous exercise of it. Thus the concentration of a due degree of power in the hands of Congress was a measure that could not be easily accomplished.

The war had continued much longer than the Americans had originally anticipated; and the natural resources of the country, mismanaged by the inexperience of the government, and its ignorance of the principles of political economy, were so much exhausted, that it became apparent the war could not be carried on without a foreign loan; and France, sufficiently embarrassed with her own affairs, was the only country to which Congress could look for pecuniary aid. Accordingly, Colonel John Laurens was employed on a mission to this country, and, besides endeavouring to negotiate a loan, was instructed to press on the French monarch the importance of maintaining a naval superiority in the American seas. The valuable counsel of Washington was afforded to the envoy on this occasion, and his letter to Colonel Laurens, containing statements and arguments in support of the application, had great influence when laid before the French king and his ministry, who recommended, in granting the loan, that the money to be appropriated to the army should be placed at the disposal of General Washington.*

While the energies of America were paralyzed by the financial difficulties of Congress, the mutinous spirit of the army, and the selfishness and apathy of several of the states, the British interest in the country seemed in a prosperous condition. General Greene was maintaining a doubtful and hazardous struggle against Cornwallis, in North Carolina; and a British detachment from New

* Sparks.
2 M 2

York, under the traitor Arnold, was ravaging the state of Virginia.

The untoward condition of American affairs could not be concealed from the British ministry, who flattered themselves that they would soon compel General Washington and his feeble army to take refuge in New England, and that they would reduce all the states south of the Hudson to submission to the British crown. But exertions on the one side, and reverses on the other, which neither had anticipated, were soon to change the relative condition of the contending parties.

From the position and strength of the hostile armies opposed on the Hudson, neither could hope to gain any decisive advantage. The American force was entirely inadequate to attack New York; and Sir Henry Clinton had no prospect of being able to force the strong posts of General Washington, in the highlands. Neither party could do more than carry on a petty and desultory warfare. Hitherto the Americans had received no direct aid from the French army. Ever since its arrival, the fleet of that nation had been blockaded at Newport; and the land forces remained in a position to co-operate with the fleet, for mutual defence.

About the middle of January, the British fleet was overtaken by a storm, off the east end of Long Island, and sustained so much loss and damage as to give the French fleet a superiority on the coast. Destouches, the French admiral, was prevailed on to seize that opportunity of sending a small force, under the command of M. de Tilly, to Chesapeake Bay, to act against Arnold, who was then pillaging Virginia; but this force returned to Newport in fifteen days from its departure, without accomplishing any thing except the capture of the Romulus, a fifty gun ship, on her way from Charleston to Chesapeake Bay.

General Washington, unwilling to relinquish the attempt against Arnold, repaired to Newport; and on the 6th of March had a conference with the French commanders, at which it was agreed that the whole fleet should immediately sail to the Chesapeake, with a detachment of troops on board; but owing to unforeseen circumstances, it was the evening of the 8th before the fleet left the harbour.

Meanwhile, due notice of the expedition was sent to General Lafayette, who had just recently been detached from the main army by General Washington, to take the command in Virginia, with instructions to co-operate with the allies. From this enterprise General Washington entertained sanguine expectations of being able to apprehend Arnold; and directed Lafayette to grant him no terms which would save him from the consequences of his crimes. However, the delay in the sailing of the fleet frustrated Washington's design.

The British admiral, Arbuthnot, having repaired his damages, pursued, and on the 16th overtook the French fleet off the capes of Virginia. An indecisive engagement ensued, in which each party claimed the victory; but the object of the French expedition was defeated, and the fleet returned to Newport.

It is necessary, here, to revert to what had been passing in Virginia, in order to understand the position of affairs in that state, at the time of Lafayette's assuming the command.

Towards the end of October, 1780, General Leslie entered Chesapeake Bay, landed at Portsmouth, and began to fortify himself there with about three thousand men. But on experiencing unexpected and increasing difficulties in the Carolinas, Cornwallis directed that officer, with his detachment, to proceed to Charleston. The invasion of Virginia, however, though interrupted, was not relinquished. Sir Henry Clinton resolved to prosecute the war with vigour, in that quarter; and in the end of the year sent the infamous Arnold to Chesapeake Bay, with a detachment of sixteen hundred men. Arnold, thirsting for plunder, sailed up James River, and on the 4th of January, 1781, landed at Westover, one hundred and forty miles from the capes, and twenty-five below Richmond.

Major-general Baron Steuben, who then commanded the American forces in that part of Virginia, thought the expedition was intended to act against Petersburg, situated on the Appomattox, which falls into James River, a little above Westover. At that place a considerable quantity of stores had been collected for the use of the southern army; and those stores the baron caused his feeble body of raw troops, scarcely amounting to three hundred men, to remove to a place of greater security.

At Westover, Arnold landed with the greater part of his troops, and marched directly towards Richmond. A few regulars who were in that vicinity, and some militia, were ordered to impede his progress, but their efforts were ineffectual. Meanwhile, Baron Steuben made every exertion to remove the stores from Richmond, carrying a part of them across the river, and a part to West Ham, at the head of the rapids.

On the day after landing at Westover, Arnold entered Richmond, with little opposition. There he halted with five hundred men, and sent Lieutenant-colonel Simcoe forward with other five hundred to West Ham, where he burned and destroyed a valuable foundery, a boring mill, a powder magazine, and a considerable quantity of military stores. Colonel Simcoe returned to Richmond, where the public property and a large quantity of rum and salt belonging to individuals were destroyed. After completing the work of destruction at Richmond, Arnold returned to Westover on the 7th; and after some skirmishing, re-embarked on the 10th, sailed down the river destroying the property on his way, and on the 20th arrived at Portsmouth, where he manifested an intention of establishing a permanent post. In this expedition, Arnold, while he destroyed a large quantity of military stores and other valuable property, stated his loss at only seven men killed and twenty-three wounded.

Baron Steuben being in no condition to attack Arnold at Portsmouth, was careful to station his troops at the most convenient passes leading from that place into the country, in order to afford the inhabitants all the protection in his power. It was while Arnold lay at Portsmouth, that General Washington formed the plan of apprehending him, which failed through the backwardness of the French to engage in it.

As Arnold's force was not sufficient to make any deep and permanent impression on the powerful state of Virginia, the British commander-in-chief resolved to increase it; and for that purpose, about the middle of March, sent General Philips with two thousand chosen men from New York to Chesapeake bay. General Philips arrived at Portsmouth on the 26th; and being the superior officer, took the command of the army in Virginia.

After employing some time in completing the fortifications of Portsmouth, General Philips began offensive operations, with a force much superior to what Congress could oppose to him in that part of the country. On the 18th of April, he embarked twenty-five hundred men on board his smaller vessels, and sailed up James River, in order to destroy every thing that had escaped the ravages of Arnold. He landed at Burrel's Ferry, and marched to Williamsburgh, the former seat of government in Virginia. A small body of militia assembled there, retreated on his approach, and he entered the place without opposition. He sent part through all the lower district of that narrow tract of land, which lies between James and York rivers, who destroyed all public stores and property which fell in their way. He then re-embarked, sailed up the river to City Point, where he landed on the 24th, and next day marched

ARNOLD'S DESCENT ON VIRGINIA

to Petersburgh, where he destroyed an immense quantity of tobacco and other property, together with the vessels lying in the river.

Baron Steuben was unable to make any effectual resistance to this ruthless work of devastation. The regular troops of the state had been sent to reinforce General Greene, and the militia then in the field did not much exceed two thousand. Even although tne whole of that number could have been collected at any one point, yet with that kind of force no enterprise of importance could be undertaken. To have hazarded a battle with the militia against regular troops would only have been to insure defeat, the loss of arms, and the consequent discouragement of the country. Baron Steuben had the mortification to see the state laid waste, without being able to relieve it ; and after some slight skirmishing he retreated to Richmond.

Arnold was detached to Osbornes, a small village on the south side of James River, fifteen miles below Richmond ; while General Philips marched to Chesterfield court-house, which had been appointed the place of rendezvous for the new levies of Virginia, where he destroyed the barracks and the public stores which had not been removed. About half-way between Osbornes and Richmond, a few small armed vessels which had been collected to co-operate with the French against Portsmouth, after a slight resistance, were scuttled, and set on fire by their crews, who joined the militia and retreated.

On the 20th of April, Philips and Arnold reunited their forces near Osbornes, and marched against Manchester, a small town on the south bank of James River, opposite Richmond, where, as usual, they set fire to the warehouses, and consumed the tobacco and other property.

At this critical and disastrous period in the history of Virginia, Lafayette arrived from the northward, to take command of the military force in that state. This illustrious friend of America had already manifested such a lively zeal for the interests of the Union as secured him the entire confidence of Washington, and of the Congress. When the attempt was meditated against Arnold at Portsmouth, Washington, as we have already seen, had appointed Lafayette to command the troops to be employed in that enterprise; but, on the abandonment of the expedition by the naval force of France, he returned from Annapolis in Maryland, where he had arrived, and proceeded to the head of Elk River, at which place he received General Washington's orders to take the command of the troops in Virginia.

When Lafayette marched to the southward on the meditated enterprise against Arnold, the troops which he commanded were drawn chiefly from the northern states; and, as it was believed the expedition would be of short duration, they were ill-provided for a southern campaign, and had imbibed strong prejudices against the climate. When they understood that the duty would be more permanent than had at first been expected, numbers of them deserted. But, appealing to their honour, Lafayette at length succeeded in inspiring his troops with the resolution of braving every danger, and enduring every privation in the cause of their country. In order to encourage them, their noble commander, as careless of fortune as he was ambitious of fame, borrowed money on his own personal credit from the merchants of Baltimore to purchase shoes, linen, and other necessaries for his detachment; and the ladies of that city, with patriotic zeal, took charge of immediately making the summer clothing of the troops.

Lafayette arrived at Richmond with his detachment on the evening before General Philips entered Manchester; and, instead of attempting to pass the river in the face of that officer, the British general marched back to Bermuda Hundreds, a point of land formed by the junction of James River and the Appomattox, destroying much valuable property on his way. Embarking his army, he sailed down the river as far as Hog's Island, where the van of his fleet arrived on the 5th of May.

On the return of the British down the river, Lafayette sent small parties to follow them and watch their motions, while he established his head-quarters behind the river Chicahominy, at some distance from Richmond. On the 7th of May, General Philips received a letter from Cornwallis, informing him of his march into Virginia, and mentioning Petersburgh as the place where he expected to meet the British troops in that province. General Philips immediately returned up the river, landed one division at Brandon, while another proceeded to City Point; and on the 9th, those two divisions met at Petersburgh, where their arrival was so unexpected that they took prisoners some of Lafayette's officers, who had been sent to that place for the purpose of collecting boats to convey his troops across the river. Meanwhile General Philips was seized with fever, and was so ill on reaching Petersburgh as to be unable to give orders. The progress of his disease was rapid, and he died four days afterwards, when the command of the British troops devolved on Arnold.

It will be recollected by the reader, that, after the battle of Guilford Court-house, Cornwallis retreated to Wilmington, where he arrived on the 7th of April, 1781. There he remained eighteen days, in order to refresh his exhausted troops; and having resolved, after much deliberation, to proceed northward, on the 25th of the month he set out on his march into Virginia, a distance of three hundred miles. In his progress he met with little opposition. Colonel Tarleton, with one hundred and eighty cavalry and sixty mounted infantry, preceded the army, and dispersed any bodies of militia that were assembling to interrupt it. On the 20th of May, Cornwallis reached Petersburgh, and took the command of the British troops in Virginia. He felt his force decidedly superior to that opposed to him, and exulted in the prospect of success. Undervaluing the talents and resources of Lafayette, his young opponent, he incautiously wrote to Europe, in a letter which was intercepted, " The boy cannot escape me."

On being informed that General Philips, in returning up the river, had landed at Brandon on the southern bank, and that Cornwallis was marching northward, Lafayette perceived that a junction of their forces was intended ; and suspecting that Petersburgh was the appointed place of meeting, he endeavoured to anticipate them in the occupation of that town. But the march of General Philips was so rapid that he entered it before him, and frustrated his design. Lafayette, with his little army, consisting of one thousand continentals, two thousand militia, and sixty dragoons, took a position at Richmond, and exerted himself in removing the military stores to places of greater security.

On the 24th of May, Cornwallis left Petersburgh, crossed James River at Westover, thirty miles below Lafayette's encampment, and being joined by a reinforcement from New York, marched at the head of upwards of four thousand veterans towards Richmond. But Lafayette evacuated that town on the 27th, and retired towards the back country, inclining his march toward the north, so that he might easily form a junction with General Wayne, who was hastening to reinforce him with eight hundred men of the Pennsylvania line. Cornwallis eagerly pursued his retreating foe as far as the upper part of Hanover county; but finding it impossible to overtake Lafayette, or to prevent his junction with General Wayne, he at length altered the course of his march, and turned his attention to more attainable objects.

In his progress he destroyed much public property. That of individuals also was plundered or consumed, under pretext of cutting the sinews of war ; so that Virginia, which had long escaped

2 N

hostile ravages, now experienced its full share of the public calamity. Cornwallis took the horses from the stables of private gentlemen, formed an efficient cavalry, and mounted many of his infantry;
so that he could move considerable detachments with uncommon
rapidity.

Being thus provided with the means of rapid marches, he planned
an expedition against Charlottesville, where the General Assembly
of Virginia was then sitting, deliberating on the means necessary
for the prosecution of the war. The Assembly had been sitting
at Richmond, but on the approach of the British army had
retired to Charlottesville, which stands on the bank of the Rivanna, high up the river. At that place were some military stores;
but the British prisoners were removed from it and conducted
towards Pennsylvania.

The force under Tarleton, in the expedition against Charlottesville, consisted of one hundred and eighty cavalry and seventy
mounted infantry of the 23d regiment, and he advanced so rapidly
towards the place of his destination, that it was by mere accident
that the inhabitants of Charlottesville heard of his approach before
he entered the town, and that all the members of the Assembly of
Virginia were not made prisoners. But Mr. Janiette, a private
gentleman, observing Tarleton's march, and suspecting his design,
mounted a fleet horse, and, by following a short and unfrequented
road, reached the town two hours before the British cavalry reached
it. The greater part of the legislative Assembly escaped and re-
assembled at Staunton, beyond the Blue-Ridge; only seven of them
were made prisoners.

Tarleton destroyed all the public stores at Charlottesville; and
sent Captain McLeod, with a troop of horse, to Mr. Jefferson's
mansion, three miles farther, in order to apprehend that gentleman
and some other individuals who were understood to be there, but
with instructions to commit no depredations. Mr. Jefferson and
his friends made their escape; but McLeod punctually obeyed his
orders; and, after remaining eighteen hours in the house, left it
and all it contained uninjured; conduct as honourable as it was
rare, especially in Virginia.

Tarleton having executed his commission at Charlottesville, hastened down the Rivanna to co-operate with Colonel Simcoe, who
had been sent with a detachment of five hundred men, chiefly
infantry, in order to surprise Baron Steuben, who was then at Point
of Fork, formed by the confluence of the Rivanna and Fluvanna,
the two great branches which constitute James River. He had

upwards of five hundred raw troops and a considerable quantity of stores under his protection, and waited for the militia to assemble to the south of James River, who had been directed to assemble at the Point of Fork.

Colonel Simcoe's progress had not been so rapid as that of Tarleton; but so skilfully had he conducted his march, that though Baron Steuben had heard of Tarleton's expedition against Charlottesville, yet he had received no notice of Simcoe's approach to his own encampment; but, as a measure of precaution, he left Point of Fork and took a position on the south side of the Fluvanna, securing all the boats on the southern bank. Colonel Simcoe's detachment unexpectedly appeared, and the baron, mistaking it for the van of the British army, retreated precipitately during the night, leaving behind him part of the stores, which were next day destroyed by Colonel Simcoe. The baron did not halt until he was thirty miles from Point of Fork.

In Virginia, the British had committed fearful devastations, and had destroyed much valuable property; but Cornwallis, though at the head of a superior army, had gained no important advantage over his opponent. He had pushed Lafayette across the Rappahannock, but was unable to prevent his junction with General Wayne, which was accomplished at Racoon Ford, on the 7th of June. Lafayette, thus reinforced, immediately repassed the Rappahannock and advanced towards the British army.

In the course of these movements, Cornwallis had got completely between Lafayette and the stores of the state, which were deposited at different places, but principally at Albemarle Old Court-house, high up the Fluvanna, on the south side of the river. These stores were an object of much importance to both armies; and, early in June, the British commander, after having dispensed with the services of Arnold, and allowed him to return to New York, directed his march to Albemarle Old Court-house. Lafayette was anxious to preserve his magazines; and while the British army was more than a day's march from Albemarle Court-house, by a rapid and unsuspected movement he suddenly appeared in its vicinity. The British general easily penetrated his design, and being between him and his magazines, took a position near the road, so that he could attack nim with advantage if he attempted to advance. During the night, however, Lafayette discovered and cleared a nearer but long disused road, and passed the British army unobserved; and in the morning, Cornwallis, with surprise and mortification, saw his adversary strongly posted between him and the stores.

Perceiving that the Americans could not be attacked unless under great disadvantages, and believing their force greater than it really was, Cornwallis abandoned his enterprise, and began a retrograde movement, and, in his night marches, fell back upwards of fifty miles. On the 17th of June, he entered Richmond, but left it on the 20th, and continued his route to Williamsburgh, where the main body of his army arrived on the 25th.

The American army followed him at a cautious distance. On the 19th, Lafayette was joined by Baron Steuben, with his detachment, which increased the American army to four thousand men: of whom two thousand were regulars, but only fifteen hundred were disciplined troops. That of Cornwallis appears to have been somewhat more numerous, and consisted entirely of veterans: it was also provided with a well-mounted body of cavalry, which had spread terror and devastation over the country, and greatly intimidated the militia.

Though Lafayette kept about twenty miles behind the main body of the British army, yet its light parties hung on its rear, and skirmishes occasionally ensued. A sharp encounter happened near Williamsburgh between the advanced guard of the Americans, under Colonel Butler, and the rear-guard of the British, under Colonel Simcoe, in which both suffered considerable loss. Part of the British army marched to Colonel Simcoe's assistance, and the Americans were obliged to retreat. Although Lafayette encouraged skirmishes and partial conflicts, yet, distrusting his new levies and militia, he cautiously avoided a general battle. While the British army remained at Williamsburgh, the Americans occupied a strong encampment twenty miles from that place.

During the various movements of the troops in Virginia, property to a great amount, both public and private, was destroyed. Among other articles, two thousand hogsheads of tobacco were burned: individuals suffered severely, and the resources of the state were considerably impaired. While the army traversed the country, carrying devastation in its train, ships of war sailed up the rivers, pillaged the farms, received fugitive negroes, and in some places laid the houses in ashes. Early in the spring, a British frigate went up the Potomac to General Washington's mansion at Mount Vernon, and demanded from the steward a quantity of provisions, which was granted in order to save the property. This compliance, however, was highly displeasing to Washington, who declared it would have been more agreeable to him to have left the enemy to take what they pleased by force, even at the risk of burning his house and property.

Though the militia showed no alacrity in taking the field, and though less resistance was made to the royal arms in Virginia than had been expected from such a powerful state, yet very little inclination manifested itself among the people to support the British cause. Some loyalists in a remote part of the province were easily reduced to unconditional submission by General Morgan, whom ill health had obliged to quit the army; but who, on this occasion, put himself at the head of a few mounted riflemen to subdue the insurgents.

For some time after entering Virginia, Cornwallis entertained the most flattering hopes of success. He was at the head of an army, which no force in that province was able to resist; and he felt no doubt of succeeding against Lafayette. But that young officer eluded his most active exertions, frustrated some of his schemes, and now hung upon him with an army, which, though still inferior, was nevertheless formidable, and continually increasing in strength. But new disappointments and more mortifying events awaited the British commander. While at Williamsburgh he received a requisition from Sir Henry Clinton for part of the troops under his command: the commander-in-chief having discovered that an attack was meditated on New York, thought his garrison insufficient for the defence of that place, and wished part of the troops in Virginia to be sent to his assistance. Cornwallis prepared to comply with Sir Henry Clinton's requisition; and believing that with the remaining troops he would be unable to maintain himself at Williamsburgh, he resolved to pass James River and retire to Portsmouth. On the 30th June he apprized the commander-in-chief of his resolution.

On the 4th of July the army marched from Williamsburgh, and encamped on the bank of James River, so as to cover a ford leading into the island of Jamestown. On the 5th and 6th, the baggage and some of the troops passed the ford; but the main body of the army kept its ground.

On the morning of the 5th of July, Lafayette left his encampment, crossed the Chicahominy, pushed his light troops near the British position, and advanced with the continentals to make an attempt on the British rear, after their main body had passed the river. On the afternoon of the 6th, Lafayette was told that the main body of the British army had crossed the ford, and that a rear guard only remained behind; an opinion which the British general

54   2 N 2

artfully encouraged by the judicious manner in which he posted
his troops. General Wayne, imagining that he had to fight a rear-
guard only, advanced boldly upon the enemy; but in a short time
he unexpectedly found himself in presence of the British army
drawn up to receive him. Instant retreat he considered impracticable, and thought the boldest course the most safe. With eight
hundred men he made a brisk attack: and for some minutes the
conflict was sharp and bloody. But Lafayette, discovering the
mistake, ordered a retreat, which was made with precipitation,
leaving two pieces of cannon in the hands of the British. The
Americans retired behind a morass, and it being nearly dark, Cornwallis, suspecting an ambuscade, ordered no pursuit. In this
encounter the Americans had one hundred and eighteen men, including ten officers, killed, wounded, or taken prisoners. The loss
of the British was not so great, amounting to five officers and about
seventy privates. In the course of the night the British passed into
the island; whence they soon afterwards proceeded to Portsmouth.

The troops required by the British commander-in-chief were
embarked; but, before they sailed, despatches arrived countermanding the order. At the same time the commander-in-chief
deprecated the thought of abandoning the Chesapeake, stating, that
as soon as the season for military operations in that quarter returned,
he would probably send thither all the disposable troops under his
command, and recommending the establishment of a defensive post
for the reception of ships of the line, either at York, or the river of
that name, or at Point Comfort in Hampton Road. Cornwallis
ordered, accordingly, Point Comfort and York to be surveyed by
engineers and officers of the navy, from whose report it appeared
that works constructed on Old Point Comfort could neither defend
the entrance into Hampton Road, nor afford protection to ships
lying there; and as it was admitted that Portsmouth was not a
station of the description required, Cornwallis thought his instructions left him no alternative but to fortify York and Gloucester, as
the only points capable of affording the requisite protection to ships
of the line. Measures were accordingly taken for seizing and fortifying those places, and for evacuating Portsmouth. Part of the
army proceeded, in boats and transports, up the Chesapeake and
York river, and on the 1st of August, took possession of Yorktown
and Gloucester Point, the former on the south, the latter on the north
side of the river. The evacuation of Portsmouth was completed;
and on the 22d the British force in Virginia concentrated at York
and Gloucester.

Here we shall leave Cornwallis and his army diligently fortifying themselves, and turn, for a while, our attention to the northward.

In the early part of the year, the affairs of Congress wore a gloomy and alarming aspect: the finances were exhausted, the troops mutinous, the army much diminished in numbers, and the soldiers who remained with the standards of their country were in a state of utter destitution. The necessity of a foreign loan and of European auxiliaries was obvious; and an early application for both had been made to France. But however well disposed that power was to grant the desired assistance, compliance was no easy matter; for the treasury had enough to do in answering the national demands necessarily made on it, and was little able to supply foreign wants. As a signal proof of friendship, however, the French monarch gave his allies a donation of six millions of livres, and promised to support them with a strong naval and military armament.

Early in May, the Count de Barras, who had been appointed to the command of the French fleet on the American coast, arrived at Boston, accompanied by the Viscount de Rochambeau, commander of the land forces. An interview between General Washington and the French commanders was immediately appointed to be held at Wethersfield, three miles from Hartford, on the 21st, but some movements of the British fleet made De Barras repair to Newport, while the two generals met at the appointed place, and agreed on the plan of the campaign. It was resolved to unite the French and American armies on the Hudson, and to commence vigorous operations against New York. The regular army at that station was estimated at only forty-five hundred men; and though Sir Henry Clinton might be able to reinforce it with five thousand or six thousand militia, yet it was believed he could not maintain the post without recalling a considerable part of the troops from the southward, and enfeebling the operations of the British in that quarter; in which case it was resolved to make a vigorous attack on the point which promised the best prospect of success.

General Washington immediately required the states of New England to have six thousand militia in readiness to march, whenever they might be called for; and sent an account of the conference at Wethersfield to Congress. His despatch was intercepted in the Jerseys and carried to Sir Henry Clinton; who, alarmed by the plan which it disclosed, made the requisition, already mentioned, of part of the troops under Cornwallis, and took diligent precaution for maintaining his post against the meditated attack.

When the American troops left their winter quarters in the month of June, and encamped at Peekskill, the army under Washington did not amount to five thousand men. This force was so much inferior to what had been contemplated when the plan of operations was agreed on at Wethersfield, that it became doubtful whether it would be expedient to adhere to that plan. But the deficiency of the American force was in some measure compensated by the arrival at Boston of a reinforcement of fifteen hundred men to the army under Count Rochambeau.

The hope of terminating the war in the course of the campaign, encouraged the states to make some exertions. Small as was their military force, it was difficult to find subsistence for their troops; and, even after the army had taken the field, there was reason to apprehend that it would be obliged to abandon the objects of the campaign for want of provisions. In that critical juncture of American affairs, when the government was without money and without credit, the finances of the Union were intrusted to Mr. Robert Morris, a member of Congress from Pennsylvania, a man of considerable capital, and of much sagacity and mercantile enterprise. He extensively pledged his personal credit for articles of the first necessity to the army; and by an honourable fulfilment of his engagements, did much to restore public credit and confidence. It was owing mainly to his exertions that the active and decisive operations of the campaign were not greatly impeded, or entirely defeated, by want of subsistence to the army, and of the means of transporting military stores.

It was Mr. Morris who planned the national bank of $400,000. Its notes were to be received as cash into the treasury of the several states, and also as an equivalent for the necessaries which the states were bound to provide for the army. In this way, and by a liberal and judicious application of his own resources, an individual afforded the supplies which government was unable to furnish.

The French troops marched from Newport and Boston towards the Hudson. Both in quarters and on the route their behaviour was exemplary, and gained the respect and good will of the inhabitants. Towards the end of June, General Washington put his army in motion; and learning that a royal detachment had passed into the Jerseys, he formed a plan to surprise the British posts on the north end of York Island; but it did not succeed; and General Lincoln, who commanded the Americans, being attacked by a strong British party, a sharp conflict ensued. General Washington marched with his main body to support his detachment, but on his advance the British retired into their works at Kingsbridge.

Having failed in his design of surprising the British posts, General Washington withdrew to Valentine's Hill, and afterwards to Dobbs's Ferry. While encamped there, on the 6th of July, the van of the long-expected French reinforcements was seen winding down the neighbouring heights. The arrival of these friendly strangers elevated the minds of the Americans, who received them with sincere congratulations. General Washington laboured by personal attentions to conciliate the good will of his allies, and used all the means in his power to prevent those mutual jealousies and irritations which frequently prevail between troops of different nations, serving in the same army. An attack on New York was still meditated, and every exertion made to prepare for its execution ; but with the determination, if it should prove impracticable, vigorously to prosecute some more attainable object.

On the evening of the 21st of July, the greater part of the American, and part of the French troops left their encampment ; and marching rapidly during the night, appeared in order of battle before the British works at Kingsbridge, at four the next morning. Generals Washington and Rochambeau, with the general officers and engineers, viewed the British lines, in their whole extent, from right to left, and the same was done again next morning. But on the afternoon of the 23d they returned to their former encampment, without having made any attempt on the British works.

At that time the new levies arrived slowly in the American camp ; and many of those who were sent were mere boys, utterly unfit for active service. The several states discovered much backwardness in complying with the requisitions of Congress, so that there was reason to apprehend that the number of troops necessary for besieging New York could not be procured. This made General Washington turn his thoughts more seriously to the southward than he had hitherto done : but all his movements confirmed Sir Henry Clinton in the belief that an attack on New York was in contemplation. As the British commander-in-chief, however, at that time, received about three thousand troops from Europe, ne thought himself able to defend his post, without withdrawing any part of the force from Virginia. Therefore he countermanded the requisition which he had before sent to Cornwallis for part of the troops under his command. The troops were embarked before the arrival of the counter order; and of their embarkation Lafayette sent notice to General Washington. On the reception of new instructions, however, as before stated, they were re-landed, and remained in Virginia.

No great operation could be undertaken against the British armies, so long as their navy had the undisputed command of the coast and of the great navigable rivers. The Americans had accordingly made an earnest application to the court of France for such a fleet as might be capable of keeping in check the British navy in those seas, and of affording effectual assistance to the land forces. That application was not unsuccessful, and, towards the middle of August, the agreeable information was received of the approach of a powerful French fleet to the American coast.

Early in March, the Count de Grasse sailed from Brest with twenty-five ships of the line, five of which were destined for the East, and twenty for the West Indies. After an indecisive encounter in the Straits of St. Lucie with Sir Samuel Hood, whom Sir George Rodney, the British admiral in the West Indies, had detached to intercept him, Count de Grasse formed a junction with the French vessels on that station, and had a fleet superior to that of the British in the West Indies. De Grasse gave the Americans notice that he would visit their coast in the month of August, and take his station in Chesapeake Bay; but that his continuance there could only be of short duration. This despatch at once determined General Washington's resolution with respect to the main point of attack; and as it was necessary that the projected operation should be accomplished within a very limited time, prompt decision and indefatigable exertion were indispensable. Though it was now finally resolved that Virginia should be the scene of action, yet it was prudent to conceal to the last moment this determination from Sir Henry Clinton, and still to maintain the appearance of threatening New York.

The defence of the strong posts on the Hudson River was intrusted to General Heath, who was instructed to protect the adjacent country as far as he was able; and for that purpose a respectable force was put under his command. Every preparation of which circumstances admitted was made to facilitate the march to the southward. General Washington was to take the command of the expedition, and to employ in it all the French troops, and a strong detachment of the American army.

On the 19th of August, a considerable force was ordered to

cross the Hudson, at Dobbs's Ferry, and take a position between Springfield and Chatham, where they were directed to cover some bake-houses, which, it was rumoured, were to be immediately constructed in the vicinity of those places, in order to encourage the belief that there the troops intended to establish a permanent post. On the 20th and 21st, the main body of the Americans passed the river at King's Ferry : but the French made a longer circuit, and did not complete the passage until the 25th. Desirous of concealing his object as long as possible, General Washington continued his march some time in such a direction as still to keep up the appearance of threatening New York. When concealment was no longer practicable, he marched southward with the utmost celerity. His movements had been of such a doubtful nature, that Sir Henry Clinton, it is said, was not convinced of his real destination till he crossed the Delaware.

Great exertions had been made to procure funds for putting the army in motion : but, after exhausting every other means, General Washington was obliged to have recourse to Count Rochambeau for a supply of cash, which he received.

On the 30th of August, at three in the afternoon, the combined American and French armies entered Philadelphia, where they were received with ringing of bells, firing of guns, bonfires, illuminations at night, and every demonstration of joy. Meanwhile, Count de Grasse, with three thousand troops on board, sailed from Cape Francois with a valuable fleet of merchantmen, which he conducted out of danger, and then steered for Chesapeake Bay, with twenty-eight sail of the line and several frigates.

Towards the end of August, he cast anchor just within the capes, extending across from Cape Henry to the middle ground. There an officer from Lafayette waited on the count, and gave him full information concerning the state of affairs in Virginia, and the intended plan of operations against the British army in that state.

Cornwallis was diligently fortifying himself at York and Gloucester. Lafayette was in a position on James River to prevent his escape into North Carolina, and the combined army was hastening southward to attack him. In order to co-operate against Cornwallis, De Grasse detached four ships of the line and some frigates to block up the entrance to York River, and to carry the land forces, which he had brought with him under St. Simon, to Lafayette's camp. The rest of his fleet remained at the entrance of the bay.

Sir George Rodney, who commanded the British fleet in the West Indies, was not ignorant that the count intended to sail for

America; but, knowing that the merchant vessels which he conveyed from Cape Francois were loaded with valuable cargoes, the British admiral believed that he would send the greater part of his fleet along with them to Europe, and would visit the American coast with a small squadron only. Accordingly, Sir George Rodney detached Sir Samuel Hood, with fourteen sail of the line to America, as a sufficient force to counteract the operations of the French in that quarter. Admiral Hood reached the capes of Virginia on the 25th of August, a few days before De Grasse entered the bay: and, finding no enemy there, sailed for Sandy Hook, where he arrived on the 28th of August.

Admiral Graves, who had succeeded Admiral Arbuthnot in the command of the British fleet on the American station, was then lying at New York with seven sail of the line; but two of his ships had been damaged in a cruise near Boston, and were under repair. At the same time that Admiral Hood gave information of the expected arrival of De Grasse on the American coast, notice was received of the sailing of De Barras with his fleet from Newport. Admiral Graves, therefore, without waiting for his two ships which were under repair, put to sea on the 31st of August, with nineteen sail of the line, and steered to the southward.

On reaching the capes of the Chesapeake, early on the morning of the 5th of September, he discovered the French fleet, consisting of twenty-four ships of the line, lying at anchor at the entrance of the bay. Neither admiral had any previous knowledge of the vicinity of the other till the fleets were actually seen. The British stretched into the bay, and as soon as De Grasse ascertained their hostile character, he ordered his ships to slip their cables, form the line as they could come up, without regard to their specified stations, and put to sea. The British fleet entering the bay, and the French fleet leaving it, they were necessarily sailing in different directions; but Admiral Graves put his ships on the same tack as the French; and about four in the afternoon, a battle began between the van and centre of the fleets, which continued till night. Both sustained considerable damage.

The fleets continued in sight of each other for five days; but De Grasse's object was not to fight unless to cover Chesapeake Bay; and Admiral Graves, owing to the inferiority of his force and the crippled state of several of his ships, was unable to compel him to renew the engagement.

On the 10th, De Grasse bore away for the Chesapeake, and anchored within the capes next day, when he had the satisfaction to find that Admiral de Barras with his fleet from Newport and four-teen transports, laden with heavy artillery and other military stores for carrying on a siege, had safely arrived during his absence.

That officer sailed from Newport on the 25th of August, and making a long circuit to avoid the British, entered the bay, while the contending fleets were at sea. Admiral Graves followed the French fleet to the Chesapeake; but on arriving there, he found the entrance guarded by a force with which he was unable to contend. He then sailed for New York, and left De Grasse in the undisputed possession of the bay.

While these naval operations were going on, the land forces were not less actively employed in the prosecution of their respective purposes. The immediate aim of the one party was to overwhelm Cornwallis and his army at Yorktown, and that of the other to res-cue him from their grasp. As soon as Sir Henry Clinton was con-vinced of General Washington's intention of proceeding to the southward, with a view to bring him back, he employed Arnold, with a sufficient naval and military force, on an expedition against New London. Arnold passed from Long Island, and on the fore-noon of the 6th of September landed his troops on both sides of the harbour; those on the New London side being under his own immediate orders, and those on the Groton side commanded by Lieutenant-colonel Eyre. As the works at New London were very imperfect, no vigorous resistance was made, and the place was taken possession of with little loss. But Fort Griswold, on the Groton side, was in a more finished state, and the small garrison made a desperate defence. The British entered the fort at the point of the bayonet; when, though opposition had ceased, a mur-derous carnage ensued. Few Americans had fallen before the British entered the works; but eighty-five were killed, sixty wounded, most of them mortally, and the remainder, seventy in number, were made prisoners. The loss of the British was consi-derable. A great quantity of valuable property was destroyed and the town much injured.

The loss sustained by the Americans at New London was great; but that predatory excursion had no effect in diverting General Washington from his purpose, or in retarding his march southward. From Philadelphia the allied armies pursued their route, partly to the head of Elk River, which falls into the northern extremity of Chesapeake Bay, and partly to Baltimore, at which places they embarked on board transports furnished by the French fleet, and the last division of them landed at Williamsburg, on the 25th of

September. General Washington, Rochambeau, and their attendants, proceeded to the same place by land, and reached it ten days
before the troops. Virginia had suffered extremely in the course
of the campaign; the inhabitants were clamorous for the appearance of the commander-in-chief in his native state, and hailed his
arrival with acclamations of joy.

Generals Washington and Rochambeau immediately repaired on
board De Grasse's ship, in order to concert a joint plan of operations
against Cornwallis. De Grasse, convinced that every exertion
would be made to relieve his lordship, and being told that Admiral
Digby had arrived at New York with a reinforcement of six ships
of the line, expected to be attacked by a force little inferior to his
own; and deeming the station which he then occupied unfavourable to a naval engagement, he was strongly inclined to leave the
bay, and to meet the enemy in the open sea.

General Washington, fully aware of all the casualties which might
occur to prevent his return, and to defeat the previous arrangements,
used every argument to dissuade the French admiral from his purpose, and prevailed with him to remain in the bay.

As De Grasse could continue only a short time on that station,
every exertion was made to proceed against Cornwallis at Yorktown, a small village on the southern bank of York River, in
which ships of the line can ride with perfect safety. A long peninsular tract of land, only eight miles broad, lies between James
and York rivers. Opposite Yorktown is Gloucester Point, which
projects considerably into the river, the breadth of which at that
place does not exceed a mile. Cornwallis had taken possession
of both these places, and diligently fortified them. The communication between them was commanded by his batteries, and by
some ships of war which lay in the river under cover of his guns.
The main body of his army was encamped near Yorktown, beyond
some outer redoubts and field-works, calculated to retard the approach of an enemy. Colonel Tarleton, with six hundred or seven
hundred men, occupied Gloucester Point.

The combined army, amounting to upwards of eleven thousand
men, exclusive of the Virginia militia, was assembled in the vicinity of Williamsburgh; and, on the morning of the 28th of September, marched by different routes towards Yorktown. About
mid-day, the heads of the columns reached the ground assigned
them; and, after driving in the outposts and some cavalry,
encamped for the night. The next day was employed in viewing
the British works, and in arranging the plan of attack. At the

YORKTOWN BATTLE GROUND

same time that the combined army encamped before Yorktown, the French fleet anchored at the mouth of the river, and completely prevented the British from escaping by water, as well as from receiving supplies or reinforcements in that way. The legion of Lauzun and a brigade of militia, amounting to upwards of four thousand men, commanded by the French general De Choisié, were sent across the river to watch Gloucester Point, and to enclose the British on that side.

On the 30th, Yorktown was invested. The French troops formed the left wing of the combined army, extending from the river above the town to a morass in front of it; the Americans composed the right wing, and occupied the ground between the morass and the river below the town. Till the 6th of October, the besieging army was assiduously employed in disembarking its heavy artillery and military stores, and in conveying them to camp from the landing place in James River, a distance of six miles.

On the night of the 6th, the first parallel was begun, six hundred yards from the British works. The night was dark, rainy, and well adapted for such a service; and in the course of it the besiegers did not lose a man. Their operations seem not to have been suspected by the besieged till daylight disclosed them in the morning, when the trenches were so far advanced as in a good measure to cover the workmen from the fire of the garrison. By the afternoon of the 9th, the batteries were completed, notwithstanding the most strenuous opposition from the besieged; and immediately opened on the town. From that time an incessant cannonade was kept up; and the continual discharge of shot and shells from twenty-four and eighteen-pounders, and ten-inch mortars, damaged the unfinished works on the left of the town, silenced the guns mounted on them, and occasioned a considerable loss of men. Some of the shot and shells from the batteries passed over the town, reached the shipping in the harbour, and set on fire the Charon of forty-four guns, and three large transports, which were entirely consumed.*

The succeeding operations of the siege are very graphically described by Dr. Thatcher, one of the surgeons of the army, in the following extract from his Military Journal:—

"The duty of our troops has been for several days extremely severe; our regiment labours in the trenches every other day and night, where I find it difficult to avoid suffering by the cold, having no other covering than a single blanket in an open field. We

* Western World.

erected a battery last night in front of our first parallel, without any
annoyance from the enemy. Two or three of our batteries being
now prepared to open on the town, his excellency General
Washington put the match to the first gun, and a furious discharge
of cannon and mortars immediately followed, and Earl Cornwallis
has received his first salutation.

"From the 10th to the 15th, a tremendous and incessant firing
from the American and French batteries is kept up, and the enemy
return the fire, but with little effect. A red-hot shell from the
French battery set fire to the Charon, a British 44 gun ship, and
two or three smaller vessels at anchor in the river, which were consumed in the night. From the bank of the river, I had a fine view
of this splendid conflagration. The ships were enwrapped in a
torrent of fire, which spreading with vivid brightness among the
combustible rigging, and running with amazing rapidity to the
tops of the several masts, while all around was thunder and lightning from our numerous cannon and mortars, and in the darkness
of the night, presented one of the most sublime and magnificent
spectacles which can be imagined. Some of our shells, overreach-
ing the town, are seen to fall into the river, and bursting, throw up
columns of water like the spoutings of the monsters of the deep.
We have now made further approaches to the town, by throwing up
a second parallel line and batteries within about three hundred
yards; this was effected in the night, and at daylight the enemy
were roused to the greatest exertions, the engines of war have
raged with redoubled fury and destruction on both sides, no cessation day or night. The French had two officers wounded, and
fifteen men killed or wounded, and among the Americans two or
three were wounded. I assisted in amputating a man's thigh.
The siege is daily becoming more and more formidable and alarming, and his lordship must view his situation as extremely critical,
if not desperate. Being in the trenches every other day and night,
I have a fine opportunity of witnessing the sublime and stupendous
scene which is continually exhibiting. The bomb-shells from the
besiegers and the besieged are incessantly crossing each other's
path in the air. They are clearly visible in the form of a black
ball in the day; but in the night, they appear like fiery meteors
with blazing tails, most beautifully brilliant, ascending majesti-
cally from the mortar to a certain altitude, and gradually descending to the spot where they are destined to execute their work of
destruction. It is astonishing with what accuracy an experienced
gunner will make his calculations, that a shell shall fall within a

few feet of a given point, and burst at the precise time, though at a great distance. When a shell falls, it whirls round, burrows, and excavates the earth to a considerable extent, and bursting, makes dreadful havoc around.

"I have more than once witnessed fragments of the mangled bodies and limbs of the British soldiers thrown into the air by the bursting of our shells; and by one from the enemy, Captain White, of the seventh Massachusetts regiment, and one soldier were killed, and another wounded near where I was standing. About twelve or fourteen men have been killed or wounded within twenty-four hours; I attended at the hospital, amputated a man's arm, and assisted in dressing a number of wounds. The enemy having two redoubts about three hundred yards in front of their principal works, enfiladed our entrenchment and impeded our approaches; it was resolved to take possession of them both by assault. The one on the left of the British garrison, bordering on the banks of the river, was assigned to our brigade of light infantry, under the command of the Marquis de Lafayette. The advanced corps was led on by the intrepid Colonel Hamilton, who had commanded a regiment of light infantry during the campaign, and assisted by Colonel Gimat. The assault commenced at eight o'clock in the evening, and the assailants bravely entered the fort with the point of the bayonet without firing a single gun. We suffered the loss of eight men killed, and about thirty wounded, among whom Colonel Gimat received a slight wound in his foot, and Major Gibbs, of his excellency's guard, and two other officers, were slightly wounded. Major Campbell, who commanded in the fort, was wounded and taken prisoner, with about thirty soldiers; the remainder made their escape. I was desired to visit the wounded in the fort, even before their balls had ceased whistling about my ears, and saw a sergeant and eight men dead in the ditch. A captain of our infantry, belonging to New Hampshire, threatened to take the life of Major Campbell to avenge the death of his favourite, Colonel Scammel; but Colonel Hamilton interposed, and not a man was killed after he had ceased to resist. During the assault, the British kept up an incessant firing of cannon and musketry from their whole line. -

" His excellency General Washington, Generals Lincoln and Knox, with their aids, having dismounted, were standing in an exposed situation, waiting the result. Colonel Cobb, one of General Washington's aids, solicitous for his safety, said to his excellency, 'Sir, you are too much exposed here, had you not better

step a little back?' 'Colonel Cobb,' replied his excellency.
'if you are afraid, you have liberty to step back.' The other
redoubt, on the right of the British lines, was assaulted at the
same time by a detachment of the French, commanded by the gallant Baron de Viominel. Such was the ardour displayed by the
assailants, that all resistance was soon overcome, though at the
expense of nearly one hundred men killed and wounded. Of the
defenders of the redoubt, eighteen were killed, and one captain
and two subaltern officers, and forty-two rank and file, captured.
Our second parallel line was immediately connected with the two
redoubts now taken from the enemy, and some new batteries were
thrown up in front of our second parallel line, with a covert way
and angling work, approaching to less than three hundred yards
of their principal forts. These will soon be mantled with cannon
and mortars, and when their horrid thundering commences, it
must convince his lordship, that his post is not invincible, and
that submission must soon be his only alternative. Our artillery-
men, by the exactness of their aim, make every discharge take
effect, so that many of the enemy's guns are entirely silenced,
and their works are almost in ruins.

   "16th.—A party of the enemy, consisting of about four hundred
men, commanded by Colonel Abercrombie, about four in the
morning, made a vigorous sortie against two unfinished redoubts
occupied by the French. They spiked up seven or eight pieces
of cannon, and killed several soldiers; but the French advanced
and drove them from the redoubts, leaving several killed and
wounded. Our New England troops here have become very
sickly; the prevalent diseases are intermittent and remittent fevers,
which are very prevalent in the climate during the autumnal
months.

   "17th.—The whole of our works are now mounted with cannon and mortars; not less than one hundred pieces of heavy ordnance have been in continual operation during the last twenty-four
hours.

   "The whole peninsula trembles under the incessant thunder-
ings of our infernal machines; we have levelled some of their
works in ruins, and silenced their guns; they have almost ceased
firing.

   "We are so near as to have a distinct view of the dreadful
havoc and destruction of their works, and even see the men in
their lines torn to pieces by the bursting of the shells. But the
scene is drawing to a close. Lord Cornwallis, realizing, at length,

the extreme hazard of his deplorable situation, and finding it in vain any longer to resist, has, this forenoon, come to the humiliating expedient of sending out a flag, requesting a cessation of hostilities for twenty-four hours, that commissioners may be appointed to prepare and adjust the terms of capitulation. Two or three flags passed in the course of the day, and General Washington consented to a cessation of hostilities for two hours only, that his lordship may suggest his proposals for a treaty, which being in part accepted, a suspension of hostilities will be continued until to-morrow.

" 18th.—It is now ascertained that Lord Cornwallis, to avoid the necessity of a surrender, had determined on the bold attempt to make his escape in the night of the 16th, with a part of his army, into the country. His plan was to leave sick and baggage behind, and to cross with his effective force over to Gloucester Point, there to destroy the French legion and other troops, and to mount his infantry on their horses, and such others as might be procured, and push their way to New York by land. A more preposterous and desperate attempt can scarcely be imagined. Boats were secretly prepared, arrangements made, and a large proportion of his troops actually embarked, and landed on Gloucester Point, when, from a moderate and calm evening, a most violent storm of wind and rain ensued. The boats with the remaining troops were all driven down the river, and it was not till the next day that his troops could be returned to the garrison at York. At an early hour this forenoon, General Washington communicated to Lord Cornwallis the general basis of the terms of capitulation which he deemed admissible, and allowed two hours for his reply. Commissioners were soon after appointed to prepare the particular terms of agreement. The gentlemen appointed by General Washington are Colonel Laurens, one of his aids-de-camp, and Viscount de Noailles, of the French army. They have this day held an interview with the British officers on the part of Lord Cornwallis ; the terms of capitulation are settled ; and being confirmed by the commanders of both armies, the royal troops are to march out to-morrow and surrender their arms. It is a circumstance deserving of remark, that Colonel Laurens, who is stipulating for the surrender of a British nobleman, at the head of a royal army, is the son of Mr. Henry Laurens, our ambassador to Holland, who, being captured on his voyage, is now in close confinement in the Tower of London."

Cornwallis, on the 19th of October, surrendered the posts of

Yorktown and Gloucester Point to the combined armies of America and France, on condition that his troops should receive the same honours of war which had been granted to the garrison of Charleston, when it surrendered to Sir Henry Clinton. The army, artillery, arms, accoutrements, military chest, and public stores of every description, were surrendered to Washington; the ships in the harbour, and the seamen, to Count de Grasse.

Cornwallis wished to obtain permission for his European troops to return home, on condition of not serving against America, France, or their allies, during the war, but this was refused; and it was agreed that they should remain prisoners of war in Virginia, Maryland, and Pennsylvania, accompanied by a due proportion of officers, for their protection and government. The British general was also desirous of securing from punishment such Americans as had joined the royal standard; but this was refused, on the plea that it was a point which belonged to the civil authority, and on which the military power was not competent to decide. But the end was gained in an indirect way; for Cornwallis was permitted to send the Bonetta sloop of war, unsearched, to New York, with despatches to the commander-in-chief, and to put on board as many soldiers as he thought proper to be accounted for in any subsequent exchange. This was understood to be a tacit permission to send off the most obnoxious of the Americans, which was accordingly done.

The officers and soldiers were allowed to retain their private property. Such officers as were not required to remain with the troops, were permitted to return to Europe, or to reside in any part of America not in possession of British troops. A considerable number of negro slaves had fled from their masters, and gone over to the royal army: these the Americans resolved to recover; but deeming it indecorous to demand the restitution of slaves, while they themselves were fighting for liberty, they expressed their claim in general language, and stipulated that any property obviously belonging to the inhabitants of the states should be subject to be reclaimed. The garrison marched out of the town with colours cased, and with the drums beating a British or German march. General Lincoln was appointed to receive the surrender, in precisely the same way in which his own had been received at Charleston. Exclusive of seamen, nearly seven thousand persons surrendered, about four thousand of whom were fit for duty. During the siege, the garrison lost, in killed, wounded, and missing, five hundred and fifty-two men.

SURRENDER OF CORNWALLIS.

By the surrender of the posts of Yorktown and Gloucester Point, the Americans gained possession of a large train of artillery, consisting of seventy-five brass, and sixty-nine iron cannon, howitzers and mortars, with a considerable quantity of arms, ammunition, military stores, and provisions. One frigate, two ships, of twenty guns each, a number of transports, and other vessels, and fifteen hundred and one seamen, surrendered to Count de Grasse, his most Christian majesty's admiral. The combined army at Yorktown may be estimated at sixteen thousand men ; consisting of seven thousand French, five thousand five hundred continentals, and three thousand five hundred militia. Their loss during the siege amounted to about three hundred killed and wounded.

General Washington felt all the importance of the conquest which he had achieved. His troops had displayed indefatigable industry, joined with much bravery ; and, in general orders of the 20th, he acknowledged their merits, thanking all the officers and men for their services. The engineers and artillery-men had particularly distinguished themselves, and were mentioned in terms of high commendation. The general offered his best acknowledgments to Count de Rochambeau and his officers and men ; the important co-operation of Count de Grasse was also duly appreciated. The capture of Cornwallis and his army raised the shout of triumph and joy throughout America, particularly in Virginia : it was like the exultation of a pastoral people over the death of a lion which had cruelly ravaged their flocks, and spread terror through their dwellings.

The attack on Cornwallis was conceived in the true spirit of military enterprise ; but a concurrence of many favourable circumstances was necessary in order to its successful execution. It was a combined effort by sea and land, carried on by different leaders, and liable to the uncertainty of winds and waves. Superiority by sea was indispensably requisite; and the whole scheme was endangered by the appearance of Admiral Hood, at Chesapeake Bay. The arrival of De Barras, the return of De Grasse after his encounter with Admiral Hood, all combined against the British, who, after behaving like brave men, were compelled to surrender themselves prisoners of war.

Sir Henry Clinton was not ignorant of the perilous situation of Cornwallis, and was anxious to relieve him ; but the fleet had sustained considerable damage in the battle with De Grasse, and some time was necessarily spent in repairing it. During that interval

2 P

four ships of the line arrived from Europe, and two from the West Indies. At length, the commander-in-chief embarked with seven thousand of his best troops, but was unable to sail from Sandy Hook till the 19th, the day on which Cornwallis surrendered. The fleet, consisting of twenty-five ships of the line, two vessels of fifty guns each, and eight frigates, arrived off the Chesapeake on the 24th, when the commander-in-chief had the mortification to be informed of the event of the 19th.

He remained on the coast, however, till the 29th, when every doubt being removed concerning the capitulation of Cornwallis, whose relief was the sole object of the expedition, he returned to New York.

While Sir Henry Clinton continued off the Chesapeake, the French fleet, consisting of thirty-six sail of the line, satisfied with the advantage already gained, lay at anchor in the bay without making any movement whatever. The grand error of the British, in the whole of this transaction, was the not sending a larger fleet from the West Indies than that which sailed under Admiral Hood.

Washington used all his influence to detain Count de Grasse some time longer on the coast, to assist in the reduction of Charleston; but the orders of his court, ulterior projects, and his engagements with the Spaniards, put it out of the power of the French admiral to continue so long in America as was required. He, however, remained some days in the bay, in order to cover the embarkation of the troops and of the ordnance to be conveyed by water to the head of the Elk. Some brigades proceeded by land to join their companions at that place. Some cavalry marched to join General Greene; but the French troops, under Count de Rochambeau, remained in Virginia, to be in readiness to march to the south or north, as the circumstances of the next campaign might require. On the 27th, the troops of St. Simon began to embark, in order to return to the West Indies; and early in November, Count de Grasse sailed for that quarter. Washington proceeded to Philadelphia, where he arrived on the 27th of November.

The capture of Cornwallis was the most decisive event of the war. The military operations in America were afterwards desultory and languid; few in number, and unimportant in their nature; injurious or fatal, indeed, to individuals, but of little public advantage or loss to either of the contending parties.

While Washington was marching against Cornwallis, the loyalists of North Carolina, under McNeill and McDougall, made themselves masters of Hillsborough, and took a number of prisoners.

McNeill and some of his followers were killed in an encounter with the Americans. McDougall was pursued, but effected his escape with a number of prisoners to Wilmington.

Late in October, Major Ross made an incursion into the country on the Mohawk at the head of five hundred men, regulars, rangers, and Indians. Colonel Willett, with about an equal force, found him at Johnstown. An engagement ensued, when part of the Americans fled without any apparent cause; but as the rest maintained their ground, the British retreated. Willett, with a select party, pursued them; and on the morning of the 30th, overtook their rear at a ford on Canada Creek. He immediately attacked them, killed a number, and put the rest to flight. Among the slain was Walter Butler, who perpetrated the massacre at Cherry Valley. He asked quarter, but was reminded of Cherry Valley and instantly despatched.

The convention of Saratoga was a severe blow to the British arms; but the surrender of Cornwallis at Yorktown was still more decisive. It produced a great change in America, and gave a new and more cheering aspect to the affairs of the Union. In the early part of the year, the cause of the States was in a drooping condition, and American freedom seemed verging to ruin. Congress was surrounded with embarrassments, and victory had fled from their standards. The success of Morgan at the Cowpens, and the exertions of Greene, dissipated the gloom in the south; but in the middle and northern provinces nothing had occurred to awaken hope and stimulate exertion. The capture, therefore, of Cornwallis and his army, which was achieved by a remarkable coincidence of good conduct and fortunate circumstances, altered the face of things. Congress, the state governments, and all classes of people, exulted with joy. A brighter sun shone on their heads, elevated their hopes, and invigorated their exertions. The clamours of the discontented were silenced, the hearts of the desponding re-animated, and the wavering confirmed in their attachment to the Union. A new impulse was given to the public mind; but, above all, the ray of peace, which seemed now to burst through the gloom of war, was grateful to their souls.

If the effects of the surrender at Yorktown were great in America, they were not less so in Europe. The government and people of Britain entertained the most sanguine hopes from the operations of the army in Virginia. The expense of the war was heavy, and every year increasing. The people murmured under the load; but were encouraged to bear with patience in the hope of being soon relieved, and ultimately reimbursed by the exclusive trade of the

subjugated provinces. Many flattered themselves that the campaign in Virginia would annihilate the power of Congress, and put
an end to the contest.

In the midst of these fond anticipations, the news of the surrender at Yorktown arrived, and struck both the ministry and people
with amazement and dismay. The blow was equally severe and
unexpected. It laid their towering hopes in the dust, and filled
them with painful apprehensions.

Parliament met on the 27th of November; and after a protracted
struggle in the House of Commons, on the 27th of February, the
opposition carried an address against the prolongation of the war
in America. Previous to this, Mr. Henry Laurens, the American
ambassador to Holland, who had been captured by the British and
confined in the Tower of London, was released.

LEE.

GENERAL GREENE.

CHAPTER XX.

Close of the War.

THE surrender of Cornwallis, although it was the event which ultimately decided the fate of the war, was not so considered at the time. Washington fully expected another campaign, and accordingly urged upon Congress the necessary preparations for rendering it an active and decisive one. The military establishment was, therefore, kept up; the states were called upon to complete their quotas of troops, money and supplies were voted, and Washington was directed to address circular letters to the governors of all the states, calling for money and troops, and reporting the actual condition of the army.

After the glorious victory at Yorktown, Lafayette, believing the favourable termination of the war to be certain, obtained permission from Congress to revisit France. He bore to his native country ample testimonials of his services from Congress, and a letter to

57   2 P 2

the king of France, commending him warmly to the favour of his sovereign.

On returning to the camp at Newburg in April, General Washington became acquainted with one of those painful incidents which result from the infuriated passions engendered by civil commotions. It was reported that on the 24th of March, Captain Huddy, who commanded the troops in a block-house in Monmouth county, New Jersey, was attacked, overpowered, and made prisoner, by a party of loyalists from New York. In a few days, he was taken out of the city by a party of refugees, led by Captain Lippincot, and hanged, with a label on his breast, declaring that he was put to death in retaliation for some of their brethren who had suffered a similar fate. Washington took up the matter seriously; submitted it to his officers, laid it before Congress, and wrote to the British general, demanding the surrender of Captain Lippincot, and threatening retaliation in case of refusal. This demand not being complied with, Washington ordered a British prisoner, of equal rank with Huddy, to be chosen by lot and sent to Philadelphia, that he might suffer as a retaliatory victim.

The lot fell on Captain Asgill, an English youth, of only nineteen years of age, and respectably connected. Great interest was made to save the life of this young gentleman; he was ultimately set free, but was long kept in a state of painful suspense.

During winter, the states laboured to prepare for another campaign; but, owing to the exhaustion of the country, and the backwardness of the people to make further sacrifices, the preparations went on slowly. Every one wished to devolve the burden on his neighbour, and every state seemed afraid of bearing more than its share of the war. Notwithstanding the late success in the southern states, and the brilliant issue of the campaign in Virginia, there was much disinclination to vigorous exertions. The troops were few in number, and almost destitute of supplies. Many of them were almost naked, and nearly all were ill-fed. Every department was without money, and without credit. Discontent was general among the officers and soldiers, and severe measures were necessary to check a mutinous spirit in the army. Fortunately for America, while the resources of Congress were exhausted and every thing was hastening to ruin, the people of Britain also had become weary of the war, and it was found expedient to change the ministry. The new servants of the crown did not inherit the military propensities of their predecessors, but were inclined to conciliation and peace.

The discontents in the army at this period of inaction and exhaustion, led to a secret combination among several of the officers, who imputed the defective administration of the national affairs to some weakness which they supposed to be inherent in republican institutions. They even went so far as to appoint one of their number to write a private letter to Washington, proposing to place him at the head of affairs with the title of KING. That such a proposition might have been carried out successfully through the agency of the army, is rendered probable by the result of almost every attempt of a similar nature which history records. But it was repelled by Washington with the strongest expressions of abhorrence; and its authors were reprehended in the severest style, in the reply which he made to the letter of the officer who had acted as the organ of the malecontents. His stern rebuke for ever silenced the aspirations of the friends of royalty in the army.

One of the last acts of the late administration was to appoint Sir Guy Carleton, afterwards Lord Dorchester, commander-in-chief in America, in the room of Sir Henry Clinton; and the new ministry continued him in that high office. He took the command at New York early in May; and being also, in conjunction with Admiral Digby, appointed a commissioner to negotiate a peace, he soon communicated to Washington copies of the votes of parliament respecting peace; and also a bill which had been introduced by the ministry to authorize his majesty to conclude a peace with the colonies of North America; and if they were met with a corresponding temper, both inclination and duty would lead him to act in the spirit of conciliation. He had addressed to Congress, he said, a letter containing the same communication; and he requested of Washington a passport for the person who was to deliver it.

Washington immediately forwarded the communications to Congress; but as the bill to enable the king to conclude peace with America had not then passed into a law; and as there was no assurance that the present commissioners were empowered to offer any other terms than those which were already rejected, as Congress was suspicious that the offers were merely intended to amuse and put them off their guard, that they might be successfully attacked when reposing in security; and as they were resolved to enter into no separate treaty, the passport was refused. Both armies, therefore, lay inactive. There was no peace, and there was no war. Sir Guy Carleton undertook no offensive operation;

and the army of Washington was too feeble to attack New York.
On the Hudson, the summer passed away in inactivity.

Early in August, Washington received a letter from Sir Guy
Carleton and Admiral Digby, informing him that negotiations for a
general peace were begun at Paris; that the independence of the
thirteen United States would be acknowledged; and that Mr.
Laurens was set at liberty; and that passports were preparing for
such Americans as had hitherto been detained prisoners in Great
Britain. This letter was soon followed by another from Sir Guy
Carleton, in which he declared that he no longer saw any object
of contest, and therefore disapproved of the continuance of hostilities either by sea or land, as tending to increase the miseries of
individuals, without any public advantage to either party. He
added, that in consequence of this opinion, he had restrained the
practice of detaching Indian parties against the frontiers of the
United States, and had recalled those who were in the field. These
communications seem to have awakened the jealousy of the French
minister in America; and, in order to allay his suspicions, Congress renewed its resolution not to enter into any discussion for a
pacification but in concert with his most Christian majesty.*

In July, the French army in Virginia marched northward, and
reached the states of New England in October. The Marquis de
Vaudreuil had been despatched with a fleet of fifteen sail of the
line, and arrived at Boston on the 10th of August, for the purpose
of transporting them to the West Indies. The troops sailed from
Boston in December, after having remained in this country two
years and a half.

Negotiations for a general peace were going on in Paris, but
were protracted by the mutual jealousies and interfering claims of
the several parties interested. Great Britain admitted the independence of the thirteen United States, and thus removed a great
cause of the war; but the boundaries of the states, and their share
in the fisheries on the banks of Newfoundland, were not so easily
adjusted, and on both of these, France and Spain seemed unfavourable to the wishes of America.

After a tedious and intricate negotiation, in which the firmness,
judgment, and penetration of the American commissioners were
exercised, preliminary articles of peace were signed on the 30th
of November; and news of the conclusion of a general peace
reached the United States early next April.

A line running through the middle of the great lakes and their

* Western World.

connecting waters, and from a certain point on the St. Lawrence to the bottom of the Bay of Fundy, was agreed to as the northern boundary of the states; and their western frontiers was to rest on the Mississippi. It was stipulated that the British creditors should be allowed to recover their debts in the United States; that Congress should recommend to the several states the restoration of the estates of the real British subjects which had been confiscated during the war; and that no further confiscation should be made.

Meantime the army under General Washington remained at Newburg, which continued to be the head-quarters till it was disbanded. During this season of inaction, the officers and soldiers had leisure to reflect on the heartless manner in which their just claims for compensation had been slighted by Congress; and on the bad prospect they had of experiencing any better treatment when the restoration of peace should render their further services unnecessary.

In December, soon after going into winter quarters, the officers had presented a petition to Congress respecting the money actually due to them, and proposing a commutation of the half-pay stipulated by the resolutions of October, 1780, for a sum in gross, which they flattered themselves would encounter fewer prejudices than the half-pay establishment. Some security that the engagements of the government would be complied with was also requested. A committee of officers was deputed to solicit the attention of Congress to this memorial, and to attend to its progress through the house.

There were members of Congress who were anxious to do justice to the army; but there were others who regarded it with jealousy and fear; and were perfectly willing to evade its claims by any means in their power. Congress was also in a divided state with regard to the disposition of the whole public debt, some members desiring to have them funded on solid continental security, while others preferred the state system.

In consequence of these divisions, the business of the army advanced slowly, and the question respecting the commutation of their half-pay remained undecided, when the intelligence was received (March, 1783) of the signature of the preliminary and eventual articles of peace between the United States and Great Britain.

The army, soured and exasperated by neglect and injustice, manifested an uneasy temper which might easily be wrought into fearful activity. Early in March, a letter was received from the com-

mittee in Philadelphia, showing that the objects which they soli·
cited had not been obtained. This occasioned a meeting of the
officers on the 10th of March, "to consider the late letter from
their representatives in Philadelphia, and what measures (if any)
should be adopted to obtain that redress of grievances which they
seemed to have solicited in vain."

On the same day an address to the army was privately circulated, which was intended to rouse the discontented spirits into
open rebellion against the government. It was in the following
terms :—

"TO THE OFFICERS OF THE ARMY.

"Gentlemen,—A fellow-soldier, whose interests and affections
bind him strongly to you, whose past sufferings have been as great,
and whose future fortunes may be as desperate as yours, would
beg leave to address you. Age has its claims, and rank is not
without its pretensions to advise ; but though unsupported by both,
he flatters himself that the plain language of sincerity and experience will neither be unheard nor unregarded.

" Like many of you, he loved private life, and left it with regret.
He left it, determined to retire from the field, with the necessity
that called him to it, and not till then—not till the enemies of his
country, the slaves of power, and the hirelings of injustice, were
compelled to acknowledge America as terrible in arms as she had
been humble in remonstrance. With this object in view, he has
long shared in your toils and mingled in your danger. He has felt
the cold hand of poverty without a murmur, and has seen the insolence of wealth without a sigh. But, too much under the direction
of his wishes, and sometimes weak enough to mistake desire for
opinion, he has till lately, very lately, believed in the justice of his
country. He hoped that, as the clouds of adversity scattered, and
as the sunshine of peace and better fortune broke in upon us, the
coldness and severity of government would relax, and that more
than justice, that gratitude, would blaze forth upon those hands
which had upheld her in the darkest stages of her passage from
impending servitude to acknowledged independence. But faith
has its limits as well as temper ; and there are points, beyond
which neither can be stretched without sinking into cowardice or
plunging into credulity. This, my friends, I conceive to be your
situation. Hurried to the very verge of both, another step would
ruin you for ever. To be tame, or unprovoked when injuries press
upon you, is more than weakness ; but to look up for kinder usage,

without one manly effort of your own, would fix your character, and show the world how richly you deserve the chains you broke To guard against this evil, let us take a review of the ground upon which we now stand, and from thence carry our thoughts forward for a moment into the unexplored field of expedient.

"After a pursuit of seven long years, the object for which we set out is at length brought within our reach. Yes, my friends, that suffering courage of yours was active once—it has conducted the United States of America through a doubtful and bloody war ; it has placed her in the chair of independence, and peace returns again—to bless whom ? A country willing to redress your wrongs, cherish your worth, and reward your services ? A country courting your return to private life with tears of gratitude and smiles of admiration ; longing to divide with you the independency which your gallantry has given, and those riches which your wounds have preserved ? Is this the case ?—or is it rather a country that tramples upon your rights, disdains your cries, and insults your distresses ? Have you not more than once suggested your wishes, and made known your wants to Congress ?—wants and wishes which gratitude and policy should have anticipated, rather than evaded. And have you not, lately, in the meek language of entreating memorials, begged from their justice what you could no longer expect from their favour ? How have you been answered ? Let the letter which you are called to consider to-morrow, reply.

"If this then be your treatment, while the swords you wear are necessary for the defence of America, what have you to expect from peace, when your voice shall sink, and your strength dissipate by division ; when those very swords, the instruments and companions of your glory, shall be taken from your sides, and no remaining mark of military distinction left, but your wants, infirmities, and scars ? Can you then consent to be the only sufferers by this Revolution ; and, retiring from the field, grow old in poverty, wretchedness and contempt ? Can you consent to wade through the vile mire of dependency, and owe the miserable remnant of that life to charity, which has hitherto been spent in honour ? If you can, go, and carry with you the jest of Tories, and the scorn of Whigs ; the ridicule, and what is worse, the pity of the world. Go, starve, and be forgotten ! But, if your spirit revolt at this ; if you have sense enough to discover, and spirit enough to oppose tyranny, under whatever garb it may assume, whether it be the plain coat of republicanism, or the splendid robe of royalty; if you have yet learned to discriminate between a people and a cause, between men and principles, awake—attend to your situation, and redress yourselves! If the present moment be lost, every future effort is in vain, and your threats, then, will be as empty as your entreaties now.

"I would advise you, therefore, to come to some final opinion upon what you can bear, and what you will suffer. If your determination be in any proportion to your wrongs, carry your appeal from the justice to the fears of government. Change the milk-and-water style of your last memorial; assume a bolder tone, decent, but lively, spirited, and determined; and suspect the man who would advise to more moderation and longer forbearance. Let two or three men who can feel, as well as write, be appointed, to draw up your last *remonstrance;* for I would no longer give it the soft, suing name of *memorial.* Let it be represented in language that will neither dishonour you by its rudeness, nor betray you by its fears, what has been promised by Congress, and what has been performed; how long and how patiently you have suffered; how little you have asked, and how much of that little has been denied. Tell them, that though you were the first, and would wish to be the last, to encounter danger; though despair itself can never drive you into dishonour, it may drive you from the field; that the wound, often irritated, and never healed, may at length become incurable, and that the slightest mark of malignity from Congress, now, must operate like the grave, and part you for ever. That, in any political event, the army has its alternative: if peace, that nothing shall separate you from your arms but death; if war, that, courting the auspices and inviting the directions of your illustrious leader, you will retire to some unsettled country, smite in your turn, and 'mock when their fear cometh on.' But let it represent, also, that should they comply with the request of your late memorial, it would make you more happy, and them more respectable. That while the war should continue, you would follow their standard into the field; and when it came to an end, you would withdraw into the shade of private life, and give the world another subject of wonder and applause—an army victorious over its enemies, victorious over itself."

Persuaded, says Marshall, as the officers were of the indisposition of government to remunerate their services, this eloquent and impassioned address, dictated by genius and by feeling, found, in almost every bosom, a kindred though latent sentiment, prepared to receive its impression. Quick as the train to which the torch is applied, the passions caught its flame, and nothing seemed to be required but the assemblage proposed for the succeeding day, to communicate the conflagration to the combustible mass, and to produce an explosion ruinous to the army and to the nation. Fortunately, the commander-in-chief was in camp. His characteristic firmness and decision did not forsake him in this crisis. The occasion required that his measures should be firm, but prudent and conciliatory—evincive of his fixed determination to oppose any rash proceedings, but calculated to assuage the irritation which was excited, and to restore confidence in government.

Knowing well that it was much easier to avoid intemperate measures than to correct them, he thought it of essential importance to prevent the immediate meeting of the officers; but knowing, also, that a sense of injury and a fear of injustice had made a deep impression on them, and that their sensibilities were all alive to the proceedings of Congress on their memorial, he thought it more advisable to guide their deliberations on that interesting subject, than to discountenance them.

With these views, he noticed, in his orders, the anonymous paper, proposing a meeting of the officers, and expressed his conviction that their good sense would secure them from paying any "attention to such an irregular invitation; but his own duty, he conceived, as well as the reputation and true interests of the army, required his disapprobation of such disorderly proceedings. At the same time he requested the general and field-officers, with one officer from each company, and the proper representation from the staff of the army, to assemble at twelve, on Saturday, the 15th, at the new building, to hear the report of the committee deputed by the army to Congress. After mature deliberation, they will devise what further measures ought to be adopted, as most rational, and best calculated to obtain the just and important object in view." The senior officer in rank present was directed to preside, and report the result of their deliberations to the commander-in-chief.

The next day a second anonymous address appeared from the same writer who had sent forth the first. He effected to consider Washington's orders as favourable to his views, as "giving system to their proceedings and stability to their resolves." But Washington took care to explain his intentions to the officers individually, and to exert his utmost influence in preventing hasty and intemperate measures. This was by no means an easy task;

for the officers were fully persuaded of the design of the government to deal unfairly with them, and it was only their reliance on their general, and their attachment to his person and character, which could induce them to adopt the measures which he recommended.

On the 15th, the convention assembled, and General Gates took the chair. The commander-in-chief then addressed them in the following terms :

GENERAL WASHINGTON'S SPEECH AT THE MEETING OF OFFICERS.

"Gentlemen,—By an anonymous summons an attempt has been made to convene you together ; how inconsistent with the rules of propriety, how unmilitary, and how subversive of all order and discipline, let the good sense of the army decide. In the moment of this summons, another anonymous production was sent into circulation, addressed more to the feelings and passions than to the judgment of the army. The author of the piece is entitled to much credit for the goodness of his pen, and I could wish he had as much credit for the rectitude of his heart ; for, as men see through different optics, and are induced by the reflecting faculties of the mind to use different means to attain the same end, the author of the address should have had more charity than to mark for suspicion the man who should recommend moderation and longer forbearance, or, in other words, who should not think as he thinks, and act as he advises.

"But he had another plan in view, on which candour and liberality of sentiment, regard to justice, and love of country has no part ; and he was right to insinuate the darkest suspicion to effect the blackest design. That the address was drawn with great art, and is designed to answer the most insidious purposes : that it is calculated to impress the mind with an idea of premeditated injustice in the sovereign power of the United States, and rouse all the resentments which must unavoidably flow from such a belief ; that the secret mover of this scheme, whoever he may be, intended to take advantage of the passions, while they were warmed by the recollection of past distresses, without giving time for cool, deliberative thinking, and that composure of mind which is so necessary to give dignity and stability to measures, is rendered too obvious, by the mode of conducting the business, to need other proofs than a reference to the proceedings.

"Thus much, gentlemen, I have thought it incumbent on me to observe to you, to show upon what principles I opposed the irregular and hasty meeting which was proposed to have been held on Tuesday last, and not because I wanted a disposition to give you every opportunity consistent with your own honour and the dignity of the army to make known your grievances. If my conduct, therefore, has not evinced to you that I have been a faithful friend to the army, my declaration of it at this time would be equally improper and unavailing. But, as I was among the first who embarked in the cause of our common country, and as I have never left your side one moment, but when called on public duty ; and as I have been the constant companion and witness of your distresses, and not among the last to feel and acknowledge your merits ; and as I have ever considered my own military reputation as inseparably connected with that of the army ; and as my heart has ever expanded with joy when I have heard its praises, and my indignation has arisen when the mouth of detraction has been opened against it, it can scarcely be supposed at this stage of the war, that I am indifferent to its interests. But, how are they to be promoted ? The way is plain, says the anonymous addresser. If war continues, remove into the unsettled country ; there establish yourselves, and leave an ungrateful country to defend itself. But who are they to defend ? Our wives, our children, our farms, and other property which we leave behind us ? or, in this state of hostile preparation, are we to take the two first (the latter cannot be removed) to perish in a wilderness with cold, hunger, and nakedness ?

"If peace takes place, never sheathe your swords, says he, until you have obtained full and ample justice. This dreadful alternative, of either deserting our country in the extremest hour of her distress, or turning our arms against it, which is the apparent object, unless Congress can be compelled into instant compliance, has something so shocking in it that humanity revolts at the idea. My God ! what can this writer have in view by recommending such measures ? Can he be a friend to the army ? Can he be a friend to this country ? Rather, is he not an insidious foe ? some emissary, perhaps from New York, plotting the ruin of both, by sowing the seeds of discord and separation between the civil and military powers of the continent ? And what a compliment does he pay to our understandings, when he recommends measures, in either alternative, impracticable in their nature.

"But here, gentlemen, I will drop the curtain, because it would be as imprudent in me to assign my reasons for the opinion, as it would be insulting to your conception, to suppose you stood in

need of them. A moment's reflection will convince every dispassionate mind of the physical impossibility of carrying either proposal into execution.

" There might, gentlemen, be an impropriety in my taking notice
in this address to you, of an anonymous production ; but the manner in which that performance has been introduced to the army,
the effect which it was intended to have, together with some other
circumstances, will amply justify my observation on the tendency
of that writing.

" With respect to the advice given by the author, to suspect the
man who shall recommend moderate measures, I spurn it, as every
man who regards that liberty and reveres that justice for which we
contend, undoubtedly must ; for, if men are to be precluded from
offering their sentiments on a matter which may involve the most
serious and alarming consequences that can invite the consideration of mankind, reason is of no use to us ; the freedom of speech
may be taken away, and, dumb and silent, we may be led like
sheep to the slaughter. I cannot, in justice to my own belief, and
what I have great reason to conceive is the intention of Congress,
conclude this address without giving it as my decided opinion, that
that honourable body entertain such exalted sentiments of the services of the army, and from a full conviction of its merits and
its sufferings will do it a complete justice. That their endeavour
to discover and establish funds for this purpose has been unwearied,
and will not cease until they have succeeded, I have not a doubt ;
but, like all other large bodies, where there is a variety of different
interests to reconcile, their determinations are slow. Why, then,
should we distrust them ; and, in consequence of that distrust,
adopt measures which may cast a shade over that glory which has
been so justly acquired, and tarnish the reputation of an army
which is celebrated all through Europe for its fortitude and patriotism ? and for what is this done ? To bring the object we seek
nearer ? No : most certainly, in my opinion, it will cast it at a
greater distance. For myself, (and I take no merit for giving the
assurance, being induced to it from feelings of gratitude, veracity,
and justice, and a grateful sense of the confidence you have ever
placed in me,) a recollection of the cheerful assistance and prompt
obedience I have experienced from you under every vicissitude of
fortune, and the sincere affection I feel for an army I have so long
had the honour to command, will oblige me to declare, in this
public and solemn manner, that in the attainment of complete justice for all your toils and dangers, and in the gratification of every

wish, so far as can be done consistently with the great duty I owe to my country, and those powers we are bound to respect, you may freely command my services to the utmost extent of my abilities.

" While I give you my assurances, and pledge myself in the most unequivocal manner to exert whatever abilities I am possessed of in your favour; let me entreat you, gentlemen, on your part, not to take any measures which, viewed in the calm light of reason, will lesson the dignity, and sully the glory you have hitherto maintained. Let me request you to rely on the plighted faith of your country, and place a full confidence in the purity of the intentions of Congress, that, previous to your dissolution as an army, they will cause all your accounts to be fairly liquidated, as directed in all the resolutions which were published to you two days ago; and that they will adopt the most effectual measures in their power to do ample justice to you for your faithful and meritorious services. And let me conjure you, in the name of our common country, as you value your own sacred honour, as you respect the rights of humanity, and as you regard the military and national character of America, to express your utmost horror and detestation of the man who wishes, under any specious pretence, to overturn the liberties of our country; and who wickedly attempts to open the flood-gates of civil discord, and deluge our rising empire in blood.

" By thus determining, and thus acting, you will pursue the plain and direct road to the attainment of your wishes; you will defeat the insidious designs of your enemies, who are compelled to resort for open force to secret artifice; you will give one more distinguished proof of unexampled patriotism and patient virtue rising superior to the pressure of the most complicated sufferings; and you will, by the dignity of your conduct, afford occasion for posterity to say, when speaking of the glorious example you have exhibited to mankind—Had this day been wanting, the world had never seen the last stage of perfection to which human nature is capable of attaining."

That eloquent and impassioned production greatly increased the sensation which had before existed; the crisis was alarming. Even in the army of a firmly established government, such a general spirit of dissatisfaction would have been unpleasant; but in a new, feeble, and tottering government, and in an army ill-trained to strict subordination, the occurrence was far more formidable.

The effect of this eloquent appeal was irresistible. No person was bold enough to oppose the advice of Washington, and the general impression was apparent. A resolution was passed " as suring him that the officers reciprocated his affectionate expressions with the greatest sincerity of which the human heart is capable. On motion of General Putnam, a committee was then appointed to prepare resolutions on the business before them, which were speedily reported and adopted. The resolutions were as follows:

" Resolved unanimously, that at the commencement of the present war, the officers of the American army engaged in the service of their country from the purest love and attachment to the rights and privileges of human nature; which motives still exist in the highest degree; and that no circumstances of distress or danger shall induce a conduct that may tend to sully the reputation and glory which they have acquired at the price of their blood, and eight years' faithful services.

" Resolved unanimously, that the army continue to have an unshaken confidence in the justice of Congress and their country, and are fully convinced that the representatives of America will not disband or disperse the army until their accounts are liquidated, the balances accurately ascertained, and adequate funds established for payment; and in this arrangement, the officers expect that the half-pay, or a commutation for it, shall be efficaciously comprehended.

" Resolved unanimously, that his excellency, the commander-in-chief, be requested to write to his excellency the President of Congress, earnestly entreating the most speedy decision of that honourable body upon the subject of our late address, which was forwarded by a committee of the army, some of whom are waiting upon Congress for the result. In the alternative of peace or war, this event would be highly satisfactory, and would produce immediate tranquillity in the minds of the army, and prevent any farther machinations of designing men, to sow discord between the civil and military powers of the United States.

" On motion, resolved unanimously, that the officers of the American army view with abhorrence, and reject with disdain, the infamous propositions contained in a late anonymous address to the officers of the army, and resent with indignation the secret attempts. of some unknown person to collect the officers together in a manner totally subversive of all discipline and good order.

" Resolved unanimously, that the thanks of the officers of the army be given to the committee who presented to Congress the late address of the army; for the wisdom and prudence with which they have conducted that business; and that a copy of the proceedings of this day be transmitted by the president to Major-general M‹Dougall; and that he be requested to continue his solicitations at Congress until the objects of his mission are accomplished."

Washington having thus, by his great personal influence, induced the officers to present their claims with moderation to Congress, now exerted the same influence in support of their application. The following letter expresses fully his views and feelings on this momentous occasion.

" The result of the proceedings of the grand convention of the officers, which I have the honour of enclosing to your excellency for the inspection of Congress, will, I flatter myself, be considered as the last glorious proof of patriotism which could have been given by men who aspired to the distinction of a patriot army; and will not only confirm their claim to the justice, but will increase their title to the gratitude of their country.

" Having seen the proceedings on the part of the army terminate with perfect unanimity, and in a manner entirely consonant to my wishes; being impressed with the liveliest sentiments of affection for those who have so long, so patiently, and so cheerfully, suffered and fought under my direction; having, from motives of justice, duty, and gratitude, spontaneously offered myself as an advocate for their rights; and having been requested to write to your excellency, earnestly entreating the most speedy decision of Congress upon the subjects of the late address from the army to that honourable body; it now only remains for me to perform the task I have assumed, and to intercede in their behalf, as I now do, that the sovereign power will be pleased to verify the predictions I have pronounced of, and the confidence the army have reposed in, the justice of their country.

" And here I humbly conceive it is altogether unnecessary (while I am pleading the cause of an army which have done and suffered more than any other army ever did in the defence of the rights and liberties of human nature) to expatiate on their claims to the most ample compensation for their meritorious services, because they are perfectly known to the whole world, and because (although the topics are inexhaustible) enough has already been said on the subject. To prove these assertions, to evince that my sentiments have ever been uniform, and to show what my ideas of the rewards in question have always been, I appeal to the archives of Congress, and call on those sacred deposits to witness for me. And in order that my observations and arguments in favour of a future adequate provision for the officers of the army may be brought to remembrance again, and considered in a single point of view, without giving Congress the trouble of having recourse to their files, I will beg leave to transmit herewith an extract from a representation made by me to a committee of Congress, so long ago as the 20th of January, 1778, and also the transcript of a letter to the president of Congress, dated near Passaic falls, October the 11th, 1780.

"That in the critical and perilous moment when the last-mentioned communication was made, there was the utmost danger a dissolution of the army would have taken place unless measures similar to those recommended had been adopted, will not admit a doubt. That the adoption of the resolution granting half-pay for life has been attended with all the happy consequences I foretold, so far as respected the good of the service, let the astonishing contrast between the state of the army at this instant and at the former period determine. And that the establishment of funds, and security of the payment of all the just demands of the army, will be the most certain means of preserving the national faith and future tranquillity of this extensive continent, is my decided opinion.

"By the preceding remarks, it will readily be imagined that, instead of retracting and reprehending (from farther experience and reflection) the mode of compensation so strenuously urged in the enclosures, I am more and more confirmed in the sentiment; and if in the wrong, suffer me to please myself in the grateful delusion. For if, besides the simple payment of their wages, a farther compensation is not due to the sufferings and sacrifices of the officers, then have I been mistaken indeed. If the whole army have not merited whatever a grateful people can bestow, then have I been beguiled by prejudice, and built opinion on the basis of error. If this country should not in the event perform every thing which has been requested in the late memorial to Congress, then will my belief become vain, and the hope that has been excited void of foundation. 'And if (as has been suggested for the purpose of inflaming their passions) the officers of the army are to be the only sufferers by this revolution; if, retiring from the field, they are to grow old in poverty, wretchedness, and contempt; if they are to wade through the vile mire of dependency, and owe the miserable remnant of that life to charity which has hitherto been spent in honour,' then shall I have learned what ingratitude is; then shall I have realized a tale which will embitter every moment of my future life.

"But I am under no such apprehensions. A country rescued

by their arms from impending ruin will never leave unpaid the debt of gratitude.

"Should any intemperate and improper warmth have mingled itself among the foregoing observations, I must entreat your excellency and Congress that it may be attributed to the effusions of an honest zeal in the best of causes, and that my peculiar situation may be my apology; and I hope I need not, on this momentous occasion, make any new protestations of disinterestedness, having ever renounced for myself the idea of pecuniary reward. The consciousness of having attempted faithfully to discharge my duty, and the approbation of my country, will be a sufficient recompense for my services."

The consequence of the proceedings of the army, and the exertions of Washington in their behalf, was a resolution of Congress commuting the half-pay into a gross sum equal to five years' full pay.

Soon after these events, a letter was received from Lafayette, announcing a general peace; and in April, official intelligence arrived of the ratification of the preliminary articles between Great Britain and France; and on the 19th of that month, the cessation of hostilities was proclaimed.

The delicate operation of disbanding an unpaid army now claimed the attention of Congress. The treasury was empty. The expenditures of the superintendent of the finances had exceeded his receipts $404,713, and the excess continued to increase rapidly.

In vain Congress urged the states to furnish their respective contingents. The foreign danger seemed passing away, and they were more remiss than ever. The financier was compelled to make further anticipations of the revenue. While he was preparing to issue his notes for three months' pay to the army, Congress issued orders to Washington to grant unlimited furloughs to the non-commissioned officers and privates who were engaged to serve during the war. This mode of disbanding the army was productive of serious alarm. The officers addressed the commander-in-chief, and communicated their views with respect to the recent promises of the government, which they had, of course, expected to be performed before they should be disbanded or dispersed.

Washington felt the whole force of this appeal. In his answer, he declared, "that as no man could possibly be better acquainted than himself with the past merits and services of the army, so no one could possibly be more strongly impressed with their present ineligible situation; feel a keener sensibility at their distresses;

59

or more ardently desire to alleviate or remove them." He added, "Although the officers of the army very well know my official situation: that I am only a servant of the public, and that it is not for me to dispense with orders which it is my duty to carry into execution, yet, as furloughs, in all services, are considered as a matter of indulgence, and not compulsion; as Congress, I am persuaded, entertains the best disposition towards the army, and as I apprehend, in a very short time the two articles of complaint will be removed, until the further pleasure of Congress can be known, I shall not hesitate to comply with the wishes of the army, under these reservations only, that officers sufficient to conduct the men who receive furloughs, will attend them, either on furlough or by detachment."

This answer was satisfactory, and the arrangements for retiring on furlough were made without further difficulty. In the course of the summer, the three years' men were also permitted to return to their homes, and in October, Congress issued a proclamation, declaring all those who had engaged for the war, to be discharged on the third of December.

The following eulogium, from the lips of one of our great statesmen, conveys a just idea of the honourable conduct of this band of patriots:

"The army was to be disbanded; but it was unpaid. It was to lay down its own power; but there was no government with adequate power to perform what had been promised to it. In this critical moment, what is its conduct? Does it disgrace its high character? Is temptation able to seduce it? Does it speak of righting itself? Does it undertake to redress its own wrongs by its own sword? Does it lose its patriotism in its deep sense of injury and injustice? Does military ambition cause its integrity to swerve? Far, far otherwise. It had faithfully served and saved the country, and to that country it now referred, with unhesitating confidence, its claim and its complaints. It laid down its arms with alacrity; it mingled itself with the mass of the community · and it waited till. in better times. and under a new government, its services might be rewarded, and the promises made to it fulfilled. We can hardly recur to this example too often, or dwell on it too much, for the honour of our country and its defenders."*

Thus the difficult problem of disbanding an unpaid army was solved by a seasonable exertion of the influence and address of

* Speeches and Forensic Arguments of Daniel Webster.

the commander-in-chief. But this could not be felt in every quar ter with equal force. In Lancaster, Pennsylvania, about eighty men were stationed, who did not hesitate to revolt against their officers, and march to Philadelphia in a body, for the purpose of obtaining a redress of grievances from the council of state at the bayonet's point.

On arriving in the city others joined them, and the whole marched to the State House, where Congress and the Executive Council of the state were assembled, placed sentinels at the doors, and sent in a written message, threatening the executive of the state with vengeance, if their demands were not granted in twenty minutes. This insult applied hardly less to Congress than to its immediate object, the executive of Pennsylvania. They were all held in durance for three hours, at the end of which period the members of Congress separated, after agreeing to re-assemble at Princeton.

Washington, on receiving intelligence of this outrage, instantly detached fifteen hundred men under General Howe, to suppress the mutiny; but before this detachment could reach the city, the disturbances were quieted. Congress, however, ordered Genera. Howe to pursue and arrest the mutineers who had retired into the country.

During the interval which elapsed between the treaty with Great Britain and his retirement into private life, Washington's attention was anxiously directed to public affairs. In particular, the peace establishment of the country occupied him; and he communicated to Congress his views respecting a competent system for the regulating and disciplining of the militia, which he justly considered essential to the future tranquillity, dignity, and respectability of the country.

The circumstances attending General Washington's retirement are thus related by Judge Marshall:

" At length the British troops evacuated New York, and a detachment from the American army took possession of that town. Guards being posted for the security of the citizens, General Washington, accompanied by Governor Clinton, and attended by many civil and military officers, and a large number of respectable inhabitants on horseback, made his public entry into the city; where he was received with every mark of respect and attention. His military course was now on the point of terminating; and he was about to bid adieu to his comrades in arms. This affect ing interview took place on the 4th of December. At noon, the principal officers of the army assembled at Frances' tavern, soon after which, their beloved commander entered the room. His emotions were too strong to be concealed. Filling a glass, he turned to them and said, 'With a heart full of love and gratitude, I now take leave of you; I most devoutly wish that your latter days may be as prosperous and happy as your former ones have been glorious and honourable.' Having drunk, he added, 'I cannot come to each of you to take my leave, but shall be obliged if each of you will come and take me by the hand.' General Knox, being nearest, turned to him. Washington, incapable of utterance, grasped his hand, and embraced him. In the same affectionate manner he took leave of each succeeding officer. The tear of manly sensibility was in every eye; and not a word was articulated to interrupt the dignified silence, and the tenderness of the scene. Leaving the room, he passed through the corps of light infantry, and walked to White Hall, where a barge waited to convey him to Powles Hook. The whole company followed in mute and silent procession, with dejected countenances, testifying feelings of delicious melancholy, which no language can describe. Having entered the barge, he turned to the company, and, waving his hat, bade them a silent adieu. They paid him the same affectionate compliment; and, after the barge had left them, returned in the same solemn manner to the place where they had assembled.

"Congress was then in session at Annapolis, in Maryland, to which place General Washington repaired, for the purpose of resigning into their hands the authority with which they had invested him. He arrived on the 19th of December. The next day he informed that body of his intention to ask leave to resign the commission he had the honour of holding in their service; and requested to know whether it would be their pleasure that he should offer his resignation in writing or at an audience.

"To give the more dignity to the act, they determined that it should be offered at a public audience on the following Tuesday, at twelve.

"When the hour arrived for performing a ceremony so well calculated to recall the various interesting scenes which had passed since the commission now to be returned was granted, the gallery was crowded with spectators, and several persons of distinction were admitted on the floor of Congress. The members remained seated, and covered. The spectators were standing, and unco vered. The general was introduced by the secretary, and con ducted to a chair. After a short pause, the president* informed him, that 'the United States in Congress assembled were prepared to received his communications.' With native dignity, improved by the solemnity of the occasion, the general rose and delivered the following address:

" 'Mr. President,—The great events on which my resignation depended, having at length taken place, I have now the honour of offering my sincere congratulations to Congress, and of presenting myself before them, to surrender into their hands the trust committed to me, and to claim the indulgence of retiring from the service of my country.

" 'Happy in the confirmation of our independence and sovereignty, and pleased with the opportunity afforded the United States of becoming a respectable nation, I resign with satisfaction the appointment I accepted with diffidence ; a diffidence in my abilities to accomplish so arduous a task, which however was superseded by a confidence in the rectitude of our cause, the support of the supreme power of the Union, and the patronage of Heaven.

" 'The successful termination of the war has verified the most sanguine expectations ; and my gratitude for the interposition of Providence, and the assistance I have received from my countrymen, increases with every review of the momentous contest.

" 'While I repeat my obligations to the army in general, I should do injustice to my own feelings, not to acknowledge in this place the peculiar services and distinguished merits of the gentlemen who have been attached to my person during the war. It was impossible the choice of confidential officers to compose my family should have been more fortunate. Permit me, sir, to recommend, in particular, those who have continued in the service to the present moment, as worthy of the favourable notice and patronage of Congress.

" 'I consider it as an indispensable duty to close this last act of my official life, by commending the interests of our dearest country to the protection of Almighty God, and those who have the superintendence of them to his holy keeping.

" 'Having now finished the work assigned me, I retire from the great theatre of action, and, bidding an affectionate farewell to this august body, under whose orders I have so long acted, I here offer my commission, and take my leave of all the employments of public life.'

* General Mifflin.
2 R

" After advancing to the chair, and delivering his commission to the president, he returned to his place, and received, standing, the following answer of Congress, which was delivered by the president.

" ' Sir,—The United States, in Congress assembled, receive with emotions too affecting for utterance the solemn resignation of the authorities under which you have led their troops with success through a perilous and a doubtful war. Called upon by your country to defend its invaded rights, you accepted the sacred charge, before it had formed alliances, and whilst it was without funds or a government to support you. You have conducted the great military contest with wisdom and fortitude, invariably regarding the rights of the civil power, through all disasters and changes. You have, by the love and confidence of your fellow citizens, enabled them to display their martial genius, and transmit their fame to posterity. You have persevered until these United States, aided by a magnanimous king and nation, have been enabled under a just Providence to close the war in freedom, safety, and independence ; on which happy event we sincerely join you in congratulations.

" ' Having defended the standard of liberty in this New World, —having taught a lesson useful to those who inflict and to those who feel oppression, you retire from the great theatre of action with the blessings of your fellow citizens. But the glory of your virtues will not terminate with your military command ; it will continue to animate remotest ages.

" ' We feel with you our obligations to the army in general, and will particularly charge ourselves with the interests of those confidential officers who have attended your person to this affecting moment.

" ' We join with you in commending the interests of our dearest country to the protection of Almighty God, beseeching him to dispose the hearts and minds of its citizens to improve the opportunity afforded them of becoming a happy and a respectable nation. And for you, we address to him our earnest prayers that a life so beloved may be fostered with all his care ; that your days may be as happy as they have been illustrious ; and that he will finally give you that reward which this world cannot give.'

" This scene being closed, a scene rendered peculiarly interesting by the personages who appeared in it, by the great events it recalled to the memory, and by the singularity of the circumstances under which it was displayed, the American chief withdrew from the hall of Congress, leaving the silent and admiring spectators deeply impressed with those sentiments which its solemnity and dignity were calculated to inspire.

" Divested of his military character, General Washington retired to Mount Vernon, followed by the enthusiastic love, esteem, and admiration of his countrymen. Relieved from the agitations of a doubtful contest, and from the toils of an exalted station, he returned with increased delight to the duties and the enjoyments of a private citizen. He indulged the hope, that, in the shade of retirement, under the protection of a free government, and the benignant influence of mild and equal laws, he might taste that felicity which is the reward of a mind at peace with itself and conscious of its own purity."*

* Marshall.

COLONEL WASHINGTON.

MADISON.

CHAPTER XXI.

Washington in Private Life. Formation of the Federal Constitution.

HE change which now took place in the situation and pursuits of Washington was remarkable. Suddenly passing from the toils of the first commission in the United States to the condition of a simple farmer, exchanging the implements of war for those of husbandry, and becoming the patron and example of ingenious agriculture, was a task that to most men would have presented insuperable difficulties. To the elevated mind of Washington, however, it was at once natural and delightful. The sensations he experienced on the total change in his habits of life are best expressed in his own words.

MOUNT VERNON

"I feel," he writes, "as a wearied traveller must do, who, after treading many a painful step with a heavy burden on his shoulders, is eased of the latter, having reached the haven to which all the former were directed, and from his house-top is looking back and tracing with an eager eye the meanders by which he escaped the quicksands and mires which lay in his way, and into which none but the all-powerful Guide and Dispenser of human events could have prevented his falling.

"I have become a private citizen on the banks of the Potomac, and, under the shadow of my own vine and my own fig-tree, from the bustle of a camp and the busy scenes of public life, I am solacing myself with those tranquil enjoyments, of which the soldier, who is ever in pursuit of fame; the statesman, whose watchful days and sleepless nights are spent in devising schemes to promote the welfare of his own, perhaps the ruin of other countries, as if this globe was insufficient for us all; and the courtier, who is always watching the countenance of his prince, in the hope of catching a gracious smile, can have very little conception. I have not only retired from all public employments, but am retiring within myself, and shall be able to view the solitary walk, and tread the paths of private life with heartfelt satisfaction. Envious of none, I am determined to be pleased with all; and this, my dear friend, being the order of my march, I will move gently down the stream of life, until I sleep with my fathers."

Agriculture, which had always been the favourite employment of Washington, was now resumed with increasing delight. The energies of his active mind were devoted to this first and most useful art. No improvements in the construction of farming utensils, no valuable experiments in husbandry, escaped his attention. He saw, with regret, the miserable system of cultivation which prevailed too generally in his native country, and wished to introduce a better. With this view, he engaged in a correspondence with some of the distinguished agriculturists in Great Britain, particularly the celebrated Arthur Young. He traced the different states of agriculture in the two countries, in a great degree, to the following obvious principles. In Great Britain, land was dear, and labour cheap. In America, the reverse took place, to such a degree that manuring land was comparatively neglected, on the mistaken, short-sighted idea, that it was cheaper to clear and cultivate new fields, than to improve and repair such as were old. To this radical error, which led to idleness and a vagabond, dispersed population, he opposed the whole weight of his influence. His example and recommendations tended to revolutionize the agriculture of his country, as his labour had revolutionized its government.

The extension of inland navigation occupied much of Washington's attention, at this period of exemption from public cares. Soon after peace was proclaimed, he made a tour as far west as Pittsburgh, and also traversed the western parts of New England and New York, and examined for himself the difficulties of bringing the trade of the west to different points on the Atlantic. Possessed of an accurate knowledge of the subject, he corresponded with the different governors of the States, and other influential characters. To them he suggested the propriety of making, by public authority, an appointment of commissioners of integrity and ability, whose duty it should be, after accurate examination, to ascertain the nearest and best portages between such of the eastern and western rivers as headed near to each other, though they ran in opposite directions; and also to trace the rivers west of the Ohio to their sources and mouths, as they respectively emptied either into the Ohio, or the lakes of Canada, and to make an accurate map of the whole, with observations on the impediments to be overcome, and the advantages to be acquired on the completion of the work.

The views of Washington in advocating the extension of inland navigation were grand and magnificent. He considered it as an effectual means of cementing the union of the States. In his letter to the governor of Virginia, he observed: "I need not remark to you, sir, that the flanks and rear of the United States are possessed by other powers, and formidable ones too; nor need I press the necessity of applying the cement of interest to bind all parts of the Union together by indissoluble bonds, especially of binding that part of it which lies immediately west of us, to the Middle States. For what ties, let me ask, should we have upon those people; how entirely unconnected with them shall we be, and what troubles may we not apprehend, if the Spaniards on their right, and Great Britain on their left, instead of throwing impediments in their way as they do now, should hold out lures for their trade and alliance? When they get strength, which will be sooner than most people conceive, what will be the consequence of their having formed close commercial connections with both or either of those powers? It needs not, in my opinion, the gift of prophecy to foretell." After stating the same thing to a member of Congress, he proceeds: "It may be asked, how we are to prevent this? Happily for us, the way is plain. Our immediate interests, as well as remote political advantages, point to it, whilst a combination of circumstances render the present time more favourable than any other to accomplish it. Extend the inland navigation of the eastern waters; communicate them as near as possible with those which run westward; open these to the Ohio; open also such as extend from the Ohio towards Lake Erie; and we shall not only draw the produce of the western settlers, but the peltry and fur trade of the lakes also, to our ports; thus adding an immense increase to our exports, and binding those people to us by a chain which never can be broken."

The Virginia legislature acted on the recommendation of General Washington to the extent of his wishes; and in consequence thereof, works of the greatest utility have been nearly accomplished. They went one step farther, and by a legislative act, vested in him, at the expense of the state, one hundred and fifty shares in the navigation of the rivers Potomac and James. The act for this purpose was introduced with the following preamble: "Whereas, it is the desire of the representatives of this Commonwealth to embrace every suitable occasion of testifying their sense of the unexampled merits of George Washington, Esq., towards his country; and it is their wish in particular that those great works for its improvement, which, both as springing from the liberty which he has been so instrumental in establishing, and as encouraged by his patronage, will be durable monuments of his glory, may be made monuments also of the gratitude of his country: Be it enacted," &c.

To the friend who conveyed to Washington the first intelligence of this bill, he replied:

" It is not easy for me to decidé, by which my mind was most affected, upon the receipt of your letter of the 6th instant, surprise or gratitude. Both were greater than I had words to express. The attention and good wishes which the Assembly have evidenced by their act for vesting in me one hundred and fifty shares in the navigation of the rivers Potomac and James is more than mere compliment. There is an unequivocal and substantial meaning annexed. But, believe me, sir, no circumstance has happened since I left the walks of public life which has so much embarrassed me. On the one hand, I consider this act as a noble and unequivocal proof of the good opinion, the affection and disposition of my country to serve me; and I should be hurt, if, by declining the acceptance of it, my refusal should be construed into disrespect, or the smallest slight upon the generous intention of the legislature, or that an ostentatious display of disinterestedness or public virtue was the source of refusal.

" On the other hand, it is really my wish to have my mind and my actions, which are the result of reflection, as free and independent as the air, that I may be more at liberty to express my sentiments, and, if necessary, to suggest what may occur to me, under the fullest conviction, that although my judgment may be arraigned, there will be no suspicion that sinister motives had the smallest influence in the suggestion. Not content, then, with the bare consciousness of my having, in all this navigation business, acted upon the clearest conviction of the political importance of the measure, I would wish that every individual who may hear that it was a favourite plan of mine, may know also that I had no other motive for promoting it than the advantage of which I conceived it would be productive to the Union at large, and to this state in particular, by cementing the eastern and western territory together; at the same time that it will give vigour to, and increase our commerce, and be a convenience to our citizens.

" How would this matter be viewed, then, by the eye of the world, and what opinion would be formed, when it comes to be related that G—— W———n exerted himself to effect this work, and that G—— W———n has received twenty thousand dollars, and five thousand pounds sterling of the public money as an interest therein ? Would not this (if I am entitled to any merit for the part I have performed, and without it there is no foundation for the act) deprive me of the principal thing which is laudable in my conduct ? Would it not in some respects be considered in the same light as a pension ? And would not the apprehensions of this induce me to offer my sentiments in future with the more reluctance ? In a word, under whatever pretence, and however customary these gratuities may be in other countries, should I not thenceforward be considered as a dependent ? One moment's thought of which would give me more pain than I should receive pleasure from the product of all the tolls, was every farthing of them vested in me."

To the governor of the state, on receiving from him an official copy of the aforesaid act, Washington replied as follows :

" Your excellency having been pleased to transmit me a copy of the act appropriating to my benefit certain shares in the companies for opening the navigation of James and Potomac rivers ; I take the liberty of returning, to the General Assembly, through your hands, the profound, and grateful acknowledgments inspired by so signal a mark of their beneficent intentions towards me. I beg you, sir, to assure them, that I am filled, on this occasion, with every sentiment which can flow from a heart warm with love to my country, sensible to every token of its approbation and affection, and solicitous to testify, in every instance, a respectful submission to its wishes.

" With these sentiments in my bosom, I need not dwell on the anxiety I feel, in being obliged, in this instance, to decline a favour which is rendered no less flattering by the manner in which it is conveyed than it is affectionate in itself. In explaining this, I pass over a comparison of my endeavours in the public service, with the many honourable testimonies of approbation which have already so far overrated and overpaid them ; reciting one consideration only, which supersedes the necessity of recurring to every other.

" When I was first called to the station with which I was honoured during the late conflict for our liberties, to the diffidence which I had so many reasons to feel in accepting it, I thought it my duty to join a firm resolution to shut my hand against every pecuniary recompense. To this resolution I have invariably adhered, and from it (if I had the inclination) I do not consider myself at liberty now to depart.

" Whilst I repeat, therefore, my fervent acknowledgments to the legislature for their very kind sentiments and intentions in my favour, and at the same time beg them to be persuaded, that a remembrance of this singular proof of their goodness towards me will never cease to cherish returns of the warmest affection and gratitude ; I must pray that their act, so far as it has for its object my personal emolument, may not have its effect ; but if it should please the General Assembly to permit me to turn the destination of the fund vested in me, from my private emolument to objects of a public nature, it will be my study in selecting these, to prove the sincerity of my gratitude for the honour conferred upon me, by preferring such as may appear most subservient to the enlightened and patriotic views of the legislature."

The wishes suggested in this letter were sanctioned by the legislature ; and, at a subsequent time, the trust was executed by conveying the shares to the use of a seminary of learning in the vicinity of each river.

Near the close of the revolutionary war, the officers of the American army, with a view of perpetuating their friendships, formed themselves into a society, to be named after the famous Roman patriot, Cincinnatus. At the head of their society General Washington was placed. By the rules of their institution, the honours of the society were to be hereditary in their respective families, and distinguished individuals might be admitted as honorary members for life. These circumstances, together with the union of the officers of the army, gave an alarm to the community; several individuals of which supposed that the hereditary part of the institution would be a germ of nobility. It was the usual policy of Washington to respect the opinions of the people, in matters indifferent, or of small magnitude, though he might think them mistaken. Having ascertained, to his own satisfaction, that a degree of jealousy pervaded the mass of the people, respecting the probable tendency of this perpetual hereditary society, he successfully exerted his influence to new-model its rules, by relinquishing the hereditary principle, and the power of adopting honorary members. The result proved the wisdom of the measure; for all jealousies of the society henceforward were done away, and the members thereof were received as brethren by the most suspicious of their fellow citizens.

When Washington, at the close of the revolutionary war became a private citizen, his country confidently anticipated every possible blessing from peace, independence, and self-government. But experience soon proved the inefficacy of existing systems for promoting public happiness, or preserving national dignity. Congress had neither the power nor the means of doing justice to public creditors, nor of enforcing the respect of foreign nations. Gold and silver vanished, commerce languished, property was depreciated, and credit expired. The lovers of liberty and independence began to be less sanguine in their hopes from the American revolution, and to fear that they had built a visionary fabric of government on the fallacious ideas of public virtue. For the first five or six years immediately following peace, the splendour which surrounded the infant states from their successful struggle in the cause of independence and self-government was daily darkening. This state of things could not be indifferent to Washington. He was among the first to discover the cause, and to point out the remedy. The inefficient support he received while commander-in-chief, proved the inefficacy of the articles of confederation for raising and supporting a requisite military force. The experience of the first years of peace proved their total inadequacy for the purpose of national government. From want of vigour in the federal head, the United States were fast dwindling into separate sovereignties, unconnected by any bond of union equal to public exigency. The enthusiasm of a popular contest, terminating in victory, began to subside, and

.he sacrifices of the Revolution soon became known and felt. The claims of those who toiled, and fought, and suffered in the arduous struggle were strongly urged, and the government had neither resources nor power to satisfy or to silence them. The federal head had no separate or exclusive fund. The members of Congress depended on the states which they respectively represented, even for their own maintenance, and money for national purposes could only be obtained by requisitions on the different members of the confederacy. On them it became necessary immediately to call forth funds to discharge the arrears of pay due to the soldiers of the Revolution, and the interest on the debt which the government had been compelled to contract. The legislatures of the different states received these requisitions with respect, listened to the monitory warnings of Congress with deference, and with silent and inactive acquiescence. Their own situation, indeed, was full of embarrassment. The wealth of the country had been totally exhausted during the Revolution. Taxes could not be collected, because there was no money to represent the value of the little personal property which had not been, and the land which could not be destroyed; and commerce, though preparing to burst from its thraldom, had not yet had time to restore to the annual produce of the country its exchangeable value. The States owed each a heavy debt for local services rendered during the Revolution, for which it was bound to provide, and each had its own domestic government to support. Under these circumstances, it is not surprising that each state was anxious to retain for its benefit the small but rising revenue derived from foreign commerce; and that the custom-houses in each commercial city were considered as the most valuable sources of income which the states possessed. Each state, therefore, made its own regulations, its tariff, and tonnage duties, and, as a natural consequence, the different states clashed with each other; one nation became more favoured than another under the same circumstances; and one state pursued a system injurious to the interest of another. Hence, the confidence of foreign countries was destroyed; and they would not enter into treaties of commerce with the confederated government, while they were not likely to be carried into effect. A general decay of trade, the rise of imported merchandise, the fall of produce, and an uncommon decrease of the value of lands, ensued.

The private letters of Washington, at this time, show his anxiety for his country's welfare, and his wisdom in pointing out a remedy. for its degradation. In one of them he observes, "The confederation appears to be to me, to be little more than a shadow without the substance, and Congress a nugatory body, their ordinances being little attended to. To me it is a solecism in politics; indeed, it is one of the most extraordinary things in nature, that we should confederate as a nation, and yet be afraid to give the rulers of that nation, who are the creatures of our own making, appointed for a limited and short duration, and who are amenable for every action, recallable at any moment, and subject to all the evils which they may be instrumental in producing, sufficient powers to order and direct the affairs of the same. By such policy the wheels of government are clogged, and our brightest prospects, and that high expectation which was entertained of us by the wondering world, are turned into astonishment; and from the high ground on which we stood, we are descending into the vale of confusion and darkness.

"That we have it in our power to become one of the most respectable nations upon earth, admits, in my humble opinion, of no doubt, if we would but pursue a wise, just, and liberal policy towards one another, and would keep good faith with the rest of the world. That our resources are ample and increasing, none can deny; but while they are grudgingly applied, or not applied at all, we give a vital stab to public faith, and will sink in the eyes of Europe into contempt."

In another, "It is one of the evils of democratic governments, that the people, not always seeing, and frequently misled, must often feel before they are set right. But evils of this nature seldom fail to work their own cure. It is to be lamented, nevertheless, that the remedies are so slow, and that those who wish to apply them seasonably are not attended to before they suffer in person, in interest, and in reputation. I am not without hopes that matters will soon take a favourable turn in the federal constitution. The discerning part of the community have long since seen the necessity of giving adequate powers to Congress for national purposes, and those of a different description must yield to it ere long."

In a letter to Mr. Jay, General Washington observed: "Your sentiments that our affairs are drawing rapidly to a crisis, accord with my own. What the event will be, is also beyond the reach of my foresight. We have errors to correct; we have probably had too good an opinion of human nature in forming our confederation. Experience has taught us that men will not adopt and carry into execution measures the best calculated for their own good, without the intervention of coercive power. I do not conceive we can subsist long as a nation, without lodging some-where a power which will pervade the whole union, in as energetic a manner as the authority of the state governments extends over the several states. To be fearful of investing Congress, constituted as that body is, with ample authorities for national purposes, appears to me the very climax of popular absurdity and madness. Could Congress exert themselves in an equal or greater proportion? Are not their interests inseparably connected with those of their constituents? By the rotation of appointment must they not mingle frequently with the mass of citizens? Is it not rather to be apprehended, if they were possessed of the powers before described, that the individual members would be induced to use them on many occasions, very timidly and inefficaciously, for fear of losing their popularity and future election? We must take human nature as we find it, perfection falls not to the share of mortals. Many are of opinion that Congress have too frequently made use of the suppliant humble tone of requisition, by applications to the states, when they had a right to assert their imperial dignity, and command obedience. Be that as it may, requisitions are a perfect nullity, where thirteen sovereign, independent, disunited states are in the habit of discussing, and refusing or complying with them at their option. Requisitions are actually little better than a jest and a bye-word throughout the land. If you tell the legislatures they have violated the treaty of peace, and invaded the prerogatives of the confederacy, they will laugh in your face. What then is to be done? Things cannot go on in the same train for ever. It is much to be feared, as you observe, that the better kind of people, having been disgusted with these circumstances, will have their minds prepared for any revolution whatever. We are apt to run from one extreme into another. To anticipate and prevent disastrous contingencies would be the part of wisdom and patriotism.

"What astonishing changes are a few years capable of producing! I am told that even respectable characters speak of a monarchical form of government without horror. From thinking, proceeds speaking; thence to acting is often but a single step. But how irrevocable and tremendous! What a triumph for our enemies to verify their predictions! What a triumph for the advocate of despotism to find that we are incapable of governing ourselves, and that systems founded on the basis of equal liberty are merely ideal and fallacious! Would to God that wise measures may be taken in time, to avert the consequences we have but too much reason to apprehend.

"Retired as I am from the world, I frankly acknowledge I cannot feel myself an unconcerned spectator. Yet, having happily assisted in bringing the ship into port, and having been fairly discharged, it is not my business to embark again on a sea of troubles.

"Nor could it be expected that my sentiments and opinions would have much weight on the minds of my countrymen. They have been neglected, though given as a last legacy in the most solemn matter. I had then, perhaps, some claims to public attention. I consider myself as having none at present."

Illumination, on the subject of enlarging the powers of Congress, was gradual. Washington, in his extensive correspondence and intercourse with the leading characters of the different states, urged the necessity of a radical reform in the existing system of government.

The time at length came when the public mind gave tokens of being prepared for a change in the constitution of the general government, an occurrence the necessity of which had long been foreseen by Washington and most of the distinguished patriots of that period. Evil had accumulated upon evil, till the mass became too oppressive to be endured, and the voice of the nation cried out for relief. The first decisive measures proceeded from the merchants, who came forward, almost simultaneously, in all parts of the country, with representations of the utter prostration of the mercantile interests, and petitions for a speedy and efficient remedy. It was shown, that the advantages of this most important source of national prosperity were flowing into the hands of foreigners, and that the native merchants were suffering for the want of a just protection, and a uniform system of trade. The wise and reflecting were convinced that some decided efforts were necessary to strengthen the general government, or that a dissolution of the union, and perhaps a devastating anarchy, would be inevitable.

The first step towards a general reformation was rather accidental than premeditated. Certain citizens of Virginia and Maryland had formed a scheme for promoting the navigation of the Potomac and Chesapeake Bay, and commissioners were appointed by these two states to meet at Alexandria, and devise some plan of operation. These persons made a visit to Mount Vernon, and while there, it was proposed among themselves, that more important objects should be connected with the purpose at first in view, and that the state governments should be solicited to appoint other commissioners, with enlarged powers, instructed to form a plan for maintaining a naval force in the Chesapeake, and also to fix upon some system of duties on exports and imports, in which both states should agree, and that in the end Congress should be petitioned to allow these privileges. This project was approved by the legislature of Virginia, and commissioners were accordingly appointed. The same legislature passed a resolution, recommending the design to other states, and inviting them to unite, by their commissioners, in an attempt to establish such a system of commercial relations as would promote general harmony and prosperity.

Five states only, in addition to Virginia, acceded to this proposition : Maryland, Delaware, Pennsylvania, New Jersey, and New York. From these states, commissioners assembled at Annapolis, but they had hardly entered into a discussion of the topics which naturally forced themselves into view, before they discovered the powers with which they were intrusted to be so limited as to tie up their hands from effecting any purpose that could be of essential utility. On this account, as well as from the circumstance that so few states were represented, they wisely declined deciding on any important measures in reference to the particular subjects for which they had come together. Before this convention adjourned, however, the commissioners agreed upon a report, in which the necessity of a revision and reform of the articles of the old federal compact was strongly urged, and which contained a recommendation to all the state legislatures for the appointment of deputies, to meet at Philadelphia, with more ample powers and instructions. This proposal was eventually carried into effect, and in conformity with it, a convention of delegates from the several states met at Philadelphia, in May, 1787.

While this proposition was under consideration, an event took place which pointed out the propriety of its adoption. The pressure of evils, in a great degree resulting from the imbecility of government, aided by erroneous opinions, which confound liberty with licentiousness, produced commotions in Massachusetts, which amounted to treason and rebellion. On this occasion, Washington expressed himself in a letter, as follows :

"The commotions and tempers of numerous bodies in the eastern country, present a state of things equally to be lamented and deprecated. They exhibit a melancholy verification of what our transatlantic foes have predicted, and of another thing, perhaps, which is still more to be regretted, and is yet more unaccountable, that mankind, when left to themselves, are unfit for their own government. I am mortified beyond expression, when I view the clouds which have spread over the brightest morn that ever dawned upon my country. In a word, I am lost in amazement, when I behold what intrigue the interested views of desperate characters, ignorance and jealousy of the minor part, are capable of effecting, as a scourge on the major part of our fellow-citizens of the Union : for it is hardly to be supposed, that the great body of the people, though they will not act, can be so short-sighted, or enveloped in darkness, as not to see rays of a distant sun through all this mist of intoxication and folly.

" You talk, my good sir, of employing influence to appease the present tumults in Massachusetts. I know not where that influence is to be found, nor, if attainable, that it would be a proper remedy for these disorders. Influence is not government. Let us have a government by which our lives, liberties, and properties, will be secured, or let us know the worst at once. Under these impressions, my humble opinion is, that there is a call for decision. Know precisely what the insurgents aim at. If they have real grievances, redress them, if possible ; or acknowledge the justice of them, and your inability to do it in the present moment. If they have not, employ the force of government against them at once. If this is inadequate, all will be convinced that the super-structure is bad, or wants support. To be more exposed in the eyes of the world, and more contemptible, is hardly possible. To delay one or the other of these expedients, is to exasperate on the one hand, or to give confidence on the other, and will add to their numbers ; for, like snowballs, such bodies increase by every move-ment, unless there is something in the way to obstruct and crum-ble them before their weight is too great and irresistible.

" These are my sentiments. Precedents are dangerous things. Let the reins of government, then, be braced and held with a steady hand, and every violation of the constitution be repre-hended. If defective, let it be amended, but not suffered to be trampled upon while it has an existence."

Virginia placed the name of Washington at the head of her dele-gates for the proposed convention. Letters poured in upon him from all sides urging his acceptance of the appointment. In an-swer to one from Mr. Madison, who had been the principal advo-cate of the measure in the Virginia legislature, General Washing-ton replied :

" Although I have bid a public adieu to the public walks of life, and had resolved never more to tread that theatre, yet, if upon any occasion so interesting to the well-being of our confederacy, it had been the wish of the Assembly that I should be an associate in the business of revising the federal system, I should, from a sense of the obligation I am under for repeated proofs of confidence in me, more than from any opinion I could entertain of my usefulness, have obeyed its call; but it is now out of my power to do this with any degree of consistency. The cause I will mention.

"I presume you heard, sir, that I was first appointed, and have since been re-chosen president of the society of the Cincinnati; and you may have understood, also, that the triennial general meeting of this body is to be held in Philadelphia the first Monday in May next. Some particular reasons, combining with the peculiar situation of my private concerns, the necessity of paying attention to them, a wish for retirement, and relaxation from public cares, and rheumatic pains, which I begin to feel very sensibly, induced me, on the 31st ultimo, to address a circular letter to each state society, informing them of my intention not to be at the next meeting, and of my desire not to be re-chosen president. The vice-president is also informed of this, that the business of the society may not be impeded by my absence. Under these circumstances, it will readily be perceived that I could not appear at the same time and place, on any other occasion, without giving offence to a very respectable and deserving part of the community, —the late officers of the American army."

The meeting of the convention was postponed to a day subsequent to that of the meeting of the Cincinnati. This removed one of the difficulties in the way of Washington's acceptance of a seat in the convention, and, joined with the importance of the call, and his own eager desire to advance the public interest, finally induced his compliance with the wishes of his friends.

The convention met in Philadelphia, in May, and unanimously chose George Washington for their president. On the 17th of September, 1787, they closed their labours, and submitted the result to Congress, with their opinion, "that it should be submitted to a convention of delegates chosen, in each state, by the people thereof, under the recommendation of its legislature, for their assent and ratification."

By this new form of government, ample powers were given to Congress, without the intervention of the states, for every purpose that national dignity, interest, or happiness required.

The ablest pens and most eloquent tongues were employed for and against its acceptance. In this animated contest, Washington took no part. Having with his sword vindicated the right of h.

country to self-government, and having with his advice aided in digesting an efficient form of government which he most thoroughly approved, it would seem as though he wished the people to decide for themselves, whether to accept or reject it.

Yet the name of Washington, at the head of such a list of worthies as would reflect honour on any country, had its proper weight with the enlightened, and with almost all the well-disposed among the less informed citizens, and the Constitution was adopted. To the eternal honour of America among the nations of the earth, it was adopted in spite of the obstacles, which in any other country would have been insurmountable ; in spite of the doubts and fears which well-meaning prejudice creates for itself, and which party so artfully inflames into stubbornness ; in spite of the vice which it has subjected to restraint, and which is therefore its immortal and implacable foe ; in spite of the oligarchies in some of the states from whom it snatched dominion ; it was adopted, and our country enjoys one more invaluable chance for its union and happiness ; invaluable ! if the retrospect of the dangers we have escaped shall sufficiently inculcate the principles we have established.*

The Constitution being accepted by eleven states, and preparatory measures being taken for bringing it into operation, all eyes were turned to Washington, as the fittest man for the office of President of the United States. His correspondents began to press his acceptance of the high office, as essential to the well-being of his country.

To those who think that Washington was like other men, it will scarcely appear possible, that supreme magistracy possessed no charms sufficient to tempt him from his beloved retirement, when he was healthy and strong, and only fifty-seven years old. But if an opinion can be formed of his real sentiments from the tenor of his life and confidential communications to his most intimate friends, a conviction will be produced, that his acceptance of the Presidency of the United States was the result of a victory obtained by a sense of duty over his inclinations, and was a real sacrifice of the latter to the former.

In a letter to Colonel Henry Lee, Washington observes :

"Notwithstanding my advanced season of life, my increasing fondness for agricultural amusements, and my growing love of retirement, augment and confirm my decided predilection for the character of a private citizen ; yet it will be no one of these

* Fisher Ames.

motives, nor the hazard to which my former reputation might be
exposed, nor the terror of encountering new fatigues and troubles,
that would deter me from an acceptance, but a belief that some other
person who had less pretence and less inclination to be excused,
could execute all the duties full as satisfactorily as myself. To say
more would be indiscreet, as a disclosure of a refusal beforehand
might incur the application of the fable, in which the fox is represented as undervaluing the grapes he could not reach. You will
perceive, my dear sir, by what is here observed, (and which you
will be pleased to consider in the light of a confidential communication,) that my inclinations will dispose and decide me to remain
as I am, unless a clear and insurmountable conviction should be
impressed on my mind, that some very disagreeable consequences
must in all human probability result from the indulgence of my
wishes."

In a letter to Colonel Hamilton, Washington observes :

"If I am not grossly deceived in myself, I should unfeignedly
rejoice, in case the electors, by giving their votes to some other
person, would save me from the dreadful dilemma of being forced
to accept or refuse. If that may not be, I am, in the next place,
earnestly desirous of searching out the truth, and of knowing whether there does not exist a probability that the government would
just as happily and effectually be carried into execution without
my aid as with it. I am truly solicitous to obtain all the previous
information which the circumstances will afford, and to determine
(when the determination can no longer be postponed) according to
the principles of right reason, and the dictates of a clear conscience, without too great a reference to the unforeseen consequence which may affect my person or reputation. Until that
period, I may fairly hold myself open to conviction, though I allow
your sentiments to have weight in them ; and I shall not pass by
your arguments, without giving them as dispassionate a consideration as I can possibly bestow upon them.

"In taking a survey of the subject, in whatever point of light
I have been able to place it, I will not suppress the acknowledgment, my dear sir, that I have always felt a kind of gloom upon
my mind, as often as I have been taught to expect I might, and
perhaps, must be called upon ere long to make the decision. You
will, I am well assured, believe the assertion, (though I have little
expectation it would gain credit from those who are less acquainted
with me,) that if I should receive the appointment, and should be
prevailed upon to accept it, the acceptance would be attended with
62

more difficulty and reluctance than I ever experienced before. It would be, however, with a fixed and sole determination of lending whatever assistance might be in my power to promote the public weal, in hopes that at a convenient and early period my services might be dispensed with ; and that I might be permitted once more to retire, to pass an unclouded evening after the stormy day of life, in the bosom of domestic tranquillity."

In a letter to General Lincoln, Washington observes, "I may, however, with great sincerity, and I believe without offending against modesty and propriety, say to you, that I most heartily wish the choice to which you allude might not fall upon me ; and that if it should, I must reserve to myself the right of making up my final decision, at the last moment, when it can be brought into one view, and when the expediency or inexpediency of a refusal can be more judiciously determined than at present. But be assured, my dear sir, if, from any inducement, I shall be persuaded ultimately to accept, it will not be, (so far as I know my own heart,) from any of a private or personal nature. Every personal consideration conspires to rivet me (if I may use the expression) to retirement. At my time of life, and, under my circumstances, nothing in this world can ever draw me from it, unless it be a conviction that the partiality of my countrymen had made my services absolutely necessary, joined to a fear that my refusal might induce a belief that I preferred the conservation of my own reputation and private ease to the good of my country. After all, if I should conceive myself in a manner constrained to accept, I call Heaven to witness, that this very act would be the greatest sacrifice of my personal feelings and wishes that ever I have been called upon to make. It would be to forego repose and domestic enjoyment, for trouble, perhaps for public obloquy ; for I should consider myself as entering upon an unexplored field, enveloped on every side with clouds and darkness.

"From this embarrassing situation, I had naturally supposed that my declarations at the close of the war would have saved me, and that my sincere intentions, then publicly made known, would have effectually precluded me for ever afterwards from being looked upon as a candidate for any office. This hope, as a last anchor of worldly happiness in old age, I had carefully preserved, until the public papers and private letters from my correspondents in almost every quarter, taught me to apprehend that I might soon be obliged to answer the question, whether I would go again into public life or not."

In a letter to the Marquis de Lafayette, Washington observes :—

"Your sentiments, indeed, coincide much more nearly with those of my other friends than with my own feelings. In truth, my difficulties increase and magnify, as I draw towards the period when, according to the common belief, it will be necessary for me to give a definitive answer in one way or other. Should circumstances render it a matter inevitably necessary to be in the affirmative, be assured, my dear sir, I shall assume the task with the most unfeigned reluctance, and with a real diffidence, for which I shall probably receive no credit from the world. If I know my own heart, nothing short of a conviction of duty will induce me again to take an active part in public affairs. And in that case, if I can form a plan for my own conduct, my endeavours shall be unremittingly exerted (even at the hazard of former fame or present popularity) to extricate my country from the embarrassments in which it is entangled through want of credit, and to establish a general system of policy, which, if pursued, will ensure permanent felicity to the Commonwealth. I think I see a path as clear and as direct as a ray of light, which leads to the attainment of that object. Nothing but harmony, honesty, industry, and frugality, are necessary to make us a great and a happy people. Happily the present posture of affairs, and the prevailing disposition of my countrymen, promise to co-operate in establishing those four great and essential pillars of public felicity."

Before the election of a President came on, so universal was the expectation that Washington would be elected, that numerous applications were made to him, in anticipation, for offices in the government, which would be in his gift. To one of such applicants he wrote, as follows :—

"Should it become absolutely necessary for me to occupy the station in which your letter presupposes me, I have determined to go into it perfectly free from all engagements of every nature whatsoever. A conduct in conformity to this resolution would enable me, in balancing the various pretensions of different candidates for appointments, to act with a sole reference to justice and the public good. This is, in substance, the answer that I have given to all applications (and they are not few) which have already been made."

For Washington, it was impossible to have rivals. Accordingly he was soon known to have been chosen President of the

United States. As a general and a patriot, he had already filled the measure of his glory ; there was no fame left for him to excel but his own, and that task, the mightiest of all his labours, was now about to be accomplished.

The following remarks on Washington's second acceptance of the office of President, occur in the recent work of Mr. Headley, entitled " Washington and his Generals."

" Though he had reached his threescore years, and pined for the rest of a quiet home, he again took on him the burdens of office. The nation prospered under his rule. Words of wisdom and piety dropped from his lips, and stretching out his arms over the Union, both the foundation and topmost stone of which he had laid, he gave it his last blessing. Had his counsels been obeyed, and all his successors followed in his footsteps, this nation would not only have stood first among the powers of the earth, but been the especial favourite of Heaven."

WASHINGTON

From a sketch, made for a portrait as large as life, painted for the state of Delaware, by D. A. Volozan.

HAMILTON.

CHAPTER XXII.

Administration of Washington. First Term.

THE impotence of the general government under the Articles of Confederation, and the dilatory and vexatious manner in which its business was of necessity conducted, had produced a great want of punctuality among the members of Congress. Although the new Constitution, which had been the theme of popular discussion ever since its promulgation, was appointed to go into operation on the 4th of March, 1787, a House of Representatives could not be formed until the 1st of April, nor a Senate until the 6th of that month. The delay thus produced was compared, by General Washington himself, to a reprieve, so great was the reluctance which he felt to enter upon his new dignity. Writing, in confidence, to General Knox, he says:

"My movements to the chair of government will be accompanied by feelings not unlike those of a culprit who is going to the place of his execution; so unwilling am I, in the evening of life, nearly consumed in public cares, to quit a peaceful abode for an ocean of difficulties, without that competency of political skill, abilities, and inclination, which are necessary to manage the helm. I am sensible that I am embarking the voice of the people, and a good name of my own on this voyage; but what returns will be made for them Heaven alone can foretell. Integrity and firmness are all I can promise; these, be the voyage long or short, shall never forsake me, although I may be deserted by all men; for, of the consolations which are to be derived from these, under any circumstances, the world cannot deprive me."

Similar sentiments were expressed in letters written about this period to General Wayne, General Schuyler, Mr. Hamilton, and others.

Twelve senators being in attendance, on the 6th of April, John Langdon, of New Hampshire, was elected president of that body, for the purpose of opening and counting the votes for President of the United States. A message, announcing the presence of a quorum, and the election of a temporary president, was then sent to the House of Representatives. That body repaired to the Senate chamber, and the votes of the electoral colleges were examined in the presence of both houses; Mr. Patterson, of New Jersey, on the part of the Senate, and Mr. Heister, of Pennsylvania, and Mr. Parker, of Virginia, on the part of the House, acting as tellers. The result, as declared by the president of the Senate, was, that George Washington was unanimously elected President, and John Adams, Vice-president of the United States. In compliance with a resolution of the House, the Senate directed that the persons elected be notified thereof. In the course of the few following days, the necessary preparations for the reception of the President and the commencement of his administration were made by the joint committee of the two houses; and Mr. Osgood, the proprietor of the house lately occupied by the president of Congress, was engaged in putting that house and its furniture in proper condition for the residence and use of the President of the United States. His temporary accommodation, at the expense of the United States, was further provided for by a joint resolution of both houses.*

Charles Thomson, the secretary of the Continental Congress,

* Marshall.

officially announced his election to the chief magistracy of the
Union to General Washington, at Mount Vernon, on the 14th of
April, 1789. Having previously determined upon the course which
he would pursue, in the event of the choice of his fellow-citizens
falling upon him, he complied with their wishes, and prepared to
set out immediately for the seat of government. Two days after
receiving notice of his election, he " bade adieu," in the words of
his diary, " to Mount Vernon, to private life, and to domestic felicity; and with a mind impressed with more anxious and painful
sensations than I have words to express, set out for New York, in
company with Mr. Thomson and Colonel Humphries, with the
best disposition to render service to my country in obedience to its
call, but with less hope of answering its expectations." He was
met on the road by a number of gentlemen of Alexandria, who
had come to invite and escort him to a public dinner in that city.
All its inhabitants united to do him honour, and their address, considered as the production of the minds and hearts of his neighbours
and friends, deserves a place in every memoir of his life.

" Again," said they, " your country commands your care.
Obedient to its wishes, unmindful of your ease, we see you again
relinquishing the bliss of retirement; and this, too, at a period
of life when nature itself seems to authorize a preference of repose!

" Not to extol your glory as a soldier; not to pour forth our
gratitude for past services; not to acknowledge the justice of the
unexampled honour which has been conferred upon you by the
spontaneous and unanimous suffrages of three millions of freemen in your election to the supreme magistracy; nor to admire
the patriotism which directs your conduct, do your neighbours
and friends now address you. Themes less splendid but more
endearing impress our minds. The first and best of citizens must
leave us: our aged must lose their ornament; our youth their
model; our agriculture its improver; our commerce its friend,
our infant academy its protector; our poor their benefactor; and
the interior navigation of the Potomac (an event replete with the
most extensive utility, already, by your unremitted exertions,
brought into partial use) its institutor and promoter.

" Farewell! Go! and make a grateful people happy; a people
who will be doubly grateful when they contemplate this recent
sacrifice for their interest.

" To that Being who maketh and unmaketh at his will, we commend you, and after the accomplishment of the arduous business

63   2 т 2

ιo which you are called, may he restore to us again the best of men, and the most beloved fellow-citizen.''

General Washington returned an answer to this address, expressing the emotions he felt at leaving them, and his desire that they might meet happily again, as they had done after the long and distressing separation occasioned by the war.   In the afternoon of the same day, he was escorted by the people to Georgetown, where a delegation from Maryland received him.   Everywhere his journey was a continued scene of public rejoicing and congratulation.   At Philadelphia, the bridge over which he crossed the Schuylkill was decorated by a laurel shrubbery on each side, and a triumphal arch of laurel was erected at each end.   The road was blocked up by masses of people, eager to catch a sight of their favourite, and at night the whole city was illuminated.   The roaring of cannon at each successive town he visited, gave notice of his approach to the people of the next, and they immediately made ready to receive him.   At Trenton, the ladies were prepared to testify, in a novel manner, their grateful sense of the deliverance from the power of a brutal enemy, which he had wrought for them twelve years before.   On the bridge over the creek which passes through the town, a triumphal arch was erected, highly ornamented with laurels and flowers ; and supported by thirteen pillars, each entwined with evergreen.   In large gilt letters, on the front of the arch, was the inscription—

"THE DEFENDER OF THE MOTHERS WILL BE THE PROTECTOR OF THE DAUGHTERS."

On another portion of the arch were conspicuously displayed the dates of the two memorable occasions in which the valour of the commander-in-chief was displayed at Trenton.   Here he was met by a party of matrons leading their daughters, clothed in white, and carrying baskets of flowers in their hands.   The latter sang, with great effect, the following ode, strewing their flowers before him when they reached the last line :

" Welcome mighty chief, once more
Welcome to this grateful shore ;
Now no mercenary foe
Aims again the fatal blow,
Aims at THEE, the fatal blow.

" Virgins fair and matrons grave,
Those thy conquering arms did save,
Build for THEE triumphal bowers ;
Strew ye fair his way with flowers,
Strew your Hero's way with flowers."

At Brunswick, the governor of New Jersey met him and accompanied him to Elizabethtown Point, the committee of Congress also forming a part of the great military parade which escorted him thither. The governor and authorities of New Jersey having taken leave of him, he embarked with the deputation from Congress, in a barge manned by thirteen branch pilots, which had been prepared by the citizens of New York. From this he landed on the 23d cf April at Murray's Wharf, which had been magnificently prepared for that purpose. There, the governor of New York received him and conducted him with military honours amid an immense concourse of people, to the apartments prepared for him. A general illumination at night followed this day of extravagant joy. Yet all these public testimonials of his popularity failed to divert the attention of General Washington from the arduous and fearful duties and responsibilities he was about to assume. His solid judgment was neither perverted nor corrupted thereby, and the proofs of confidence thus afforded, while they certainly gave him reason for present rejoicing, filled him with anxieties for the future. In his journal, speaking of the escort which accompanied him from Elizabethtown Point to New York, he says: "The display of boats which attended and joined on this occasion, some with vocal and others with instrumental music on board, the decorations of the ships, the roar of cannon, and the loud acclamations of the people, which rent the air as I passed along the wharves, filled my mind with sensations as painful (contemplating the reverse of this scene, which may be the case after all my labours to do good) as they were pleasing."

Two days before the arrival of General Washington, Mr. Adams, having arrived in New York, was inducted into the chair of the vice-president. Upon taking his seat, he addressed the Senate in a neat speech, in which he alluded to the formation of the new government and character of the chief magistrate elect, in the following terms:

"It is with satisfaction that I congratulate the people of America on the formation of a national constitution, and the fair prospect of a consistent administration of a government of laws; on the acquisition of a House of Representatives chosen by themselves, of a Senate thus composed by their own state legislatures; and on the prospect of an executive authority in the hands of one whose portrait I shall not presume to draw. Were I blessed with powers to do justice to his character, it would be impossible to increase the confidence or affection of his country, or make the smallest addition to his glory. This can only be effected by a discharge of the present exalted trust, on the same principles, with the same abilities and virtues which have uniformly appeared in all his former conduct, public or private. May I, nevertheless, be indulged to inquire, if we look over the catalogues of the first magistrates of nations, whether they have been denominated presidents or consuls, kings or princes, where shall we find one whose commanding talents and virtues, whose overruling good fortune have so completely united all hearts and voices in his favour? Who enjoyed the esteem and admiration of foreign nations and fellow-citizens with equal unanimity? Qualities so uncommon are no common blessings to the country that possess th m. By these great qualities and their benign effects, has Provide ice marked out the head of this nation with a hand so distinctly visible, as to have been seen by all men, and mistaken by none."*

On Thursday, April 30th, the preliminaries being adjusted, the two houses of Congress assembled in the Senate chamber, whither General Washington was conducted by the joint committee, and introduced to the chair. All then proceeded to the gallery in front of the Senate chamber, where the chancellor of the state of New York administered the oath in the presence of both houses, and in view of a great concourse of people, who greeted his entry upon the duties of office, with loud and long-repeated applause. Returning to the Senate chamber, he delivered the following address:—

"Fellow citizens of the Senate and House of Representatives:— Among the vicissitudes incident to life, no event could have filled me with greater anxieties, than that of which the notification was transmitted, by your order, and received on the 14th day of the present month. On the one hand, I was summoned by my country, whose voice I can never hear, but with veneration and love, from a retreat which I had chosen, with the fondest predilection, and, in my flattering hopes, with an immutable decision, as the asylum of my declining years; a retreat which was rendered every day more necessary, as well as more dear to me, by the addition of habit to inclination, and of frequent interruptions to my health, to the gradual waste committed on it by time. On the other hand, the magnitude and difficulty of the trust to which the voice of my country called me, being sufficient to awaken, in the wisest and most experienced of her citizens, a distrustful scrutiny into his qualifications, could not but overwhelm with despondence one who,

* Marshall.

inheriting inferior endowments from nature, and unpractised in the duties of civil administration, ought to be peculiarly conscious of his own deficiencies.   In this conflict of emotions, all I dare aver is, that it has been my faithful study to collect my duty from a just appreciation of every circumstance by which it might be affected.   All I dare hope is, that if, in executing this task, I have been too much swayed by a grateful remembrance of former instances, or, by an affectionate sensibility to this transcendant proof of the confidence of my fellow-citizens ; and have thence too little consulted my incapacity, as well as disinclination, for the weighty and untried cares before me, my error will be palliated by the motives which misled me, and its consequences be judged by my country, with some share of the partiality in which they originated.

"Such being the impressions under which I have, in obedience to the public summons, repaired to the present station ; it would be peculiarly improper to omit, in this, my first official act, my fervent supplications to that Almighty Being who rules over the universe ; who presides in the councils of nations, and whose providential aids can supply every human defect, that his benediction may consecrate to the liberties and happiness of the people of the United States, a government instituted by themselves for these essential purposes, and may enable every instrument employed in its administration to execute with success the functions allotted to his charge.   In tendering this homage to the great Author of every public and private good, I assure myself that it expresses your sentiments not less than my own ; nor those of my fellow-citizens at large, less than either.   No people can be bound to acknowledge and adore the invisible hand which conducts the affairs of men, more than the people of the United States.   Every step, by which they have advanced to the character of an independent nation, seems to have been distinguished by some token of providential agency ; and, in the important revolution just accomplished in the system of their united government, the tranquil deliberations and voluntary consent of so many distinct communities, from which the event has resulted, cannot be compared with the means by which most governments have been established, without some return of pious gratitude, along with an humble anticipation of the future blessings which the past would seem to presage.   These reflections, arising out of the present crisis, have forced themselves too strongly on my mind to be suppressed. You will join with me, I trust, in thinking that there are none under the influence of which the proceedings of a new and free government can more auspiciously commence.

" By the article establishing the executive department, it is made the duty of the president, 'to recommend to your consideration such measures as he shall judge necessary and expedient.' The circumstances under which I now meet you, will acquit me from entering into that subject, farther than to refer to the great constitutional charter, under which you are assembled; and which, in defining your powers, designates the objects to which your attention is to be given. It will be more consistent with those circumstances, and far more congenial with the feelings which actuate me, to substitute, in place of a recommendation of particular measures, the tribute that is due to the talents, the rectitude, and the patriotism, which adorn the characters selected to revise and adopt them. In these honourable qualifications, I behold the surest pledges, that, as on one side, no local prejudices or attachments, no separate views nor party animosities, will misdirect the comprehensive and equal eye, which ought to watch over this great assemblage of communities and interests ; so, on another, that the foundations of our national policy will be laid in the pure and immutable principles of private morality, and the pre-eminence of free government be exemplified by all the attributes which can win the affections of its citizens, and command the respect of the world. I dwell on this prospect, with every satisfaction which an ardent love of my country can inspire : since there is no truth more thoroughly established than that there exists, in the economy and course of nature, an indissoluble union between virtue and happiness, between duty and advantage, between the genuine maxims of an honest and magnanimous policy, and the solid rewards of public prosperity and felicity ; since we ought to be no less persuaded, that the propitious smiles of Heaven can never be expected on a nation that disregards the eternal rules of order and right, which Heaven itself has ordained : and since the preservation of the sacred fire of liberty, and the creating of the republican model of government, are justly considered as deeply, perhaps, as finally staked, on the experiment intrusted to the hands of the American people.

" Besides the ordinary objects committed to your care, it will remain with your judgment to decide, how far an exercise of the occasional power delegated by the fifth article of the Constitution, is rendered expedient at the present juncture, by the nature of objections which have been urged against the system, or by the degree of inquietude which has given birth to them. Instead of undertaking particular recommendations on this subject, in which I could be guided by no lights derived from official opportunities, I shall again give way to my entire confidence in your discernment and pursuit for the public good; for, I assure myself, that, whilst you carefully avoid every alteration which might endanger the benefit of a united and effective government, or which ought to await the future lessons of experience; a reverence for the characteristic rights of freemen, and a regard for the public harmony, will sufficiently influence your deliberations on the question, how far the former can be more impregnably fortified, or the latter be safely and advantageously promoted.

"To the preceding observations, I have one to add, which will be most properly addressed to the House of Representatives. It concerns myself, and will, therefore, be as brief as possible. When I was first honoured with a call into the service of my country, then on the eve of an arduous struggle for its liberties, the light in which I contemplated my duty required that I should renounce every pecuniary compensation. From this resolution, I have in no instance departed: and being still under the impressions which produced it, I must decline, as inapplicable to myself, any share in the personal emoluments which may be indispensably included in a permanent provision for the Executive Department; and must, accordingly, pray, that the pecuniary estimates for the station in which I am placed, may, during my continuance in it, be limited to such actual expenditures as the public good may be thought to require.

"Having thus imparted to you my sentiments, as they have been awakened by the occasion which brings us together, I shall take my present leave; but not without resorting once more to the Benign Parent of the human race, in humble supplication, that, since he has been pleased to favour the American people with opportunities for deliberating in perfect tranquillity, and dispositions for deciding, with unparalleled unanimity, on a form of government for the security of their union, and the advancement of their happiness; so, His divine blessing may be equally conspicuous in the enlarged views, the temperate consultations, and the wise measures, on which the success of this government must depend.

"GEORGE WASHINGTON."

In answer to the speech of the president, the Senate prepared an address, which was presented to him on the 14th.

"SIR,—We, the Senate of the United States, return you our sincere thanks for your excellent speech delivered to both houses of Congress; congratulate you on the complete organization of the federal government, and felicitate ourselves, and our fellow-citizens on your elevation to the office of President: an office highly important, by the powers constitutionally annexed to it, and extremely honourable, from the manner in which the appointment is made. The unanimous suffrage of the elective body, in your favour, is peculiarly expressive of the gratitude, confidence, and affection, of the citizens of America; and is the highest testimonial at once of your merit and their esteem. We are sensible, sir, that nothing but the voice of your fellow citizens could have called you from a retreat, chosen with the fondest predilection, endeared by habit, and consecrated to the repose of declining years. We rejoice, and with us all America, that, in obedience to the call of our common country, you have returned once more to public life. In you, all parties confide: in you, all interests unite: and we have no doubt that your past services, great as they have been, will be equalled by your future exertions; and that your prudence and sagacity, as a statesman, will tend to avert the dangers to which we were exposed, to give stability to the present government, and dignity and splendour to that country, which your skill and valour as a soldier so eminently contributed to raise to independence and empire.

"When we contemplate the coincidence of circumstances, and the wonderful combination of causes, which gradually prepared the people of this country for independence; when we contemplate the rise, progress, and termination of the late war, which gave them a name among the nations of the earth, we are, with you, unavoidably led to acknowledge and adore the Great Arbiter of the universe, by whom empires rise and fall. A review of the many signal instances of Divine interposition, in favour of this country, claims our most pious gratitude: and permit us, sir, to observe, that, among the great events which have led to the formation and establishment of a federal government, we esteem your acceptance of the office of president as one of the most propitious and important.

"In the execution of the trust reposed in us, we shall endeavour to pursue that enlarged and liberal policy to which your speech so happily directs. We are conscious that the prosperity of each state is inseparably connected with the welfare of all, and that, in promoting the latter, we shall effectually advance the former. In full persuasion of this truth, it shall be our invariable aim to divest ourselves of local prejudices and attachments, and to view the

·great assemblage of communities and interests committed to our charge with an equal eye. We feel, sir, the force, and acknowledge the justness of the observation, that the foundation of our national policy should be laid in private morality: if individuals be not influenced by moral principles, it is in vain to look for public virtue ; it is, therefore, the duty of legislatures to enforce, both by precept and example, the utility, as well as the necessity, of a strict adherence to the rules of distributive justice. We beg you to be assured, that the Senate will at all times cheerfully co-operate in every measure which may strengthen the Union, conduce to the happiness, or secure and perpetuate the liberties of this great, confederated republic.

"We commend you, sir, to the protection of Almighty God, earnestly beseeching him long to preserve a life, so valuable and dear to the people of the United States ; and that your administration may be prosperous to the nation, and glorious to yourself."

The address of the House, in answer to the president's speech, as reported by Mr. Madison, and accepted by the house, was as follows:—

"Sir,—The representatives of the people of the United States present their congratulations on the event by which your fellow-citizens have attested the pre-eminence of your merit. You have long held the first place in their esteem ; you have often received tokens of their affection ; you now possess the only proof that remained of their gratitude for your services, of their reverence for your wisdom, and of their confidence in your virtues ; you enjoy the highest, because the truest honour, of being the first magistrate, by the unanimous choice of the freest people on the face of the earth.

"We well knew the anxieties with which you have obeyed a summons, from a repose reserved for your declining years, into public scenes, of which you had taken your leave for ever. But the obedience was due to the occasion. It is already applauded by the universal joy which welcomes you to your station ; and we cannot doubt, that it will be rewarded with all the satisfaction with which an ardent love for your fellow-citizens must review successful efforts to promote their happiness.

"This anticipation is not justified merely by the past experience of your signal services. It is particularly suggested by the pious impressions under which you commence your administration, and the enlightened maxims by which you mean to conduct it. We feel, with you, the strongest obligations to adore the Invisible Hand, which has led the American people through so many difficulties; to cherish a conscious responsibility for the destiny of republican liberty; and to seek the only sure means of preserving and recommending the precious deposit, in a system of legislation, founded on the principles of an honest policy, and directed by the spirit of a diffusive patriotism.

"The question arising out of the fifth article of the Constitution will receive all the attention demanded by its importance; and will, we trust, be decided under the influence of all the considerations to which you allude.

"In forming the pecuniary provisions for the executive department, we shall not lose sight of a wish resulting from motives, which give it a peculiar claim to our regard. Your resolution, in a moment critical to the liberties of your country, to renounce all personal emolument, was among the many presages of your patriotic services, which have been amply fulfilled; and your scrupulous adherence now, to the law then imposed on yourself, cannot fail to demonstrate the purity, while it increases the lustre of a character which has so many titles to admiration.

"Such are the sentiments which we have thought fit to address to you. They flow from our own hearts; and we verily believe, that, among the millions we represent, there is not a virtuous citizen whose heart will disown them.

"All that remains is, that we join in our fervent supplications for the blessings of Heaven on our country, and that we add our own, for the choicest of these blessings, on the most beloved of her citizens."

The President, the Vice-president, with the two Houses of Congress, proceeded, after the ceremony of inauguration, to St. Paul's Chapel, where Divine service was performed by the chaplain to Congress, after which the President was re-conducted to his house by a committee appointed for that purpose.

In the evening, a very ingenious and splendid show of fireworks was exhibited. Between the Fort and the Bowling-Green stood conspicuous a superb and brilliant transparent painting, in the centre of which was the portrait of the President, represented under the emblem of Fortitude; on his right hand was Justice, representing the Senate of the United States, and on his left, Wisdom, representing the House of Representatives.

The following animated account of the commencement of the domestic life of General Washington in his new position, we extract from the "Recollections and Private Memoirs of the Life and Character of Washington," by his honoured relative, G. W. P. Custis, Esq. It will afford an interesting and not uninstructive comparison of the states of society at the commencement of the constitutional government, and at the present time.

"In the then limited extent and improvement of the city, there was some difficulty in selecting a mansion for the residence of the chief magistrate, and a household suitable to his rank and station. Osgood's house, a mansion of very moderate extent, was at length fixed upon, situated in Cherry street. There the President became domiciled. His domestic family consisted of Mrs. Washington, the two adopted children, Mr. Lear as principal secretary, Colonel Humphreys, with Messrs. Lewis and Nelson, secretaries, and Major William Jackson, aid-de-camp.

"Persons visiting the house in Cherry street at this time of day, will wonder how a building so small could contain the many and mighty spirits that thronged its halls in olden days. Congress, cabinet, all public functionaries in the commencement of the government, were selected from the very elite of the nation. Pure patriotism, commanding talent, eminent services, were the proud and indispensable requisites for official station in the first days of the republic. The first Congress was a most enlightened and dignified body. In the Senate were several of the members of the Congress of 1776, and signers of the Declaration of Independence —Richard Henry Lee, who moved the Declaration, John Adams, who seconded it, with Sherman, Morris, Carroll, &c.

"The levees of the first President were attended by these illustrious patriots and statesmen, and by many others of the patriots, statesmen, and soldiers, who could say of the Revolution, "magna pars fui;" while numbers of foreigners and strangers of distinction crowded to the seat of the general government, all anxious to witness the grand experiment that was to determine how much rational liberty mankind is capable of enjoying, without said liberty degenerating into licentiousness.

"Mrs. Washington's drawing-rooms, on Friday nights, were attended by the grace and beauty of New York. On one of these occasions, an incident occurred which might have been attended by serious consequences. Owing to the lowness of the ceiling in the drawing-room, the ostrich feather in the head-dress of Miss McIver, a belle of New York, took fire from the chandelier, to the no small alarm of the company. Major Jackson, aid-de-camp to the President, with great presence of mind, and equal gallantry,

flew to the rescue of the lady, and, by clapping the burning
plumes between his hands, extinguished the flame, and the drawing-room went on as usual.

"Washington preserved the habit, as well in public as in private life, of rising at four o'clock, and retiring to bed at nine. On
Saturdays he rested somewhat from his labours, by either riding
into the country, attended by a groom, or with his family in his
coach drawn by six horses.

"Fond of horses, the stables of the President were always in the
finest order, and his equipage excellent, both in taste and quality.
Indeed, so long ago as the days of the vice-regal court of Lord
Botetourt, at Williamsburg, in Virginia, we find that there existed
a rivalry between the equipages of Colonel Byrd, a magnate of the
old regime, and Colonel Washington—the grays against the bays.
Bishop, the celebrated body-servant of Braddock, was the master
of Washington's stables. And there were what was termed *muslin horses* in those old days. At cock-crow, the stable-boys were
at work; at sunrise Bishop stalked into the stables, a muslin hand-
kerchief in his hand, which he applied to the coats of the animals,
and, if the slightest stain was perceptible upon the muslin, up
went the luckless wights of the stable-boys, and punishment was
administered instanter; for to the veteran Bishop, bred amid the
iron discipline of European armies, mercy for any thing like a
breach of duty was altogether out of the question.

"The President's stables in Philadelphia were under the direction of German John, and the grooming of the white chargers will
rather surprise the moderns. The night before the horses were
expected to be rode, they were covered entirely over with a paste,
of which whiting was the principal component part; then the animals were swathed in body-cloths, and left to sleep upon clean
straw. In the morning the composition had become hard, was
well rubbed in, and curried and brushed, which process gave to
the coats a beautiful, glossy, and satin-like appearance. The hoofs
were then blacked and polished, the mouths washed, teeth picked
and cleaned; and, the leopard-skin housings being properly adjusted, the white chargers were led out for service. Such was the
grooming of ancient times.

"There was but one theatre in New York in 1789, (in John
street,) and so small were its dimensions, that the whole fabric
might easily be placed on the stage of one of our modern theatres.
Yet, humble as was the edifice, it possessed an excellent company
of actors and actresses, including old Morris, who was the associate

of Garrick, in the very outset of that great actor's career at Good-mans-fields. The stage boxes were appropriated to the President and Vice-president, and were each of them decorated with emblems, trophies, &c. At the foot of the play-bills were always the words ' *Vivat Respublica*.' Washington often visited this theatre, being particularly gratified by Wignell's performance of *Darby*, in the *Poor Soldier*.

"It was in the theatre in John street, that the now national air of ' Hail Columbia,' then called the ' President's March,' was first played. It was composed by a German musician, named Fyles, the leader of the orchestra, in compliment to the President. The national air will last as long as the nation lasts, while the meritorious composer has been long since forgotten.

"It was while residing in Cherry street that the President was attacked by a severe illness, that required a surgical operation. He was attended by the elder and younger Doctors Bard. The elder being somewhat doubtful of his nerves, gave the knife to his son, bidding him ' cut away—deeper, deeper still; don't be afraid; you see how well he bears it.' Great anxiety was felt in New York, at this time, as the President's case was considered extremely dangerous. Happily, the operation proved successful, and the patient's recovery removed all cause of alarm. During the illness a chain was stretched across the street, and the sidewalks laid with straw. Soon after his recovery, the President set out on his intended tour through the New England states.

"The President's mansion was so limited in accommodation that three of the secretaries were compelled to occupy one room—Humphreys, Lewis, and Nelson. Humphreys, aid-de-camp to the commander-in-chief at Yorktown, was a most estimable man, and at the same time a poet. About this period he was composing his ' Widow of Malabar.' Lewis and Nelson, both young men, were content, after the labours of the day, to enjoy a good night's repose. But this was often denied them ; for Humphreys, when in the vein, would rise from his bed at any hour, and, with stentorian voice, recite his verses. The young men, roused from their slumbers, and rubbing their eyes, beheld a great burly figure, ' *en chemise*,' striding across the floor, reciting, with great emphasis, particular passages from his poem, and calling on his room-mates for their approbation. Having in this way, for a considerable time, ' murdered the sleep' of his associates, Humphreys, at length, wearied by his exertions, would sink upon his pillow in a kind of dreamy languor. So sadly were the young secretaries annoyed by the frequent outbursts of the poet's imagination, that it was remarked of them by their friends, that, from 1789 to the end of their lives, neither Robert Lewis, nor Thomas Nelson, were ever known to evince the slightest taste for poetry."*

The first care of the president was directed to the attainment of such a knowledge of the state of the governmental affairs under the Articles of Confederation, as would enable him to administer properly the executive department. While Congress was making the necessary arrangements for the new government, the old institutions continued, and to the temporary heads of departments the president turned to obtain this information. Their reports showed that there was ample room for the exercise of all the firmness, integrity, and talents of even Washington himself. Another man would have shrunk back in despair at the prospect which now presented itself to Washington, only to call forth his energy in surmounting its difficulties. There were very many objects to be contemplated, the documents respecting which could not be found in the official records. The conflict respecting the Constitution had been so sharp and exciting as to engender much animosity, and though its friends formed a majority of the people, two states still remained out of the Union, and the discontent and ill-feeling existing in the others required the utmost circumspection on the part of the administration. In the west, there appeared a disposition to separate from the confederacy, in order to obtain certain advantages, which, it was supposed, would be granted to a separate republic in the west, but which Congress would not be able to obtain. British agents suggested that if the people there would separate themselves from their Atlantic brethren, the aid of the governor of Canada would be afforded them in seizing and fortifying the Balize, at the mouth of the Mississippi, against the power of Spain, whose capricious agents frequently denied the right of navigating that river, and interdicted commerce with New Orleans. Spain also had her agents employed in tampering with the people of the west. They suggested that the Mississippi afforded the only highway by which the produce of the west could reach the markets of the world, that the future wealth and prosperity of that section of country depended upon its free navigation, and intimated that that which would be readily accorded to an independent empire established in the interior, could never be granted to them while they remained connected with the Atlantic states. The animosity felt against England by the inhabitants generally, precluded

* National Intelligencer.

all fears from her machinations, but those of Spain were more formidable.*

The Indian relations of the country also demanded consideration. The savage tribes were now far more formidable than they had been to the early colonists. Instructed first by the French in the use of firearms and swords, they had cast aside their primitive weapons before the Revolution commenced, and during its continuance they had acquired no little knowledge of discipline. They had always been possessed of natural courage, and they nearly supplied by superior cunning what they lost by their inferiority in bodily strength when compared with the descendants of the Europeans. In the south, the Creek Indians, whose fighting men amounted to six hundred, were at war with Georgia. Their chief was a half-breed named McGillivray, whose feelings against the colonists were embittered by the confiscation of the property of his father, a white man who had been a Tory. The state of Georgia claimed a tract of land on the Oconge River, under a purchase which the Indians denied to be valid. The northern Indians were supposed to be able to bring five thousand fighting men into the field, and of these nearly one third were at open war with the United States, and the residue far from friendly. The regular force of the states numbered less than six hundred men. In addition to the policy of accommodating differences by negotiation which the government was in no condition to terminate by the sword, a real respect for the rights of the natives, and a regard for the claims of justice and humanity, disposed the President to remove all causes of quarrel by treaties, and his message to Congress on this subject evinced his preference of pacific measures.

With the different nations of Europe, the United States were at peace, but there existed controversies of a delicate nature with some of them, which, it was feared, would involve the infant republic in serious difficulties. Spain not only denied the right to navigate the Mississippi, but claimed a large territory as her property under the title of an alleged conquest from Great Britain, the extent of which could not be precisely ascertained. An attempt on the part of the old government to settle the matter by treaty had failed, and all the watchfulness and prudence of the executive was necessary to resist the violent discontent of the western people, which furnished Spain with additional motives for perpetuating the evil of which they complained. The mutual ill-feeling between the people of the United States and the inhabitants of England led the colonists to consider

* Marshall.

AMERICAN COMMISSIONERS NEGOTIATING THE TREATY.

the commercial regulations of the British government as the offspring of jealousy, and induced them to look to the sinister influence of Britain for the cause of all their other troubles, and produced similar effects in England. The temper displayed on both sides, from the close of the Revolution until the formation of the new government, was such as to render the idea of a renewal of the war, at no distant period, far from improbable.

Frederic the Great of Prussia had been early applied to by the merican government, which solicited him to join in a treaty of neutrality, "as the monarch best calculated to set an example to the other powers of Europe." The admiration which the career and character of Washington had inspired in the bosom of the king, extended itself to the whole American nation: he acceded to their request without hesitation, and Franklin, Jefferson, and Adams, concluded a treaty with the Prussian ambassadors at the Hague, in 1785, the terms and stipulations of which, based on considera. tions of the purest philanthropy, form a most honourable memorial of the good understanding between two of the most illustrious men of the age.

With Portugal, an attempt to conclude a commercial treaty had failed, and the Barbary powers manifested a hostile disposition. The emperor of Morocco, indeed, had concluded a treaty, and exhibited no intention of violating it, but peace was yet to be purchased from Algiers, Tunis, and Tripoli.

During its first session, the national legislature was principally occupied in providing revenues for the long-exhausted treasury, in establishing a judiciary, in organizing the executive departments in detail, and in framing amendments to the Constitution, agreeably to the suggestion of the President. The members immediately entered upon the exercise of those powers so long refused under the Articles of Confederation. They imposed a tonnage duty as well as duties on various imported articles, steadily keeping in sight, however, the navigating interest of the country, which had hitherto been almost wholly at the mercy of other nations. Higher tonnage duties were imposed on foreign than on American bottoms, and goods imported in vessels belonging to citizens of the United States paid ten per cent. less duty than the same goods brought in those owned by foreigners. These discriminating duties were intended to counteract the commercial regulations of foreign nations, and encourage American shipping. To aid in the management of the affairs of government, three executive departments were established, styled Departments of War, Foreign Affairs, and of the Treasury, with a secretary at the head of each.

The heads of these departments, in addition to the duties specially assigned them, were intended to constitute a council, to be consulted by the President whenever he thought proper ; and the executive was authorized by the Constitution to require the opinion, in writing, of the principal officers in the executive departments, on subjects relating to the duties of their offices. In framing the acts, constituting these offices, and defining their duties, it became an important subject of inquiry in what manner, or by whom these important officers could be removed from office. This was a question as new as it was momentous, and was applicable to all officers of executive appointment. In the long and learned debates on the subject, in Congress, there arose a very animated opposition to such a construction of the Constitution as to give this power to any

65

one individual. Whatever confidence might be placed in the chief magistrate then at the head of the government, equal confidence could not be expected in his successors, and it was contended that a concurrence of the Senate was as necessary and proper, in the removal of a person from office, as in his appointment. Some of the members of the House of Representatives were of opinion that they could not be removed without impeachment. The principal question, however, on which Congress was divided, was, whether they were removable by the President alone, or by the President, in concurrence with the Senate. A majority, however, in both houses, decided that this power was in the President alone. In the House, the majority in favour of this construction was twelve. This decision of a great constitutional question has been acquiesced in, and in its consequences has been of greater importance than almost any other since the establishment of the new government. From the manner in which this power has been exercised, it has given a tone and character to the executive branch of the government, not contemplated, it is believed, by the framers of the Constitution, or by those who constituted the first Congress under it. It has greatly increased the influence and patronage of the President, and in no small degree made him the centre, around which the other branches of the government revolve.*

In a free country, where the private citizen has both the right and the inclination to take an interest in the public concerns, it is natural that political parties and civil contentions should arise. These will be more or less violent, angry, and hostile, according as a sense of common security from external dangers leaves no cause for united action, and little anxiety for the common peace. A natural consequence of this strife of parties is the exercise of the passions—pride, interest, vanity, resentment, gratitude—each contributing its share in irritating and prolonging the controversy. In the beginning of the Revolution, the people of the United States divided themselves into the two great classes of Whigs and Tories; then they again separated upon the question of absolute independence. Other questions arose during the war relative to its conduct, and the qualifications of the leaders of the army. Independence achieved, the minds of the people were agitated about the nature of the government, which all saw to be necessary for their own happiness, and for the better enabling them to prosecute with foreign countries peaceful negotiations, or the operations of war. Many saw, in too close a union, dangers as great and conse-

* Pitkin.

quences as distasteful as in their entire separation. It was believed by many, that the extent of the country, the great diversity of character, habits and pursuits, among the several states, presented insuperable obstacles to a closer union than that afforded by the Articles of Confederation. Some were almost exclusively commercial, others agricultural ; some were disposed to engage in manufacturing pursuits ; some had domestic slavery firmly connected with their domestic relations, and were disposed to look favourably on the extension of the institution ; others regarded involuntary servitude as a curse, and desired its abolition. It was not to be wondered at, that with such points of diversity, many should suppose that a single government could not administer the affairs of all, except by a greater delegation of power than would be submitted to by the American people. While some looked wholly to these apprehended consequences of a close union and a single government, others chiefly regarded the dangers arising from disunion, domestic dissensions, and even war. One party dreaded consolidation ; the other anarchy and separation. Each saw, in the object of its dread, the destruction of good government, though one party looked too exclusively to its characteristic of *order*, the other to that of *civil liberty*. These were the thoughts of the people, widely differing, but all equally honest. But the politicians addressed themselves to these prejudices, often with unworthy motives. Local prejudices, self-interest, fears, in some cases from an anticipated loss of consequence, in the event of a transfer of sovereignty from the individual states to the general government, all combined to make many violent in their expressions of opposition to the plan. Apprehensions of violence and disorder, and fears from individual popularity in a circumscribed sphere, led others to desire consolidation. With these, ranked others who were fond of the pomp and show of authority which would attend a powerful government, and still others, who, having claims upon the country, supposed that they would have much stronger hopes of being paid themselves, and of seeing the debts due abroad liquidated, if a system of government were established which could be certain to raise a revenue for these objects. On the formation of the Constitution, the community settled down into two great parties, Federalists and Anti-federalists, or Democrats ; the first believing that the most imminent danger to our peace and prosperity was in disunion ; and that popular jealousy, always active, would withhold the power which was essential to good order and national safety ; the other party believing that the danger most to be apprehended was in too close a union, and that their most powerful opponents wished a consolidated and even a monarchical government.

There were many who had been accustomed to reflect upon government and political relations previously to the war of independence, when the constitution of Great Britain being by far the best that had ever existed, they may naturally be supposed to have conceived for it a degree of homage and respect which it could not now inspire. The speculations on political rights, to which the contest with Great Britain and the debates on the question of independence gave rise, greatly favoured the doctrines of political equality and the hatred of power, in any form that could control the public will. There are, in the heart of every man, principles which readily prepare him for republican doctrines, and after a few years, some of the speculative politicians began to think that the free, simple, and equal government which was suited to the tastes and habits of our people, was also the best in theory. The great body of the people were partial to the form of government to which they had been accustomed, and wished for none other, though the leading statesmen differed upon this point. Some preferred the republican form in theory, and believed that no other would be tolerated in practice ; and others regretted that they were obliged to yield so far to popular prejudice as to forego the form they deemed best, but determined to avail themselves of every opportunity of improving the existing government into that form. Nor were they without hopes that by siding with the general government in every question of power between that and the separate states, and with the executive in all questions between that and the legislature, and by continually increasing the patronage of the executive by means of an army, a navy, and the multiplication of civil offices, they would ultimately obtain their object.*

It was in the midst of this society, so agitated and disturbed, that Washington, without ambition, without any false show, from a sense of duty rather than inclination, and rather trusting in truth than confident of success, undertook actually to found the government decreed by the new-born Constitution. He rose to his high office invested with an immense influence, which was acknowledged and received even by his enemies.

Washington's natural inclination, says Guizot,† was rather to a democratic social state than to any other. Of a mind just rather than expansive, of a temper wise and calm, full of dignity, but

* Tucker's Life of Jefferson.
† Essay on the Character and Influence of Washington.

free from all selfish and arrogant pretensions; coveting rather respect than power, the impartiality of democratic principles, and the simplicity of democratic manners, far from offending or annoying him, suited his tastes, and satisfied his judgment. He did not trouble himself with inquiring whether more elaborate combinations, a division into ranks, privileges, and artificial barriers, were necessary to the preservation of society. He lived tranquilly in the midst of an equal and sovereign people, finding its authority to be lawful and submitting to it without effort.

But when the question was one of political and not social order, when the discussion turned upon the organization of the government, he was strongly federal, opposed to local and popular pretensions, and the declared advocate of the unity and force of the central power.

He placed himself under this standard, and did so to insure its triumph. But still his elevation was not the victory of a party, and awakened in no one either exultation or regret. In the eyes, not only of the public, but of his enemies, he was not included in any party, and was above them all; "the only man in the United States," said Jefferson, "who possessed the confidence of all;— . . . there was no other one who was considered as any thing more than a party leader."

It was his constant effort to maintain this honourable privilege. "It is really my wish to have my mind, and my actions, which are the result of reflection, as free and independent as the air. . . . If it should be my inevitable fate to administer the government, I will go to the chair under no pre-engagement of any kind or nature whatsoever. . . . Should any thing tending to give me anxiety present itself in this or any other publication, I shall never undertake the painful task of recrimination, nor do I know that I should ever enter upon my justification. . . . . All else is but food for declamation. . . . . Men's minds are as various as their faces; and, where the motives of their actions are pure, the operations of the former are no more to be imputed to them as a crime, than the appearance of the latter. . . . . Differences in political opinions are as unavoidable, as, to a certain point, they may, perhaps, be necessary."* A stranger also to all personal disputes, to the passions and prejudices of his friends, as well as his enemies, the purpose of his whole policy was to maintain this position, and to this policy he gave the true name, "the just medium!"

* Washington's Writings, vols. ix. x.

2 X

It is much, continues the great statesman of France, to have the wish to preserve a just medium ; but the wish, though accompanied with firmness and ability, is not always enough to secure it. Washington succeeded in this as much by the natural turn of his mind and character, as by making it his peculiar aim ; he was, indeed, really of no party, and his country, in esteeming him so, did no more than pay homage to truth.

A man of experience and a man of action, he had an admirable wisdom and made no pretension to systematic theories. He took no side beforehand ; he made no show of the principles that were to govern him. Thus, there was nothing like a logical harshness in his conduct, no committal of self-love, no struggle of rival talent. When he obtained the victory, his success was not to his adversaries either a stake lost, or a sweeping sentence of condemnation. It was not on the ground of the superiority of his own mind that he triumphed, but on the ground of the nature of things and of the inevitable necessity that accompanied them. Still his success was not an event without a moral character, the simple result of skill, strength, or fortune. Uninfluenced by any theory, he had faith in truth, and adopted it as the guide of his conduct. He did not pursue the victory of one opinion against the partisans of another ; neither did he act from interest in the event alone, or merely for success. He did nothing which he did not think to be reasonable and just ; so that his conduct, which had no systematic character that might be humbling to his adversaries, had still a moral character, which commanded respect.

Men had, moreover, the most thorough conviction of his disinterestedness ; that great light to which men so willingly trust their fate ; that vast power, which draws after it their hearts while at the same time it gives them confidence that their interests will not be surrendered, either as a sacrifice or as instruments to selfishness and ambition. A striking proof of his impartiality was afforded in the choice of the persons who were to form his cabinet under the law for the formation of the executive departments. Before he had assumed the duties of the office to which he had been chosen, he had received letters from different persons making application for offices which would be in his gift as President. Many of these were persons whom he was disposed to favour ; but an extract from an answer to one of them will show what rule he had adopted for his government in this respect : " Should it become absolutely necessary for me to occupy the station in which your letter presupposes me, I have determined to go into it perfectly free from all engagements of any kind whatsoever. A conduct in con-formity to this resolution would enable me, in balancing the various pretensions of different candidates for appointments, to act with a sole reference to justice and the public good. This is in substance the answer that I have given to all applications (and they are not few) which have already been made. Among the places sought after in these' applications, I must not conceal that the office to which you particularly allude is comprehended. This fact I tell you merely as a matter of information. My general manner of thinking, as to the propriety of holding myself totally disengaged, will apologize for my not enlarging farther on the subject. Though I am sensible that the public suffrage, which places a man in office, should prevent him from being swayed, in the execution of it, by his private inclinations, yet he may assuredly, without violating his duty, be indulged in the continuance of his former attachments."

In making the selection of the persons who were to take a share in his administration, Washington exerted all the means he possessed to search out and nominate those persons who would discharge the duties of their respective offices to the best interest and highest credit of the American union. The unmingled patriotism of his motives would receive its clearest demonstration from a view of all his private letters on this subject : and the success of his endea-vours is completely attested by the abilities and reputation which he drew into the public service.

At the head of the Department of Foreign Affairs, since denomi-nated the Department of State, he placed Thomas Jefferson. The Democratic party—not the turbulent and coarse democracy of an-tiquity or the middle ages, but the great modern democracy— never had a more faithful, or more distinguished representative than Jefferson. A warm friend of humanity, liberty, and science ; trusting in their goodness as well as their rights ; deeply touched by the injustice with which the mass of mankind have been treated, and the sufferings they endure, and incessantly engaged with an admirable disinterestedness, in remedying them, or preventing their recurrence ; accepting as a dangerous necessity, almost as one evil opposed to another, and exerting himself not merely to restrain, but to lower it ; distrusting all display, all personal splendour, as a tendency to usurpation ; of a temper, open, kind, indulgent, though ready to take up prejudices against, and feel irritated with the enemies of his party ; of a mind bold, active, ingenious, inquir-ing, with more penetration than forecast, but with too much good sense to push things to the extreme, and capable of employing, against a pressing danger or evil, a prudence and firmness which would perhaps have prevented it, had they been adopted earlier or more generally.*

Mr. Jefferson, in 1784, had been appointed to succeed Dr. Franklin at the court of Versailles, where he had acquitted himself to the satisfaction of his countrymen, and to the delight of the people among whom he represented them. Having lately obtained permission to return for a short time to the United States, he was, while on his passage, nominated to this important office, and on his arrival in Virginia, found a letter from the President, giving him the option of becoming secretary of Foreign Affairs, or of retaining his station at the court of France. In reply to it, Mr. Jefferson said that his inclinations led him to prefer his former station in France, to which it had been his intention to return. "But," he added, " it is not for an individual to choose his post. You are to marshal us as may be best for the public good ; and it is only in case of its being indifferent to you that I would avail myself of the option you have so kindly offered in your letter. If you think it better to transfer me to another post, my inclination must be no obstacle ; nor shall it be, if there is any desire to suppress the office I now hold, or to diminish its grade. In either of these cases be so good as to signify to me, by another line, your ultimate wish, and I shall conform to it accordingly. If it should be to remain at New York, my chief comfort will be to work under your eye ; my only shelter, the authority of your name ; and the wisdom of measures to be dictated by you and implicitly executed by me."

Mr. Madison united his solicitations to those of the President, and Mr. Jefferson finally assumed the duties of the station.

The important and intricate task which would devolve principally upon the Secretary of the Treasury, of re-creating the public credit, drawing order and arrangement from the chaotic confusion in which the finances of America were involved, and of devising means which should render the revenue productive, and commensurate with the demand, was confided to Alexander Hamilton.

Hamilton deserves to be ranked among those men who have best understood the vital principles and essential conditions of government ; not merely of a nominal government, but of a government worthy of its mission and of its name. In the Constitution of the United States, there is not an element of order, strength, and

* Marshall, Guizot.

durability to the introduction and adoption of which he did not powerfully contribute. Perhaps he believed the monarchical form preferable to the republican. Perhaps he sometimes had doubts of the success of the experiment attempted in his country. Perhaps, also, carried away by his vivid imagination and the logical vehemence of his mind, he was sometimes exclusive in his views, and went too far in his inferences. But, of a character as lofty as his mind, he faithfully served the republic, and laboured to found and not to weaken it. His superiority consisted in knowing, that, naturally, and by a law inherent in the nature of things, power is above, at the head of society ; that government should be consti tuted according to this law ; and that every contrary system or effort brings sooner or later trouble and weakness into the society itself. His error consisted in adhering too closely, and with a somewhat arrogant obstinacy, to the precedents of the English constitution, in attributing, sometimes, in these precedents, the same authority to good and to evil, to principles and to the abuse of them, and in not attaching due importance to, and reposing sufficient confidence in, the variety of political forms and the flexibility of human society. There are occasions in which political genius consists, in not fearing what is new, while what is eternal is respected.

The Department of War was already filled by General Knox, whose character was remarkable for integrity and ability, but who was too apt to submit himself to the influence of others, especially to those of lofty minds, like Hamilton, to whose political school he belonged. The office of Attorney-general was given to Edmund Randolph, a Democrat in politics, distinguished in the profession of the law, at one time governor of Virginia, and an active member of the convention which framed the Constitution. He was a restless spirit, who scarcely justified the reliance placed in his probity and good faith by the President.

During the first session of Congress, twelve articles were agreed to by both Houses, and submitted to the states as amendments to the Constitution. Of these, ten were ratified, by the constitutional majority of the states. A national judiciary was also estab.ished during this session, consisting of a Supreme Court, circuit and district courts.

The organization of the judiciary has remained nearly the same, with a short interval, during which another plan was tried and abandoned, to the present time. Much debate was had during this session, on the subject of designating a place for the permanent seat of the national government, but the session closed without a decision. The salaries of the President, Vice-president, the secre-taries, and the judiciary were fixed, but not without difficulty. A law was passed, placing the states of Rhode Island and North Carolina on the same footing with the states of the Union until the 15th of January, 1790, in order to allow another opportunity, by ratifying the Constitution, of entering the new confederacy.

Congress did not lose sight of the principal object in view, in forming the new government, the support of public credit. Just before they rose, a resolution passed the House of Representatives directing the Secretary of the Treasury to prepare a plan for this purpose, and report the same to the next session. The President, by a resolution of both houses, was requested to recommend to the people of the United States a day of public thanksgiving and prayer, to be observed by acknowledging with grateful hearts the many and signal favours of Almighty God, especially by affording them an opportunity peaceably to establish a constitution of government for their safety and happiness. Having fixed the first Monday in January, 1790, for their next meeting, Congress adjourned the 29th of September.

"A government," says Marshall, "supported in all its depart-ments by so much character and talents, at the head of which was placed a man whose capacity was undoubted, whose life had been one great and continued lesson of disinterested patriotism, and for whom almost every bosom glowed with an attachment bordering on enthusiasm, could not fail to make a rapid progress in conciliating the affection of the people. That all hostility to the Constitution should subside ; that public measures should receive universal ap-probation; that no particular disgusts and individual irritations should be excited, were expectations which could not reasonably be indulged. Exaggerated accounts were indeed circulated of the pomp and splendour which were affected by certain high officers, of the monarchical tendencies of particular institutions, and of the dispo-sitions which prevailed to increase the powers of the executive. That the doors of the Senate were closed, and that a disposition had been manifested by that body to distinguish the President of the United States by a title, gave considerable umbrage, and were repre-sented as evincing inclinations in that branch of the legislature un-friendly to republicanism. But the apprehensions of danger to liberty from the new system, which had been impressed on the minds of well-meaning men, were visibly wearing off; the popu-larity of the administration was communicating itself to the govern-

meat, and the materials with which the discontented few were fur
nished, could not yet be efficaciously employed.

The more violent opponents of the new government, indeed, were
still actively employed in endeavouring to excite the feelings of
the people against it by all manner of false reports and distorted
versions of facts. Partly with reference to these effusions of
malice, the President, in a letter to Dr. Stuart of Virginia, uses the
following language :—" While the eyes of America, perhaps of the
world, are turned to this government, and many are watching the
movements of all those who are concerned in its administration, I
should like to be informed through so good a medium of the public opinion of both men and measures, and of none more than myself; not so much of what may be thought commendable parts, if
any, of my conduct, as of those which are conceived to be of a different complexion. The man who means to commit no wrong,
will never be guilty of enormities, consequently he can never be
unwilling to learn what are ascribed to him as foibles. If they are
really such, the knowledge of them in a well-disposed mind will
go halfway towards a reform. If they are not errors, he can
explain and justify the motives of his actions.

" At a distance from the theatre of action, truth is not always
related without embellishment, and sometimes is entirely perverted,
from a misconception of the causes which produce the effects that
are the subjects of censure. This leads me to think that the system which I found it indispensably necessary to adopt on my first
coming to the city, might have undergone severe strictures, and
have had motives very foreign from those that govern me assigned
as causes thereof. I mean, first, returning no visits; secondly,
appointing certain days to receive them generally, not to the exclusion, however, of visits on any other days, under particular circumstances; and thirdly, at first entertaining no company and afterwards, until I was able to entertain any at all, confining it to official characters. A few days evinced the necessity of the two first
in so clear a point of view, that, had I not adopted it, I should
have been unable to attend to any sort of business, unless I had
applied the hours allotted to rest and refreshment to this purpose;
for, by the time I had done breakfast, and thence till dinner, and
afterwards till bed-time, I could not get relieved from the ceremony
of one visit, before I had to attend to another. In a word, I had
no leisure to read or to answer the despatches that were pouring
in upon me from all quarters.

" With respect to the third matter, I early received information through very respectable channels, that the adoption thereof was not less essential than that of the other two, if the President was to preserve the dignity and respect that were due to the first magistrate. For a contrary conduct had involved the late presidents of Congress in insuperable difficulties, and the office, in this respect, in perfect contempt; for the table was considered as a public one, and every person who could get introduced conceived that he had a right to be invited to it. This, although the table was always crowded, (and with mixed company, and the President considered in no better light than as a *maitre d'hotel,*) was in its nature impracticable, and as many offences given as if no table had been kept.

" The citizens of this place were well acquainted with this fact, and the principal members of Congress, in both Houses, were so well convinced of the impropriety and degrading situation of their President, that it was the general opinion that the President of the United States should neither give nor receive invitations; some from a belief, independent of the circumstances I have mentioned, that this was fundamentally right, in order to acquire respect. But to this I had two objections, both powerful in my mind; first, the novelty of it I knew would be considered as an ostentatious mimicry of sovereignty; and secondly, that so great a seclusion would have stopped the avenues to useful information from the many, and made me more dependent on that of the few. But to hit on a discriminating medium was found more difficult than it appeared to be at first view; for if the citizens at large were begun with, no line could be drawn; all, of decent appearance, would expect to be invited, and I should have plunged at once into the evil I was endeavouring to avoid. Upon the whole, it was thought best to confine my invitations to official characters and to strangers of distinction. This line I have hitherto pursued. Whether it may be found best to adhere to it or to depart from it, must in some measure be the result of experience and information.

" So strongly had the citizens of this place imbibed an idea of the impropriety of my accepting invitations to dinner, that I have not received one from any family, though they are remarkable for hospitality, and though I have received every civility and attention possible from them, since I came to the city, except to dine with the governor on the day of my arrival; so that if this should be adduced as an article of impeachment, there can be at least one good reason adduced for my not dining out; to wit, never having been asked to do so."

In June, 1790, he wrote again to Dr. Stuart, explaining the line of conduct he had adopted for the accommodation of those who were disposed to call upon him. It combined, he said, public advantage with private convenience, and in his judgment was unexceptionable in itself. Referring to a person who represented, according to Dr. Stuart, that there was more pomp used at the President's levees than at St. James's, and that the President's bows were more distant and stiff, General Washington humorously writes, "That I have not been able to make bows to the taste of poor Colonel B——, (who, by the by, I believe, never saw one of them,) is to be regretted; especially, too, as, upon those occasions, they were indiscriminately bestowed, and the best I was master of. Would it not have been better to have thrown the veil of charity over them, ascribing their stiffness to the effects of age, or to the unskilfulness of my teacher, rather than to pride and dignity of office, which, God knows, has no charms for me? For I can truly say, I had rather be at Mount Vernon with a friend or two about me, than to be attended at the seat of government by the officers of state and the representatives of every power in Europe.

" These visits are optional. They are made without invitation. Between the hours of three and four every Tuesday I am prepared to receive them. Gentlemen, often in great numbers, come and go, chat with each other, and act as they please. A porter shows them into the room, and they retire from it when they please, and without ceremony. At their first entrance they salute me, and I them, and as many as I can talk to, I do. What pomp there is in all this, I am unable to discover. Perhaps it consists in not sitting. To this, two reasons are opposed : first, it is unusual; secondly, which is a more substantial one, because I have no room large enough to contain a third of the chairs which would be sufficient to admit it. If it is supposed that ostentation, or the fashions of courts, (which, by the by, I believe, originate oftener in convenience, not to say necessity, than is generally imagined,) gave rise to this custom, I will boldly affirm, that no supposition was ever more erroneous ; for if I were to give indulgence to my inclinations, every moment that I could withdraw from the fatigue of my station should be spent in retirement. That it is not, proceeds from the sense I entertain of the propriety of giving to every one as free access as consists with that respect which is due to the chair of government; and that respect, I conceive, is neither to be acquired nor preserved but by observing a just medium between too much state and too great familiarity.

"Similar to the above, but of a more sociable kind, are the visits, every Friday afternoon, to Mrs. Washington, where I always am. These public meetings, and a dinner once a week tc as many as my table will hold, with the references to and from the different departments of state, and other communications with all parts of the Union, are as much, if not more than I am able to undergo ; for I have already had, within less than a year, two severe attacks, the last worse than the first. A third, more than probably, will put me to sleep with my fathers. At what distance this may be I know not. Within the last twelve months, I have undergone more and severer sickness than thirty preceding years afflicted me with. I have abundant reason, however, to be thankful that I am so well recovered."

That Washington should expatiate at such length on this topic, may seem strange in our day, when the nature and object of the ceremonial arrangements are so well understood, but at the time he wrote they were the subject of grave party questions.

Anxious to visit New England, to observe in person the condition of the country, and the dispositions of the people towards the government and its measures, the President was disposed to avail himself of the short respite from official cares afforded by the recess of Congress, to make a tour through the Eastern States. This intention was received with favour by his friends, who anticipated the best effects from such a token of regard, from one who so fully enjoyed their love and esteem. He left New York on the 15th of October, and arrived there again on the 13th of November, having passed through Connecticut and Massachusetts, as far as Portsmouth in New Hampshire, going and returning by different routes. It was pleasing to him to contemplate once more the theatre on which many interesting military scenes had been exhibited, and to review the ground on which his first campaign as commander-in-chief of the American army had been made. The progress of society, the improvements in commerce, agriculture and manufactures, filled him with grateful emotions, which the temper, circumstances, and dispositions of the people were calculated to heighten still more. His re-appearance in the high station he now filled, brought back to recollection the perilous transactions of the war; and the reception universally given him attested the unabated love which was felt for his person and character, and indicated the growing popularity, in that part of the Union at least, of the government he administered. Constituted authorities, corporate bodies, religious and learned institutions, particular trades and occupations, the militia and all classes of people, vied with each other by affectionate addresses, by illuminations, by military parade, by triumphal processions, and by various preparations, decorated by genius and by taste, in testifying the sentiment which glowed in their bosoms, and to which his presence gave increased activity.

The addresses which were presented evinced a strong attachment to the government, and decided approbation of its measures. They connected his past services with his present situation, and manifested the general conviction that, in returning to a public station, the private wishes of his heart had yielded to a sense of duty to his country.   The sincerity and warmth with which he reciprocated the affection expressed for his person was well calculated to preserve the sentiments which were generally diffused.   "I rejoice with you, my fellow-citizens," said he, in answer to an address from the inhabitants of Boston, "in every circumstance that declares your prosperity ; and I do so most cordially, because you have well deserved to be happy.   Your love of liberty ; your respect for the laws ; your habits of industry ; and your practice of the moral and religious obligations, are the strongest claims to national and individual happiness.   And they will, I trust, be firmly and astingly established."

Just before his departure from New York, President Washington received from the Count de Moustiers, the minister of France, official notice that he was permitted by his court to return to Eu rope.   By the orders of his sovereign he added, "that his majesty was pleased at the alteration which had taken place in the government, and congratulated America on the choice they had made of a President."   As from himself, he observed that the government of this country had been hitherto of so fluctuating a nature that no dependence could be placed on its proceedings ; in consequence of which foreign nations had been cautious of entering into treaties, or engagements of any kind with the United States, but that in the present government there was a head to look up to, and power being placed in the hands of its officers, stability in its measures might be expected.   The disposition of the French monarch to cultivate the good will of the new government was also manifested in the choice of the new minister, Colonel Ternan, who was named as a person who would be particularly acceptable to America, and whose appointment was preceded by the compliment of ascertaining the sense of the President respecting him.   Soon after his return to New York, the President was informed of the ill success which had attended his first attempt to negotiate a peace with the Creek Indians.

General Lincoln, Mr. Griffin and Colonel Humphries had been deputed by him on this mission, soon after his inauguration. These met with McGillivray, and other chiefs of the nation, with about two thousand men at the Rock Landing, on the frontiers of Georgia. The negotiations were soon broken off by McGillivray, whose personal interests and connection with Spain were supposed to have been the real cause of their abrupt and unsuccessful termination. The next year brought round an accomplishment of the President's wishes, which had failed in the first attempt. Policy and interest concurred in recommending every prudent measure for detaching the Creek Indians from all connection with the Spaniards, and cementing their friendship with the United States. Negotiations carried on with them in the vicinity of the Spanish settlements, promised less than negotiations conducted at the seat of government. To induce a disposition favourable to this change of place, the President sent Colonel Willet, a gallant and intelligent officer of the late army, into the Creek country, apparently on private business, but with a letter of introduction to McGillivray, and with instructions to take occasional opportunities to point out the distresses which a war with the United States would bring on the Creek nation, and the indiscretion of their breaking off the negotiation at the Rock Landing; and to exhort him to repair with the chiefs of his nation to New York, in order to effect a solid and lasting peace. Willet performed these duties with so much address that McGillivray, with the chiefs of his nation, was induced to come to New York, where fresh negotiations commenced, which, on the 7th of August, 1790, terminated in the establishment of peace.

So fully had the benefit of the new system begun to be felt and realized, that during the recess of Congress, the state of North Carolina ratified the Constitution, and in May, 1790, the President had the pleasure of witnessing the completion of the Union under the new government by the adoption by Rhode Island of the Constitution.

At the opening of the next session, the President congratulated Congress on the favourable prospect of public affairs; and among other things recommended to their attention the important subject of providing for the common defence, by the establishment of a good militia system, and the promotion of such manufactures as would render America independent of others for essentials, particularly military supplies. He also recommended the adoption of all proper means for the advancement of agriculture, commerce, and manufactures, and the promotion of science and literature; and above all, that provision should be made for the support of the public credit.

The report of the Secretary of the Treasury respecting public credit was submitted to the House on the 15th of January. The public debt of the United States was estimated by the secretary at more than fifty-four millions of dollars. Of this sum the foreign debt, principally due to France and the Hollanders, constituted eleven millions and three quarters, including more than a million and a half of interest; and the domestic liquidated debt, including about thirteen millions of arrears of interest, more than forty millions; and the unliquidated debt, two millions. The secretary recommended the assumption of the debts of the several states, to be paid equally with those of the Union, as a measure of sound policy and substantial justice. These were estimated at twenty-five millions of dollars. Doubts were expressed by the secretary whether, in addition to all other expenses, it was in the power of the United States to make a secure and effectual provision for the payment of the interest of so large a sum, on the terms of the original contracts. He therefore submitted to the House several plans for the modification, security, and payment of the domestic debt.

This important subject was under the consideration of Congress until the 4th of August, 1790, when a law making provision for the debt of the United States was passed. By this act, a new loan of the whole domestic debt was proposed on the following terms:—two-thirds of the principal to draw an interest of six per cent. after January 1st, 1791; and the other third to draw the same interest, after the year 1800; the arrears of interest to draw three per cent. after January, 1791. The debt drawing six per cent. to be redeemable by payments not exceeding, in one year, eight per cent. on account both of principal and interest; and the three per cents. were made redeemable at the pleasure of the government. By the same act, Congress assumed twenty-one millions and a half of the state debts; and this sum was apportioned among the states, having regard to the amount of the debts of each. The sum thus assumed was also to be loaned to the United States by individuals holding certain evidences of state debts, but on terms somewhat different from those of the domestic debt. Four-ninths was to bear an interest of six per cent. commencing on the 1st of January, 1792, two-ninths to draw the same interest after the year 1800, and the other three-ninths an interest of three per cent. from January, 1792.

The report of the secretary gave rise to long and serious debates. In the national legislature much difference existed as to the mode and manner of providing for the payment of so large a debt, deemed of little value under the old federal government; and particularly on the question of assuming the state debts. The public creditors, as well as the community at large, had waited with no small degree of solicitude, for the first financial report from the Secretary of the Treasury, and this solicitude was rather increased than diminished by the proceedings of Congress on the subject. It was generally expected that some provision would be made for the payment of this debt under the new government; and the propriety of making a discrimination between the original holders and the purchasers, had been suggested in private circles as well as in the public papers.*

The report of the secretary adverting to the fact that many of the holders of the evidences of the debt had purchased them for a fourth or fifth of their nominal value, examined the question whether any discrimination should be made between such purchasers of the debt and the original creditors; and its author was clearly of opinion, that no discrimination could be made without a breach of public faith, and even lessening the value of the debts still remaining in the hands of the original holders. In an early stage of the proceedings on the report, this question was submitted to the House of Representatives.

N the 11th of February, Mr. Madison proposed that where the public securities had been alienated, the present holders should receive the highest market price of such securities, and the residue should be paid to the original proprietors.

After a spirited debate, which called forth nearly all the talents of the house, Mr. Madison's motion was lost by a vote of thirty-six to thirteen. The irredeemability of the debt, except to the amount of eight per cent., on account of both principal and interest, occasioned also much opposition and debate. The most serious debate, however, was upon the assumption of the state debts, a measure which created divisions both in and out of Congress, the effects of which were long felt in the administration of the general government. The debts of the states were very unequal. Those

* Pitkin.

of Massachusetts and South Carolina amounted to more than ten millions and a half, while the debts of all the other states were only estimated at between fourteen and fifteen millions. The first proposition on this subject in the House of Representatives, was to assume the whole of these debts. In committees of the whole, a small majority at first voted in favour of this plan; but when the members from North Carolina took their seats in Congress, the subject was recommitted, and the decision reversed. Propositions were afterwards made to assume specific sums from each, but were negatived. These various propositions occasioned long and violent debates among the members from different states, and led to an inquiry into the origin of the state debts, and to a comparative view of the different exertions and expenses of the states themselves in the struggle for independence. The assumption of specific sums from each, was finally carried in the Senate by a majority of two, and was concurred in by the House of Representatives by a majority of six.

In the course of the debate, Mr. Sedgwick declared that the insurrection which had taken place in Massachusetts was occasioned by the burden of taxes necessarily imposed on the people of that state to pay a debt incurred merely for national purposes. Fisher Ames, in an eloquent speech on the occasion, held the following language: "Were the state debts contracted for the war? It appears, by the books in the public offices, that they were. Will any one say, that the whole expense of defending our common liberty ought not to be a common charge? Part of this charge was contracted by Massachusetts before Congress assumed the exercise of its powers. The first ammunition that repulsed the enemy at Lexington and made such havoc at Bunker Hill was purchased by the state, and appears in the form of the state debt." The assumption was negatived at first, but its friends persevered in their purpose, and it was finally carried. Previous to its final decision, a bill had been passed, fixing the temporary seat of government at Philadelphia, until 1800, and after that time permanently on the river Potomac. This subject had long been agitated in the old Congress, and until this session all attempts to settle it had failed. Many have supposed, and on the authority of Mr. Jefferson the supposition is confirmed, that this decision was the effect of a compromise on the question of assumption.

During this session of Congress, a cession of western lands was made by North Carolina; the territory south of the Ohio river was formed into a territorial government; an enumeration of the inhabitants was directed to be made on the first Monday in August, 1790 ; and a uniform rule of naturalization was established. A fund for sinking the national debt was established. Rhode Island having adopted the Constitution in May, 1790, the union of all the states under the new government was completed. Congress adjourned on the 12th of August, to meet in Philadelphia on the first Monday in the following December.

As we have already mentioned, a treaty of peace was concluded in August of this year, with the Creek Indians, which restored tranquillity to the people of Georgia. The pacific overtures made to the Indians of the Wabash and the Miamis had not been equally successful. The western frontiers were still exposed to their incursions ; and there was much reason to apprehend that the people of Kentucky and of the western counties of the Middle States, could only be relieved from the horrors of savage warfare by an exertion of the military strength of the Union. In the opinion of the President, the emergency required the immediate employment of a force competent to the object, and which should carry terror and destruction into the heart of the hostile settlements. The people of the west, however, declared their opinion in favour of desultory military expeditions, and Congress indulged their wishes. The desire of the executive for a military establishment equal to the exigency, was not regarded, and the distresses of the frontier inhabitants therefore still continued.

The conduct of Spain in relation to the disputed boundary and its pretensions to the navigation of the Mississippi was such as to give ground to fear that its dispositions towards the United States were unfriendly. Between the United States and England, the non-execution of several articles of the treaty of peace still furnished matter for reciprocal crimination, which there was the more difficulty in removing because there was no diplomatic intercourse maintained between them. Under the old government, Mr. Adams's mission had been treated with neglect, and the new administration was not disposed to subject itself to a similar mark of disrespect. Mr. Gouverneur Morris was instructed, as an informal agent to the British government, to sound its views respecting amicable and permanent arrangements of the matters in dispute. But, Mr. Morris remarked, "that there never was, perhaps, a moment in which this country (Britain) felt herself greater, and, consequently, it is the most unfavourable moment to obtain advantageous terms from her in any bargain." He conducted his mission with ability and address, but was unable to bring it to a happy conclusion.

The communications laid before the American government at the same time, by Major Beckwith, an English gentleman who had come in an informal manner to learn the dispositions of the American government towards England and Spain, between which a rupture was expected, gave the executive an explanation of the delays which had been practised with Mr. Morris. He was persuaded that a disposition existed in the cabinet of London to retain things in their actual situation until the intentions of the American government should be ascertained with respect to the war supposed to be approaching. If America would make a common cause with Great Britain against Spain, the way would be smoothed to the attainment of all their objects; but if America should incline towards Spain, no adjustment of the points of difference between the two nations would be made. He therefore determined to hold himself free to pursue, without reproach in the expected war, such a course as the interest and honour of the United States might dictate. The want of official authenticity in the communications of Mr. Beckwith was therefore signified to that gentleman as a reason for reserve on the part of the government, and the powers given to Mr. Morris were withdrawn. It was determined that things should remain in their actual situation until a change of circumstances should require a change of conduct. Scarcely had this resolution been adopted, when the dispute between Britain and Spain was adjusted, and thus both the fear of inconveniences and the hope of advantages which might result to America from war between the two powers was terminated.

By his incessant application to public business and the consequent change of active for sedentary habits, the constitution of the President seemed much impaired, and during the second session of Congress he had, for the second time since entering upon the duties of his office, been attacked by a severe disease which reduced him to the brink of the grave. Exercise, and a temporary relief from the cares of office being essential to the restoration of his health, he determined for the short interval afforded by the recess of the legislature, to retire from the fatigues of public life to the tranquil shades of Mount Vernon. Previously, however, he made a visit to Rhode Island, which not having been a member of the Union at the time of his late tour through New England, had not been visited by him at that time.

His final departure from New York was not less affecting than his arrival had been, when he came to assume the reins of government. It was always his habit, says Custis in his " Recollections,' to endeavour to avoid the manifestations of affection and gratitude that met him everywhere. He strove in vain, he was closely watched, and the people would have their way. He wished to slip off unobserved from New York, and thus steal a march upon his old companions .n arms. But there were too many of the dear glorious old veterans of the Revolution at that time of day in and near New York to render such an escape even possible.

" The baggage had all been packed up ; the horses, carriages, and servants ordered to be over the Ferry to Paulus Hook by daybreak, and nothing was wanting for departure but the dawn. The lights were yet burning, when the President came into the room where his family were assembled, evidently much pleased in the belief that all was right, when, immediately under the windows, the band of the artillery struck up Washington's March. 'There,' he exclaimed, ' it's all over ; we are found out. Well, well, they must have their own way.' New York soon after appeared as if taken by storm ; troops and persons of all descriptions hurrying down Broadway toward the place of embarkation, all anxious to take a last look on him whom so many could never expect to see again.

" The embarkation was delayed until all the complimentary arrangments were completed. The President, after taking leave of many dear and cherished friends, and many an old companion in arms, stepped into the barge that was to convey him from New York for ever. The coxswain gave the word ' let fall ;' the spray from the oars sparkled in the morning sunbeams ; the bowman shoved off from the pier, and, as the barge swung round to the tide, Washington rose, uncovered, in the stern, to bid adieu to the masses assembled on the shore ; he waved his hat, and, in a voice tremulous from emotion, pronounced Farewell. It may be supposed that Major Bauman, who commanded the artillery on this interesting occasion, who was first captain of Lamb's regiment, and a favourite officer of the war of the Revolution, would, when about to pay his last respects to his beloved commander, load his pieces with something more than mere blank cartridges. But ah ! the thunders of the cannon were completely hushed when the mighty shout of the people arose that responded to the farewell of Washington. Pure from the heart it came ; right up to Heaven it went, to call down a blessing upon the Father of his Country.

" The barge had scarcely gained the middle of the Hudson when the trumpets were heard at Paulus Hook, where the governc : and the chivalry of Jersey were in waiting to welcome the chief to those well-remembered shores. Escorts of cavalry relieved each other throughout the whole route, up to the Pennsylvania line; every village, and even hamlet, turned out its population to greet with cordial welcome the man upon whom all eyes were fixed, and in whom all hearts rejoiced.

"What must have been the recollections that crowded on the mind of Washington during this triumphant progress! Newark, Brunswick, Princeton, Trenton! What a contrast between the glorious burst of sunshine that now illumined and made glad every thing around these memorable spots, with the gloomy and desolate remembrances of '76! Then his country's champion, with the wreck of a shattered host, was flying before a victorious and well-appointed foe, while all around him was shrouded in the darkness of despair; now, in his glorious progress over the self-same route, his firm footstep presses upon the soil of an infant empire, reposing in the joys of peace, independence, and happiness.

"Among the many who swelled his triumph, the most endeared to the heart of the chief were the old associates of his toils, his fortunes, and his fame. Many of the revolutionary veterans were living in 1790, and, by their presence, gave a dignified tone and character to all public assemblages; and, when you saw a peculiarly fine-looking soldier in those old days, and would ask, ' to what corps of the American army did you belong?' Drawing himself up to his full height, with a martial air, and back of the hand thrown up to his forehead, the veteran would reply, ' Life Guard, your honour.'

"And proud and happy were these veterans in again beholding their own good Lady Washington. Greatly was she beloved in the army. Her many intercessions with the chief for the pardon of offenders; her kindness to the sick and wounded; all of which caused her annual arrival in camp to be hailed as an event that would serve to dissipate the gloom of the winter quarters.

"Arrived at the line, the Jersey escort was relieved by the cavalry of Pennsylvania, and, when near to Philadelphia, the President was met by Governor Mifflin and a brilliant cortege of officers, and escorted by a squadron of horse to the city. Conspicuous among the governor's suite, as well for his martial bearing as for the manly beauty of his person, was General Walter Stewart, a son of Erin, and a gallant and distinguished officer of the Pennsylvania line. To Stewart, as to Cadwallader, Washington was most warmly attached; indeed, those officers were among the very choicest of the contributions of Pennsylvania to the army and cause of independence. Mifflin, small in stature, was active, alert, ' every inch a soldier.' He was a patriot of great influence in Pennsylvania in the 'times that tried men's souls,' and nobly did he exert that influence in raising troops, with which to reinforce the wreck of the grand army at the close of the campaign of '76.

" Arrived within the city, the crowd became intense ; the President left his carriage and mounted the white charger ; and, with the governor on his right, proceeded to the city tavern in Third street, where quarters were prepared for him, the light infantry, after some time, having opened a passage for the carriages. At the city tavern the President was received by the authorities of Philadelphia, who welcomed the chief magistrate to their city as to his home for the remainder of his presidential term. A group of old and long-tried friends were also in waiting. Foremost among these, and first to grasp the hand of Washington, was one who was always nearest to his heart, a patriot and public benefactor, Robert Morris.

" After remaining a short time in Philadelphia, the President speeded on his journey to that home where he ever found rest from his mighty labours, and enjoyed the sweets of rural and domestic happiness amid his farms and at his fireside of Mount Vernon."

The meeting of Congress soon summoned him to Philadelphia. He met the legislature with a speech consistent with his former views and policy, breathing the purest intentions of a devoted patriot. Though he was unanimously applauded by Congress, a different feeling was very soon excited, and the friends of state rights and limited government startled into decided opposition by the projects of the Secretary of the Treasury. One of his propositions, to tax domestic distilled spirits, was warmly resisted, and engendered able and protracted debates. Its opponents contended that imposts collected on any domestic manufacture wore the semblance of a foreign power intruding itself into their particular concerns, and excited serious apprehensions for state importance and for liberty.* Pennsylvania, Maryland, North Carolina, and Virginia, protested against it in strong and energetic terms. Another and more important scheme proposed by the head of the Treasury excited more discussion, while it awakened warmer feelings, and commenced a metaphysical debate which still continues, and is hardly likely to terminate among a people all equally free, and equally at liberty to participate in the administration of their own government. This was the scheme of a national bank, which arrayed parties in fierce opposition, and divided the cabinet to a

* Marshall.

degree that menaced its total rupture. Jefferson and Randolph were of opinion that Congress, in passing the bill, transcended the powers vested in them by the Constitution. General Hamilton, on the other hand, maintained it to be purely constitutional.

It was not an easy task to unite two men of such opposite natures as Hamilton and Jefferson, and make them act in concert in the same cabinet. The critical state of affairs at the first adoption of the Constitution, and the impartial preponderance of Washington alone could accomplish it. He applied himself to it with consummate perseverance and wisdom. At heart, he felt a decided preference for Hamilton and his views. "By some," said he, "he is considered an ambitious man, and, therefore, a dangerous one. That he is ambitious I readily grant, but his ambition is of that laudable kind which prompts a man to excel in whatever he takes in hand. He is enterprising, quick in his perceptions, and in his judgment intuitively great."

 UT it was only in 1798, in the freedom of retirement, that Washington spoke so explicitly. While in office, and between his two secretaries, he maintained towards them a strict reserve, and testified the same confidence in both. He believed both of them to be sincere and able; both of them necessary to the country and to himself. Jefferson was to him, not only a connecting tie, a means of influence with the popular party which rarely became the opposition; but he made use of him in the internal administration of his government as a counterpoise to the tendencies, and especially to the language, sometimes extravagant and inconsiderate, of Hamilton and his friends. He had interviews and consultations with each of them separately, upon the subjects which they were to discuss together, in order to remove or lessen beforehand their differences of opinion. He knew how to turn the merit and popularity of each with his own party, to the general good of the government, even to their own mutual advantage. He skilfully availed himself of every opportunity to employ them in a common responsibility. And when a disagreement too wide, and passions too impetuous, seemed to threaten an immediate rupture, he interposed, used exhortation and entreaty, and by his personal influence, by a frank and touching appeal to the patriotism and right-mindedness of the two rivals, he postponed the breaking forth of the evil which it was not possible to eradicate. On the bank question, he required from each his arguments in writing, and after maturely weighing them both, he gave the sanction of his signature

68

co the act passed by Congress for its incorporation. From the moment of the incorporation of the Bank of the United States, parties assumed the almost perfect forms of organization and principles by which they are marked in our own day. The arguments and imputations of the republican party, however, were not so much intended to apply to Washington and his measures as to Colonel Hamilton, who was considered and acknowledged by all as the head of the federal party. This fact was sufficiently proved when Washington, at the close of the session of Congress, made an excursion into the Southern States. His reception by men of all parties was ample testimony of the fact that he united all hearts, and that, however the measures or the constitution of government might be censured and disapproved, none would refuse to pour the grateful homage of free hearts into the bosom of their veteran chief.

The first session of the second Congress assembled on the 24th of October, 1791, at Philadelphia. The most important bill which came under their notice, was one for the apportionment of the representation : the Federalists taking sides in favour of a limited representation, while the Republicans contended for an increase of the numbers of the House, sufficient to allow what they termed a full representation of the people. On the 8th of May, Congress adjourned, having previously passed a bill augmenting the army to five thousand men. This was made necessary by the misfortunes connected with the war with the north-western Indians. The first expedition sent against them had been put under command of General Harmar, who was defeated with considerable loss in the neighbourhood of Chilicothe. General St. Clair was sent on a second expedition, but was also defeated with great loss. General Wayne was then selected to conduct another campaign, but the season was so far advanced before he was enabled to commence operations, that he did little more than march to the intended theatre of operations. Here he erected a fort called Fort Recovery, and employed himself during the winter in disciplining his troops, and making preparations for advancing early into the Indian settlements.

On the 8th of August, 1794, he reached the confluence of the Au Glaize and the Miamis of the Lakes, without opposition. This was thirty miles from the British post on the Miamis of the Lakes, near which about two thousand Indians were collected. General Wayne's legion was about equal in number, and the militia force joined with it amounted to eleven hundred men

WAYNES VICTORY

From the 14th to the 19th, Wayne moved cautiously down the Miami, and on the 20th a battle took place.

The Indians had advanced into a thick wood, in front of the British works, and had taken a position inaccessible to cavalry, and of very difficult access to infantry. They were formed in three lines, near enough to support each other, and greatly extended in front. On the discharge of the first rifles, the legion was instantly formed, the front ordered to advance with trailed arms, and with their bayonets to drive the enemy from their hiding places, then deliver their first fire, and press the fugitives so briskly as not to allow them time to load. So rapid was the charge, and so entirely was the enemy broken by it, that in the course of one hour they were driven more than two miles, through thick woods, and within gunshot of the British fort. General Wayne remained for three days in front of the field of battle, laying waste the houses and cornfields, above and below, and within pistol-shot of the British fort. In the conflagration, the houses and stores of Colonel McKee, an English trader, who had encouraged the savages to continue the war, were reduced to ashes. On the 28th, the army returned to Au Glaize and destroyed all the villages and corn within fifty miles of the river. The confidence which the Indians had acquired from their former victories was destroyed by this total defeat. They found themselves not only vanquished, but driven from their country, with the prospect of famine from the total destruction of their cornfields. Their calamities disposed them to peace, and a treaty was concluded in August, 1795, by General Wayne, which put an end to the Indian wars, at that period, with the United States.

2 Z

CHAPTER XXIII.

Administration of Washington. Second Term.

HE administrative talents of Washington were once more to be exercised for the service of his country. With great reluctance he had consented not to decline a second election, and on the 5th of March, 1793, he took the oath of office, and entered upon the second term of his administration. He had again received the unanimous vote of the electors. Mr. Adams was re-elected to the Vice-presidency, having received seventy-seven votes of one hundred and thirty-two, the whole number. Fortunate was it for America that she possessed in the person of her chief magistrate, at this time, a man of so much wisdom, firmness, and weight of character. Hitherto the discussions and divisions which had occupied the

attention of the President and Congress had grown out of the domestic arrangements and circumstances, and were more fitted to warn and teach, than to bring danger upon the people. But on the breaking out of the French Revolution, principles and views were developed which, without respect to time, place, or national peculiarity, were held up as perfectly new and unexceptionable models, whose universal applicability was stoutly and presumptuously asserted. The directors of that revolution required a universal assent to their favourite doctrine that the new political wisdom of the great people of France must be cordially and thankfully received, and defended with united powers against all opponents in every part of the earth.

Towards France and her revolution Washington deported himself on the great truth that every nation possessed a right to govern itself according to its own will, to change its institutions at discretion, and to transact its business through whatever agents it might think proper. But as war had just commenced between France and Great Britain, his correct, sound judgment, instantly decided that a perfect neutrality was the right, the duty, and the interest of the United States; and of this he gave public notice by a proclamation, in April, 1793. Subsequent events have proved the wisdom of this measure, though it was then reprobated by many. The war between the late enemies and friends of the United States revived revolutionary feelings in the breasts of the citizens, and enlisted the strongest passions of human nature against one, and in favour of the other. A wish for the success of France was almost universal; and many were willing to hazard the peace of their country, by taking an active part in the war in her favour. The proclamation was at variance with the feelings and the passions of a large portion of the citizens. To compel the observance of neutrality, under these circumstances, was no easy matter. Hitherto Washington had the people with him; but in this case a large proportion was on the other side. His resolution was nevertheless unshaken; and at the risk of popularity he persisted in promoting the real good of his fellow-citizens, in opposition to their own mistaken wishes and views.

The President was soon openly and violently assaulted in the public prints for the proclamation of neutrality. All governments were said to be hostile to liberty, and many insinuations were made against the administration, under the general class of those who abetted the tyranny of kings, or refused to succour a free people struggling for liberty against a combination of tyrants. These dis-

positions were greatly increased by the arrival of Mr. Genet, the first
minister plenipotentiary from the Republic of France to the United
States.   He landed April 8th, 1793, at Charleston, South Carolina,
the contiguity of which to the West Indies fitted it to be a convenient resort for privateers.   By the governor of the state, William
Moultrie, and the citizens, he was received with ardour approaching to enthusiasm.   During his stay, which was for several
days, he received unequivocal proofs of the warmest attachment to
his person, his country, and its cause.   Encouraged by these evidences of the good wishes of the people for the success of the
French Revolution, he undertook to authorize the fitting and arming
of vessels in that port, enlisting men, and giving commissions to
vessels to cruise and commit hostilities on nations with which the
United States were at peace.   The captures made by these cruisers
were to be tried, condemned, and sold, under the authority of
Genet, who had not yet been recognised as a public minister by
the government.

Similar marks of enthusiastic attachment were lavished on
Genet as he passed through the country between Charleston and
Philadelphia.   At Gray's Ferry, over the Schuylkill, he was met by
crowds who flocked to do honour to the first ambassador of a
republican allied nation.   On the day after his arrival in Philadelphia, he received addresses from societies and the inhabitants,
who expressed their gratitude for the aids furnished by the French
nation to the United States in their late struggle for liberty and
independence, and unbounded exultation at the success of the
French arms.   Genet's answers to these addresses were well calculated to preserve the idea of a complete fraternity between the
two nations, and that their interests were the same.

After Genet had been thus accredited by the citizens of Philadelphia, he was presented to the President and received with expressions of a sincere and cordial regard for his nation.   In the
conversation which took place on the occasion, Mr. Genet gave
the most explicit assurances that France did not wish to engage
the United States in the war between his country and Great Britain.

While Mr. Genet was receiving these flattering marks of attention
from the people, the British minister preferred a long catalogue
of complaints against his proceedings at Charleston.   This was
founded on the acts already mentioned, which were calculated to
make the United States instruments of hostility in the hands of
France, against those with whom she was at war.   These were
farther aggravated by actual hostilities in the territories of the

United States. The ship Grange, a British vessel, was captured by the French frigate L'Ambuscade, within the capes of the Delaware, while on her way from Philadelphia to the ocean. Of this ship, and of other illegal prizes, which were in the power of the American government, the British minister demanded restitution.

The cabinet council of Washington was unanimous that every independent nation was exclusively sovereign in its own territories, and that the proceedings complained of were unwarranted usurpations of sovereignty, and violations of neutrality; and therefore must in future be prevented. It was also agreed that the efficacy of the laws should be tried against those citizens of the United States who had joined in the offences complained of. The restitution of the Grange was also agreed to ; but on the propriety of enforcing the restitution of prizes made on the high seas, there was a diversity of sentiment, the Secretaries of the Treasury and of War being for it, and the Secretary of State and the Attorney-general against it. The principles on which a concurrence of sentiment had taken place being considered as settled, the Secretary of State was desired to communicate them to the ministers of France and of Britain ; and circular letters were written to the governors of the several states requiring them to co-operate with force, if necessary, to execute the rules which had been agreed upon.

Mr. Genet was highly dissatisfied with these determinations, and considered them as subversive of the treaty between the United States and France. His representations induced a re-consideration of the subject; but on the most dispassionate review of it, no reason appeared for an alteration of any part of the system. The minister of France was further informed, that in the opinion of the President, the vessels which had been illegally equipped should not depart from the ports of the United States.

Mr. Genet, adhering to his own construction of the treaty between France and the United States, would not acquiesce in those decisions of the government. Intoxicated with the flattering attentions he had received, and ignorant of the firmness of the executive, he seems to have expected that the popularity of his nation and its cause would enable him to undermine the executive, or render it subservient to his views.

About this time, two citizens of the United States, who had been engaged in Charleston by Mr. Genet to cruise in the service of France, were arrested by the civil authority, in pursuance of the determination formed by government to prosecute persons who had offended against the laws. Mr. Genet demanded their release as

69   2 z 2

French citizens, in the most extraordinary terms. This was refused, but on trial they were acquitted by the verdict of a jury.

The minister of the French republic was encouraged to this line of opposition by a belief that the sentiments of the people were in his favour. So extravagant was their enthusiastic devotedness to France; so acrimonious were their expressions against all the powers at war with the new republic, that a person less sanguine than Mr. Genet might have cherished the hope of being able to succeed so far with the people as, with their support, ultimately to triumph over the opposition he experienced. At civic festivals, the ensigns of France were displayed in union with those of America; at these the cap of liberty passed from head to head, and toasts were given expressive of the fraternity of the two nations. The proclamation of neutrality was treated as a royal edict, which demonstrated the disposition of the government to break its connections with France, and dissolve the friendship which united the people of the two republics. The scenes of the revolutionary war were brought into view; the effects of British hostility against the United States, and of French aids both in men and money in their favour, were painted in glowing colours. The enmity of Britain to the United States was represented as continuing undiminished; and in proof of it, their detention of the western posts, and their exciting from these stations the neighbouring Indians to make war on the frontier settlers, were urged with great vehemence, and contrasted with the amicable dispositions professed by the French republic. It was indignantly asked, should a friend and an enemy be treated with equal favour? By declamations of this kind daily issuing from the press, the public mind was so inflamed against the executive, that Genet, calculating on the partialities of the people, openly insulted the government; and adhering to his own construction of the treaty, that he had a right to do as he had done, threatened to appeal to the sovereign people against their President.

To preserve neutrality in such a crisis was no easy matter. Washington, adhering to the principles avowed in his late proclamation and imbodied in the Declaration of Independence, "that the United States would hold all mankind enemies in war and friends in peace," exerted all his authority and influence to keep the balance even between the belligerents.

It was at length resolved by Washington to instruct Mr. Morris, the minister of the United States at Paris, to request the recall of Mr. Genet; and that Mr. Morris should be furnished with all the necessary documents to evince the propriety of the request. What

MONROE.

was asked was granted; and Mr. Genet's conduct was disapproved by his government. Mr. Fauchet was appointed his successor, who was succeeded by Mr. Adet. The successors of Genet continued to tread in his footsteps, but with less violence. They made frequent complaints of particular cases of hardship, which grew out of the war and out of the rules which had been adopted by the executive with regard to ships of war, cruisers and their prizes. They complained particularly that in the treaty with Great Britain the principle of " free ships making free goods" was given up, and urged the injustice, while French cruisers were restrained by treaty from taking English goods out of American bottoms, that English cruisers should be liberated from the same restraint. In vain did the executive show a willingness to relieve France from the pressure of a situation in which she had voluntary placed herself. Private explanations were made, that neither the late treaty made with Britain, nor the arrangements growing out of it, furnished any real cause of complaint to France.

The French republican government had requested the recall of Gouverneur Morris, and General Washington had appointed Mr. Monroe to represent the American interests in France, in May, 1794. He was received with distinguished favour by the government and people of that country, but his political principles differed from those of General Washington, whose views of neutrality were but poorly conformed to by the course of the minister. Mr. Monroe was therefore recalled by the President in 1796. He published a volume explaining and vindicating his views and proceedings, and censuring the policy of the administration towards the French republic, but he did not suffer political differences to estrange his affections from Washington, nor to prevent his acknowledging the merits and perfect integrity of that great man.

With the same conciliatory view which occasioned the mission of Monroe, Washington appointed General Pinckney minister plenipotentiary to the French republic, "to maintain that good understanding, which, from the commencement of the alliance, had subsisted between the two nations, and to efface unfavourable impressions, banish suspicion, and restore that cordiality which was at once the evidence and pledge of a friendly union." The Directory having inspected his letter of credence, announced their haughty determination, "not to receive another minister from the United States until, after a redress of grievances demanded of the American government, which the French republic had a right to expect from it." This was followed by a written mandate to General Pinckney, to quit the territories of the republic. To complete the system of hostility, American vessels, wherever found, were captured by French cruisers.

With Spain, however, the President succeeded in amicably adjusting all controversies the same year that brought round peace with the Indians. Some of the western settlers had been willing to sacrifice country, allegiance, and every thing to their interest. Others had been disposed to force their way down the Mississippi, to the gulf of Mexico, though the waters should be crimsoned with blood. But the more moderate and judicious citizens, adhering to the government, and knowing their present inability to force the free navigation of the Mississippi, made up their mind to wait events, and patiently submit to a present inconvenience in hopes of a change for the better. These hopes were realized sooner than they expected. The war between republican France and Spain taught the latter the importance of the friendship of the United States. Among other daring projects of the new republic of France, was one to revolutionize Spanish America, by the aid of the western American settlers, co-operating with a French force, to be introduced through Georgia or Florida and commanded by Mr. Genet. But Washington, though zealous for the free use of the Mississippi, would not permit a foreign nation to attack the Spanish settlements from the United States; and a scheme which, with his connivance alone, would probably have been successful, was thus defeated. How far this magnanimous policy influenced the court of Madrid to seek the friendship of the United States, is not known, but we can hardly suppose it to have been without effect, as almost at the same time the commissioners of Spain, at Philadelphia, gave hints of the practicability of expediting the negotiations which had, with little interruption, been protracted without any prospect of termi-

nation for nearty fifteen years. These hints were attended to, and
Mr. Thomas Pinckney was appointed envoy extraordinary to his
Catholic majesty. Shortly after his arrival in Madrid, he concluded a treaty with the king of Spain, in which the claims of the
United States on the important points of boundary and the navigation of the Mississippi, were fully conceded. Thus the justice,
moderation, and good faith of the government finally succeeded in
procuring important advantages for the United States without either
war or dishonour.*

Two years after the ineffectual attempt made by the American
government through its informal agent Mr. Morris, to bring about
a better understanding with the court of St. James, the British
ministry, finding that the new government had become everywhere
respected for stability and energy, appointed of their own accord,
as minister to the United States, Mr. Hammond. This advance
induced the President soon after to send Mr. Thomas Pinckney to
the court of Great Britain, in a similar diplomatic capacity.

In America, the tide of popular opinion ran as strongly against
Britain as in favour of France. The former was accused of insti-
gating the Indians to acts of hostility against the United States ; of
impressing their sailors, of illegally capturing their ships, and of
stirring up the Algerines against them. The whole of this hostility
was referred to a jealousy of the growing importance of the United
States. Motions were made in Congress for sequestering debts to
the British subjects, for entering into commercial hostility with
Great Britain, and even for interdicting all intercourse with her, till
she pursued other measures with respect to the United States.
Every appearance portended immediate war between the two countries. ' The passionate admirers of France wished for it ; while
others, more attached to British systems, dreaded a war with Great
Britain, as being likely to throw the United States into the arms of
France. In this state of things, when war seemed inevitable, the
President composed the troubled scene by nominating John Jay, in
April, 1794, envoy extraordinary to the court of London. By this
measure a truce was obtained, which led to an adjustment of the
points in controversy between the two countries. The exercise of
the constitutional right of the President to negotiate, virtually suspended all hostile legislative measures; for these could not with
delicacy or propriety be urged, while the executive was in the act
of treating for an amicable adjustment of differences.

A treaty between the United States and Great Britain was the

* Ramsay.

result of this mission. This was pronounced by Mr. Jay " to be the best that was attainable, and which he believed it for the interest of the United States to accept." While the treaty was before the Senate for consideration, a member, contrary to the rules of that body, furnished an editor of a newspaper with a copy of it. This being published, operated like a spark of fire applied to combustible materials. The angry passions which for some short time had been smothered, broke out afresh. Some went so far as to pronounce the treaty a surrender of their power to their late enemy, Great Britain, and a dereliction of their tried friend and ally, France. The more moderate said, that too much was given and too little received. Meetings of the people were held at Boston, New York, Philadelphia, Baltimore, Charleston, and several other places, in which the treaty was pronounced to be unworthy of acceptance, and petitions were agreed upon and forwarded to the President, urging him to refuse his signature to the obnoxious instrument.

These agitations furnished matter for serious reflection to the President, but they did not affect his conduct, though they induced a reiterated examination of the subject. In a private letter to a friend, after reciting the importance of the crisis, he added,— " There is but one straight course, and that is to seek truth and to pursue it steadily." It is probable that he had early made up his mind to ratify the treaty as better than none, and infinitely better than war; but regretted that it was so generally disliked, and considered by many as made with a design to oppress the French republic. Under the weight of his high responsibility, he consoled himself, " that in time when passion shall have yielded to reason, the current may possibly turn." Peace with all the world was his policy, where it could be preserved with honour. War he considered as an evil of such magnitude as never to be entered upon without the most imperious necessity. The mission of Mr. Jay was his last effort for the preservation of peace with Great Britain. The rejection of the treaty which resulted from this mission, he considered as the harbinger of war; for negotiation having failed to redress grievances, no alternative but war was left. By this prudent conduct the rising states were preserved in peace. But the bickerings of the citizens among themselves, and their animosities against Great Britain, still continued. The popularity of the President for the present was diminished; but this he had anticipated. In a letter to General Knox, he observes:

" Next to a conscientious discharge of my public duties, to

carry along with me the approbation of my constituents would be the highest gratification of which my mind is susceptible. But the latter being secondary, I cannot make the former yield to it, unless some criterion more infallible than partial (if they are not party) meetings, can be discovered as the touchstone of public sentiment. If any person on earth could, or the Great Power above would erect the standard of infallibility in political opinions, no being that inhabits this terrestrial globe would resort to it with more eagerness than myself, so long as I remain a servant of the public. But as I have hitherto found no better guide than upright intentions, and close investigation, I shall adhere to them while I keep the watch."

After the treaty was duly ratified, an attempt was made to render it a dead letter by refusing the appropriations of money necessary to carry it into effect. Preparatory to this, a motion was made for the adoption of a resolution to request the President to lay before the House of Representatives a copy of his instructions to Mr. Jay, together with the correspondence and other documents relative to the treaty with Great Britain. This involved a new question, where the treaty-making power was constitutionally lodged? The debate was animated and vehement. Appeals were made both to reason and passion. After a discussion of more than twenty days, the motion was carried in the affirmative by a majority of twenty-five votes. When the resolution was presented to the President, he replied "that he would take time to consider it." His situation was peculiarly delicate: the passions of the people were strongly excited against the treaty ; the popularity of the demand being solely for information ; the large majority by which the vote was carried ; the suspicions that would probably attach in case of refusal—that circumstances had occurred in the course of the negotiation, which the President was afraid to publish, added to other weighty considerations, would have induced minds of an ordinary texture to yield to the request. With Washington, popularity was only a second object. To follow the path of duty and the public good was a primary one. He had sworn to "preserve, protect, and defend the Constitution." In his opinion, the treaty-making power was exclusively given by the people in convention to the executive, and the public good required that it should. be so exercised. He therefore sent an answer to the House, in which he stated coolly, and forcibly, the reasons why the House of Representatives, which has no part in the treaty-making power, cannot be constitutionally entitled to the papers called for; and concluded with saying: " A first regard to the Constitution and to the duty of my office, under all the circumstances of this case, forbids a compliance with your request."

Though the call for papers was unsuccessful, the favourers of the resolution for that purpose opposed the appropriations necessary to carry the treaty into effect; but from the firmness of the President, the ground was altered. The treaty was ratified, and proclaimed to the public as constitutionally obligatory on the citizens. To refuse appropriations for carrying it into effect would not only incur the high responsibility of breaking the public faith, but make a schism in the government between the executive and legislative departments. After long and vehement debates, in which argument and passion were both resorted to, with the view of exposing the merits and demerits of the treaty, the resolution for bringing in the laws necessary to carry it into effect was carried by a majority of three. Though, in this discussion, Washington had no direct agency, yet the final result in favour of the treaty was the consequence of the measures he had previously adopted. For having ratified the treaty and published it to the world as the law of the land, and having in his answer to the request of the House of Representatives, proved that he had a constitutional right so to do, the laws necessary for giving effect to the treaty could not be withheld without hazarding the most serious consequences.

The treaty which was thus carried into operation, produced more good and less evil than was apprehended. It compromised ancient differences, produced amicable dispositions, and a friendly intercourse. It brought round a peaceable surrender of the British posts, and compensation for American vessels illegally captured. Though it gave up some favourite principles, and some of its articles relative to commerce were deemed unequal, yet from Britain, as a great naval power, holding valuable colonies and foreign possessions, nothing better, either with or without the treaty, could have been obtained.

After the lapse of ten years has cooled the minds both of the friends and the enemies of the treaty, most men will acknowledge that the measures adopted by Washington with respect to it, were founded in wisdom; proceeded from the purest patriotism; were carried through with uncommon firmness: and finally eventuated in advancing the interests of his country.

Gradually the first cabinet of Washington had become entirely changed. Mr. Jefferson retired first at the end of the year 1793

PICKERING.

Mr. Randolph was appointed to succeed him, and the office of attorney-general vacated by Mr. Randolph was filled by Mr. Bradford, of Pennsylvania. Thirteen months afterwards, Mr. Hamilton resigned his post at the head of the Treasury, owing to the inadequate amount of his salary. The same cause induced the resignation of the Secretary of War, General Knox. Oliver Wolcott, of Connecticut, succeeded Hamilton, and Timothy Pickering succeeded General Knox. In August, 1795, Mr. Randolph retired from the office of Secretary of State. Mr. McHenry was then called to the head of the War Department, while Mr. Pickering was transferred to the office of Secretary of State. Colonel Pickering's highest eulogy has been spoken by the eloquent lips of John Randolph. That gentleman, on the floor of Congress, spoke of him as one " whom, whatever may be said of him, all will allow to be an honest man. The other day, when on the compensation question, he was speaking of his own situation; when his voice faltered, and his eyes filled at the mention of his poverty, I thought I would have given the riches of Dives himself for his feelings at the moment; for his poverty was not the consequence of idleness, or extravagance, or luxury, nor of the gambling spirit of speculation: it was an honourable poverty, after a life spent in laborious service, and in the highest offices of trust under government, during the war of independence as well as under the present Constitution."

The violent opposition to the excise law by a portion of the people, particularly in the interior of Pennsylvania, where meetings were held, and the revenue officers threatened with personal injury, induced Congress, in May, 1792, to pass an act authorizing the President to call out the militia to assist in executing the laws, if he should deem proper. The President, being reluctant to employ military force, issued a proclamation exhorting the people to. desist from all illegal acts and meetings, but these efforts proved ineffectual. The discontents continued, until, in August, 1794, the "whisky insurrection" had assumed so serious a character in Western Pennsylvania, that an army of volunteers and militia was formed to suppress it, numbering about fifteen thousand men. The insurgents did not venture to meet this force, the insurrection ceased, and the excise law was enforced.

The third Congress of the United States, which first assembled in December, 1793, was about equally divided between the two great political parties. During the interval between the final adjournment of the third Congress and the meeting of the fourth, a treaty was made with Algiers, by Mr. Donaldson, acting under Colonel Humphreys, the United States consul at Portugal. The terms were disadvantageous, but the best that could be obtained. When the first session of the fourth Congress was commenced, it was found that the friends of the administration had increased their majority in the Senate, while the House of Representatives showed a majority in opposition. In the answer to the President's speech, the House of Representatives refused to adopt a report returned by their committee, until some expressions of *undiminished* confidence were changed. Their measures in opposition to the British treaty expressed still further their dissatisfaction with the measures of the administration. Several important acts were adopted at this session, among which was one establishing agencies among the Indian tribes, and another making provision for the sale of the public lands. Another provided for the relief and protection of American seamen, and on the last day of the session, June 1st, 1796, Tennessee was admitted into the Union.

After the adjournment of Congress, the third election for President engaged the public attention. General Washington was earnestly solicited to be a candidate for re-election, but positively declined. He had been forced, as it were, from the enjoyment of private life, by the power of public opinion, and considerations of national usefulness; but he had yielded to this coercion with painful reluctance. He had conducted the ship of state through the stormy tempests of domestic discord and foreign aggression, and now that he supposed her safely moored, he turned his eyes to the shades of Mount Vernon, with longings for tranquillity and repose. Another motive had much weight with him in the formation of this resolution: the establishment, by a precedent, of a wholesome limit to executive power, which the Constitution had left open to an indefinite practice.

In September, 1796, he announced his intention to the people, in his memorable Farewell Address. In this document he made a last effort to impress upon his countrymen those great political truths which had been the guides of his own administration, and could alone form a sure and solid basis for the happiness, the independence, and the liberty of the United States. The sentiments of veneration with which this address was generally received were manifested in almost every part of the Union. Some of the state legislatures directed it to be inserted at large in their journals; and nearly all of them passed resolutions expressing their respect for the President, their high sense of his exalted services, and the emotions with which they contemplated his retirement from office.

The person in whom alone the voice of the people could be united having declined a re-election, the two great parties in the United States respectively brought forward their chiefs, and every possible effort was made by each to obtain the victory. By the federalists, Mr. John Adams and Mr. Thomas Pinckney, the late minister to England, were supported as President and Vice-president; the republican party united in support of Mr. Jefferson. In November, while the election was pending, and parties were so nearly balanced that neither scale could be perceived to preponderate, Mr. Adet, the minister of France, addressed a letter to the Secretary of State, which he also caused to be immediately published, in which he recapitulated the numerous complaints which had been urged by himself and his predecessors against the government of the United States; reproached that government in terms of great asperity with violating those treaties which had secured its independence, with ingratitude to France, and with partiality to England. He also announced orders of the Directory to suspend his ministerial functions with the federal government, a suspension which was not, however, to be regarded as a rupture between France and the United States, but as a mark of just discontent, which was to last until the government of the United States returned to sentiments and to measures more conformable to the interests of the alliance, and to the sworn friendship between the two nations. It can scarcely be doubted that this extraordinary proceeding was intended to influence the people in the election of a new President, but if it produced any effect upon the result of that election, it was to render more determined and more vigorous the exertions of the friends of that candidate whose election Mr. Adet deprecated.*

On the 7th of December, 1796, Washington met Congress fo the last time. His address on the occasion was highly dignified.

* Marshall.

He congratulated Congress on the internal situation of the **United** States ; on the progress which had been made for preserving peace with the Indians and meliorating their condition, and after stating the measures which had been adopted in execution of the treaties with Britain, Spain, and Algiers, and the negotiations which were pending with Tunis and Tripoli, he observed:—" To an active external commerce, the protection of a naval force is indispensable. This is manifest with regard to wars in which a state is itself a party. But besides this, it is in our own experience, that the most sincere neutrality is not a sufficient guard against the depredations of nations at war. To secure respect to a neutral flag, requires a naval force, organized and ready to vindicate it from insult or aggression. This may even prevent the necessity of going to war, by discouraging belligerent powers from committing such violations of the rights of the neutral party, as may first or last leave no other option. From the best information I have been able to obtain, it would seem as if our trade to the Mediterranean, without a protecting force, will always be insecure, and our citizens exposed to the calamities from which numbers of them have but just been relieved.

" These considerations invite the United States to look to the means, and to set about the gradual creation of a navy. The increasing progress of their navigation promises them, at no distant period, the requisite supply of seamen, and their means in other respects favour the undertaking. It is an encouragement likewise, that their particular situation will give weight and influence to a moderate naval force in their hands. Will it not then be advisable to begin without delay, to provide and lay up the materials for the building and equipping of ships of war, and to proceed in the work by degrees, in proportion as our resources shall render it practicable, without inconvenience, so that a future war of Europe may not find our commerce in the same unprotected state in which it was found by the present ?"

He then recommended the establishment of national works for manufacturing implements of defence ; of an institution for the improvement of agriculture ; and pointed out the advantages of a military academy, of a national university, and the necessity of augmenting the salaries of the officers of the United States.

In respect to the disputes with France, he observed :—" While in our external relations some serious inconveniences and embarrasments have been overcome, and others lessened, it is with much pain and deep regret I mention, that circumstances of a very un·

welcome nature have lately accrued. Our trade has suffered and is suffering extensive injuries in the West Indies, from the cruisers and agents of the French republic, and communications have been received for its minister here, which indicate the danger of a further disturbance of our commerce by its authority; and which are in other respects far from agreeable.

"It has been my constant, sincere, and earnest wish, in conformity with that of our nation, to maintain cordial harmony and a perfectly friendly understanding with that republic. This wish remains unabated, and I shall persevere in the endeavour to fulfil it, to the utmost extent of what shall be consistent with a just and indispensable regard to the rights and honour of our country; nor will I easily cease to cherish the expectation that a spirit of justice, candour, and friendship, on the part of the republic, will eventually ensure success.

"In pursuing this course, however, I cannot forget what is due to the character of our government and nation, or to a full and entire confidence in the good sense, patriotism, self-respect, and fortitude of my countrymen."

This address was concluded in the following pathetic terms:

"The situation in which I now stand for the last time, in the midst of the representatives of the people of the United States, naturally recalls the period when the administration of the present form of government commenced; and I cannot omit the occasion to congratulate you and my country on the success of the experiment, nor to repeat my fervent supplications to the Supreme Ruler of the universe, and sovereign arbiter of nations, that his providential care may still be extended to the United States; that the virtue and happiness of the people may be preserved; and that the government which they have instituted for the protection of their liberties may be perpetual."

The pleasing emotions which are excited in ordinary men on their acquisition of power, were inferior to those which Washington felt on the resignation of it. To his tried friend, General Knox, on the day preceding the termination of his office, he observed in a letter: "To the weary traveller who sees a resting place and is bending his body thereon, I now compare myself. Although the prospect of retirement is most grateful to my soul, and I have not a wish to mix again in the great world, or to partake in its politics, yet I am not without regret at parting with (perhaps never more to meet) the few intimates whom I love. Among these be assured you are one."

3 A 2

The numerous calumnies of which Washington was the subject, drew from him no public animadversions, except in one case. A volume of letters, said to be from General Washington to John Parke Custis and Lund Washington, were published by the British, in the year 1776, and were given to the public as being found in a small portmanteau, left in the care of his servant, who, it was said by the editors, had been taken prisoner in Fort Lee. These letters were intended to produce in the public mind impressions unfavourable to the integrity of Washington's motives, and to represent his inclinations as at variance with his profession and duty. When the first edition of these spurious letters was forgotten, they were republished during Washington's civil administration, by some of his fellow-citizens who differed from him in politics. On the morning of the last day of his Presidency he addressed a letter to the Secretary of State, in which, after enumerating all the facts and dates connected with the forgery, and declaring that he had hitherto deemed it unnecessary to take any formal notice of the imposition, he concluded as follows :—" But as I cannot know how soon a more serious event may succeed to that which will this day take place, I have thought it a duty that I owed to myself, to my country, and to truth, now to detail the circumstances above recited, and to add my solemn declaration that the letters herein described are a base forgery, and that I never saw or heard of them until they appeared in print. The present letter I commit to your care, and desire it may be deposited in the office of the Department of State as a testimony of the truth to the present generation and to posterity."

The moment now approached which was to terminate the official character of Washington, and in which that of his successor, John Adams, was to commence. The old and new President walked in together to the House of Representatives, where the oath of office was administered to the latter. On this occasion Mr. Adams concluded an impressive speech with a handsome compliment to his predecessor, by observing that though he was about to retire, " his name may still be a rampart and the knowledge that he lives a bulwark against all open or secret enemies of his country."

The immense concourse of citizens who were present gazed with love and affection on the retiring Washington, while cheerfulness overspread his countenance and joy filled his heart, on seeing another invested with the high authorities he so long exercised, and the way opened for his returning to the long-wished-for happiness of domestic private life. After paying his respects to the new

President, he set out for Mount Vernon, the scene of enjoyment which he preferred to all others. His wishes to travel privately were in vain; for wherever he passed, the gentlemen of the country took every occasion of testifying their respect for him. In his retirement he continued to receive the most flattering addresses from legislative bodies, and various classes of his fellow-citizens.

During the eight years' administration of Washington, the United States enjoyed prosperity and happiness at home; and, by the energy of the government, regained among foreigners that importance and reputation, which, by its weakness, they had lost. The debts contracted in the Revolutionary War, which, from the imbecility of the old government, had depreciated to an insignificant sum, were funded; and such ample revenues provided for the payment of the interest and the gradual extinction of the principal, that their real and nominal value were, in a little time, nearly the same. The government was so firmly established as to be cheerfully and universally obeyed. The only exception was an insurrection in the western counties of Pennsylvania, which was quelled without bloodshed. Agriculture and commerce were extended far beyond what had ever before taken place. The Indians on the frontiers had been first compelled by force to respect the United States, and to continue in peace; and afterwards a humane system was commenced for teaching them to exchange the tomahawk and scalping-knife for the plough, the hoe, the shuttle, and the spinning-wheel. The free navigation of the Mississippi had been acquired with the consent of Spain, and all differences compromised with that power. The military posts which had been long held by Britain within the United States, were peaceably given up. The Mediterranean was opened to American vessels in consequence of treaties made with the Barbary powers. Indeed, differences with all powers, either contiguous to or connected with the United States, had been amicably adjusted, with the exception of France. To accomplish this very desirable object, Washington made repeated advances; but it could not be obtained without surrendering the independence of the nation, and its right of self-government.

THE NEW TOMB OF WASHINGTON.

CHAPTER XXIV.

𝕷𝖆𝖘𝖙 𝕯𝖆𝖞𝖘 𝖔𝖋 𝖂𝖆𝖘𝖍𝖎𝖓𝖌𝖙𝖔𝖓.

HE season of repose which now awaited him was as welcome as it was necessary to Washington. On returning to Mount Vernon, he resumed agricultural pursuits. These, with the society of men and books, gave to every hour innocent and interesting employment; and promised a serene evening of his life. Though he wished to withdraw not only from public office, but from all anxiety respecting public affairs, yet he felt too much for his country to be indifferent to its interests. He heard with regret the repeated insults offered by the French Directory to the United States, in the person of their ministers, and the injuries done to their commerce, by illegal capture of their vessels. These indignities and injuries, after a long endurance and a rejection of all advances for an accommodation, at length roused the government, in the hands of Mr. Adams, to adopt vigorous measures. To be in readiness to repel a threatened invasion, Congress authorized the formation of a regular army. As soon as the adoption of this

SUMMER-HOME AT MOUNT VERNON.

measure was probable, the eyes of all were once more turned on Washington as the most suitable person to be at its head. Letters from his friends poured in upon him, urging that he should accept the command. In one received from President Adams, it was observed, "We must have your name, if you will in any case permit us to use it; there will be more efficacy in it than in many an army." A letter from the Secretary of War, written four days afterwards, concludes with asking, " may we flatter ourselves, that, in a crisis so awful and important, you will accept the command of all our armies. I hope you will, because you alone can unite all hearts and all hands, if it is possible that they can be united." In reply to this letter, Washington writes, "It cannot be necessary for me to premise to you, or to others who know my sentiments, that to quit the tranquillity of retirement, and enter the boundless field of responsibility, would be productive of sensations which a better pen than I possess would find it difficult to describe. Nevertheless, the principle by which my conduct has been actuated through life, would not suffer me, in any great emergency, to withhold any services I could render when required by my country; especially, in a case where its dearest rights are assailed by lawless ambition and intoxicated power, in contempt of every principle of justice, and in violation of solemn compact, and of laws which govern all civilized nations; and this, too, with the obvious intent to sow thick the seeds of disunion, for the purpose of subjugating our government, and destroying our independence and happiness.

"Under circumstances like these, accompanied by an actual invasion of our territory, it would be difficult for me at any time to remain an idle spectator, under the plea of age or retirement. With sorrow, it is true, I should quit the shades of my peaceful abode, and the ease and happiness I now enjoy, to encounter anew the turmoils of war, to which possibly my strength and powers might be found incompetent. These, however, should not be stumbling-blocks in my own way."

President Adams nominated Washington with the rank of lieutenant-general, to the chief command of all the armies raised and to be raised in the United States. His commission was sent to him by Mr. McHenry, the Secretary of War, who was directed to repair to Mount Vernon, and to confer on the arrangements of the new army with its commander-in-chief. To the letter which President Adams sent with the commission by the Secretary of War, Washington in two days replied as follows:

"I had the honour, on the evening of the 11th instant, to receive from the hand of the Secretary of War, your favour of the 7th, announcing that you had, with the advice and consent of the Senate, appointed me 'Lieutenant-general and commander-in-chief of all the armies raised, or to be raised, for the service of the United States.'

"I cannot express how greatly affected I am at this new proof of public confidence, and the highly flattering manner in which you have been pleased to make the communication. At the same time, I must not conceal from you my earnest wish, that the choice had fallen upon a man less declined in years, and better qualified to encounter the usual vicissitudes of war.

"You know, sir, what calculation I had made relative to the probable course of events on my retiring from office, and the determination I had consoled myself with, of closing the remnant of my days in my present peaceful abode. You will therefore be at no loss to conceive and appreciate the sensations I must have experienced, to bring my mind to any conclusion that would pledge me, at so late a period of life, to leave scenes I sincerely love, to enter upon the boundless field of public action, incessant trouble, and high responsibility.

"It was not possible for me to remain ignorant of, or indifferent to, recent transactions. The conduct of the Directory of France towards our country; their insidious hostility to its government; their various practices to withdraw the affections of the people from it; the evident tendency of their acts, and those of their agents, to countenance and invigorate disaffection; their disregard of solemn treaties and the laws of nations; their war upon our defenceless commerce; their treatment of our ministers of peace; and their demands, amounting to tribute, could not fail to excite in me corresponding sentiments with those my countrymen have so generally expressed in their affectionate addresses to you. Believe me, sir, no one can more cordially approve of the wise and prudent measures of your administration. They ought to inspire universal confidence, and will, no doubt, combined with the state of things, call from Congress such laws and means as will enable you to meet the full force and extent of the crisis.

"Satisfied, therefore, that you have sincerely wished and endeavoured to avert war, and exhausted to the last drop the cup of reconciliation, we can with pure hearts appeal to Heaven for the justice of our cause; and may confidently trust the final result to that kind Providence who has heretofore and so often signally favoured the people of these United States.

" Thinking in this manner, and feeling how incumbent it is upon every person of every description, to contribute at all times to his country's welfare, and especially in a moment like the present, when every thing we hold dear and sacred is so seriously threatened; I have finally determined to accept the commission of commander-in-chief of the armies of the United States ; with the reserve only that I shall not be called into the field until the army is in a situation to require my presence, or it becomes indispensable by the urgency of circumstances.

" In making this reservation, I beg it to be understood, that I do not mean to withhold any assistance to arrange and organize the army, which you may think I can afford.   I take the liberty also to mention that I must decline having my acceptance considered as drawing after it any immediate charge upon the public ; or that I can receive any emoluments annexed to the appointment, before entering into a situation to incur expense."

The time of Washington, after the receipt of this appointment, was divided between agricultural pursuits and the cares and attentions which were imposed by his new office.   The organization of the army was, in a great measure, left to him.   Much of his time was employed in making a proper selection of officers and arranging the whole army in the best possible manner to meet the invaders at the water's edge ; for he contemplated a system of continued attack, and frequently observed, "that the enemy must never be permitted to gain foothold on the shores of the United States." Yet he always thought that an actual invasion of the country was very improbable.   He believed that the hostile measures of France took their rise from an expectation that these measures would produce a revolution of power in the United States, favourable to the views of the French republic ; and that when the spirit of the Americans was roused, the French would give up the contest. Events soon proved that these opinions were well founded ; for no sooner had the United States armed, than they were treated with respect, and an indirect communication was made that France would accommodate all matters in dispute on reasonable terms. Mr. Adams embraced these overtures, and made a second appointment of three envoys extraordinary to the French republic.   These, on repairing to France, found the Directory overthrown and the government in the hands of Bonaparte, who had taken no part in the disputes which had brought the two countries to the verge of war.   With him negotiations were commenced and soon terminated in a pacific settlement of all differences.   The joy to which this event gave birth was great; but in it General Washington did not partake, for before accounts arrived of this amicable adjustment, he had ceased to be numbered with the living.

On the 13th of December, 1799, his neck and hair were sprinkled with a light rain while he was out of doors attending to some improvements on his estate. In the following night he was seized with an inflammatory affection of the windpipe, attended with pain and a difficult deglutition, which was soon succeeded by fever and a laborious respiration. He was bled in the night, but would not permit his family physician to be sent for before day. About 11 o'clock, A. M., Dr. Craik arrived, and rightly judging that the case was serious, recommended that two consulting physicians should be sent for. The united powers of all three were exerted in vain; in about twenty-four hours from the time he was in his usual health, he expired without a struggle, and in the perfect use of his reason.

In every stage of his disorder he believed that he should die, and he was so much under this impression, that he submitted to the prescriptions of his physicians more from a sense of duty than from any expectation of relief. After he had given them a trial, he expressed a wish that he might be permitted to die without further interruption. Towards the close of his illness, he undressed himself and went to bed, to die there. To his friend and physician, Dr. Craik, he said, "I am dying, and have been dying for a long time, but I am not afraid to die." The equanimity which attended him through life, did not forsake him in death. He was the same in that moment as in all the past, magnanimous and firm; confiding in the mercy and resigned to the will of Heaven. He submitted to the inevitable stroke with the dignity of a man, the calmness of a philosopher, the resignation and confidence of a Christian.

On the 18th, his body, attended by military honours, and the offices of religion, was deposited in the family vault on his estate.

In December, 1837, the remains of this great father of our nation, after a slumber of thirty-eight years, were again exposed by the circumstance of placing his body once, and for ever, within the sarcophagus of marble, made by Mr. Struthers, of Philadelphia. The body, as Mr. Struthers related, was still in wonderful preservation; the high pale brow wore a calm and serene expression, and the lips, pressed together, had a grave and solemn smile.

When intelligence reached Congress of the death of Washington, they instantly adjourned until the next day, when John Marshall, then a member of the House of Representatives, and since Chief

THE OLD TOMB OF WASHINGTON.

Justice of the United States and biographer of Washington, addressed the speaker in the following words:

"The melancholy event which was yesterday announced with doubt, has been rendered but too certain. Our Washington is no more. The hero, the patriot, and the sage of America; the man on whom in times of danger every eye was turned and all hopes were placed, lives now only in his own great actions, and in the hearts of an affectionate and afflicted people.

"If, sir, it had even not been usual openly to testify respect for the memory of those whom Heaven has selected as its instruments for dispensing good to man, yet such has been the uncommon worth, and such the extraordinary incidents which have marked the life of him whose loss we all deplore, that the whole American nation, impelled by the same feelings, would call with one voice for a public manifestation of that sorrow, which is so deep and so universal.

"More than any other individual, and as much as to any one individual was possible, has he contributed to found this our wide spreading empire, and to give to the western world independence and freedom.

"Having effected the great object for which he was placed at the head of our armies, we have seen him convert the sword into the ploughshare, and sink the soldier into the citizen.

"When the debility of our federal system had become manifest and the bonds which connected this vast continent were dissolving, we have seen him the chief of those patriots who formed for us a Constitution, which, by preserving the Union, will, I trust, substantiate and perpetuate those blessings which our Revolution had promised to bestow.

"In obedience to the general voice of his country, calling him to preside over a great people, we have seen him once more quit the retirement he loved, and in a season more stormy and tempestuous than war itself, with calm and wise determination, pursue the true interests of the nation, and contribute more than any other could contribute to the establishment of that system of policy which will, I trust, yet preserve our peace, our honour, and our independence. Having been twice unanimously chosen the chief magistrate of a free people, we have seen him, at a time when his re-election with universal suffrage could not be doubted, afford to the world a rare instance of moderation, by withdrawing from his high station to the peaceful walks of private life. However the public confidence may change and the public affections fluctuate with respect to others, with respect to him they have, in war and in peace, in public and in private life, been as steady as his own firm mind, and as constant as his own exalted virtues. Let us then, Mr. Speaker, pay the last tribute of respect and affection to our departed friend. Let the grand council of the nation display those sentiments which the nation feels. For this purpose, I hold in my hand some resolutions which I take the liberty of offering to the House.

"Resolved, That this House will wait on the President in condolence of this mournful event.

"Resolved, That the Speaker's chair be shrouded with black, and that the members and officers of the House wear black during the session.

"Resolved, that a committee, in conjunction with one from the Senate, be appointed to consider on the most suitable manner of paying honour to the memory of the man, first in war, first in peace, and first in the hearts of his fellow-citizens."

The Senate, on this melancholy occasion, addressed to the President the following letter :

"The Senate of the United States respectfully take leave, sir, to express to you their deep regret for the loss their country sustains in the death of General George Washington.

"This event, so distressing to all our fellow-citizens, must be peculiarly heavy to you, who have long been associated with him in deeds of patriotism. Permit us, sir, to mingle our tears with yours. On this occasion, it is manly to weep. To lose such a man at such a crisis, is no common calamity to the world. Our country mourns a father. The Almighty Disposer of human events has, taken from us our greatest benefactor and ornament. It becomes us to submit with reverence to him 'who maketh darkness his pavilion.'

"With patriotic pride we review the life of our Washington, and compare its events with those of other countries, who have been pre-eminent in fame. Ancient and modern times are diminished before nim. Greatness and guilt have too often been allied; but his fame is whiter than it is brilliant. The destroyers of nations stood abashed at the majesty of his virtues. It reproved the intemperance of their ambition, and darkened the splendour of victory. The scene is closed, and we are no longer anxious lest misfortune should sully his glory; he has travelled on to the end of his journey, and carried with him an increasing weight of honour; he has deposited it safely where misfortune cannot tarnish it, where malice cannot blast it. Favoured of Heaven, he departed without exhibiting the weakness of humanity. Magnanimous in death, the darkness of the grave could not obscure his brightness.

"Such was the man whom we deplore. Thanks to God, his glory is consummated. Washington yet lives on earth in his spotless example; his spirit is in Heaven.

"Let his countrymen consecrate the memory of the heroic general, the patriotic statesman, and the virtuous sage. Let them teach their children never to forget, that the fruits of his labours and his example are their inheritance."

To this address, the President returned the following answer:—

"I receive with the most respectful and affectionate sentiments, in this impressive address, the obliging expressions of your regret for the loss our country has sustained in the death of her most esteemed, beloved, and admired citizen.

"In the multitude of my thoughts and recollections on this melancholy event, you will permit me to say, that I have seen him in the days of adversity, in some of the scenes of his deepest distress, and most trying perplexities. I have also attended him in the highest elevation, and most prosperous felicity, with uniform admiration of his wisdom, moderation, and constancy.

"Among all our original associates in that memorable league of this continent in 1774, which first expressed the sovereign will of a free nation in America, he was the only one remaining in the general government. Although with a constitution more enfeebled than his, at an age when he thought it necessary to prepare for

72   3 B 2

retirement, I feel myself alone bereaved of my last brother, yet I derive a strong consolation from the unanimous disposition which appears in all ages and classes, to mingle their sorrows with mine, on this common calamity to the world.

" The life of our Washington cannot suffer by a comparison with those of other countries, who have been most celebrated and exalted by fame. The attributes and decorations of royalty could only have served to eclipse the majesty of those virtues which made him, from being a modest citizen, a more resplendent luminary. Misfortune, had he lived, could hereafter have sullied his glory only with those superficial minds, who, believing that character and actions are marked by success alone, rarely deserve to enjoy it. Malice could never blast his honour, and envy made him a singular exception to her universal rule. For himself, he had lived long enough to life and to glory; for his fellow-citizens, if their prayers could have been answered, he would have been immortal; for me, his departure is at a most unfortunate moment. Trusting, however, in the wise and righteous dominion of Providence over the passions of men and the results of their actions, as well as over their lives, nothing remains for me but humble resignation.

" His example is now complete; and it will teach wisdom and virtue to magistrates, citizens, and men, not only in the present age, but in future generations, as long as our history shall be read. If a Trajan found a Pliny, a Marcus Aurelius can never want biographers, eulogists, or historians."

The committee of both Houses appointed to devise the mode by which the nation should express its grief, reported the following resolutions, which were unanimously adopted.

" Resolved, by the Senate and House of Representatives of the United States of America, in Congress assembled, That a marble monument be erected by the United States at the capitol of the city of Washington, and that the family of General Washington be requested to permit his body to be deposited under it, and that the monument be so designed as to commemorate the great events of his military and political life.

" And be it further resolved, that there be a funeral from Congress Hall to the German Lutheran church, in memory of General George Washington, on Thursday the 26th instant; and that an oration be prepared at the request of Congress, to be delivered before both houses that day; and that the President of the Senate and Speaker of the House of Representatives, be desired to request one of the members of Congress to prepare and deliver the same.

"And be it further resolved, that the President of the United States be requested to direct a copy of these resolutions to be transmitted to Mrs. Washington, assuring her of the profound respect Congress will ever bear for her person and character, of their condolence on the late afflicting dispensation of Providence : and entreating her assent to the interment of the remains of General Washington in the manner expressed in the first resolution.

"And be it further resolved, that the President of the United States be requested to issue his proclamation, notifying to the people throughout the United States, the recommendation contained in the third resolution."

To the letter of President Adams, which transmitted to Mrs. Washington the resolution of Congress that she should be requested to permit the remains of General Washington to be deposited under a marble monument, to be erected in the city of Washington, she replied very much in the style and manner of her departed husband, and in the following words : " Taught by the great example which I have so long had before me, never to oppose my private wishes to the public will, I must consent to the request made by Congress, which you have had the goodness to transmit to me ; and in doing this, I need not, I cannot say, what a sacrifice of individual feeling I make to a sense of public duty."

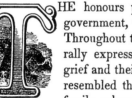HE honours paid to Washington at the seat of government, were but a small part of the whole. Throughout the United States, the citizens generally expressed, in a variety of ways, both their grief and their gratitude. Their heartfelt distress resembled the agony of a large and affectionate family, when a bereaved widow and orphan children mingle their tears for the loss of a husband and father.

We cannot better conclude this volume than by extracting from the works of Fisher Ames the sketch of the character of Washington, contained in the eulogium upon him pronounced by that statesman before the legislature of Massachusetts. It is less impassioned than many similar passages which we might select, much less so than the well-known character of Mr. Ames as a most brilliant orator would lead us to expect. At the time it was delivered, however, the numerous funereal honours already paid to the memory of the beloved dead, had already made a great demand upon the public sensibility. Mr. Ames chose rather to dwell on the political events and acts which illustrated his character than to draw tears for his loss.

"It is not impossible," he said, "that some will affect to con-sider the honours paid to this great patriot by the nation, as exces-sive, idolatrous. and degrading to freemen who are all equal.   I answer, that rcfusing to virtue its legitimate honours would not pre-vent their being lavished in future, on any worthless and ambitious favourite.   If this day's example should have its natural effect, it will be salutary.   Let such honours be so conferred only when, in future, they shall be so merited ; then the public sentiment will not be misled, nor the principles of a just equality corrupted.   The best evidence of reputation is a man's whole life.   We have now, alas, all of Washington's before us.   There has scarcely appeared a really great man whose character has been more admired in his lifetime, or less correctly understood by his admirers.   When it is comprehended, it is no easy task to delineate its excellences in such a manner as to give the portrait both interest and resemblance ; for it requires thought and study to understand the true ground of the superiority of his character over many others, whom he resembled in the principles of action and even in the manner of acting.   But perhaps he excels all the great men that ever lived in the steadiness of his adherence to his maxims of life, and in the uniformity of all his conduct to those maxims.   Those maxims, though wise, were yet not so remarkable for their wisdom as for their authority over his life, for if there were any errors in his judgment, and he displayed as few as any man, we know of no blemishes in his virtue.   He was the patriot without reproach : he loved his country well enough to hold his success in serving it an ample recompense. Thus far, self-love and love of country coincided : but when his country needed sacrifices that no other man could, or perhaps would be willing to make, he did not even hesitate.   This was virtue in its most exalted character.   More than once he put his fame at hazard, when he had reason to think it would be sacrificed, at least in this age.   Two instances cannot be denied : when the army was disbanded, and again when he stood, like Leonidas at the pass of Thermopylæ, to defend our independence against France.

"It is indeed almost as difficult to draw his character as to draw the portrait of virtue.   The reasons are similar; our ideas of moral excellence are obscure, because they are complex, and we are obliged to resort to illustrations.   Washington's example is the happiest, to show what virtue is; and to delineate his character, we naturally expatiate on the beauty of virtue ; much must be felt and much imagined.   His pre-eminence is not so much to be seen in the display of any one virtue, as in the possession of them all, and in the practice of the most difficult. Hereafter, therefore, his characte. must be studied before it will be striking, and then it will be ad mitted as a model, a precious one to a free republic.

"It is no less difficult to speak of his talents. They were adapted to lead, without dazzling mankind; and to draw forth and employ the talents of others without being misled by them. In this he was certainly superior, that he neither mistook nor misapplied his own. His great modesty and reserve would have concealed them if great occasions had not called them forth; and then, as he never spoke from the affectation to shine, nor acted from any sinister motives, it is from their effects only that we are to judge of their greatness and extent. In public trusts, where men, acting conspicuously, are cautious, and in those private concerns, where few conceal or resist their weakness, Washington was uniformly great, pursuing right conduct from right maxims. His talents were such as to assist a sound judgment and ripen with it. His prudence was consummate, and seemed to take the direction of his powers and passions; for, as a soldier, he was more solicitous to avoid mistakes that might be fatal than to perform exploits that are brilliant; and as a statesman to adhere to just principles, however old, than to pursue novelties; and therefore, in both characters, his qualities were singularly adapted to the interest and were tried in the greatest perils of the country. His habits of inquiry were so far remarkable, that he was never satisfied with investigating, nor desisted from it, so long as he had less than all the light that he could obtain upon a subject, and then he made his decision without bias.

" This command over the partialities that so generally stop men short, or turn them aside in their pursuit of truth, is one of the chief causes of his unvaried course of right conduct in so many difficult scenes, where every human action must be presumed to err. If he had strong passions, he had learned to subdue them, and to be moderate and mild. If he had weaknesses, he concealed them,' which is rare, and excluded them from the government of his temper and conduct, which is still more rare. If he loved fame, he never made improper compliances for what is called popularity. The fame he enjoyed is of the kind that will last for ever; yet it was rather the effect, than the motive of his conduct. Some future Plutarch will search for a parallel to his character. Epaminondas is perhaps the brightest name of all antiquity. Our Washington resembled him in the purity and ardour of his patriotism; and like him, he first exalted the glory of his country. There, it is to be hoped, the parallel ends, for Thebes fell with Epaminondas. But such comparisons cannot be pursued far, without departing from the similitude. For we shall find it as difficult to compare great men as great rivers; some we admire for the length and rapidity of their currents, and the grandeur of their cataracts; others for the majestic silence and fulness of their streams; we cannot bring them together to measure the difference of their waters. The unambitious life of Washington, declining fame, yet courted by it, seemed, like the Ohio, to choose its long way through solitudes, diffusing fertility; or like his own Potomac, widening and deepening his channel, as he approaches the sea, and displaying most the usefulness and serenity of his greatness towards the end of his course. Such a citizen would do honour to any country. The constant veneration and affection of his country will show that it was worthy of such a citizen.

"However his military fame may excite the wonder of mankind, it is chiefly by his civil magistracy that his example will instruct them. Great generals have arisen in all ages of the world, and perhaps most of them in despotism and darkness. In times of violence and convulsion they rise, by the force of the whirlwind, high enough to ride in it, and direct the storm. Like meteors, they glare on the black clouds with a splendour, that, while it dazzles and terrifies, makes nothing visible but the darkness. The fame of heroes is indeed growing vulgar: they multiply in every long war; they stand in history and thicken in their ranks almost as undistinguished as their own soldiers.

"But such a chief magistrate as Washington appears like the pole star in a clear sky, to direct the skilful statesman. His presidency will form an epoch and be distinguished as the age of Washington. Already it assumes its high place in the political region. Like the milky-way, it whitens along its allotted portion of the hemisphere. The latest generations of men will survey, through the telescope of history, the space where so many virtues blend their rays, and delight to separate them into groups and distinct virtues. As the best illustration of them, the living monument, to which the first of patriots would have chosen to consign his fame, it is my earnest prayer to Heaven that our country may subsist even to that late day in the plenitude of its liberty and happiness, and mingle its mild glory with Washington's."

APPENDIX.

WASHINGTON'S FAREWELL ADDRESS TO THE PEOPLE OF THE UNITED STATES.

Friends and fellow-citizens,

The period for a new election of a citizen to administer the executive government of the United States being not far distant, and the time actually arrived when your thoughts must be employed in designating the person who is to be clothed with that important trust, it appears to me proper, especially as it may conduce to a more distinct expression of the public voice, that I should now apprize you of the resolution I have formed, to decline being considered among the number of those, out of whom a choice is to be made.

I beg you, at the same time, to do me the justice to be assured, that this resolution has not been taken, without a strict regard to all the considerations appertaining to the relation which binds a dutiful citizen to his country ; and that in withdrawing the tender of service which silence in my situation might imply, I am influenced by no diminution of zeal for your future interest ; no deficiency of grateful respect for your past kindness ; but I am supported by a full conviction that the step is compatible with both.

The acceptance of, and continuance hitherto in the office to which your suffrages have twice called me, have been a uniform sacrifice of inclination to the opinion of duty, and to a deference for what appeared to be your desire. I constantly hoped that it would have been much earlier in my power, consistently with motives which I was not at liberty to disregard, to return to that retirement from which I had been reluctantly drawn. The strength of my inclination to do this, previous to the last election, had even led to the preparation of an address to declare it to you ; but mature reflection on the then perplexed and critical posture of our affairs with foreign nations, and the unanimous advice of persons entitled to my confidence, impelled me to abandon the idea.

I rejoice that the state of your concerns, external as well as internal, no longer renders the pursuit of inclination incompatible with the sentiment of duty or propriety ; and am persuaded, whatever partiality may be retained for my services, that in the present circumstances of our country, you will not disapprove my determination to retire.

The impressions with which I first undertook the arduous trust, were explained on the proper occasion. In the discharge of this trust, I will only say that I have, with good intentions, contributed towards the organization and administration of the government, the best exertions of which a very fallible judgment was capable. Not unconscious, in the outset, of the inferiority of my qualifications, experience, in my own eyes, perhaps still more in the eyes of others, has strengthened the motives to diffidence of myself ; and, every day, the increasing weight of years admonishes me more and more, that the shade of retirement is as necessary to me as it will be welcome. Satisfied that if any circumstances have given peculiar value to my services, they were temporary, I have the consolation to believe that, while choice and prudence invite me to quit the political scene, patriotism does not forbid it.

In looking forward to the moment which is to terminate the career of my political life, my feelings do not permit me to suspend the deep acknowledgment of that debt of gratitude which I owe to my beloved country, for the many honours it has conferred upon me ; still more for the steadfast confidence with which it has supported me ; and for the opportunities I have thence enjoyed of manifesting my inviolable attachment, by services faithful and persevering, though in usefulness unequal to my zeal. If benefits have resulted to our country from these services, let it always be remembered to your praise, as an instructive example in our annals, that under circumstances in which the passions, agitated in every direction, were liable to mislead amidst appearances sometimes dubious, vicissitudes of fortune often discouraging—in situations in which, not unfrequently, want of success has countenanced the spirit of criticism—the constancy of your support was the essential prop of the efforts, and a guarantee of the plans by which they were effected. Profoundly penetrated with this idea, I shall carry it with me to my grave, as a strong incitement to unceasing vows, that heaven may continue to you the choicest tokens of its beneficence —that your union and brotherly affection may be perpetual—that the free constitution, which is the work of your hands, may be sacredly maintained—that its administration in every department may be stamped with wisdom and virtue—that, in fine, the happiness of the people of these states, under the auspices of liberty, may be made compiete by so careful a preservation, and so prudent a use of this blessing as will acquire to them the glory of recommending it to the applause, the affection, and adoption of every nation which is yet a stranger to it.

Here, perhaps, I ought to stop. But a solicitude for your welfare, which cannot end but with my life, and the apprehension of danger, natural to that solicitude, urge me, on an occasion like the present, to offer to your solemn contemplation, and to recommend to your frequent review, some sentiments which are the result of much reflection, of no inconsiderable observation, and which appear to me all-important to the permanency of your felicity as a people. These will be offered to you with the more freedom, as you can only see in them the disinterested warnings of a parting friend, who can possibly have no personal motive to bias his counsel. Nor can I forget, as an encouragement to it, your indulgent reception of my sentiments on a former and not dissimilar occasion.

Interwoven as is the love of liberty with every ligament of your hearts, no recommendation of mine is necessary to fortify or confirm the attachment.

The unity of government which constitutes you one people, is also now dear to you. It is justly so; for it is a main pillar in the edifice of your real independence; the support of your tranquillity at home; your peace abroad; of your safety; of your prosperity; of that very liberty which you so highly prize. But, as it is easy to foresee, that from different causes, and from different quarters, much pains will be taken, many artifices employed, to weaken in your minds the conviction of this truth; as this is the point in your political fortress against which the batteries of internal and external enemies will be most constantly and actively (though often covertly and insidiously) directed; it is of infinite moment, that you should properly estimate the immense value of your national union to your collective and individual happiness; that you should cherish a cordial, habitual, and immoveable attachment to it; accustoming yourselves to think and speak of it as of the palladium of your political safety and prosperity; watching for its preservation with jealous anxiety; discountenancing whatever may suggest even a suspicion that it can, in any event, be abandoned; and indignantly frowning upon the first dawning of every attempt to alienate any portion of our country from the rest, or to enfeeble the sacred ties which now link together the various parts.

For this you have every inducement of sympathy and interest., Citizens by birth, or choice, of a common country, that country has a right to concentrate your affections. The name of American, which belongs to you in your national capacity, must always exalt the just pride of patriotism, more than any appellation derived from local discriminations. With slight shades of difference, you have the same religion, manners, habits, and political principles. You have, in a common cause, fought and triumphed together ; the independence and liberty you possess, are the work of joint counsels, and joint efforts, of common dangers, sufferings and successes.

But these considerations, however powerfully they address themselves to your sensibility, are greatly outweighed by those which apply more immediately to your interest. Here, every portion of our country finds the most commanding motives for carefully guarding and preserving the union of the whole.

The *north*, in an unrestrained intercourse with the *south*, protected by the equal laws of a common government, finds in the productions of the latter, great additional resources of maritime and commercial enterprise, and precious materials of manufacturing industry. The *south*, in the same intercouse, benefiting by the same agency of the *north*, sees its agriculture grow, and its commerce expand. Turning partly into its own channels the seamen of the *north*, it finds its particular navigation invigorated ; and while it contributes, in different ways, to nourish and increase the general mass of the national navigation, it looks forward to the protection of a maritime strength, to which itself is unequally adapted. The *east*, in a like intercourse with the *west*, already finds, and in the progressive improvement of interior communications by land and water will more and more find a valuable vent for the commodities which it brings from .abroad, or manufactures at home. The *west* derives from the *east* supplies requisite to its growth and comfort—and what is perhaps of still greater consequence, it must of necessity owe the *secure* enjoyment of indispensable *outlets* for its own productions, to the weight, influence, and the future maritime strength of the Atlantic side of the Union, directed by an indissoluble community of interest as *one nation*. Any other tenure by which the *west* can hold this essential advantage, whether derived from its own separate strength, or from an apostate and unnatural connection with any foreign power, must be intrinsically precarious.

While then every part of our country thus feels an immediate and particular interest in union, all the parts combined cannot fail to find in the united mass of means and efforts, greater strength, greater resource, proportionably greater security from external danger, a less frequent interruption of their peace by foreign nations ; and, what is of inestimable value, they must derive from union an exemption from those broils and wars between themselves, which so frequently afflict neighbouring countries not tied together by the same government ; which their own rivalships alone would be sufficient to produce, but which, opposite foreign alliances, attachments and intrigues, would stimulate and imbitter. Hence likewise, they will avoid the necessity of those overgrown military establishments, which under any form of government are inauspicious to liberty, and which are to be regarded as particularly hostile to republican liberty. In this sense it is, that your union ought to be considered as a main prop of your liberty, and that the love of the one ought to endear to you the preservation of the other.

These considerations speak a persuasive language to every reflecting and virtuous mind, and exhibit the continuance of the Union as a primary object of patriotic desire. Is there a doubt whether a common government can embrace so large a sphere ? Let experience solve it. To listen to mere speculation in such a case were criminal. We are authorized to hope that a proper organization of the whole, with the auxiliary agency of governments for the respective subdivisions, will afford a happy issue to the experiment. It is well worth a fair and full experiment. With such powerful and obvious motives to union, affecting all parts of our country, while experience shall not have demonstrated its impracticability, there will always be reasons to distrust the patriotism of those, who, in any quarter, may endeavour to weaken its bands.

In contemplating the causes which may disturb our union, it occurs, as matter of serious concern, that any ground should have been furnished for characterizing parties by *geographical* discriminations,— *northern* and *southern*—*Atlantic* and *western ;* whence designing men may endeavour to excite a belief that there is a real difference of local interests and views. One of the expedients of party to acquire influence within particular districts, is to misrepresent the opinions and aims of other districts. You cannot shield yourselves too much against the jealousies and heart-burnings which spring from these misrepresentations : they tend to render alien to each other those who ought to be bound together by fraternal affection. The inhabitants of our western country have lately had a useful lesson on this head : they have seen, in the negotiation by the executive, and in the unanimous ratification by the Senate of the treaty with Spain, and in the universal satisfaction at the event throughout the United States, a decisive proof how unfounded were the suspicions propagated among them of a policy in the general government and in the Atlantic States, unfriendly to their interests in regard to the Mississippi. They have been witnesses to the formation of two treaties, that with Great Britain and that with

Spain, which secure to them every thing they could desire, in respect to our foreign relations, towards confirming their prosperity. Will it not be their wisdom to rely for the preservation of these advantages on the union by which they were procured? will they not henceforth be deaf to those advisers, if such there are, who would sever them from their brethren, and connect them with aliens?

To the efficacy and permanency of your union, a government for the whole is indispensable. No alliances, however strict, between the parts can be an adequate substitute; they must inevitably experience the infractions and interruptions which all alliances, in all times, have experienced. Sensible of this momentous truth, you have improved your first essay, by the adoption of a Constitution of government better calculated than your former for an intimate union, and for the efficacious management of your common concerns. This government, the offspring of our own choice, uninfluenced and unawed, adopted upon full investigation and mature deliberation, completely free in its principles, in the distribution of its powers uniting security with energy, and containing within itself a provision for its own amendment, has a just claim to your confidence and your support. Respect for its authority, compliance with its laws, acquiescence in its measures, are duties enjoined by the fundamental maxims of true liberty. The basis of our political systems is the right of the people to make and to alter their constitutions of government. But the constitution which at any time exists, until changed by an explicit and authentic act of the whole people, is sacredly obligatory upon all. The very idea of the power and the right of the people to establish government, presupposes the duty of every individual to obey the established government.

All obstructions to the execution of the laws, all combinations and associations under whatever plausible character, with the real design to direct, control, counteract, or awe the regular deliberations and action of the constituted authorities, are destructive of this fundamental principle, and of fatal tendency. They serve to organize faction, to give it an artificial and extraordinary force, to put in the place of the delegated will of the nation the will of party, often a small but artful and enterprising minority of the community; and, according to the alternate triumphs of different parties, to make the public administration the mirror of the ill-concerted and incongruous projects of faction, rather than the organ of consistent and wholesome plans digested by common councils, and modified by mutual interests.

However combinations or associations of the above description may now and then answer popular ends, they are likely, in the course of time and things, to become potent engines, by which cunning, ambitious, and unprincipled men, will be enabled to subvert the power of the people, and to usurp for themselves the reins of government; destroying afterwards the very engines which have lifted them to unjust dominion.

Towards the preservation of your government and the permanency of your present happy state, it is requisite, not only that you steadily discountenance irregular oppositions to its acknowledged authority, but also that you resist with care the spirit of innovation upon its principles, however specious the pretext. One method of assault may be to effect, in the forms of the Constitution, alterations which will impair the energy of the system; and thus to undermine what cannot be directly overthrown. In all the changes to which you may be invited, remember that time and habit are at least as necessary to fix the true character of governments as of other human institutions:—that experience is the surest standard by which to test the real tendency of the existing constitution of a country:—that facility in changes, upon the credit of mere hypothesis and opinion, exposes to perpetual change from the endless variety of hypothesis and opinion: and remember, especially, that for the efficient management of your common interests, in a country so extensive as ours, a government of as much vigour as is consistent with the perfect security of liberty is indispensable. Liberty itself will find in such a government, with powers properly distributed and adjusted, its surest guardian. It is, indeed, little else than a name, where the government is too feeble to withstand the enterprises of faction, to confine each member of the society within the limits prescribed by the laws, and to maintain all in the secure and tranquil enjoyment of the rights of person and property.

I have already intimated to you the danger of parties in the state, with particular references to the founding them on geographical discriminations. Let me now take a more comprehensive view, and warn you in the most solemn manner against the baneful effects of the spirit of party generally.

This spirit, unfortunately, is inseparable from our nature, having its root in the strongest passions of the human mind. It exists under different shapes in all governments, more or less stifled, controlled, or repressed; but in those of the popular form, it is seen in its greatest rankness, and is truly their worst enemy.

The alternate domination of one faction over another, sharpened by the spirit of revenge natural to party dissension, which, in different ages and countries, has perpetrated the most horrid enormities, is itself a frightful despotism. But this leads at length to a more formal and permanent despotism. The disorders and miseries which result, gradually incline the minds of men to seek security and repose in the absolute power of an individual; and, sooner or later, the chief of some prevailing faction, more able or more fortunate than his competitors, turns this disposition to the purposes of his own elevation on the ruins of public liberty.

Without looking forward to an extremity of this kind, (which nevertheless ought not to be entirely out of sight,) the common and continual mischiefs of the spirit of party are sufficient to make it the interest and duty of a wise people to discourage and restrain it.

It serves always to distract the public councils, and enfeeble the public administration. It agitates the community with ill-founded jealousies and false alarms; kindles the animosity of one part against another; foments occasional riot and insurrection. It opens the door to foreign influence and corruption, which finds a facilitated access to the government itself through the channels of party passions. Thus the policy and the will of one country are subjected to the policy and will of another.

There is an opinion that parties in free countries are useful checks upon the administration of the government, and serve to keep alive the spirit of liberty. This, within certain limits, is probably true; and, in governments of a monarchical cast, patriotism may look with indulgence, if not with favour, upon the spirit of party. But in those of the popular character, in governments purely elective, it is a spirit not to be encouraged. From their natural tendency, it is certain there will always be enough of that spirit for every salutary purpose. And there being constant danger of excess, the effort ought to be, by force of public opinion, to mitigate and assuage it. A fire not to be quenched, it demands a uniform vigilance to prevent it bursting into a flame, lest, instead of warming, it should consume.

It is important, likewise, that the habits of thinking in a free country should inspire caution in those intrusted with its administration, to confine themselves within their respective constitutional spheres, avoiding in the exercise of the powers of one department, to encroach upon another. The spirit of encroachment tends to consolidate the powers of all the departments in one, and thus to create, whatever the form of government, a real despotism. A just estimate of that love of power and proneness to abuse it which predominate in the human heart, is sufficient to satisfy us of the truth of this position. The necessity of reciprocal checks in the exercise of political power, by dividing and distributing it into different depositories, and constituting each the guardian of the public weal against invasions of the others, has been evinced by experiments ancient and modern: some of them in our country, and under our own eyes. To preserve them must be as necessary as to institute them. If, in the opinion of the people, the distribution or modification of the constitutional powers be in any par ticular wrong, let it be corrected by an amendment in the way which the Constitution designates. But let there be no change by usurpa tion ; for though this, in one instance, may be the instrument of good, it is the customary weapon by which free governments are destroyed. The precedent must always greatly overbalance in permanent evil, any partial or transient benefit which the use can at any time yield.

Of all the dispositions and habits which lead to political prosperity, religion and morality are indispensable supports. In vain would that man claim the tribute of patriotism, who should labour to subvert these great pillars of human happiness, these firmest props of the duties of men and citizens. The mere politician, equally with the pious man, ought to respect and to cherish them. A volume could not trace all their connections with private and public felicity. Let it simply be asked, where is the security for property, for reputation, for life, if the sense of religious obligation *desert* the oaths which are the instru ments of investigation in courts of justice ? And let us with caution indulge the supposition that morality can be maintained without re ligion. Whatever may be conceded to the influence of refined edu cation on minds of peculiar structure, reason and experience both forbid us to expect that national morality can prevail in exclusion of religious principle.

It is substantially true, that virtue or morality is a necessary spring of popular government. The rule, indeed, extends with more or less force to every species of free government. Who that is a sincere friend to it can look with indifference upon attempts to shake the foundation of the fabric ?

Promote, then, as an object of primary importance, institutions for the general diffusion of knowledge. In proportion as the structure of a government gives force to public opinion, it should be enlightened.

As a very important source of strength and security, cherish public credit. One method of preserving it is to use it as sparingly as possi ble, avoiding occasions of expense, by cultivating peace, but remember ing, also, that timely disbursements, to prepare for danger, frequently prevent much greater disbursements to repel it ; avoiding likewise he accumulation of debt, not only by shunning occasions of expense, out by vigorous exertions in time of peace to discharge the debts which unavoidable wars may have occasioned, not ungenerously throwing upon posterity the burden which we ourselves ought to bear. The execution of these maxims belongs to your representatives, but it is necessary that public opinion should co-operate. To facilitate to them the performance of their duty, it is essential that you should practically bear in mind, that towards the payment of debts there must be revenue; that to have revenue, there must be taxes; that no taxes can be devised which are not more or less inconvenient and unpleasant; that the intrinsic embarrassment inseparable from the selection of the proper objects, (which is always a choice of difficulties,) ought to be a decisive motive for a candid construction of the conduct of the government in making it, and for a spirit of acquiescence in the measures for obtaining revenue, which the public exigencies may at any time dictate.

Observe good faith and justice towards all nations; cultivate peace and harmony with all. Religion and morality enjoin this conduct; and can it be that good policy does not equally enjoin it? it will be worthy of a free, enlightened, and, at no distant period, a great nation, to give to mankind the magnanimous and too novel example of a people always guided by an exalted justice and benevolence. Who can doubt but, in the course of time and things, the fruits of such a plan would richly repay any temporary advantages which might be lost by a steady adherence to it; can it be that Providence has not connected the permanent felicity of a nation with its virtue? the experiment, at least, is recommended by every sentiment which ennobles human nature. Alas! is it rendered impossible by its vices?

In the execution of such a plan, nothing is more essential than that permanent, inveterate antipathies against particular nations, and passionate attachments for others, should be excluded; and that, in place of them, just and amicable feelings towards all should be cultivated. The nation which indulges towards another an habitual hatred, or an habitual fondness, is in some degree a slave. It is a slave to its animosity or to its affection, either of which is sufficient to lead it astray from its duty and its interest. Antipathy in one nation against another, disposes each more readily to offer insult and injury, to lay hold of slight causes of umbrage, and to be haughty and intractable when accidental or trifling occasions of dispute occur. Hence, frequent collisions, obstinate, envenomed, and bloody contests. The nation, prompted by ill-will and resentment, sometimes impels to war the government, contrary to the best calculations of policy. The government sometimes participates in the national propensity, and adopts through passion what reason would reject; at other times, it makes the animosity of the nation subservient to projects of hostility, instigated by pride, ambition, and other sinister and pernicious motives. The peace often, sometimes perhaps the liberty, of nations has been the victim.

So, likewise, a passionate attachment of one nation for another produces a variety of evils. Sympathy for the favourite nation, facilitating the illusion of an imaginary common interest in cases where no real common interest exists, and infusing into one the enmities of the other, betrays the former into a participation in the quarrels and wars of the latter, without adequate inducements or justification. It leads also to concessions to the favourite nation, of privileges denied to others, which is apt doubly to injure the nation making the concessions; by unnecessarily parting with what ought to have been retained: and by exciting jealousy, ill will, and a disposition to retaliate in the parties from whom equal privileges are withheld: and it gives to ambitious, corrupted, or deluded citizens, who devote themselves to the favourite nation, facility to betray or sacrifice the interests of their own country, without odium, sometimes even with popularity; gilding with the appearances of a virtuous sense of obligation, a commendable deference for public opinion, or a laudable zeal for public good, the base or foolish compliances of ambition, corruption, or infatuation.

As avenues to foreign influence in innumerable ways, such attachments are particularly alarming to the truly enlightened and independent patriot. How many opportunities do they afford to tamper with domestic factions, to practise the arts of seduction, to mislead public opinion, to influence or awe the public councils!—such an attachment of a small, or weak, towards a great and powerful nation, dooms the former to be the satellite of the latter.

Against the insidious wiles of foreign influence, (I conjure you to believe me, fellow citizens,) the jealousy of a free people ought to be *constantly* awake; since history and experience prove, that foreign influence is one of the most baneful foes of republican government. But that jealousy, to be useful, must be impartial; else it becomes the instrument of the very influence to be avoided, instead of a defence against it. Excessive partiality for one foreign nation, and excessive dislike for another, cause those whom they actuate to see danger only on one side, and serve to veil and even second the arts of influence on the other. Real patriots, who may resist the intrigues of the favourite are liable to become suspected and odious; while its tools and dupes usurp the applause and confidence of the people, to surrender their interests.

The great rule of conduct for us, in regard to foreign nations, is, in extending our commercial relations, to have with them as little *political* connection as possible. So far as we have already formed engagements, let them be fulfilled with perfect good faith. Here let us stop.

Europe has a set of primary interests, which to us have none, or a

74

very remote relation. Hence, she must be engaged in frequent controversies, the causes of which are essentially foreign to our concerns. Hence, therefore, it must be unwise in us to implicate ourselves, by artificial ties, in the ordinary vicissitudes of her politics or the ordinary combinations and collisions of her friendships or enmities.

Our detached and distant situation invites and enables us to pursue a different course. If we remain one people, under an efficient government, the period is not far off when we may defy material injury from external annoyance; when we may take such an attitude as will cause the neutrality we may at any time resolve upon, to be scrupulously respected; when belligerent nations, under the impossibility of making acquisitions upon us, will not lightly hazard the giving us provocation; when we may choose peace or war, as our interest, guided by justice, shall counsel.

Why forego the advantages of so peculiar a situation? why quit our own to stand upon foreign ground? why, by interweaving our destiny with that of any part of Europe, entangle our peace and prosperity in the toils of European ambition, rivalship, interest, humour, or caprice?

It is our true policy to steer clear of permanent alliances with any portion of the foreign world; so far, I mean, as we are now at liberty to do it; for let me not be understood as capable of patronizing infidelity to existing engagements. I hold the maxim no less applicable to public than to private affairs, that honesty is always the best policy.

I repeat it, therefore, let those engagements be observed in their genuine sense. But, in my opinion, it is unnecessary, and would be unwise to extend them.

Taking care always to keep ourselves, by suitable establishments, on a respectable defensive posture, we may safely trust to temporary alliances for extraordinary emergencies.

Harmony, and a liberal intercourse with all nations, are recommended by policy, humanity, and interest. But even our commercial policy should hold an equal and impartial hand; neither seeking nor granting exclusive favours or preferences; consulting the natural course of things; diffusing and diversifying by gentle means the streams of commerce, but forcing nothing; establishing with powers so disposed, in order to give trade a stable course, to define the rights of our merchants, and to enable the government to support them, conventional rules of intercourse, the best that present circumstances and mutual opinion will permit, but temporary, and liable to be from time to time abandoned or varied as experience and circumstances shall dictate constantly keeping in view, that it is folly in one nation to look for disinterested favours from another; that it must pay with a portion of its independence for whatever it may accept under that character; that by such acceptance, it may place itself in the condition of having given equivalents for nominal favours, and yet of being reproached with ingratitude for not giving more. There can be no greater error than to expect, or calculate upon real favours from nation to nation. It is an illusion which experience must cure, which a just pride ought to discard.

In offering to you, my countrymen, these counsels of an old and affectionate friend, I dare not hope they will make the strong and lasting impression I could wish; that they will control the usual current of the passions; or prevent our nation from running the course which has hitherto marked the destiny of nations; but if I may even flatter myself, that they may be productive of some partial benefit, some occasional good; that they may now and then recur to moderate the fury of party spirit, to warn against the mischiefs of foreign intrigue, to guard against the impostures of pretended patriotism; this hope will be a full recompense for the solicitude for your welfare by which they have been dictated.

How far, in the discharge of my official duties, I have been guided by the principles which have been delineated, the public records and other evidences of my conduct must witness to you and to the world. To myself, the assurance of my own conscience is, that I have, at least, believed myself to be guided by them.

In relation to the still subsisting war in Europe, my proclamation of the 22d of April, 1793, is the index to my plan. Sanctioned by your approving voice, and by that of your representatives in both houses of Congress, the spirit of that measure has continually governed me; uninfluenced by any attempts to deter or divert me from it.

After deliberate examination, with the aid of the best lights I could obtain, I was well satisfied that our country, under all the circumstances of the case, had a right to take, and was bound in duty and interest to take, a neutral position. Having taken it, I determined, as far as should depend upon me, to maintain it with moderation, perseverance, and firmness.

The considerations which respect the right to hold this conduct, it is not necessary on this occasion to detail. I will only observe that, according to my understanding of the matter, that right, so far from being denied by any of the belligerent powers, has been virtually admitted by all.

The duty of holding a neutral conduct may be inferred, without any thing more, from the obligation which justice and humanity impose on every nation, in cases in which it is free to act, to maintain inviolate the relations of peace and amity towards other nations.

The inducements of interest for observing that conduct will best be referred to your own reflections and experience. With me, a predominant motive has been to endeavour to gain time to our country to settle and mature its yet recent institutions, and to progress, without interruption, to that degree of strength and consistency which is necessary to give it, humanly speaking, the command of its own fortunes.

Though in reviewing the incidents of my administration, I am unconscious of intentional error ; I am nevertheless too sensible of my defects not to think it probable that I may have committed many errors. Whatever they may be, I fervently beseech the Almighty to avert or mitigate the evils to which they may tend. I shall also carry with me the hope that my country will never cease to view them with indulgence ; and that, after forty-five years of my life dedicated to its service, with an upright zeal, the faults of incompetent abilities will be consigned to oblivion, as myself must soon be to the mansions of rest.

Relying on its kindness in this as in other things, and actuated by that fervent love towards it, which is so natural to a man who views in it the native soil of himself and his progenitors for several generations ; I anticipate with pleasing expectation that retreat in which I promise myself to realize, without alloy, the sweet enjoyment of partaking, in the midst of my fellow citizens, the benign influence of good laws under a free government—the ever favourite object of my heart, and the happy reward, as I trust, of our mutual cares, labours, and dangers.

VALUABLE

HISTORICAL, THEOLOGICAL,

AND

MISCELLANEOUS

BOOKS,

PUBLISHED BY

LEARY, GETZ & Co.

No. 224 North Second Street,

PHILADELPHIA.

————◆————

☞ Any Book in this Catalogue will be sent by mail, postage receipt of the Retail Price in money or in postage sta

————◆————

☞ *Persons desiring to act as Agents for the sale of these*
necessary information relating to the business by add

3

Pilgrim's Progress.—A new Pictorial Edition. With a life of the Author, with Scott's full and explanatory Notes. Illustrated by fine Engravings. 12mo., cloth, gilt. (*very large type*,) 1.00

Do   do   arabesque, gilt, ... 1.25
Do   do   red morocco, full gilt, ... 2.00

The Family Sabbath Day Miscellany. — Comprising over three hundred Religious Tales and Anecdotes, original and select, with occasional Reflections, for the use of Families on the Lord's Day. By C. A. Goodrich. 12mo., Numerous Engravings, cloth, gilt, ... 1.00

Do   do   arabesque, gilt, ... 1.25
Do   do   red morocco, full gilt, ... 2.00

Life of Christ, to which is added the Lives and Sufferings of his Holy Evangelists and Apostles. By Rev. John Fleetwood, D. D., with an Introduction by Prof. S. Seager. 12mo., 460 pages, numerous Engravings, cloth, gilt, ...1.00

Do   do   arabesque, gilt, ... 1.25
Do   do   red morocco, full gilt, ... 2.00

The Christian's Legacy—or, Bible Directory. By Rev. Wm. Jackson; with an appendix containing a compendium of the Holy Bible; designed for making the reading and study of the Scriptures more easy, 12mo., twenty-five full ... engravings, cloth, gilt, ... 1.00

Do   do   ... que, gilt, ... 1.25
Do   do   red morocco, full gilt, ... 2.00

Knapp's Female Biography—Containing short Biogra of Distinguished Women, in different Nations and Ages. By S. L. Knapp. Illustrated with Elegant Engravings, 12mo, cloth, gilt,.... 1.00

Do   do   arabesque, gilt,.................................... 1.25
Do   do   red morocco, full gilt, ...2.00

The Historical Cabinet—Containing authentic Accounts of many Remarkable and Interesting Events which have taken place in modern times. Carefully Collected and Compiled from various sources, and not to be found in any one work heretofore published. 12mo, over 500 pages. Illustrated with fifty Engravings, cloth, gilt, ... 1.00

Do   do   arabesque, gilt,................................... 1.25
Do   do   red morocco, full gilt, ... 2.00

The Young Man's Book of Knowledge—Containing a Familiar view of the Importance of Religion, the Works of Nature, Logic, Eloquence, the Passions, Matter and Motion, Magnetism, Mechanical Powers, Hydrostatics, Hydraulics, Optics, Acoustics, Electricity, Galnism, Geometry, Geography, Astronomy, Chronology, History, &c., By Thomas Tegg. To which is added an Epitome of American , and appropriate Reflections on the Prosperity, Influence, and ice of the United States. Illustrated with fine Engravings, cloth, ... 1.00

do   arabesque, gilt, ... 1.25

Nights' Entertainments; or, the Thousand s. A new edition, translated and arranged for Family o, nearly one hundred Engravings, cloth, gilt, ... 1.00

arabesque, gilt, ...1.25

The Glory of America—Comprising Memoirs of the Lives and Glorious Exploits of some of the most Distinguished Officers engaged in the Revolutionary and Late Wars with Great Britain. Illustrated with numerous Engravings, cloth, gilt, ...1.00
  Do   do   arabesque, gilt, ...1.25

Old Christianity against Papal Novelties; including a Review of Dr. Milner's end of Controversy. By Gideon Ouseley. In one large duodecimo volume, 406 pp., cloth, gilt. "A Book that should be in the hands of every American Christian," 1.00
  Do   do   arabesque, gilt, ...1.25

The Closing Scene; or, Christianity and Infidelity Contrasted, in the Last Hours of Remarkable Persons. By Rev. Erskine Neale, A. M. One handsome duodecimo volume, cloth, gilt. With two handsome Engravings representing the Christian's and the Infidel's Death-beds, ...1.00
  Do   do   arabesque, gilt, ...1.25

St. Pierre's Studies of Nature—Translated by Henry Hunter, D. D., who observes in his preface:—"St. Pierre has enabled me to contemplate the Universe with other eyes—has furnished new arguments to combat Atheism—has established beyond the power of contradiction, the doctrine of a Universal Providence—has excited a warmer interest in favour of suffering humanity, and has disclosed sources unknown of intellectual enjoyment," cloth, gilt,............................ 1.00
  Do   do   arabesque, gilt, ... 1.25

Combe on the Constitution of Man.—The Constitution of Man considered in relation to external objects, by George Combe. A reprint from the late Edinburgh Edition. Complete in 1 volume, 12mo., cloth, gilt, ... 1 00

The Complete Cook and Confectioner—Containing seven hundred plain and practical receipts in Cooking, Baking, Boiling, Roasting and Frying Fish, Meats, Seasoning, Cooking Vegetables, Preparing Salads, Clarifying, Making of Pastry, Puddings, Gruels, Gravies, &c. Also, five hundred plain and practical receipts in Confectionery, for making all kinds of Cakes, Candies, Jellies, Preserves, Sugar Boiling, Ice Creams, every description of Plain and Ornamental Cakes, Ornaments, Syrups, Artificial Yeasts, Fancy Biscuits, Rolls, Muffins, Tarts, Pies, &c. By Sanderson and Parkinson. 12mo., cloth, gilt, ...1.00

Simms' Life of General Nathanael Greene—Major General in the Army of the Revolution; with interesting and Authentic Accounts of some of the most Important Events in the Revolutionary Struggle. By W. Gilmore Simms. In one handsome 12mo. volume, beautifully illustrated by colored Engravings. Arabesque, gilt, ... 1.25

History of the Devil.—Containing his Origin; a State of his Circumstances: his Conduct, Public and Private: the various turns of his affairs from Adam down to the present time; the various methods he takes to converse with Mankind; with the manner of his making Witches, Wizards and Conjurers; and how they see their souls to him, &c., &c. The whole interspersed with many of the Devil's Adventures, to which is added a description of his Dwelling, called Hell. By De Foe, author of "Robinson Crusoe." One volume, 12mo., cloth, ... 1.00

3

Pilgrim's Progress.—A new Octavo Pictorial edition. To which is added THE TRAVELS OF THE UNGODLY, or the Life and Death f Mr Badman, contained in no other edition. Also containing a Life of Bunyan, and Scott's numerous and full explanatory notes. Very large type, being the most readable edition published in the United States. Illustrated with fine engravings, and bound in neat plain cloth,.... 2.00

Do	do	arabesque, gilt,.....................................	2.50
Do	do	'red morocco, full.gilt, ...	3.00
Do	do	super extra antique, ...	5.00

Fleetwood's Life of Christ, with the Lives, Transactions and Sufferings of his Holy Evangelists, Apostles and other Primitive Martyrs; and a History of the Jews, brought down to the destruction of Jerusalem. By the Rev. John Fleetwood, D. D. To which is added a continuation of the History of the Jews to the present time. One large octavo volume, embellished with twenty-five fine coloured Engravings, strongly and neatly bound,. 2.50

Do	do	red morocco, full·gilt,.............	3.00
Do	do	super extra antique,...............................	5.00

Burder's History of all Religions.—From the Earliest Records to the Present Time. By Wm. Burder, B. A. Greatly improved as a Book of Reference, by the insertion of a Full Account, Historical, Doctrinal, and Statistical, of the Principal Religious Denominations of the United States. By the Rev. Joel Parker, D. D. Embellished with numerous elegant Engravings. One large octavo volume, of 700 pages, beautifully bound, in embossed morocco, ...·............. 3.00

Do	do	super extra antique,...............................	5.00

Frost's Lives of Eminent Christians.—This Work contains the Lives of One Hundred and Twenty-five Persons, of both sexes, remarkable for their Piety and Philanthropic Deeds; illustrated with numerous Portraits. One volume 8vo. arabesque,........................ 2.50

Do	do	red morocco, full gilt,...........	3.00
Do	do	super extra antique,........................	5.00

The Perpetual Keepsake; being the New Testament very beautifully printed on fine white paper, large type, and profusely illustrated by Engravings, originally designed and engraved expressly for this magnificent work, by W. Croome and J. H. Brightly. Intended expressly for a Presentation Book. Beautifully bound in red morocco, full gilt, ... 2.50

Do	do	super extra antique, ...5.00

Pictorial Cottage Testament; Same Work as above described, bound in arabesque, ... 1.50

Christian Martyrology; or, Sufferings of the Early Christians, being an Authentic and Genuine Historical Account of the principal Persecutions against the Church of Christ, in different parts of the World, by Pagans and Papists. One large octavo volume, of over 250 pages, illustrated with twenty-four full page coloured Engravings, and bound in arabesque, gilt, ...1.50

do.	do.	red morocco, full gilt,.......................2.00

4

Rotteck's History of the World.—A General History or the World from the earliest period. Embracing an account of the Origin and Manners and Customs of all the Nations of the Earth, the Rise and Progress of Judaism, Paganism, and Christianity, &c., &c. By Charles Von Rotteck, LL. D. With a continuation, containing an account of the various Revolutions and Wars in all parts of the World, to the PRESENT TIME. By Charles J. Peterson. Four volumes in one, making more than 1700 large octavo pages, illustrated with fifty highly finished Historical Engravings. Handsomely bound in arabesque, gilt, ... 3.50

Do   do   2 vols., sheep, library, ... 4.00

Frost's Pictorial History of America. — Remarkable

Events in the History of America, from the Discovery to the Present time. By John Frost, LL. D. Embellished with 700 Engravings. This splendid work contains an account of the Conquest of Mexico, by Cortez. The Conquest of Peru, by Pizarro and Almagro. The Conquest of Florida, by De Soto. The Discovery and Settlement of the United States and Canada. King Philip's War. The Seven Years' War. The American Revolution. The War of 1812. The War with the French Republic. The several Indian Wars, and the late War with Mexico. Complete in one volume of 1600 large octavo pages, beautifully bound in arabesque, gilt, ... 3.50

Do   do   2 vols., sheep, library, ... 4.00

Pictorial History of the United States, from the Discovery of America to the Formation of the States, and from thence to the Present time. By C. B. Taylor. One large volume of over 600 pages, illustrated by over one hundred handsome Engravings, and bound in arabesque, gilt, ... 2.00

Lives of Remarkable and Eccentric Characters.—

Lives of Remarkable and Eccentric Characters, of all Ages and Countries; comprising Heroes, Conquerors, Statesmen, Authors, Artists, Extraordinary Humorists, Misers, Mountebanks, Kings and Queens, Jugglers and other Curiosities of Human Nature, compiled from authentic materials. One large octavo volume of 800 pages, illustrated by several hundred Engravings, and beautifully bound, ... 2.50

Do   do   super extra antique, ... 5.00

Frost's Pictorial Life of Washington.—Pictorial Life of

George Washington: embracing a complete history of the Seven Years' War, the Revolutionary War, Formation of the Federal Constitution, and the Administration of Washington. By J. Frost, LL. D. One elegant large octavo volume, with upwards of one hundred Engravings, by Croome and Devereux, and six handsomely executed on steel. Bound in arabesque morocco, gilt. 3.00

Do   do   red morocco, full gilt, ... 3.50

Do   do   super extra antique, ... 5.00

Life and Speeches of Henry Clay.—This work is in

tended to trace clearly the career of Mr. Clay from his entrance on the stage of public life, down to the period of his death. The Biography comprises 200 pages, and his speeches about 1100. With an authentic Portrait on steel, and also a view of his birth-place. One large octavo volume; large, clear type, handsomely bound, ... 8 00

Do   do   2 vols., sheep, Library, ... 3.50

Whitefield's Life and Sermons.—The Life and Sermons of Rev. George Whitefield. A new, revised, and improved edition, with an introduction by Rev. C. E. Stowe, D. D. In one large octavo volume of 666 pages, printed on fine white paper, with clear. type, and embellished with a Portrait on Steel, and several other beautiful Engravings. Bound in handsome and durable leather, ... 2.50
Do   do   super extra antique,............................ 5.00

Edmondson's Short Sermons.—Containing one hundred and forty short, plain and practical Sermons on important Subjects. By Jonathan Edmondson, with an Introduction by Rev. J. P. Durbin, D.D. A new and improved edition, 8vo., cloth, containing an authentic Portrait of the Author, beautifully engraved on steel,........................ ...... 1.50
Do   do   sheep, library,...... ...... 2.00
Do   do   super extra antique,............................. 5.00

Evans' Sermons.—Sermons of Christmas Evans, a New Translation from the Welsh, with a Memoir and Portraiture of the Author. By Rev. Joseph Cross. 8vo., sheep, library,.................. 1.50

The Wonders of Nature Displayed; or, 365 Reflections on the Works of God's Providence. By Sturm. This work contains a subject for reflection for every day throughout the year, intended to draw out the better feelings of man's nature in thankfulness to the great "Architect of the Universe" for the manifold blessings heaped upon sinful man throughout all the various walks of life. One volume, 8vo., 486 pp., cloth, gilt,.. 1.50

Josephus' Works.—The Works of Flavius Josephus, containing twenty books of Jewish Antiquities, seven books of the Jewish War, and the Life of Josephus, written by himself. Translated from the original Greek, according to Havercamp's accurate edition, together with Explanatory Notes and Observations. By the late Wm. Whiston, A. M., 8vo., arabesque,... ... 2.50

Lord Byron's Works.—The Complete Poetical Works of Lord Byron, with a Memoir of his Life. A new and beautiful edition in one volume octavo, handsomely illustrated with eight elegant Steel Engravings, ... 2.50

Todd's Johnson and Walker's Dictionary.—Containing also Walker's Key to the classical pronunciation of Greek, Latin, and Scripture proper names. In one handsome royal octavo volume, of nearly 1200 pages, double columns, neatly bound in plain leather. Being the best and cheapest edition in the English language,.................... 2.50

Chambers' Information for the People.—Information for the People. A popular Encyclopædia. By Wm. and Robert Chambers. With numerous additions, and more than six hundred Engravings. Complete in two imperial octavo vols. of 850 pages each. Handsomely bound in sheep. Library style,............. .... 5.00

The Modern Stair Builder's Guide, and Practical System of Hand-railing, embracing all its necessary details, and Geometrically illustrated with twenty-two Steel Engravings; together with the use of the most important Principles of Practical Geometry. By Simon De Graff, Architect. One quarto volume, bound in extra cloth, ... 3.00

6

Platt's Book of Curiosities.—Containing Ten Thousand Wonders and Curiosities of Nature and Art, and of remarkable and astonishing Places, Beings, Animals, Customs. Experiments, Phenomena, &c., &c., of both Ancient and Modern Times, on all parts of the globe, comprising authentic accounts of the most wonderful Freaks of Nature and Arts of Man. Complete in one large octavo volume of nearly 1000 pages, and handsomely illustrated with numerous Engravings. Beautifully bound in arabesque, gilt back,.. 2.50

Memoirs of Rev. George Whitefield.—By Rev. John Gillies, with an Introduction by Prof. C. E. Stowe, D. D., of Andover, Mass. An entirely new and enlarged edition, with many improvements, and containing a beautifully engraved Steel Portrait. One duodecimo volume, bound in embossed cloth... 1.00
  *** This work is bound to match with, and is a necessary companion to, "Stevens's History of Methodism."

Dr. Buchan's Family Physician.—Domestic Medicine; or, a Treatise on the Prevention and Cure of Diseases by Regimen and Simple Medicines, with the latest Corrections and Improvements, and full directions in regard to Air, Exercise, Bathing, Clothing, Sleep, Diets, &c., and the general management of the Diseases of Women and Children. To which is annexed, a complete Family Dispensatory, for the use of Private Practitioners. By Wm. Buchan, M. D. With considerable Additions and Corrections, by an American Physician. One handsome large, 8vo. volume, strongly bound, and illustrated with a fine Portrait of Dr. Buchan, ... 2.50

Peterson's History of the War of 1812, and with Mexico. Illustrated with two hundred Engravings, 8vo., arabesque,.......... 2.50

Peterson's History of the American Revolution.—By Charles J. Peterson. Magnificently illustrated with about two hundred Engravings, 8vo., arabesque, ... 2.50

Peterson's History of the United States Navy, from the formation of the Navy to the close of the Mexican War. One handsome octavo volume, with more than one hundred Engravings, embracing Portraits of all the Prominent Officers, Sketches of Naval Engagements, &c. In arabesque, gilt,... 2.50

The Heroic Women of History.—This valuable work furnishes a vast amount of Historical Information concerning the most Prominent Women of all ages and countries. Numerous Engravings, and handsomely bound,.. 2.50

Moore's History of the Indian Wars.—The Indian Wars of the United States, from the Discovery to the Present Time, with accounts of the Origin, Manners, Superstitions, &c., of the Aborigines. By William V. Moore. 8vo., arabesque, ... 2.00

Scott's Life of Napoleon.—The Life of Napoleon Bonaparte, Emperor of the French, with a Preliminary view of the French Revolution. By Sir Walter Scott. Complete in one large octavo vol., with handsome Engravings, ...2.50

Bnnyan's Pilgrim's Progress.—18mo., with 8 fine plates. Cloth, gilt,.. 50

Bunyan's Holy War.—18mo., with 8 fine plates, cloth, gilt,.. 50

Bunyan's Minor Works—Containing Grace Abounding to the Chief of Sinners; Heart's Ease in Heart's Trouble; The World to Come, or Visions of Heaven and Hell; and the Barren Fig-Tree, or the Doom and Downfall of the Fruitless Professor. Complete in one volume, cloth, gilt, ... 50

The Dialogues of Devils—On the many vices which abound in the Civil and Religious World. By Rev. John Macgowan, V. D. M. 18mo., cloth, gilt, ... 50

Temperance Tales; or, Six Nights with the Washingtonians. (With Cruikshank's eight celebrated Plates of the "Bottle.") By T. S. Arthur. 2 vols. in one, 18mo., cloth, gilt,............................ 50

The Ladies' Guide in Needle Work.—A Gift for the Industrious, Containing Instructions in Canvass Work, Knitting, Netting and Crochet Work, Millinery and Mantua Making, Embroidery and Applique. Numerous Engravings, 18mo., cloth, gilt,...................... 50

Willison's Afflicted Man's Companion.—Improved edition. 18mo., cloth, gilt,.. 50

The Pastor's Wife.—A Memoir of Mrs. Sherman, of Surrey Chapel, London. Edited by her husband, the Rev. James Sherman, Pastor of Surrey Chapel. Unabridged edition, 18mo., cloth, gilt,... 50

Drew on the Immortality and Immateriality of the Soul. 18mo., cloth, gilt,... 50

Dick's Philosophy of a Future State.—18mo., cloth, gilt,.. 50

Young's Night Thoughts.—18mo., cloth, gilt,.......... 50

The Course of Time.—By Robert Pollok, A. M., with an enlarged Index, and an Analysis prefixed to each book. One volume, 18mo., cloth, gilt,.. 50

Cobbett's Sermons.—18mo., cloth, gilt,...................... 50

Cobbett's Advice to Young Men.—A Book that every Young Man should read. 18mo., cloth, gilt,............................ 50

Zimmerman on Solitude.—18mo., with Portrait of the Author. Cloth, gilt,.. 50

8

Doddridge's Rise and Progress of Religion in the
Soul.—Thick 18mo., cloth, gilt,... 50

Baxter's Saint's Everlasting Rest.—18mo., with Portrait of the Author, cloth, gilt,.. 50

Baxter's Call to the Unconverted.—18mo., cloth,.. 50

Jay's Family Prayers.—18mo., cloth,...................... 50

Camp Meeting Chorister, (Methodist Hymn Book,) neat sheep, ... 25

The Devil upon Two Sticks.—Translated from the French of M. Le Sage, with a Memoir of the Author. Asmodeus' Crutches, and Dialogues between two chimneys of Madrid,.............................. 50

Original Poems, for Infant Minds, by the Taylor Family. 18mo., cloth, gilt,.. 50

The Life and Essays of Dr. Franklin—written by himself. A book that every young man in the United States should read. One volume, 18mo., with numerous plates, cloth, gilt,................... 50

Stories of the War of 1812, and with Mexico.—A beautiful Juvenile Book, commemorative of these Important Events in the History of our Country. Elegantly illustrated, 16mo., cloth, gilt,... 50

Tom Thumb.—The Life and Adventures of Tom Thumb. One of the best and most Entertaining Books published for Children, containing 16 Engravings,.. 50

Dr. Dodd's Lectures to Young Men.—Discourses to Young Men. Illustrated with numerous highly interesting Anecdotes. A neat 24mo. volume, cloth, with Plates,......................... 50

Combe on the Constitution of Man—Fine Edition, 18mo., cloth, gilt,.. 50

he Vicar of Wakefield.—By Dr. Goldsmith, 18mo., cloth, gilt,... 50

Æsop's Fables.—Select Fables from Æsop and others. Illustrated with 200 Engravings. 18mo., cloth, gilt, ... 50

The Lights and Shadows of Scottish Life.—By Professor Willson. New edition, 18mo. cloth,............................50

Life and Times of the Duke of Wellington.—Illustrated with 41 Engravings. 18mo., cloth, gilt,...................... 50

Life of the Notorious Stephen Burroughs.—Containing many incidents in the Life of this Wonderful Man, never before published; newly corrected and revised edition. 18mo. cloth, gilt,...... 50

The Farmer's Barn Book—By Clater, Youatt, Skinner and Mills. Containing the Causes, Symptoms, and Treatment of all the Diseases incident to Oxen, Sheep, and Swine; the Anatomy and Physiology of Neat Cattle, with an Essay on the Use of Oxen and the Breed of Sheep; Stable Management, Treatment of the Diseases of Horses; Plain and Practical Directions in the choice and purchase of Horses; with Directions how to ascertain the good qualities, and detect the faults of Carriage, Cart and Saddle Horses. 12mo, cloth, gilt, illustrated with numerous Engravings,.. 1.00
Do   do   arabesque, gilt,.................................... 1.25

The New American Pocket Farrier and Farmer's Guide in the Choice and Management of Horses, Neat Cattle, Sheep and Swine; Including a Description of their Internal Structure—their Digestive System; the Diseases to which they are liable, with their causes, symptoms, and most approved methods of cure. From the writings of Youatt, Lawrence, Hines, White, Clater, and others. To which is added a variety of Agricultural and Miscellaneous Receipts. 18mo., cloth, gilt,......... 50

Every Man his own Farrier.—Containing ten minutes' advice, How to Buy a Horse; to which is added, how to use your horse at home, or on a journey, and what remedies are proper for all diseases to which he is liable. 18mo., boards,.................................... 15

Every Man his own Cattle Doctor.—Containing a Treatise on the Diseases of Horses, Cattle, Dogs, Sheep and Swine, with their Causes, Symptoms and Cure. 18mo., boards, ... 15

Shakspeare's Complete Works.—The Complete Works of Wm. Shakspeare, comprising his Plays and Poems, with Dr. Johnson's Preface, a Glossary, an account of each Play, and a Memoir of the Author. By Rev. Wm. Harness, M. A. Embellished. Complete in one large royal octavo volume, bound in sheep, marble edges,.......... 2.50

True Republican.—Containing the Constitution of the United States, Declaration of Independence, a fine Portrait of each of the Presidents—also the Constitutions of the principal States in the Union, and the Inaugural Addresses and first Annual Messages of each of the Presidents, &c. One large volume, 12mo., of about 500 pages. Arabesque, gilt,.. 1.25

Life of General Anthony Wayne, of the Revolutionary War. Illustrated with beautiful Engravings. Complete in one volume, 18mo., cloth, gilt,.. 50

Life of General Francis Marion, the great Partisan Chief of the War of Independence. Illustrated with beautiful Engravings. Complete in one volume. 18mo., cloth, gilt,........................ 50

Lives of Generals Wayne and Marion.—Both complete in one volume, with numerous Engravings, handsomely bound, roan, gilt, 18mo.,.. 75

Robinson Crusoe.—A new edition, 18mo., cloth, gilt, 8 plates,... 56

10

Mrs. Barwell's Advice to Mothers on the Treatment

of Infants, with directions for Self-Management before, during and after Pregnancy. Addressed to Mothers and Nurses. Revised, enlarged, and adapted to the Habits and Climate of the United States, by a Physician of New York, under the approval and recommendation of Dr. Valentine Mott. 12mo., cloth,.. 50

Paul and Virginia, to which is added *Elizabeth*, or *the Exiles of Siberia*. Two volumes complete in one. 18mo., fancy cloth,.. 50

Fanny Dale, or A Year after Marriage, by T. S. Arthur;

to which is added *The Young Music Teacher*, by T. S. Arthur. Two vols., complete in one. 18mo., fancy cloth,............................... 50

The Lady at Home, or Leaves from the every Day-Book

of an American Woman, by T. S. Arthur. To which is added Elizabeth, or the Exiles of Siberia. Two volumes complete in one. 18mo., fancy cloth,... 50

Alonzo and Melissa; or, The Unfeeling Father, A Tale

Founded on Fact. With one exception, and that is "Charlotte Temple," Alonzo and Melissa has probably been read more than any other Tale ever published in the United States. 18mo., cloth, gilt,............... 50

Love and Romance; or, Charlotte and Lucy Temple. Two

volumes in one. "Susannah Rowson, the authoress, has, by her interesting style, drawn more tears (for who has not shed tears over Charlotte Temple?) than any other authoress or author of modern times." In one neat volume, 18mo., cloth, gilt,.............................. 50

The American Joe Miller; or, the Jester's Own Book.

18mo., cloth, gilt,.. 50

Leary's Ready Reckoner, and Coin Book in Dollars and

Cents; to which is added the Coins of different parts of the world, with their value. Also, forms of Notes, Bills, Receipts, Petitions, &c.; also Interest Tables, at 6 per cent., from $1,00 to $12,000; together with other useful Tables,.. 15

Charlotte Temple—A Tale of Truth, by Mrs. Rowson,

18mo., boards,.. 15

Lucy Temple.—A Sequel to Charlotte Temple, 18mo.,

boards, ... 15

Etiquette Letter-Writer.—Being the Complete Art of

Fashionable Correspondence. 18mo., boards,..................... 15

Jack Lawrence, the Sailor Boy.—By the Author of

Jack Halyard. 1 vol., 18mo., boards, ... 15

The Laughing Philosopher.—Or Book of Fun,........ 15

Hocus Pocus.—Or the whole Art of Legerdemain explained.

18mo., boards,... 15

Parlor Library, comprising the following six volumes, in a handsome case, bound to match, in scarlet morocco, full gilt.

SABBATH DAY MISCELLANY,
CHRISTIAN'S LEGACY,
PILGRIM'S PROGRESS,
HISTORICAL CABINET,
KNAPP'S FEMALE BIOGRAPHY,
FLEETWOOD'S LIFE OF CHRIST,.........*Price*, for the set, 12.00

Cottage Cabinet Library; six vols., 18mo., in a neat case.

PILGRIM'S PROGRESS,
DREW ON THE SOUL,
DODDRIDGE'S RISE AND PROGRESS,
DIALOGUES OF DEVILS,
BAXTER'S SAINT'S REST,
DICK'S FUTURE STATE. ....*Price*, for the set, 3.00

Young Folks' Cabinet Library; six vols., 18mo., in a neat case.

ARTHUR'S TEMPERANCE TALES,
LIFE AND ESSAYS OF DR. FRANKLIN,
ÆSOP'S FABLES,
ROBINSON CRUSOE,
LIFE OF WELLINGTON,
ORIGINAL POEMS BY JANE TAYLOR......*Price*, for the set, 3.00

Young Lady's Cabinet Library; six vols., 18mo., in a neat case.

LADIES' GUIDE IN NEEDLE WORK,
LOVE AND ROMANCE,
ALONZO AND MELISSA,
PASTOR'S WIFE,
LIGHTS AND SHADOWS OF SCOTTISH LIFE,
VICAR OF WAKEFIELD......................*Price*, for the set, 3.00

Young Man's Cabinet Library; six vols., 18mo., in a neat case.

COBBETT'S ADVICE TO YOUNG MEN,
COMBE ON MAN,
ZIMMERMAN ON SOLITUDE,
LIFE OF STEPHEN BURROUGHS,
DEVIL ON TWO STICKS,
POLLOK'S COURSE OF TIME...............*Price*, for the set, 3.00

12   *

STANDARD ROMANCES.

32mo., Roan, Gilt.

The following series of the old English classics is neatly brought out. Each volume is in a convenient form, and may be carried in the pocket. They are bound in handsome and durable roan binding, gilt backs, and sold at lower prices than any other editions in America.

Children of the Abbey.—3 vols. in one, 32mo., roan, gilt, 75

Robinson Crusoe.—Complete edition. 32mo., with plates, roan, gilt,.. 75

The Bandit's Bride, or the Maid of Saxony. A very interesting romance, by Louisa Sydney Stanhope. Complete in one volume, 32mo., roan, gilt,... 75

Cottage on the Cliff.—A new and unabridged edition, to match the Children of the Abbey,.. 75

Cook's Voyages.—Illustrated with numerous Engravings. Complete edition. 2 vols. in one, 32mo., roan, gilt,..................... 75

Arabian Nights' Entertainments.—70 Plates. 32mo., roan, gilt,.. 75

Scottish Chiefs.—By Miss Jane Porter. 3 vols. in one, 32mo., roan, gilt,.. 75

Gil Blas.—4 vols. in one, 32mo., roan, gilt,.................. 75

Don Quixotte.—4 vols. in one, 32mo., roan, gilt,......... 75

The Mysteries of Udolpho.—3 vols. in one, 32mo., roan, gilt,.. 75

Romance of the Forest.—2 volumes in one, roan, gilt, 50

Thinks I to Myself.—A Serio-Ludicro-Comico-Tragico Tale. 1 vol., 32mo., roan, gilt,.. 25

Peter Wilkins' Visit to the Flying Islanders.—1 vol. 32mo., roan, gilt, ... 25

SCHOOL BOOKS.

Roy's Hebrew and English Dictionary.—A complete
Critical and Pronouncing Dictionary, containing all the words in the
Holy Bible, both Hebrew and Chaldee, with the vowel points, the prefixes
and affixes, as they stand in the original text; together with their deri-
vation, literal and etymological meaning, as it occurs in every part of
the Bible, and illustrated by numerous citations from the Targum, Tal-
mud, and Cognate dialects. By W. L. Roy, Professor of Oriental Lan-
guages. Complete in one royal octavo volume, bound in half Russia.
Price 5.00

Booth's New Pictorial United States.—For Primary
Schools, 244 pages, 18mo., neatly bound, with Questions. This is the
best History of the United States now published for the use of Primary
Schools, ... 50

The Central School Reader.—Compiled by the Female
Association of Friends for the Improvement of Juvenile Books. One of
the best books published for Select Schools and Academies. Also designed for Family Use. 12mo., ... 1.00

Wilmsen's Reader; or, the Children's Friend. One hundred and sixtieth edition. One of the best books ever published for
Children between the ages of eight and twelve years. 12mo.......... 75

Murray's English Reader.—12mo., half arabesque,... 25

Murray's Introduction.—12mo., boards,.................. 12½

Chapin's New Classical Spelling Book.—12mo., boards,
Price 12½

Cordery's Colloquies in Latin, improved with Exercises
and Vocabulary. 12mo., ... 38

Public School Singing Book, by A. F. Cox, suited for
Schools, Academies and Seminaries. 32mo., boards,................ 12½

Kelley's New Juvenile Primer,............................... 3

The Washington Primer.—A beautiful Book for Young
Children, ... 2

Testament.—A good School edition. 18mo., half arabesque,
Price. 25

14

STANDARD WORKS

In fine Bindings, suitable for Presentation Books, printed on fine White Paper, and beautifully Illustrated.

Bunyan's Pilgrim's Progress.—Octavo, large type, 16 Engravings, bound in English morocco, full gilt sides, back and edges, 3.00
THE SAME WORK, super extra antique,.. 5.00

Fleetwood's Life of Christ and his Apostles, with a History of the Jews, up to this time. Octavo, 25 engravings, bound in English Morocco, full gilt sides, back and edges, ... 3.00
THE SAME WORK, super extra antique, ... 5.00

The Perpetual Keepsake; being the **New Testament,** got up in very handsome style, large type, fine white paper. with initial letters and full page engravings, expressly designed and executed for this work. Octavo, bound in English morocco, full gilt sides, back and edges, ... 2.50
THE SAME WORK, super extra antique,.. 5.00

The Family Fire-Side Book; or Monuments of Temperance. Octavo, 10 steel plates, bound in English morocco, full gilt sides, back and edges,.. 2.50
THE SAME WORK, super extra antique,.. 5.00

Frost's Lives of Eminent Christians.—Octavo, 16 engraved portraits, bound in English morocco, full gilt sides, back and edges, ... 3.00
THE SAME WORK, super extra antique,.. 5.00

Burder's History of all Religions.—Octavo, 24 plates, bound in super extra antique,.. 5.00

Whitefield's Life and Sermons.—Octavo. Steel portrait and 16 engravings. Bound in super extra antique, ... 6.00

Platt's Book of Curiosities, or Wonders of the World, in Nature, Art, Science, &c., &c. Octavo, 24 engravings. bound in super extra antique,.. 5.00

Frost's Pictorial Life of Washington—Octavo, six fine steel plates and 100 engravings, bound in super extra antique,..... 5.00
THE SAME WORK, Red morocco, full gilt....................... 3 00

Lives of Remarkable and Eccentric Characters.—Octavo, over 100 engravings, bound in super extra antique,............. 5.00

Christian Martyrology, or Sufferings of the early Christians. Octavo, 24 engravings, bound in English morocco, full gilt sides, back and edges..................................... 2.00

Edmondson's Short Sermons, containing one hundred and forty plain and practical Sermons. Octavo, steel portrait, bound in super extra antique,..................................... 5.00